Gospel (on the Road to) Emmaus

Volume Two

Edward Joseph Clemmer

authorHOUSE®

AuthorHouse™
1663 Liberty Drive
Bloomington, IN 47403
www.authorhouse.com
Phone: 1-800-839-8640

© 2011 Edward Joseph Clemmer. All rights reserved.

No part of this book may be reproduced, stored in a retrieval system, or transmitted by any means without the written permission of the author.

First published by AuthorHouse   3/11/2011

ISBN: 978-1-4567-7378-6 (sc)
ISBN: 978-1-4567-7379-3 (hc)
ISBN: 978-1-4567-7360-1 (e)

Library of Congress Control Number: 2011901580

Printed in the United States of America

Diary of St. Maria Faustina Kowalska: Divine Mercy in My Soul © 1987 Marian Fathers of the Immaculate Conception, Stockbridge, MA 01263. Used with permission.

Cover Art: Robert Zünd,
Der Gang nach Emmaus, 1877
Oil on canvas, 119,5 x 158,5 cm
Kuntzmuseum, St. Gallen, Switzerland

This book is printed on acid-free paper.

Because of the dynamic nature of the Internet, any web addresses or links contained in this book may have changed since publication and may no longer be valid. The views expressed in this work are solely those of the author and do not necessarily reflect the views of the publisher, and the publisher hereby disclaims any responsibility for them.

Volume Two

**Index of Psalms and Canticles
Psalm/Canticle: Verses
(Chapter and Page)**

Ps 2:1-11 (Ch. 29, p. 134)
Ps 2:1-12 (Ch. 40, p. 520)
Ps 18:1-51 (Ch. 30, p. 137) Cf. Only
Ps 22:23-32 (Ch. 28, p. 92)
Ps 22:1-31 (Ch. 37, p. 422)
Ps 26:1-12 (Ch. 30, p. 137) Cf. Only
Ps 31:1-24 (Ch. 32, p. 206)
Ps 42-43:1-11, 1-5 (Ch. 38, p. 446)
Ps 46:1-11 (Ch. 38, p. 450)
Ps 47:1-9 (Ch. 39, p. 483)
Ps 57:1-12 (Ch. 30, p. 137) Cf. Only
Ps 59:1-17 (Ch. 36, p. 358)
Ps 63:1-11 (Ch. 38, p. 448)
Ps 65:2-6 (Ch. 28, p. 92)
Ps 68:1-35 (Ch. 36, p. 360)
Ps 69:2-37 (Ch. 33, p. 242)
Ps 72:1-20 (Ch. 40, p. 522)
Ps 78: 5-7, 34-37; 40-47; 48-55; 56-61; 62-69, 72 (Ch. 30, p. 152)
Ps 78:52-72 (Ch. 36, p. 364)
Ps 87:1-7 (Ch. 40, p. 524)
Ps 103:1-22 (Ch. 39, p. 481)
Ps 104:1-35 (Ch. 39, p. 484)
Ps 110:1-7 (Ch. 35, p. 324)
Ps 113:1-9 (Ch. 35, p. 326)
Ps 114:1-8 (Ch. 35, p. 327)
Ps 115:1-18 (Ch. 34, p. 295)
Ps 116:10-19 (Ch 35, p. 325)
Ps 117:1-2 (Ch. 35, p. 328)
Ps 118:1-29 (Ch. 27, p. 49)
Ps 118:19-29 (Ch. 31, p. 176)
Ps 122:1-9 (Ch. 31, p. 177)
Ps 124:1-8 (Ch. 33, p. 242)
Ps 135:8-14 (Ch. 31, p. 175)
Ps 140:2-14 (Ch. 33, p. 241)
Ps 147:12-20 (Ch. 35, p. 327)
The Wisdom of God's Favour as to a Son: Proverbs 3:1-12
    (Ch. 42, p. 555) Cf. Only
Canticle of Isaiah: Isaiah 54:1-10 (Ch. 28, p. 90)
Canticle of Two Blind Men: Matthew 20:29-34 (Ch. 29, p. 123)

Canticle of Paul: Colossians 1:12-20 (Ch. 34, p. 294)
Canticle of John: Revelation 4:11, 5:9-14 (Ch. 34, p. 296)

CONTENTS

Volume Two

27) More Sermons at the River Jordan: The Virtue of Poverty and the Use of Possessions— Renunciation, Simplicity of Life and Reliance on God. 1
    1 — Readings: Luke 12:13-21; Luke 12:22-31, Matthew 6:25-33, Luke 12:32-34, Matthew 6:19-21
    11 — Readings: Luke 13:10-17, 14:1-6; Luke 14:7-24; Luke 14:25-33
    26 — Readings: Luke 15:11-32, Luke 16:1-15; Matthew 6:1-4, Luke 16:19-31
    49 — Prayer Reflection: Psalm 118:1-29

28) Marriage and Celibacy are Permanent Vows: Two Paths for the Contemplation of God's Promises of His Eternal Life and Eternal Love . . . 53
    53 — Readings: Matthew 19:3-12, 13-15, Mark 10:2-12, 13-16, Luke 16:18, 18:15-17; 1 Corinthians 7:1-16, 17, 24, 25-40
    80 — Readings: John 11:1-54
    90 — Prayer Reflection: Isaiah 54:1-10, Psalms 65: 2-6, 22:23-32

29) The Final Journey to Jerusalem: On the Road to the Revolution, and to the Cross and the Glory. 95
    95 — Readings: John 11:55-57; Matthew 19:16-30, Mark 10:17-31, Luke 18:18-30; Matthew 20:1-16
    109 — Readings: Matthew 20:17-19, 20-28, Mark 10:32-34, 35-45, Luke 18:31-34; Luke 18:35-43, Mark 10:46-52, Matthew 20:29-34; Luke 19:1-10, 11-28
    134 — Reflective Prayer: Psalm 2:1-11

30) Saturday Evening, 9th Nisan (1st April, 30 CE): A Resurrection Dinner Party 137

137 — Readings: John 12:1-8, 9-12; Psalms 26:1-12, 18:1-51, 57:1-12

152 — Prayer Reflection: Psalm 78: 5-7, 34-37; 40-47; 48-55; 56-61; 62-69, 72

156 — Concluding Prayer

Part Three
Grand Liturgy of the Lord in God's New and Eternal Creation

---

31) Sunday Afternoon, 9th Nisan (2nd April, 30 CE): Jesus Humbly Enters Jerusalem as King on the Colt of an Ass—He Makes His Way Straight for the Temple, to His Father's House, in Triumph and in Peace 161

161 — Readings: John 12:12-19, Matthew 21:1-11, Luke 19:28-44, Mark 11:1-11

175 — Reflective Prayer: Psalms 135:8-14, 118:19-29, 122:1-9

32) The Next Day, on Monday, 10th Nisan (3rd April, 30 CE), Jesus Works Tirelessly in His Father's House, to God's Great Honour and Glory— But at the Beginning Early in the Morning, Jesus Openly Declares God's War Against the Chief Priests and Religious Authorities by Assaulting the Moneychangers in the Temple, and at the End of the Workday He Leaves— Then, on Tuesday Morning and Afternoon, the 11th Nisan (4th April, 30 CE), He Returns for the Ongoing Revolution 179

179 — Readings: Mark 11:12-14, Matthew 21:18-19; Matthew 21:12-13, Mark 11:15-18, Luke 19:45-46, John 2:13-17; Luke 19:47-48, 21:37-38; John 2:18-22, 23-25, Matthew 21:14-17, Mark 11:19

189 — Readings: Mark 11:20-21, Matthew 21:20-22, Mark

11:22-25; Matthew 21:23-27, Mark 11:27-33, Luke 20:1-8; Matthew 21:28-32; Matthew 21:33-46, Mark 12:1-12, Luke 20:9-19; Matthew 22:1-15

206 — Reflective Prayer: Psalm 31:1-24

33) Wednesday Morning and Afternoon, the 12th Nisan (5th April, 30 CE)—Christ in the Temple among the Pharisees and Scribes, Those Scholar-Hypocrites of the Law, Snakes and Sons of Snakes, and Opponents to the True Devotees of God's Law to Love: Jesus and His Children of the Resurrection. 211

211 — Readings: Luke 20:20-26, 27-40, Matthew 22:15-22, 23-33, Mark 12:13-17, 18-27; Matthew 22:34-40, Mark 12:28-34; Luke 20:41-44, Matthew 22:41-46, Mark 12:35-37

230 — Readings: Luke 20:45-47, 21:1-4, Mark 12:38-40, 41-44; Matthew 23:1-39

241 — Reflective Prayer: Psalms 140:2-14, 124:1-8, 69:2-37

34) Wednesday Evening, the 13th Nisan (5th April, 30 CE)— The Restoration of the Kingdom of God in Christ is Near, as Also Was the Basis for, and the Origin of, the Written Gospel: And Although Everyone's Been Invited, the Jews First, They're Still Not Fully Understanding—Except for the First One from among the Hundreds of Thousands—She Had Been Listening to the Mystery in the Lord's Dialogues and Revelations: Mary of Magdala, the Sister of Martha and Lazarus from Bethany!. .247

247 — Readings: Matthew 24:1-44, Mark 13:1-37, Luke 21:5-36

279 — Readings: Matthew 25:1-46

287 — Readings: Matthew 26:1-16, Mark 14:1-11, Luke 22:1-6

294 — Prayer Reflection: Colossians 1:12-20; Psalm 115:1-18; Revelation 4:11, 5:9-14

35) Thursday, the 13th/14th Nisan (6th April, 30 CE)—Christ in Jerusalem, the Daytime and Evening of His New Creation: The First Day of His Feast of Unleavened Bread, the New Covenant in His Body and Blood 298

    298 — Readings: John 12:20-50; Matthew 26:17-19, Mark 14:12-16, Luke 22:7-13

    308 — Readings: John 13:1-20; Mark 14:17-25, Matthew 26:20-29, Luke 22:14-30, John 13:21-30

    318 — Readings: John 13:31-38, 14:1-31, Mark 14:26, Matthew 26:30, Luke 22:31-39

    324 — Prayer Reflection: Psalms 110:1-7, 116:10-19; Psalms 113:1-9, 147:12-20; Psalms 114:1-8, 117:1-2

36) Friday, the 14th Nisan (7th April, 30 CE), Early in the Dark Morning Long Before Daybreak—Going to His Father, Jesus Now on His Way to the Mount of Olives with His Disciples, and Going to the Ambush There in the Garden 329

    329 — Readings: John 15:1-27, 16:1-33, Mark 14:27-31, Matthew 26:31-35, John 17:1-26, 18:1

    351 — Readings: Matthew 26:36-46, Mark 14:32-42, Luke 22:39-46; Matthew 26:47-56, Mark 14:43-52, Luke 22:47-54, John 18:2-11

    358 — Prayer Reflection: Psalms 59:1-17, 68:1-35, 78:52-72

37) Friday, the 14th Nisan (7th April, 30 CE)—The Long Eve of Darkness and Our Day of Shame: Our Lord's Day of Glory and of God's Retribution: The Conviction, Passion, Death, and Burial of Jesus Christ 368

    368 — Readings: Mark 14:53-54, Matthew 26:57-58, Luke 22:54-55, John 18:12-24; John 18:25-27, Mark 14:66-71, Matthew 26:69-74, Luke 22:56-61, Mark 14:72, Matthew 26:75, Luke 22:62; Luke 22:63-65, Matthew 26:67-68, Mark 14:65; Luke 22:66-71, Mark 14:55-64, Matthew 26:59-66, Luke 23:1, Mark 15:1, John 18:28

    394 — Readings: Matthew 27:1-10; Luke 23:1-7, Mark 15:1-5, Matthew 27:11-14, John 18:28-38; Luke 23:8-12; Luke 23:13-19, John 18:39-40, Mark 15:6-11,

Matthew 27:15-18; Matthew 27:19; Mark 15:11-14, Matthew 27:20-25, Luke 23:20-23; John 19:1, Mark 15:15, Matthew 27:26, Luke 23:16; John 19:2-3, Matthew 27:27-30, Mark 15:16-19; John 19:4-15, Luke 23:24; Mark 15:20, Matthew 27:31; John 19:16, Luke 23:25, Mark 15:15, Matthew 27:26

406 — Readings: John 19:17, Mark 15:21-22, Matthew 27:32-33, Luke 23:26-32; John 19:18, 23-24, 19-22, Mark 15:23-26, Matthew 27:34-37, Luke 23:33-34, 38, 44; Mark 15:29-33, Matthew 27:39-45, Luke 23:35-37, 39-43; John 19:25-27; Mark 15:40-41, Matthew 27:55-56, Luke 23:40; Mark 15:34-37, Matthew 27:46-50, John 19:28-30, Luke 23:46; Luke 23:45, Mark 15:38, Matthew 27:51-52, 53; Mark 15:39, Matthew 27:54, Luke 23:47, 48; John 19:31-37; Mark 15:42-47, Matthew 27:57-61, John 19:38-42, Luke 23:50-56; Matthew 27:62-66

422 — Reflective Prayer: Psalm 22:1-31

38) Easter Sunday, the 16th/17th Nisan (9th April, 30 CE)—After the Friday Preparation Day for Passover and the Sabbath Rest, from Early Easter Morning unto That Late Evening: On the Third Day, We All Are Now Sent into the New Creation of the Lord from Its First Day 427

427 — Readings: John 20:1, Matthew 28:1, Mark 16:1-2, Luke 24:1, Matthew 28:2-4, John 20:2; John 20:3-10; John 20:11a, Mark 16:3-4, Luke 24:2-4, Mark 16:5-7, Matthew 28:5-7, Luke 24:5-8, Mark 16:8, John 20:11b-13; John 20:14-18, Mark 16:9-11, Matthew 28:9-10, 8, Luke 24:9-12; 1 Corinthians 15:5; Matthew 28:11-15; Mark 16:12-13, Luke 24:13-35; Mark 16:14, Luke 24:36-43, John 20:19-25, Acts 10:40-41

446 — Reflective Prayer: Psalms 42-43:1-11, 1-5; 63:1-11; 46:1-11

39) The First Fifty Days in the Lord's New Creation: From Easter Sunday to Pentecost (9th April to 28th May, 30 CE)—Days after the Resurrection of the Lord to the Coming of the Holy Spirit; And Both Resurrection and Pentecost Are Concurrent with Our Baptism into Christ's Death and in the Birth of the Church 452

    452 — Readings: Matthew 27:50-53, Acts 10:40-41, Mark 16:14, 1 Corinthians 15:3-5; John 20:24-31, 21:1-25; Matthew 28:16-20, Mark 16:15-20; 1 Corinthians 15:6-7; Luke 24:44-53, Acts 1:1-14; 1 Corinthians 15:8, Acts 9:1-9, 22:6-21, 26:2-6, 23:6-7, 26:7-18, 19-32; Galatians 3:23-29, Ephesians 4:7-8, 3:1-3, 2:11-22, 3:5-11, Philemon 1-25

    475 — Readings: Acts 1:15-26, 2:1-13; Proverbs 8:1-36, Genesis 1:1-2, Ephesians 3:14-21; 1 Corinthians 12:4-11

    481 — Reflective Prayer: Psalms 103:1-22; 47:1-9; 104:1-35

40) From the Nativity of Our Lord Jesus Christ (Winter Solstice 8 BCE) to the Birth of the Church   (The Spring of 30 CE)—the Christian Family and Christian Ecumenism: the Born, the Unborn, and the Reborn 489

    489 — Readings: Luke 2:1-21, 22-40; Matthew 1:18-25, 2:1-23

    512 — Readings: Acts 2:14-36, 37-47; Acts 10:1-43, 44-48, 11:15-26

    520 — Reflective Prayer: Psalms 2:1-12, 72:1-20, 87:1-7

Part Four
Sin, Faith, and Salvation through Jesus Christ; with Our True Repentance, Mutual Faithfulness, and God's Grace

41) The Gospel (on the Road to) Emmaus: Epilogue Our Personal Journey of Faith with Jesus in Our Time of Grace Cared for by an Intimate and Loving God: Father, Son, and Holy Spirit . . .529
   529 — Readings: Genesis 1:1—3:24; John 1:1-18; Revelation 21:1—22:21
   553 — Final Prayer: the Divine Praises

42) Faith Post-Pentecost: Lead Us Not into Temptation, but Deliver Us from Presumption and Doubt. 555
   555 — Readings: Proverbs 3:1-12, Hebrews 12:1-29, John 7:2-18
   601 — Concluding Prayer

Endnotes: 605

Appendix 631

Synopses of the Forty-two Chapters

Chapter 27

More Sermons at the River Jordan: The Virtue of Poverty and the Use of Possessions—Renunciation, Simplicity of Life and Reliance on God

Readings: Luke 12:13-21; Luke 12:22-31, Matthew 6:25-33, Luke 12:32-34, Matthew 6:19-21

In the course of another day's preaching by Jesus at the other side of the Jordan,[1] a man from the crowd shouted out to him with urgency, "Teacher, tell my brother to share our inheritance with me."[2] And in my general experience of Maltese culture, this often happens to be a bitterly familiar and problematic issue when multiple siblings need somehow to divide even one or several properties in allegedly equal parts of inheritance. So the authoritative reply that Jesus first makes to this man and to his brother, who both were there together in the crowd, should come as no surprise to us, as Jesus raised his voice just a bit and said:

> My friend, who appointed me as your judge or arbitrator
> to divide property between the two of you?[3]

So now you know what some Maltese, on occasion, pray for along with their other sincere petitions, pledges, promises, and bribes

---
[1] John 10:40
[2] Luke 12:13; Luke 15:2
[3] Luke 12:14; Galatians 4:1-7; Luke 15:11-12

to God! But also, Jesus now had called this man his "friend," which was not simply a rhetorical appellation, but a genuine sentiment of the Lord's for this man from the crowd, for the Lord's aspirations for this friend's true vocation. However, what Jesus did say next would be quite startling for everyone, as the Lord intended it to be: even then for the disciples, just as much as it is for us today, and certainly not only in Malta, when unfortunately it seems that there is nothing more divisive than inherited property to be divided among siblings to bring out the quiet ugliness in some families.[4] So, just as the man had called out previously to Jesus from the crowd, Jesus now turned his attention back to the entire crowd, as he shouted out what must have been quite a lightning bolt, if ever there was a thunder jolt:

> Watch out, and guard against any kind of greed; for although a person may be rich beyond his needs, life is not made secure through one's possessions.[5]

Just imagine if Jesus had said this today, as he still does, in tiny Malta, like nearly anywhere else in the affluent world: we plunge into debt to buy or build the ideal house; we claw and fight to obtain the best jobs or income of others; we deprive our children of their freedom and of their childhood as we push them through a make-or-break competitive educational system, as we also preferably put them in private schools if we can. We insist to have that particular new car; the latest mobile-phone or communications technology; or another gold chain, or bracelet, or piece of expensive jewellery. We spend lavishly, oftentimes without a second thought, on our weekly or daily entertainment, or on our dining out. We worry about our financial investments or lack of them; our secure or insecure jobs; our likely or unlikely pensions; and our public or private resources, should any actual or potential need arise for expensive medical care. Yet, more of us, and more and more of our children, are becoming obese from the plentiful food we consume or push upon our children; or from the alcohol we consume, or our children are consuming along with recreational drugs and sex at increasingly tender ages; and each year we grow fatter from the sedentary consumerism we avidly take up,

---

4   Romans 13:12-13
5   Luke 12:15; Matthew 19:24, Mark 10:25, Luke 18:25; Romans 13:11

that pervasively surrounds us daily as normalized globalization and modern living.

Then again in Malta, for example, how many engaged couples are there who would want to start their married life in an unfurnished rented flat? Don't they prefer, instead, to purchase/build their perfect property, with its detached house/villa/farmhouse, and then add in their complete sets of new movable household furniture to the bank mortgage and loans they both have committed their full-time plus part-time jobs to paying off? Or how many Maltese are there who would ever make do without a car, even if they easily can afford one? Isn't the representative case, instead, more likely to be like this one?

> A certain self-employed person living alone bought a new car for business and personal use because someday the old one might not run. However, this person also kept the old car because the new one some day might develop problems. So even with two cars she was insecure! Then, when she could ill-afford the running expenses and insurance for both cars, she decided to give the old car away to someone without a car, allegedly as charity, but certainly for the greater security of debt relief. The charity excuse, however, relieved her from the insecurity of not having two cars!

By the way, this woman also had a sister who worked as much as possible, so to retain her job and income, but her health was badly affected; but then if she had any time away from work, she panicked that others might take her job. Again, much like her sister's two cars, neither activity she required for herself, work and freedom from work, brought her security when either one was present; and in their absence, without work or stressed from overwork, her insecurity increased just the same. Such, sometimes, is the conflicted madness of our insecurities and worries over possessions and wealth.

Then also in Malta there was a popular public personality who once said of herself that she could never allow that she be seen wearing anything else in jeans than the current hip-hugging midriff-baring fashion. Like her or our jeans, our mobile flip-phones, iPhones,

BlackBerries, and notepad computers also have become fashion statements just as much as they are tools of work and communication, in the same way that our CDs, DVDs, and more recent generations of technology for Xbox or Play Station have become mandatory forms of entertainment. It would seem that no one wants to live without all of their possessions, or even without just some small bit of their affluence and technology, let alone even ignoring or forgetting about our most rudimentary items of life: food, clothing, and property. Although Jesus did not oppose the proper use of possessions and wealth,[6] here he most certainly opposed possessions as if they were something intrinsic to our real security; and especially with solicitous regard to our salvation, he opposed any kind of greed:[7] for things, for aspirations, for persons, for self.

Oftentimes, as we may observe, the insecurities of the rich lead them to accumulate ever more riches, and to demand even greater protection for their accumulated wealth and acquired styles of high-living. In 2007, global wealth realized as investment assets under management reached $109.5 trillion (or 76 trillion Euro), with 35% of this global wealth owned by 1% of the world's richest households; yet, also among these 1% are included the exclusive superrich, the top 0.001%, the one in every 100,000 global households, who collectively owned 20% of total global investment assets. On the other hand, one in every five households, the bottom 20% of the world, possessed only 1% of total global wealth. Comparing individual households, the global wealth of the superrich is 400,000 times greater than the wealth of the world's poorest households. Also in 2007, despite the available global assets, approximately $13,000 (or 9,000 Euro) per person, five million children died before reaching their fifth birthday. As for the poor and dispossessed, sometimes even their insecurities may lead them towards the envy or hatred of others; or, for some, their lustful pursuit of money and retribution even may lead them into various criminal behaviours against society. Then, either because of the greed of the poor; or because of their perceived genuine need; or because of the greed of others who take advantage

---

6   Luke 16:9
7   Luke 12:15

of their poverty; the poor may be victimized once again: by becoming targets of ransom by unscrupulous usurers, or from someone's ambitious exploitation of others for quick money around centres of affluence: through gambling addictions, or through prostitution, or through selling drugs or contraband out of desperation.

So, quietly now, with the huge crowd before Jesus, still bewildered by his statement that possessions do not guarantee security,[8] he told them all, and all of us, a clarifying parable. However, for this crowd, Jesus now would introduce them to the startling goal of their detachment not only from the good things they possessed, but also from themselves.[9] And also, he would try to lead them to absolute trust in God: for them to make a committed attachment only to God, to Jesus in his eventual cross,[10] and to what are truly treasures in God's sight:

> Once there was a rich man, and his land produced a super abundant harvest.[11] So he thought to himself, "What shall I do, since I haven't any space to store all these crops?"[12] Then he told himself, "This is what I will do: I'll tear down my barns and build larger ones, and there I'll store my grain and all my goods in them,[13] and I'll say to my soul deep down: Soul, you have many good things stored up for so many years to come; take it easy now, eat, drink, and be merry!"[14] But God said to him, "You fool! This very night your soul will be demanded from you; and as to this hoard you have prepared, to whom will it belong?"[15] So it will be for the one who stores up for himself what is treasure, but not what makes himself rich in the sight of God.[16]

---

8   Luke 12:15; Luke 18:26, 28-30
9   Luke 14:26
10 Luke 14:27
11 Luke 12:16; Luke 12:30, 27-28, 17:5-6
12 Luke 12:17; Luke 12:22-23, 26
13 Luke 12:18; Luke 12:24
14 Luke 12:19, James 5:5; Wisdom 2:6-9, 1-4; Luke 12:29
15 Luke 12:20; Luke 12:25
16 Luke 12:21; Luke 12:34

In the parable Jesus has just told them, he describes a person who is not in any kind of desperate material need, but one who has much more materially than he would ever need. His wealth, in fact, is so great that there is no place to keep it, and if he wishes he can do whatever he wants with it, which for many persons is the very rationale for their power through wealth. But if this person could never use all that he had, then this surplus wealth in itself becomes unjustifiable, except perhaps for our giving it away, which superficially becomes the communist argument against capitalism. But to justify their excessive personal wealth, capitalists and philanthropists both claim that the investments of their private wealth benefit the public welfare.

However, like most hoarders, for capitalists and for the rich man of the parable, what seems to provide their greatest security is not actually using their excess wealth, but simply knowing that it would always be there, if ever and whenever they should feel need of it. Such a person wants not only a life assurance policy against any hardship or suffering, but also the promise for a life of full material comfort, if not absolute luxury.[17] If today the complementary aspects of socialism and capitalism are commonly practiced, and usually simultaneously, by family systems, by social communities, and by nation states, then although a greater moral burden is placed certainly upon the rich,[18] the clear caveat given by the Lord is that there must not be in us greed of any kind.[19]

So logically, the only relevance of wealth for this person in the parable, and perhaps also for the capitalist of today, was to support his irrational belief that he controlled life, as if it were the welfare of his soul but not its true destiny, by retaining possessions far beyond even any personal need, which certainly is madness before the absolute God.[20] Therefore, this person's only felt need was the presumption of the power of his possessions, even against any of

---

17	Luke 14:27, 33
18	Luke 18: 18, 22-27
19	Luke 12:15
20	Psalm 62:10-11

God's sure demands.[21] But in the end, he would be wanting for what God had expected of him, because all that remains to anyone after death is their soul, which belongs only to God, and also left behind is the record of their good or bad works. And for everyone after death, even one's possessions no longer are one's own, but they become the spoils of inheritance, or their wealth is transferred to the state.

For anyone, in fact, the only riches of significance are from God, one's riches for eternal life. So what ultimate riches did this man's wealth accumulate for his soul? There seemed to be none, unfortunately. But here, Jesus leaves each one of us alone to take stock of ourselves, for each one of us to zero in to ask of ourselves that "million-dollar" question, "What riches have we stored up by our lives for the glory of God, and ultimately for the welfare of our souls, or for the good of the souls of others?"[22]

The Lord, however, did not immediately continue with his expansion of this parable for the crowds at hand,[23] because many of them had not yet understood and some would never understand;[24] and, as the Lord does for everyone who receives his mercy, he also was insisting upon central matters for Christian life: our careful reflection, our necessary prayer, our humble repentance, and, as in this case, a very large change for most of us in our attitudes and lifestyles. The irony would be that while Jesus may have declined to arbitrate the division of property between the two brothers,[25] quite consistently Jesus would go on to advocate, at first privately for his disciples, and later quite publicly, that they separate themselves completely from all of their possessions.[26] Thus it was, after Saint Augustine had clothed himself in the Lord by baptism,[27] that he organized religious life into common communities of monastic rule for men and women, separately; and, accordingly, Augustine concluded in his Confessions, to paraphrase King David's psalm, "O

---

21   Matthew 25:35-36, John 15:17, 1 John 4:17-21; Psalm 62:12-13
22   Luke 12:21, 33; Psalm 62:8
23   Luke 12:16, Matthew 13:34-35, Luke 12:22
24   Matthew 13:13, Mark 4:11-12, Luke 8:10
25   Luke 12:14
26   Luke 12:33; Luke 14:33, 25-27
27   Romans 13:14, Galatians 3:27; Matthew 6:28

Lord, you made us for yourself; and our hearts are not at rest until they rest in thee."[28] Indeed, this affirmation of Augustine proves that there is no solace in possessions. And put most simply in paraphrase, all of us otherwise are just miserable souls, in need of one thing only: namely, the possession of Christ through God's graces.[29] So, in fact, this very morning, from a bit of "God's Wisdom," a friend has told me, "Who except God can give you peace? Has the world ever been able to satisfy the heart?"

It was on the same day of this parable of the "rich fool,"[30] when Jesus could take time to be alone with the disciples away from the crowd, that Jesus expanded upon and sharpened the issues from his parable. So then, Jesus now spoke to them with particular care and affection because, as they were his true disciples, he also made them truly his friends:[31]

> That is why I am telling you [**command**] don't worry about your life and what you will eat, or about your body and what you will wear,[32] for surely [**explanation & instruction**] the soul is more than food, and the body more than clothing![33] Notice the ravens [**explanation & illustration**]: they neither plant seeds nor gather in a harvest; they have neither storehouses nor barns, yet [**instruction**] God feeds them; and you are worth much more than birds![34] [**Exhortation**]: Can any of you, by worrying about it, lengthen your life-span by a single moment [**instruction**]?[35] Therefore [**conclusion & instruction**], if even the smallest things of life are beyond your control, why do you worry about the rest?[36]

---

28 Luke 12:34; Psalm 62:2-3, 6-7; 2 Corinthians 5:1-5
29 Psalm 62:12-13
30 Luke 12:16-21
31 John 15:14, 8
32 Luke 12:22, Matthew 6:25; John 3:6; John 15:20, 16:2
33 Luke 12:23, Matthew 6:25; John 8:23; Ephesians 5:30, 1 Corinthians 15:53-57
34 Luke 12:24, Matthew 6:26; Luke 12:7; Psalm 104:10-18, Luke 13:15
35 Luke 12:25, Matthew 6:27; Psalms 90:4c-6, 102:12
36 Luke 12:26; Luke 10:41-42

[**Exhortation**]: And why be anxious about clothes?[37] Notice [**illustration**] how the wild flowers grow: they never toil to make clothes by weaving or spinning; but I tell you, not even Solomon in all the splendour of his riches was as finely robed as one of these.[38] Now [**explanation**] if that is how God clothes the wild grass—that [**illustration & instruction**] today blooms but is thrown into the furnace tomorrow—will he not [**conclusion**] provide much more for you [**encouragement**]?[39] [**Exhortation**]: O how little faith you have![40]

As for you as my disciples, [**command**] you must not be preoccupied about eating or drinking, or about what to wear; don't worry [**exhortation**] about these things.[41] All the nations of the world seek them [**recognition & empathy**], and your Father knows [**recognition**] well that you need them [**empathy & encouragement**].[42] Instead [**command**], set your hearts on his kingdom and his righteousness, and [**encouragement**] he will provide you these other things as well.[43] So [**conclusion**], don't worry about tomorrow [**command & exhortation**]: tomorrow will take care of itself [**explanation**],[44] and [**empathy & instruction**] each day has trouble enough of its own.[45]

There is no need [**exhortation**], little flock [**encouragement**],[46] for you to be afraid any longer, for

---

37 Matthew 6:28
38 Luke 12:27, Matthew 6:28-29; 1 Kings 10:4-5, 23, 25
39 Luke 12:28, Matthew 6:30; Matthew 6:34; Psalms 102:4-6, 103:15-18, Isaiah 40:6-10; Isaiah 17:11, 30:33, 31:9, 10:17-22; 2 Corinthians 9:8-9, Psalm 112:1, 9
40 Luke 12:28, Matthew 6:30; Luke 17:5-6, Matthew 17:20, Mark 11:23-24
41 Luke 12:29, Matthew 6:31; Luke 22:35, 10:3-4, 21:8-12, 16-19
42 Luke 12:30, Matthew 6:32; Psalm 112:10
43 Luke 12:31, Matthew 6:33; Psalm 103:19-22, Luke 12:19-21
44 Matthew 6:34; Wisdom 2:23
45 Matthew 6:34; Job 14:1-2, Wisdom 2:5, 24-3:1; Ephesians 5:16; 1 John 5:19
46 Psalm 23:1, Isaiah 40:11

[**explanation & encouragement**] your Father is pleased to give you the kingdom.[47] [**Command**]: Sell your possessions and give away all the proceeds as alms to the poor.[48] [**Exhortation**]: Do not store up treasures for yourselves on earth, where [**illustrations & instruction**] moth and decay destroy them,[49] and thieves can break in and steal.[50] [**Explanation & exhortation**]: Obtain money bags for yourselves that do not wear out, a treasure in heaven that never finishes, where no thief can reach to steal it, nor moth destroy it [**illustrations & instruction**].[51] For [**conclusion & instruction**] where your treasure is, there also your heart will be.[52]

Jesus sets out for us fundamental principles for Christian living by giving sets of commands, instructions, exhortations and explanations, combined with his empathy, encouragement, vivid illustrations, and forceful conclusions. He commands us not to worry about life, or about food or clothes; to set our hearts on God's kingdom and his righteousness; and to sell all of our possessions, and to give away the proceeds to the poor. He carefully explains that our souls are more important than our mortal flesh; that God will provide for us what he knows we need, not only food and clothes, but mainly, primarily and of sole importance, God gives us his kingdom in heaven. And then by his exhortations, Jesus also encourages everyone not to worry; to have faith; and to rely on God's providence to deal with our inevitable troubles derived from human needs and spiritual evils.

The Father's recognition and the empathy of Jesus are platforms for the illustrations and metaphors that Jesus uses. He draws the

---

47   Luke 12:32; John 6:44, Hebrews 6:17-20
48   Luke 12:33, 18:22; Acts 2:44-45, 3:32, 34-35; Luke 12:42-44; 1 John 5:12, 3:16. 4:21
49   Matthew 6:19; Job 14:13, 28
50   Matthew 6:19; Matthew 24:42-44, 25:13; 1 John 2:15-16
51   Luke 12:33, Matthew 6:20; John 14:23, 1-3; 2 Corinthians 4:18, 1 John 2:17
52   Luke 12:34, Matthew 6:21; Sirach 15:17, Deuteronomy 30:15-20; Psalm 62:9, Philippians 3:10; 1 Kings 10:24, 2 Chronicles 1:10, Wisdom 1:3-6; 2 Chronicles 6:34-42, 7:1, Isaiah 31:9, 30:33, 10:17, Luke 12:49

listener to common observations in the natural and human world; but masterfully he also includes the hopeful promises of God, made to us throughout the scriptures; and Jesus also refers to his previous words and teachings. Finally, the Lord's conclusions are very practical and basic rules of thumb. If God is in control, then we shouldn't be preoccupied with trying to be in control: instead, trust in God. Because we are ever so much more important to God than birds and wild flowers, which also are cared for by God, so certainly he will provide for us. It is the present moment that God gives to each of us for the focus of our human activity; so what tomorrow will be also is in God's hands, which is where we should leave it. And foremost of all his conclusions, Jesus finally presents us with a challenge: Since God alone is the real treasure of our hearts and souls, while all earthly possessions are only phantom treasures, which of the two then do we choose? Like sin or grace,[53] it's ultimately an all or none proposition for us: earthly possessions, or God.

Readings: Luke 13:10-17, 14:1-6; Luke 14:7-24; Luke 14:25-33

During this time the Lord generally stayed with his flock on the far side of the Jordan,[54] but Jesus did not simply stay put. The crowds came to him for six days of the week, but the last day of the week was the Sabbath of the Lord.[55] On that holy day, kept entirely for the Lord because the Lord makes us holy,[56] people would go to synagogue,[57] and they would stay in their homes.[58] However, the Son of Man had nowhere to lay his head;[59] for not even a nanosecond was to be lost for his gaining for us our salvation. On one of these Sabbath excursions, when Jesus was teaching in a local synagogue,[60] they were crushed into a standing-room-only crowd, where there was a crumpled and crippled woman; and as noted by Saint Luke,

---

53   1 John 5:16-18
54   John 10:11, 40
55   Exodus 20:10-11, 23:12, Luke 13:15
56   Deuteronomy 5:15, Exodus 31:13
57   Leviticus 23:3
58   Exodus 35:2-3
59   Luke 9:58, Matthew 8:20; Isaiah 41:3-4
60   Luke 13:10

the physician turned evangelist: she had been deformed so badly by the spirit of Satan for eighteen years that she was entirely unable to stand erect.[61] In many ways, however, we are entirely like her, just as Christ also would become like her for every man:[62] if we are not now physically deformed like her through the power of sin, then we may be injured or deformed still by many torturous years of chronic spiritual turmoil and suffering.

This woman, perhaps, would have remained hidden to everyone if only she had been quietly crumpled on some back bench on the women's side of the synagogue. But, as was more likely, she had been standing because of the overflowing crowds hoping to see and hear Jesus; so it would have been difficult for anyone not to stare at the sight of this woman's miserable physical condition; perhaps it was some grave scoliosis or from polio. Also like so many others who had come,[63] she must have been praying for Jesus to touch her. But as soon as Jesus saw her, and to emphasize for everyone the urgency of their condition of sin, without any delay in mercy, and in the perfection God had intended for us by the Sabbath,[64] he called her over to himself,[65] no doubt to her surprise, and said:

Woman, you are relieved of your infirmity.[66]

In this same moment, Jesus firmly and reassuringly laid his hands upon her, and she stood up straight at once; and after another dumbfounded instant of eternal joy, she shouted out her praises of glory to God.[67] There was no recompense she could make to God, however great her praises, except that by this grace,[68] she could repay the Lord in due course, at the resurrection of the righteous.[69]

---

61 Luke 13:11
62 Isaiah 52:14
63 Luke 13:14
64 Ezekiel 20:12, Exodus 20:11, Genesis 2:2-3, Romans 8:19-21, Revelation 21:5-7, 1-2
65 Isaiah 43:1; Luke 14:13, 16-21
66 Luke 13:12
67 Luke 13:13
68 Luke 19:13, Matthew 25:14
69 Luke 14:14

It is only the Spirit of God that allows someone to recognize God's glory,[70] but that day the Spirit of God was not in the official in charge of the synagogue, at least, not yet. At once, he spoke out to the assembly in fierce indignation against the Lord's healing on the Sabbath.[71] His immediate bias was inclined towards a strict interpretation of the Law, which ignored the essence of the Sabbath: for in fact, the first Sabbath after creation was the most eminent symbol of the eschatological perfection and fulfilment that would be brought about by God in the end times. For the synagogue official, the seeming contradictions at this moment posed by God's rule-breaking, particularly by his generosity to this sinful crippled woman on the Sabbath, shattered his orderly illusions of self-righteousness according to strict observance of the Law, and this event now challenged his neatly-cornered and rigidly-structured concept of God's immutable laws; and, not incidentally, this public work of Jesus threatened to undermine his own established post of leadership and authority—a possession of power he held by not recognizing Jesus, and that he was not about to relinquish to the Lord.[72]

So this official, with the quick public justice of a football referee, called a foul against the manifestation of God's perfection and mercy through his Son, and he said to the crowd, "There are six days when work is suppose to be done; so come on those days to be cured, but not on the Sabbath."[73] And in this crowd, there were many enemies of God who also vehemently agreed with this obstinately unbelieving leader of the synagogue. But Jesus sought to heal on the Sabbath precisely because of God's loving intention: whatever helps humanity, individually or as a whole, become more whole and perfect is a participation in that perfection and fulfilment of creation to come.[74] And no one ever achieves God's redemption and mercy,[75] except in faith through Christ—not by church rank or by abiding God's rules, as if the kingdom of God ever were obtained

---

70 John 10:26, 37-38
71 Luke 13:14
72 Luke 14:31-33
73 Luke 13:14
74 Romans 8:21
75 Romans 4:4-5

through the privileges or attributes we possess, as if we were taking some kind of civil-service qualification or school examination! Nonetheless, everyone also would have their personal judgment to endure,[76] as well as their passage to righteousness via suffering the cross.[77] For God, the healing of this crippled woman was never a question of simple fairness, but of mercy and of fidelity to God's plan for creation: therefore, the Sabbath, in fact, was the perfect day for God's healing, for making whole any part of imperfect humanity, just as someday from the "new creation" now for this woman, except for those who refused it, the whole of humanity would be made perfect and perfectly whole in the end-time.[78]

So the Lord answered this synagogue official and all of his linesman co-objectors by saying:

> You hypocrites! Is there anyone of you who does not untie his ox or ass from the manger on the Sabbath and lead it out to drink?[79] And this woman, a daughter of Abraham,[80] whom Satan has bound now for eighteen years—was it not right to liberate her from her bondage on the Sabbath?[81]

After eighteen years, the crippled woman, indeed, might have waited another day, but for this perfect day, the Sabbath, there was not another day to wait. And after Jesus had said this, all of his adversaries were utterly humiliated in a riot of confusion;[82] but the people[83] [of God] rejoiced at the wonderful works of Jesus.[84]

Then on another Sabbath day, Jesus went to eat at the home of

---

76 Matthew 25:37-40
77 Matthew 27:32, Luke 23:26-27, 9:23
78 2 Peter 3:13, Romans 8:19
79 Luke 13:15; Luke 2:7, Matthew 1:23; Isaiah 56:9-11
80 John 8:33-34; Isaiah 41:8, 44:2-3
81 Isaiah 50:8, John 8:35-36, Luke 23:53-54; Exodus 13:21-22, 6:7-8, Leviticus 26:12, Genesis 15:1-17, 22:17, 24:60, 35:10-11, Isaiah 9:1-3, Matthew 4:16, Luke 1:79, 2:32, Acts 22:6-11; Isaiah 50:11
82 Luke 13:17; Exodus 14: 23-28
83 Romans 9:22-24
84 Luke 13:17; Exodus 14:29-31; Acts 2:22-24, 18-21, Matthew 1:23

one of the leading Pharisees, and there the people were observing Jesus very carefully, in order to catch him out.[85] However, because of their hostility Jesus had come there specifically to take his case directly to the hearts of his enemies. And at this dinner, directly in front of Jesus at table, there was a man suffering from edema,[86] which was an abnormal swelling of the body or limbs due to an accumulation of serous fluid. At one point, as the scholars of the Law and the Pharisees were discoursing with Jesus and trying to catch him out, Jesus replied to them point-blank:

> Is it, or is it not lawful to cure on the Sabbath?[87]

But not wishing to be cornered, they all kept silent.[88] So Jesus broke the silence by taking hold of the suffering man; and without a moment's hesitation, he healed him; and then Jesus dismissed him from their presence.[89]

However, they all still maintained a deadly silence. But as Jesus also had captured everyone's attention, returning to his previously familiar argument, he forcefully asked them:

> If your son or ox falls into a well, who among you would not immediately pull him out on the Sabbath day?[90]

But they were not willing to surrender their battle against God on his conditions, nor were they willing to concede any of their objections against his terms for peace.[91] Instead, they very stubbornly clung to their war,[92] so they were entirely unable to answer his question.[93]

Then, but only for just a moment, Jesus skipped over his dinner host for this party; and instead, he next focused on the host's invited guests. Noticing how they had picked places of honour at the table,

---

85 Luke 14:1; Matthew 22:15
86 Luke 14:2
87 Luke 14:3
88 Luke 14:4
89 Luke 14:4
90 Luke 14:5; Luke 13:15, Matthew 12:11; Isaiah 50:2
91 Luke 14:31-32
92 Luke 14:24; Acts 4:11, Romans 9:33, Isaiah 28:16
93 Luke 14:6

Jesus told them the following parable:[94]

> When someone invites you to a wedding banquet, do not assume to take the place of honour at table, for someone more distinguished than you may have been invited.[95] The host, who invited both of you, may come to you and say, "Give up your place to this man," and to your embarrassment you would have to take the lowest place.[96] No, instead: when you are invited, go and take the lowest place, so that when your host comes to you, he may say, "My friend, move up to a better place," and then you will enjoy honour with your companions at the table.[97] For everyone who exalts himself will be made humble; and everyone who humbles himself will be made great.[98]

And now, without a break in his thought, Jesus turned back to his host, who had invited him, and said to him in public, and with fraternal admonishment:

> When you give a lunch or a dinner, do not invite your friends, or your brothers, or your relatives, or your wealthy neighbours, just so they may invite you back and in this way you will be repaid for your courtesy.[99] No, instead: when you give a banquet or celebration, invite the poor, and the crippled, and the lame, and the blind.[100] Indeed, you will be fortunate when they cannot pay you back because repayment will be made to you when the virtuous rise from the dead.[101]

When one of the guests heard this (and also thought himself justified), he said to Jesus, "Blessed is the one (including himself) to dine in the kingdom of God." Like ourselves, this guest correctly

---

94	Luke 14:7; Matthew 23:6, Mark 12:39
95	Luke 14:8
96	Luke 14:9
97	Luke 14:10
98	Luke 14:11; Matthew 23:11-12; John 13:12-15, Luke 9:48, 22:26-27
99	Luke 14:12
100	Luke 14:13; Luke 14:21-22
101	Luke 14:14; Revelation 21:7

understood the Lord's analogy of the kingdom of God compared to a great banquet; unfortunately, his understanding of the entry requirements to the banquet was less sufficient,[102] and likewise, perhaps we lack some understanding, too. So, now for everyone, Jesus then presented some clarifying caveats, but in the form of a supplementary parable:

> There was a man who gave a great feast, and he had invited many people.[103] When it was time for the feast, he sent his servant to announce to those invited, "Come, everything is ready now."[104] But everyone excused themselves, one right after the other.[105] The first one said, "I bought a field, and I must go to check it out; so I'm sorry, but really I must decline."[106] Another one said, "I have purchased five yoke of oxen and just now I am going to try them out; so please consider me excused."[107] And another said, "I have just taken a wife, and therefore, I'm sure you understand why I cannot come."[108] The servant returned and reported all of this to his master.[109]
>
> Then the master of the house flew into a rage and he commanded his servant, "Hurry and go into the streets and alleys of the town,[110] and bring back in here the poor and the crippled, and the lame and the blind."[111] The servant reported, "Sir, your orders have been carried out, but there is still room for more."[112] So the master told his servant, "Go to the open roads and country

---

102 Luke 7:28
103 Luke 14:16; Matthew 22:2, Revelation 19:7-9, 21:14
104 Luke 14:17; Luke 4:18-19, 21, Matthew 4:23, Mark 1:38, Luke 9:35; Revelation 22:12, Matthew 25:34
105 Luke 14:18
106 Luke 14:18
107 Luke 14:19
108 Luke 14:20
109 Luke 14:21
110 Isaiah 60:14
111 Luke 14:21; 1 Corinthians 1:28
112 Luke 14:22

lanes and force people to come in, so that my home will be full.[113] For, I tell you, none of those who were invited will taste my banquet."[114]

Although everyone is invited to the great banquet in God's kingdom for the wedding of the Bride and the Lamb,[115] for this celebrated union of the saints consummated with their God, the places of honour have been designated already: they are intended, first of all, for the chosen people of Israel,[116] out of the special favour of God's covenant with his people.[117] This is not an injustice, but simply the favour of God's mercy to whomever he chooses.[118] However, none of the Jews were to presume their privilege to take those honoured seats; nor was anyone else for that matter to be so presumptuous for their place in God's kingdom. The host for this glorious celebration, our Father in heaven, also has invited guests of lesser distinction—not only those other Jews despised by their fellow Jews: the dispossessed, the crippled, the lame, and the blind;[119] but also all of the Gentiles. In fact, the places of honour at the feast would be taken forcibly from the city of Israel; and they would be given only to a surviving remnant,[120] and also then to the Gentiles of the countryside,[121] made righteous through their faith in Jesus.[122]

Therefore, for some of these chosen people, especially for those of greater social prestige,[123] they would have been quite shocked to find their places of honour taken away from them, and placed at the bottom of the kingdom at the great feast in heaven, if they were fortunate. Or perhaps even more to their amazement, if the truth were repressed but not unknown to their soul,[124] they could be abysmally

---

113	Luke 14:23
114	Luke 14:24; Genesis 3:15, 23-24, Revelation 2:7, 22:14
115	Ephesians 5:22-27, Revelation 21:2
116	Romans 9:6-8
117	Romans 9:4-5
118	Romans 9:14-16, 18
119	Luke 14:13
120	Romans 10:21, 11:5
121	Luke 20:16-18, Romans 11:11-12; Luke 16:31, Ephesians 1:19-20
122	Romans 4:25
123	Luke 14:7; Matthew 23:6, Mark 12:39, Luke 11:43
124	1 John 3:19-21, 2:22-23,28, 1:8-10

worse off: if their rightful place, in fact, were the highest place in Hades; then they would not even taste the banquet, nor even have the lowest seat in the house, let alone take their presumed places of honour.[125] But unless we strive for perfect holiness,[126] we too, in fact, may risk this worst of all possible fates. Although any place in God's kingdom is an honourable place, for anyone to be really great, and not simply be least in the kingdom of God and just barely be there by the skin of their teeth, they must seek the very lowest place among men; and they must live neither for honours nor for glories. Instead, we must place ourselves wholly and humbly in God's service to our companions and fellow travellers through life, especially to the poor, the crippled, and the lame, all those who could never hope to repay us,[127] except through their persistence, and our perseverance, as once we also were like them, together unto our mutual hope to live forever with the Lord in the communion of saints.

Some humble persons, by their most exemplary lives of holiness, are recognized by the whole church by their honourable placement in the church's official canon of the saints, the bridal registry of the Lamb of God: for example, such persons as Mother Teresa of Calcutta,[128] whose work focused mainly on the poorest of the poor and on the dying. Oftentimes, the Lord himself chooses to elevate even the most obscure of humble servants among us to great renown according to his purposes for the honour and glory of God.[129] For indeed, after the master would fill the house from the streets and

---

125   Romans 2:4-8, 9:6; Luke 14:24, 9
126   1 Peter 2:4-10
127   Luke 14:13-14
128   Born in Skopje, present-day Macedonia, on 26th August 1910, from a family [Bojaxhiu] of Albanian descent, she was baptized "Gonxha Agnes" the following day. Living at the crossroads of the Balkans, south of Kosovo and north of Greece, as a young child this territory was controlled by Serbia and Bulgaria until it became part of the former confederation of Yugoslavia. She first arrived to Calcutta on 6th January 1929, eventually becoming an Indian citizen. When she died on 5th September 1997, her Missionaries of Charity sisters numbered over 4,000; and her Society had established 610 foundations in 123 countries.
129   Romans 9:17

alleys of the town,[130] there still would be room for many others from the highways and the byways,[131] so that God's house eventually would be as entirely full as he designed it to be from the onset of creation.[132] But unfortunately, there would be no more room, not even one vacant space, for any of the others who were left outside and far away.[133]

After the Sabbath had passed, the very next morning, the Lord hit the road on foot, and with his usual bare provisions.[134] But behind him, there were large crowds of people who followed along,[135] as Jesus now led the way: once again going back to the far side of the Jordan,[136] while indirectly taking his meandering and resolute journey towards his final destination in Jerusalem.[137] However, the crowds accompanying him were travelling with their families and friends, and it seems they went on the journey with all of their provisions for every possible contingency—perhaps, if not enough to supply a customary daytrip to the beach by Maltese villagers after their weeklong celebration of their yearly festival, then surely, it seemed, enough to provide for even the surplus needs of an army on the march. With great annoyance, the Lord recognized this as they walked together, as his thoughts raced ahead to the cross, and as from behind him their noise pounded in his head. If any of these people were going to follow in his true footsteps as disciples, just to start this task, let alone to finish this project, they would need to begin first by jettisoning their possessions.

Suddenly Jesus turned around to the crowd behind him on the road, and he squarely faced their brazen self-reliance in possessions,[138] used in place of God to assuage their insecurities and uncertainties

---

130 Luke 14:21
131 Luke 14:22-23
132 Isaiah 55:11
133 Romans 2:9-11; Luke 16:26
134 Luke 9:3; Luke 14:33, 12:29-31
135 Luke 14:25
136 John 10:40
137 Luke 9:51; Luke 18:31-33
138 Luke 14:25

in life.[139] Bluntly and firmly, Jesus addressed their many claims to various possessions with these words:

> If any man comes to me, he cannot be my disciple without hating [loving me more than[140]] his father and mother, his wife and children, his brothers and sisters, and yes, even his own life.[141] Whoever does not carry his own cross and come after me cannot be my disciple.[142]
>
> Is there any one of you, if he intends to build a tower, who does not first sit down and figure out what it will cost to see if he would have enough money to complete it?[143] Otherwise, if he lays the foundation and then finds himself unable to finish the work, everyone who sees what happened would laugh at him and put him to shame,[144] and they would say, "This man began to build, but he did not have enough resources to finish."[145]
>
> Or again, what king marching to war would not first sit down and decide whether with ten thousand troops he could stand up against another king steadily advancing upon him with twenty thousand troops?[146] If not,[147] then while the other king still remained a long way off,[148] he would send envoys to sue according to the terms of peace.[149] In the same way, none of you, unless he renounces all of his possessions, can be my disciple.[150]

We may understand that when we die we have no choice except

---

139 Psalm 49:1-7
140 Matthew 10:37
141 Luke 14:26; Matthew 10:39; Psalm 34:13, 23
142 Luke 14:27; Luke 9:23, Matthew 16:24, Mark 8:34; Luke 18:24, 23:26; John 21:18, 21-22; 1 Corinthians 1:18, 27-28; Psalm 56:14
143 Luke 14:28; Psalm 48:13-14
144 Luke 14:29; Psalm 34:6
145 Luke 14:30; Psalms 49:8-9, 90:17
146 Luke 14:31; Psalms 68:22, 27:3
147 Psalms 20:7-8, 74:12
148 Psalm 20:9-10
149 Luke 14:32; Psalms 34:5, 91:5-9
150 Luke 14:33; Psalms 34:11, 49:13-21

to give up all our possessions, and then perhaps with even some or great regret, or even with fierce reluctance. But it may be even more traumatic to consider that, in fact, we must give up all of our possessions even while very much alive, with whatever life is ahead of us now, and not just when we die; or, if possible, it even would be best to do this from the beginning of our lives.[151] There is no ambiguity whatsoever, nor flexibility, about these declarations coming from Jesus, if we harbour any hope of being the Lord's disciple. If we are going to build that tower or find peace against the Lord's advancing armies, then we need spiritual resources,[152] not the strength of our possessions: instead, we must give up all our possessions and suffer the cross. As obviously reflected in the psalms, the Lord is the warrior King, Son of David; and Saint Matthew only slightly tones down the harsher narration provided here by Saint Luke. But the stark reality of God's truth, like a boxer's punch to the gut, comes to us not simply from the opinion of Luke the evangelist, nor from just the human reflections of King David, but from the forcefully clear wisdom of the Lord.[153]

This, however, completely turns on its head our usual aspirations: instead of our preoccupations with wealth and our natural attachments to persons, we are called to the virtue and practice of poverty—not for the purpose of some kind of transcendental mysticism, but out of our total allegiance and devotion to God, to love nothing more than God himself, and especially not less than ourselves. And if we love God, then also we must love our brother and sister in need.[154] But we don't love them—we love ourselves more—if we only love them from our surplus; but rather, we love God most perfectly when we love someone from the whole of our worldly means, and not by waiting first until we're dead to disperse our legacy, while clinging meanwhile to our fortunes. We may most readily do this for our wife or husband, for our children, and for our close relatives; but what about our loving Christ above all, for example by beginning with the world's most hungry and the poorest of the poor, nearly one-

---

151 Matthew 5:3
152 Matthew 25:1-4
153 Matthew 22:41-44
154 Luke 10:29-37; 1 John 4:20-21, 3:17-18

third of humanity?[155] Strangely, it's often easier than we think: the very instant I finished writing out this question, the Daughters of the Sacred Heart phoned me at home to purchase common household consumables for their mission campaign. So now I have a half-year supply of toilet paper and laundry detergents; and children orphaned from AIDS in Kenya, India, and Korea have some little additional help from me! We never know from day to day, or from week to week, what opportunities are provided for us to provide such help. On another day like many others of its type, now this morning as I am writing this in the afternoon, I responded to a small request for financial help from two religious sisters on Republic Street, Valletta, the main pedestrian boulevard of Malta's Capital, so that they could provide for the care of the elderly at a community residence they staffed. Such opportunities present themselves continuously: we only have to respond.

And sometimes, much closer to home, there was a man who lived for twenty traumatic years in an abusive marriage. Those years included the initially shocking insight and panic, after ten years into the troubled marriage, that there was a monstrous problem. The next ten years included in various combinations: genuine efforts at conflict resolution through every form of intervention; very deep anger and periodic "madness" in the affliction; and in the later and final years a combination of professional counselling and disciplined psychotherapy. He had hoped to love his wife, and had totally loved his four sons, then running in age from twelve to eighteen, when, in the end, he left his ex-wife, his children, his family life and home with all of its possessions in America, and he left them all to his ex-wife and children. Then, with paternal leadership, he shouldered all of his legal and moral obligations to support his family; and from his homelessness he also paid the staggering child support, out of what would be his future earnings for the remainder of his ordinary working life; and he also paid off accumulated debts which was only made possible in part by significant gifts from his father.

Then, after a civil divorce, this man humbly and graciously also obtained a church annulment. At the same time, he also had

---

155   Matthew 25:34-36

relinquished even his native country and culture to take up new blessings from the Lord: a temporary full-time job in his academic profession in Malta for four years; and, in particular, a new Maltese wife and her home and family. He assisted her for ten years through her only son's drug addiction, and through her son's marriage and the ultimately tragic motorcycle accident that ended her son's life just five weeks after her son's only child, her granddaughter, had been born to her son and his foreign wife.

This man also took up full-time household management: laundry, dishes, and shopping; and management of his wife's part-time supplementary business. He provided support for his wife's full-time job; he encouraged her in her work and retirement, through her diabetes and heart-bypass surgery, in her family relationships with her only maiden-sister, and in the care of her father (his father-in-law) until he died at nearly a hundred-years of age; and he took on occasional part-time economic activities. Apart from an entire life-time of previous blessings, the greatest blessing of all, so far, has been the opportunity given to me from the Lord to write this book. But, in order for me to do this, first of all, I had to give up all of my possessions. Eventually, I also would have to give up all my anger and resentments towards my previous wife, but not until within his healing gifts I also had praised the Lord's blessings to me. Even so, ultimately I have learned that anyone's firm repentance, particularly my own, is only our total commitment to the continual process of our becoming a "New Creation" in Christ,[156] whereby the only possession we must cling to is our embrace of the cross that we share with the person of Christ, who with the Father provides us with everything we need.[157]

Also, in God's providence and love for us, there is now another blessing and instruction from the Lord both for me,[158] and for you.[159] On 13 July 2010, after my having "finished" writing this book and

---

[156] Romans 12:1-2, 5; Colossians 3:2-4, 1:15-18
[157] Luke 14:27, 33; Colossians 1:19-20, John 17:24-26, Colossians 1:11-14, 3:9-10
[158] Luke 14:8-9
[159] Matthew 19:21, John 15:13-17

as I was revisiting this point of the text in its preparations prior to the manuscript's submission for publication, from a newspaper interview I first learned of a new religious community living in Sicily practically on my Maltese doorstep.[160] Brother Antonio, Sister Letizia, and Sister Effatah, were hitch-hiking through Malta travelling without money. All of us have been called towards our respective seats in the celebrated "party that doesn't end,"[161] but these three souls and their community, the Little Brothers and Sisters (v.v.) of Jesus and Mary, known as Poor Friars or Poor Nuns (without money), have been far more virtuous than I in their poverty and in their obedience to the will of God. As a manifestly contradictory "sign" for us in the world,[162] their poverty is the measure of their faith.[163] Founded by Brother Voluntino Verde (v.v.), the consecrated "voluntini" are dedicated to a radical witness of the Gospel by their practice of absolute poverty (not touching money); and for whatever they need, they trust solely upon God's everyday providence, as they embrace God's will above all possessions. Even their very lives they have given back to God.

An Australian of Maltese descent, Brother Antonio Maria Speedy, formerly Michael Farrugia, originally encountered the community in Catania as they were asking for alms; although he had lost his faith in school, university, work, alcohol, and drugs, eventually he found the will of God in the Poor Friars.[164] The Sicilian Sister Letizia Maria Vera exchanged her worldly wealth (her diplomas, her job, her friends, her parish commitments, her car, her capital worth of more than 100,000 euro) for the kingdom of heaven: seeking first the will of her Father in heaven and also embracing poverty.[165] German born Sister "Effatah" Maria Teresa took her religious name from the gospel of Mark, "Be opened."[166] Originally a Protestant Evangelical,

---

160 www.timesofmalta.com/articles/view/20100713/local/hitch-hiking-to-heaven
161 Luke 14:16
162 Luke 9:23-24, 12:15, 14:33; 1 Corinthians 1:25, 2:4-16
163 Luke 9:3, Luke 12:29-31, Matthew 6:31-34
164 2 Corinthians 8:4-5, 9-11
165 Matthew 7:21, 19:21
166 Mark 7:34-35

she went on the Camino de Santiago pilgrimage in Spain and frequently encountered the passage from Matthew's gospel where the Lord instructs the disciples to travel light;[167] and she felt guilty about carrying her heavy backpack. There, in December 2002, she encountered the Poor Friars, who had travelled to Spain from Sicily carrying no money and no food. Back in Germany, she lost her inner peace completely; leaving her planned studies and her boyfriend behind, with her artificial leg she biked to Sicily, where she was welcomed by the Poor Friars: after three months of prayer she converted to Catholicism and received her Confirmation, 23 June 2004; and eventually she completed her exploration, year-trial, and two-year novitiate. The Poor Friars Community combines the way of St. Francis, "The Lord has revealed to me, it be His will I be crazy in the world," with the contemplative mode of the Carmelites, and so the order also is dedicated to Our Lady of Carmel, which was the feast that was being celebrated yesterday, as now I write, 17 July 2010. By this instruction, the Lord has reminded me to keep my focus upon the will of God above everything; that I must never seek to possess anything or anyone other than God; and, again, Our Lady is the best example of this discipline and desire.

Readings: Luke 15:11-32, Luke 16:1-15; Matthew 6:1-4, Luke 16:19-31

After these Sabbath expeditions,[168] Jesus once again arrived with his troop of disciples back at base camp on the far side of the Jordan.[169] Already large crowds were gathering to hear what Jesus had to say: the Pharisees and scribes had captured strategic places for themselves in the front,[170] while some of the others, who were public sinners and tax collectors, were creeping forward trying to edge closer to Jesus,[171] as best they could on the grassy meadow;[172]

---

167 Matthew 10:9-10
168 Luke 13:10, 14:1
169 John 10:40; Acts 13:24, Luke 3:7-8; Isaiah 29:1-3, 42:13-18, Zechariah 10:3-5
170 Luke 11:54
171 Isaiah 55:1-3; John 7:37, 6:65
172 Psalm 23:1-2

and immediately the Pharisees and scribes objected.[173] Perhaps this explains why front row seats so often are empty in church: no one wants to be taken as a Pharisee, or be recognized as a sinner! Even so,[174] it makes no difference to the Lord. Because he wants us to come closer to him, we shouldn't blush to take our seats before the Lord: either in his presence in the Eucharist in front of his tabernacle, or with the person of Christ through the priest in the confessional.

The Pharisees and scribes began to grumble, but not just about this encroachment upon their listening post; they were complaining about the very presence of tax collectors and sinners in their midst; and taking their legal notes, they were scandalized that Jesus welcomed such obvious sinners to eat at his table:[175] even literally at dinner table, as sinners like these had done frequently on previous occasions;[176] and now figuratively at table, in their listening to his word;[177] or pre-figuratively at table, for his later sacrifice on the cross and in the gift of himself in the Eucharist![178] So then Jesus told them, and also all of us, a parable about a man, our heavenly Father, and two of his sons; and apparently either one of the sons could be anyone of us. But like the Pharisees and the tax collectors in front of him, one son seemed to be a righteous grumbler, although a potential saint, while the other one was a blatant sinner. This is what Jesus had to say about both sons:

> A man had two sons.[179] The younger one said to his father, "Father, give me now the share of your estate that should come to me."[180] So the father divided his property between both sons.[181] A few days later, the younger son sold his part of the property, gathered

---

173 Luke 15:1-2
174 Matthew 9:13, Isaiah 55:6-8
175 Luke 15:2, 7; Luke 22:14; Psalm 23:5
176 Matthew 9:11, 11:19
177 John 6:63
178 1 Corinthians 11:26; John 6:52-53
179 Luke 15:11
180 Luke 15:12; Luke 12:13-14; Galatians 3:16, Genesis 24:7, 12:7; Colossians 3:16
181 Luke 15:12; Colossians 1:12-14; Genesis 27:27-30

up his money, and left for a distant country where he squandered his entire inheritance on a life of dissolute sensuality.[182] Then after he had spent everything, a severe famine struck that country,[183] so that without any means of support he was in dire straits.[184]

So he hired himself out as a day labourer to one of the local inhabitants who sent him out to his farm to tend the pigs.[185] He craved to fill his stomach with the empty pods of the broad beans given to the pigs to eat, but no one gave him anything.[186] Then at last he came to his senses, and thought, "All my father's hired workers have more food than they can ever eat, but I am here starving to death.[187] I will leave this place and go to my father and say, 'Father, I have sinned against heaven and against you;[188] I do not deserve to be called your son; but regard me as one of your hired workers.'"[189] So he got up and went back to his father.[190]

While he was still a long way off, his father saw him, and moved with pity he ran to embrace his son, and kissed him.[191] The son told him, "Father I have sinned against heaven and against you; I do not deserve to be called your son."[192] But his father ordered his servants, "Quickly, fetch the finest robe and put it on him; put a ring on his finger and sandals on his feet.[193] Then take the calf we have been fattening, and slaughter it; we are

---

182   Luke 15:13; Acts 7:6, Genesis 15:13; Luke 12:21, 19, 29-31, 23; Luke 16:1-3
183   Acts 7:11-12, Genesis 42:1-2, Luke 15:17
184   Luke 15:14; Psalm 102:1-2, 10-12
185   Luke 15:15; Exodus 1:11-14; Leviticus 11:4-8, 10:10
186   Luke 15:16; Exodus 3:7-9
187   Luke 15:17; Exodus 16:1-3, Deuteronomy 8:3-5, Hebrews 12:5-6; John 6:35
188   Luke 15:18; Psalm 38:19; Psalm 38:20-23, Luke 15:1-2
189   Luke 15:19; Luke 10:2, John 15:15-16
190   Luke 15:20; Exodus 15:13, Hebrews 4:16
191   Luke 15:20; Psalm 102:20-21; Luke 15:4, 8
192   Luke 15:21; Hebrews 2:6, Romans 9:16
193   Luke 15:22; John 19:1-5

going to celebrate with a feast![194] Because this son of mine was dead, but now he has come alive; he was lost, but now he has been found."[195] And they began the celebration.[196]

Meanwhile the older son had been out in the fields.[197] On his way back, when he approached the house,[198] he heard the sound of music and dancing coming from inside.[199] So, he called over one of the servants, and he asked him, "What's going on."[200] The servant told him, "Your brother has returned,[201] and your father has slaughtered the fattened calf because he has him back safe and sound."[202] At this he became angry and refused to enter the house; so his father came out and begged him to come inside.[203]

He shouted back to his father,[204] "Look, all these years I have worked like a slave for you;[205] and not once did I ever disobey your commands;[206] yet never did you offer me so much as a goat to celebrate with my friends.[207] However when this son of yours returns,[208] after swallowing up your property with prostitutes,[209]

---

194   Luke 15:23; John 19:6, 15-16, Romans 9:14-15
195   Luke 15:24; Luke 15:5-6, 9
196   Luke 15:24; Luke 15:7, 10
197   Luke 15:25; Luke 20:14, 16
198   2 Corinthians 5:1, Ephesians 2:6, Revelation 21:22, Ephesians 2:20-22, 1 Peter 2:6-8
199   Luke 15:25; Luke 20:17-19
200   Luke 15:26
201   Luke 15:1-2
202   Luke 15:27; John 10:27-30; John 3:16, 1 John 4:9-10; Luke 20:13, 15, John 20:17
203   Luke 15:28; Luke 13:25; Psalm 23:6, 1 Peter 2:4-5, Psalm 118:22; John 2:17, Psalm 69:9
204   Luke 15:29; Romans 9:20
205   Luke 15:29; Isaiah 29:24, 30:1-3; 1 Corinthians 9:19, 4:9-13, John 13:12, Philippians 2:7
206   Luke 15:29; Isaiah 28:13, Luke 18:20-22;
207   Luke 15:29; Leviticus 16:7-9, Hebrews 10:4-10, 13-14
208   Luke 15:30; Luke 15:4-10
209   Luke 15:30; Hosea 1:2, 2:4-7

for him you slaughter the calf we had been fattening!"[210]
The father said to him, "My son, you are here with me always, and everything I have is yours.[211] But it is right for us now to celebrate and rejoice,[212] because your brother was dead and has come to life; he was lost and has been found."[213]

This parable of the Lord is an allegory about the central mystery of our salvation. It is about God the Father, and his two sons;[214] however, not simply about the two explicit sons of the parable. In fact, these sons represent only one collective person, each of us, but disparate paths for the same sheepfold, or like two sides of the same coin:[215] the younger son presents the prototypic ideal for any potential repentant sinner, while the older son is the frequent, prototypical reality for Jewish non-repentance with their longer public history with God than Gentiles,[216] but not every Israelite or just the Pharisees and scribes in general. For, at one time or another, the older son applies to every man or woman who, like Esau to Jacob, through sin has sold their birthright from God.[217] The only human exception is Our Lady, who was preserved from sin through the grace of her son. Christ, as the Son of God, then actually is the second of the father's two sons beyond ourselves in the parable, but implicitly so: in the parable Jesus hides himself temporarily from everyone, disguised as the calf soon to be slaughtered for our sins, which would be the central action and focal point for our soul's salvation,[218] and who also is the centrepiece of the father's homecoming celebration for the repentant younger son.[219]

210　Luke 15:30; Luke 15:1-2, 13, 23; Acts 8:32, Hebrews 10:11-12, John 6:53-57; Hosea 2:18
211　Luke 15:31; Matthew 28:20, John 15:4-5, 14:2-3, 8:29
212　Luke 15:32; John 6:50, Isaiah 28:16, 1 Corinthians 11:26; 1 Peter 2:6-10; Hosea 2:21-22, Genesis 27:46
213　Luke 15:32; Luke 15:4-5, 1 Peter 2:25, John 10:11, 1 Timothy 1:15-16; Psalm 102:29
214　Luke 15:11
215　Luke 15:4,8
216　Romans 9:4-5
217　Genesis 25:32-34; Romans 9:12-13, Genesis 25:23, Romans 9:23-24
218　Luke 23:44-46, John 19:28-30, Luke 12:49-50
219　Luke 15:23, 30

However, entitlement to our heavenly inheritance, as has been promised to us by the Father,[220] only comes through the unmerited mercy of Christ, but also, in justice to the cross of Christ, we will be judged according to our deeds and our faith in him.[221] The truth is that all of us as sinners have squandered our inheritance, and that, except for Christ's timely intervention by the will of the Father, we all are in absolutely dire straits. Unfortunately, many of the Pharisees and scribes, as interpreters of the Law, and according to their interpretation of the rules, stubbornly refused to recognize the dire condition of their sinfulness. Because they were in charge of the fields of the Lord's vineyard,[222] they may have thought that God's house automatically belonged to them,[223] as if it were their property.[224] At one time or another, as sinners we have demanded from God even our bodies and souls believing them both to be our own exclusive possessions,[225] which is the fiction of self-indulgence and consumption that the world holds out for us as its ideal, as it loudly promotes the death of God.

In fact, although everything we have is from God, by our sin it has been our choice to squander God's property: our body, our soul, our earthly wealth, and our heavenly inheritance, and we do this all the while we reside in a distant country in this life far from our true home in heaven.[226] In the ideal case, when we do experience sin in ourselves, we may feel a desperate insufficiency and hunger,[227] and in this blessed knowledge of our inadequacy we also come to realize our total dependency upon God.[228] But also in a moment of grace, above all we experience our sin as an offence, against God's holiness vested in the saints, and as an infinite insult, against the perfect goodness of our Creator.[229] But then by grace we also humbly repent

---

220   Luke 15:12
221   John 14:1
222   Luke 20:9, 15:25,
223   Luke 15:1-2, Matthew 20:15-16
224   Luke 15:12
225   Luke 15:12
226   Luke 15:13
227   Luke 15:16
228   Luke 15:17
229   Luke 15:18; Revelation 4:11, Romans 12:2, Ephesians 4:22-24, Matthew

by bending our will to God's, who gives life to the dead and calls into being what does not exist:[230] that is, we repent when we return to the Father and accept sight unseen whatever work in this life the Lord in his mercy surely will give us as his hired labourer;[231] and we all agree to work only for the same usual daily wage, our inheritance in God's house.[232] However, that inheritance is not earned by us as a wage; for instead, Christ, the Father's other son, was hired for the wages of our sins;[233] so that for us, our inheritance through faith in Christ is entirely God's free gift.[234]

As soon as the younger son engaged this attitude—or this grace—of repentance, and accordingly he left his former life behind him and started off towards his father's house, the father sees his son when the son is still far from home. Although the actual journey home spans an entire lifetime, as a repentant son we are already safely on our way: because God, our Father in heaven, is not just some impersonal abstraction and "master of the universe" somewhere up in the clouds; but he shows himself to be a constant and loving father to all of his children, a person of strong emotions and decisively clear actions in our lives on earth.[235] This father of the parable not only feels great empathy for his son's pitiful condition (and ours), in our Father's compassion he joyfully runs to his son (and to us when we repent through Christ's generosity[236]), and he embraces him (and us) and kisses him.[237] In reply, the younger son resolutely and humbly greets his father (and ours) with this sequence of sinful admissions: of his guilt, of his injury against all holiness, and of his self-offence against his very sonship.[238]

But it was precisely this first step that the Pharisees and scribes

---

        5:48, 19:21
230   Romans 4:17
231   Luke 15:19; Matthew 20:1, 1 Peter 4:10, Ephesians 4:7-8, 1; Luke 12:48
232   Matthew 20:2, 14
233   Romans 6:23
234   Romans 4:4-5, 16, 5:16-17, Ephesians 2:4-10; John 13:6-8
235   Psalm 103:11-14
236   Matthew 20:15
237   Luke 15:20
238   Luke 15:21

rejected now: by their dissociation with sinners, they refused to admit any guilt.[239] As someone told me just this morning from God's Wisdom: "He who busies himself with the sins of others, or judges his brother on suspicion, has not yet even begun to repent or to examine himself so as to discover his own sins." They were like many people of today—and not just the neurotics in our midst—who do everything in their power to avoid any feelings of guilt. However, just because we don't feel guilt, it doesn't mean we're not guilty; or on the other hand, as may be the case for neurotics, they often feel guilty when, in fact, they are not. So for former sinners—and the neurotics among us—we should remember the younger son in the parable: along with his receiving the father's gracious forgiveness, the son also humbly accepts himself to be his father's son—although immediately the father interrupts his son's further thought to be treated as one of the hired servants![240] The job for the hired servant already was taken up by God's Son.[241]

In fact, like all repentant sinners, he would no longer be a hired servant;[242] the former slave of sin was not treated as such, as a household member without status. But he would regain his status as son, as also we are "adopted" sons.[243] The father provided his servants to fetch for his son a robe of the finest linen,[244] a ring for his finger,[245] and sandals,[246] which they, not himself, placed on his son. Here the father had refused his son's request to be treated as a servant. If his son had become a servant, then the father could not be a father anymore, but he would have become only a master for his former son. Our Father in heaven is a true father for us; he becomes our master only if we are unrepentant sinners. In place of his former life submerged in sensuality,[247] the returning son now

---

239 Luke 15:2
240 Luke 15:21, 18-19; Galatians 4:6-7
241 Romans 4:5, 24-25, 6-8, Psalm 32:1-2; Hebrews 5:1-10, John 13:15-16, 15:15
242 Luke 15:15
243 Galatians 4:1-5
244 Luke 15:22; Isaiah 61:10; 1 Peter 2:9-10, Revelation 5:10
245 Luke 15:22; Hosea 2:21-22, Revelation 19:7
246 Luke 15:22; Mark 6:9; 2 Peter 1:3-4
247 Luke 15:13; 1 Peter 4:2-3

would be surrounded by the secure comfort of God enveloping his senses;[248] his finger was surrounded by the sign of their mutual pledges of eternal fidelity; and for walking the rest of his journey home, his sandals would fit him perfectly.[249] Although we haven't yet arrived home to our inheritance either, like the younger son we are also safely on our way by virtue of Jesus,[250] who as the Lamb of God is the calf that is slaughtered for the feast;[251] but we are safe only if we have returned to God.[252] And then with God our Father the whole of heaven rejoices at the assurance of our arrival: as the feast already begins without the younger son,[253] ahead of his and our own homecoming, because once we were dead and lost to eternity;[254] but now that we are alive in Christ,[255] we can be found among the descendants of Abraham's descendant,[256] numbered like the stars of the heavens to possess eternal life—the only possession that really matters.[257]

So now, as repentant sinners, we are not lost; but we can be found among the sheepfold as true servants of God.[258] But Christ, as the approaching wolf, will scatter those hired men, the Pharisees and scribes, who are not being shepherds,[259] but who work only for money.[260] These were far from safe; in fact, many of them, unfortunately,[261] as casualties of their spiritual warfare,[262] would never be going home.[263] In the parable, while the younger son was safely

---

248   Psalms 103:2-4, 32:7, 10
249   Psalm 32:8
250   2 Peter 3:13-14
251   Luke 15:23; Revelation 5:9, 7:10
252   Luke 15:20
253   Luke 15:24
254   Luke 15:24
255   Romans 6:4-7
256   Galatians 3:16
257   Luke 15:24, 9:25; 1 Timothy 6:18-19; Revelation 7:9, Genesis 22:17
258   Romans 9:25-28
259   John 10:12; John 10:2-5
260   John 10:13; Luke 16:13-14, John 2:13-16
261   2 Peter 3:9
262   Romans 7:21-25; 2 Peter 3:7, 10
263   John 8:21, Luke 19:45-46, Jeremiah 7:11, 5-10

on his way back home, the older son had been out in the fields,[264] which is a metaphor for the religious authorities God had charged to make productive the house of Israel. But under the Pharisees and scribes, the broken walls and ravaged state of those non-productive fields resembled more battlefields and trenches than the Lord's wheat fields and vineyards.[265]

Even so, the older son like the younger son was on his way back to his father's house, but when the older son only approached the house and was not himself inside our heavenly Father's house, he heard even from a distance those joyfully boisterous celebrations coming from inside.[266] With his sinful "no-good" younger brother far away squandering his portion of his father's inheritance,[267] the older brother had believed, as he was the one in charge of the fields, that he had been perfectly obedient. In fact, he was like the Pharisees and scribes as "perfect" upholders of God's laws; but they were not God's true sons, just as the elder son was a perfect servant, but not the son he should have been. He also believed that he knew everything that was going on in the household. So it was a double shock to learn from one of the servants that (1) he didn't know what was happening,[268] and (2) the father was celebrating his brother's forthcoming safe return.[269] At this, he threw a tantrum outside of his father's house and waged war against God, although his father in begging the older son to come inside was offering him, and as Christ was offering the Pharisees and scribes, the terms for peace:[270] namely, their repentance: not by being simply "servants" of God, although perfect ones, but by being God's "sons," joint-heirs with Christ.[271] We are brothers with Christ; as his Father is our Father, and his God is our God.[272]

---

264   Luke 15:25
265   Psalms 80:13-16, 89:41-42
266   Luke 15:25
267   Luke 15:12
268   Luke 15:26
269   Luke 15:27
270   Luke 15:28; Luke 14:31-32
271   Romans 8:14-17
272   John 20:17; 1 John 3:1

Otherwise all of God's opponents would be liable to the wrathful prison sentences demanded by the judge,[273] and master. However, the older son seems not to budge, much like the Pharisees and scribes; like them, he rebukes the father's and God's requirements for justice and peace. He had been the perfect servant, and he objects to the settlement: "I've slaved for you and never once have I broken your commands,"[274] although only Jesus can claim this perfection not to be a sinner;[275] and for the Pharisees and scribes, as slaves of the details of the Law, their sin entitles them to the full wrath of God,[276] because they were not being true sons of God. The older son's greatest objections are threefold: first, with no sense of guilt about himself, he finds the absence of a celebration in his honour as unjust; then there is no sense that his brother's sin can be forgiven; and ultimately, he fails to recognize the slaughter of the calf.[277] And likewise, the Pharisees and scribes failed to understand Christ's holocaust of himself as truly necessary for everyone's salvation from their sins, as sons of the Father. Why was the father so stingy with his elder son, never giving a kid goat to rejoice with his friends, when he had slaved all these years as such a perfectly obedient boy? Because his elder son wanted that his father would behave like a master; but he was a father, and not a master. A father wants to be in the midst of his children's rejoicing; he would give his elder son even a fattened calf, only if he were there with him and his friends, rejoicing with them in their midst. That is a father; he could never be a master, because he was a father. And the father wanted his son to be just that: a son, and not a perfectly obedient servant. Sometimes in our religious rigidities we fail to note this important distinction.

It is only through grace that anyone comes to understand more fully how their undeserved place as God's son (or daughter) was earned through the passion and death of Christ.[278] So, for many of the Pharisees and scribes, both in their opposition to grace and in their

---

273   Luke 12:57-59; Acts 5:39
274   Luke 15:29
275   1 John 1:10, 2:5-6
276   Romans 4:14-15, 6:20; Luke 16:17, Romans 6:6, 18, 22
277   Luke 15:30
278   Luke 16:16; Romans 8:29, Ephesians 1:4-8, Romans 6:14

reliance on the Law,[279] this cornerstone for God's house and for the salvation of sinners was a stumbling block unto their destruction.[280] In the father's final plea to his elder son, Christ reminded the Pharisees and scribes of their inheritance: of being eternally with God, and along with God their possessing everything he has;[281] which they risked throwing all away through their intransigence.[282] Lastly, but never finally,[283] in the father's parting words to the elder son, Jesus demolishes the original objection of the Pharisees and scribes to the sinners in their midst:[284] it was right for them to celebrate with Jesus at his table,[285] for these dead brothers of theirs have come to life by their faith in Jesus;[286] and although once these sinners were lost, they have been found;[287] and as Jesus knew both their hearts and those of the others, unlike the Pharisees and scribes,[288] these brother "sinners" were justified.[289]

Then by very clever comparison and contrast, Jesus continued his critique against the Pharisees and scribes, so that he could underline for his disciples the kind of shrewdness they must have to gain eternal life for themselves, and also for others.[290] He would implicitly describe the religious authorities as dishonest stewards who abused their positions over God's property only so to create more money for themselves;[291] and also he would attack their reliance on the Law, apart from the necessity of Jesus himself, for the forgiveness of their sins.[292] At the same time, for the disciples, Jesus would indicate that their approaching stewardship would require their effective use of

---

279   Luke 16:16-17; Romans 2:17-23, 3:19-26, Galatians 2:21
280   Luke 20:17-18; Acts 4:11, 1 Corinthians 1:23, Isaiah 28:16, Psalm 118:22
281   Luke 15:31
282   Luke 15:28
283   1 John 1:9; Romans 4:16, 23-25
284   Luke 15:1-3
285   Psalm 149:5
286   Romans 6:11-13
287   Luke 15:32
288   Luke 16:15; Romans 2:27-29
289   Romans 10:4, 9:33, 5:21, 8:30
290   Luke 16:9, 12; Luke 11:52, Matthew 23:13, 15
291   Luke 16:13; Luke 20:47, John 2:16
292   Luke 15:23, Psalm 51:21

worldly wealth as well as their responsible management of God's wealth, the spiritual property that he would be entrusting to them.

So now, Jesus told the disciples, as the future religious leaders of his church,[293] a parable about a rich man's steward.[294] Meanwhile the Pharisees, as God's soon to be unemployed religious leaders, were carefully listening to overhear what Jesus was saying for whatever evidence they could find against him.[295] This then is what Jesus said; and indeed, our heavenly Father is like a very rich man who makes ours everything he has;[296] for his great wealth of mercy and grace to us through his Son is priceless,[297] and rich beyond measure:[298]

> There was a rich man whose steward was reported to him for squandering his property.[299] He called for him and said, "What is this I hear about you? Prepare the balance sheet for your stewardship, because you cannot be my manager anymore."[300] The steward thought to himself, "Now that my master is taking my position as manager away from me, what shall I do? I'm not strong enough to dig ditches, and I am too ashamed to go begging.[301] Aha! I know what I'll do: when I am dismissed from my post,[302] there will be friends to welcome me into their homes."[303]
>
> So, one by one he called in all his master's debtors. To the first he said, "How much do you owe my master?"[304] "One hundred barrels of olive oil," replied the first. The steward said, "Here is your bond; sit down quickly and

---

293   Luke 12:42-44, Acts 20:28
294   Luke 16:1
295   Luke 16:14; Luke 11:54; Psalm 49:17-21
296   Luke 15:31; Luke 19:26, Matthew 25:29
297   Matthew 13:45-46, 1 Corinthians 6:20
298   Ephesians 1:3, 2:4-7
299   Luke 16:1; Mark 4:22, 25
300   Luke 16:2; Luke 1:52
301   Luke 16:3
302   Luke 12:40, 42
303   Luke 16:4
304   Luke 16:5

write fifty."³⁰⁵ To another he said, "And you, how much do you owe?" This one replied, "One-thousand bushels of wheat." To him the steward said, "Here, take your bond and write one for eight-hundred."³⁰⁶ The master of the dishonest steward praised him for his shrewdness; because the children of this world are more astute with their own matters than are the children of light (with theirs).³⁰⁷

And so I tell you, use money, as dishonest as it is, to win friends for yourselves, so that when it becomes exhausted you will be welcomed into eternal dwellings.³⁰⁸ The person who can be trusted in small matters can also be trusted in great ones; and whoever is dishonest in trivial matters is also dishonest in great ones.³⁰⁹ Therefore: if you can't be trusted with dishonest wealth, then who will trust you with true wealth?³¹⁰ If you can't be trusted with what belongs to someone else, then who will give you what actually is yours?³¹¹ No servant can be the slave of two masters: he will either hate one and love the other, or treat one with respect and the other with scorn; you cannot be the slave of both God and money.³¹²

When the Pharisees, who loved money, heard all of this, they laughed and sneered at Jesus.³¹³ He said to them:

You are the very ones who pass yourselves off as virtuous in the sight of others, but God knows your hearts; for

---

305	Luke 16:6; Hebrews 7:5, Numbers 18:21, 25-26, 29, Luke 11:39-42, Matthew 23:23; Luke 19:45-46, Jeremiah 50:6-7, Zechariah 11:4-5; 1 Peter 1:18-19, 1 Corinthians 7:23
306	Luke 16:7; Matthew 23:2-3, Luke 16:17; Matthew 19:3, Mark 10:2-4, Deuteronomy 24:1, Matthew 19:8, Luke 16:18; Romans 7:1-4
307	Luke 16:8; John 12:36, Philippians 2:15; Luke 19:12-13, Galatians 6:9, Luke 19:27
308	Luke 16:9; Hebrews 10:34
309	Luke 16:10
310	Luke 16:11; Revelation 21:26
311	Luke 16:12
312	Luke 16:13; Matthew 6:24
313	Luke 16:14; Luke 16:13, 1 Peter 2:23

what is thought of great value by men is an abomination in the sight of God.[314]

The Pharisees and scribes, like the dishonest steward of the parable, were unscrupulous usurers. Everyone was in debt to the steward's master: due to our sins, our obligatory justice to offending God required expiation, although only God's son could provide that. However, until Christ paid the price, Levites were obliged to offer temple sacrifices and the Israelites were obliged to support them with their tithes; and the Levites themselves were obligated to present to the Lord a tithe of the tithes—and it was to be the best 10 percent of their earnings, as they too were not exempt from their guilt from sin. The dishonest steward collected from his master's debtors an excess, sometimes an exorbitant amount above what was actually due. In the first debtor's case,[315] the excess was 100 percent since the dishonest steward reduced the amount owed to his master by 50 percent. Similarly, the Pharisees and scribes were making fortunes on the religious obligations of the Israelites; but at the same time, they themselves did not honor their obligations to God because of their greed and their failures to observe God's law. Furthermore, in their greed, as religious lawyers they would ingratiate themselves with others:[316] by encouraging hefty payments against the remission of guilt for sins, and oftentimes by their satisfying clients through finding the right loopholes in the law,[317] as in the case of providing for divorce. But then, like these latter clients, many of the Pharisees and scribes were guilty of adultery along with their other sins; and as dishonest stewards of God's people,[318] money was their god and material riches were their abominable idolatry.[319] Although they may have gathered wealth and the respect of men through their usurious hypocrisies, they actually despised God's law and God's justice (or his mercy), and they were despicable in God's sight.[320]

---

314 Luke 16:15; Luke 12:21
315 Luke 16:6
316 Luke 16:4
317 Luke 16:5-7; Matthew 15:9
318 Luke 16:1
319 Luke 16:13-14
320 Luke 16:15

On the other hand, as for the disciples, they were to be God's slaves and not slaves of money.[321] Seeking God's kingdom was to be their primary task,[322] but they also needed to use tainted money to its best advantage for spiritual wealth, ideally by using it all up before being welcomed into God's kingdom.[323] The quickest and best way to do this, in fact, would be to sell everything one has; to give the proceeds as alms to the poor [This certainly would win friends among the poor, although the rich may be dismayed at the thought!]; and then to follow the Lord.[324] But the kingdom of God would not be realized over night;[325] and not even necessarily during one's lifetime on earth.[326] So, the disciples would be responsible for their use of money, as small, trivial and tainted as it was, to achieve the honest purposes of God's work; and their administration of such matters was in parallel to their management of true wealth, the great mysteries of God's kingdom.[327]

However, at this moment, what Jesus intended by his caution was even more specific: for among the disciples there was one person specifically in charge of the community purse, namely, Judas Iscariot; and in his role with such insignificant matters, Judas now was regularly skimming the funds for his personal use;[328] and later on, after such patterns of dishonesty, he would also gravely mishandle the true wealth of the kingdom of God in his midst,[329] [and just so, in his grace and person Jesus now lives within us[330]]; but for Judas, Satan would enter into him finally. Then, for God's purpose of accomplishing his great work,[331] as we all do because of our own sin,[332] Judas eventually would hand Jesus over to the chief

---

321 Luke 16:13
322 Luke 12:31, Matthew 6:33
323 Luke 16:9
324 Luke 18:22, 12:33
325 Luke 11:2
326 Luke 19:11, 12-13, 20-22
327 Luke 16:10-11
328 John 12:4-6
329 Luke 17:20-21; Luke 15:31
330 1 John 3:6
331 Luke 22:3-6, 1 John 3:5; Matthew 26:9, 14-16, Mark 14:5, 10-11
332 Mark 8:37; John 12:25, Matthew 16:25-26, 10:32-33

priests and temple scribes for thirty pieces of silver.

But even so, Jesus now was trying to save Judas from his fatal choices towards perdition.[333] His great sin was not yet his; just as his final destiny in eternity was not yet sealed through his fatal choices.[334] If the betrayal of Judas would have happened with his repentance, or if it had not happened at all, no one would have thwarted Jesus from accomplishing his great end.[335] There were plenty of other unfortunate souls like Judas for the betrayal, with insufficient faith in Jesus and the mercy of his cross, who would ultimately reject Jesus as their King,[336] especially among the Pharisees. Likewise, all of us have betrayed Christ by sinning; and also the sins of the entire world (including our own sins) and the sins for the whole of time were always known to God, but also in horror known to Jesus were those who still would not repent. So, if ever we should sin, what is crucial is not that we have sinned,[337] but that we have repented, which requires the actions and deeds of our calling, not simply our good thoughts and words, or merely our avoidance of sin: for Christ has died already for our sins,[338] and our true inheritance is derived from this act and from our faith in Abraham's descendant, in Jesus;[339] and this inheritance belongs only to the children of Abraham,[340] that is, to those who also are Christ's children of the Light.[341]

But since the Pharisees risked refusing the gift of God's mercy,[342] like Judas would do, or as any of the other disciples could have done but didn't refuse in their repentance,[343] Jesus, like a shepherd, was going after the numerous strays;[344] and he was determined for the

---

333   Luke 16:13; Matthew 16:26; Luke 15:4, 8
334   Luke 16:9; Luke 22:48, Acts 1:18
335   John 18:37, 19:11; John 17:4-5, 1
336   Luke 19:14, 27
337   Romans 11:32
338   Acts 2:36-39; Romans 5:6-11
339   Psalm 52:10-11
340   Romans 9:7-13, Galatians 4:28; Genesis 15:5-6
341   John 12:36, Luke 16:8; Genesis 15:4-5, Ephesians 5:5-14; 1 John 1:7
342   Romans 5:15-18
343   John 17:10, Philippians 3:9-10
344   Luke 15:4, 7; Matthew 10:6, 15:24, 9:36, Mark 6:34; Isaiah 40:11, Ezekiel 34:11-12

salvation of his entire flock.³⁴⁵ So, after the Pharisees just sneered at Jesus when he had attacked their love for money,³⁴⁶ Jesus then warned them immediately about their certain fate,³⁴⁷ if they (or even, if we) should not repent, by now telling the Pharisees (and us) yet another parable about themselves³⁴⁸ (or possibly, even about some of us):

> Once there was a rich man who used to dress in purple and fine linen and who feasted magnificently every day.³⁴⁹ And lying in front of his gate outside the door of his house, there also was a beggar named Lazarus who was covered with sores.³⁵⁰ He longed to eat his fill from the scraps that fell from the rich man's table; and even the dogs would come to lick his sores.³⁵¹ The poor beggar eventually died and was carried by the angels to the bosom of Abraham [at the banquet in heaven];³⁵² the rich man died and (directly) was buried.³⁵³ From his place of torment in the underworld, he looked up and saw Abraham in the distance far away, with Lazarus at his side.³⁵⁴
>
> So he cried out, "Father Abraham! Have pity on me and send Lazarus to dip (even just) the tip of his finger in water to cool my tongue, for I am tortured in these flames!"³⁵⁵ Abraham replied, "My child, remember that during your lifetime all good things came to you, just as every misery came to Lazarus; but here he now is comforted, while you are there in agony.³⁵⁶ And that's not all: between us and you there has been fixed a great

---

345   Romans 9:16-18; Ezekiel 33:11
346   Luke 16:14; Psalms 41:12-13, 52:8-9
347   Romans 9:22-24
348   Romans 11:11-12
349   Luke 16:19
350   Luke 16:20
351   Luke 16:21; Luke 14:12-13
352   Luke 16:22; Luke 14:21; Matthew 8:11; John 1:18, 13:23, Luke 22:14-18, Matthew 22:2, Revelation 19:9; Psalm 23:6
353   Luke 16:22; Luke 14:24
354   Luke 16:23; Luke 13:28, 14:15; Psalm 23:5
355   Luke 16:24; Matthew 3:9-10, John 8:33-37
356   Luke 16:25

abyss, so that anyone who might wish to go from our side to yours, or from your side to ours, is prevented from crossing."[357]

The rich man replied, "Then I beg you, father, send Lazarus to my father's house,[358] where I have five brothers, to warn them so that they, at least, do not come to this place of torment."[359] But Abraham answered, "They have Moses and the prophets; let them listen to them."[360] "Oh no, father Abraham," said the rich man, "but if someone only comes to them from the dead, they will repent."[361] Then Abraham said to him, "If they do not listen to Moses and the prophets,[362] they will not be persuaded even if someone were to rise from the dead."[363]

Like the Pharisees with their long-flowing robes and prime positioning at feasts,[364] this rich man of the parable went about his life of privilege consumed in self-gratification by his passion for fine clothes and sumptuous dining,[365] just as today's elite, the rich and famous and the fashionable of the world, are often so preoccupied. But the rich man had no excuse in his abundance for not knowing of Lazarus and helping him; Lazarus was on his doorstep, just as today through televised "live-aid" programs and news globalization, the poor of the world are figuratively on ours. In fact, the beggar we see even under our feet could be the unemployed or elderly neighbour living on our block, the homeless person we see on our way to work, or another illegal immigrant landing on our shores. But the rich man (and we like him: if we are not poor, we are rich) ignored Lazarus, except for knowing his name, as if he were the standard fixture of his doorway. The rich man nearly always stumbled over him whenever

---

357 Luke 16:26; Revelation 20:1-3, 10
358 Luke 16:27
359 Luke 16:28
360 Luke 16:29; Luke 9:30-31, 35
361 Luke 16:30
362 Luke 16:31; Luke 24:25-27
363 Luke 16:31; Luke 24:5-7
364 Matthew 23:5-6
365 Luke 12:22-23, 21:34

he left or entered his house; or perhaps he just sent out others to do his work while he leisurely stayed at home undisturbed in his private space, with the barrios outside his gate.

But everyone dies, the poor and rich alike,[366] although some rich may feel, think, and live as if there is no existence beyond this life;[367] or, if they were believers, perhaps they thought themselves virtuous because of their riches,[368] and so they expected continuing entitlement to their luxurious lifestyles after they had died. Whichever way it was for this rich man,[369] it would be his unpleasant surprise to discover his afterlife in hell without relief or parole, while at the same time he saw poor Lazarus enjoying the heavenly banquet. But after death the experience of hell comes too late for those suffering its torments. So, this parable of the Lord was a corrective warning to the Pharisees, and to all of those Israelites who may have failed to listen to Moses and the prophets,[370] even though many still would not be convinced after Christ had risen from the dead.[371]

An implicit meditation on this parable is provided for us by Saint Maria Faustina Kowalska, when she describes in her diary her experience of a special grace afforded to her. In this experience of total darkness, the "Terror of the Soul,"[372] she described herself as if she were "poised on the summit of a lofty mountain on the very brink of a precipice" (Diary, #98, p. 55). In fact, Sister Faustina's position on the mountain was closer to her actual holiness with God, although through this grace she experienced God as far away; and she was plunged into the depths of the rich man's experience of God's anger and total abandonment in the abyss of his sin in hell.[373] Every

---

366 Luke 16:22; Ecclesiastes 9:11-12
367 Isaiah 22:13, 1 Corinthians 15:32; Luke 12:19
368 Luke 18:11-12; Ecclesiastes 2:24-25, 3:13, 9:7-10
369 Luke 18:25-27
370 Deuteronomy 32:22, Lamentations 4:11; Jeremiah 7:20, Ezekiel 8:18, 15:6-7; Matthew 3:12
371 Luke 16:31; 1 Corinthians 15:12-19; John 4:48, 20:29
372 Kowalska, Saint Maria Faustina. (2003). Diary: Divine Mercy in My Soul. Stockbridge, Massachusetts, USA: Marians of the Immaculate Conception, (Notebook I, 95-101, pp. 52-57).
373 Luke 16:23; Psalm 116:3-4

person, while still alive, lives on the edge of this potential precipice when tempted to sin.[374] Yet, only by the mercy and grace of God are we preserved from its awful depths; but because God is present with us, we need not fear.[375] Christ tells us this through Sister Faustina and the scriptures: "Fear not, my daughter, I am with you" (Diary, #103, p. 58).[376] At times Christ seemed like a ghost to her, but he was not a ghost: for when the soul is in its purity, as Sister Faustina writes in her diary, "It feels the lightest touch of grace and is very faithful to God" (Diary, #115, p. 64).[377]

However, her experience of the soul's rejection from God "becomes a fire which penetrates every nerve to the marrow of the bone" (Diary, #98, p. 56). This was the torture of the flames experienced by the rich man as he cried out for water from just a single fingertip of Lazarus.[378] Sister Faustina writes, "Jesus, You alone know how the soul, engulfed in darkness, moans in the midst of these torments and, despite all this, thirsts for God as burning lips thirst for water. It dies and withers; it dies a death without death; that is to say, it cannot die" (Diary, #101, p. 56). It seems the soul would wish itself not to exist, but instead it is doomed to eternal torment at the loss of God's presence forever; and as a kind of post-traumatic torture, it suffers only "the memory of the love with which God formerly surrounded it" (Diary, #101, p. 56). It is then that the agony of the rich man's soul reaches its climax when it no longer looks for help from anyone. Sister Faustina writes, "It shrinks into itself and loses sight of everything; it is as though it has accepted the torture of being abandoned" (Diary, #98, p. 56).[379]

But the obverse of this hell must be true; for those who aren't in hell there must be resurrection to life,[380] for in God's justice there cannot be a hell without its alternative, heaven. If we should remain in our sin, then we should be in terror after the Lord's parable of

---

374	Psalm 118:5
375	Psalms 23:4, 118:6-7
376	Matthew 14:26-31; Luke 12:32; Psalm 118:6
377	Psalm 103:17-18
378	Luke 16:24
379	Luke 16:26
380	Luke 16:31

the rich man and Lazarus, or after Sister Faustina's experience of her "Terror of the Soul." But instead, because God draws near to us as his children of the Light, we have the consolation of our "intimacy with God" (Diary, #95, p. 52), not terror from our sins. Sister Faustina describes her intimacy with God as "lights" which become stronger and more frequent as the soul "is crystallized" and penetrated by the light (Diary, #95, p. 52).[381] She writes of a "superior light" to the surrounding darkness, "This light which has touched the soul is alive within it, and nothing can either quench or diminish it" (Diary, #95, p. 52). These spiritual fires are enkindled by our love for God, in contrast to the unquenchable torments of the infernal fires enkindled by our sins; the former are fueled by our constant hope and joyful craving for union with God; the latter are fueled by total and constant despair.

Sister Faustina, much like Lazarus as if he actually had been dispatched to warn the rich man's five brothers from the grave,[382] writes of her experience: "It seemed to me that I had come back from the other world. I feel an aversion for everything that is created; I snuggle to the heart of God like a baby to its mother's breast" (Diary, #104, p. 58).[383] In parallel to Sister Faustina's statement, just as I was finishing this chapter's final review, through the Holy Spirit another bit of "God's Wisdom" came to me today, 29 July 2010, once again from a friend who says: "Your life consists in drawing nearer to God. To do this you must endeavour to detach yourself from visible things and remember that in a short time they will be taken from you." The rich man, however, had sought comfort from his material possessions and magnificent dinners,[384] which was in direct contrast to Sister Faustina's finding her sole comfort in God.[385] On the other hand, Lazarus implicitly and humbly had accepted from God his miserable state in life without possessions;[386] although he sincerely prayed to God for modest scraps from the rich man's table; he also

---

381   Revelation 21:11
382   Luke 16:30
383   Luke 12:34
384   Luke 16:19
385   1 Peter 2:2
386   Luke 16:25

very likely had thanked God even for the blessings of the dogs for licking his sores;[387] and undoubtedly, Lazarus firmly placed his only hope and longing for salvation in his whole-hearted obedience to God.[388]

Like this poor beggar Lazarus, Sister Faustina had not only understood that she was "not of this earth" (Diary, #107, p. 59), her value orientation had shifted nearly entirely from matters of little importance to the great ones, where true wealth is found, but the trivial matters are given their proper due.[389] Regarding this consequence of her experience, she writes, "My communion is more with heaven than with earth, though I in no way neglect my duties" (Diary, #107, p. 59). And like Sister Faustina, although we stand on the mountain top above the perilous precipice the whole while we are alive,[390] we also must place our trust in God, as we of little faith so often have difficulty doing, and redirect our gaze always upwards towards our constant help from heaven.[391] Otherwise, without our faith and full devotion to God, we may not be strong enough for the spiritual warfare,[392] and without the mercy of God we may perish when we die.[393] And if we should fail in small graces not of our own provision, how can we be entrusted with larger graces, so that we may be given what is ours?[394] But, even if in God's mercy it should be our grace that we are not destined for God's wrath, nonetheless many persons, always potentially like ourselves, do finish up as the Lord had warned the Pharisees: like the formerly complacent rich man starring out from the depths of the great abyss of hell, from where throughout eternity he was alone, so completely and forever abandoned by God.[395]

387	Luke 16:21
388	Psalm 119:14
389	Luke 16:10, 13
390	Psalms 24:3, 39:8, 103:4
391	Psalm 62:7; Luke 18:7-8
392	Ephesians 6:10-13, Luke 13:23-24
393	1 Thessalonians 5:8-9
394	Luke 16:11-12, 15:11-12, 12:13-15
395	Luke 16:23; Mark 10:23, Luke 18:25, Matthew 19:24

Prayer Reflection: Psalm 118:1-29

Antiphon: Give thanks to the Lord, for he is good,
    his mercy endures forever.[396]

    Let the house of Israel say:
        "His mercy endures forever."[397]
    Let the house of Aaron say:
        "His mercy endures forever."[398]
    Let those who fear the Lord say:
        "His mercy endures forever."[399]

    In danger I called on the Lord;
        he answered me and set me free.[400]
    The Lord is with me; I am not afraid;
        what can anyone do against me?[401]
    The Lord is at my side as my helper;
        I shall look down in triumph on my foes.[402]
    It is better to take refuge in the Lord
        than to put one's trust in man.[403]
    It is better to take refuge in the Lord
        than to put one's trust in princes.[404]

---

396   Psalm 118:1; Luke 15:24; Ephesians 2:5
397   Psalm 118:2; Luke 15:4; Matthew 10:6
398   Psalm 118:3; Luke 16:1
399   Psalm 118:4; Luke 14:15
400   Psalm 118:5; Luke 13:11-12; Luke 13:16
401   Psalm 118:6; Luke 15:30; Luke 12:32
402   Psalm 118:7; Luke 14:5
403   Psalm 118:8; Luke 14:26
404   Psalm 118:9; Luke 12:19

All the nations surrounded me;
   in the Lord's name I crushed them.[405]
They surrounded me on every side;
   in the Lord's name I crushed them.[406]
They swarmed around me like bees;
   they blazed like a fire among the thorns;
   in the Lord's name I crushed them.[407]
I was hard pressed and was being defeated,
   but the Lord helped me.[408]
The Lord is my strength and courage;
   he came to me as my saviour.[409]

There are joyful shouts of deliverance
   in the tents of the victors:
   the Lord's right hand strikes with power.[410]
The Lord's right hand is raised in battle;
   the Lord's right hand has triumphed.[411]
I shall not die, but I shall live
   and declare his deeds.[412]
Although the Lord chastised me harshly,
   he did not hand me over to death.[413]

405	Psalm 118:10; Exodus 15:3
406	Psalm 118:11; Exodus 15:4
407	Psalm 118:12; Luke 14:1; Exodus 15:7
408	Psalm 118:13; Luke 15:1
409	Psalm 118:14; Exodus 15:2
410	Psalm 118:15; Luke 13:17
411	Psalm 118:16; Exodus 15:6
412	Psalm 118:17; Luke 15:17; 1 Corinthians 15:56-57
413	Psalm 118:18; Luke 13:15; 1 Corinthians 15:55

Open to me the gates of holiness;
   I will enter and thank the Lord.[414]
This is the Lord's own gate,
   where the just may enter.[415]
I praise you, Lord, for you have answered me;
   you, my saviour, have given me victory.[416]
The stone which the builders rejected
   has become the cornerstone.[417]
By the Lord has this been done;
   it is wonderful in ours eyes.[418]
This is the day the Lord has made;
   let us rejoice in it and be glad.[419]
O Lord, hosanna [grant salvation]![420]
   O Lord, give us success.[421]

Blessed is he who comes in the name of the Lord;
   we bless you from the house of the Lord.[422]
The Lord is God and has given us light;
   go forward in procession with leafy branches
   up to the horns of the altar.[423]
You are my God, I give you thanks;
   my God, I praise you.[424]

Antiphon: Give thanks to the Lord, for he is good;
   his mercy endures forever.[425]

414	Psalm 118:19; Luke 14:27, 33; Matthew 7:13-14
415	Psalm 118:20; Luke 13:24; John 10:9
416	Psalm 118:21; Luke 16:31; John 10:27-28
417	Psalm 118:22; Luke 16:1; Luke 20:17-18
418	Psalm 118:23; Luke 19:37
419	Psalm 118:24; Luke 24:6
420	Psalm 118:25; Matthew 21:9, Mark 11:9-10, John 12:13
421	Psalm 118:25; Luke 15:23; Luke 12:15
422	Psalm 118:26; Luke 13:35; Luke 19:38
423	Psalm 118:27; Ephesians 5:2, 8
424	Psalm 118:28; Luke 24:46-47
425	Psalm 118:29; Ephesians 1:18

Glory be to the Father,
 and to the Son,
  and to the Holy Spirit,
 as it was it the beginning,
  is now,
   and ever shall be world without end. Amen.

Chapter 28

Marriage and Celibacy are Permanent Vows: Two Paths for the Contemplation of God's Promises of His Eternal Life and Eternal Love

Readings: Matthew 19:3-12, 13-15, Mark 10:2-12, 13-16, Luke 16:18, 18:15-17; 1 Corinthians 7:1-16, 17, 24, 25-40

It would not be just another routine, yet always-purposeful day for Jesus and his disciples near Bethany on the far side of the Jordan.[1] On that day, in fact, in the Great Spiritual Civil Wars, Christ would provide the thunderously profound revelation of God's New Covenant Law on marriage. But, according to the battle plan the Pharisees and scribes had devised for that day, they had hoped this day would be a turning point in their counter-offensive against Jesus.[2] Their objective was to drive a wedge of opinion between the assembled followers of Jesus,[3] so that, at last, the crowds might be roused to oppose him (and each other) with some convincing and, perhaps, undeniable force. By initiating their action against Jesus, the Pharisees and scribes had hoped to drive as many as possible of his supporters back into their ideological political-religious camp.[4]

This particular divide-and-conquer strategy is still recognizable after almost 2000 years, in the expression of that tactic by enemies

---

[1] Matthew 19:1, John 10:40, 1:28, Mark 10:1
[2] Luke 14:31-33
[3] Matthew 19:2, John 10:42
[4] John 15:19, 17:14

of Christ in today's world: someone just "tests" Jesus by initiating some skirmish against him,[5] so as to provoke an open revolt in faith against the Christ. Ironically, at the hands of the Pharisees, Jesus later would be the one to stand accused of inciting a revolt.[6] But now, although any one of many handy issues were possible,[7] in this case and at this moment, the authorized interpreters of the Law of Moses[8] chose to "test" Jesus about his position on divorce! As their reasoning went, whatever position Jesus would take on this particular issue should be a "lose-lose" political situation for him because every position seemed guaranteed for them to foster divisive and sharply antagonistic disputes. For throughout human history, marriage and divorce have been central issues in every religious and secular culture the whole world over, just as they are today for hundreds of millions of husbands and wives in their personal lives. This is basic human anthropology.

But the anti-divorce position Jesus would declare now, both for Jews and Christians alike, and the consequences of that position—then against his life and also now against Christ in our 21st century society—would be the death penalty: just as earlier it had been for John the Baptist, when Herodias had worked her design for John's beheading over the same issues.[9] Just as, in their political pragmatism as Herodians, these same religious authorities had been personal supporters of Herod regarding his divorce from his first wife, Phasaelis, and of his marriage to his niece, Herodias, who then had been the wife of his brother, Herod Philip, so now these legal-eagle Pharisees were still in league with Herod Antipas,[10] the adulterer,[11] and the politically and morally elusive, and very self-absorbed "fox."[12] Even so, and also despite the attempted use of this alliance by the Pharisees to stimulate Herod's animosity against Jesus,

---

5   Matthew 19:3, Mark 10:2; Jeremiah 20:10
6   Luke 23:13-14
7   Luke 20:20, 22, 33
8   Matthew 23:2-3
9   Matthew 14:3-4, Mark 6:17-18, Luke 3:19
10 Mark 3:6, 8:15, Luke 13:31
11 Matthew 3:7, Mark 6:21
12 Luke 13:32

as a political cover for their plots,[13] unlike Herod's base instincts for survival, Jesus chose to march deliberately towards his victory goal: his glorification according to his death by crucifixion; and, by glorification from the Father, his subsequent resurrection from the dead.[14] And so, although the Lord's death was according to God's ultimate plan for our salvation, while the hearts of the Pharisees were hardened by their blind insincerity, they approached Jesus in order to trap him, as they imagined, in some useful contradiction: either one seemingly made by Jesus against the Law, according to their judgment and public perception; or one implicitly made against Herod, or seemingly blatant in its overt political opposition as they hoped. And so, openly in front of the crowd, they cunningly put to him their critical question:

> Does our law provide any justification whatsoever for a man to divorce his wife?[15]

At first, Jesus simply replied to them with his own test question, since they acknowledged no law except for what is specified in the Pentateuch:

> What did Moses command you?[16]

Under the Law, although divorce had been taken for granted, the grounds for divorce had never been emphasized. Sufficient grounds for divorce were presumed to be always necessary,[17] but even seemingly quite liberal grounds were permitted, as in the case for an Israelite, if in war he had taken a female captive to be his wife.[18] So, although the Law did not readily specify conditions for divorce, sometimes it was quite specific about its prohibitions to divorce: for example, as a deterrent against the injustice of a man's unsolicited rape of an un-betrothed woman, which, if this were discovered for an unmarried man, also imposed the Mosaic "justice" of marriage

---

13   Luke 23:4-8, 10, 12-15, 23-24
14   John 3:14, 4:34, 6:39-40, 17:4-5; Luke 9:29-31; 1 Corinthians 15:56-58, 22-23
15   Matthew 19:3; Mark 10:2
16   Mark 10:3
17   Deuteronomy 24:1
18   Deuteronomy 21:14

upon the couple.[19] The Law also spoke against remarriage to the former spouse, if the former spouse had remarried after divorce.[20] This would seem to provide support in the Law for regarding the valid subsequent marriage as clearly sacred and as supported by God's grace after the previous divorce. In fact, this would be true only if the former and original marriage relationship did not have the support of God's grace, so making it invalid. Then, if this former marriage had been invalid, logically on the basis of its continuing and perpetual non-validity, and interrupted by an intervening marriage, God's grace also would not have been extended to the hypothetical re-marriage of these former partners to each other, if in some hypothetical future the second marriage also would have been dissolved. But, in fact, if divorce ever had been permissible before God, then there actually would be no limit to the potential cycles of divorce and remarriage, which has been a very human inclination: for example, given the case of the Samaritan woman with Jesus near Jacob's well, who had five husbands, and the man she was with was not her husband.[21]

However, there is a far more parsimonious explanation for Mosaic Law's not allowing former spouses to be remarried to each other, if one party had remarried after divorce: quite simply, the prohibition sought to avoid additional compounding of any religious and social chaos introduced by divorce in the first place. This is like today's Maltese situation (and also in the Philippines): where under a "Catholic" cultural imposition, there is no civil divorce in Malta, under the social supposition that having no divorce means less chaos. In Malta, couples still legally separate and form new unions, although generally without the legal benefit of marriage. However, like the Mosaic permission for divorce, Malta recognizes the civil divorces of other nation-states and also provides for the civil annulments of Maltese civil- or church-marriages—but under current Maltese law, civil annulment processes are suspended if a church annulment is under review; and there are no civil annulments for Catholic church-marriages in Malta if a church annulment is fully processed

---

19   Deuteronomy 22:28-29
20   Deuteronomy 24:2-4
21   John 4:15-18

and is not granted, which very seldom is granted in Malta relative to Maltese civil annulments; the ratio of granted church annulment to civil annulment is less than 1:5 in Malta.[i] In Malta, if due process is respected, civil annulments for various recognized church-marriages may be granted, but only when church annulments are not applied for by either party, or are discontinued before a decision is reached by a church tribunal;[22] but then, universally, one's church status also may become irregular by a positive civil annulment because the Catholic Church does not recognize the annulment of a valid church-marriage by any power or civil process.[23] Therefore, in Malta one applies for a church annulment, and not a civil annulment, if one hopes to abide faithfully to the church's teaching and discipline. The procedure for all Catholic church-annulments also requires clear evidence that the former relationship is irreparable; for example, in the United States the proper sequence requires that one's case for a civil divorce must have been initiated before filing as a petitioner for a Catholic church-annulment.[24] The Mosaic permission for divorce in the Law had attempted to deal with mankind's universal heterosexual instability; but also its permissions seemed to ignore or contradict the divine intention for marriage permanence. Because of the great human demand for alternatives to conflicted marriages and the human demand for solutions, the Law, in part, had sought to justify new alternative relationships to original marriage partners; but more so, as we shall see, it had attempted to remedy the injustices perpetrated by divorce.

Without arguing any of the absent (non-supportive) finer

---

22   This is according to 1995 amendments to the Marriage Act, Chapter 255 (article 30.1 and 30.2), which also recognizes the civil effects of Catholic [and Anglican] marriages celebrated in Malta (article 21.1) and the civil effects of the nullity of a Catholic marriage by its competent church tribunal (subject to the procedural and substantive provisions of article 24), when one of the parties is domiciled in, or a citizen of, Malta (article 23.1).

23   Canon Law 1141, 1075, 1134

24   In the United States, the civil effect of nullity of a Catholic marriage by a church tribunal would require the parallel judgment of divorce provided by the competent civil court, generally of the party's State of residence at the time of filing for divorce.

points of the Law, the Pharisees replied to Jesus with their general legal conclusion:

> Moses allowed us to draw up a writ of dismissal, and so, to divorce.[25]

But Christ was a greater authority than Moses. He was with God, as the Word and as God, in the beginning of creation,[26] so that when Jesus answered the Pharisees' question about divorce, he referred them to the Law in the earliest chapters of Genesis; there his words in Genesis and those words that followed now in his discourse, as the Father taught him to say,[27] were both God's law:

> Because your hearts were so stubbornly obdurate Moses wrote this commandment allowing you to divorce your wives, but it was not like this from the beginning.[28] Have you not read that from the beginning the Creator "made them male and female?"[29] And that he said, "This is why a man shall leave his father and mother and be joined to his wife, and the two shall become one flesh."[30] They are no longer two, but one flesh.[31] Therefore what God has united, no human being must untie.[32] I tell you this: any man who divorces his wife and she has not been unfaithful [I am not speaking of an illicit marriage][33] and marries another; he commits adultery.[34]

When Moses laid down the condition of the writ, he was actually restricting the wide and indiscriminate interpretation of the current practice. Men, in their hardheartedness, were sending off

---

25 Mark 10:4, Matthew 19:7; Deuteronomy 24:1
26 John 1:1
27 John 8:28
28 Mark 10:5, Matthew 19:8
29 Matthew 19:4, Mark 10:6; Genesis 1:27
30 Matthew 19:5, Mark 10:7-8; Genesis 2:24; Ephesians 5:31
31 Mark 10:8, Matthew 19:6
32 Mark 10:9, Matthew 19:6
33 Matthew 19:9, 5:32
34 Matthew 19:9; Exodus 20:14, Leviticus 18:20, Matthew 5:27-28; 2 Corinthians 1:18

their wives without giving them a writ, which bound them forever to a life a tragedy. No one could help these women in any way, because while they remained the property of their husbands, if they were assisted by any other man, the woman and man could both incur the punishment for adultery, namely death,[35] even though these women were not supported at all by their husbands who had sent them off in the first place. Moses was restricting this sending off of wives against their being provided the writ by their husbands.[36]

And so, after the disciples returned to the house where Jesus and the disciples were staying, they questioned him further about this new command.[37] No one, not the disciples and especially not the Pharisees, had quite expected this command. So, once more Jesus told the disciples:

> Whoever divorces his wife and marries another, he commits adultery against her;[38] if she divorces her husband and marries another, she commits adultery;[39] and the man who marries a woman divorced from her husband also commits adultery.[40]

The Lord had made very clear by this that the marriage bond between the couple and blessed by God was indissoluble: the bond was sacred not just for the couple, but also any third party intruders against this grace would be guilty of violating this bond by any remarriage after the couple had divorced. Marriage now was to be a profound celebration and direct reflection of the New Covenant of God with mankind,[41] the great mystery of the relationship between Christ, who declared himself the bridegroom, and his bride, the church; and John the Baptist, who stood by his side and listened, was his best man.[42] It is by baptism that we have entered into this

---

35 Leviticus 20:10
36 Deuteronomy 24:1-4
37 Mark 10:10
38 Mark 10:11; Matthew 19:9, Luke 16:18
39 Mark 10:12; 1 Corinthians 7:10-11
40 Luke 16:18; Matthew 5:32
41 1 Corinthians 11:3, Ephesians 5:21-30, Romans 12:5, 1 Corinthians 10:16-17, 12:12, 6:15-20
42 Ephesians 5:32; John 2:1-5, Revelation 21:2, John 3:29; Matthew 9:15,

New Covenant of Christ's death and resurrection, so that then we are now like a married woman bound by law to her living husband; namely, we belong to Christ, who, although he was put to death for our sins, is raised from the dead and is fully alive in our bodies, so that through his grace, baptized into the church and in the marriage covenant when we enter into it, we bear fruit: always as disciples, with our spouses, and sometimes, with children.[43]

The disciples, still in their amazement and only partially understanding this mystery, said: "If that is the way it is between a husband and wife, it would be better [for persons] not to marry."[44] Then in reply, initially to the second part of their statement (that is, about celibacy, "better not to marry"), Jesus told them:

> This word of mine is not for everyone to accept, but only for those to whom God has granted it.[45] For there are different reasons why men do not marry: some are eunuchs because they were born that way; some are eunuchs because they were made that way by others; and then there are eunuchs who have made themselves that way for the sake of the kingdom of heaven. Whoever can accept this teaching, ought to accept it.[46]

In his reply, Jesus actually had addressed both marriage and celibacy as graces: eunuchs are both incapable of marriage and they are celibate. And because neither marriage nor celibacy is for everyone, there are conditions where the grace for marriage does not exist, and therefore, when the marriage itself would be invalid and, in fact, the sacrament does not exist before God. Three reasons were given by the Lord why some persons are incapable of marriage, why they may not have this grace from God; and these reasons are strikingly consistent with modern psychology: the first reason was because of genetic or biological dispositions—some persons were

---

22:2, 25:1
43 1 Corinthians 7:4, Romans 7:2-4; 1 Corinthians 6:17, 19, Romans 8:11; Genesis 1:28, John 15:1-5, 8
44 Matthew 19:10
45 Matthew 19:11
46 Matthew 19:12

born that way; the second reason was because of personal dispositions from experience or from social environments—some persons were made that way by others; and thirdly, some men do not marry because some make themselves eunuchs—that is, by their personal interaction with the grace of God, some (men or women) choose celibacy, either permanently by the unmarried or temporarily by the already married,[47] for the sake of the kingdom of heaven.[48] This third point does not make a marriage invalid, but it is a condition favouring celibacy, or even religious life for widows or widowers post marriage, in that marriage/re-marriage may be against one's freely accepted vocation to God. Accordingly, the celibate person or the formerly married person now celibate puts aside yet another possession,[49] namely, his/her sexual pro-creative function and marriage, in order to advance fruitfully God's work on earth. This exceptional grace is not for everyone, but the one who does have this grace is advised by the Lord to embrace the gift.

Although the Lord gives an elevated status to celibacy for the sake of the kingdom of heaven, he is not anti-marriage. Rather, Jesus very much supported what today has been regarded as the "traditional" marriage, like the original Adam and Eve, a monogamous union between a man and a woman. But, historically and anthropologically such "traditional" marriages were not always so "traditional," although through the original design of marriage at the beginning of creation, in their union a man and a woman participate in the work of God's hand. Abraham had been the father of many nations: through his son Ishmael born of Hagar, the Egyptian maidservant given to Abraham by his wife Sarai;[50] and through his son Isaac born of his wife, Sarah, as God renamed her when she was blessed with Abraham's son Isaac in their old age.[51] But, as Abraham's wife, Sarai in fact was outraged by this violation of Hagar against her marriage;[52] and the Lord favoured Abraham's wife Sarah: both as God's blessing

---

47 1 Corinthians 7:5-7
48 Matthew 19:11
49 Luke 14:33, Matthew 13:43-44; 1 Corinthians 7:8-9
50 Genesis 16:2-3
51 Genesis 17:15
52 Genesis 16:4-5

of the basic principle of the marriage covenant, as well as giving rise in their marriage to the fulfilment of the covenant promise through their son Isaac.[53]

Through offspring by Isaac's only wife Rebekah, the younger son Jacob inherited God's blessing for the fulfilment of the Lord's oath with Abraham.[54] But the twelve tribes of Judah were descendants of Jacob's two wives, Leah and Rachel, the daughters of Laban, and their respective maid-servants, Zilpah and Bilhah, as Jacob's two concubines.[55] Although Jacob initially had been tricked into polygamy by Laban, Jacob accepted both wives. And even though clearly Jacob preferred his true love, Rachel, he certainly never divorced Leah, whose son Judah would be the progenitor of King David and of his descendant, namely, the Christ;[56] furthermore, when Jacob's oldest son Reuben lay with his father's concubine, Bilhah, that adultery was an offence against the body of Israel.[57] At this time in human history, God had blessed these non-monogamous unions.

King David also had taken several wives,[58] but he sinned only when he took Uriah's wife, Bathsheba, and conceived a son by her, and then he sinned again when he attempted to cover up his sin against Uriah and Bathsheba's marriage by arranging for Uriah's death in the frontlines of battle. When King David repented of his sins, God forgave him, but the newborn son conceived through his passion for another man's wife died of an illness after seven days.[59] Not so for the second son conceived with Bathsheba in David's compassion for his wife, as she mourned their first son's death; for in David's love of Bathsheba, now as his wife, this son was loved by God and became King Solomon.[60] Even in this period of polygamous human history, the expanded marriage bond had been made sacred and was in accord with the covenant promise. Even then God's faithfulness to

---

53 Genesis 17:16
54 Genesis 26:3-4
55 Genesis 35:23-26
56 Genesis 49:10
57 Genesis 35:22, 49:4
58 2 Samuel 12:8
59 2 Samuel 12:18
60 2 Samuel 12:24

the covenant always had excluded adultery or divorce because such offences against marriage were offences against the grace of God.

But now, Christ had corrected the liberalization of Moses to allow divorce; and the reason was that Christ's faithfulness to the fulfilment of the covenant always had respected the marriage covenant, in fact, doing so beginning with Adam and Eve.[61] And by his reference to the way it had been in the beginning,[62] as far as marriage goes, Christ was anti-divorce and anti-polygamy, as well as pro-marriage (monogamy) and pro-celibacy. For now, in our relationship with Jesus, the New Covenant also required a new sign of our mutual and reciprocal faithfulness: commitment through marriage for some, for others celibacy for the sake of the kingdom, and for those without the grace for either, neither one.[63] In this new law of Christ, Jesus also grants that some are incapable of marriage, perhaps never capable of it, or only incapable of it at the time one entered into marriage and therefore its non-validity continuing for its subsequent duration.

Sometimes, the absence of that grace in a marriage is revealed through the help of one's testimony, and the testimony of others, through the official process of one's obtaining a Catholic church-annulment. In the absence of divorce, the concept of annulment may be confusing, but essentially it is this: although a marriage has taken place, the marriage sacrament may be invalid because marriage was not entered into freely, either because one or both parties in the marriage were born that way or because they were made that way by others;[64] and/or one or both parties may not have understood the person whom they were marrying when they got married, or one or both persons may not have understood what marriage was about.[ii] The consequence of these invalidating elements, when so determined by the church, officially recognizes that God, in fact, did not bind the couple to that originally invalid marriage; and therefore, a person would be free to enter into a new marriage relationship in the church, either without any limitations, or within the provisions

---

61　Genesis 3:15; 1 Corinthians 15:21-23, Romans 7:4
62　Matthew 19:4-6, Genesis 2:21-25
63　Matthew 19:12
64　Matthew 19:12

of the judgments of the marriage tribunal regarding the required capacity of persons for sacramental marriage: for example, the potential requirement for professional psychological counselling before remarriage in the church.

Sometimes the discovery of grace in marriage can be a long and painful journey. Originally, I was married in Fort Wayne, Indiana (USA) according to the Rite of the Roman Catholic Church on 29th December 1971 at twenty-three years of age. Another twenty-three years later, approximately eighteen months after a petition for divorce had been filed, the Judgment of Divorce became Absolute in Essex County according to the laws of the Commonwealth of Massachusetts (USA) on 15th March 1994, but it only was registered eight months later at Salem County on 14th November 1994. In 1995, Case No. T-086-95 for my marriage annulment was initiated before the Marriage Tribunal for the Diocese of Fort Wayne—South Bend (Indiana), in the diocese where our marriage had taken place. Then the following year, having been in Malta since 12th October 1992, I married my wife, Joan Zammit, at the Civil Marriage Registry in Malta on 3rd September 1996. In August 1997, the Marriage Tribunal informed me of the grounds for the case, and subsequently I made my submissions for the case twice: first, in late 1997, there was a twenty-one-page single-spaced document that I had completed by myself; later there was a shorter comprehensive document prepared with me and written by the Maltese Marriage Tribunal in 1998. The first document had been a challenge and grateful opportunity for me to write; the second document, more than the first, was a great joy to complete.[65]

Then concluding on 12th March 1999, the Marriage Tribunal in America issued a declaration of nullity of marriage on the basis of its affirmative decision. Therefore, the bond of my previous marriage, the *ligamen*, no longer was in effect. Before this moment, although against the norm I had married Joan and lived with her before that judgment of the church, I had accepted the original gift of Joan from God, as both in faith and in good conscience I also had recognized the context for the genuine invalidity of her first marriage, yet to be

---

[65] 1 Corinthians 5:7-8

affirmed by the church; also I had accepted that, given her individual psychology and life circumstances, I should not pressure her to pursue a church annulment.[66] But, only upon the removal of her *ligamen*, either through the affirmative judgment of a Marriage Tribunal or through the death of her previous spouse still living,[67] only then could our mutual embrace of new-found grace and gifts from God eventually be officially recognized and confirmed by the church.[68] Well, unexpectedly for us, by virtue of her first husband's death on 5th August 2008, at last her *ligamen* was removed; we had learned of her former husband's death thirty days later, the day after our 12th wedding anniversary. Through God's mercy, and five years after my taking up the Gospel Emmaus, and after fifteen years together as a couple, the Lord now had provided us the opportunity to apply to the Curia for the registration of our marriage in the church. In only a matter of months, we were re-married in the church, at Santa Barbara's in Valletta (Malta) on 8th December 2008, the feast of the Immaculate Conception; and now, as I continue my third round of editing this book, it is nearly one year later, our first Marian anniversary.

In the early Christian church at Corinth (Greece), Saint Paul found himself as mediator for a proper balance on issues of celibacy, marriage, and divorce, against the exaggerated asceticism some Corinthians were adopting. At first, Paul quotes the proposition of their written letter as if to agree that "it is a good thing for a man not to touch a woman,"[69] however he immediately rebuts this proposition. In cases where the natural inclination to sex would otherwise lead to sexual immorality, Paul pragmatically and universally is in favour of marriage: "Because of cases of immorality, every man should have his own wife; and every woman her own husband."[70] And then, in the context of this natural sex-drive, Paul asserts that husbands and wives have fundamental sexual duties to each other: "the husband must give his wife what she expects, and likewise the wife should do

---

66   Acts 15:28-29, Romans 5:1-5, 13:8, 1 Corinthians 7:16-17, 18-24
67   1 Corinthians 7:39
68   2 Corinthians 5:7-10
69   1 Corinthians 7:1
70   1 Corinthians 7:2

the same for her husband."[71] Paul continues his thought: "The wife has no rights over her own body, but rather her husband has them; in the same way, the husband has no rights over his own body, but they belong to the wife."[72]

Before marriage everyone has authority and responsibility from God over his or her own body,[73] but not so in marriage, when spouses give themselves completely to each other: sexually, most certainly, but not only in physical love. This surrender of their bodies is not tyranny, as certain modern advocates of women's rights might claim; but along with its exclusivity, this surrender of their body completely to their spouse is mutual obedience to love and justice. Any temporary exclusion and denial of sex by spouses to each other was to be avoided, except by mutual consent, and then only for an agreed upon time— not so long as to allow Satan's sufficient and inevitable temptations to get a foothold into the marriage; but if spouses agreed upon such sexual abstinence, then this deprivation was permissible, but only in the further context of allowing time for the couple to be together in prayer.[74] This was Paul's only concession to the Corinthians for their proposition of sexual asceticism; and his concession to them for a clearly defined period of abstinence was not a command, but quite definitely it was only a cautious permission.[75]

Within marriage, it would be immoral for spouses to withhold intercourse from each other for any lengthy period or without a mutual agreement for doing so. The absence of intercourse over time within marriage could be a symptom of a disordered marriage, and it could contribute to active immoralities against the marriage because of the natural sex-drive. Against the ascetic restrictions the Corinthians had advocated, Saint Paul recognized these lethal dangers of sexual abstinence within marriage; but also he recognized marriage as a gift from God, just as his celibacy was his special gift from God. So, just as others had their gifts, celibacy was not for everyone, but neither

---

71	1 Corinthians 7:3
72	1 Corinthians 7:4, 6:20; Luke 9:24
73	1 Corinthians 6:19, Genesis 1:27
74	1 Corinthians 7:5
75	1 Corinthians 7:6

was marriage. Paul writes, "I should like everyone to be like me, but everyone has his own particular gifts from God, one with a gift of one kind and the other with a gift for the opposite."[76]

As for the personal choice Paul had made for himself, Paul takes up this preference of his for the never-married or those not married now, for virgins and widows (male or female): "I say, it is a good thing for them to remain as they are, as I do."[77] But immediately Paul again places his balance: "But if they cannot control their sexual urges, they should get married—because it is better to marry than to burn with passion."[78] Also, it is an irony that marriage too, like the sexual urge, comes with its natural afflictions.[79] So, against the uncontrollable sexual urge, Paul once more balances this captivity by the deliberately chosen bondage in marriage one embraces under one's faithful commitment within the Lord's covenant.[80] To the married or prospectively married, Paul reminds them of the Lord's commands regarding a valid marriage: "A wife should not separate from her husband—or if she does leave him, she must either remain single or become reconciled to her husband—and a husband must not divorce his wife."[81] This principle applies then to marriages between any two baptized Christians because through baptism we belong to the New Covenant and there is only one baptism and one faith in the one Lord of all, even if there are different expressions of that faith in the separated Christian churches.

But if a baptized Christian should be married to an unbaptized spouse, Paul on his own (and not from the Lord) extended this principle of non-separation to them too, provided that the relationship was a peaceful and sanctifying one: "If a brother has a wife who is an unbeliever, and she is content to live with him, he must not send her away; and if any woman has a husband who is an unbeliever, and he is willing to live with her, she must not leave

---

76 1 Corinthians 7:7
77 1 Corinthians 7:8, 1
78 1 Corinthians 7:9
79 1 Corinthians 7:28, Luke 9:23
80 Philippians 2:5-8
81 1 Corinthians 7:10-11; Matthew 19:6, 9, Mark 10:9, 11-12, Luke 16:18; John 1:35, 43, 2:1, 11

him."[82] For, as Paul reminded them, it is through the believing wife or husband that the unbelieving spouse is made holy; and, in fact, their children also are holy;[83] that is, they are blest by God, which added weight to his argument, as well as other weighty arguments about having children. But first, before we get to those matters, once again Paul provided the balance, the exception, to this rule of non-separation, which is the basis for the Pauline privilege.[84] This allows a Christian spouse to separate from a non-baptized spouse; and on this basis, the former marriage is dissolved by dispensation, so that the spouse may remarry in the church. Paul writes: "If the unbelieving partner separates, then let him separate; for the brother or sister is not bound in such circumstances: God has called you to a life of peace."[85] Also, in this particular dispensation reserved to the Pope, the so-called "Petrine privilege" permits the dissolution of a marriage between any baptized and un-baptized spouse, if either party wants to marry a Catholic. If the Pope does decide to act favourably for this dispensation in such a case, this would be done so as to favour the Christian faith of the Catholic fiancé or fiancée.[86]

And also, it was right for Saint Paul to remind married couples about the holiness of their children, even within a Christian marriage with a non-believing spouse.[87] Shortly after Jesus had discussed these matters of marriage and divorce with his disciples,[88] while they were now heading towards Jerusalem, people were bringing their children to Jesus, so that he might bless and touch them and pray over them, but the disciples began shooing them all away.[89] When Jesus saw this he was quite indignant, and so he told everyone there:

> Let the little children come, and do not prevent them
> from coming to me; for the kingdom of heaven belongs

---

82 1 Corinthians 7:12-13
83 1 Corinthians 7:14
84 Canon 1143-1150
85 1 Corinthians 7:15
86 "In a doubtful matter the privilege of faith possesses the favor of the law" (Canon Law 1150).
87 1 Corinthians 7:14
88 Mark 10:10-12, Matthew 19:10-12
89 Mathew 19:13, Mark 10:13, Luke 18:15

to such as these.[90] For I tell you solemnly, anyone who does not accept the kingdom of God like a child will never enter it.[91]

Then Jesus embraced the children, placed his hands on them, and blessed them,[92] and then he went on his way.[93]

Jesus did mean for us to trust him entirely, to follow him with the simplicity and total unreservedness of a child. But here Jesus also was addressing all married couples worldwide, especially couples with even just a single partner who is professing to be Christian:

> Do not prevent the little ones from coming to me:[94] not through abortion, not by the forced sterilization of single-child families, not through birth-control devices or pills, nor through prolonged sexual abstinence; not because of the ordinary or presumed risks of bringing a child to full-term or because of unknown or potential dangers of childbirth for the mother's life, nor because of anxieties about parenting or fears about a child's difficult existence in the hostile world; for God's kingdom belongs to children such as these. Amen, I tell you: anyone who does not accept a child like the kingdom of heaven will never enter it.[95]

You can be sure of this: God will bless all of his children:[96] and all our natural born or adopted children, and our grandchildren too. But if from Paul's cautious permission to the Corinthians even any brief sexual abstinence within marriage required the couple's first coming together in prayer, in place of their physical love;[97] then by extension a couple's shared prayer would be an even greater necessity if any considerations other than sexual abstinence are being considered

---

90　Matthew 19:14, Mark 10:14, Luke 18:16
91　Mark 10:15, Luke 18:17
92　Matthew 19:15, Mark 10:16
93　Matthew 19:15
94　Matthew 19:14, Mark 10:14, Luke 18:16
95　Mark 10:15, Luke 18:17
96　Matthew 19:15, Mark 10:16
97　1 Corinthians 7:5

by either partner as a means for morally valid and presently urgent family planning.[98] In sincere prayer and genuine openness to the Holy Spirit, directions and means are found for holy decisions.[99] If couples are so divided so as not to be able to pray together, then at least one partner, or other persons along with Christ,[100] needs to pray hard to avoid any imminent tragedies of sin.[101]

The early Christian church was caught up in the dilemma of marriage versus celibacy: marriage (with its heterosexuality reserved exclusively between spouses) was the very image of Christ in relationship to the church as his bride;[102] while celibacy excluded marriage or any other acts of a sexual nature (be they heterosexual, homosexual, or masturbation), so that in celibacy the person could dedicate himself/herself exclusively in mind and body to the service of the kingdom of God.[103] However, despite many potential conflicts, the ministers of many protestant Christian denominations regularly take wives; and sometimes women of those denominations are ordained as ministers, priests, or bishops, which disregards gender. In the Roman Rite of the Catholic Church, as a general rule a married man may be ordained as a deacon, but not as a priest; and occasionally one may even find a married cleric, but the rare married priest very likely was ordained and married before his becoming Roman Catholic.

We also may observe that a former priest has left the priesthood, or a religious sister has left her convent, sometimes in order to take up his/her marriage vocation, usually after his or her dispensation from religious vows. In 2004 (compared to 1970) with 1.114 billion (up +70%) Catholics worldwide, there were 405,450 priests (down slightly -3.4%) and 54,620 and 776,269 religious brothers or sisters, respectively, (down -31.2% and -22.7%), all overtly dedicated to celibacy in the Lord. In 2004 there also were 31,524 permanent deacons (up +10,202%), either married or unmarried, and 45% of

---

98 Luke 17:20-21; 1 Thessalonians 4:3-8
99 Matthew 18:19
100 Matthew 18:20
101 Matthew 7:11, Luke 11:13
102 Ephesians 5:21-33
103 Luke 18:29-30, Matthew 19:29-30, Mark 10:29-31

these were in the United States, where there were even greater declines than worldwide: in priests (down -26.5%), in lay religious brothers (down -37.0%), and in lay religious sisters (down -48.1%); and compared to 1965 (five years earlier when I had been in seminary), 2004 declines for the U.S. in religious brothers and sisters were even greater still (down -55.7% and -61.0%). Always, the survival of the human species has never required marriage of everyone, only of some; but for the continued and basic survival and propagation of the faith, many celibate persons in the Lord are required absolutely, along with full and generous dedication and the ecclesial company of some married persons, too.

Saint Paul's position was that everyone should continue before God in the state in which he was called,[104] namely, the married should stay married and virgins should remain celibate. Unlike married persons, who have from the Lord a clear commandment of commitment in married life to their spouses,[105] Paul offers no commandment as such from the Lord about virgins,[106] any unmarried (and celibate) daughters or men, who have greater options for choice before God, either choosing marriage or celibacy in the Lord. However, Paul does provide his clear opinion, rooted in his faithfulness and the Spirit of God,[107] and based upon the respective gifts from the Lord for married or celibate persons:[108]

> If you are bound to a wife, do not seek a separation; but if you are free of a wife, do not look for one.[109] However, if you do marry, it is not a sin; nor is it a sin if a young girl gets married; but such persons will experience troubles in their married life in the world, and I would like to spare you that.[110] What I mean, brothers, is that our time is growing short; and those having wives should

---

104   1 Corinthians 7:17, 24
105   1 Corinthians 7:10-11; Matthew 19:9, Mark 10:11-12, Luke 16:18
106   1 Corinthians 7:25
107   1 Corinthians 7:25, 40
108   1 Corinthians 7: 7
109   1 Corinthians 7:27
110   1 Corinthians 7:28

live as though they had none.[111] And those weeping should live as though they had nothing to weep for; those enjoying life as though they were not rejoicing; those whose life is buying things should live as though they owned nothing;[112] and those who have to use the world, should not become engrossed in it.[113] For the world as we know it is passing away.[114]

In the context of the impending distress of his age, Paul thought that married or unmarried persons should remain as they were, not only because of the coming persecutions,[115] but because immanently the world was passing away to be remade in Christ,[116] as is still slowly being done today, nearly 2000 years later, with 17% of the world's population nominally Catholic. Then Paul more explicitly explained his pastoral preference for celibacy over marriage:

> I would like to see you free of anxieties: an unmarried man can devote himself to the Lord's affairs, being anxious about how best to please the Lord.[117] But a married man is worried about the world's affairs,[118] and he devotes himself to pleasing his wife;[119] and [sometimes between the two] he is torn in both directions,[120] [as well as torn apart between them and the Lord]. Also an unmarried woman, or a young girl, can devote herself to the Lord's affairs, so that she may be holy in both body and spirit.[121] But on the other hand, a married woman is preoccupied about the world's affairs and

---

111   1 Corinthians 7:29
112   1 Corinthians 7:30
113   1 Corinthians 7:31; 1 John 2:15-16
114   1 Corinthians 7:31; 1 John 2:17
115   Mark 10:30; Matthew 5:10-12, 10:22-23; 2 Corinthians 12:10, 2 Timothy 3:1
116   1 Corinthians 7:26, 31;
117   1 Corinthians 7:32
118   1 Corinthians 7:33; Matthew 20:5
119   1 Corinthians 7:33; Luke 14:20
120   1 Corinthians 7:34
121   1 Corinthians 7:34

how she can please her husband.¹²² But I am telling you this only to help you—not to put a halter around your necks—simply for the sake of propriety, and only that you may give yourself completely and unreservedly to the Lord.¹²³

Furthermore, the potentially critical dilemma regarding celibacy was given astute attention by Paul for either the father of a daughter, or for a man engaged to his girl. But, once again, Paul supported celibacy as preferable to marriage—provided that certain conditions not limiting such celibacy were met:

> If anyone thinks he is behaving improperly toward his virgin: such as if a father feels that it would not be fair to his daughter to let her grow too old for marriage, or when an engaged couple decides not to marry, if the man feels that he is not acting properly towards his betrothed; and if the moment for acting is critical or passions are too strong, and he feels that they ought to marry, then he is free to do as he wishes; and there would be no sin if they should get married.¹²⁴ On the other hand, if anyone has firmly made up his mind, without compulsion and in complete freedom of choice, to keep his virgin as she is and not to give or take her in marriage, then he will be doing a good thing.¹²⁵ So then, a man who sees that his daughter is married, or a man who marries his girl, does well; but the man who keeps his daughter unmarried, or who chooses not to marry her, will do even better.¹²⁶

And then, similarly as he did for never-married persons, Paul addresses the potential remarriage of widows, but in this he encourages his preference, even-handedly for both groups, that widows also should remain unmarried:

122	1 Corinthians 7:34
123	1 Corinthians 7:35
124	1 Corinthians 7:36
125	1 Corinthians 7:37
126	1 Corinthians 7:38

> A wife is bound to her husband as long as he is living; but if he dies, then she is free to marry whomever she wishes, but it must be a marriage to a Christian man.[127] However, she would be more blessed, in my opinion, if she stayed as she is—and I think that I too have the Spirit of God.[128]

In the spring of 1966, then as a seventeen-year-old seminarian, I took the train from Syracuse, Indiana, the town closest to the seminary, for a weekend trip to the Dominican novitiate in Winona, Minnesota.[129] Initially around 7:00 a.m. I missed the train, while I stood on the railway platform at an undesignated stop by myself. As the train rushed by, my anticipation turned to dismay; but after a phone call to the seminary, and one strategic car-chase later, I just managed to catch the train at its next local stop. From there I made my way 240 km on to Chicago, where another train took me across Illinois to Dubuque, Iowa, another 270 km; and then the same train turned northward 160 km along the Mississippi River, and crossed the state line another 80 km into Minnesota, where I got off at Winona. It was a long and arduous journey taking the full day's light. But this would be my introductory visit to the Dominican monastery before I would engage my first and only year at Dubuque, one of the two required years of college study before entering the novitiate. This monastery visit also would be my first personal experience with the Dominicans face-to-face beyond my second-hand associations through my mother's sister, then a Racine (Wisconsin) Dominican; and because of my closeness to her, more as if my dearest older sister by five years than an aunt, she also inspired my Dominican aspirations. However, on my own vocational journey, I was nearing the end of my four-year diocesan-seminary formation at Lake Wawasee under the Crosier Fathers and Brothers, a religious order transplanted to America from its Netherlands roots, then having religious houses in Fort Wayne, Indiana, my birthplace, and also in Onamia, Minnesota; but now with their headquarters in Phoenix, Arizona.

---

127   1 Corinthians 7:39
128   1 Corinthians 7:40
129   Matthew 19:12

The weekend at the Dominican monastery in Minnesota was notable for its welcoming participation in the life of the religious community, and for the opportunity it afforded a small group of us to discuss religious vocation issues with the priests and novices. Besides the quiet and the brotherhood, the prayer and the liturgy, and the meals in common, while at one meal we listened to a community member reading aloud to us from a John le Carré novel; and besides the reflections and homilies of our casual semi-retreat, perhaps for me the most important moment was the personal discussion I had while cornered away with one of the novices as we all met together in a group. Mostly I listened to this mid-twenty-year-old novice as he described his conflicted, but committed choice to leave behind his fiancée, abruptly, for his novitiate years within the monastery enclosed entirely away from outside contacts with the world, except for ourselves as its exceptional guests.[130] Along with the intensity of his serious pursuit of his potential vocation to religious life, he also freely shared with me the painful ambivalence in his heart that combined with his prayerful devotion to God's will.

A year later, the forceful memory of my meeting this particular novice graphically co-existed with my eventual decision to leave the seminary, but only when I initially understood my actual hope and longing for some type of ideal "loving-wife".[131] And then, only a few months after that gradual insight, once again I returned to the monastery for the initiation of some of my former college associates into their first novitiate year with the Dominicans. I don't remember ever learning anything more about the older novice I had met the previous year, whether or not he continued in his religious vocation, or if he had returned to his girl.[132] But I also will always remember one of the new novices among my close associates, one who was already fluent in reading the theologians Karl Rahner and Hans Küng in their original German: he did become a Dominican priest; and his glowing smile on his face that day, when he entered the religious life as a novice, still lingers fondly and admirably in my mind.

---

130   Luke 18:29-30, 1 Corinthians 7:36-38
131   1 Corinthians 7:7-9
132   1 Corinthians 7:36

The most disturbing factor for my generation[133] was the Vietnam War; but also the critical liberating factor of my generation for my Roman Catholic faith was Vatican II (the Second Vatican Council, 1962-1965), although for others, including large numbers of laity and religious, it disturbed their religious routine. But then, some of my thirty seminary classmates eventually were ordained: one today is still a Diocesan priest and now is a Monsignor for a very large parish; while another classmate left the priesthood only a few years after his ordination, and then was married. My spiritual director in seminary also eventually left the priesthood; and then he taught mathematics at university in Colorado before he was married. One of the religious brothers, who instructed us in athletics, also left the religious life; but then he was drafted immediately into the army, as also was an ex-seminarian schoolmate, who had been two years ahead of me, Terry Ruth. Terry was killed on 8 September 1968, at age twenty-two, in Hua Nghia, South Vietnam, a ground casualty of hostile small arms fire. Terry was a nervously intense, kind, and dedicated personality, who shared my seminary life and our competition for the piano practice-room. His senior-year classmates offered this vivid memory of Terry in the school's 1964 yearbook, *Cumque*:

> The symphony and the hockey stick, the textbook and the beaming smile—all these are part of Terry Ruth. Terry has reserved himself a seat high on the honour roll during all four years here, and his keen perception and riotous sense of humour leave everyone he meets in better spirits than before. The seniors will never forget "T. Ruth," the sophomore, passing out cookies up and down the (dormitory) hall at eleven o'clock at night.[134]

For Terry, ever so generous and humble, his ironic nickname, "T. Ruth," was a loving analogy to the ferocious dinosaur king, "T. Rex" (*Tyrannrosaurus Rex*).[135] But only by chance and God's design, unlike Terry, I had managed to escape the ravages of the military draft with my quite sufficiently high lottery number for my birth year

---

133   1 Corinthians 7:26
134   Matthew 14:15-16
135   Matthew 10:16

and date: 238th out of the 365 ranked possibilities. After twenty-five years, in August 1992, when I was in Washington, DC for a few days, I sought out Terry's name on the Vietnam War Memorial, where I successfully located it on Panel 44W, Line 6. There, as I stood before Terry's name engraved on the solemn black marble wall, during a period of my life that was particularly stressful and spiritually very dangerous for me without a home and jobless,[136] I lingered for a while to remember Terry and to pray for him. Yet, there also were others who had persisted in their religious vocations during those times of crisis in the 1960s: in particular, there was the Reverend Father Thomas Scheets, O.S.C., who had been my favourite and most significant teacher in seminary.

In 1975, nine years after I had attended, the seminary closed its doors on the shores of Lake Wawasee, Indiana; and eventually Father Tom would go to a parish in Pueblo, Colorado, St. Leander, where he eagerly had made his ideal transition to pastoral work among the Hispanic and American Indian parishioners that he had cared for so lovingly; that is, until his final devotion to the cross, in early August of 1996. Then, a twenty-year-old paranoid schizophrenic, who was living with his mother and grandmother across the street from the parish rectory, suddenly stopped taking his medication. Immediately, the inevitable voices came to the young man: "You will be killed if you do not kill someone!" Over the weekend, when the voices got worse, the very concerned mother took her son to the doctor on Monday. But, through an unusual set of circumstances, neither that doctor, nor two others, nor the local hospital's psychiatric ward could act, or would not act. Then, on Wednesday, the young man hopped in his mother's car and drove around the neighbourhood looking for someone to kill. But his voices kept saying, "Not that one!" Finally, he panicked; he went home; and he took a paring knife from the kitchen. Then he went across the street to the rectory, where he killed two priests: Father Tom, who at that time was sixty-five-years-old, and a retired priest, who also was living there.[137] It was the 7th of

---

136 John 10:1-3, Luke 15:3-6, John 8:31-33, 37-38, 10:4, 6:63, Luke 15:21-24; Luke 19:10, 5-6, John 17:24
137 Fr. Tom's brother, Fr. Francis (Bud) Kelly Sheets, OSC relayed these events to me personally twice: first in July 1997, when I was visiting in

August, the day after the feast of Our Lord's transfiguration.

Yet, here, in these sad events, the Lord reminds us that although, if we follow him, our commitment to his cross must come first; then there also will be the resurrection.[138] For Father Tom, and for all of us, on 4 August 1996 (Year A), during the previous Sunday's liturgy for the 18th Sunday in Ordinary Time, Saint Paul had posed this question in his letter to the Romans:

> Who will separate us from the love of Christ? Trial, or distress, or persecution, or hunger, or nakedness, or danger, or the sword?[139]

To Paul's partial list of violence against the body of Christ, we also may add small arms gunfire for Terry Ruth, and a paring knife for Father Tom. Similarly, on a daily basis around the world, there is catastrophic violence and murder. In Paul's letter, Paul also had quoted the psalm verse that is ironic and prophetic commentary, but this verse was omitted from that Sunday's second reading:

> As the scripture says, "For your sake we are being massacred all day long, treated as sheep to be slaughtered."[140]

However, in the beginning of the gospel that Father Tom had read on his final Sunday, we also witness Jesus in his response to his hearing about the death of John the Baptist, beheaded by a blade of the knife: Jesus withdrew by boat to a deserted place by himself, but the crowds followed him.[141] And there, in that remote place, also in anticipation of his gift of Eucharist and of his sacrifice on the cross, he gave us and the crowds his promise of his eternal presence with us, by the sign of his feeding the crowds from five loaves and two fish, but also by his critically telling his disciples, and his would be future disciples:

Fort Wayne, and then once again ten years later, in October 2007.
138 Luke 9:30-32, Mark 9:9-10, Luke 9:23
139 Romans 8:35
140 Romans 8:36, Psalm 44:22
141 Matthew 14:13

> There is no need for them [the crowds] to disperse.
> Give them something to eat yourselves.[142]

Both Terry Ruth and Father Tom had done this by their lives; but also, by their deaths, as they were united with the Lamb of God in Christ's immeasurable act of love.[143] The example of their love, by their taking someone else's place in death from among the living, feeds our lives and allows them to say:

> Yet, in all this we are more than conquerors because of him [Jesus] who has loved us.[144]

With and through the lives of Terry and Tom, Christ also had lived with us. Now that they are gone, we have been left behind with the Lord's same charge to his disciples, namely, for all of us now to feed the body of Christ ourselves. Some of us, including myself, did not continue with our potential vocations to religious life; and for everyone who did, vocations took their unexpected turn. Our generation, like every generation, had its turmoil and anxieties, just as now, for example, there are evil sources and roots for today's international terrorism and the wars in Iraq and Afghanistan. But in our time,[145] my colleagues also had been devoted to the mystery of our calling in the Lord,[146] whether called to marriage in the world or to celibacy in the religious life.[147] Ultimately, yesterday as well as today, Christ has been our only liberator.[148] And graciously and mercifully Christ also sends us his gifts, and especially our particular cross, that he also shares with us; before, later on, unto God's glory, he then shares with us his resurrection.[149]

---

142 Matthew 14:16
143 Revelation 7:13-14
144 Romans 8:37-39; John 10:14-15, 15:12-13, Matthew 28:20
145 1 Corinthians 7:26-31, 2:6
146 1 Corinthians 7:35, 2:7, 1:18
147 1 Corinthians 7:7, Matthew 19:11; Romans 8:28
148 Luke 18:31; Romans 8:29
149 Matthew 20:19, Mark 10:34, Luke 18:33; 1 Corinthians 2:9, Romans 8:30

Readings: John 11:1-54

Jesus remained with his disciples and taught the crowds in the region where John had baptized,[150] near Bethany across the Jordan,[151] until the two sisters, Martha and Mary,[152] about 30 km away at home in Bethany near Jerusalem,[153] sent the Lord this message, succinct and clear, about their brother Lazarus, who lived together with them their celibate lives in the house:[154] "Master, the man you love is sick."[155] Although Lazarus had been sick for quite a while, the sisters sent their present message only when it now seemed that death was imminent for their gravely ill brother; and that the time was certainly near for the Lord to act. And they knew where to find Jesus, as Jesus and his many disciples were part of one body, forming the large, social network of continuous word-of-mouth or direct communications with Jesus about each other's activities.

Martha, Mary, and Lazarus, in fact, were among the Lord's closest and dearest of personal friends.[156] But even so, when Jesus heard that Lazarus was sick, he did not rush off in a hurry, as we might have done in such an emergency, and as Martha and Mary had done with their dispatch of an urgent message to signal Jesus, if he intended to prevent Lazarus from dying.[157] But instead of rushing off, Jesus did quite the contrary: he intentionally stayed put for yet another two days,[158] as if to ensure that Lazarus was most emphatically dead.[159] Yet, upon his receiving their message, Jesus calmly and reassuringly told his disciples simply:

> This sickness will not end in Lazarus' death, but it will be for God's glory, so that (in the end) through it, the

---

150	Matthew 3:5-7, 11
151	John 10:40, 1:28
152	Luke 10:38-39
153	John 11:18
154	John 11:1
155	John 11:3
156	John 11:5
157	John 11:21, 32
158	John 11:6
159	John 11:17

Son of God (also) will be glorified.[160]

The disciples never imagined the truth of what Jesus actually meant by his seeming dismissal of any concern for Lazarus' illness; for God's glory in Lazarus was to be the immediate precursor for the Lord's yet to be understood death and resurrection, and another true sign from God for our eternal life in Christ.[161]

For soon, the raising of Lazarus from the dead by Jesus would be the final straw for the Pharisees and the Sanhedrin;[162] but to the glory of the Father's gifts to us, by his grace and in his Son,[163] this would enable Christ to accomplish his Father's will;[164] the raising of Lazarus would lead, namely, to the first glorification of God's Son, to the redemption of our sins through his death on the cross;[165] this then would be followed by his second glorification, this by the Father through his Son's resurrection as firstborn of the dead;[166] and thirdly, by virtue of his original glorification, the Lord's glory from before the beginning of the world, Jesus would be enthroned soon as our King in heaven.[167] Then, finally at the end of time, and for our own final glorification or condemnation,[168] Jesus would come at last in his entire glory to judge all the living and the dead;[169] these last Jesus also judges upon their death,[170] at the thieving hour on their personal Day of the Lord.[171]

After the two days had passed, seemingly just running in place,[172]

---

160 John 11:4
161 John 11:25-26, 6:47-51
162 John 11:47
163 John 17:4
164 John 11:53
165 John 17:1
166 Revelation 1:5, 1 Corinthians 15:20
167 Matthew 19:28, 25:31, 26:64; John 17:5
168 John 5:29, Mark 8:38
169 Matthew 24:30, 25:32
170 2 Corinthians 5:10, 6:1-2
171 Matthew 24:43-44, Luke 12:36, 39-40; 1 Thessalonians 5:2; Luke 12:33, 1 John 2:28
172 John 11:6

just standing still but full of the usual activity of the Lord,[173] Jesus suddenly and simply said, "Let's go to Judea."[174] With quite a bit of surprise, and with some initial alarm, the disciples dissuasively asked, "Rabbi, the Jews were just trying to stone you a little while ago;[175] and now, you want to go back there again?"[176] But Jesus replied:

> Are there not twelve hours in a day?[177] If one walks in the daytime, he does not stumble because he has the light of this world to see by.[178] But if one walks at night, he stumbles because there is no light in him to guide him.[179] Our friend Lazarus is sleeping;[180] but I am going to wake him up.[181]

But the disciples had misunderstood this figure of speech of Jesus. So the disciples said to him, "Lord, if he is resting, surely then he will get better."[182] They thought that he had meant ordinary sleep, not death.[183] So, Jesus then told them plainly:

> Lazarus is dead.[184] And for your sake I am glad that I was not there with him, so that you may believe. Let's go to him.[185]

When Jesus said this, Thomas, the one called Didymus, misunderstood Jesus once more. He thought that Jesus had meant to test their faith right then by having the disciples join him now in death with Lazarus in Judea. Later on, this same Thomas would doubt the word of all the others, that the Lord himself on Easter was risen from the dead, without his first having put his hand and fingers

---

173　Matthew 8:20
174　John 11:7
175　John 10:31, 39; John 8:59
176　John 11:8
177　John 11:9; John 9:4
178　John 11:9; John 9:5
179　John 11:10; Matthew 15:14, John 9:40-41; 1 John 1:5-7, 2:8
180　John 11:11; Matthew 9:24, Mark 5:39, Luke 8:52
181　John 11:11
182　John 11:12
183　John 11:13
184　John 11:14
185　John 11:15

into the wounds of Christ.[186] But now, with this grand irony, the eagerly zealous Thomas called out to his fellow disciples, "Let's also go and die with him."[187]

Then, in what appears to be a moment of "group mind" [Freud, 1923], seemingly carried away in their strong group-reinforced identifications with the person of Jesus, immediately and nearly unconsciously they followed Jesus to the last man like dazed automatons; and, in the attraction of the dynamism and charisma of Jesus, they marched off in unison with him to their imagined deaths in Judea. This is not unlike the psychology we witness today among some groups following their terrorist leaders according to the paths of their extreme political-religious ideologies. However, in actually following Jesus, eventually there would be a time for many of the disciples when their martyrdoms would be very real, and not imaginary. Actually, Jesus now had been preparing them for their future: when their following of the Lord to their deaths would not be some automatic emotion, but rather a fully conscious choice and commitment to the will of God. And through their determined hope in Christ, by his promises and by their utter conviction in his cross and resurrection, these present events involving Lazarus would lead the disciples to their subsequently greater faith in Jesus, and in God's mercy, to their ultimate resurrection to eternal life with the Lord.[188]

When Martha heard that Jesus was coming, she went to meet him as he had arrived, just outside the village of Bethany.[189] She likely was the first one who told the Lord that Lazarus had been in the tomb already for four days.[190] Martha also told Jesus, "Lord, if you had been here, my brother would not have died,[191] but I know that, even now, whatever you ask of God, God will give you."[192] Then Jesus told her:

186	John 20:25
187	John 11:16
188	John 11:15
189	John 11:20, 30
190	John 11:17
191	John 11:21
192	John 11:22

Your brother will rise.[193]

And Martha replied, "I know he will rise at the resurrection on the last day."[194] But Jesus told her:

> I am the resurrection and the life; whoever believes in me, even if he dies, he will live,[195] and whoever lives and believes in me will never die. Do you believe this?[196]

Martha replied, "Yes, Lord. I have come to believe that you are the Christ, the Son of God, the one who was to come into the world."[197] After saying this and remaining there with Jesus, Martha secretly called her sister Mary, who was in the house,[198] saying to her, "The Master is here, and he is calling for you."[199]

When Mary heard this, she immediately got up and hurried out of the house to meet the Lord,[200] without speaking a word to the Jews who had come from nearby Jerusalem to comfort Mary and Martha about their brother.[201] As Mary rushed out, because the Jews in the house presumed that she was going to the tomb to weep for her brother, they followed her there.[202] When Mary arrived to the place where Jesus was,[203] upon seeing him, she threw herself at his feet saying,[204] "Lord, if you had been here, my brother would not have died."[205] Sometimes persons, in sorrow and anger over death, similarly cry against God, "If you exist, you would not have let my loved one die." But the cries of both Mary and Martha for their brother expressed more their trust in God, not such despair. At the sight of Mary's weeping, and with her also the weeping of the many

---

193 John 11:23
194 John 11:24
195 John 11:25
196 John 11:26
197 John 11:27
198 John 11:20
199 John 11:28
200 John 11:29
201 John 11:18-19
202 John 11:31; Luke 22:39
203 John 11:32; Luke 22:40
204 John 11:32; Luke 22:41
205 John 11:32; John 11:21; Luke 22:42

Jews who had come with her, Jesus became greatly distressed,[206] not only in his empathy with the others;[207] but also in anticipation of his own passion and death for our sins;[208] and because of the many who did not believe;[209] so Jesus cried out an anguished sigh from deep within his heart.[210]

And then, choking softly, he firmly asked Mary and Martha:

Where have you put him?[211]

And they replied with their invitation, "Sir, come and see."[212] And Jesus wept.[213] When the Jews from Jerusalem saw this, they said, "See how much he loved him!"[214] But some of them also remarked, "He opened the eyes of the blind man,[215] couldn't he have done something to prevent this man's death?"[216] But still sobbing, Jesus went to the tomb: it was a cave, with its opening closed by a stone.[217] And he told them:

Take away the stone.[218]

Martha, the dead man's sister, replied, "Lord, there will be a great stench by now [from the corpse]; it has been four days now since he has died."[219] But Jesus, gently upholding her faith, reminded her:

Didn't I tell you that if you believed you will see the glory of God?[220]

206	John 11:33
207	Luke 22:43
208	John 12:27; Luke 22:44
209	John 10:25, 11:15, 26, 40, 42, 45-46
210	John 11:33
211	John 11:34; John 20:15
212	John 11:34
213	John 11:35; Luke 22:45
214	John 11:36
215	John 9:7, 3, 11:40
216	John 11:37; John 11:21, 32; Luke 22:46
217	John 11:38
218	John 11:39; John 20:1-2
219	John 11:39
220	John 11:40; John 6:29; John 20:8-9

By this, Jesus meant not only his raising of Lazarus, but also through himself with the Father,[221] the resurrection of all believers.[222]

And so, they took away the stone from the tomb; then, Jesus raised his eyes towards heaven,[223] and so that everyone could hear him, he loudly said:

> Father, I thank you for hearing me.[224]

But, in a seeming side remark intended for the disciples and his followers nearby, immediately, Jesus also said:

> I know indeed that you always hear me; but I have said this for the sake of all those who stand around me;[225] so that they may believe that it was you who sent me.[226]

After saying this, he then cried out in a loud voice:

> Lazarus, come out.[227]

The dead man came out, with his hands and feet bound in burial bands, and his face wrapped in cloth.[228] At this, Jesus simply told them:

> Untie him, and let him go free.[229]

Many of the Jews, who had come to visit Mary, when they saw what Jesus had done, began now to believe in him.[230]

However, some of the others went to the Pharisees and told them what Jesus had done.[231] They also had done this when Jesus

---

221 John 5:21, 10:30
222 John 6:40, 17:2-3, Matthew 22:32
223 John 11:41, 17:1
224 John 11:41; John 5:19
225 John 11:42; John 11:16, 19; John 16:32, 19:25-26
226 John 11:42; John 5:20, 8:54
227 John 11:43; John 8:51, 6:63; John 8:31-32, 14:6
228 John 11:44
229 John 11:44; John 8:36
230 John 11:45, 42; John 6:47-50, 40, 5:21, 25-26, 28
231 John 11:46; John 12:42

had restored the sight of the man born blind, whom he had sent to the pool of Siloam to wash;[232] and the paralytic man near the Sheep Gate in Jerusalem himself had done so after Jesus had cured him of his illness of thirty-eight years.[233] And in each case the authorities had censured Jesus for curing on the Sabbath,[234] and they also had censured both men Jesus had cured: one for carrying his mat on the Sabbath,[235] and the other was thrown out of the temple, while his parents feared the same fate.[236] But now, over this raising of Lazarus from the dead by Jesus, the chief priests and Pharisees convened the Sanhedrin, the entire Jewish leadership, in an emergency session; and they asked themselves, "What are we going to do about this man working all of these signs?[237] If we let him alone, everyone will believe in him, and the Romans will come and destroy our holy temple and take away our nation."[238] Soon everyone would have their answers to their questions, when they destroyed the temple of Christ's body:[239] for the greatest of his signs was yet to come, so that all might come to believe in Jesus as the Son of God, everyone from Nicodemus to the disciples,[240] the one body of Christ,[241] joined with his bride as the entire people of God, from both Jews and Gentiles.

But among the Sanhedrin there was one, Caiaphas, who was high priest that year,[242] and he spoke out, "You have grasped nothing of this situation; nor do you see that it is better for one man to die for the people, than for the whole nation to perish!"[243] He had said this not on his own; but it was in his capacity as high priest for that year

---

232 John 9:13, 7
233 John 5:15, 8-9
234 John 5:10, 12, 9:14-16
235 John 5:10-11
236 John 9:20-22, 32-38
237 John 11:47; John 2:9-11; 4:48-50, 51-54; 5:1, 5, 15-18; 6:11-14; 6:19, 25-33; 9:1-7; 11:43-44
238 John 11:48; John 6:14-15, Matthew 24:1-2
239 John 2:18-19, 21-22; Mark 14:58, 1 Peter 2:4-6
240 John 3:14-15; 8:28; 19:39-40; 20:1-2, 9; 20:3-7, 11:48, 20:8
241 1 Corinthians 12:12-13, 27; 1 Peter 2:10; John 11:52
242 John 11:49; Hebrews 5:1-2
243 John 11:49-50

that he had prophesied Jesus to die for the nation,[244] and not only for the nation, but to gather into one the dispersed children of God.[245] In fulfilment of the old covenant, Christ would be both high priest and holocaust of the new covenant: as high priest according to the order of Melchizedek,[246] he offered himself,[247] and by his sacrifice he established for us a new covenant for the forgiveness of our sins.[248] So, stemming from man's original fall from grace,[249] the Sanhedrin, in God's providence for humankind, from that day forward planned to kill Jesus.[250] According to the divine plan, Caiaphas, as high priest, more prophesied than advised the slaughter of Jesus. Soon the sins of the nation, and of us all, would be laid on his back,[251] as Jesus willed completely that he would be the scapegoat, the one to be slaughtered for all our sins.[252]

Because the Jews would kill him now, Jesus no longer could walk in public among the Jews.[253] And also, because the Jews would kill him if they could, the disciples now escorted Jesus into a region near the desert,[254] but unknowingly as proscribed by the Lord for the ritual of the live goat sent away into the desert for the atonement of sin:[255] they went with Jesus to the town of Ephraim,[256] about 25 km north of Jerusalem and about 20 km northwest of Jericho. There from around the first day of spring,[257] Jesus remained near the desert with his disciples,[258] until he would come at last to Jerusalem for the

---

244 John 11:51
245 John 11:52
246 Hebrews 5:10, 7:17, 21
247 Hebrews 7:27, 10:5
248 Hebrews 8:6-12, 10:14-23
249 Genesis 3:15
250 John 11:53
251 Isaiah 53:6
252 Leviticus 16:6-10, 20-22; Hebrews 10:7, Psalm 40:9, John 6:38, 7:19
253 John 11:54
254 John 11:54
255 Leviticus 16:10, 21-22; Isaiah 53:11
256 John 11:54
257 Isaiah 40:3, 6-7, Psalm 90:6, 102:12-17
258 John 11:54; Luke 7:24, 26, 9:18-19, John 9:13, 17, 4:17-19, 28-29; Matthew 11:7, 13-14, 10, 19, 17:12, Luke 13:33; Luke 12:4, 27-28, 17:20-21, Matthew 13:31, John 12:24, Isaiah 53:10, Psalm 65:10-14; Luke 17:6, 1

final Passover of the Lamb of God.[259]   But in his raising Lazarus from the dead, Jesus was prophesizing for us the fulfilment of his new covenant promises to be accomplished through his own death and resurrection.[260] And when we enter into this covenant through our baptism, we reciprocate these promises of the Lord through his covenant by our own perpetual vow;[261] and furthermore, we extend our previous baptismal promises in this new covenant of the Lord whenever we embrace, by the new grace in the Lord, our further commitment either to marriage or to celibacy.[262]

Saint Faustina in her Diary (Notebook 1, #199, p. 106) described her thoughts just prior to her profession of religious vows at the end of her novitiate:

> When I think of my perpetual vows and who it is that wants to be joined with me, for hours I become absorbed in the thought of Him. How can this be; you are God and I—I am your creature. You, the Immortal King and I, a beggar and misery itself! But now all is clear to me; your grace and your love, O Lord, will fill the gulf between You, Jesus, and me.

During her profession of vows on 1 May 1933 in Warsaw, Poland, only 39 days after Hitler's legal dictatorship had been established in the first days of spring in neighbouring Germany, Sister Maria Faustina heard these words of Jesus speaking to her: "My spouse, our hearts are joined forever. Remember to whom you have vowed" (Diary, #239, p. 118). And four days later, she saw the Lord all covered with wounds, and then Jesus spoke to her once again: "Look at whom you have espoused" (Diary, #252, p. 124).

When we choose to embrace our commitment to the Lord in baptism, and whenever we do so in our baptism then again through marriage or celibacy in particular, we also are choosing to embrace

---

	Corinthians 15:36-37, 42-44, 50-53
259	Exodus 12:21-27, Leviticus 23:4-8, John 1:29, 35-37
260	Acts 13:32-39, Colossians 2:12
261	John 11:25-26; Romans 8:9-13
262	Romans 8:35-39; Colossians 3:18-24, John 13:16, 5-7

our union with the sufferings of Christ and his cross. But at the time of her perpetual vows, Saint Faustina had not yet experienced first hand the coming horrors of her generation, with its great holocaust and World War II. As Faustina lay prostrate and she was sprinkled with the waters of her baptism, along with the other sisters taking their vows, then the officiating priest, like the Lord calling Lazarus, called out, "Rise, you who are dead to the world, and Jesus Christ will enlighten you" (Diary, Footnote 69, p. 663). When the Lord wills it, also through our union with his sufferings and the cross, our share in his resurrection will follow. Therefore, let us now reflect on this great love of the Lord for each of us, as individuals in the way of Christ, no matter and whatever may be, or may become, our personal and societal histories.

Prayer Reflection: Isaiah 54:1-10, Psalms 65: 2-6, 22:23-32

Antiphon: They are no longer two, but one flesh.[263]
    Raise a glad cry, Jerusalem,[264] you barren one who bore no
        children, rejoice! Break forth and shout in jubilation,
        you who were not in labour;
    for more numerous are the children of the deserted wife
        than are the children of her who has a husband,
        says the Lord.[265]

Enlarge the space for your tent:
    spread out your tent cloths unsparingly;
    lengthen your ropes and make firm your tent-stakes.[266]
For you shall spread abroad to the right and to the left;
    your descendants shall dispossess the nations,
        and they shall people the desolate cities.[267]

---

263   Matthew 19:6
264   Galatians 4:26
265   Isaiah 54:1
266   Isaiah 54:2; John 11:52
267   Isaiah 54:3; Galatians 3:16-17, 22, 29

Fear not, you shall not be put to shame;
> you need not blush, for you shall not be disgraced;
> the shame of your youth you shall forget;
> no longer will you remember the reproach of your
> > widowhood.[268]

For he who has become your husband is your Maker;
> his name is the Lord of hosts;
> your redeemer is the Holy One of Israel;
> > he is called God of all the earth.[269]

The Lord calls you back, like a wife forsaken and grieved
> in
> > spirit,
> a wife married in youth and then cast off, says your
> > God:[270]

For a brief moment I abandoned you,
> but with great tenderness I will take you back;[271]
> In an outburst of wrath, for a moment I hid my face
> > from you,
> > > but with enduring love I take pity on you,
> > > says the Lord, your redeemer.[272]

This is for me like the days of Noah,
> when I swore that the waters of Noah should never
> > again deluge the earth;
> so I have sworn not to be angry with you, or to rebuke
> > you.[273]

Though the mountains leave their place and the hills be
> shaken,
> > my love shall never leave you nor my covenant of
> > peace be
> > > shaken,
> > says the Lord, who has mercy on you.[274]

---

268 Isaiah 54:4; 1 Corinthians 7:8, 25-26, 39-40
269 Isaiah 54:5; Isaiah 62:5, Revelation 21:2, 9
270 Isaiah 54:6; Hosea 1:2-3, 6, 8-9
271 Isaiah 54:7; Hosea 2:4, 8-9, 16-18, 21
272 Isaiah 54:8; Mark 10:9; Hosea 2:22, 25, 1 Peter 2:10, Romans 9:25-26, Hosea 1:7, 2:20, John 11:46, 53
273 Isaiah 54:9; 1 Peter 3:21
274 Isaiah 54:10; John 11:40

Antiphon: Father, I thank you for hearing me.[275]

 It is right, O God, for us to sing your praise in Zion;[276]
  we must pay our vows to you.[277]

 Because you hear our prayers,
  to you all flesh must come.[278]
 With its burden of sins,
  our offences are too heavy for us;
  only you can pardon them.[279]

 Blessed are the chosen ones you call
  to dwell in your courts;
 May we be filled with the good things of your house,
  the blessings of your holy temple![280]

 You keep your pledge with awesome deeds of justice,[281]
  O God our saviour,
  the hope of all the ends of the earth
  and of far distant islands.[282]

Antiphon: I will proclaim your name to the assembly;
  in the community of your people, I will praise you:[283]

 "You who fear the Lord, praise him: all you descendants
  of
 Jacob,
  give him glory; worship him, you people of Israel![284]

---

275 John 11:41
276 Psalm 65:2; Isaiah 38:20
277 Psalm 65:2; Psalm 66:13, Luke 15:23, 32; Matthew 19:9-12, Philippians 2:8, John 6:38-40
278 Psalm 65:3; John 11:43, Isaiah 38:10
279 Psalm 65:4; John 11:49-50, Isaiah 38:17
280 Psalm 65:5; John 11:25, Isaiah 38:16
281 Psalm 65:6; John 11:44, 51, Isaiah 38:18
282 Psalm 65:6; John 11:52, Isaiah 38:19
283 Psalm 22:23
284 Psalm 22:24; Romans 11:26-27, 32

For God has not spurned or disdained the misery of this
>   poor
> wretch,
>   did not turn away from me, but he heard my cry for
>   help![285]
> I will offer praise in the great assembly;
>   I will fulfil my vows of sacrifice before those who fear
>   the
>   Lord.[286]
>
> The lowly shall eat their fill;
>   those who seek the Lord shall praise him:
>   'May your hearts enjoy life forever!'"[287]
>
> All the ends of the earth will remember the Lord and
>   turn to
>   him;
>   all the families of nations shall worship him.[288]
>
> For kingship belongs to the Lord,
>   and he rules the nations.[289]
> To him alone shall bow down all who sleep in the earth;
>   all who have gone down into the dust will kneel in
>   homage.[290]
>
> And my soul shall live for the Lord;
>   and my descendants also will serve you.[291]
> Let the coming generation of the Lord be told
>   that they may proclaim to a people yet unborn:
>   "The Lord saved his people!"[292]

---

285   Psalm 22:25; John 11:3
286   Psalm 22:26; John 11:49-50
287   Psalm 22:27; John 11:45
288   Psalm 22:28; John 12:3
289   Psalm 22:29; John 12:15
290   Psalm 22:30; John 12:1-2
291   Psalm 22:31; Matthew 19:14
292   Psalm 22:32; Romans 8:16-17, Psalm 102:19-23

Glory be to the Father,
 and to the Son,
  and to the Holy Spirit,
as it was in the beginning,
 is now,
  and ever shall be world without end. Amen.

Chapter 29

The Final Journey to Jerusalem: On the Road to the Revolution, and to the Cross and the Glory

Readings: John 11:55-57; Matthew 19:16-30, Mark 10:17-31, Luke 18:18-30; Matthew 20:1-16

As the Jewish Passover drew near, many countryside people went up to Jerusalem so that they could take part in the purification ceremonies before the feast.[1] The period for ritual purification lasted seven days, and, as its final day, included the preparation day for Passover,[2] which feast began at sunset on the 14th day of the first month (Abib) of the Jewish calendar, or Nisan, as Abib was called after the Babylonian captivity.[3] During this solemn period of purification, persons also refrained from intercourse and from touching anything unclean,[4] such as a human corpse.[5] And from the beginning of Passover, that is from the evening of the 14th Nisan, for another seven days until the evening of the 21st, the feast of unleavened bread also was celebrated.[6] But before this particular Passover feast, now in

---

1   John 11:55; Luke 14:23, Matthew 22:9-10
2   Exodus 12:4-5, John 19:41-42
3   Exodus 12:2-6, 11-14, 13:3-5, Deuteronomy 16:1-2
4   Exodus 19:10-11, 15; John 2:19, Matthew 20:19, Mark 10:34, Luke 18:33; Hebrews 8:7-13, Romans 8:33-34, Hebrews 10:29, 22
5   Numbers 9:6-12, 19:11-12, 13-22; Mark 15:42-43, Luke 23:50-54, John 19:38-42
6   Exodus 12:18, 13:6-7, 34:18, Deuteronomy 16:3-4

the year 30 CE, people were on the look out for Jesus; and as they stood about in the temple area in Jerusalem, they murmured to one another, "What do you think? Do you suppose he won't come to the feast?"[7] For already the chief priests and Pharisees had given their orders: that if anyone should know the whereabouts of Jesus, they were obliged to inform them of it immediately, so that they could arrest him.[8]

But at this moment, as Jesus and his disciples were setting out from the rugged, prayerful highlands near Ephraim,[9] just like many of the others who also were on their pilgrimage journey to Jerusalem via Jericho at sea-level,[10] there was a rich young man,[11] a Jewish official from one of the leading families,[12] who approached Jesus on the road, and on the run to catch up with him;[13] and then he knelt humbly before Jesus;[14] and barely catching his breath after the chase, the youth asked his vital question, "Good Master, what good deed must I do to inherit eternal life?"[15] Now this was a bold and insightful question, and it derived from the young man's sensitivity to the Lord's true calling for him. He knew that he had some kind of specific calling, just as at some time or conscious moment we too may become aware of our own special calling from God. Yet, there was something he couldn't quite distinguish very well: a clear conflict between his certain inclination towards God and his unconscious reservations to God's call.

The question of the young man, in its simplest stock form, would seem to be: "How do I get to heaven?" and this almost would be like asking for travel directions to some unfamiliar destination. But then, this young man's question was distinguished by its reference to two "goods": first, Our Lord, addressed as "Good Master," and then

---

7 John 11:56; John 12:27, 10:10, 7:28-30
8 John 11:57
9 Mark 10:17; John 11:54
10 John 11:55; Luke 18:35, 19:1
11 Matthew 19:22
12 Luke 18:18
13 Matthew 19:16, Mark 10:17
14 Mark 10:17
15 Matthew 19:16, Mark 10:17, Luke 18:18; Luke 10:25

the young man's question about his own "good deed." His question to the Lord was distinguished further by references to "eternal life" and to what he "must do" to inherit it. In response, Jesus answered him directly, succinctly and completely, but first Jesus expands the young man's questions:

> Why do you call me good?[16] And why ask me about the good?[17] There is only One, God, who alone is good.[18] But if you wish to enter into life, keep the commandments.[19]

Jesus, in his reply, also expanded upon the true nature of the "good," which was the young man's most important starting point; and then Jesus continued with what was by now his and God's stock answer to this familiar standard question: namely, to "keep the commandments."[20] However, we are not made righteous by our keeping of the Law, but by our faith in Jesus Christ,[21] who is the Law.[22]

We have no goodness apart from God, who is the source of all goodness and grace;[23] and the institutional church was established by Christ as a fountain to us for his life and grace.[24] In any calling from God, with that grace of his in our hearts, we also are able to recognize God's goodness and mercy.[25] Our initial response to this calling involves our apperception of the divine goodness, but the full journey of our vocation in the cross of Christ,[26] when finally and truly we decide to make it, leads to even greater perceptions

---

16   Mark 10:18, Luke 18:19
17   Matthew 19:17
18   Matthew 19:17, Mark 10:18, Luke 18:19
19   Matthew 19:17; 1 Timothy 1:8-12; Psalm 119:9
20   Exodus 20:1-17, Leviticus 22:31, Deuteronomy 5:6-21, 29; 1 Kings 3:14, 6:12, 9:6-8, 11:38; 2 Kings 17:13-14, 1 Chronicles 29:17-19
21   Romans 4:25, Galatians 2:15-16
22   John 15:12, Matthew 5:17, 20, Hebrews 3:12, 18-19, 4:1-2, 11-12, John 7:16, 19
23   1 Chronicles 29:14-16
24   Matthew 16:18, 13
25   1 Timothy 1:13-14
26   Galatians 2:19-20

and understanding of the profound mysteries and depths of God's goodness and mercy. This call is never something that we can produce from our own "goodness," nor is it ours because we are good; for it is never based on merit, but only upon God's generosity and faithfulness. We are all sinners,[27] even when we are called in the mystery of his special grace,[28] for God alone is good.[29]

But when we respond in gracious gratitude to God's grace, we seek to reciprocate the mystery of his absolute goodness—but naturally we can only fall short of any perfect reciprocity, which is impossible for us, but not with God for us.[30] Because of God's goodness, it is true for everyone's calling to holiness that we must keep the commandments,[31] a task which only would be simple justice in our regard to God's infinite goodness.[32] But even so, despite our appreciable human limitations, and because of God's goodness, God also recognizes that we are imperfect in this task even before he calls us.[33] Eventually, after God has made us perfect,[34] as we become more perfect as Christ was perfect, we reach eternal life.[35] However, even though some saints are greater in their perfection than others,[36] all saints by their faith and by the fullness of their holiness in Christ entirely give glory to God.[37]

But the particular calling of this young man, sincerely kneeling before the Lord, was more than just to keep permanent one's vows to the commandments. At first, however, he thought his vocation might lay in being even more diligent in observing some of them, so he asked Jesus, "Which ones should I keep?"[38] Initially, as Jesus also does with us, he still gave the youth his stock answer:

---

27 1 Timothy 1:15-16
28 Isaiah 55:6-11
29 1 Timothy 1:17
30 Romans 8:31; Matthew 19:26, Mark 10:27, Luke 18:27
31 Hebrews 10:26-29
32 1 Chronicles 29:20-22, Hebrews 10:4-5
33 1 John 1:9
34 1 John 4:12, 17-19, 9-11, Philippians 3:12
35 1 John 5:12, 1-3
36 Luke 14:8, 9:46-48
37 Philippians 3:14-16
38 Matthew 19:18

You know the commandments.[39] "Don't commit adultery; don't kill; don't steal; don't bear false witness;[40] don't defraud;[41] honour your father and your mother;[42] and love your neighbour as yourself."[43]

Immediately, the young man replied to Jesus, "Teacher,[44] all of these I have observed from my youth."[45] The young man knew from the spirit of God in his soul that there must be something more expected of him; so still pursuing his vocation until he should understand it, he asked of Jesus: "What do I still lack?"[46] This, now, was the critical question Jesus had been waiting for, from him and from anyone called to serve the Lord most perfectly. Jesus looked into the young man's serious eyes and into the depths of his soul's sincerity, where he loved him; only then Jesus clearly offered him the gift, telling him point blank exactly what necessary "good deed" was needed: [47]

You are lacking in one thing.[48] If you wish to be perfect,[49] there is still one thing left for you to do:[50] go and sell everything you own and give the money to the poor, and you will have a treasure in heaven. Then come, follow me."[51]

When the young man heard this answer from the Lord, his face suddenly dropped, and he was very much visibly shaken.[52] No

---

39 Mark 10:19, Luke 18:20; Exodus 20:12-16, Deuteronomy 5:16-20; Luke 10:26; Psalm 119:10
40 Luke 18:20, Matthew 19:18, Mark 10:19
41 Mark 10:19
42 Matthew 19:19, Mark 10:19, Luke 18:20
43 Matthew 19:19; Romans 13:9-10, 8, Galatians 5:14; Leviticus 19:18, Matthew 22:39, Mark 12:31, Luke 10:27
44 Mark 10:20
45 Mark 10:20, Luke 18:21
46 Matthew 19:20; Hebrews 4:12
47 Mark 10:21; Matthew 19:16
48 Mark 10:21; Psalm 119:2
49 Matthew 19:21
50 Luke 18:22
51 Matthew 19:21, Mark 10:21, Luke 18:22; Luke 12:33; Psalm 119:14
52 Mark 10:22; Luke 12:34

one knows from this existential moment of his true calling, just as whenever the moment comes for ourselves, whether or not this young man ever did take up his vocation, but it seems not: for he went away quite sad, because he was very rich and he had many possessions.[53] Just at his life's most critical moment of understanding, decision, and commitment, he seemed to choke on the worldly thorns of his wealth.[54] Our answerable responsibility to the Lord is to answer the Lord's call whenever it is given, whether in our lifetime we may be hired at dawn or at five o'clock, until eventually, after our period of service, we collect the usual daily wage from the Lord in the evening of our life.[55] However, should it happen that we would refuse this call, to our own detriment and peril, the Lord's harvest still would not be thwarted;[56] and if necessary, our personal mission and our rejected responsibility would be taken away from us and given to someone else.[57]

But still, Jesus did not give up on the young man, as Jesus, sometimes repeatedly, also does not so easily give up on us;[58] and so, Jesus now looked directly at him, threading his thought right through the eye of the needle of this young man's heart, and he said:

> How hard it is for those who have wealth to enter the kingdom of God![59] Yes, it is easier for a camel to pass through the eye of a needle than for a rich man to enter the kingdom of God.[60]

---

[53] Matthew 19:22, Mark 10:22, Luke 18:23; Matthew 13:44-46, Luke 8:14-15

[54] Matthew 13:22, Mark 4:7, 18-19, Luke 8:14

[55] Matthew 20:1-8

[56] Matthew 25:26, Isaiah 55:11

[57] Matthew 25:29; Matthew 13:12, Mark 4:25, Luke 8:18, 19:26

[58] While God's commitment to us is perfect in his "goodness," our personal commitment to follow the Lord on our theological road to Jerusalem, to our cross with Jesus and beyond his resurrection and ours from the dead of sin, depends upon our acceptance of that critical moment of grace: when we recognize our inherent sinfulness, but also our complete liberty from sin by Jesus when we align ourselves with God's perfect will.

[59] Luke 18:24; Mark 10:23

[60] Luke 18:25; Matthew 19:24

At these words from Jesus, the man left, then in a crisis of anguished attachment and disappointment; and afterwards, as Jesus looked around,[61] he seemed to be searching already to find the youth's replacement for God's work. But more specifically, he was looking over the entire crowd (and perhaps at us) for anyone who would surrender his wealth in exchange for the kingdom of God.[62] At that moment, Jesus then also had identified the problem in his midst as much closer to home; equally, it was more subtle than the wealth of just this one young man, or of the others in the crowd; so, he pointedly told his disciples:

> Amen, I say to you most solemnly, it will be hard for those who have riches to make their way into the kingdom of heaven.[63] Again I say to you, it is easier for a camel to pass through the eye of a needle than for a rich person to enter the kingdom of God.[64]

When the disciples heard this, and now for their second time, they were even more astonished than in their having heard it from the Lord for the first time,[65] mainly because now the Lord directed his statement with his full emphasis at themselves, and not just at the rich young man who had left. Although, like everyone else among the crowd, they commonly had understood wealth in this life to be a sign of God's blessings; indeed, unlike everyone else, they had given up everything to follow the Lord! But also, and primarily, they had expected that Jesus would restore the throne of King David to the house of Israel—and in his doing so, they also expected that money and wealth would be a natural and necessary by-product for the temporal restoration of the kingdom of God on earth, let alone a means for eternal life in heaven. So now, in this moment, the disciples were confused entirely and they were profoundly incredulous; so they asked Jesus: "In that case, who then can be saved?"[66]

61	Mark 10:23
62	Mark 8:36-37, Matthew 16:26
63	Matthew 19:23
64	Matthew 19:24; Luke 8:14
65	Matthew 19:25, Mark 10:26
66	Matthew 19:25, Mark 10:26, Luke 18:26

Jesus, speaking to them gravely with his eyes, gazed directly now right through his disciples,[67] to the core of their hearts and to the spiritual centre of their souls,[68] and then, firmly in the intention of his love, but softly in his gentle invitation to their choice, he said:

> For human beings this is impossible,[69] but not for God;[70] things that are impossible for men are possible for God,[71] for everything is possible with God.[72]

But Peter, still stunned like the others, spoke up then for all of the disciples about this matter, "What about us?" he said to Jesus. "We left all that we had to follow you."[73] Indeed, because Peter had a mother-in-law,[74] he specifically had a wife; but he had left everything, including his wife and family, to follow the Lord, whom Peter also had trusted as his pearl of great price and the hope of his salvation.[75]

In every age, including our own, there have been people who have left everything, in the name of God, to follow even leaders of blasphemous religious cults, such as Jim Jones of the USA, or even quasi-religious political leaders of international terrorist groups, such as the Saudi-born Osama Bin Laden, just to mention only two of the many false prophets and Messiahs of my times.[76] But not unlike the followers of today's false Messiahs, similarly Peter had professed Jesus to be the Christ;[77] and as the Messiah, the disciples thought that Jesus would overthrow the Roman occupation, and that therefore, finally, Jesus would restore the throne of King David in Jerusalem.[78]

---

67 Matthew 19:26, Mark 10:27, 23, 21
68 John 2:25; John 4:14, 7:37-38, 4:10, 28
69 Matthew 19:26
70 Mark 10:27
71 Luke 18:27
72 Matthew 19:26, Mark 10:27; Luke 6:40, 2 Corinthians 7:1, Hebrews 10:14; 1 John 4:12, Colossians 3:14, Philippians 1:6
73 Matthew 19:27, Mark 10:28, Luke 18:28
74 Matthew 8:14, Mark 1:30, Luke 4:38
75 Matthew 13:45-46
76 Matthew 24:23-24
77 Matthew 16:16, Mark 8:29, Luke 9:20
78 John 6:15, Matthew 21:5, 9, 25:31

In fact, they would cherish this vibrant belief in the restoration of the kingdom to Israel right up to the very last moment, right before the Lord's ascension from the earth to his glory in heaven.[79]

And now, because the disciples all were expecting remuneration for their personal sacrifices, but as yet without their comprehending the true nature of the Lord's approaching sacrifice for our sins, Peter continued to speak on everyone's behalf as he asked the Lord, "So then, what are we to have?"[80] So, Jesus said to all of them:

> Amen, I tell you solemnly, you who have followed me: in the age when all is made new,[81] and when the Son of Man is seated on his throne of glory,[82] you will yourselves sit on twelve thrones to judge the twelve tribes of Israel.[83]

Although Jesus now was referring to himself as enthroned in heaven, the twelve disciples did not as yet understand this intended meaning. Rather, according to their biased mindset for the "coming revolution," they still saw Jesus as their divine earthly King—and they imagined themselves as key officials in their new-found positions of power and wealth in the kingdom. But Jesus then continued speaking without any interruption of his thought:

> There is no one, who has left house, brothers and sisters, father and mother, (wife)[84] and children, or land(s) for my (name's)[85] sake[86] and for the sake of the gospel[87]/kingdom of God,[88] who will not be repaid a hundred times over:[89] houses, brothers, sisters, mothers, children, and land—and not without accompanying

---

79 Acts 1:6
80 Matthew 19:27
81 Matthew 19:28; Romans 8:22, Revelation 21:1; 2 Corinthians 5:17
82 Matthew 19:28, 25:31, 26:64, 16:27
83 Matthew 19:28; Revelation 21:14; Matthew 20:20-21, 24
84 Luke 18:29
85 Matthew 19:29
86 Mark 10:29; Matthew 10:39, Luke 9:24, 17:33
87 Mark 10:29; Mark 8:35, John 12:25
88 Luke 18:29
89 Matthew 19:29, Mark 10:30; Luke 8:8, Matthew 13:8, Mark 4:8

persecution[90]—now in this present age and in the world to come;[91] and there, he also will inherit[92] eternal life.[93] But many who (now) are first will be last, and the last will be first.[94]

And again, for the time being, the disciples gave these words of Jesus their revolutionary interpretation: namely, that their investment in the revolution would be repaid a hundred times over, both on earth and in heaven; so that even then the disciples continued to misinterpret the real kingdom of God. Yet, these words from the Lord had been instructions of encouragement, even though they also seemed to allow the radical suggestion for the revolution: that the leaving of wives and children or other family, for the sake of the gospel, would be preferable to traditional family life; and it is. But also, because human civilization would collapse if there were no family life of any kind, family life within marriage was blest by God, and not abandoned by Christ.[95] So here, Jesus was expressing the choice of himself, more than any other personal attachment or relationship, as the ideal: for the particular and occasional grace to the religious life,[96] yes; but also in the inevitable divisions that would occur within family households because of Christ,[97] when one then must choose God, even over one's natural family.[98]

But for both the unmarried and married followers of Christ, in the growing communion of saints both in this life and in the next, there would be houses and land, as lived by the common communities of the early church,[99] and also there would be their

---

90 Mark 10:30; Matthew 5:10-12, 10:22-23; 2 Corinthians 12:10, 2 Timothy 3:1
91 Mark 10:30, Luke 18:30; Ephesians 2:19
92 Matthew 19:29; Revelation 21:7; Matthew 16:26, Mark 8:36, Luke 9:25
93 Matthew 19:29; Mark 10:30, Luke 18:30; Matthew 19:23, 2 Corinthians 12:9
94 Matthew 19:30, Mark 10:31; Matthew 20:16; Matthew 19:23
95 Matthew 19:4-5
96 Matthew 19:12
97 Luke 12:52-53, Matthew 10:21, 34-36
98 John 7:1-6, 8
99 Acts 4:32-35

places in heaven.[100] For those who had left their families behind for the Lord's sake: there would be in the Lord enough brothers and sisters and other mothers;[101] and even many others would become the Lord's spiritual children of the Light,[102] through one's life lived in dedication to the Lord's gospel. But in the end, especially for those who had left everything to follow the Lord,[103] for them there would be everlasting life.[104] These were not today's false promises for Paradise, such as those we witness made to misguided suicide bombers,[105] who then blow themselves and others to bits in their murderous revolutions. Sadly, at the moment that I was writing this, in September 2008, in yet another tragic example, just yesterday a truck-bomb in Islamabad, Pakistan destroyed the Marriott Hotel, killing dozens and wounding hundreds, when the blast of that explosion also brought down the ceiling in a banquet room of the hotel during a meal to mark the end of the Ramadan fast. Now, as I review this chapter again on 1st December 2009, with the United States 14 trillion dollars in debt, President Obama has committed 30,000 additional troops to Afghanistan.

But the Lord, also with similar revolutionary fervour, did say to his disciples: whoever would loose his life for Christ's sake and for the gospel would save it; while those trying to save their life for this world, would forfeit it in the next.[106] And indeed, therefore, it would not be easy especially for a rich man to enter the kingdom of God.[107] But along with the privilege of following the Lord into eternal life by keeping his commandments,[108] there would be its required costs: there would be persecutions,[109] indeed, its requisite cross,[110] and its

---

100   John 14:1-3
101   Luke 8:21
102   John 12:36
103   Matthew 19:27, Mark 10:28, Luke 18:28
104   Matthew 19:29; John 6:64-68, 10:26-30
105   Matthew 24:11
106   Matthew 16:25-26, Mark 8:35-36, Luke 9:24-25
107   Matthew 19:24, 7:14
108   Matthew 19:17, 1 John 3:23, John 13:34, 15:17
109   Mark 10:30
110   Matthew 16:24, Mark 8:34, Luke 9:23

many personal sacrifices,[111] including, ultimately and necessarily, the giving up of life itself.[112] And, to be first in God's kingdom, one also would have to put one's self last to serve the rest;[113] just as very soon Jesus would be taking his place humbly upon the cross for all of us.[114] Nevertheless, despite all the disciples had seen and had tried to understand during their engagement with the Lord,[115] going on now for close to two and one-half intensive years after the Lord's baptism,[116] they still seemed not to grasp any of this—not yet.

But Jesus, with his seemingly inexhaustible patience, once again began to explain to the disciples what the kingdom of God was like. So this time, in order to facilitate their comprehension and reflection, he told the Twelve this parable:

> The kingdom of heaven is like the owner of an estate who went out early in the morning to hire day-labourers for his vineyard.[117] He agreed to pay them one denarius, the usual wage for a day's work, and he sent them into his vineyard.[118] Going out about the third hour (around nine o'clock), he saw others standing around the marketplace and having no work to do,[119] and he said to them, "You too go into my vineyard, and I will pay you a fair wage."[120] And so they went. Later he went out again about the sixth hour (around noon), and again about the ninth hour (mid-afternoon), and he did the same.[121] Then at about the eleventh hour (around five o'clock), when he went to the marketplace again, he still found others standing around idle, and he said to them,

---

111 Matthew 19:21, 29
112 Luke 23:46
113 Matthew 20:27, John 13:3-5
114 Philippians 2:7-9
115 Ephesians 5:31-32
116 Matthew 3:11-17
117 Matthew 20:1
118 Matthew 20:2
119 Matthew 20:3
120 Matthew 20:4
121 Matthew 20:5

"Why are you standing here wasting the whole day?"[122] They answered him, "No one has hired us." And he said to them, "You go into my vineyard, too."[123]

When evening came, the owner of the vineyard said to his foreman, "Call the workers and give them their wages,[124] but start with the hired workers who arrived last, and end with those hired first."[125] So, when those came forward who were hired about the eleventh hour (in the late afternoon), they each received the usual full-day's wage, one denarius.[126] So, when the group who were first showed up, they thought they would be paid even more, yet each one of them was given one denarius, the standard daily wage.[127] They took it, but they grumbled against the landowner.[128] They said to him, "This last group only worked for an hour, yet you have treated them the same as us, as if they had worked, as we did, all day long in the scorching sun!"[129] The owner, addressing one of them, said, "My friend,[130] I'm not cheating you. We agreed on one denarius, didn't we?[131] So take what is yours and go. What if I choose to pay this last hired man as much as you![132] Don't I have a right to do whatever I want with what is mine? Or why should you be envious because I am generous?"[133] Thus, the last will be first, and the first will be last.[134]

In God's kingdom, the compensatory wages would not be the wealthy fortunes of earthly kings: but instead, very simply: for

---

122	Matthew 20:6
123	Matthew 20:7; Matthew 9:37-38
124	Matthew 20:8; Leviticus 19:13, Deuteronomy 24:14-15, Matthew 20:13
125	Matthew 20:8
126	Matthew 20:9
127	Matthew 20:10
128	Matthew 20:11
129	Matthew 20:12
130	Matthew 20:13; John 15:14
131	Matthew 20:13
132	Matthew 20:14
133	Matthew 20:15
134	Matthew 20:16

everyone, those wages would be just one silver denarius, a coin less than four (3.85) grams or just 0.136 ounces, and equivalent to a common labourer's full-day's wages. And this wage, the "enjoyment of God," would be the same even for the latecomers, let alone the leading pioneers like the disciples; and no matter whether they joined in God's work early or late in life, or earlier or later in human history. For everyone who responds to the Lord's calling,[135] as long as they persevere from that new-found moment of treasured grace unto the very end,[136] they would be paid, in the full generosity of Christ's gift, the usual wages the Lord had agreed to pay everyone for their full-day's or part-day's labor of lifetime-work devoted to God's calling,[137] once God initially calls us from anytime of the day;[138] and we hear and respond to his call in justice, even if we should not yet understand this call from him.[139]

What God gives us, eternal life, was never earned by anyone, except by Christ who earned it for us.[140] But to receive it, we must hear and answer God's call. Not everyone who was asked to go into the vineyards actually went, after they had been standing around in the marketplace of the world, wasting their lives not only in this world, but also their lives for the next. As for the twelve disciples, just because they had been called first did not diminish God's gifts for those who would be called later. Everyone, who arrives to work the vineyards of the Lord and who does so when they are called,[141] they each are to be given their full wage, from what only belongs to God. It also becomes ours only because the Lord agreed to give it to us, to entrust us with his property, in exchange for our sins.[142] This wage is made fair not by any works of ours,[143] but only when we believe in Christ and in his work on the cross for our salvation.[144]

135	Matthew 21:28-31, John 6:65
136	Philippians 1:29, Hebrews 3:13
137	1 Corinthians 15:58
138	Matthew 20:2
139	John 6:45-48
140	John 6:50-51, Romans 5:17-18
141	John 15:16-17, Romans 8:28-30
142	Luke 19:12-13, Matthew 25:14, 20:15
143	Romans 4:4-5, 11:6
144	John 6:64-65, 66-70, 3:14-16

And in God's justice,[145] we are obliged to labour for God in the vineyard, once our eyes and hearts have been opened fully to his grace and mercy,[146] and we comprehend through this grace that we are called. For this same reason, the disciples would be obligated so as to give glory to this generosity from God, although this grace was not restricted by anyone's primacy,[147] but it was given freely, only by God, to whomever he willed to give it, including even those who are called late in life by the Lord.[148] As long as we are ready to listen and to act upon the Lord's mercy and grace to us, the final wages of the Lord for those who persevere, paid to us wholly through his work of salvation, are the same for everyone hired by the Lord to work for his ongoing human harvest: eternal life with the Lord, in the kingdom of God.[149]

Readings: Matthew 20:17-19, 20-28, Mark 10:32-34, 35-45, Luke 18:31-34; Luke 18:35-43, Mark 10:46-52, Matthew 20:29-34; Luke 19:1-10, 11-28

Somewhere between Ephraim and still north of Jericho, as they all were on the road going up to Jerusalem,[150] Jesus went before them leading the way while the disciples followed behind:[151] however, for the moment, envision a revised interpretation: suddenly, Jesus broke into a downhill sprint and raced ahead of them. They all were amazed at this;[152] and not knowing what this peculiar behaviour of the Lord could mean, those who did follow the Lord were afraid.[153] In this case, I have shifted Mark's original intention as an evangelist, that the disciples were feeling apprehensive about the Lord's journey, to provide the new context of Saint Paul, with the Lord rushing ahead as he strives to take hold of his victory prize for us. It was as if Jesus

---

145 Matthew 19:26
146 Matthew 20:34, Mark 10:51-52, Luke 18:42-43; John 20:3-9
147 Matthew 19:28
148 Matthew 20:15; Romans 9:15-16, 18, 22-24
149 Matthew 25:34
150 Matthew 20:17, Mark 10:32
151 Mark 10:32
152 Mark 10:32
153 Mark 10:32

also was challenging them to a race to Jerusalem,[154] "Many that are first will be last, and the last will be first!"[155] While the Lord himself was not crazy, as the world would have defined him, the fear of the disciples was grounded in the realities of their present destination. Somewhere along this route, the Lord did take the disciples aside; but for the sake of our familiar analogy, let us consider our not so crazy and imagined reconstruction. When the Twelve, clueless and largely out of breath, finally caught up with Jesus, he quietly took them off to the side of the road where they could be by themselves after the chase;[156] and there he firmly told them what was going to happen to him.[157] Like an athletics coach, surrounded by his team of distance runners, Jesus told them the harsh truth, despite their reservations:

> Look here and listen up! We now are going up to Jerusalem,[158] and everything written by the prophets about the Son of Man is to be fulfilled:[159] he will be handed over to the chief priests and scribes, and they will condemn him to death;[160] they will hand him over to the pagans (Gentiles), who will mock him, maltreat him with insults and by spitting at him;[161] and after they have scourged him, they will put him to death (by crucifying him);[162] but on the third day, he will rise again.[163]

However, the disciples understood none of these things; his words to them remained for them quite obscure; they had no idea whatsoever what Jesus could mean by what he had said.[164] At least

---

154 Philippians 3:10-15
155 Mark 10:31; Matthew 20:27-28, Mark 10:44-45
156 Matthew 20:17, Mark 10:32
157 Mark 10:32
158 Matthew 20:18, Mark 10:33, Luke 18:31
159 Luke 18:31; Luke 24:27, 32
160 Matthew 20:18, Mark 10:33
161 Mark 10:34, Luke 18:32
162 Matthew 20:19, Mark 10:34, Luke 18:33
163 Matthew 20:19, Mark 10:34, Luke 18:33; Psalm 16:10, Hosea 6:2, Jonah 2:1, Matthew 12:40, 16:4, Luke 11:29
164 Luke 18:34; Isaiah 42:16

twice before, Jesus had made explicit these same predictions: several times, beginning first from after the time when the disciples were returning to Galilee from Caesarea Philippi near the source of the Jordan River, where Jesus had named Simon the "rock" of his church;[165] and again in Galilee, soon after their coming down the mountain of the transfiguration of the Lord.[166] But now, once more, as Jesus spoke to the disciples, what he had said still did not make any sense to them: in part, because again they were afraid to ask; but primarily, because his words did not fit their plans, or their schemas, for what they had imagined, or thought, the Messiah would be as their king.[167] Soon their political-religious aspirations would be confronted, as the larger entourage also following the Lord shortly caught up with Jesus and the disciples ahead, who had been alone further down the road.

Amongst their group was the mother of James and John, Zebedee's sons. She was, perhaps, like competitive mothers in almost all other societies: she was very proud of her two sons; after all, they were "apostles,"[168] and as their mother she wanted only the best futures for her sons. So, when she heard through her aspiring sons that, after the revolution, as they imagined it to be, when Jesus sat on his throne as King, the disciples would sit on twelve thrones to judge the tribes of Israel,[169] she, and they, became relatively anxious for the high ambitions she had shared with her sons, when she also learned from them that the Lord also had said, "The first would be last, and the last would be first."[170] At least, through her sons, that is how she gathered and interpreted what seemed to be the unfair arrangement the Lord presumably had said. On the other hand, as for James and John, having prompted their mother, they also knew that their dear mother would do for them whatever she could do to promote their careers with Jesus.

So the mother of James and John approached the Lord, with

---

165   Matthew 16:13, 21
166   Matthew 17:22-23
167   Isaiah 33:17
168   Luke 6:13
169   Matthew 19:28
170   Matthew 19:30, 20:16

both of her sons, her Lord's "Sons of Thunder,"[171] in tow behind her. Before she made her request of the Lord, she graciously bowed to him with her well-planned formality and respect.[172] But James and John were the first to speak, "Teacher, we'd like you, as a favour, to do for us whatever we ask you to do."[173] For a long time now, a running squabble had been going on with James and John versus Peter, as the three of them regularly had been singled out by the Lord's favour,[174] and even those three may have been pitted against the other nine disciples, ever since Christ had named Simon the "rock" of his church.[175] Although Jesus knew what James and John and their mother had intended, he put the explanation for their request back into their political tennis-court, saying to them what he asks from all who approach him [just as I had done, and the Lord had asked of me in my soul in my conversation with him at the start of this journey on 12th September 2003]:

What is it that you want me to do for you?[176]

Then James and John and their mother spoke, nearly simultaneously. Their mother said, "**Promise that these two sons of mine will sit**, one at your right and the other at your left, **when you are King!**"[177] And James and John boldly requested the same thing, "**Allow us, in your glory, to sit with you**, one at your right and the other at your left."[178] Jesus, at first, replied gently and factually:

You don't know what you are asking for.[179]

But then Jesus firmly continued:

Can you drink the cup that I **must** drink,[180] or **be baptized** with the baptism with which I **must** be

---

171 Mark 3:17
172 Matthew 20:20
173 Mark 10:35;
174 Matthew 17:1
175 Matthew 16:18
176 Matthew 20:21, Mark 10:36; Mark 10:51, Luke 18:41, Matthew 20:32
177 Matthew 20:21
178 Mark 10:37
179 Matthew 20:22, Mark 10:38
180 Matthew 20:22, Mark 10:38; Matthew 26:36-45, John 18:11

baptized?[181]

James and John both answered, "We can."[182] Then, unconditionally, Jesus accepted their commitment, but only to part of their request,[183] namely, to the "cup" and to the "baptism," without prejudice for the gift to Peter or the others:

> Very well; indeed, you will drink the cup that I must drink,[184] and you shall be baptized, in the way in which I must be baptized;[185] but as for seats at my right or at my left, they are not mine to give, but they belong to those for whom my Father has prepared them.[186]

Undoubtedly, but not so for James and John in the kingdom, whomever the Father might have designated to be seated at the right and left of Christ in his glory as King, if such placements actually did exist in heaven, as I had originally presumed, very likely one of those seats would have been reserved for the Lord's mother, Mary, as the Queen of Heaven.[187] And later, at the cross, the Lord also would entrust his mother to John's care while she remained upon the earth,[188] until her assumption body and soul into heaven, where already she reigns like the risen Lord, both in her body and in spirit. Fittingly enough, in parallel with Mary's Son of Man, Jesus, as the new Adam,[189] Mary herself, as the new Eve, would become, through her divine Son, the mother of all the living.[190] Then, as I first had speculated, if there should be another person besides Our Lady seated at the other hand of Christ, whoever it could be was anyone's best guess; but if another human being was so determined

---

181 Mark 10:38
182 Matthew 20:22, Mark 10:39; Mark 14:50-52, John 18:15-16; Acts 12:2, John 21:22, 18-19
183 John 14:14
184 Matthew 20:23, Mark 10:39
185 Mark 10:39; Luke 12:50
186 Matthew 20:23, Mark 10:40
187 Revelations 12:1
188 John 19:26-27
189 Romans 5:14-21
190 Genesis 3:20, 15, Revelation 12:5, 13, 17; Romans 6:22-23

by the Father, perhaps it could be Abraham;[191] or someone yet to be born before the end of time. Given mankind's salvation history with Christ at its centre,[192] I hadn't imagined that there could be any greater historic figures than both Mary and Abraham,[193] for the Father's likely choices, if there were seats in heaven right along side the Blessed Trinity.

However, there are no relative placements in heaven, where for human beings the consequences of our sins have been remitted in their entirely by the merits of Christ. Jesus himself, when he had spoken earlier with reference to his own mother had said, "But even more blessed (than she) are those who hear the word of God and keep it,"[194] all those whom Jesus also regarded then and now to be his mother or brother or sister, anyone who hears and puts into practice the will of God.[195] Even the least in the kingdom of heaven would be greater than the greatest, John the Baptist, "no one greater than all the children born to women,"[196] as Jesus had described John. So, in heaven, as Jesus has informed us, there only is the perfect participation of the saints in God's own life for eternity, their glorious state of "beatific vision," when we will behold God "face to face."[197] The kingdom of God simply cannot be some physical place, or even a spiritual space with neatly numbered seats and place-cards. For, in heaven there are no differences between least and greater saints in their identical states of perfection with God.

But, indeed, there are and have been a great many differences between individual souls in their readiness to enjoy the vision of God as he is: where "the last shall be first; and the first shall be last.["][198] Individual differences pertain regarding our required purification, either in this life and/or in the next, as a consequence of our sins: even

---

191 Genesis 22:15-18, Luke 16:22-23, 27-31
192 Genesis 15:1-6, 17:1,5,15-19, 18:1-2,9-14; Luke 1:26-33, 34-38, 49, 55; Romans 4:3-5, Luke 1:45
193 Revelation 12:1; Luke 16:22, Galatians 3:6-9, 29
194 Luke 11:28
195 Luke 8:20-21, Matthew 12:49-50
196 Luke 7:28, Matthew 11:11
197 Psalm 17:15; 1 Corinthians 13:12; Revelation 21:4
198 Matthew 19:30, 20:16

all who have only barely escaped the fires of hell will eventually enjoy the singular perfection of their holiness in God, if they have taken their journey with Jesus to Jerusalem, right to the Lord's cross.[199] That same cross has established the privilege of the Immaculate Conception for his mother, who was conceived without original sin and preserved from any further sin as a consequence of her Son's perfect mediation for her.[200] The rest of us are all sinners, but even the worst of sinners is subject to the perfect redemption of Christ, provided that the sinner accepts his grace. The last shall be first: those who have put aside the world, or who have been cast aside by the world, so they may put into action the will of God most perfectly and without sinning: these shall enter heaven more imminently. Then the first shall be last: even those who may have been rich in the world, but who by divine mercy still share in God's life by some measure of their true repentance by embracing his cross: possibly unto the final judgment,[201] these may require a relatively longer and appropriate period of after-death purification (purgatory) before their ultimate fullness of life with God.

When the other ten disciples overheard these requests from James and John and their mother, and they also had overheard the apparent concessions granted to James and John by the Lord, quickly they aligned themselves with Peter and became indignant at the two brothers.[202] But immediately, Jesus called over all of the disciples;[203] and then, as he now spoke to them, he addressed what was to be the centrepiece of his New Covenant revolution:

> You know how it is among the pagans (Gentiles): that their so-called rulers lord it over them, and their great ones make their authority over them felt.[204] But it should not be this way among you. No; if anyone wishes to be

---

199 John 3:12-16
200 Luke 1:28 [κεχαριτωμένη (kecharitōmenē), highly favoured, endowed with grace, "gratia plena"]
201 Matthew 25:31-32, 23:39, 26:62-64, 25:44-46
202 Matthew 20:24, Mark 10:41; Mark 9:33, Luke 9:46
203 Philippians 2:1-5
204 Matthew 20:25, Mark 10:42; John 18:33-40; John 12:31, 11:49-50, 19:12, 15-16; Colossians 1:16, Romans 13:1-7, Ephesians 6:12, Luke 10:18, 20

great among you, he will be your servant;[205] for whoever wants to be first among you must be your slave.[206] Just so, the Son of Man did not come to be served but to serve, and to give his life as a ransom for many.[207]

Eventually, when Jesus would return to the Father,[208] he would preside as King in his glory.[209] But his kingdom would not belong to this world;[210] although, even now, he was working to establish the kingdom of God and his Father's will on the earth, as it is and would be in heaven.[211] And Jesus would accomplish everything, ultimately on the cross, by drinking his "cup" and by suffering his "baptism" of death, as a ransom for our sins, for many.[212] But unfortunately, because some would remain in their sins, not all would be saved, even though Christ desires everyone's salvation.[213] Later on, except for John, all the apostles would share this same cup and baptism of the Lord's death, by their martyrdom. As for James, John, and Peter: in 43 or 44 CE, James would be beheaded by the sword under the jurisdiction of Herod Agrippa I during the reign of Roman Emperor Claudius. Then twenty years after the death of James in Jerusalem, Peter would be crucified in Rome under Nero. And John would be the last of the apostles to die, but by natural causes at Ephesus, and five years after his initial exile on the island of Patmos under Emperor Domitian, and seventy years after the death of the Lord; but John also shared in the passion and death of Jesus as the suffering witness to the suffering Christ,[214] and as a faithful suffering witness to the persecutions of his companions and the elect of the early Church.[215]

---

205 Matthew 20:26, Mark 10:43; Mark 9:34-37, Luke 9:47-48
206 Matthew 20:27, Mark 10:44; John 13:12-15; John 6:33, 31-32
207 Matthew 20:28, Mark 10:45; 1 Timothy 2:5-6, John 11:49-50, Job 33:24, 1-33, Psalm 49:8-10, Isaiah 35:10, 51:11, Matthew 26:26-28; Exodus 30:11-16, Matthew 17:24-27
208 Luke 24:51
209 Matthew 25:31; Luke 19:12
210 John 18:36
211 Matthew 6:10
212 Matthew 20:28, Mark 10:45
213 1 Timothy 2:4, John 8:24
214 John 18:15, 24, 28, 19:1-3, 14-18, 25-30
215 Revelation 6:9-11

After these present events on the road to Jerusalem, the Lord still would continue to distinguish James, John, and Peter from the rest of the disciples, as he also had done so many times before, and as he would do most especially on the night before he died in the garden of Gethsemane.[216] Those three disciples in training, Peter, James, and John, were privileged by their vocations, planned for them by God, which they accepted as fully-faithful willing servants of the Lord: James eventually would be the first of the apostles to be martyred for the faith; John, by the end of his life at Ephesus, would have been head of the churches of Asia Minor, teacher, and evangelist; and Peter would become the Vicar of Christ and Servant of Servants, in the footsteps of the Lord, also by the pattern of Peter's suffering the Lord's crucifixion, and in his feeding of the Lord's sheep.[217]

But now, as the Lord intervened into these internal squabbles among his disciples, Jesus focused his disciples on the central mystery of himself, as the suffering servant, where without him none of us could ever hope to go.[218] And Jesus re-explained for them that we all should follow by heeding his example. Blessed indeed are those whose vocation from the Lord also is to suffer and to serve;[219] while some, also in their sensitivity and their charity, are dutifully privileged to accompany others who suffer in their crosses and to bear up their sufferings in Christ.[220] Even so, despite the Lord's example, on the night before he died, Christ still would find it necessary to pray for the unity of all believers,[221] which Saint Paul also would continue to encourage, as later Paul described the sources for Christian unity in his great letter to the Ephesians for the universal church.[222] And now, with the coming uncertainty, fear, and remorse proximate in the disciples during and following the approaching passion events, they all would need each other's support through their next period of transitional trauma and confusion, until the Lord once again would

---

216 Matthew 26:37, Mark 14:33
217 John 21:15-19
218 John 8:21-22, 28-29, 1 Timothy 2:5-6, John 1:16-17, 8:31-32, 51, 7:28-29
219 Ephesians 4:7-8, Matthew 20:28, Romans 6:5, 10-13
220 Mark 15:21, Matthew 27:32, Luke 23:26
221 John 17:11
222 Ephesians 4:1-6

return after his resurrection from the dead, as he had said he would, to provide his direct reassurance and guidance.

At this time, like most all of us, the disciples were still imperfect as saints; they were however disciples, not because they were saints, but because they were called to become saints.[223] In parallel to each of the three very explicit predictions made by Jesus about his death, he always also raised the ideal for the disciples, for them to aspire to be servants, or slaves, for all the rest.[224] By this the Lord was showing them, and us, that surrendering one's life to the cross and giving one's life in service to others are necessarily tandem events. And when Jesus, here, indicates these twin roles of theirs by his own example, he also makes the implicit contrast to the Roman emperor Tiberius Caesar, who at that time was the principal ruler who, indeed, made himself to be felt throughout the known Gentile world. One easily could misunderstand Jesus, if one's heart were not open to the true meaning of the Lord's words, as if he were primarily a revolutionary who intended to overthrow Caesar's subjugation of Israel. In fact, however, this had been the general Jewish perception and expectation; and, in fact, insurrection later becomes one of the charges levelled by the Jews against the Lord in their final appeal made to Pilate for the Lord's Roman crucifixion.[225]

However, it also would be such an exquisitely divine irony that Barabbas [also, by name, a son of the father, our heavenly Father: Barabbas],[226] an actual revolutionary against Rome, would be released by Pilate to the crowds, instead of Jesus, the supposed revolutionary, according to the Lord's ransom, his life for the many.[227] Unlike the great rulers of the Roman Empire, who were like so-called "gods" as rulers and made their retributions felt,[228] God instead sends us his Son, the true Son of God, as a true ransom for the full retributions of

---

223   John 15:8, 16; 1 Peter 1:10
224   Luke 9:22, 23-24; Luke 9:44, 46-48; Matthew 20:18-19, 25-28, Mark 10:33-34, 42-45
225   Luke 23:2, John 18:29-33
226   Galatians 4:4-7, Colossians 1:18, Romans 8:29
227   John 18:39-40, 19:12, 15-16
228   Matthew 20:25, Mark 10:42

our sins.[229] If we find this difficult to believe, either that Jesus is God's Son or that our sins are forgiven because he died for us, then perhaps we may be thinking of God according to our human dispositions, as if God were like Caesar, or some other despotic potentate.[230] If this is so for us; although if then our own faith may be weak, or even if this anthropomorphic construction of God in others may have weakened or destroyed our faith, every good is possible with God,[231] especially by his mercy and love.[232] God's vengeance will be wrathful only for those who are finally disobedient, for those who are inactive to accepting his mercy for all.[233]

Perhaps for us this problem of faith is just as it was then for the disciples. Given their insufficient faith, the truly amazing story of our ransom by the Lord, was for now completely beyond their comprehension.[234] They had relied more on their sight and ambition than on their faith and service; and accordingly, they had been rendered unseeing, metaphorically, actually blind to the Lord's words because of their not yet sufficient faith.[235] But the disciples also had lots of company: there were many other persons of struggling faith, just like themselves, along the road on their journey to Jerusalem. But on the way, with the Lord's help to gather their attention to the discovery, the disciples soon were about to witness some remarkable examples of faith: to most persons it seemed that they were only lowly blind beggars, or in another instance, just a wealthy tax collector for the Romans, surely another sinner if ever there was one. However, along that road and amongst the crowds, they were exactly who the Lord was looking for: in their faith, any true sons of Abraham that Jesus could find.[236]

According to the various parallel accounts by three evangelists

---

229   John 17:3-5, 12:28-30, 10:17-18, 8:49-50, 7:18, 6:37-40, 5:36; John 6:27, 4:34, 3:35, 14-16
230   Matthew 20:25, Mark 10:42; Luke 19:21, Matthew 25:24; John 3:17
231   Matthew 19:26, Mark 10:27, Luke 18:27; Luke 24:46-47
232   1 Peter 1:16; 1 Corinthians 2:8-9, 12-16
233   Matthew 9:13; Luke 19:15, 23, Matthew 25:25-27
234   Luke 24:25-27; Isaiah 53:1-12
235   2 Corinthians 5:7-9
236   John 8:39-40, 56-58

of these events which followed, when Jesus drew near to Jericho,[237] or after Jesus and the disciples had come to Jericho and they were leaving the city with a large crowd following behind them,[238] there was a blind man sitting along the roadside begging;[239] or his name was Bartimaeus, son of Timaeus;[240] and/or there were two blind men sitting at the side of the road as they left Jericho.[241] Obviously, the three different accounts may be regarded independently, or they each may be evaluated according to the intentions of the evangelist. The difficulty of ascertaining historicity arises when comparisons are raised across evangelists. Now, while it seems by these accounts that there may have been one event, or two or three events; accordingly, there also may have been one, two or three, or four blind men. If there had been a single event, then there could have been only one location: either before entering Jericho, or after leaving the city. As for the single-man hypothesis, the first blind man, not specifically identified by name, strongly resembles Bartimaeus, the blind man who is named; but these may or may not be the same person because of their split locations; or then again, perhaps, there only may have been some confusion about the actual location and the timing of the event for a single blind man.

But alternatively, if these three versions were a series of different events, one or two or three locations could have been involved; or there might have been two, three, or four blind men. Or there may have been two individual blind men only at different locations, or two blind men at the same location beyond Jericho. Or there may have been three blind men between two locations, or four blind men among three locations. There is no clear reconciliation for this seeming hair-splitting other than to recognize the difficulty of establishing some historical unity across the synoptic accounts. However, perhaps more relevantly, it also seems that the Lord did intend to replicate these events in order to emphasize his point clearly; and if so, that would have required two, or three, or four

---

237   Luke 18:35
238   Mark 10:46
239   Luke 18:35
240   Mark 10:46
241   Matthew 20:29-30

persons: Matthew alone provides two, who, although they had been blind, were men of remarkable faith. Yet, also essential to the common purpose of the three accounts, there were many others along the road who were not physically blind; however, due to their lack of faith, they were spiritually unseeing; nonetheless, there also were other unidentified faithful, who may have followed Jesus "faithfully." Yet, even then, the disciples, like so many if not most of the others, were learning and growing in their faith; and like many or most of us, they were not yet complete in their faith: sufficient to the absolute faith in which we are called.

However, cutting through the ambiguities of the three narratives, perhaps this is the true story [reconstructed according to the common intentions that the evangelists shared with the Lord] when the Lord came to Jericho, as if in a single journey: it seems most certain that Jesus saw only two blind men of absolute faith along the road.[242] The first man was unnamed, when the disciples and Jesus were entering Jericho;[243] and the second man, when they were leaving Jericho, was Bartimaeus, another case like the first blind man.[244] As Jesus was on his way into the city, the first blind man heard such a noisy disturbance that he had to ask the crowd passing in front of him, "What's happening?"[245] They told him, "Jesus the Nazarene is passing by."[246] So he shouted out, "Jesus, Son of David, have pity on me!"[247] But the man was out of sight, behind the crowd standing along the edge of the road, where the people were in front of him; and they turned around and scolded him for his irritating disturbance, telling him to keep quiet, but he kept calling out all the louder, "Son of David, have pity on me!"[248] But, right there in front of them all, Jesus stopped and ordered them to bring the blind man over to him.[249] And, making way for the man to pass and leading

---

[242] Matthew 20:30
[243] Luke 18:35
[244] Mark 10:46
[245] Luke 18:36
[246] Luke 18:37
[247] Luke 18:38
[248] Luke 18:39
[249] Luke 18:40

him on, when he drew close to Jesus, Jesus asked him:

What do you want me to do for you?[250]

And he replied, "Sir, let me see again."[251] This also should be our confident prayer to God. And while Jesus touched his eyes without a beat lost between them, Jesus told him simply and quietly:[252]

Have sight; your faith has saved you.[253]

Immediately his sight returned, and he followed Jesus praising God; and with him, all the people who saw this, they also gave glory to God.[254]

Then, after this first event, Jesus and his disciples had passed through Jericho and they were on their way out of the city; and as if to prove that lightening does indeed strike the same place twice, when the Lord wants to emphasize his point: they came to the blind Bar-timaeus, who had been begging on the roadside as he sat.[255] When this son-of-Timaeus heard that this crowd was with Jesus from Nazareth, he also began to cry out and say, "Jesus, Son of David, have pity on me."[256] Although, like the case before, many rebuked him and told him to keep silent, he kept calling out almost constantly and even still louder, "Son of David, have pity on me."[257] Once again, Jesus stopped and simply said:

Call him.[258]

So, as the Lord does for us, those nearby called the blind man, saying to him, "Be cheerful! Take courage! Get up; he is calling you!"[259] At this, Bar-timaeus, threw off his cloak, jumped to his feet,

---

250 Luke 18:40-41; Mark 10:35-36
251 Luke 18:41
252 Matthew 20:34
253 Luke 18:42; Matthew 20:34; 2 Corinthians 5:7
254 Luke 18:43
255 Mark 10:46
256 Mark 10:47; Luke 18:37-38
257 Mark 10:48; Luke 18:39
258 Mark 10:49
259 Mark 10:49

and came to Jesus.[260]   In reply, Jesus then said to him:

> What do you want me to do for you?[261]

And, as we too should answer, the blind man answered, "Rabbuni [Teacher]: let me see again."[262] Jesus, as he touched his eyes,[263] told him:

> Go; your faith has saved you.[264]

At once, he regained his sight; and he also followed Jesus along the road.[265]

So now, in my gospel representation, we may have a further summary of these same events, as presented according to Matthew's gospel; it seems also to be Matthew's hymn of praise to God, as if the narrative story forms a canticle:

> As they left Jericho with a large crowd following Jesus,[266]
>   there had been two blind men sitting on the road;
> when they heard that Jesus of Nazareth was passing by,
>   they began to shout, "Lord! Have pity on us, Son of David!"[267]
> Although the crowd scolded them and told them to stay quiet,
>   they only shouted the more loudly,
>   "Lord! Son of David, have pity on us!"[268]
>
> Jesus stopped and called them over,
>   when he said to them,
>   "What do you want me to do for you?"[269]

---

260   Mark 10:50
261   Mark 10:51; Luke 18:41
262   Mark 10:51; Luke 18:41
263   Matthew 20:34
264   Mark 10:52; Luke 18:42
265   Mark 10:52; Luke 18:43
266   Matthew 20:29; Luke 18:35, Mark 10:46
267   Matthew 20:30; Luke 18:37-38, Mark 10:47
268   Matthew 20:31; Luke 18:39, Mark 10:48
269   Matthew 20:32; Luke 18:41, Mark 10:51

They told him, "Lord! Let our eyes be opened."[270]
Jesus felt pity for them;
> so when he touched their eyes,
> immediately their sight returned;
> and they followed him.[271]

Praise be to God![272]

But originally, when Jesus had come to Jericho, he had intended just to pass through; but in fact, he then stayed on for a while, before leaving town later that day.[273] There had been a man in the town named Zacchaeus, who was one of the senior-most tax collectors; so, as manager at the top of his tax-collection pyramid, he also had become a very wealthy man.[274] And, because he had been hearing about Jesus, Zacchaeus was eager to see for himself who Jesus was; so he showed up for the Lord's parade through town, but because he was a man of very short stature, he could not see above the crowd.[275] However, he cleverly ran ahead of the crowd and climbed into a sycamore tree in order to at least catch a glimpse of Jesus, who was about to pass that way.[276] Now, sycamore trees can have a very sizeable trunk, making it difficult for anyone to put one's arms around it; but because its thick lateral branches often are low-hanging, if one could manage to climb onto a limb, or if one wedged oneself above a limb and between the trunk higher up the tree, the tree would easily support a person. So, Zacchaeus climbed the sycamore tree. Soon his determination and bold initiative would be rewarded.

When Jesus reached the place along the road where Zacchaeus was, Jesus looked up into the tree and he called out to him:

> Zacchaeus, come down quickly, because today I must stay at your house.[277]

---

270 Matthew 20:33; Luke 18:41, Mark 10:51; Psalm 119:18
271 Matthew 20:34
272 Psalm 24:3-8
273 Luke 19:1, 5
274 Luke 19:2
275 Luke 19:3
276 Luke 19:4
277 Luke 19:5

Zacchaeus hurried down as fast as he could.[278] Perhaps, he even may have peeled some of the fragile bark off the sycamore tree; or maybe he scattered some of its hand-sized leaves, left over from the previous winter as the first few days of spring had recently just begun.[iii] When Zacchaeus had dropped to the ground, at once he welcomed Jesus with joy.[279] But everyone else, when they saw what was happening, they all grumbled, "He [Jesus] has gone to stay as a guest at the house of a sinner!"[280] But Zacchaeus, short as he was, stood there and publicly defended himself with the Lord, "Look, Sir! I am going to give half of my property to the poor; and if I have ever extorted anything from anyone, I will pay him back four-times the amount."[281] Then, in response to him, and also so that all the others could hear,[282] Jesus loudly said:

> Today, salvation has come to this house, because this man also is a descendant of Abraham.[283] For the Son of Man has come to seek out and save what was lost.[284]

Once, the Lord came for dinner as a guest in my father's house.[285] He had come implicitly one Sunday afternoon with his Dominican priest,[286] who was in Fort Wayne, Indiana, the city of his birthplace, and my hometown, for a brief visit with his own family, after returning from the Bolivian missions in La Paz and Cochabamba. Father Ralph had accepted a dinner invitation to our house through my mother's sister, Mary Ann, at that time a Dominican postulant, and also on behalf of my own aspirations, then, to the Dominican missions in Bolivia. So, besides me at age thirteen and my aunt, at the Sunday dinner table there also were my mother's parents (my godparents), my mother and father, and all five

---

278   Luke 19:6
279   Luke 19:6
280   Luke 19:7; Luke 18:11; Psalm 1:1, Luke 18:9-10
281   Luke 19:8
282   Psalm 1:6
283   Luke 19:9; John 8:39, Genesis 15:6; Galatians 3:7, 26, 16, Matthew 1:1, Romans 4:13, 16, 20-25
284   Luke 19:10; Matthew 15:24, 18:11, Luke 15:4-6, 19:5, 9
285   Luke 19:5
286   Hebrews 13:1-2, Matthew 18:20, Luke 24:30

of my younger siblings. At the centrepiece of this meal, my father, with great enthusiasm, had prepared stuffed Cornish rock hens, an unusual and unfamiliar delicacy for a salesman's large family, perhaps which then I ate for my very first time. For my father, his work also involved the wholesale food industry, selling to hotels, restaurants, schools, and hospitals; and throughout his life, well-prepared and finer quality food had been his family's experience; and, for him, at home for his family or in his job, putting good food on the table was his preoccupation.

However, being on the cusp of the not yet imagined Second Vatican Council, and during those early nineteen-sixties, at the start of the receding golden-age of America's period of greatest wealth in its history, our unassuming Dominican dinner guest plainly was embarrassed; and he seemed to be greatly offended by this extravagance compared to the daily life of his Quechua and Aymara Indians, who often worked the nationalized tin mines of Bolivia. So perhaps, or as some of us then thought it must have seemed to Father Ralph, my father would have done better to have served the Lord by serving ordinary chicken, and to have given half the meal's intended expense to the Bolivian missions.[287] More than 40 years after our dinner, 83% of Bolivia's population is still Quechua, Aymara, or mestizo; and national per capita income today is less than $2.50 per day, but certainly not so for those of European origin in Bolivia; and today the tin mines are closed. Today,[288] the class struggle in Bolivia threatens the integrity of the country as governors of the largely white eastern provinces want autonomy from the mostly indigenous western highlands. The kingdom of God has not yet fully appeared in Bolivia, or in a great deal of the world, or even in our part of the world, as we all should hope.[289] And now,[290] just yesterday, Evo Morales, the pro-indigenous socialist Bolivian President, has been re-elected with an overwhelming mandate for his social reforms.

---

287 John 12:4-5, Luke 19:8
288 As I had written in my previous editing of this chapter, it was then 3rd October 2008.
289 Luke 19:11, 11:2, 19:13
290 As I am writing this now, perhaps for the last time reviewing this chapter, it is the 7th December 2009.

However, at the time of my family's dinner celebration with Father Ralph, my father had ample reason for his choices of menu. They were not symptoms of relative luxury, as some of us at table had supposed; but rather, hidden from us then and beyond our imaginations, they were my father's private and humble expressions of generosity, in his gratitude to God,[291] by his heartfelt welcome to Christ the Lord.[292] The great mystery of this expression of praise, except for the occasional hint or leakage from my father, would not be clarified for the family until several decades had passed: for unknown to us, my father had escaped the infernos of hell. The Japanese had attacked Pearl Harbor on the 7th December 1941, causing the United States to enter the Second World War. Six months later in June 1942, my father, Benjamin,[293] who was the youngest of six children, graduated from secondary school; and following a brother and sister into the American Navy, he enlisted on 12th March 1943. Eleven months later in February 1944, as the war in the Pacific progressed, at nineteen years of age, my father found himself 3500 km southwest of Hawaii, actually slightly nearer to Tokyo only 3200 km to the northwest, when he landed on the northernmost island of the Kwajalein Atoll, on Roi-Namur, where U.S. troops first made their landing in the Marshall Islands, the very spot which had been the original source for the surprise Japanese attack on Pearl Harbor.

The two islands of Roi-Namur were joined by a narrow causeway: Namur, the larger island, had the width and breadth of 12 football fields; the island of Roi was only half that size, termed a "three-quarter mile square junk pile" after both islands were secured initially on February 1st. However, eleven days later, during the night of 11th-12th February, the Japanese managed to get some of their aircraft repaired and made flyable. When they headed for the tiny, but strategic, Roi-Namur Islands, they dropped a bomb, or two, on Roi, nearby to where my father's company, the 20th Engineers and Seabees, was billeted; and one incendiary bomb landed in their ammunition dump. Although the high-flying air raid lasted only five

---

291   Luke 9:51-56
292   Matthew 19:16, Revelation 21:3, 1 John 5:18, Matthew 19:17
293   Genesis 35:18, 42:3-4, 19-20, 43:13-16, 29, 44:1-2, 12-17, 27-31, 45:1-2, 9-15, 46:6-7

minutes, the subsequent bombardment from the multiple explosions of ammunition and TNT lasted for four hours. One eyewitness recounted: there were "solid sheets of flame;" tracer ammunition "lit up the sky as far as we could see;" and red-hot fragments rained down from the sky for a full-half hour, "like so many hailstones, burning and piercing the flesh when they hit." For my father and over the entire island, the result was apocalyptic.[294] According to my father, after the bomb hit and exploded, as best as he could, he ran to find a shell hole in the ground to protect himself from the blasts. But, literally, as he fell into one of these holes, he found its bottom was covered with red-hot metal materials; and, before he could remove himself from it, he was burned. Later on, he was awarded the Purple Heart for the wounds he suffered; however, not many of my father's shipmates actually survived the blasts.[295]

Afterwards, when my father returned to his camp in the morning light, he discovered a large piece of shrapnel embedded in a cardboard box, inches away from where his head had been. And thereafter, for many weeks, the daily routine began for searches of the island for secluded enemy, while Navy planes, that were small enough to land on the island's airstrip, made their daily flights around the atoll searching for enemy, until they all were eliminated. But, my father, as one destined by God's providence to survive amongst his shipmates,[296] he never wanted to talk about these matters throughout his life, except until now,[297] for, in his interior soul, these experiences were simultaneously a hellish horror, and a mysterious mercy from God.[298] Perspicaciously, my aged mother asked my eighty-three-year-old father, "What did you do for four long hours to survive the holocaust?" He said, "The marines had bunkers with their guns and I just jumped into one of these bunkers with a marine. The marines normally would not allow anyone in a bunker with them,

---

294	Revelation 20:7-10
295	Matthew 24:40
296	Matthew 24:22
297	Two years ago, 2nd December 2007 personal narration, of my father to my mother, in answer to the question about what had happened, put to him by my forty-eight-year-old "baby" sister, Teresa.
298	Luke 15:18-24, 14:12-14

but, coincidentally, this marine happened to be from Fort Wayne, and he was a classmate of mine, Jim Hayes. He let me share his bunker. I didn't even know Jim was on the island until I had jumped into the bunker with him."[299] And today, over sixty-four years later, Jim and Dad attend the same church,[300] still bunker buddies with the Lord.[301]

But now, because Jesus soon would be close to Jerusalem, those who followed him on the road imagined that the kingdom of God would be appearing right then and there,[302] in fact, as soon as they would be arriving in Jerusalem.[303] So, while the people still were listening to the Lord as he declared his mission of salvation to them in front of Zacchaeus,[304] Jesus then went on, accordingly, to tell them this parable:[305]

> There was a man of noble birth, who went off to a distant country to be made king, and afterwards he would return.[306] At once, he summoned ten of his servants and he gave them ten gold coins telling them, "Engage in trade with these until I get back."[307] But his fellow countrymen hated him, and they sent a delegation following behind him to announce their message: "We do not want this man to be our king."[308] But on his return, after he had obtained his kingship, he again summoned the servants to whom he had given the money, to find out what profit they had made through

---

299 Matthew 6:27, 24:40, 10:29, 24:22
300 Galatians 2:20, John 21:19-23; 1 John 3:2
301 Now, 8th December 2009, my father has bunkered up with the Lord, for eternity on 20th October 2009; at Dad's funeral, I also learned that Jim Hayes was still among the living, although unwell.
302 Luke 19:11; Luke 17:20-21
303 Luke 19:36-37, 38, Matthew 21:8-9, Mark 11:9-10, John 12:13; Psalm 118:25-26, Luke 19:9-10
304 Luke 19:9-10
305 Luke 19:11-12
306 Luke 19:12; Luke 2:11-14; Luke 20:9; Matthew 25:14, 31
307 Luke 19:13; Matthew 25:15-18
308 Luke 19:14; Luke 19:7, 15:1-2, 5:30; Psalm 129:5

trading.[309]

The first one came forward and said, "Sir, your gold coin has brought in ten more."[310] The king replied, "Well done, my good servant, bravo! Because you proved yourself faithful in such a very small matter, I am placing you in charge of ten cities."[311] Then the second one came forward and reported, "Sir, with your gold coin, I have earned five more."[312] To this servant he also said, "And you, take charge of five cities."[313] Next there came another, who said, "Sir, I'm returning your gold coin; I put it away safely in a handkerchief, for I was afraid of you because you are a demanding person: you take up what you have not put down, and you harvest what you did not plant."[314] The king said to him, "A wicked servant you are! With your own words I shall condemn you! You knew that I was a demanding person, picking up what I did not lay down, and reaping what I have not planted.[315] Why didn't you put my money in a bank, at least? Then when I returned, I could have taken it out with interest."[316]

And to those who were standing by, he said, "Take away the gold coin from him, and give it to the man who has ten"[317] But they said to him, "Sir, he already has ten gold coins!"[318] He replied, "I tell you: to everyone who has, more will be given; but from the man who has not, even the little bit he has will be taken away.[319] But now, as for these enemies of mine who did not want me

---

309 Luke 19:15; Matthew 18:23-24, 25:32; Matthew 25:19
310 Luke 19:16; Matthew 25:20
311 Luke 19:17; Matthew 25:21
312 Luke 19:18; Matthew 25:22
313 Luke 19:19; Matthew 25:23
314 Luke 19:20-21; Matthew 25:24-25
315 Luke 19:22; Matthew 25:26
316 Luke 19:23; Matthew 25:27
317 Luke 19:24; Matthew 25:28
318 Luke 19:25
319 Luke 19:26; Matthew 25:29; Isaiah 22:15, 19-24

for their king,[320] bring them right here before me and execute them in my presence."[321]

After saying this, and providing no commentary,[322] Jesus proceeded on his journey up to Jerusalem.[323] Jesus, of course, was that nobleman of David's royal lineage;[324] born for the cross as Son of Man,[325] and so to be our King;[326] but Jesus was telling the crowd implicitly that also he would not be the earthly king that they had desired him to be: the one they had hoped would restore King David's throne to Israel against the Romans.[327] Instead, Jesus would be going off elsewhere: to a place seemingly distant from his earthly country, back to his Father in heaven, where he would be made King; and afterwards, as King he would be coming back.[328] But for now, before Jesus assumed his dominion over the whole of creation, in Jerusalem soon his only crown would be made of thorns;[329] and before taking up his eternal throne in heaven,[330] as daily we are reminded by the crucifix in our homes and churches, Jesus would be ascending to his glory of the cross in Jerusalem first;[331] and only lifted up from there,[332] would he establish his heavenly kingdom throughout the ends of the earth.[333]

But before this nobleman, Son of God, went away to be made King, he has given everyone a royal commission,[334] in both senses of the word: both a payment and a mission. The gold coin that we each receive from the Lord, whenever he summons us to receive it, most

---

320   Luke 18:32-33; Isaiah 22:13-14; Acts 4:25-27, Psalm 2:1-2
321   Luke 19:27; Luke 19:14, 7; Matthew 25:30; Isaiah 22:25
322   Matthew 13:10-12, 25:29
323   Luke 19:28
324   Matthew 1:1, 16-17
325   John 18:37
326   Luke 19:12
327   Psalm 126:1-4
328   Psalm 96:13, 10
329   Mark 15:17
330   Ephesians 1:21
331   Isaiah 65:17-19, 66:13; Isaiah 24:23, Luke 23:44-45
332   John 3:14, 19:19-20
333   Psalms 22:28, 72:8, 86:9
334   Luke 19:13; 1 Peter 2:9

certainly from our baptism and in some particular moment of faith, is also a moment of grace to fill our souls,[335] refined pure as gold by the victory of salvation gained for us on the cross through the blood of the Lamb of God.[336] For with this precious coin, the Lord has paid the unattainable price for our sins;[337] and in exchange for his mortal life, he has traded away our sins in return for his grace to us. But with the Lord's giving us this grace, we also then must engage in similar trading through our daily union with the cross of Christ,[338] so that in our life's transactions through the cross, the fortune of the Lord's good gift to us, for only God is good,[339] results in gains for the Lord's wealth, not just for ourselves, but also to the benefit of others for the glory of God.[340] For any grace we receive as individuals from the Lord is quite dynamic: never intended for us alone, nor ever meant to remain forever static, the Lord entrusts us with the hard-earned investment of his sacrifice on the cross, and he expects us to bring home dividends from our use of his capital.[341]

At the very least, the Lord expects to collect interest on his redemption from our use of his grace among men.[342] But the more industrious of the Lord's servants give greater glory to God by the more illustrious gains of their trading. In exchange for their faithfulness, the Lord will entrust them with even greater responsibilities and rewards,[343] just as the Lord had done with Saint Paul, whose grace in life was to be a servant to the whole human race.[344] However, there are two ways we can squander the Lord's gold coin: if we choose to revert to sin, certainly;[345] but also if we put the gift aside and fail to use it or are inactive with it, that is, if we should keep this grace

---

335	Colossians 1:22
336	Revelation 3:18, 5:6-10
337	Colossians 2:14, Ephesians 1:14
338	Luke 19:13; Romans 6:3-4, Luke 9:23, Philippians 3:10, Romans 12:1-2
339	Luke 18:18-19
340	Romans 6:5-6
341	Luke 19:15, Philippians 3:12
342	Luke 19:23
343	Luke 19:16-19, 12:42-44
344	Colossians 1:23
345	Luke 11:35-36; Hebrews 10:26-27, 39

hidden under a handkerchief,[346] or under a bowl or under a bed,[347] and we don't follow the Lord's commission to uncover his gold coin.[348] Each coin should gleam like the shinning of a lamp, and it must be brought into the open for all to see,[349] so that the grace of the Lord may return to him, not empty-handed,[350] but as a bountiful harvest,[351] to be seen by men to the glory of God.[352] Otherwise, if it remains hidden, then even the little grace one has from the Lord will be taken away and given to others of greater enterprise.[353]

Although almost everyone now following the Lord wanted him to be King, even if for the wrong reasons, there were others trailing the Lord as temple spies, particularly the Pharisees and scribes, who did not want Jesus to be their King.[354] They were different altogether from those who followed the Lord initially as his servants,[355] who eventually prove to be faithful or wicked servants.[356] No, these others, as his enemies, were firmly opposed to the Lord; and consequently, they were firmly opposed to the kingdom of God. But in the conclusion to his parable, Jesus gives them a warning: the King demands that all his enemies, who did not want him King, are to be killed before him in his sight, right then and there.[357] Here the style of Christ, as King, resembled the more familiar justice of Caesar, who made his power felt throughout the Roman Empire.[358] But, if we are inactive followers of Christ; or if we are his explicit enemies, because in our sin we do not want Jesus for our King; then regarding our salvation, we may be in serious trouble with God. We all have been warned.

346	Luke 19:20
347	Luke 8:16
348	Luke 19:13
349	Mark 4:22, Luke 8:17
350	Exodus 23:15-16, 34:20, Deuteronomy 16:16-17; Luke 20:10-11
351	Matthew 20:1-2; John 15:8
352	Matthew 9:38, Luke 10:2
353	Luke 19:26, 8:18
354	Luke 19:14
355	Luke 19:13
356	Luke 19:22
357	Luke 19:27
358	Matthew 20:25

Therefore, we need to ask ourselves two questions: Do we follow Jesus wholeheartedly? And do we really want Jesus to be our King? If our answers should be negative or lukewarm,[359] then we may be like many of the Pharisees and scribes, who would be the primary targets for the Lord's last days of evangelization in his final mission to Jerusalem. But for the time being, the Lord had placed his superabundant generosity ahead of his exercising any equally appropriate justice,[360] the wrath he had warned against for any of us, all who were his murderers to-be, for those who still did not want Jesus as their King.[361]

Reflective Prayer: Psalm 2:1-11

Antiphon: Here is a King of my own choosing,
    who will rule on Mount Zion.

> Why are the nations rebelling in protest?
>   Why this useless murmuring amongst the peoples?[362]
> The kings of the earth are in revolt,
>   princes plot together against the Lord and his
>   Anointed,
>   the King he chose:[363]
> "Come," the rebels say, "let us break their shackles
>   and cast off their chains,"[364]
> by which in his retribution
>   we are shackled and bound.[365]

---

359   Revelation 3:16
360   1 Timothy 2:4, 2 Timothy 2:13; 2 Peter 3:15
361   John 10:10, 12:47-48; Luke 20:14-16, 19:26, 20:17-19
362   Psalm 2:1; Luke 19:7; Luke 18:36-39
363   Psalm 2:2; Luke 19:14; John 8:40-42, 44, Acts 4:27
364   Psalm 2:3; Luke 18:20; John 8:24, 1 Timothy 1:8-10
365   Psalm 149:8-9; John 8:34-36; Colossians 2:15

Gospel (on the Road to) Emmaus / 135

The One, from his throne in heaven, laughs;
> he derides them, mocking to scorn their feeble plans.[366]

The Lord speaks to them in anger,
> striking them with terror in his rage:[367]

"Myself, I AM, have installed my King
> on Zion, my holy mountain."[368]

I, the King, will announce the decree of the Lord,
> what he said to me: "You are my Son,
> today your Father has begotten you.[369]
> Only ask it of me, and I will make the nations your inheritance,
> put the very ends of the earth in your possession.[370]

With an iron hand you shall shepherd them,
> shatter them like a potter's jar."[371]

So, you kings, pay attention now and understand;
> heed my warning, you rulers on the earth![372]

Serve the Lord with fear,
> with trembling bow down in homage,
> lest God be angry and push you from the way
> in a sudden blaze of anger.[373]

Happy are all who put their trust in God.[374]

Antiphon: Whoever wishes to be first among you
> will be the slave of all.[375]

366	Psalm 2:4; John 11:57; John 10:30
367	Psalm 2:5; Luke 19:22; John 10:36-38
368	Psalm 2:6; Mark 10:45; Exodus 3:14, Psalm 24:3, John 18:4-8
369	Psalm 2:7; Matthew 20:18; John 10:58
370	Psalm 2:8; Matthew 19:29; Genesis 22:17-18
371	Psalm 2:9; Matthew 19:21, Luke 19:8; Isaiah 64:7-8
372	Psalm 2:10; Luke 19:27; Isaiah 66:16, 24, Psalm 21:9-10
373	Psalm 2:11; Matthew 20:20; Matthew 20:24-26
374	Psalm 2:11; Mark 10:52; John 18:36, Psalm 23:6
375	Mark 10:44

> Glory be to the Father,
>   and to the Son,
>   and to the Holy Spirit,
>   as it was in the beginning,
>   is now,
>   and ever shall be world without end. Amen.

Chapter 30

Saturday Evening, 9th Nisan (1st April, 30 CE): A Resurrection Dinner Party

Readings: John 12:1-8, 9-12; Psalms 26:1-12, 18:1-51, 57:1-12

In Jericho, when Zacchaeus had welcomed Jesus and the disciples as guests into his home,[1] all together they had celebrated his faith and virtuous repentance,[2] except for Judas Iscariot in his gnawing restlessness and in the hidden interiors of his soul.[3] But there along with Zacchaeus, all of the faithful also had found joyful peace and restful solitude in the Lord's presence,[4] away from the murmurings of the self-righteous crowds going up to Jerusalem for the feast.[5] Nonetheless, Jesus had thoroughly pursued them all,[6] implicitly including Judas;[7] and so Jesus had given them all quite specific warning if they, like the Pharisees and scribes, should not want him for their King,[8] soon to be enthroned upon the cross.[9] For many of the Lord's opponents, whom the Lord had sought out to

---

1 Luke 19:5-6; Psalm 26:8
2 Luke 19:8-10; Luke 18:13-14; Psalm 26:6-7
3 Psalm 34:16
4 Psalm 26:1-3
5 Luke 19:7, 14; Matthew 9:13, 12:7, Luke 18:9-10; Psalm 26:11
6 Luke 15:4, 8
7 John 6:64-65, 10:2-3
8 Luke 19:27; Psalm 26:9-10
9 Luke 18:31-33, John 19:19

save,[10] Zacchaeus was exactly their spiritual antithesis; even though for them, in their antithesis to the will and Spirit of God,[11] Zacchaeus seemed to be their idealized abomination to holiness: a tax collector for the hated Romans.[12] Yet, for this reason, Zacchaeus (no less than us) was the ideal case for Jesus to demonstrate God's mercy with his grace and his presence.[13] Zacchaeus, in his gratitude for the Lord's favour, truly was a humble sinner and a model host.[14] And in his wholehearted and gracious generosity that he displayed towards the Lord's invitational request to stay at his house,[15] Zacchaeus must have provided a very lavish dinner celebration for Jesus and his disciples;[16] and Zacchaeus also would have been privileged to enjoy some lengthy conversations with Jesus in his own home. Moreover, it seems, Jesus and his disciples must have stayed overnight with Zacchaeus. And according to the pattern established early on by the Lord,[17] they would have remained in that house, or homes, now the blessed household of Zacchaeus,[18] before moving on to their next stop in another town or village.[19]

But now, when Jesus would move on with his disciples from Jericho to Bethany, it would be an uphill walking distance of more than seven hours, and the journey also occurred before the Sabbath day.[20] When the Sabbath would have intervened, the crowds would have paused from their pilgrimage to Jerusalem, in order to observe the required Sabbath day's rest; for everyone then, even a journey of slightly more than one kilometre would not have been allowed.[21] Also, this standard Sabbath observance would occur at the Lord's Bethany rest-stop; certainly it would have allowed Jesus, Lord of the

---

10	Luke 19:10
11	Luke 24:44-50
12	Luke 5:30, 15:1-2, 20:20-25
13	Luke 19:9-10
14	Psalm 26:4-5
15	Luke 19:5
16	Luke 15:6, 23-24; Psalm 26:12
17	Matthew 10:11, Mark 6:10, Luke 10:7-8
18	Luke 10:5-6
19	Luke 19:5, John 14:23
20	Exodus 31:13-17, 35:2-3, Genesis 1:31, 2:1
21	Acts 1:12; Genesis 2:2-3, Exodus 20:11, 31:15-17, Deuteronomy 5:12-15

Sabbath,[22] important and necessary time for prayer.[23] But for this penultimate Sabbath day,[24] from its Friday evening initiation until its conclusion after the Sabbath day, it would be the Lord's last and final preparation, a Sabbath rest and prayerful reflection for all, before the singular bloom of his creative ministry, before Jesus engaged his ultimate week of "New Creation," the Lord's six full liturgical nights and days that would culminate in his chosen passion, death, and burial on the sixth day before his great and final Sabbath rest,[25] the day before his resurrection on the first new day of his revolutionary spiritual creation,[26] announced to us on the Easter Sunday, and that we also would celebrate on subsequent Sundays as our Paschal Lamb's victory over our sin and death. But from Jericho, Jesus had resumed his journey to Jerusalem in advance of the crowds, and most likely under the dark of night, because Jesus manages to leave Jericho only with his core disciples, quite intentionally, alone with them and completely unnoticed.[27]

So now, very quietly, without any fanfare or curious crowds pressing to see him, Jesus slips into Bethany where Lazarus lived, it seems, perhaps, going directly to his home. In any case, whenever Jesus showed up there in Bethany, perhaps in the morning hours or even just at daybreak, after Jesus would have arrived, it would have been sometime during daylight before the Sabbath that would begin after sunset on our Friday,[iv] one week before the Passover meal was to be consumed on the Friday evening of 15th Nisan.[28] This date for the celebrated Passover meal occurred after the death of the Lord, and it would be concurrent with the Sabbath observance.[29] The Passover date was determined by the 1st Nisan start of the new year, by the first day after the first new moon following the Spring equinox; and that first "day" began according to the definition in the Hebrew

---

22 Luke 6:5; Exodus 20:11
23 Psalm 18:1-51
24 Matthew 12:8, Colossians 1:15-16, Genesis 1:1, 31, 2:1-4; Exodus 31:15, Colossians 1:19-20
25 Luke 23:54, Matthew 27:62; John 19:14, 31, 42
26 Colossians 3:9-11, 1:15, 2:6-17
27 Luke 19:27-28, John 11:57
28 John 12:1, Mark 14:12, Luke 22:7-8, 14-15, Matthew 26:17-19
29 Mark 14:2, John 18:28, 19:14, 31, 42

liturgical calendar in Genesis: "evening came and morning came, the first day;"[30] and accordingly, for each Hebrew day, the darkness of night was followed by the light of day, so that a new day always began after sunset twilight. In 30 CE (Hebrew Year 3790), according to its astronomical determination, the 1st Nisan began on Thursday 23rd March (Julian calendar).[v] However, there is a discrepancy between the new moon's astronomical determination and its phasis; and when the preceding month has been 29 days (as was Adar in this instance), lag between the new month's observational determination and its astronomical calculation could vary one day, or even two.[31] This accounts for the actual one day difference for the start of Nisan in 30 CE between its astronomical and its liturgical determinations. The astronomical determinations provide universal comparisons between chronological systems; but, for their religious significance, we also must recognize the differences in calibration actually afforded by the Hebrew liturgical calendar, which Nisan dates my chapter labels have retained. Therefore, Jesus entered the house of the Last Supper when it was evening, on astronomical 15th Nisan, which was the liturgical start of 14th Nisan,[32] just as the Passover lamb was to be sacrificed on 14th Nisan between the two evenings, as Jesus would be sacrificed as the Lamb of God,[33] during his passion between Thursday evening and Friday late afternoon. So, the Lord's Thursday evening meal preceded the Jewish celebration of the actual Passover meal on Friday evening 15th Nisan; the Lord's Paschal sacrifice would be on 14th Nisan, Friday 7th April 30 CE, as the Lord's grand seven-day liturgy was being accomplished.[34]

The liturgical days of the Hebrew Calendar proceed from the darkness of one evening until nautical twilight of the following day; but the days of the Roman and Jerusalem civil calendar, which were Julian calendar days and also provide for us our nominal days

---

30 Genesis 1:5
31 Benjamin W. Bacon in his "Notes on Gospel Chronology" (Journal of Biblical Literature, Vol. 28, No. 2 (1909), pp. 130-148) allows potentially as much as 36 hours between astronomical new moon and phasis.
32 John 13:1, Mark 14:17, Matthew 26:20, Luke 22:13-14
33 John 1:35
34 John 19:30, 1 Corinthians 5:7

of the week, proceeded from midnight to midnight, which is the familiar custom for our Gregorian dating of the days and hours. In the conversion of the Julian date to the Gregorian date, days of the week remain equivalent, but the hypothetical Gregorian date lags two days behind the Julian date for 30 CE; for 2010 CE, the Julian date now lags behind the Gregorian date by thirteen days. When Jesus arrived in Bethany seven days before Passover, it was still day time on Friday (8th Nisan astronomically, or liturgical 7th Nisan), 31st March (Julian calendar). When the Sabbath began on that Friday evening, it became astronomical 9th Nisan, which then continued as the Jewish liturgical day 8th Nisan into Saturday until the conclusion of that Sabbath at twilight. Then the dinner at Bethany Saturday evening was initiated on astronomical 10th Nisan, as the first day of the week, whose liturgical celebration continued as 9th Nisan into daytime Sunday, when this initial evening to evening day of creation also would be marked by the Palm Sunday entrance of Our Lord into Jerusalem, with his sudden departure from the city when evening came,[35] before the advent of the second liturgical day on Sunday evening (astronomical 11th Nisan, or liturgical 10th Nisan), which Jesus continues with his purification of the Temple on Monday morning.[36] The Friday evening of Holy Week concludes the sixth day of its New Testament creation when the Sabbath rest begins (on astronomical 16th Nisan, or the liturgical 15th Nisan), the start of the seventh day; that Friday solemnity also was our most solemn Christian preparation day because of the Lord's Passover sacrifice, that entered immediately into its celebration of the Sabbath Passover.[37]

In Bethany, only very recently before this, Jesus had raised Lazarus from the dead;[38] so now, this fact also becomes principal to the Lord's reasons for returning to Lazarus in Bethany. For after the Sabbath in the Lord's coming to Bethany, from that Saturday evening supper, one complete liturgical week before Easter Day would now begin; and from that Saturday evening Bethany supper, the daytime

---

[35] Mark 11:11
[36] Mark 11:15, 19
[37] Luke 23:54, Matthew 27:62; John 19:14, 31, 42
[38] John 11:1, 17, 41-44

half of the final octave of that Holy Week would begin precisely with the early morning hour, perhaps to the very minute of the Lord's resurrection on the first day, Easter Sunday![39] Even so, along the route to Jerusalem, starting from the week before his transfiguration, Jesus had been telling his disciples explicitly about his death and resurrection;[40] and soon these things would happen exactly as he had been predicting them;[41] but because nearly everyone failed to comprehend the Lord's explicit meaning of his predictions,[42] this became another reason for the Lord's coming to Bethany now as he did. For, as the Lord wished, if anyone could be led to understand, logically and spiritually, his approaching death and resurrection before it happened, and even be led to their rational and spiritual explanation after they had occurred, then it should have been clear by his own death and resurrection and through the present sign and person of his dear friend Lazarus, together with the ample help of the two sisters of Lazarus, Mary and Martha, the Lord's closest family.[43] Indeed, although the Lord's visit to Bethany anticipated his own death, its foremost meaning specifically was this: for the Lord to celebrate with us his forthcoming resurrection, and ours. This was his emphatic point,[44] just as Jesus had told Martha before he had raised her brother Lazarus from the dead, namely: that for everyone who believes in me, I, Jesus, am the resurrection and the life.[45] And equally, through the Lord's celebrations with Lazarus now at dinner, he intended to make explicit this meaning of our true discipleship in Jesus, as we are remade as a new creation in Christ.[46]

Bethany lay just to the east of the Mount of Olives; a Sabbath's walking distance outside of Jerusalem and its temple walls, whose imposing structures began to rise from its foundations at eye level just to the west across the Kidron Valley from the Mount of Olives.[47]

39	John 20:1; John 1:4-5, 9; 1 John 1:5-7; John 11:9-10, 12:35-36, 46
40	Luke 9:22-23, 28-31
41	Matthew 20:18-19, Mark 10:33-34, Luke 18:31-34
42	Luke 18:34
43	John 11:3, Mark 3:33-35, Luke 8:21
44	Jeremiah 24:7
45	John 11:25-26, 40; John 8:28, 3:14-15
46	1 Corinthians 15:49, Ephesians 4:24; Romans 8:14-25
47	John 11:18; Mark 13:1, Matthew 24:1, Luke 21:5

So, this is the proximate context for Jesus: his ultimate mission in Jerusalem,[48] when later that day, on Saturday after the Sabbath, in nearby Bethany they specifically had prepared a dinner there in the Lord's honour: for Jesus, he intended it to anticipate his death and resurrection, and also ours;[49] but for the others, they initially understood it, as the Lord also had understood it, to be in celebration of Jesus having raised Lazarus from the dead.[50] This dinner celebration was not the later event at the house of Simon the Leper, despite the obvious shared commonalities between events; there would occur yet this other dinner for the Lord, again in Bethany, four days later, on the Wednesday evening, just two days (the Thursday and Friday) before the Friday evening start of Passover.[51] No, this particular dinner celebration in Bethany was the first, held just four days before Simon's, whose was the last before Passover would begin; and, most likely, this first dinner was held at the home of Lazarus.

Wherever household in Bethany this Saturday evening dinner may have been held, after the traditional Sabbath had ended, Martha helped serve it; and Lazarus, appropriately, sat with the Lord at the head table.[52] Also Mary, the sister of Martha and Lazarus,[53] especially honoured Jesus then while he still was reclining at table: she very gratefully proceeded to anoint his weary, not-yet-finished-travelling-to-Jerusalem feet with part of a whole pint of spikenard,[54] an expensive aromatic ointment, which was like spices that Jews used customarily for their burial preparations of the body.[55] Very likely this ointment was readily available to Mary because of her brother's earlier pre-resurrection burial.[56] And, as Mary surrounded the Lord's feet with her hair, which flowed ever so gracefully to her lap, the sweet scent of the perfume filled the entire house.[57]

48	John 19:18
49	Luke 15:23-24; Romans 6:3-6
50	John 12:2; John 11:2; Luke 15:32, 22:30
51	Matthew 26:2, 6, Mark 14:1,3; John 12:1
52	John 12:2;
53	John 11:2
54	John 12:3; Psalm 147:11
55	John 12:7, John 19:39-40
56	John 11:2, 17
57	John 12:3

But one of the disciples, Judas Iscariot, who later betrayed the Lord, interrupted Mary, almost reflexively; as in that instant Judas had hoped that there still would be some chance to realize a sizeable profit from the remainder of the unspent ointment. So, in an implicitly accusatory, but nearly pious mercenary tone, Judas remarked, "Why wasn't this ointment sold for three hundred denarii [300 days-wages], and the money given to the poor?"[58] However, Judas cared not at all for the poor; he had said this only because he was in charge of the purse for the disciples;[59] for quite simply, he was only an ordinary thief, who used to help himself to their common funds.[60] But, not quite before Judas had finished speaking, Jesus jumped at his hypocrisy; and with barely contained, yet subtle disgust for Judas in the Lord's voice, Jesus also came to Mary's defence; while clearly, at the same time, Jesus also planted implicit instructions to Mary for her later behaviour.[61]

And so, accordingly, explicitly hinting to everyone for their meditations about his approaching death, Jesus said:

> Leave her alone! Let her keep what she has for the day of my burial.[62]

Jesus had directed his words, sharply, to Judas; but he added specifically for him a very pointed subtext: Jesus not only dismisses the unfair criticism of Mary by Judas, but also Jesus justifies now her later use for this ointment; but then, he also warned Judas, although Jesus had said this to everyone, by also turning the consequences of the approaching betrayal of Judas back upon Judas, and also even-handedly, and justly so,[63] upon all the rest of us who also have betrayed the Lord by our sins:

> You will always have poor people with you, but you will not always have me.[64]

---

58   John 12:5; Luke 20:24
59   Luke 16:10; John 12:4, Matthew 26:25, 14-15, 27:3-5
60   John 12:6
61   Luke 23:55-56, 24:1, John 20:1
62   John 12:7
63   Acts 2:22-23, 36
64   John 12:8; John 12:25; Luke 17:3-4

There is a double meaning intended here by Jesus. Soon, he no longer would be walking among them: his first meaning. But also for Judas, the moment was fast approaching when, in the hypocrisy of his sin,[65] Judas would abandon Jesus: his second meaning, for Jesus had not abandoned Judas. Just as Jesus seeks everyone's salvation, he had sought to save Judas; and so, Jesus did not now condemn him, but he would do so on the last day,[66] if Judas persisted in his tragic course. For, in his very last, Judas would reject the mystery of his potential conversion and of his actual forgiveness through the cross of Christ;[67] if only with the grace of faith he had believed.[68] But, as it is possible for any of us to seize this grace of repentance, as Judas in counterexample unfortunately would fail to do, we must strive to accept and to behold the cross with the resurrection, simultaneously; with all of our strength of mind, heart, and soul,[69] we must wholly embrace them both.[70] This explains the Lord's rationale, as he had intended for everyone's benefit, when on this post-Sabbath evening one week before Easter Jesus had pre-celebrated his death and resurrection from the dead, which is, along with the present overt post-resurrection celebration of Lazarus,[71] our share with the Lord to eternal life if we hold out to the end.[72] Of all the protagonists in this particular gospel episode, Lazarus had experienced the most profound of transformations.[73] He had been sick and had died, just as we all do because of the spiritual illness and death that is our sins; but then, after Lazarus was in the tomb for four days, in the righteousness of his faith in Jesus, the Lord had raised him to a new life![74] Radically and foremost by his full discipleship, Lazarus now visibly displayed for everyone what spiritual life every disciple may

---

65   John 8:24
66   John 12:47-48
67   John 14:26-27, 17:12, Acts 1:16, Psalm 41:10; Matthew 18:21-27, Psalm 103:12-14, Matthew 10:33
68   John 6:47, 40
69   Matthew 22:37-40
70   Luke 23:39-43; Psalm 118:10-14
71   Psalm 118:15-19
72   2 Peter 3:17-18
73   Psalm 118:1-4
74   John 11:39; Psalm 118:5-9

anticipate in the life of the yet to be risen Lord:[75] through his restored earthly life, in the passion and resurrection of Christ, Lazarus now revealed a new humanity from Jesus, the life and resurrection,[76] that had come to him from God, as it does to all true disciples.[77]

As a consequence of this manifestation of God's glory, Lazarus also had become a popular curiosity for some people, ranking equally high, right along with the Lord, in their various pursuits of entertainment; just as today people sometimes run after so-called psychics, gurus, or other public personalities associated with unexplained mysteries, esoteric religious beliefs, or purported claims of the occult. So, when a crowd of the Jews learned that Jesus now had come to Bethany, when the Sabbath had finished they went there to the house also trying to see Lazarus, just as much as they then may have hoped to see the Lord.[78] However, because of Lazarus, many of the Jews were leaving their leaders and believing in Jesus.[79] Therefore, as an illustrious disciple, Lazarus had become a key figure in the Christian revolution; so politically and socially, because of God's glory, Lazarus also had become a marked man. The chief priests now would be including him along with Christ in their immediate murder plans.[80] Ironically, once again for Lazarus, his earthly life was now in complete jeopardy;[81] but also because of the death and resurrection of the Lord, and by his shared life in Christ, Lazarus was also destined for eternal life.[82]

Martha, too, had changed, as now she had grown in the simple everyday practice of her faith. Once, at an earlier time before this moment, Martha had pleaded with the Lord for his help: to get her sister, Mary, to help her in the serving of her dinner guests.[83] But now, Martha had learned that her true and only sufficient joy comes

---

75	1 Corinthians 15:44-45
76	John 14:6, 11:25-26
77	Romans 6:5, 1 Corinthians 15:46-50
78	John 12:9
79	John 12:11
80	John 12:10
81	1 Corinthians 15:3-4
82	1 Corinthians 15:20
83	Luke 10:40

from her serving the Lord. So at this dinner, Martha was fully engaged in serving the meal,[84] not only gladly, but also without any of her previous hang-ups or anxieties![85] Indeed, if we wholeheartedly serve the Lord, there can be no anxiety.[86] And so it was that, now, Martha was completely secure and at peace in her having learned her role of service to others,[87] even if only as a simple waitress or as a simple cook, just as she had learned from the Lord's example, who had come as a slave for all, and not to be served.[88] Now, as Martha was grounded more firmly in the Lord's perspective, she no longer had any complaints to make regarding her sister, or about any of her sister Mary's profound contemplations on the Lord's words and deeds.[89] As together Martha and Mary demonstrate, service to others and contemplation in the Lord are both necessary roles for modern housewives and mothers, as well as proper roles for women and men professionals with careers, either in or out of religious life.

And Mary, the sister of Lazarus and Martha,[90] as was typical of her, had been absorbed in her meticulously listening to the Lord; so that now the sweet-smelling memory of her present deed to the Lord would linger in her hair from that Saturday evening, and it would continue to grace her constant and newest reflections on Jesus' words.[91] Because of this, and because whatever Mary heard and understood she typically put into action, in just four days, on the Wednesday, she would be the first person, after John the Baptist, and beyond the prophets and with the mother of our Lord,[92] to fully recognize the meaning intended by the Lord's being "Lamb of God."[93] And afterwards, in another two days, on the Friday later called Good, Mary would be looking on from a distance, together with

---

84 John 12:2; Luke 17:8-9
85 Luke 10:41
86 1 John 4:18
87 Matthew 20:26-27, Luke 17:10
88 Matthew 20:28, John 13:4-5
89 John 12:3, 13:8, Luke 10:42
90 Luke 10:39
91 John 12:7-8
92 Luke 2:41-42, 49-51, John 1:35-36, 2:1-4;
93 Matthew 26:6-7,12-13, Mark 14:3, 8-9; John 1:29-30, Exodus 12:21, 2-11, Luke 22:15-16

the other friends,[94] to behold Jesus upon the cross at Golgotha.[95]

With Mary's meditations upon her Lord's *Via Crucis*, and upon his hands and feet nailed in suffering to the wood of a tree, her thoughts would blaze back and forth to this present moment of Saturday evening, and to the forthcoming Wednesday evening, when both times she had anointed the feet of her King and had wiped them with her hair, remembering all that the Lord had said and done when they had celebrated her brother's and the Lord's resurrections.[96] On this approaching Friday, she also would persevere in her faith and hope.[97] For Mary, indeed, it would be quite an astonishing week, from this Saturday evening before Easter to the next Sunday morning and Easter Day![98] But she would learn of the Lord's resurrection only on his third day;[99] when then, her steadfast hope in the gospel would somersault to an unbounded joy in her Lord and in her God's confirmation of his promised triumph over death and sin, unto eternal life.[100]

Judas too had changed; he hadn't always been so hardened, as now he was by his advancing corruption. Once, out of the many dozens of disciples, Judas had been chosen by the Lord to be one of the twelve apostles; and along with the foundation of the others in Jesus, he was sent to preach the Kingdom of heaven.[101] He had been chosen by God to participate fully in the Lord's salvation ministry; he had not been chosen so, as to become a traitor in his destiny, or because he was corrupt. No, in this we all have been the same as Judas. At one time or another, all of us have been corrupted by our misfortunes of sin, when also we have been traitors to the Lord; and, unfortunately, some of us still may be continuing to slide down this destructive path. Corruption first begins with the little things; but then, step by step, by denial after denial, it worms its way into our

---

94 Luke 23:49
95 John 19:17; Numbers 21:5, 8, John 3:14-15, 12:32
96 Psalm 57:2-6
97 Psalm 16:7-8, Isaiah 25:6-9; Psalm 57:7-12
98 John 12:2, 20:19, Luke 24:37-43
99 Luke 18:31-33
100 Acts 2:23-32, Psalm 16:9-11; John 5:24
101 Luke 6:12-16, Mark 3:13-19, Matthew 10:7-15, 1 Peter 2:4-6

hearts of flesh, gradually turning them, by degree after degree, into icy hearts of stone. At first, the corruption seems to be just a small deception, such a little lie; but it begins to steal your soul, until denial after denial one becomes just like Judas. In reality, towards the end, while Judas was just an ordinary thief, his soul had vanished to the thievery of sin. He really cared nothing for the poor, but only about himself, as he helped himself to whatever he wanted from the use of other people's money, money he had stolen by his misappropriations from its proper use,[102] for the works of God.[103]

And like Judas, sometimes people also callously steal from employers,[104] or from their spouses,[105] or from any one of their many other victims.[106] So also, it is possible for any of us, like Judas, that we could deny God's will for us by our creeping infidelities until, in the end, we also finally may refuse to see ourselves as God and others see us, after corruption has wrecked its horrible toll on our oblivious souls and on the natural and spiritual lives of the innocents we have slaughtered around us.[107] Just as our striving for holiness is not intended by God for our benefit alone, but it also is for the benefit of others in God's glory, let there be no mistake about sin: if we continue to choose it, the evil of sin is never isolated to its perpetrator, as if somehow we could ever get away with our sin because, "If I want to sin, it might only harm me."[108] No, sin not only harms me, but as we see around us, in the misery of an entire world suffering from the abuses and misuses of wealth and power, our collective and personal sin has nailed the Son of God, and our neighbour, to the cross; and God (Father, Son, and Holy Spirit) deserves infinitely better than this from us.[109] Originally, Judas was without remorse or any intention of reform; but later he would come to regret his betrayal of an innocent man.[110] Yet, without his embracing the forgiveness of Jesus through

---

102 Luke 16:9-12
103 John 12:6; Luke 19:13
104 Matthew 20:1, Luke 19:15
105 Matthew 5:27-28, 31-32
106 Mark 10:19
107 Luke 17:1-2, Luke 23:41
108 Romans 14:7, Deuteronomy 29:15-20
109 Matthew 22:37-40
110 Matthew 27:3-4

the cross and resurrection, before this week was over, Judas would be body and soul in the grave.[111] Only God knows how many others like him, then and now, up to now and past our time, also would die in their sins.[112]

And in Bethany on this week before Easter, also in the background beyond the Lord's immediate circle of disciples and those others who knew him personally, there were the crowds. Many were just late-coming sightseers;[113] others were sincere followers of Jesus;[114] and, like the hardened Pharisees, some also were determined enemies of the Lord.[115] Some of us, in fact, out of the seemingly anonymous crowd of billions of persons ever to have lived, may deeply enjoy a real personal friendship with the Lord, as he truly lives among us and within us:[116] we keep his commandments;[117] our personal prayer with God is rich and intimate, just as we love the scriptures and the community prayers of the church;[118] and we contemplate and experience the Lord's presence through and within his sacraments.[119] But that is not enough: if we don't follow the Lord in his mystery of salvation by fully embracing holiness in his cross;[120] unless we do share with the Lord in his suffering and glory,[121] bringing God's holiness and grace to others,[122] that requires our most active love for the poor.[123]

At other times, we can be like the ambivalent crowds: one minute, as we make the journey with Jesus to Jerusalem, some of us cheer the Lord along the road;[124] but in another fickle minute we are still part

---

111	Matthew 26:24, 27:5, Acts 1:18; John 12:25
112	John 8:24
113	John 12:9; Luke 23:8
114	John 12:26;
115	John 11:53, 12:10-11; Matthew 22:41-44, Psalm 110:1
116	Luke 17:20-21, 1 John 3:2, 4:12
117	John 15:10, 1 John 3:23-24; Luke 18:21
118	John 6:63, Luke 24:27
119	John 6:51, 20:23
120	Luke 9:23, 14:27
121	John 16:33, Galatians 6:14; Luke 14:33
122	John 12:8
123	John 12:6; 1 John 3:18-19; Luke 18:22-23, 19:8, 12:32-34
124	Luke 19:11

of the sinful mob shouting out for his crucifixion before Pilate.[125] Or again, in one minute we think we want Jesus for our King;[126] but then in another unstable minute we won't commit ourselves completely to the Lord.[127] Sometimes, even defiantly, some of us do not want Jesus for our King;[128] but actually we may wish him dead,[129] or we may proclaim him so in our specific personal and pragmatic philosophies,[130] or in some moment of our spiritual realization we may find ourselves to be dead, without his life in us.[131] Or, in an action of spiritual recourse, we might find ourselves standing with Mary Magdala at the entrance of the tomb wanting the Jesus, whom we still believe to be dead, "They have taken my Lord away, and I don't know where they have put him."[132] However, God is alive, and Jesus is quite transcendent.[133] Our only hope for God's mercy,[134] if ever we should be so estranged from God, or if we are much less of a disciple of Jesus than we ought to be, is for us to pray.[135] If we can pray, then by our joining our will to the grace of God,[136] God always does hear us.[137] Then, our Father in heaven gives good things to everyone who asks of him.[138]

---

125 John 19:15
126 John 6:15, 12:13
127 Matthew 22:37-39
128 Luke 19:14
129 Luke 20:14-15
130 John 10:20
131 John 12:35-36; Colossians 1:21-23; Luke 19:27
132 John 20:13
133 John 1:4-5, 14; 1 John 2:2, John 14:1-3; Revelation 21:3
134 John 9:32-41
135 John 14:12-13
136 John 4:34, 6:38; Matthew 7:21, 12:50, 6:9-10
137 1 John 5:5-8, Luke 19:10, John 14:14
138 Matthew 7:11, 7-10

Prayer Reflection: Psalm 78: 5-7, 34-37; 40-47; 48-55; 56-61; 62-69, 72

Antiphon: Do not forget the works of the Lord.

> God set up a decree in Jacob,
>   established his laws in Israel;
> and what he commanded of our ancestors,
>   they were to teach their children;[139]
> that the next generation might come to know them,
>   children yet to be born;
>   and in turn they were to recite them to their
>   children.[140]
> In this way, they too will put their trust in God,
>   not forgetting what he has done,
>   and always keeping his commandments.[141]
>
> When God slew them, they began to seek him
>   and inquired after him again,[142]
> remembering that God was their rock,
>   the Most High God, their redeemer.[143]
> But they flattered him with their mouths
>   and lied to him with their tongues,[144]
> because their hearts were not constant toward him;
>   they were not faithful to his covenant.[145]

---

139 Psalm 78:5; Hebrews 8:8, Jeremiah 31:31
140 Psalm 78:6; Hebrews 8:9, Jeremiah 31:32
141 Psalm 78:7; Hebrews 8:10, Jeremiah 31:33
142 Psalm 78:34; Luke 19:27
143 Psalm 78:35; Luke 19:9
144 Psalm 78:36; Luke 18:36-37
145 Psalm 78:37; Luke 18:39

Antiphon: Do not forget the works of the Lord.

> How often they rebelled against God in the desert,
>   grieved him in the wasteland.[146]
> Again and again they tested God,
>   provoked the Holy One of Israel.[147]
> They did not remember his power,
>   the day he redeemed them from the foe,[148]
> when he displayed his wonders in Egypt,
>   his marvels in the plain of Zoan.[149]
>
> God changed their rivers to blood;
>   their streams they could not drink.[150]
> He sent insects that devoured them,
>   frogs that destroyed them.[151]
> He gave their harvest to the caterpillar,
>   the fruits of their labour to the locust.[152]
> He killed their vines with hail,
>   their sycamores with frost.[153]

---

146 Psalm 78:40; Exodus 15:22-24, 16:1-3, 17:1-3, 19:1-2, 20:1, 18-21; Deuteronomy 32:18
147 Psalm 78:41; Exodus 32:1-6; Deuteronomy 32:19
148 Psalm 78:42; Exodus 32:15-20, Deuteronomy 9:15-21
149 Psalm 78:43; Exodus 19:10-15, Luke 18:33; Hebrews 12:18-29
150 Psalm 78:44; Exodus 7:19-21
151 Psalm 78:45; Exodus 8:12-13, 17-20, 7:25-29, 8:1-11
152 Psalm 78:46; Exodus 10:3-15
153 Psalm 78:47; Exodus 9:25

Antiphon: Do not forget the works of the Lord.

> He exposed their flocks to deadly hail,
>> their cattle to lightning.[154]
> He unleashed against them his fiery breath, roar, fury,
>> and distress, storming messengers of death.[155]
> He cleared a path for his anger;
>> he did not spare them from death;
>> he delivered their beasts to the plague.[156]
> He struck all the firstborn of Egypt,
>> love's first child in the tents of Ham.[157]
>
> God led forth his people like a shepherd;
>> he guided them through the desert like sheep.[158]
> He led them on secure and unafraid,
>> but the sea swallowed up his enemies.[159]
> He brought them to his holy land,
>> the mountain his right hand had won.[160]
> God drove out the nations before them;
>> he apportioned them a heritage by lot,
>> and settled the tribes of Israel in their tents.[161]

---

[154] Psalm 78:48; Exodus 9:22-23
[155] Psalm 78:49; Exodus 9:24, 26
[156] Psalm 78:50; Exodus 9:1-6
[157] Psalm 78:51; Exodus 11:1-7, 12:1-14, 24-30
[158] Psalm 78:52; John 12:1; Exodus 12:37-42, 13:17-22
[159] Psalm 78:53; John 12:3; Exodus 14:1-4, 10-14, 21-31
[160] Psalm 78:54; John 12:2; Exodus 15:17-18
[161] Psalm 78:55; John 12:9; Exodus 23:23-24, 34:13-14; Numbers 26:52-56, 33:50-54, 34:13-15, Joshua 14:1-5, 24:1-14

Gospel (on the Road to) Emmaus / 155

Antiphon: Do not forget the works of the Lord.

> But still they tested, rebelled against the Most High God,
>> and they did not observe his decrees.[162]
> They turned back from God, deceitful like their ancestors;
>> they proved themselves false like a bow with no tension.[163]
> They enraged God with their high places;
>> with their idols they goaded him.[164]
>
> God heard and grew angry;
>> he rejected Israel completely.[165]
> He forsook the shrine at Shiloh,
>> the tent where he dwelt with humans.[166]
> He gave up his might into captivity,
>> his glorious ark into the hands of the foe.[167]

Antiphon: Do not forget the works of the Lord.

> God abandoned his people to the sword;
>> he was enraged against his heritage.[168]
> Fire consumed their young men;
>> their young women heard no wedding songs.[169]
> Their priests fell by the sword;
>> their widows made no lamentation.[170]
> Then the Lord awoke as from sleep,
>> like a warrior from the effects of wine.[171]

---

162 Psalm 78:56; Joshua 24:15-28
163 Psalm 78:57; John 12:4-5; Judges 2:10-12
164 Psalm 78:58; John 12:6; Deuteronomy 7:5-11, 12:2-5; Judges 2:13, 1 Peter 4:1-6
165 Psalm 78:59; John 12:7
166 Psalm 78:60; John 12:8; Joshua 18:1
167 Psalm 78:61; 1 Samuel 4:1-11
168 Psalm 78:62; Hebrews 10:26; Judges 2:14-15, Deuteronomy 28:15, 36-37, 47-51, 63-68, Jeremiah 24:10, 25:4-7, Revelation 18:21
169 Psalm 78:63; Hebrews 10:27; Jeremiah 25:8-10, Revelation 18:22-23
170 Psalm 78:64; John 12:10; Jeremiah 25:33-38, Revelation 18:24
171 Psalm 78:65; Hebrews 8:12, 10:17, Jeremiah 31:34; Deuteronomy 32:30,

He put his enemies to flight;
  everlasting shame he dealt them.[172]
He rejected the tent of Joseph,
  chose not the tribe of Ephraim.[173]
God chose the tribe of Judah,
  Mount Zion which he favoured.[174]
He built his shrine like the heavens,
  like the earth which he founded forever.[175]
He shepherded them with a pure heart,
  and he guided them with skilled hands.[176]

Glory be to the Father,
 and to the Son,
   and to the Holy Spirit,
as it was in the beginning,
 is now,
   and ever shall be world without end. Amen.

Concluding Prayer

Let us pray:

God our Father, in obedience to you, your only Son accepted death on the cross for the salvation of humankind. We acknowledge the mystery of your cross on earth: because through your Son, he is the first-born of all the living; and because, when we follow Jesus, we are privileged to share in your cross as your adopted sons and daughters. Increase our courage, multiply our determination, and energize our faith, so that we may daily and steadfastly embrace both your commandments of love and the cross. Through the glory of

---

Jeremiah 25:15-32, 1 Peter 4:12, 16-18, Romans 5:8-11, Revelation 19:11-13

172 Psalm 78:66; John 12:11; Deuteronomy 32:31
173 Psalm 78:67; Deuteronomy 33:7
174 Psalm 78:68; John 19:17; Deuteronomy 32:48-50, 1 Peter 4:13, 19
175 Psalm 78:69; John 19:18; Exodus 34:10; Jeremiah 31:38-40, Revelation 21:9-27
176 Psalm 78:72; John 17:12; Exodus 34:11; Jeremiah 33:14-18, 1 Corinthians 11:26, 1 Peter 2:9-10, John 14:15-21

your cross, may we, at last, also receive the gift of your redemption in heaven; through the mystery of your love and mercy, and by your skilful guidance, safely bring to the glory of the resurrection all those your Son alone has redeemed by his sacrifice on the wood of the cross. We ask this through our Lord Jesus Christ, your son who lives and reigns with you and the Holy Spirit, one God, for ever and ever. Amen.

[Based upon Opening and Communion Prayers & their adaptation and amplification, liturgy for Triumph of the Cross, September 14th]

Part Three

**Grand Liturgy of the Lord
in God's New and Eternal Creation**

Chapter 31

Sunday Afternoon, 9ᵀᴴ Nisan (2ᴺᴰ April, 30 CE): Jesus Humbly Enters Jerusalem as King on the Colt of an Ass—He Makes His Way Straight for the Temple, to His Father's House, in Triumph and in Peace

Readings: John 12:12-19, Matthew 21:1-11, Luke 19:28-44, Mark 11:1-11

For Jesus and his disciples, after last evening's dinner celebrations in Bethany,[1] which was held on the first day of the week on Saturday evening, Sunday morning was not spent in bed, as many of us might have wished for ourselves after some of our weekend Saturday night revelries. But, in the pattern that would be set for the week ahead,[2] Jesus and the disciples most likely had not even a bed for the night! Instead, more likely than not, they would have spent Saturday night by themselves under the stars, gathered together near Bethany among the olive groves on the Mount of Olives. For there in the quiet, the timing for the Lord's next move did not depend upon any demands pressed upon him: not by the immediacy of random curiosity seekers;[3] not even by the unstoppable rising of the sun at daybreak on Sunday, that continued the first day of the week; but much more precisely: it depended upon God's specific timing

---
[1] John 12:2
[2] Luke 21:37
[3] John 12:9

for our redemption;[4] and then only after Jesus had finished with making his current preparations of privileged instruction for his specially chosen twelve disciples;[5] and also after his private prayer and their community prayer together with Jesus. Although these various activities of this Sunday morning have not been recorded for us, it would be sometime after mid-day, as is noted for us by each evangelist, that Jesus then would set out from the Mount of Olives for Jerusalem.[6]

As for Jesus, although he had been ready for the coming week, and he was eager in his anticipation for it,[7] he would be very troubled by its approach,[8] and only partly because he had anticipated his death and physical torments;[9] but mostly Jesus was troubled by the spiritual horror he also felt from the weight of our sins,[10] and even more he would be troubled with grief for those who, later on, should still reject their salvation from him.[11] Except for the Lord's innocence and his final free surrender of himself into the hands of darkness,[12] any other man would have been troubled knowingly awaiting certain execution, as if on death-row. However, it is we, not the Lord, who would have been condemned, except for the Lord's intention with the Father to deliver us from our condemnation.[13] Jesus, in surrender to the will of God, in his obedience to his Father,[14] and to our Father,[15] was committed totally to his mission. The disciples, like everyone else, because of their sinfulness, and we because of our own sinfulness,[16] were living under a death-sentence,[17] soon to be

---

4	Romans 5:6; Exodus 12:6
5	John 15:16, Luke 22:28
6	Matthew 21:1, Mark 11:1, Luke 19:28-29, John 12:12
7	Luke 12:49-50
8	John 12:27, Mark 14:34-36
9	Mark 10:33-34, Matthew 20:18-19, Luke 18:31-34, John 12:27
10	Luke 22:42-44
11	Luke 22:44-47, John 8:21, 24, 9:41, 12:37-41
12	Isaiah 53:8-10, Romans 5:7; Luke 22:53, John 10:18, 19:11, 6:38
13	Hebrews 9:15-24
14	John 1:29, 32-34, 3:17, 35, 5:36, 6:38, 8:16, 10:18; Philippians 2:8
15	John 4:23, 5:21, 6:37, 8:18, 14:8-9, 20:17
16	Romans 3:23
17	Luke 23:39-41

lifted from us by the Lord.[18]

Only Jesus would be able to remove our collective guilt; yet, the disciples were still in the dark about the week ahead.[19] As psychoanalysis and cognitive science might define such non-awareness, the disciples seemed to be only pre-consciously aware of the nature of redemption that lay in store for themselves, and for the rest of humankind, in the coming week.[20] Simply, the disciples had presumed that on Friday evening they would be celebrating the Passover with the Lord, as they routinely had done for two previous years;[21] and just as their ancestors had done throughout Jewish history for some1280 previous years of Passover commemorations, or for nearly 64 generations since the Children of Israel had made their exodus out from Egypt at God's powerful hand under the leadership of Moses, and against the might of the Pharoah, Ramesses II Usermaatre-setpenre.[22] The disciples did not understand yet that this moment now was the reason for their perpetual keeping of the feast.

For this year in 30 CE, the feast would be different from all the rest; yet it also would be the very same: for on this Passover there would be the fulfilment of the original institution of the feast. Soon, because of the blood of the Lord as the Lamb of God,[23] the wrath of God would forever pass over our sins;[24] and instead of death, as in Egypt it once had come to every first-born creature unprotected by the sign of the blood of the Passover lamb, soon now, never again would any destructive blow fall upon us.[25] But this would be so for each of us, only if we truly repented of our sins; and if we believed in God's only Son (Jesus) and in the one who sent him

---

18	Romans 8:1-11
19	Luke 18:34
20	Colossians 1:22, 2:14; 1 John 4:16
21	John 2:13, 6:4
22	Exodus 3:1-10, 12:24-27, 13:8; Deuteronomy 6:21-23
23	John 1:29, 35-37
24	Romans 5:5-8, Hebrews 8:12, 10:16-17
25	Exodus 12:13; Isaiah 60:18, Jeremiah 31:40, Zechariah 14:11, Revelation 22:3; Psalms 88:11, 103:4, 107:20, Revelation 9:11

(the Father),[26] as Jesus was the Son of Man and the first-born of all creation;[27] and then, only if we persevered in this faith.[28] But, in the context of this proximate Passover, at the Lord's supper the gift of the Eucharist would be substituted for the lamb of the perpetual institution of Passover,[29] which would be replaced by the new and eternal covenant established in the blood of Christ,[30] the gate of the sheepfold, whose pierced and lashed body, and whose blood as the Lamb of God, would be splattered and smeared across both doorposts and the lintel of the cross.[31]

And afterwards on the third day, because of this sacrifice, God the Father would bestow on Jesus the seal of this New Covenant to eternal life in his Son: first of all, by the resurrection of Christ, and then upon his ascension to the Father as King;[32] just as earlier the Lord had raised Lazarus from the dead,[33] and the Father had sealed the Lord with glory, and the Son had glorified the Father; and also just as the Father had heard the Lord's prayer for their collaborative work of raising from the dead and back to life the only son of the widow from the village of Nain, after the youth's mother also had experienced the death of her husband;[34] and just as today, when all of us once were dead because of sin, but we now hear the voice of the only Son of God and keep his commands;[35] so that, if so, we now live in the spirit of the one God through the Son,[36] who, as the victorious Paschal Lamb, is the entire source of life for all the living.[37] Then, on the last day, when the Son of Man is seated on

---

26	John 5:24
27	Colossians 1:15
28	Colossians 1:23; Hebrews 10:23-39
29	Exodus 12:14
30	Hebrews 5:10, 7:22, 9:11-12
31	1 Corinthians 11:23-26, Exodus 12:7, John 10:1-3, 9; John 10:11, 15, 17
32	1 Corinthians 15:20; Acts 2:32, 5:31, 11:18; John 12:28-30, Matthew 16:21, 17:1-9, 3:16-17; Philippians 2:9
33	John 11:42
34	Luke 7:13-15; John 14:10-11, 5:19-21, 30
35	John 10:27-30
36	Philippians 3:11, Luke 20:35-36
37	John 5:24-29; Luke 7:14, John 11:43, 10:25-30, 4:21, 23-24, 14:15-17, 21, 23; Romans 5:17-19

his throne of glory, in the life of Christ we may ascend to our proper places in heaven, but with our glorified body reunited now with our soul, and we with God among the resurrection of the just.[38]

So, finally now, the time had come for Jesus to go with his disciples to Jerusalem from the nearby Mount of Olives. For the previous leg of their journey, from Jericho to Bethany, they had climbed uphill by more than 1000 metres, from some 360 metres below sea level at Jericho over a distance of about thirty-four kilometres, or an average ascent of thirty metres per kilometre.[39] Thanks to our daily interdependence with the Lord for his grace,[40] we have this opportunity, each and every day and one day at a time, to journey with the Lord to his cross. Over a lifetime, our journey is likely to resemble the Lord's uphill trek with his disciples from Jericho to Jerusalem, let alone the final way of the cross itself from inside the city of Jerusalem to the crucifixion on Calvary outside its walls;[41] but ultimately, our journey with the Lord to his cross is one of triumph and peace. And now, from the Lord's location on the eastern slope of the Mount of Olives, Jerusalem still lay on the heights above, only about three kilometres ahead of them, out of sight over the summit to the west. Bethphage, ahead of them, had come into view from the road,[42] and Bethany also was in sight downhill from behind, about one kilometre to the southeast.[43] Then, there on the outskirts of Bethphage, Jesus sent two of his disciples into the village, now facing them.[44] Foreknowingly, Jesus told them:

> Go off to the village opposite you, and as soon as you enter it, you will find a tethered donkey,[45] and with her a tethered colt that no one yet has ridden; untie

---

38	Matthew 25:31-34, 1 Corinthians 15:42-49
39	Luke 19:28; Isaiah 56:7
40	John 15:1, 4-5
41	John 19:17, Luke 23:26
42	Matthew 21:1
43	Mark 11:1, Luke 19:29
44	Matthew 21:1, Mark 11:1, Luke 19:29
45	Matthew 21:2

it [them][46] and bring it [them] to me.[47] If anyone says [anything][48] to you, "What are you doing,[49] by untying it?"[50] Say, "The Master needs it[51] [them],[52] and will send it [them] back directly."[53]

So, the disciples went on ahead and did exactly what Jesus had told them,[54] finding everything to be just as he had told them it would be.[55] When they had gone off as messengers,[56] there in the village they found a colt tethered near a door in the open street, and they untied it.[57] [It seems, when they did this, that they may have already untied the donkey.][58] But, as they were untying the colt, some men standing there said, "What are you doing, untying that colt?"[59] And, as well, among them the owner had asked them, "Why are you untying that colt?"[60] The disciples gave them the answer that Jesus had told them,[61] "The Master needs it,"[62] "and he will send it [them] back here at once,"[63] and so the men let them go.[64] When the disciples brought [the donkey and][65] the colt to Jesus, they laid their cloaks on [their] its back[s]; and helping Jesus up onto the colt,[66] he then sat on it [them].[67] This took place to fulfil what

---

46	Matthew 21:2
47	Matthew 21:2, Mark 11:2, Luke 19:30
48	Matthew 21:3
49	Mark 11:3
50	Luke 19:31
51	Luke 19:31
52	Matthew 21:3
53	Matthew 21:3, Mark 11:3
54	Matthew 21:6
55	Luke 19:32
56	Luke 19:32
57	Mark 11:4
58	Matthew 21:2, 7
59	Mark 11:5
60	Luke 19:33
61	Mark 11:6
62	Luke 19:34, 31
63	Matthew 21:3, Mark 11:3
64	Mark 11:6
65	Matthew 21:7
66	Luke 19:35
67	Matthew 21:7, Mark 11:7

had been written through the prophet,[68] Zechariah. At this time, the disciples had not understood this action of the Lord; but later on they would understand, only after Jesus had been glorified, when they did remember that these things had been written about him in the scriptures, and that, in fact, this then had happened to him.[69]

And indeed, also as King David had placed his son Solomon, as a humble servant of God,[70] on David's own mule, and then at Gihon David had Solomon anointed King,[71] so now also Jesus entered Jerusalem, but not on a royal mule, but in humility on the borrowed colt of a donkey. But, he would follow Solomon's route, in direct fulfilment of God's promise to King David that his heir, that is, the Christ, would make David's royal throne and sovereign dynasty secure forever:[72]

> Say to daughter Zion:[73]
> [Rejoice, heart and soul, O daughter Zion,
>   shout for joy, O daughter Jerusalem!][74]
> Fear no longer, daughter of Zion;[75]
> "Behold, your king comes to you;[76]
> [See, your king is approaching;][77]
> See, your king comes,[78]
>
> he is humble, and he rides on a donkey[79]
> [he is vindicated and victorious,
>   meek, and riding on a donkey,][80]

---

68 Matthew 21:4, John 12:14
69 John 12:16
70 1 Kings 1:33; Luke 22:27
71 1 Kings 1:38, 28-48
72 2 Samuel 7:12-13, 1 Chronicles 17:11, Acts 2:25-31, Psalm 132:11, 17-18, Isaiah 11:1; Matthew 21:42, Psalm 118:22-23, Isaiah 28:16
73 Matthew 21:5; Isaiah 62:11
74 Zechariah 9:9
75 John 12:15; Isaiah 40:9
76 Matthew 21:5
77 Zechariah 9:9
78 John 12:15
79 Matthew 21:5
80 Zechariah 9:9

and on a colt, the foal of a beast of burden."[81]
[on a colt, the foal of a beast of burden.][82]
seated on the colt of a donkey.[83]

At first, it seems that Matthew, or whoever may have been the evangelist, has interpreted Zechariah's portrayal of the messianic king on the basis of a linguistic conjunction of nouns: apparently, as if the Lord rode on both the donkey and a colt, rather than taking the Hebrew parallelism of the noun's apposition, as the Lord's actual and more plausible riding of the animal: on the single foal of the donkey, as described by John and also by the other evangelists Mark and Luke; for, practically, no person rides two such animals simultaneously. But beyond linguistics and this presumed parsimony, both Matthew and John, as apostolic sources, were historical eyewitnesses to the same event, where either one or two animals had been involved; but, because both conditions are exclusive, only one condition may be true, but not both. Certainly, if one insisted that two animals had been involved, the colt would have been mounted by the Lord. Perhaps, one might conjecture, that the donkey had been included only by Matthew, although it was omitted by the others, because then the donkey had accompanied the colt, while only the colt was ridden by the Lord. One also might presume that the foal would have been more comfortable with humans by its being accompanied by the donkey, presumably the colt's mother. And indeed, the Lord did send two disciples, whichever two of the twelve they may have been in their anonymity, like any and all of us as disciples; so, with two disciples, there were available two persons to lead each of the two beasts of burden; so, as one might argue, the donkey may have facilitated the foal's journey to Jerusalem with the Lord.

But the whole matter of the prophecy of Zechariah is meant to show how the King Jesus enters his city riding on a lowly donkey (or colt). The lowly King enters his city to save the ungrateful city. Oftentimes in our stubbornness, most of us may be reluctant to

---

81   Matthew 21:5
82   Zechariah 9:9
83   John 12:15

embrace fully the contradiction of the cross;[84] for indeed, it does entail our sacrifice and, ultimately in faith, the passionately obedient surrender of our lives totally to God, in just thanksgiving for his all-consuming love.[85] Besides the Lord, his mother was the only other person to have done so perfectly; she alone was as pure as the colt; and if there also had been a donkey,[86] we have been that donkey, stubborn and disobedient. We are instructed by these events to do whatever God wills for us; for, we are to be for the Lord his obedient beasts of burden,[87] along with the Lord's other designated team members, together in our Christian and world communities. Therefore, in our thanksgiving for God's mercy,[88] sin should no longer have a place in the daily equation we now write through God's grace for our lives in our love of God.[89]

Meanwhile, back on the road at the outskirts of Bethphage, Jesus and his disciples were no longer alone. Soon they were surrounded by great crowds: people, who were going up to Jerusalem, were gathering around them from behind; while others were streaming out of the village on to the road in front of the Lord. Among the first to know of the Lord's approach to Jerusalem may have been the villagers of Bethphage, as the messages from the two disciples,[90] to the men near the donkey and the colt in their small hillside village,[91] travelled faster than the disciples could walk, with people quickly running and shouting to their neighbours, and to everyone they had met along the way, "Jesus is coming."[92] Furthermore, as Jesus was waiting on the road, some people had passed him by, and then they had hurried on up to Jerusalem along with some of the other villagers. Both groups had left for the city in haste to inform the crowds, who

---

84   1 Corinthians 1:18, 23-25
85   1 Peter 4:2, Psalm 118:1
86   Matthew 21:2-7
87   Genesis 49:10-11
88   Romans 9:15-16
89   Mark 12:28-31, Matthew 22:40, Mark 12:32, Luke 10:26, Mark 12:33, Luke 10:28, Mark 12:34, John 15:12, 17, 13:35; 1 Thessalonians 1:2-6, 2 Corinthians 6:16-7:1
90   Luke 19:31-32
91   Mark 11:5, Luke 19:33-34
92   Isaiah 55:3-6, Revelation 21:9-10, 22:14, Romans 8:24-25

had come up earlier to the festival, that right now Jesus was on his way into the city.[93]   Many of those already in Jerusalem had been with Jesus at Bethany when he had called Lazarus out of the tomb and had raised him from the dead; so that these people also had been telling others about how they had witnessed this.[94] Therefore, because the people had heard that Jesus had given this sign,[95] when they now heard that Jesus was coming to Jerusalem, they all joyfully rushed out to meet Jesus as their King, who at that moment was on his way into the city, on the road from Bethphage.[96]

As Jesus road along,[97] the people were spreading their cloaks on the road in front of him,[98] and others were cutting palm branches from the trees,[99] or leafy branches from the fields,[100] and they were spreading them on the road;[101] while those coming up from Jerusalem took palm branches as they went out to meet him.[102] Both groups, now going up to the city and coming down from the city, came together on the downhill slope of the Mount of Olives, where the whole multitude of disciples converged and began to praise God aloud with joy for the mighty deeds they had seen from the Lord,[103] and especially for his having raised Lazarus from the dead. In their proclamation of Jesus as King,[104] those in front of Jesus leading the way and those following from behind together they cried out:[105]

> Hosanna [grant salvation!] to the Son of David!
> Blessed is he who is coming in the name of the Lord;

---

93   John 12:12
94   John 12:17, 11:45
95   John 11:47-48; Matthew 16:4, Luke 11:29, Matthew 12:39-42, 1 Kings 1:38-40
96   John 12:18; Acts 2:36, Psalms 110:1, 16:9-11, 2:6; Matthew 25:1
97   Luke 19:36
98   Matthew 21:8, Mark 11:8, Luke 19:36
99   Matthew 21:8
100 Mark 11:8
101 Matthew 21:8
102 John 12:13
103 Luke 19:37
104 Luke 19:38
105 Matthew 21:9, Mark 11:9

> Hosanna in the highest heavens.[106]
>
> Hosanna! Blessed is he who comes in the name of the Lord![107]
> Blessed is the kingdom of our father David that is to come!
> Hosanna in the highest heavens![108]
>
> Blessed is the king who is coming in the name of the Lord.
> Peace in heaven and glory in the highest.[109]
>
> Hosanna! Blessed is he who is coming in the name of the Lord,
> the king of Israel.[110]

And today, after the Eucharistic Prayer at Mass, but before the bread and wine is consecrated and they become the body and blood of the Lord, we also likewise exclaim the "Sanctus" in our worship of our King:[111]

> Holy, holy, holy Lord, God of power and might.[112]
> Heaven and earth are full of your glory.[113]
> Hosanna in the highest.
> Blessed is he who comes in the name of the Lord.
> Hosanna in the highest.

But for many of the Pharisees, even though secretly some of the others had been disciples of Jesus, this was insurrection.[114] So, some of the hostile Pharisees in the crowd said to Jesus, "Teacher, check

---

106   Matthew 21:9; Psalm 118:25-26
107   Mark 11:9
108   Mark 11:10; Luke 1:68-75
109   Luke 19:38; Luke 2:14, 1:76-79
110   John 12:13
111   1 Corinthians 11:23-26, Acts 2:42, 46-47
112   Revelation 5:12
113   Revelation 4:11
114   John 11:48

your disciples!"[115] But in curt reply, he told them:

> I tell you, if they keep silent, the stones will cry out![116]

Then, further to this obstinacy of the Pharisees and the Lord's reply to them, as Jesus drew near to Jerusalem, when he saw the city he wept over it,[117] saying:

> If you too had only recognized on this day the way to peace! But in fact it is hidden from your eyes![118] Yes, a time is coming when your enemies will raise fortifications all around you, when they will encircle you and hem you in on every side; they will dash you and the children inside your walls to the ground; they will not leave one stone standing on another within you,[119] because you did not recognize the moment of your visitation.[120]

Although it would have been possible for Jesus to have entered Jerusalem from the eastern gate, by coming into Jerusalem from the Portico of Solomon, it seems more likely that Jesus approached the city from a southern gate, entering from the gate near the spring of Gihon;[121] and he retraced the same route that Solomon had taken when he had been anointed King.[122] And like Solomon,[123] when Jesus finally entered Jerusalem, the whole city was thrown ferociously into a raucous turmoil; and, with such a shaking of the city to its very foundations,[124] much like an earthquake, the people asked, "Who is this?"[125] And the crowds roared their answer, "This is Jesus

---

115 Luke 19:39; Luke 19:14
116 Luke 19:40; Revelation 19:6
117 Luke 19:41; Jeremiah 14:17, 9:17; Luke 1:51-52
118 Luke 19:42, Zechariah 9:10; John 12:40, Isaiah 6:10; Acts 28:25-28; Luke 13:34, 12:46-52, Jeremiah 11:9-12
119 Luke 19:43; Matthew 24:2, Mark 13:2, Luke 21:6
120 Luke 19:43-44; Luke 13:35, Jeremiah 9:16-21; Luke 2:22-38
121 Genesis 49:22
122 1 Kings 1:38-40; 2 Samuel 7:12, 1 Chronicles 17:11
123 1 Kings 1:41, 45
124 Psalm 68:35
125 Matthew 21:10; Matthew 2:1-3

the prophet, from Nazareth in Galilee."[126] Then the Pharisees, in their alarm,[127] said to one another, "You see, you are registering no progress at all! Look, the whole world is running after him!"[128] It seems that eventually Jesus made his way through the Royal Portico's Triple Gate, and into the Court of the Gentiles; then from there, apparently while still riding the colt and surrounded by the crowds, he went directly into the temple;[129] and once he arrived inside, he looked carefully all around him;[130] but because it was very late in the day, he then quickly left his Father's house, and went back out to Bethany with the Twelve,[131] for another night near to Jerusalem, but under God's starry heavens somewhere on the eastern far-side of the Mount of Olives.

First of all, Jesus had come to the temple as a clearly visible sign of his total obedience to God the Father,[132] even in such humble fidelity to God unto death on a cross,[133] which today is his great lesson for us in obedience,[134] to God's commandments,[135] to our baptismal promises,[136] to our marriage vows,[137] or to our religious vows,[138] and to any other of God's special assignments he has in mind for us.[139] And Jesus surveyed there the area in the temple,[140] as if to take into his gaze the whole of salvation history and the temple's purpose:[141] for he knew that soon the temple of his body would be

---

126   Matthew 21:11; Matthew 2:4-6, 22-23
127   John 11:47-48; Matthew 2:16-18
128   John 12:19
129   Mark 11:11
130   Mark 11:11; Luke 15:4, 19:27; John 10:1, 7-12, Matthew 21:13; John 11:57, 56, Luke 2:49-50
131   Mark 11:11
132   John 8:28-29
133   Philippians 2:8, 1 Peter 5:6
134   Romans 1:3-6; Romans 1:16-17, Hebrews 11:8-10
135   1 John 2:5-6; John 14:21, 23
136   1 Peter 3:21
137   1 Peter 3:1, 7
138   1 Peter 5:4
139   John 21:17-19, 1 Peter 1:14-16; Exodus 19:6, Leviticus 11:44, 19:2, 20:7, 26; 1 Peter 2:21
140   Mark 11:11
141   John 2:17; 2 Samuel 7:4-13, 2 Kings 25:8-9, 2 Chronicles 36:15-21,

destroyed on the cross, but also he knew that it would be restored by his resurrection from the dead, as the new temple we now share in the body and spirit of Christ.[142] And as Jesus now looked about his Father's house, not only did he envision the early morning crowds who would gather there for his teaching in the remaining days ahead,[143] but from his present moment of eternity and of ours,[144] along with the same clarity of his purpose as he had discussed with Moses and Elijah at the Lord's transfiguration,[145] Jesus also foresaw the entire multitudes of future saints who would be assembled before him as King in the heavenly New Jerusalem.[146]

But now, Jesus was like some relentless but patient military general on his mighty war-stead,[147] but only seated humbly on the donkey's colt and declaring his terms for peace.[148] After now securing his temple base for his forthcoming operations of the week,[149] his quickest and most direct exit would have been by the single eastern gate (Shushan, or today's Golden Gate) along Solomon's Portico;[150] and so, as it seems it must have been the way, Jesus promptly withdrew from Jerusalem to Bethany,[151] and he eluded the crowds. Jesus had accomplished his work for that day; but for the morrow on Monday morning, he would begin again quite early, in fact, at the crack of dawn;[152] and then, on that morrow in front of the Pharisees and scribes, it would be the children's turn for their "hosannas,"[153] made in their innocently clear and honest imitation of the proclamations from the adults on this Sunday afternoon; for indeed, the Lord's fulfilment

---

      Haggai 1:9, Zechariah 1:16; John 2:19-22, Matthew 21:42, Ephesians 2:20-22
142   John 2:19, 1 Peter 2:4-6, 3:18, Mark 14:58; Ephesians 4:16, 3:18-19
143   Luke 21:37
144   Romans 8:28-30, Revelation 3:5, 13:8
145   Luke 9:30-31, Acts 3:18
146   Revelation 21:10, 14:1, 3
147   Revelation 19:11-16; Psalms 45:4-5, 21:9-13, 45:6
148   Zechariah 9:9, Genesis 49:10-11; Zechariah 9:11-17
149   Isaiah 62:1-5, 10-12
150   John 10:23, 39
151   Mark 11:11
152   Luke 21:38
153   Matthew 21:15-16; John 8:13-14

of the covenant was near at hand.[154] So very soon, just on the Friday of this most sacred of weeks, humankind's covenant of peace with God would rest in Jerusalem through the Lord's victorious triumph of his holy cross over death and sin,[155] and in its potential for us: through our faith in Jesus and in our humble obedience to his cross,[156] Jesus was leading us to our resurrection, in likeness to the Lord's on Easter Sunday,[157] and with him in that glory unto our eternal life.[158]

Reflective Prayer: Psalms 135:8-14, 118:19-29, 122:1-9

Antiphon: Great is the Lord, our God,
        transcending all other gods.[159]

    The Lord struck down Egypt's firstborn,
        man and beast alike,[160]
    he sent signs and wonders
        into the heart of Egypt,
        against Pharaoh and all his officials.[161]

    He struck down many nations in their greatness,
        slaughtered mighty kings in their splendour:[162]
    Sihon, king of the Amorites,[163]
        Og, king of Bashan,[164]
        all the kingdoms of Canaan.[165]
    He gave their land as a heritage,
        a birthright to his people Israel.[166]

---

154   John 2:18-22
155   Psalm 76:1-6, Hebrews 2:7-9
156   1 Peter 1:2
157   1 Corinthians 15:35-49, John 12:24, 25-26
158   1 Peter 1:3-5, 24-25
159   Psalm 135:5, Exodus 18:11; Psalms 95:3-4, 15:1, Exodus 19:12-13, 16-19, 40:35, Hebrews 12:21-24, Luke 1:26-33
160   Psalm 135:8; John 11:55; Exodus 12:29-30
161   Psalm 135:9; John 12:1, 12; Exodus 7:3-5, 34:10
162   Psalm 135:10, 136:17-18; 2 Peter 3:10-13, Revelation 16:1, 13-20
163   Deuteronomy 2:30-36
164   Deuteronomy 3:1-8
165   Psalm 135:11, 136:19-20; John 12:14-15; Exodus 34:11
166   Psalm 135:12, 136:21-22; John 12:16; Exodus 15:13

> Lord, your name endures forever,
>> your renown is unforgotten from age to age.[167]
> For the Lord vindicates his people,
>> and shows mercy to his servants.[168]

Antiphon: Joyful shouts of deliverance
>> are heard in the tents of the victorious.[169]

> Open for me the gates of victory:
>> I will enter and give thanks.[170]
> This is the Lord's own gate,
>> where the upright may enter.[171]
> I thank you for you answering me
>> and making yourself my Saviour.[172]

> The stone which the builders rejected
>> has become the cornerstone.[173]
> This is the Lord's work;
>> it is a marvel in our eyes.[174]
> This is the day the Lord has made,
>> a day for us to rejoice and be glad.[175]
> O Lord, we beg you, grant us salvation!
>> We beg you, Lord, give us victory![176]

---

167 Psalm 135:13, 136:23; John 12:17; Exodus 15:11-12
168 Psalm 135:14, 136:24; John 12:18; Exodus 15:13
169 Psalm 118:15, Revelation 21:12
170 Psalm 118:19; Matthew 21:10; Revelation 22:14, 7:9-10
171 Psalm 118:20; Matthew 21:11; Revelation 3:12
172 Psalm 118:21; Luke 19:37; Hebrews 3:1
173 Psalm 118:22; Luke 19:39-40; Hebrews 3:6
174 Psalm 118:23; Luke 19:41; Hebrews 2:16, Revelation 15:3-4
175 Psalm 118:24; Luke 19:42; Hebrews 2:17, Revelation 14:3, 5:9-10
176 Psalm 118:25; Mark 11:9; Hebrews 2:18, Revelation 6:17, 7:2-4

Blessed is he who comes in the name of the Lord.
   We bless you from the house of the Lord.[177]
The Lord is God and gives us light;
   link your processions, with leafy branches in hand
   up to the horns of the altar.[178]

You are my God, I give you thanks,
   all praise to you, my God;
   thank you for hearing me
   and making yourself my Saviour.[179]
Give thanks to the Lord for he is good,
   his faithful love endures forever.[180]

Antiphon: I rejoiced when I heard them say,
   "Let us go up to the house of the Lord."

I rejoiced when they said to me,
   "Let us go to God's house."[181]
And now, at last, our feet are standing
   at your gates, Jerusalem![182]
Jerusalem, built as a city,
   walled all about in one united whole.[183]

Here the tribes go up,
   the tribes of the Lord,
   as it was decreed for Israel,
   to give thanks to the name of the Lord.[184]
For here are set the thrones of judgment,
   the thrones of the house of David.[185]

---

177   Psalm 118:26; Matthew 21:9; Revelation 21:22
178   Psalm 118:27; Mark 11:8; Revelation 21:23
179   Psalm 118:28; Luke 19:38; Revelation 5:12
180   Psalm 118:29; Matthew 21:1-3; Exodus 15:18, Revelation 5:13
181   Psalm 122:1; Luke 19:33-35; Hebrews 2:10-13
182   Psalm 122:2; Mark 11:11; Revelation 9:10-11
183   Psalm 122:3; Luke 19:43-44; Revelation 9:12
184   Psalm 122:4; Matthew 21:4-5; Revelation 14:1
185   Psalm 122:5, Luke 22:28-30; Mark 11:10; Revelation 20:12, 22:12

>   Pray for the peace of Jerusalem:
>   "May those who love you prosper![186]
>   May peace reign within your ramparts,
>   prosperity within your towering palaces!"[187]
>   For love of my brethren and friends,
>   I say, "Peace upon you!"[188]
>   For love of the house of the Lord, our God
>   I will pray for your well-being.[189]

Antiphon: This is God's dwelling place;[190]
>   he has made it holy;[191]
>   and it will stand firm forever.[192]

>   Glory be to the Father,
>   and to the Son,
>   and to the Holy Spirit,
>   as it was in the beginning,
>   is now, and ever shall be,
>   world without end. Amen.

---

186   Psalm 122:6; John 11:56; 2 Peter 3:14
187   Psalm 122:7; John 12:19; Revelation 21:1-2
188   Psalm 122:8; John 20:19; Revelation 21:3
189   Psalm 122:9; John 20:21; Revelation 21:4
190   Revelation 21:9; Revelation 21:3, 2 Corinthians 6:16, Ezekiel 37:26-27
191   Hebrews 10:10; Ezekiel 37:28
192   Matthew 16:16-18, Revelation 22:13; 2 Corinthians 7:1

Chapter 32

The Next Day, on Monday, 10th Nisan (3rd April, 30 CE), Jesus Works Tirelessly in His Father's House, to God's Great Honour and Glory—But at the Beginning Early in the Morning, Jesus Openly Declares God's War Against the Chief Priests and Religious Authorities by Assaulting the Moneychangers in the Temple, and at the End of the Workday He Leaves—Then, on Tuesday Morning and Afternoon, the 11th Nisan (4th April, 30 CE), He Returns for the Ongoing Revolution

Readings: Mark 11:12-14, Matthew 21:18-19; Matthew 21:12-13, Mark 11:15-18, Luke 19:45-46, John 2:13-17; Luke 19:47-48, 21:37-38; John 2:18-22, 23-25, Matthew 21:14-17, Mark 11:19

Now on the very next day,[1] after yesterday's triumphant procession, with great throngs of people accompanying Jesus as he humbly entered Jerusalem on his way to the temple,[2] just as there is first the Entrance Rite that begins our Eucharistic celebrations,[3] but for Jesus and his disciples its now being just after sunrise early

---
1   Mark 11:12
2   Hebrews 10:19-21, Isaiah 40:11
3   Psalm 66:13, Hebrews 10:5-7

Monday morning,[4] they were quietly returning to Jerusalem, and to the Lord's week of liturgy,[5] when along their way from their base outpost, as they were starting out by themselves near Bethany on the Mount of Olives, Jesus was hungry.[6] It seems that he had eaten nothing from the night before, perhaps not even a bite to eat since his procession to the temple yesterday from mid-day or late afternoon; certainly he had not eaten after his grand entrance and sudden departure from Jerusalem with his disciples, which was from sometime around sundown yesterday, as the liturgical day was about to end.[7] Similarly, before the Second Vatican Council, the communion fast for morning Mass used to begin for us from midnight, although now the communion fast for any liturgy is just an hour. So also now for Jesus, instead of eating,[8] it seems that from yesterday evening he had preferred to pray late into the night,[9] as he would do throughout that week on the Mount of Olives;[10] and just as after his baptism from John or from one of John's disciples,[11] Jesus had fasted not just for one night, but before initiating the mission entrusted to him by the Father, he had fasted and prayed for forty days in the desert, before he began to preach his witness of the Father's love for us, along with the Father's witness of his Son's: that the Kingdom of God was near.[12]

So, just as at that very first time at the beginning of his ministry, Jesus now had prayed and fasted, and also for the same reasons:[13] that is, so as not to fall into temptation,[14] which comes to everyone

---

4 Mathew 21:18; 1 Thessalonians 5:2-6
5 Luke 2:41-47, 48-50, 21:37-38; John 7:53, 8:1-11; 1 John 3:2-3; Hebrews 3:1, 7-19, John 3:14-16, 8:28
6 Mathew 21:18, Mark 11:12; Matthew 4:2-4, 6:16-18, 31, 33, 9:14-15, 10:7, 9-10, 11:18-19, 12:1, 14:16-21, 15:32-38, 16:8-10, 20:27-28, 21:18-19, 22:1-4, 24:45-47, 25:14-15
7 Mark 11:11; John 6:15
8 John 6:27, 4:34
9 Mark 1:35, Matthew 14:23, Luke 6:12, John 18:1-2
10 Mark 14:32, Luke 22:39
11 Luke 3:19-22
12 Matthew 4:2, Luke 4:2; Matthew 4:17, John 8:17-18, 17:26
13 Luke 4:1-2
14 Luke 22:39-41; 1 Corinthians 10:12

throughout life, but especially towards its very end.[15] Soon enough there would be some chance for everyone to catch a bite to eat in Jerusalem,[16] if indeed the Lord had wanted to take something to eat later in the city; but Jesus was hungrier now for more than just breakfast.[17] Because very soon, at this available time, he would engage his Liturgy of the Word at temple,[18] just as we do now at church. But first, also as we do after the initial entrance in the Celebration of the Eucharist,[19] there comes the Penitential Rite;[20] so, along this path to Jerusalem with the disciples, the Lord next called us to reform and to bear fruit, just as God had done through all of his prophets, particularly through John the Baptist and Isaiah,[21] but now emphatically through Jesus himself.[22] In light of our need for repentance,[23] and so that Jesus could clearly make his point of reminding us about his own real hunger for our full fruitfulness in him,[24] at a distance Jesus spotted a fig tree in leaf by the road; and he went over to it, to see if he could find anything on it.[25] But when he reached it, since it was not the time for figs, a metaphor for our complicity with sin within the seasonal time for our salvation,[26] although now the Lord's work for us had been ongoing for nearly three years,[27] Jesus found nothing on the fig tree but leaves.[28]

In reply, Jesus said to the fig tree, as if then he had been speaking to the Pharisees and scribes,[29] or actually to anyone of us, and especially to one of his disciples among the twelve, anyone who might have resisted grace and risked a life in sin and error without

---

15 Matthew 4:3-10, Luke 4:13, 22:40; John 4:34, 17:4, 9, 15, 20
16 John 6:51
17 John 6:35, Luke 12:49-51; Psalm 63:2
18 Luke 21:37, Psalm 63:3-4
19 Hebrews 10:25
20 Hebrews 10:22-24
21 John 1:23-27, Luke 3:3-6, Isaiah 40:3-10
22 Jeremiah 23:5-6, Romans 5:17-19
23 Luke 3:9
24 John 15:1-6
25 Mark 11:13, Matthew 21:19; Luke 13:6
26 Romans 13:11, Colossians 1:10, Romans 12:1-2, 7:1, 4
27 Luke 13:7
28 Mark 11:13, Matthew 21:19; Luke 13:6
29 Matthew 7:15, 20, Luke 6:45, Matthew 12:34-36

producing good fruit,[30] he cursed their lack of fruit:[31]

May no one ever eat of your fruit again![32]

The disciples overheard Jesus say this curse,[33] although they hadn't yet noticed that immediately the fig tree had begun to wither,[34] that is, they would not do so until early the next morning on their return journey to Jerusalem, when again they would re-walk this same route.[35] Even though Jesus now had cursed the fig tree, he would not now curse people, because in God's compassion and mercy he had come specifically to save them;[36] but, as Jesus did do, he now would warn them of God's wrath to come,[37] as also he would do in his parting words for the scribes and Pharisees in the Lord's sevenfold indictment of their hypocrisy,[38] and for anyone for whom the curse of God would be their damnation; because God's curse is not simply some "Old Testament" phenomenon.[39] But, if damnation should be anyone's final curse from God,[40] it would happen at the Lord's word,[41] just as Jesus now had cursed the barren fig tree.[42] However, not understanding what Jesus had intended by what he had just done, for he also had intended to strengthen their faith,[43] the group of disciples continued on to the temple with Jesus, where now all of the people were thronging to hear him, their also having gotten up, and about business, and out to the temple so early in the morning.[44]

30	John 6:70-71, 13:21, 27, 15:6, 2, Luke 3:9
31	Luke 6:43-44, Matthew 7:17-19, 12:33; John 15:1-2, 16-17
32	Mark 11:14, Matthew 21:19
33	Mark 11:14
34	Matthew 21:19; Hebrews 6:7-8
35	Mark 11:20-21
36	Luke 13:7-8; Matthew 26:28, 20:28, Romans 5:18, Matthew 9:13, Romans 11:32, Isaiah 53:6
37	Luke 13:9; Romans 11:22
38	Matthew 23:13, 15-33
39	Genesis 3:14, Deuteronomy 11:26-28; Revelation 20:10, 14-15, 22:3-5
40	Matthew 25:33, 41
41	Luke 19:27
42	Mark 11:14; Genesis 3:15, Revelation 12:17-18, 19:1-3, 21:8
43	Matthew 21:21-22, Mark 11:22-24
44	Luke 21:38; John 8:2, Luke 12:1-2

But, however early it must have been, when the Lord arrived with his disciples at the temple in Jerusalem,[45] from much earlier still, well ahead of the crowds, the temple money changers and vendors for animal sacrifices already had prepared their stalls and tables, just as is done daily for the "Monti," which is a hawkers' street market in my capital city of Valletta, Malta. So, in the temple area, Jesus found people there from sun-up selling all sorts of cattle, sheep, and pigeons; and seated there as well also were the money changers,[46] all ready for their day's commerce in temple sacrifices. Then Jesus, making a whip out of cords,[47] drove everyone who was engaged in the buying and the selling,[48] out of the temple,[49] along with the sheep and the oxen.[50] And as he also overturned the tables of the money changers and knocked over the seats of those who were selling doves,[51] he scattered all of their coins.[52] Furthermore, he did not permit anyone to carry anything through the temple area: [53] he allowed nothing that had been purchased or that was intended for selling, neither furniture nor equipment, not even personal belongings.[54] And to those who sold doves,[55] Jesus told them:

> Take these out of here, and stop making a marketplace of my Father's house.[56]

Then he taught them all,[57] saying:

> According to scripture,[58] isn't it written?[59] "My house

---

45	John 2:13, Mark 11:15
46	John 2:14
47	John 2:15
48	Matthew 21:12, Mark 11:15
49	Luke 19:45
50	John 2:15; Hebrews 10:5-9, Romans 12:1, John 4:23-24
51	Matthew 21:12, Mark 11:15
52	John 2:15; Psalm 68:1
53	Mark 11:16
54	Nehemiah 13:7-9, 19, John 19:31, 42, 20:1-2
55	John 2:16; Luke 2:21, Matthew 1:21, Luke 2:22-24
56	John 2:16
57	Mark 11:17
58	Matthew 21:13, Luke 19:46
59	Mark 11:17

shall be called a house of prayer,[60] for all peoples."[61] But you (are turning it into)[62] have made it "a bandits' den."[63]

When his disciples heard this, they recalled the words from scripture, "I am eaten up with Zeal for your house."[64] But soon afterwards, when these words of Jesus came to the ears of the chief priests and scribes, these only wanted to kill him.[65]

So, on that day, and on every day while Jesus was teaching in the temple, the chief priests and teachers of the Law, in the company of the senior leaders of the people, were seeking some way to do away with him.[66] But, as yet, they could not see through to finding some way to accomplish their purpose because all of the people were hanging on to his words spellbound, so deeply transfixed were they by the word of God, and their not wanting to miss a single word from him;[67] so that the authorities not only were afraid of Jesus, they also feared the people.[68] Now this is quite a model to follow from the Lord, for our contemporary preachers of the word of God, and also for us as listeners of his effective word![69] However, what the Lord told the people throughout most of that Monday in his teaching in the temple has not been documented for us,[70] except for certain specific details,[71] which would be significant indeed! Instead, for now, what we are allowed to know would be as if we had not been there, or as the void would be for us now if we were not seeking the Lord. So, for this particular day, we have been allowed to witness only the impact of the words of Jesus, and not their substance, both

---

60   Matthew 21:13, Luke 19:46
61   Mark 11:17, Isaiah 56:7; 1 Kings 8:43
62   Matthew 21:13
63   Mark 11:17, Luke 19:46, Jeremiah 7:11; Ezekiel 34:8-10; John 10:27-29
64   John 2:17, Psalm 69:9; Luke 12:50; Luke 2:46, Mark 14:58; Ezekiel 34:11-16
65   Mark 11:18; John 10:8-11
66   Luke 19:47; John 11:49-50
67   Luke 19:48
68   John 11:48; Luke 20:3-6, 19:39-40, 20:17-19, 11:47-51
69   Hebrews 4:12, John 12:48, 6:63-65, 12:49-50
70   2 Corinthians 4:3-4
71   John 2:19, Matthew 21:16; Luke 18:17

for those who believed in him, as we also should be entranced by his every word, and for those non-believers, in their hatred for Jesus but in accord with God's plan, who simply wanted to find some way to kill him.[72]

For the present moment, we are allowed to imagine what this lack of faith might be for us, as if now we were living without our intimacy with the Lord,[73] and without any impact of the Lord's word on us as actual believers. For in today's world, there are persons of faith, or persons opposed to the faith; and should we try to fall between, Jesus sought to sharpen this division of alternative positions clearly, like his separation of sheep from goats,[74] in order to direct us now more forcefully towards our choice: for us either to freely accept, or to freely reject, his invitation to the banquet.[75] In some countries, such as in today's China where one-eighth of humanity lives with atheism as its official state policy, or in some African, Middle-Eastern, or Asian national states with Islam their official and protected state religion, the teaching of Christianity, or even the ownership or distribution of bibles, may be regarded as a criminal offence punishable by prison or hefty fines. Just so, recently in one such Islamic country, a male teacher had been reported to the local civil authorities by his students, and he was arrested for defamation of the Qur'an. His crime: he had attempted a zealous exposition and reading of the Bible in his comparative literature class with his students.

But even without this kind of cultural and state opposition to Christianity, such as may be found in states where only one of various religious expressions or even atheism is protected, or even where the constitutional state religion may be either Catholic or Protestant, individuals still can choose not to believe in the Christian faith. Persons and groups may be indifferent, or in opposition to Christ; or they may be brutally intolerant regarding any religion,

---

72   John 6:63-64
73   John 14:19-20, 15:10, 14-15; Romans 6:12, 1 Corinthians 6:16-17; 1 John 3:6, 4:6, Revelation 21:2-3
74   Matthew 25:32
75   Matthew 22:1-3; John 6:47-51, Revelation 22:14-15, 21:8

or the alternative religion of others. Sometimes public forms of religious expression are limited by laws or courts; even prayer, religious symbols, or types of clothing may be banned, even in secular Western states: like the BA airhostess who was not allowed to carry a small crucifix around her neck, or the nun in the UK who had been serving there in a hospital for over thirty years, but was accused of religious discrimination and alleged health violations because she did not want to remove the crucifix from her neck, and the sister then was transferred. But, despite such obstacles, the Lord, as Wisdom and Understanding,[76] still may suddenly call upon any of us by the gates or at the entryways of our cities;[77] or already the Lord stands before us, if only we should hear his voice and open the door as he knocks, in order for us to let him into our house, so that we may mutually dine together with the Lord.[78] Whenever the Lord does knock, he waits for us to freely open our hearts to him, so that he can lay his heart into ours, where his love and his life may dwell within us: particularly so at the celebration of the Eucharist, and in the reading of sacred scriptures, or in community prayer and religious song; or however else the Lord may choose to come to us,[79] whenever it is we may realize, perhaps without any expectations at all, that the Lord has come, quietly and eagerly, just as also now in our Emmaus journey,[80] he is knocking softly for us at the door of our hearts.[81]

Now at this time, both with yesterday afternoon and in this morning's temple entrance, Jesus had come into his Father's house forcefully and with authority; while the Pharisees and teachers of the Law, with their blind disdain, their envy, and their alarm, regarded Jesus in the temple as an unwelcome intruder into God's sacred territory, which they had regarded as wholly their own exclusive province;[82] and with the social and spiritual power-politics of

---

76   Luke 2:46-47
77   Proverbs 8:1-9
78   Revelation 3:20
79   Mark 7:24
80   Luke 24:31-32
81   Proverbs 8:34-36; Luke 19:44
82   Matthew 23:1-3, 15:3, Mark 7:9-13, Matthew 15:13-14

their religious authority, they sought to keep God's Son out of their territory, and his followers too, if they could. Yet, although Jesus was not undermining their authority,[83] readily he was attacking their lack of faith and virtue.[84] So, when the Jews eventually did come to intervene, they said to Jesus, "What sign can you show us to justify your acting like this?"[85] And Jesus answered them, saying:

Destroy this temple, and in three days I will raise it up.[86]

Then, with not so subtle scoffing and unreserved scepticism, the Jews replied, "It has taken forty-six years to build this temple,[87] and you are going to raise it up again in three days?"[88] But Jesus was talking about the sanctuary of his body,[89] so that then what Jesus meant was unclear even to his disciples. However, when Jesus was raised from the dead, his disciples remembered that he had said this, and they came to believe the scripture and the word he had spoken.[90]

But now, as Jesus taught in the temple, the blind and the lame also came to him, and he cured them.[91] And we now are exactly like them, because at one time or even at various times, no one in their spiritual pilgrimage through life is immune from their blindness or lameness; but likewise, when we do recognize and admit our sinfulness and we do go to Jesus, he cures us. However, the chief priests and scribes stubbornly persisted in their spiritual blindness and unbelief,[92]

---

83 Matthew 23:2
84 Matthew 23:3
85 John 2:18; Matthew 12:38-40, 16:1, 4, Luke 11:29, Jonah 2:3-11, 1, Romans 5:6, 4:25
86 John 2:19; Mark 14:57-59, Matthew 26:61
87 In the next Chapter 33, this is the specific evidence from St. John's gospel that provides proof for an earlier cleansing of the Temple at the beginning of the Lord's public ministry, where the evangelist John properly places that event, against the potential (but false) single-cleansing hypothesis incorporated here.
88 John 2:20
89 John 2:21; Hebrews 9:1, 10:19-21
90 John 2:22; John 20:6-9; Luke 24:27, 18:31-34
91 Matthew 21:14
92 John 9:32, 39-41, 12:39-41

and they hardened their positions against the accumulated manifest evidence from God. So, later in this day, even though they saw the wonderful things God was doing, and when even the children were shouting and crying aloud in the temple, "Hosanna to the son of David!" they became angry and indignant. [93] And with their clearly suggestive reprimand against any blasphemous recognition of his Messianic kingship in their voice, they told Jesus, "Do you hear what they are saying?"[94] But with even greater clarity to the honour and glory of God, Jesus answered them, "Yes,"[95] to which he added, in contrast to many of the adults:

> Have you never read this: "Out of the mouths of infants and babes in arms you [God] have brought forth praise?"[96]

So, while Jesus was in Jerusalem for the feast of Passover, many believed in his name when they saw the signs he was doing.[97] Yet, Jesus did not trust himself to any of them because he knew people all too well;[98] for he never needed anyone to explain to him human nature, and he could tell exactly what someone had in him.[99] And, at last, when evening came that day,[100] Jesus left them and went out of the city back to Bethany, where he spent the night.[101] For tomorrow, like in the beginning of God's creation, it would be another day for sowing seeds of grace in the Lord's new creation,[102] and also for the Lord's vineyards and fig trees to be pruned,[103] for those destined to bear present and future fruits.[104]

---

93 Matthew 21:15; Matthew 22:41-45
94 Matthew 21:16; Luke 19:39, 24:27
95 Matthew 21:16; Matthew 11:25, Luke 10:21, 23-24
96 Matthew 21:16; Luke 19:40, Matthew 18:2-3; Psalm 8:3
97 John 2:23, 12:42
98 John 2:24
99 John 2:25, 12:43
100 Mark 11:19
101 Matthew 21:17
102 John 12:24; Matthew 13:4-8
103 John 15:3, 7-8
104 Genesis 1:11-13; John 15:4-6, Matthew 3:10, 21:19, 33-34, Revelation 14:14-20; John 12:24-25, Matthew 13:23

Gospel (on the Road to) Emmaus / 189

Readings: Mark 11:20-21, Matthew 21:20-22, Mark 11:22-25; Matthew 21:23-27, Mark 11:27-33, Luke 20:1-8; Matthew 21:28-32; Matthew 21:33-46, Mark 12:1-12, Luke 20:9-19; Matthew 22:1-15

Early the next morning, now on Tuesday, when Jesus and the disciples again were returning to Jerusalem from Bethany, they passed by yesterday's fig tree once more; but this time as they passed it by, they saw that the fig tree had withered to its roots.[105] Peter was the first to notice this and to remember it,[106] as he exclaimed, "Rabbi, look, the fig tree that you cursed has withered away."[107] When the other disciples saw this, they too were astounded; and they asked one another and the Lord, "How did the fig tree dry up so quickly?"[108] Then, pausing there on the hillside of the Mount of Olives, Jesus answered them:

> Remember this![109] If you have faith in God,[110] if you believe and do not doubt, not only will you be able to do what I have done to this fig tree, but you will be able to say to this mountain,[111] "Get up and throw yourself into the sea."[112] If in your heart you do not doubt, but you believe that what you say will happen,[113] then it will be done for you.[114] Therefore, I tell you:[115] if you have faith, you will receive everything you ask for in prayer.[116] Everything you ask and pray for, believe that you have it already, and it will be yours.[117] And when

---

105 Mark 11:20, 13
106 Mark 11:21, 14
107 Mark 11:21
108 Matthew 21:20; Matthew 12:43-45, John 14:23, 15:5-7
109 Matthew 21:21, Mark 11:22
110 Mark 11:22; Mark 10:27, Luke 18:27
111 Matthew 21:21
112 Matthew 21:21, Mark 11:23; Matthew 17:20, Luke 17:5-6
113 Mark 11:23
114 Matthew 21:21, Mark 11:23; James 1:6, 8; Romans 4:22, 21, Genesis 15:1-6, 22:6-12, John 3:16
115 Mark 11:24
116 Matthew 21:22; Mark 9:23, John 15:7
117 Mark 11:24; John 11:40-42

you stand to pray, forgive anybody whatever grievances you have against them, so that your heavenly Father also may forgive you your failings too.[118] [But if you don't forgive, your Father in heaven won't forgive you your failings either.[119]]

At first when Jesus had cursed the fig tree, he directed us to the negative threat of God's wrath against those of us who don't bear fruit. But also with this same case, Jesus actually was providing his disciples with a positive example for their faith. For, with faith in God, the disciples would be able to do not only what Jesus had done to the fig tree, but anything else, even seemingly as fantastic or impossibly far-fetched like throwing the Mount of Olives into the sea; but Jesus demonstrates, by the efficacy of his curse, that with such a faith in God we also can be confident that everything we ask for in prayer will be given to us. Certain terms and conditions, however, do apply according to this morning's renewed Penitential Rite: namely, sufficient faith and our acts of forgiveness and acts of reconciliation, regarding grievances we have against others and those derived from our own failings; and our prayers must conform to the will and love of God. For our acts of faith and our prayers to conform to the will of God, when we pray we must discern the will of God, at least in our hearts, if not also by our minds; and then for us to possess sufficient faith, after our initial reconciliations, we must pray hard for the grace of God's action in us;[120] and then, for us to bear fruit, as Mother Teresa of Calcutta reminds us, we need to begin prayer with the silence:

> The fruit of silence is prayer;
> the fruit of prayer is faith;
> the fruit of faith is love;
> the fruit of love is the silence.

Faith, like prayer, is not like history or science, where the course of human interactions or the laws of nature determine the potential

---

118	Mark 11:25; Matthew 5:23-24, 6:14; Matthew 6:12, Luke 11:3-4; Romans 4:5, James 2:20-24
119	Mark 11:26, Matthew 6:15
120	1 Corinthians 13:13; Romans 9:21, Ephesians 2:8-10; James 1:19-25

probabilities or the actual outcomes for the world's events. But in faith, as also in history or science, one cannot speak with certain knowledge; that is, we can possess knowledge of the past and present, as either history or as science, which themselves provide functional probabilities for future human actions [i.e., the social sciences] and reliable predictions for the natural world [i.e., the physical sciences], but there is no such determinism in faith. In faith and prayer, we only can have absolute trust in God about our potential future, regarding what in essence for us is humanly indeterminate, but divinely is wholly determinate.[121] Ordinary history depends upon the interactive fate of variously determined events; and the natural sciences also depend upon valid understanding of determinable events. But our personal salvation history depends upon our absolutely free response to God's grace, freely given to us by God, which is wholly determined by God and, through God's gift of faith, also by our prayer. Our faith in God, our certain trust and confidence about his past, present and future for us and our hope for the destiny of others, comes from God. And our hope for God's ready fulfilment of our prayer proceeds from this confidence—not as some form of human expectation or human wish fulfilment—but our hope proceeds from our faith in God's love,[122] and our grateful recognition of God's certain accomplishment of our prayer through God's love.[123]

Sometimes when we pray, we are inclined to overlook our own failings, often blindly so,[124] while at the same time we may harbour malicious thoughts or grudges towards others, whose failings against us we would never overlook.[125] And yet, undoubtedly, all our failings have offended God's love, even if now our past forgiven or our present offences may have become largely unconscious to us;[126] but these are not likely to go unnoticed by others.[127] Yes, we should pray for ourselves and for others, for God's forgiveness; but first of all we must

---

121	Hebrews 11:1, 2 Corinthians 5:7
122	1 John 4:9-10, John 3:34-35, 5:19-21, 6:40, 10:29-30, 16:26-27
123	1 John 4:16
124	Matthew 7:3
125	Matthew 7:4, 5:22
126	John 3:20
127	John 3:21

forgive anybody,[128] especially our known enemies,[129] against whom we hold very real grievances, not just potentially imagined ones; for, our human nature being what it is, God's grievances against us have always been real,[130] and not potential.[131] Real faith requires that we forgive others their faults against us, because in our faith we also recognize that God has forgiven us our sins.[132] If he has already done so,[133] we must acknowledge our confidence in God's potential forgiveness for others by our forgiving them first. Our forgiveness and mercy to others should become the centre of our fidelity to God and of our faith in him.[134] For, when we forgive others from our hearts,[135] then God not only forgives us our faults,[136] but then we also can be confident that he answers our prayers.[137]

In their resistance to the Lord, the chief priests, elders, and scribes of the Law were being quite stubborn and intransigent;[138] just as, often enough, most of us can be, or even now, perhaps as we may be at this very moment in our lives. However, despite all such obstinacy, the Lord, certainly knew how to capture everyone's full attention, just as he had intended: first of all, on Sunday, now the afternoon before yesterday, he had marched into the temple with his masses of supporters; and then, again on yesterday morning, on Monday, he had evicted from the temple anyone who had been engaged, in their temple commerce, in any kind of buying or selling. So, now, on this early Tuesday morning, when Jesus had arrived on his own schedule to the temple in Jerusalem,[139] the priests, elders, and scribes already were prepared for confrontation and were waiting

---

128   Mark 11:25
129   Matthew 5:44
130   Hebrews 12:5-6
131   Hebrews 12:12-13; Matthew 21:14
132   Colossians 2:11-15
133   Matthew 5:45
134   Matthew 5:23-24
135   Luke 23:33-34, 46, Acts 7:59-60, 1 Peter 2:23; Matthew 18:21-22; Genesis 4:1-8, 17-19, 23-24, 25-26, Exodus 3:15, Isaiah 53:10-12
136   Matthew 6:12
137   Hebrews 7:25, 9:24
138   Matthew 21:28-31, 34-39, 22:2-6, 23:30-37
139   Matthew 21:23, Mark 11:27, Luke 20:1

for him, if only they could catch him! After a short time, they finally found Jesus, who had been walking about in the temple from place to place,[140] where already he had been occupied with his teaching and his preaching of the Good News;[141] and they asked him, "Tell us:[142] what right do you have for doing these things? And who gave you this authority to do them?"[143] Replying instantly, Jesus said:

> And I will ask you a question, just one, and if you should answer it for me, I'll tell you my authority for doing these things.[144] So tell me,[145] where did John's baptism come from? Was it from heaven or from man?[146]

The scribes of the Law, leading elders, and chief priests had come *en masse* united in their temple procession to challenge the Lord; but in his astute response to them Jesus simply had offered them a profound challenge of his own; and immediately with that question of his, Jesus fractured their group, as now they began to argue among themselves:[147]

> What shall we say? If we say "from heaven," he will say to us, "Why didn't you believe John?"[148] But if we say, "It's of human origin,"[149] then all the people will stone us,[150] for all of them regard John, and they believe with conviction,[151] that he was a prophet.[152]

For the chief priests and temple elders and scribes of the Law, to them this seemed to be a loose-loose situation: if they answered "from God," they would be subject to the rebuke of Jesus; and if they

---

140 Mark 11:27
141 Matthew 21:23, Luke 20:1
142 Luke 20:2
143 Matthew 21:23, Mark 11:28, Luke 20:2
144 Matthew 21:24, Mark 11:29, Luke 20:3
145 Mark 12:30, Luke 20:3
146 Matthew 21:25, Mark 11:30, Luke 20:4; Matthew 3:1-3, 7-10
147 Matthew 21:25, Mark 11:31, Luke 20:5
148 Matthew 21:25, Mark 11:31, Luke 20:5
149 Matthew 21:26, Mark 11:32
150 Luke 20:6
151 Luke 20:6
152 Matthew 21:26, Mark 11:32, Luke 20:6; Matthew 11:10, Luke 7:27

said "from man," they feared the likely provocation of the crowd.[153] Yet, if they had made an honest appraisal and commitment to the will of God over the issue of this question, it could have led them to their salvation.[154] However, and perhaps most crucially, because of their given authority and power,[155] they were still unwilling to yield to the gate of grace and to say from where John's baptism of repentance had come;[156] so, in their self-same unity in their non-repentance and in disregard of God's grace, they simply said to Jesus, "We don't know."[157] So, crisply, Jesus told them:

> Neither will I tell you my authority for doing these things.[158]

But even so, and at the same time because of their reluctance to believe in him, in his mercy and his generosity, and in their best interests, Jesus then immediately told them this supportive, yet also highly critical parable, as if he were their father to his sons.[159] Even though Jesus now would skilfully corner them in their guilt, he also would leave them a way out from their self-made trap, provided that they also followed his lead:[160]

> What is your opinion? There was a man who had two sons. He went to the older son and said, "My boy, go out and work in the vineyard today."[161] He answered, "I don't want to," but later, thinking better of it, he changed his mind and went.[162] Then the father went to the other son and gave him the same order. "Yes, sir," he replied, but he did not go.[163] Therefore, which

---

153   Matthew 21:26, Mark 11:32
154   John 10:2, 9
155   Matthew 23:2
156   Luke 20:7
157   Matthew 21:27, Mark 11:33
158   Matthew 21:27, Mark 11:33, Luke 20:8
159   Hebrews 5:5, 12:5-6
160   John 10:3-4
161   Matthew 21:28; Matthew 20:1
162   Matthew 21:29
163   Matthew 21:30; 2 Timothy 2:25-26

of the two sons,[164] in your opinion,[165] did the father's will?[166]

They answered him, "The first one." Then Jesus replied:

> In truth I tell you, tax collectors and prostitutes are entering the kingdom of God ahead of you.[167] For John the Baptist came to you, showing you the way of uprightness,[168] and you did not believe him, but the tax collectors and prostitutes did; and yet, even after seeing that, you refused to change your minds afterwards and to believe in him.[169]

Today, we are all called by our baptism,[170] and by our true repentance, to go out and to work in the Lord's vineyard—and it is not just the priests and nuns or religious brothers who are called. However, as religious authorities, the chief priests and elders of the temple and the Pharisees and scribes had an even greater responsibility to their calling, as is true in the church today, especially for bishops and pastors in their particular labours in the vineyard for the household of God throughout the world. But whenever we sin, and whenever sin holds an attraction for us in our personal lives, we are saying implicitly, "I don't want to go and work." This is particularly true regarding the scandalous sin of some priests. However, there is a crucial difference, between our sinning and its otherwise sometimes seductively experienced attraction, which is given by our choice of action:[171] we have not chosen sin if, after thinking better of our desires or of sin's false attractions, instead of sinning, we change our minds and wills for God, and we go into his vineyard along the path committed to righteousness.[172] However, we would not be doing God's will, whatever his particular calling

---

164 Matthew 21:31
165 Matthew 21:29
166 Matthew 21:31
167 Matthew 21:31; Luke 19:2, 8-9, 7:37-39, 47-48
168 Matthew 21:32; Luke 3:7-9, 7:33-34
169 Matthew 21:32; Luke 7:29-30
170 Romans 6:4
171 Romans 6:16
172 Romans 5:19, 6:17-19

may have been, or remains for each of us to do,[173] if we should say, even genuinely, "Yes, I will go," but then actually we don't go; because we are liars, and we remain in sin.

And if, supposedly, our sin should be hidden from others through our outward appearances, because in our social worlds we attempt to negotiate a more flattering truth for our actual moral status; yet even so, the moral truth is still known to God.[174] For unlike our social worlds, the reality of our moral status before God and before men is independent of our own thoughts or the thoughts of others on the matter.[175] With the exception of Jesus and his mother, all humans are guilty of sin; and except for grace, the weight of this guilt and of sin's debilitation generally renders us unfit,[176] both for working in the vineyard and for entering into the kingdom of heaven. This would have seemed to be objectively so for persons plainly recognized as public sinners in the Lord's day: such as the local Roman tax collector, who also may have secured exaggerated wealth from socially unjust and corrupt practices; and for the neighbourhood prostitute, who, along with her clients, through their poisonous immoralities of the body, also would have shared in their several corruptions of various hearts, souls, minds, and personal relationships. But such true self-evaluations, before God and men,[177] are rarely honestly made.[178] Nonetheless, only God is truly capable of objectivity about any person's real moral status.[179] For, in contrast to religious leaders of the temple, the chief priests, elders, and scribes, even tax collectors and prostitutes were entering the kingdom of heaven ahead of them; because those public sinners, in their remorse, initially had recognized their sin and had asked for God's mercy;[180] and then also in their penitence, they truly

---

173 John 10:14-15
174 Luke 16:15, 2 Corinthians 5:11
175 Matthew 10:33
176 Matthew 5:13
177 Matthew 25:31-32
178 Luke 18:13-14
179 Luke 6:37, 41, 15:4, 19:7, 10; John 12:48, Matthew 25:15; Romans 3:23-24, 2 Corinthians 13:5; 1 John 3:18-19
180 Luke 18:13, 19:1-3; Luke 7:36-39

had acted in faith:[181] first of all by breaking with sin,[182] and then afterwards by repentance, by expressing God's forgiveness in their lives through their acts of love.[183]

However, unlike examples of the true way of righteousness,[184] in such tax collectors like Zacchaeus (of Jericho) and Matthew (the apostle and future evangelist) or in reformed prostitutes like Mary Magdalene,[185] or provided for us in the example of Saint Paul,[186] or even in the lives of the Carmelite Saints Teresa of Avila and Therese of Lisieux, or in any of the saints as archetypes in "the way of perfection,"[187] be it their "little way,"[188] or a great one,[189] the temple authorities in Jerusalem would have nothing of this. Instead, in blunt opposition to the fruitful care for God's vineyard entrusted to them,[190] these authorities obstinately preferred to reject God's grace surrounding them,[191] also despite its obvious manifestations among allegedly "obvious" sinners;[192] and instead, they wanted to kill Jesus.[193] And yet, for any of these leaders to transcend guilt,[194] just as it is for any of us as sinners, they only had to place themselves, as we must place ourselves, loyally and completely in the hands of God's son,[195] and wholly at his mercy,[196] while trusting entirely in his justice for the righteous.[197]

---

181   Luke 19:4; Luke 7:50
182   Luke 19:5-6; John 8:3-5, 10-11; 1 John 3:6-7
183   Luke 19:8; Luke 7:47-48; 1 John 3:15-16, 18-19
184   Matthew 21:31; John 10:37-38
185   Luke 19:2, Matthew 9:9-13, Mark 16:9
186   1 Timothy 6:11-12
187   St. Teresa of Avila. (1583/1964). The way of perfection. [E. Allison Peers, trans. & ed.] Image Books: Garden City, New York.
188   Beevers, John [Trans.] (1957). The autobiography of St. Therese of Lisieux: The story of a soul. Image Books: Garden City, New York, p. 110.
189   John 21:21-22
190   Isaiah 5:3-6, Matthew 20:16, 21:43; Hebrews 12:3
191   John 8:34-38
192   Matthew 21:32
193   Luke 19:47; Hebrews 12:4
194   Luke 15:1-4
195   John 19:18; 1 John 1:9
196   John 19:34, 1 John 5:6; Numbers 20:11, John 7:37-38, 1 John 4:10-13
197   Matthew 24:45-51; Isaiah 40:10-11, 41:2-3; Luke 17:9-10

Then, for those who are saved through the Lord's forgiveness,[198] in his proclaimed Good News,[199] we are made capable of love,[200] so that unto the honour of God we may negotiate the kingdom of heaven in his vineyards on earth, in our social worlds and in our interpersonal lives.[201] Saint Therese, also known as the "Little Flower of the Child Jesus," in her autobiography (p. 110) writes:

> Love has so worked within me,[202] that it has transformed my soul into itself....If I glance at a book, no matter how good and moving it is, my heart at once contracts and I read without understanding or, if I understand, I cannot meditate on it. When I'm in this state, the Bible and *The Imitation* come to my rescue. In them I find hidden manna, a pure and substantial food.[203] But, above all, the Gospels help me in my prayers.[204] They are always showing me new ways of looking at things, and I am always finding hidden and mysterious meanings in them.[205] I understand and, by experience, I know that the Kingdom of God is within us.[206] Jesus has no need of books or doctors of the Church to guide souls. He, the Doctor of doctors, can teach without words.[207] I have never heard Him speak,[208] but I know that he is within me.[209] He guides me and inspires me every moment of the day.[210] Just when I need it, a new light shines on my problems.[211] This happens not so much during my hours of prayer as when I'm busy with

---

198 Isaiah 40:2
199 Luke 8:1, Matthew 3:2, 4:17, 23, 9:35, 24:14
200 Luke 8:2, Philippians 2:13-14
201 Colossians 3:2-4, Isaiah 42:1-4; Matthew 25:14-15
202 2 Corinthians 5:14-15
203 John 6:48-51, 63
204 John 15:16
205 2 Timothy 3:16
206 Luke 17:21, Colossians 1:26-27, 3:4
207 1 John 2:27
208 John 1:14; 1 John 1:1; Acts 9:3-6
209 John 14:21-23
210 2 Timothy 3:17
211 Matthew 11:28-29; John 1:9

my daily work.[212]

And so it must be for each of us wherever we may labour daily in the vineyard, and as also now I continue trying to tell our story of the Lord's Good News.

But for the unjust, as the Lord now would warn the chief priests and the scribes of the Law, God's justice also will be allotted with the full fury of his vengeance.[213] So, immediately, and with the authority of his kingship,[214] Jesus continued to speak in parables to his enemies assembled before him in the temple.[215] And now with his fair warning,[216] he told these shepherds of Israel:

> Listen to another parable.[217] There was a man, a landowner,[218] who planted a vineyard;[219] he fenced it in with hedging, dug out a trough in it for a winepress, and built a watchtower.[220] Then he leased it to tenants, and went abroad for a long time.[221] When the vintage time drew near,[222] he sent his servant/s to the tenants to collect from them his share of the produce from the vineyard.[223] But they seized the first man,[224] thrashed him and sent him away empty-handed.[225] The landowner persevered,[226] however, and he sent a second servant,[227] whom they also beat about the

---

212   Matthew 11:30; Philippians 2:13-16
213   Hebrews 10:30-31
214   Matthew 21:10-11, Revelation 19:16
215   Mark 12:1, Luke 20:9
216   Hebrews 12:25
217   Matthew 21:33
218   Matthew 21:33; Matthew 20:1
219   Matthew 21:33, Mark 12:1, Luke 20:9
220   Matthew 21:33, Mark 12:1, Isaiah 5:1-2; Revelation 19:15, Isaiah 63:1-6; Genesis 49:11, Mark 11:1-2, Jeremiah 25:30-38, Joel 4:13-21
221   Matthew 21:33, Mark 12:1, Luke 20:9
222   Matthew 21:34
223   Matthew 21:34, Mark 12:2, Luke 20:10; Hebrews 6:7-8, Matthew 22:7
224   Mark 12:3
225   Mark 12:3, Luke 20:10
226   Luke 20:11
227   Luke 20:11, Mark 12:4

head and treated shamefully,[228] and sent away empty-handed.[229] Still persevering, the landowner sent a third servant, but him they wounded and then they threw him out.[230]

One by one the tenants seized his servants, thrashing one, killing another and stoning a third.[231] He sent yet another servant, and him they killed,[232] and he sent more servants,[233] then even a larger number of others,[234] and some they beat and the rest they killed,[235] in the same way as they had done with the others.[236] Then the owner of the vineyard said, "What am I to do?"[237] But he still had someone left: his beloved son.[238] So finally,[239] he thought, "I will send my dear son to them. Perhaps,[240] surely,[241] they will respect him."[242] And he sent his son to them last of all.[243] But when the tenants saw him, they put their heads together and said to each other, "This is the heir.[244] Come on! Let's kill him so that the inherited property will become ours."[245] So they seized him,[246] and threw him out of the vineyard,[247] and there

---

228   Mark 12:4
229   Mark 12:4, Luke 20:11
230   Luke 20:12
231   Matthew 21:35
232   Mark 12:5
233   Matthew 21:36
234   Mark 12:5, Matthew 21:36
235   Mark 12:5
236   Matthew 21:36
237   Luke 20:13
238   Mark 12:6
239   Matthew 21:37
240   Luke 20:13
241   Mark 12:6
242   Luke 20:13
243   Matthew 21:37, Mark 12:6; Matthew 3:17, Genesis 22:2
244   Hebrews 1:1-2, 9:16-17
245   Matthew 21:38, Mark 12:7, Luke 20:14; Genesis 4:8
246   Matthew 26:50, Mark 14:46
247   Hebrews 13:11-12, John 19:17

they killed him.[248]

For a few moments of stunned silence,[249] Jesus paused, and then, calmly, he asked the chief priests and Pharisees:

> What will the owner of the vineyard do,[250] to those tenants when he comes?[251]

But, out of their own mouths they swiftly condemned themselves when they answered Jesus,[252] "He will bring those wretched men to a wretched end and lease the vineyard to other tenants, who will deliver his produce to him at the proper seasons."[253]

Indeed!

said Jesus:

> He will come and put those tenant farmers to death and turn over the vineyard to others.[254]

Upon hearing this, the people exclaimed, "God forbid! Let it not be so!"[255] But Jesus looked at them long and hard, and he asked them:[256]

> What then is the meaning of this scripture?[257] Have you not read this passage?[258] Or did you never read it?[259]

> The stone which the builders rejected

---

248 Matthew 21:39, Mark 12:8, Luke 20:15; Luke 11:50-51, Matthew 5:17-18; 1 Kings 19:9-10, 13-14, Mark 15:29-31, Romans 8:3
249 Isaiah 29:9-10
250 Mark 12:9, Luke 20:15
251 Matthew 21:40
252 Luke 19:22
253 Matthew 21:41; Matthew 12:37, 33-34, 3:7-8
254 Mark 12:9, Luke 20:16; Romans 11:18-22
255 Luke 20:16
256 Luke 20:17
257 Luke 20:17; Psalm 118:22-23
258 Mark 12:10
259 Matthew 21:42

> has become the cornerstone;[260]
> this has been the Lord's doing,
>   and we marvel at what we see.[261]
>
> Therefore, I say to you, the kingdom of God will be taken away from you and given to a people that will produce its fruit.[262] Anyone who falls on that stone will be dashed to pieces; and it will crush anyone on whom it falls.[263]

When the chief priests and Pharisees heard these parables, they knew that Jesus was speaking about them.[264] And because Jesus had addressed this parable to them, right then and there they would have put their hands on him; they would have arrested him on the spot;[265] but because they also feared the crowds, who regarded Jesus as a prophet,[266] they left him and went away.[267]

God was persistent in his long-suffering patience towards Israel and its shepherds;[268] and Jesus would be the culmination of a long line of prophets whose righteous blood would be shed at their hands: from Abel, son of Adam and Eve,[269] murdered at the hands of their son Cain in his fields,[270] to Zechariah, the son of Jehoiada,[271] who was stoned to death between the sanctuary and the altar of the temple,[272] like so many other witnesses to faith.[273] There would be many others

---

260   Luke 20:17, Mark 12:10, Matthew 21:42; Isaiah 28:16, Acts 4:11-12, Ephesians 2:20
261   Matthew 21:42, Mark 12:11; Acts 13:40-41, Habakkuk 1:5, Isaiah 29:14
262   Matthew 21:43
263   Luke 20:18; Luke 20:17, Isaiah 8:14-15, 1 Peter 2:7-8; Romans 9:28, 33
264   Matthew 21:45
265   Luke 20:19
266   Matthew 21:46; Matthew 21:26
267   Mark 12:12; Matthew 22:2, 5
268   2 Chronicles 36:15-16, Luke 20:13, Romans 2:4
269   Genesis 3:20
270   Genesis 4:3-5, 8; Hebrews 11:4, Genesis 4:10-12, 1 John 3:12; Matthew 23:31-33, 21:43, Isaiah 66:24
271   2 Chronicles 24:20-22; not Zechariah 1:1
272   Matthew 23:35
273   Hebrews 11:37, Acts 7:52; 2 Maccabees 6:18-30, Isaiah 53:1-12; 2 Maccabees 7:1-41, Luke 2:34-35, John 19:25; Matthew 2:16

to follow the Lord:[274] like Stephen,[275] and Paul,[276] and Peter,[277] and all saints enduring their great trials.[278] But God had sent Jesus to his people, not only as a prophet, but as the prophet—that is, as the long-awaited and expected Messiah, just as God's faithful promises had been foretold in the scriptures,[279] and just as the religious leaders had been all too keenly aware, as was shown by their anxious inquiries about this promise made to John the Baptist by the priests, Levites and Pharisees sent to John by the authorities.[280] And Christ's shedding of his blood was different from his predecessors, for as the son of God and the son of David,[281] only he could make uprightness of our unrighteousness through his perfect righteousness and perfect sacrifice for our sins, and by our faith in him.[282]

Jesus, by this one sacrifice in this one faith we share with the prophets,[283] would not only make righteous the blood of the prophets, as Christ did, but he also would sanctify all righteous blood shed upon the earth throughout the whole of human history,[284] including the blood of those prophets, wise men and women, and scribes or writers and journalists, who today are sent into the world by Christ: including those who have been slaughtered, or others scourged, by those who oppose his name;[285] including the millions of holocaust victims during various 20th/21st century wars, ethnic cleansings, and abortions;[286] including the world's abominable immolations of an estimated 1.8 million children yearly to the sex industry, another 5.7 million children who are sold into slavery, and 1.2 million more who are subject to human trafficking, and many of them without a trace.

---

274 Hebrews 12:1-2
275 Acts 7:51, 53-60
276 Acts 22:1-15, 29-30, 23:1-6, 11; 2 Corinthians 4:11-18, 5:1
277 John 21:14-19, 1 Peter 4:12-13, 1:7-12, 2 Peter 3:2-9
278 Revelation 7:9, 13-14
279 Deuteronomy 18:15-19, John 7:18
280 John 1:19-27
281 Romans 1:3-4
282 Romans 3:21-26
283 Acts 2:1-6, 14-36; Romans 4:3, 18-25
284 Matthew 23:35
285 Matthew 23:34; Matthew 5:11-12, John 3:18-20
286 Jeremiah 31:15, Mathew 2:17-18, 24:19-22, Revelation 16:13-14

Among the righteous prophets of our times,[287] also are included the blood of those drowned at sea in their dangerous migrations from Africa to Europe, or their survivors languishing in foreign camps or in immigrant ghettos, or who are beaten up in alien places because of their skin colour or ethnic designations; and the voiceless innocents around the world who are blown to bits by bombs or shredded to death by rockets or bullets or machetes; and those wasted away through hunger and deprivation—all on an everyday basis, in the relentless names of various ethnic hatreds and political or sectarian interests, or in other people's envy and struggle for power, or in someone else's desire to create or maintain their personal agendas or wealth, out of self-interest or lively greed. But, together with the Lord's witness, these international prophets of today warn us about the tragedy of our disinterest to their horrible plights; and they inform us about our fundamental obligation to assist these people in their human and their spiritual needs.[288]

After the religious authorities, in their angry frustration of that moment, had departed,[289] Jesus replied to their walk-out and to their persistent disbelief in him with yet another parable clearly addressed to them,[290] but which now was quite simply and quite summarily spoken to the remaining crowds packing the temple, including some of the Pharisees acting as spies,[291] and to the rest of us:

> The kingdom of heaven may be compared to a king who gave a feast for his son's wedding.[292] He sent his servants to call the invited guests to the feast, but they refused to come.[293] So he sent some other servants to them, saying, "Tell those who have been invited: Look, I have my banquet all prepared; my oxen and fattened cattle have been slaughtered; and everything is ready.

---

287 John 3:21
288 Matthew 25:40-46
289 Mark 12:12; Deuteronomy 18:20-22, 13:2-6, 18:13-15; Exodus 20:1-17, Matthew 5:17-20
290 Matthew 22:1; Luke 14:15-16
291 Matthew 22:15
292 Matthew 22:2; Luke 15:25-26
293 Matthew 22:3; Luke 15:28-30

Come to the wedding feast!"[294] But they were not interested and they ignored the invitation: one went off to his farm, and another went to his business.[295] The rest seized his servants, beat them up, and killed them.[296] The king was furious: he sent his troops, destroyed those murderers, and burnt their town.[297]

Then he said to his servants: "The wedding feast is ready, but those who were invited were not worthy to come.[298] So, go to the main crossroads and invite to the feast everyone you can find."[299] So these servants went out into the streets and collected together anyone they could find, both bad and good alike;[300] and the entire wedding hall was filled with guests.[301] But when the king came in to meet the guests, he noticed a man there who wasn't dressed in his wedding clothes,[302] and he said to him, "My friend, how did you get in here without a wedding garment?"[303] And the man fell absolutely speechless.[304] Then the king said to his attendants,[305] "Tie up his hands and feet, and throw him into the darkness outside,[306] where there will be wailing and gnashing of teeth."[307]

Then, with one final penetrating gaze directed towards the Pharisees, Jesus concluded by saying:

294	Matthew 22:4; Luke 14:17, 15:27, 23-24
295	Matthew 22:5; Luke 14:18-20
296	Matthew 22:6; Matthew 21:33-39; Revelation 16:15
297	Matthew 22:7; Luke 14:24; Matthew 21:40-41; Revelation 16:16
298	Matthew 22:8; Luke 14:21-22; Revelation 21:9-14
299	Matthew 22:9; Luke 14:23; Matthew 10:11-16
300	Matthew 22:10; Matthew 13:26, 38, 30, 40-43; Matthew 19:16-21
301	Matthew 22:10; John 14:2-3
302	Matthew 22:11; Revelation 19:8, 21:2, 22:14-15; Ephesians 5:26, Matthew 28:19, John 15:3, 13:10, Ephesians 5:27, John 3:5, 1 Peter 1:3-5
303	Matthew 22:12; Matthew 25:10-11
304	Matthew 22:12; Matthew 22:41, 46
305	Matthew 22:13; Matthew 25:1-4, Luke 12:35; John 9:5, 1 John 1:5-7, John 12:36, Matthew 5:14-16
306	Matthew 22:13; Matthew 25:8
307	Matthew 22:13; Matthew 8:11-12, Luke 13:28, Matthew 25:30

Although many are invited, not all are chosen.[308]

And immediately the Pharisees went off, to work out with each other how they might trap Jesus in what he said.[309] But potential disaster loomed for these shepherds and false prophets in Jerusalem, just as the prophet Jeremiah had warned, and as they then should have realized: for "Yahweh would raise an upright branch for David."[310] Yet, despite the treachery of the Lord's many enemies, Jesus was not alone.[311]

Reflective Prayer: Psalm 31:1-24

Antiphon: I have come from heaven,
> not to do my own will,
> but to do the will of him who sent me.[312]

> In you, O Lord, I take refuge,
>   let me never be put to shame,
>   in your saving justice deliver me.[313]
> Incline your ear to me;
>   make haste to rescue me!
>   Be for me a rock of refuge,
>   a fortified citadel to save me.[314]
> You are my rock, my fortress stronghold;
>   true to your name, lead me and guide me.[315]

---

308 Matthew 22:14; John 15:16-17; Romans 9:7-16
309 Matthew 22:15; Matthew 21:38
310 Jeremiah 23:5-6, 1-4, 7-24; John 8:24, 7:33-34; Romans 11:5-6, Ephesians 2:11-13, 19-20, Romans 11:16-24
311 John 8:29
312 John 6:38
313 Psalm 31:1; Mark 11:15; Philippians 3:17, Acts 9:20-25
314 Psalm 31:2; Mark 12:8; Mark 15:22
315 Psalm 31:3; Luke 20:17; Matthew 16:18

Free me from the hidden nets they have spread for me,
> for you, O Lord, are my refuge.[316]
Into your hands I commend my spirit,
> you have redeemed me.[317]
God of truth, you hate
> those who worship ineffectual idols;
> but I put my trust in Yahweh.[318]
I will be glad and rejoice in your faithful love;
> once you have witnessed my misery,
> and have seen my soul's distress,[319]
you will not abandon me into enemy hands,
> but will set my feet free to roam in an open space.[320]

Antiphon: The will of him who sent me
> > is that I should lose nothing of all he has given to me,
> > but that I should raise it up on the last day.[321]

Have mercy on me, O Lord,
> for I am in trouble;
> tears gnaw away at my eyes,
> and eat my soul deep within me.[322]
My life is worn out by sorrow,
> my life with sighs;
> my strength gives way under affliction,
> my bones are consumed.[323]

316	Psalm 31:4; Mark 11:28; Matthew 6:26
317	Psalm 31:5; Mark 12:11; John 19:28-30
318	Psalm 31:6; Matthew 22:5; John 4:23
319	Psalm 31:7; Luke 20:10; Colossians 1:12-13
320	Psalm 31:8; Mark 11:27; Colossians 1:14, Romans 8:1
321	John 6:39
322	Psalm 31:9; Matthew 22:9-10; 2 Corinthians 5:1,5
323	Psalm 31:10; Mark 11:18; 2 Corinthians 4:16, 5:2-4

In the face of the sheer number of my enemies,
   I am made a reproach,
   a contemptible sight to my neighbours,
   a horror to my friends;
   and when people see me in the street,
   they quickly run away.[324]
I am forgotten, like a corpse,
   like a shattered dish to be thrown away.[325]
I have heard the whispered slander of the crowd;
   I am surrounded by terror everywhere I turn,
   as they conspire together against me,
   plotting to take my life.[326]

But as for me, I put my trust in you, O Lord;
   I say, "You are my God."[327]
Every moment of my life is in your hands;
   rescue me from my enemies,
   from the clutches of my pursuers.[328]
Let your face shine on your servant;
   save me in your faithful love.[329]
Do not let me be disgraced,
   for I have called on you, O Lord;
   but instead, put the wicked to shame,
   reduce them to silence in Sheol.[330]
Strike dumb their lying lips,
   arrogant lips that attack the just
   in contempt and scorn.[331]

---

[324] Psalm 31:11; Matthew 21:45; John 16:32, Acts 22:30
[325] Psalm 31:12; Matthew 21:39; John 16:31, Acts 23:1-2
[326] Psalm 31:13; Matthew 21:38; Acts 25:11
[327] Psalm 31:14; Matthew 21:28-29; Acts 26:8
[328] Psalm 31:15; Matthew 21:46; Acts 26:32
[329] Psalm 31:16; Luke 19:47-48; Acts 26:13, 2 Corinthians 3:18
[330] Psalm 31:17; Matthew 22:11-13; Acts 26:28-29
[331] Psalm 31:18; Matthew 22:15; John 3:36, Philippians 3:19

Antiphon: It is my Father's will that whoever
> sees the Son and believes in him should have eternal life,
> and that I should raise that person up on the last day.[332]

> Yahweh, what great quantities of good things
> you have in store for those who fear you;
> that you bestow on those who trust in you,
> for all humanity to see.[333]

In the shelter of your presence you safely hide them,
> far from the plotting of men;
> you shield them within your tent,
> far from disputing tongues.[334]

Blessed be the Lord who has shown me
> the miracles of his wondrous love,
> has been for me a fortified city.[335]

> Once in a state of terror I cried,
> "I am cut off from your sight,"
> yet you heard my plea for help
> when I cried out to you.[336]

Love the Lord, all you faithful:
> Yahweh guards his loyal servants,
> but he repays the arrogant
> in full with interest.[337]

Be strong, take courage,
> all who put your hope in the Lord.[338]

---

332 John 6:40
333 Psalm 31:19; Matthew 22:4; Philippians 3:20, 1 Corinthians 2:9, Romans 9:23-24
334 Psalm 31:20; Luke 19:45-46; Acts 9:15-16
335 Psalm 31:21; Matthew 21:14-16; Acts 9:3-6
336 Psalm 31:22; Matthew 21:32; John 15:2, Acts 27:14-15, 18-20
337 Psalm 31:23; Matthew 22:7; Acts 23:11
338 Psalm 31:24; Mark 11:24; Ephesians 3:12, Acts 27:22-26

Antiphon: Everyone whom the Father gives me will come to me; I certainly will not reject anyone who comes to me.[339]

> Glory be to the Father,
> and to the Son,
> and to the Holy Spirit,
> as it was in the beginning,
> is now, and ever shall be,
> world without end. Amen.

Blessed and praised be the Lord,
from Whom comes all the good
that we speak and think and do.
Amen.[340]

---

339 John 6:37
340 St. Teresa of Avila, Ibid., p. 280; Acts 17:28, 24-27

Gospel (on the Road to) Emmaus / 211

Chapter 33

Wednesday Morning and Afternoon, the 12th Nisan (5th April, 30 CE)—Christ in the Temple among the Pharisees and Scribes, Those Scholar-Hypocrites of the Law, Snakes and Sons of Snakes, and Opponents to the True Devotees of God's Law to Love: Jesus and His Children of the Resurrection

Readings: Luke 20:20-26, 27-40, Matthew 22:15-22, 23-33, Mark 12:13-17, 18-27; Matthew 22:34-40, Mark 12:28-34; Luke 20:41-44, Matthew 22:41-46, Mark 12:35-37

The Pharisees and scribes of the Law, in their seemingly fearless and blindly single-minded determination,[1] had resolved to attack the Lord with wave after wave of cleverly constructed assaults,[2] until, at last by their manoeuvres, they should succeed; and indeed, together with the chief priests and the leading citizens,[3] those thieves would succeed to kill him.[4] But, just as at the Passover feast of twenty-four years earlier,[5] when the Lord had been twelve

---

1 Matthew 13:14-15, John 9:39-41
2 Matthew 22:15, Mark 14:1-2
3 Matthew 26:57-59
4 John 10:10; Luke 19:45-48, Matthew 27:20; John 8:37, 39-51, 58, 10:29-30
5 The birth of the Lord will be explained in Chapter 40, as 21st December

years old,[6] Jesus now was to be found in his Father's house,[7] where once again he was sitting in the Temple among the teachers, listening to them, and asking questions of them.[8] But also, in parallel to that time of his early adolescence, in these final days for doing his Father's work,[9] the Lord not only was in his authority,[10] just as he had been Yahweh's King in his youth; but also this time, Jesus was occupied with, and fully in command of, God's planned implementation of our salvation history.[11] Three days ago, when Jesus had come to his Father's house in royal procession,[12] and on the following day, on Monday, when Jesus had cleansed the Temple,[13] he had come into Jerusalem in his manifest authority as King,[14] and he had come as God's humble high priest of the new covenant,[15] as the promised Messiah, who was God's beloved Son; and by his sacrifice at this approaching Passover, he also would be for us our eternal unconquerable light.[16]

But during his public life before now, Jesus had celebrated two previous Passovers with his disciples, and both of those feasts are unified with this third feast; and this unity of Passover celebrations is exemplified most clearly in the gospel of Saint John. While all four of the evangelists describe the Lord's driving of merchants out from the Temple, uniquely John's gospel places this first of two similar-

---

	(the winter solstice) in 8 BCE.
6	Luke 2:41, 48-50
7	Luke 2:49
8	Luke 2:46, 21:37-38
9	John 2:13-17, Zechariah 12:2a, 14:21, 4-5, 13:1, 12:9-10, John 19:37, Isaiah 52:7-8
10	Matthew 21:23, Mark 11:27-28, Luke 20:1-2; John 1:19-34, 8:25-29; Mark 11:29-30, 1:1-4, 7-11
11	John 18:33-37, 3:35, 8:42, 14:10, 17:4, 23, 25; Luke 2:41-43, 49-51
12	John 12:12-13, Luke 19:36-38, Matthew 21:8-11, Mark 11:8-11
13	Matthew 21:12, Mark 11:15-16, Luke 19:45-46, John 2:13-16
14	Isaiah 9:5-6
15	Hebrews 9:11, 7:11-28, 8:1-7
16	Genesis 3:15, 22:14-18, Exodus 12:1-6, 12-13, 21-27, 13:2, 12-15, Luke 2:22-23, Deuteronomy 18:15, 18-19, Matthew 17:5-6, Deuteronomy 18:16-17, 4:11-13, John 1:14, Matthew 17:7-9, Mark 9:10; Luke 1:76-79, 1 John 1:5-7, 1 Peter 2:9; Acts 26:17-18, Luke 1:68-72, Acts 26:23, Luke 2:32, John 16:33, 1:5, 12:31-32, 35-36

appearing events towards the beginning of the Lord's public life, rather than among the events of Holy Week, where we may have come to expect it from the Synoptic evangelists; and accordingly my own gospel narrative had included this initial Temple cleansing from John as if it had been part of this later event. However, as now will be provided, the Lord, indeed, had driven moneychangers and sellers from the Temple twice: not only at this Passover in 30 CE, but also for the first time before Passover in 28 CE. Both of these cleansing events would have raised the immediate attention and ire of temple authorities,[17] who on the day after this final cleansing in preparation for his sacrifice,[18] now only yesterday on Tuesday had inquired of Jesus what authority was his for acting like this?[19]

Working against the single-event hypothesis for one Temple cleansing, in the first such event described by John, there is unique dialogue between Jesus and the Temple authorities: first, their telling Jesus that he should provide them with a "sign" to show he should act like this, although the Synoptic accounts do provide for their subsequent questioning of his authority;[20] and secondly, there is their specific reply to Jesus indicating that "forty-six years" had passed since the building of the Temple,[21] which refers not to its completion, but to the current moment of its ongoing reconstruction, because the reconstruction would not be finished for another thirty-six years, not until 64 CE. And shortly thereafter, in 70 CE, the Temple would be destroyed completely during the siege of Jerusalem by the Romans under Titus.[22] The prior restoration of the Temple under Herod the Great had begun in January of 19 BCE; so, allowing for a full forty-six years of ongoing reconstruction (19 + 27 = 46 BCE/CE years), John's gospel would be describing a first Temple cleansing by the Lord around Passover in the spring of 28 CE. And at that

---

17 Malachi 3:1-3, John 1:6-8, 19-27, Matthew 3:7; Revelation 6:17, Amos 5:18, John 9:4
18 Hebrews 7:26, 9:12
19 Matthew 21:23, Mark 11:27-28, Luke 20:2
20 John 2:18-19, 3:1-2; Mark 11:28, Matthew 21:23, Luke 20:2; 1 Corinthians 1:22-23, John 5:43-44, 7:48-52, Acts 2:22-24, Matthew 16:1-4
21 John 2:20
22 John 11:48; Matthew 24:2, Mark 13:2, Luke 21:6, 20

Passover, the "sign" that Jesus told the authorities that he would give for his actions would be his final sacrifice and his resurrection from the dead, "Destroy this Temple, and in three days I will raise it up."[23] This "sign" would reveal the glory of God's love for us that the Father provides through the power of his glorified Son,[24] who is himself the Temple of God;[25] it would be his "sign of Jonah,"[26] which the Lord's recent resurrection of Lazarus also predicts.[27]

For John, the Lord's dramatic first appearance to the Temple in Jerusalem in 28 CE shows the glory of the Lord who dwells among us.[28] Unlike the glory of God reflected in the radiant face of Moses or in the Meeting Tent of the Lord,[29] and in the absence of an account of the transfiguration of Jesus in John's gospel, but also like Moses as Matthew and Luke had described how the Lord's face in the transfiguration was changed like the sun and his clothing became brilliant as lightening,[30] but now still in veiled glory,[31] with John's theology for the cleansing of the Temple, the Spirit-filled presence of the Son in the sanctuary of his body fills the dwelling place of God,[32] as the perfect reflection of the Father,[33] and as the light of the world.[34] It also had been around this first Passover of 28 CE that Nicodemus, a Pharisee and a notable leader of the Jews among

---

23   John 2:19, 21-22
24   John 1:14, 10:17-18; 1 Corinthians 1:23-24, Ephesians 1:18-20, Philippians 3:10-11, Colossians 2:12-13
25   1 Corinthians 2:7-9, John 12:23, 28, 13:31-32, 16:14, 17:1, 5, 10; 1 John 4:9, John 1:14, Leviticus 26:11-12, 1 Corinthians 3:16-17, Revelation 21:3, 22-23, Ephesians 2:20-22, John 1:32-34, 4:23-24, Colossians 1:17-20
26   Matthew 16:4, 12:38-40
27   John 11:40; John 20:15-16; Acts 2:27, John 11:25-26, 39, 20:1
28   John 2:23, 1:14; 1 John 1:1-2
29   Exodus 25:8, 22, 29:43, 34:29-35, 40:34-35; Leviticus 26:11-12, Deuteronomy 4:7;
30   Matthew 17:2, Luke 9:29-31
31   John 2:23-24; 1 Corinthians 13:12; 2 Corinthians 3: 7, 13, 18, 4:6, Revelation 22:4
32   John 2:21, Exodus 27:20, Leviticus 24:2-4; Revelation 21:22-23
33   John 1:18, 6:46, 8:54, 10:30, 14:7, 9
34   1 John 1:5; John 1:9, 8:12, 9:5, 11:9-10, 12:35-36; Isaiah 6:1-4, John 12:39-41

the Sanhedrin, had come to Jesus secretly at night,[35] and it was to him that Jesus then had explained his purpose for coming as the Son of Man.[36] Even then Jesus had urged Nicodemus to become his public disciple,[37] by which coming into the open light for all to see Nicodemus finally did do, but then he did so only eventually and only gradually,[38] which in God's freedom and grace was his faithful course towards God,[39] unlike the path towards destruction chosen by many of his colleagues and peers, who refused to believe even in the works Jesus did.[40]

Then, one year later on,[41] John describes the Passover of 29 CE, in terms of its immediately preceding central events: by the feeding of the five thousand with five barley loaves and two fish on remote shores on the Sea of Galilee near Tiberias;[42] and on the following day, by the Lord's Bread of Life discourse in the synagogue at Capernaum,[43] after somehow the Lord had rejoined the disciples, suddenly there near the shore before daybreak, by meeting them and their boat by his walking there several kilometres across the Sea of Galilee.[44] And then, in Capernaum, Jesus had told everyone there, including the incredulous Jewish authorities among them, of the unity between the "bread" of a future Eucharist and the "flesh" of his Passover passion and sacrifice, "the bread that I shall give is my flesh, for the life of the world."[45] Its fulfilment would be accomplished only now during the Lord's Passover in 30 CE, in his final "Passover of glory."[46] The Lord's passion, unto the life of the world and out of

---

35	John 3:1-2; John 12:42
36	John 3:13-17; Hebrews 9:22-24
37	John 3:18-21
38	John 7:50-52, 19:39; Matthew 21:28-32
39	John 5:24, 10:27, 8:28
40	John 8:24, 43, 47; John 11:25-26, 8:51-53, 10:37-38
41	John 6:4
42	John 6:14-15, 23; Matthew 14:13, Mark 6:32, Luke 9:12-13
43	John 6:30-33, 48-50
44	John 6:16-21, Mark 6:52
45	John 6:51, 55-58; Luke 22:14-20
46	John 12:27-28, Luke 22:21-23, John 13:27-32

his love for us,[47] would proceed from within this "Passover" meal:[48] after his initial liturgy of the word,[49] and from that very moment in his new covenant liturgy when Jesus in the Eucharist would give us his body to eat; and at that same meal, when Judas, unto his own condemnation and in his treachery unto nailing the Lord's flesh to the cross by the death of the Lord,[50] would take the bread given to him from the hand of Jesus, as Jesus would tell him, "What you are going to do, do quickly."[51] Eucharist is bound intrinsically to the cross and resurrection, which we celebrate until Christ comes again: Christ has died; Christ is risen; Christ will come again.[52]

And, very shortly now, the Pharisees and scribes once again would be astounded at the Lord's intelligence and by his replies; just as, perhaps, some of them had been astonished when they may have witnessed the Lord personally in his youth;[53] and just as almost six months ago, near mid-October during the month of Tishri, when all of them had been astonished by the Lord's teaching at the Jewish harvest festival of Tabernacles, or Shelters.[54] Then, as Jesus also would do now, he had challenged the Pharisees and Temple scribes in their arrogance for political power, because of their presumptions of strength derived from the prestige of their positions of religious authority and from their heritage as sons of Abraham.[55] It was then, at that time nearly six months ago, that they had marvelled at the Lord's teaching, with its dramatic power, its overwhelming logic, and its simple clarity,[56] without Jesus ever being schooled to read,[57] and without his undertaking any training in the Law under

---

47	John 6:51, 13:1
48	Exodus 12:9-11, 14, Luke 22:15, 19-20, 1 Corinthians 10:16
49	John 15:3
50	1 Corinthians 11:26-27, John 13:10-11, Luke 22:21-22
51	John 13:27
52	1 Corinthians 11:26, Colossians 3:1-4; 1 Thessalonians 4:13-15
53	Luke 2:47
54	John 7:11-13
55	John 7:48-49; John 8:33, 39, 53, Matthew 3:9
56	In my opinion, I would suggest that these are the same reasons in the unity of the Spirit for my support of the modern gospel account of Maria Valtorta as from the Lord, as and how she claims them to be derived.
57	John 7:15; Maria Valtorta (Chapter 38) also provides that Mary alone

their formal tutelage, but from God the Father himself.[58] Even so, in approximately 48 hours,[59] when they would have crucified their King,[60] the great Day of the Lord would fall upon all of them,[61] upon all of those supposed scholars of the Law,[62] but also, unto our salvation for those who believed in him,[63] upon all of us sinners.[64]

At first, the Pharisees decided to send their disciples to Jesus,[65] together with some Herodians,[66] who were supporters of the political dynasty arising from Herod the Great. The Pharisees, in their strict reliance on observance of Jewish Law and traditions,[67] and in their fervent theocratic nationalism,[68] were not the natural allies of the Herodians, except that they both had shared historical hatred of the Hasmoneans; and along with this shared animosity, the Pharisees also engaged a presently pragmatic self-preservation of their religious and political status through favours they curried from Herod Antipas. It was now thirty-four years after the death of Herod the Great; but they had not forgotten how within the month before he died, Herod had suppressed an uprising by the Pharisees.[v] On 13th March 4 BCE, Herod had executed its ringleaders, two of their most learned doctors of the Law, Judas son of Sariphaeus and Matthias son of Margalothos: first, Judas and Matthias were burned alive; with their execution, some thirty-eight other rash, young followers were executed by the axe or the bowstring; and then Herod dismissed the High Priest, his father-in-law Simeon Boethus, and in his stead appointed his brother-in-law, Joazar ben Boethus.

---

	and entirely, and resolutely against the custom for synagogue training, had home-schooled her child Jesus in preparation for his maturation.
58	John 7:16-17
59	Matthew 27:45, John 3:14-15
60	Matthew 27:41-42, Luke 23:36-38, John 19:19-22
61	Matthew 27:51
62	Matthew 22:29, 23:10
63	John 1:11-13, 3:14-15
64	John 8:56; Hebrews 11:17-18, 13, Numbers 24:1-9, 23:18-24, 24:15-24, Hebrews 9:24-28
65	Luke 20:20; Matthew 23:15, John 8:44
66	Matthew 22:16; Mark 3:6, Luke 13:31-33
67	Mark 2:24, 3:1-2, 7:1-4; Romans 4:13-14, 7:4-6
68	Luke 17:20-21, John 11:47-53; John 1:45, Acts 1:6; Luke 19:11, Mark 11:9-11, John 12:19

Then only five days before Herod died, he executed Antipater, his eldest son by Doris, his first of ten wives, after Antipater had been imprisoned at home for his attempted patricide. Then, when Mariamme II also became implicated in the plot, Herod divorced her, his sixth wife of 19 years, who had been the very attractive daughter of Simeon Boethus from Alexandria, and Herod also struck their son, Herod-Philip, out of succession, who had been the next in line after Antipater. Three years before this, Herod's sister Salome had stoked the king's imagination regarding the family's internecine intrigues. Consequently, in 7 BCE, Herod also executed Alexander and Aristobulus for alleged attempted patricide; both princes had been the surviving sons by Mariamme I, Herod's Hasmonean queen and his second wife. Twenty-two years before this, in 29 BCE, Salome also had succeeded to manipulate her brother to execute Mariamme I, the wife that Herod had loved, although she had come to hate him; with her, Herod also executed Mariamme's mother, Alexandra; and then, in Salome's plotted good riddance, Herod executed Salome's aged husband Joseph, his paternal uncle.

Upon Herod's engagement to Mariamme I in 42 BCE, Doris was banished; and he married Mariamme I in 37 BCE. When she had been only recently wed, Herod also took his third and fourth wives: an unknown niece in 37 BCE, and an unknown cousin around 34/33 BCE, neither of whom bore him any children. But just within two years after Herod had executed Mariamme I, he quickly took up with three adolescent replacement wives. First there was his fifth wife Malthace, which for him may have been an intentionally explicit violation of the prohibition of Jewish-Samaritan intermarriage to help him erase his sorrowful memory of Mariamme I. And he also discovered "love again" with his sixth wife Mariamme II, who had been a striking local beauty from the Jewish Diaspora in Alexandria. Then there was Herod's seventh wife, Cleopatra of Jerusalem (she was not the famous daughter of the Ptolemies). Eleven years later in 16 BCE, Herod took another set of three wives: eighth wife Pallas, ninth wife Phaedra, and tenth wife Elpis; each, respectively, would produce one child: a son Phasael and daughters Roxane and Salome. First wife Doris also returned to Herod's court in 14 BCE, until she was banished for the second time around 7/6 BCE. Mariamme II was divorced no later than 6 BCE. Malthace barely survived Herod before she died.

For the Lord in 30 CE, it now was twenty-four years after Archelaus, Herod's first son born to his Samaritan wife Malthace, had been banished as King of Judea. And Herod's powerful sister, Salome, also had been dead for twenty years, and having left her estate to the Roman Empress. But ever since the death of Herod the Great, Herod Antipas, Herod's second son by his fifth wife Malthace, remained tetrarch of Galilee and Peraea;[69] and his half-brother Philip, son of Herod the Great and of his seventh wife Cleopatra of Jerusalem, was still tetrarch of Ituraea and Trachonitis, the Transjordan.[70] Herod Antipas had married the first wife of his half-brother Herod-Philip, Herodias, the daughter of Aristobulus, who had been the son of Herod the Great and Mariamme I, while his half-brother, son of Herod the Great and Mariamme II, was still living. And for marrying his brother's wife, Herod Antipas had been roundly chastised by John the Baptist, whom Herodias, in her ire, managed to arrange for John's head on a plate.[71] Likewise the Pharisees also had tried to entrap the Lord on this same issue,[72] perhaps implicitly hoping to elicit even greater anger and hatred from the Herodians.[73] Yet, to the religious dismay of the Pharisees who permitted divorce, the Lord's sharp position against divorce, rooted in Genesis,[74] had been even more conservative than the criticism John had levelled at Herod Antipas based upon Leviticus,[75] whose criticism of Antipas, and implicitly Herodias, also had been based upon propinquity, for with Herodias Antipas had married his niece.

Therefore, already now during Holy Week of 30 CE, Jesus found great antipathy and political disfavour among the supporters of

---

69   Luke 3:1
70   Luke 3:1
71   Matthew 14:3-8, Mark 6:17-18, 22-25
72   Matthew 19:3, Mark 10:2-5
73   Mark 3:6
74   Matthew 19:4-6, Mark 10:6-9; Genesis 1:27, 2:24
75   Leviticus 18:16, 20:21; Deuteronomy 25:5-6, Matthew 22:24, Mark 12:19, Luke 20:28

Herod Antipas and his sycophants,[76] equal to if not greater than their hatred for John the Baptist.[77] But Herod Antipas, as an ally of Rome, ruled Galilee, the residence of Jesus, and Peraea to the east of the Jordan River; while Pontius Pilate had been the Roman procurator of Judea, its governor now for four years.[78] And according to the Pharisees' plan,[79] they wanted to draw all these localized civil forces of the Roman Empire into their campaign against the Lord.[80] So, it was in this context, and now specifically with several Herodians close at hand, that the Pharisees approached Jesus as he was teaching in the Temple; and there they asked him:

> Master, we know that you are an honest man,[81] that you say and teach what is right;[82] that you are not afraid of anyone's opinion, because human rank means nothing to you;[83] you favour no one, but teach the way of God according to the truth.[84] Therefore, tell us your opinion.[85] Is it permissible to pay taxes to Caesar or not?[86] Should we, or shouldn't we, pay them?[87]

But Jesus, aware of their malice,[88] cunning,[89] and hypocrisy,[90] said to them:

> You hypocrites![91] Why are you testing me?[92] Show

---

76 Mark 6:21, 8:15; Matthew 14:1-5; Luke 3:19-20, 23:8, 10-12
77 Luke 3:7, 20:34; Matthew 3:7, Luke 20:27
78 Luke 3:1
79 Matthew 22:15, Mark 12:13
80 Luke 20:20; Mark 8:15; Luke 23:2, 7, 12; John 11:48
81 Matthew 22:16, Mark 12:14;
82 Luke 20:21
83 Matthew 22:16, Mark 12:14; Matthew 20:25, Mark 10:42, Luke 22:25; Matthew 20:26-28, John 18:36, Philippians 2:6-8
84 Mark 12:14, Matthew 22:16; John 18:37, 17:17-19
85 Matthew 22:17
86 Matthew 22:17, Mark 12:14, Luke 20:22
87 Mark 12:14
88 Matthew 22:18
89 Luke 20:23
90 Mark 12:15
91 Matthew 22:18; Matthew 23:13, Luke 12:1
92 Mark 12:15; Luke 11:37, 52-54

me the coin that you pay for the tax.[93]

And they handed him a Roman silver denarius.[94] Then Jesus asked them:

> Whose portrait is this? Whose title is on it?[95]

And they replied, "Caesar's."[96]

Now, it was against Jewish Law to make images of any person, such as would be found on coins; or to make images of creatures of the earth, heavens, or seas; or to bow down to them or to serve them as gods or idols;[97] and as now was done beginning from Julius Caesar, when the emperor had been installed midst the state pantheon of Roman gods. But, in the ancient world, coinage was more than an ingenious medium of economic colonialism and foreign exchange for subsidizing armies: with stamped images of its various rulers on its coins, it also was the basic propaganda tool of mass media communications for the projection of power by the political authority of the day, who, at that time already for nearly sixteen years throughout the Roman Empire, was Tiberius Caesar.[98] So, Jesus said to them:

> Very well then,[99] pay to Caesar what belongs to Caesar—and to God what belongs to God.[100]

They were amazed at Jesus when they heard this.[101] Also, as they were unable to catch Jesus in anything he ever had to say in public, they were finally silenced in their questions.[102] So then, they now left him alone, and they went away.[103]

93	Matthew 22:19, Mark 12:16; Luke 20:24
94	Matthew 22:19
95	Matthew 22:20, Mark 12:16, Luke 20:24
96	Matthew 22:21, Mark 12:16, Luke 20:24
97	Exodus 20:2-5, Deuteronomy 4:16-18, 5:7-9
98	Luke 3:1
99	Matthew 22:21, Luke 20:25
100	Matthew 22:21, Mark 12:17, Luke 20:25
101	Matthew 22:22, Mark 12:17, Luke 20:26
102	Luke 20:26
103	Matthew 22:22

Shortly, later that afternoon,[104] some Sadducees also came to Jesus with another line of attack.[105] While the Pharisees, more so, had been a populist religious party, the Sadducees, generally, were from the wealthy upper aristocratic and priestly families; and they limited the basis for their religious views more strictly to the Torah, namely, to the written Law attributed to Moses: the first five biblical books of Genesis, Exodus, Leviticus, Numbers, and Deuteronomy. But the Sadducees, in their interpretation of the Law, also denied that there was any resurrection of the body.[106] Yet, even so, a clear hope in the resurrection already had been expressed within Judaism,[107] although within Judaism its full revelation would be achieved only in Christ.[108] Later on, Saint Paul would describe this very hope, also clearly in opposition to the teaching of the Sadducees: one's salvation cannot be achieved through the Law, but it comes to everyone only through the death and resurrection of Christ.[109] As such, therefore, Christianity would not be a different religion from Judaism;[110] but, in fact, in fulfilment of the old covenant, it is its continuation,[111] and under Christ its replacement by himself as the mediator of the new covenant, with its promise of eternal life, for both body and soul,[112] provided for us entirely through the glory of the Lord's death and resurrection.[113]

So then, now in their turn, the Sadducees approached Jesus in the temple with their contrived question:

104	Matthew 22:23
105	Matthew 22:23, Mark 12:18, Luke 20:27; Matthew 16:6
106	Matthew 22:23, Mark 12:18, Luke 20:27; Acts 23:8
107	2 Maccabees 7:9, Daniel 12:2-3
108	Acts 23:6-8, 24:1, 14-15, 20-21, 25:13-15, 23, 26:1-8; 1 Corinthians 15:12-26
109	Romans 5:20-21, 6:3-11, 7:4, 8:28-30; Hebrews 2:5-9, 14-17
110	Hebrews 3:1-6, 12; Matthew 5:17-18, Luke 24:44-47
111	John 4:21-22, Ephesians 2:11-22, Romans 9:24, 8, Galatians 4:4-7, John 8:33-37; 1 Corinthians 11:23-27
112	1 Corinthians 6:19, 14
113	Hebrews 12:22-25; 1 Corinthians 15:35, 42-44, 56-57; Romans 8:18, 2 Corinthians 4:16-18, 5:1, Philippians 3:20-21, Colossians 3:1-4; Mark 16:9-12, Luke 24:13-16, Mark 16:13-14, Luke 24:9-11, John 20:19, 26, Luke 24:36-43; 1 Corinthians 15:3-8, Acts 22:6

> Master, Moses prescribed for us,[114] if a man dies childless, that his brother must marry the widow, his sister-in-law, so as to bring forth descendants for his brother's name.[115] Now, we had this case here where there had been seven brothers living together: the first one married, then he died having no children, but he left his wife to his brother.[116] So, the second brother married the widow, but he also died leaving no children; then the same thing happened with the third.[117] And so on to the seventh brother, they married the widow and died leaving no children.[118] Then finally, last of all, the woman herself died.[119] Now at the resurrection, when they all rise again,[120] whose wife among the seven will she be, since the woman had been married to all the brothers?[121]

When they had finished, after Jesus had listened to them in anticipation and with much improvised patience, he broke his silence to them with this steely reply:

> Surely,[122] aren't you misled, because you understand neither the scriptures nor the power of God?[123] The children of this world take wives and husbands, marrying and remarrying;[124] but those who are judged worthy of a place in the other world and in the resurrection of the dead neither marry nor are given in marriage.[125] For when the dead rise to life, men and women do not

---

114 Mark 12:19, Luke 20:28; Deuteronomy 25:5-6
115 Matthew 22:24, Mark 12:19, Luke 20:28
116 Matthew 22:25, Mark 12:20, Luke 20:29
117 Matthew 22:26, Mark 12:21, Luke 20:30-31
118 Matthew 22:26, Mark 12:22, Luke 20:31
119 Matthew 22:27, Mark 12:22, Luke 20:32
120 Mark 12:23
121 Matthew 22:28, Mark 12:23, Luke 20:33
122 Mark 12:24
123 Matthew 22:29, Mark 12:24; John 5:39-40; Ephesians 1:19-21, Colossians 2:15
124 Luke 20:34; Luke 14:20, 16:18; 1 Corinthians 7:1-2, 8-11
125 Luke 20:35

marry;[126] no,[127] because they can no longer die;[128] for they are the same as the angels in heaven,[129] and being children of the resurrection they are children of God.[130] And now, as for the resurrection of the dead,[131] have you never read in the Book of Moses,[132] where Moses himself implies that the dead rise again,[133] in the passage about the bush,[134] what God himself said to you,[135] how God spoke to Moses and said:[136] I am,[137] the God of Abraham, the God of Isaac and the God of Jacob?[138] Now,[139] he is God, not of the dead, but of the living;[140] for to him everyone is alive.[141] You are completely mistaken.[142]

Then some of the scribes—these were not the Sadducees, but scribes who were Pharisees— shouted out their bravos to Jesus, saluting their agreement, "Well put, Teacher;"[143] but for the Sadducees, on the other hand, they did not dare, and would not ever dare, to ask Jesus any more questions.[144]

---

126   Matthew 22:30
127   Mark 12:25
128   Luke 20:36; Romans 7:1-2, Revelations 21:4, 7-8, 1 John 3:14-15, 1 Corinthians 15:25-26
129   Matthew 22:30, Mark 12:25, Luke 20:36; John 6:63, 1 Corinthians 15:45-49
130   Luke 20:36; John 1:12-13; 1 John 3:2, Ephesians 2:6
131   Matthew 22:31, Mark 12:26
132   Mark 12:26
133   Luke 20:36
134   Mark 12:26, Luke 20:37
135   Matthew 22:31
136   Mark 12:26
137   John 8:58; Exodus 3:14, John 4:34; John 8:24, 26, 18:4-6
138   Matthew 22:32, Mark 12:26, Luke 20:37; Exodus 3:6, 15, 1 John 4:9
139   Luke 20:38
140   Matthew 22:32, Mark 12:27, Luke 20:38; Isaiah 38:16-17, 18-20, Ephesians 1:22-23, Revelations 21:2-3
141   Luke 20:38; John 6:51, 54, 57-58, Revelation 1:17-18, Ephesians 2:4-5, Romans 6:10-11, 1 Corinthians 15:22, Colossians 2:13, 1 Thessalonians 4:14; 1 John 1:1-3
142   Mark 12:27; Acts 23:8
143   Luke 20:39; Acts 23:6-7
144   Luke 20:40

Gospel (on the Road to) Emmaus / 225

But, when the Pharisees heard that Jesus also had silenced their rivals, the Sadducees,[145] they now were greatly alarmed by the Lord's partisan victory, because with the Lord's axe planted firmly against the roots of the Sadducees over the resurrection of the dead,[146] very well they could be the next casualty. They not only needed to win over public opinion and dwindling followers for themselves,[147] they also needed an effective religious pretext to put Jesus to death. So, the Pharisees got together,[148] and in order to justify themselves in their actions, just as another lawyer in an earlier incident had sought to justify himself along the Lord's journey to Jerusalem,[149] they now arranged once again to put Jesus to the test,[150] intending to catch him out, that dreamer, in some apostasy as a capital offence.[151] Yet, soon enough that afternoon, at first a welcomed word, the Pharisees would hear directly from the Lord that he entirely supported their authority, together with the other scribes, in the chair of Moses.[152] However, ultimately, and also unequivocally, Jesus then would reject their role to provide guidance, because the Pharisees and scribes were hypocrites.[153]

Yet, before this happened, according to the plan of the Pharisees, they tried to conceal their intended attack by recruiting one of their members to put forward their question, without obviously exposing their plot: a scribe, who had listened to the debates with Jesus, so this particular scribe was well-informed of the arguments, and because he had appreciated respectfully that Jesus had given the Sadducees a

---

145	Matthew 22:34; Luke 20:26
146	Matthew 3:10
147	John 11:47-48, 12:19, Luke 11:30, Matthew 12:40; John 5:44, 12:43, Matthew 23:5, 28; Matthew 6:1, 5, 16, 7:15, 9:10-11, 14; Luke 13:30, 16:15, 18:9, 14; Matthew 10:32-33, 23:33, Genesis 3:1, 15
148	Matthew 22:34
149	Luke 10:25-29
150	Matthew 22:34
151	Deuteronomy 13:1-11
152	Matthew 23:1-2
153	Matthew 12:1-2, 9-12, 20:28, John 10:11, 19:31, 42, Matthew 12:13-14; Matthew 12:22-24, John 8:44, 47; Matthew 15:1-2, 7-9, 12-13, 19-20; Matthew 16:1-4, 5-6, 11-12; Matthew 21:28-32, 33, 40-45; Matthew 23:3, 13-36

good answer.[154] So, the Pharisees in their deception pushed forward this dedicated and sincere teacher of the Law; but he also was driven by God's design and grace,[155] when he asked Jesus, "Master,[156] which of all the commandments is the first,[157] the greatest commandment of the Law?"[158] Then, like Moses coming down from Mount Horeb,[159] Jesus replied, but as the Son of Man come down from heaven, now face to face with his people.[160] And from there, in God's sacred dwelling place in his high holy City,[161] Jesus, also like Yahweh on Mount Sinai,[162] proclaimed:

> This is the first: "Listen, Israel, the Lord our God is the one, only Lord,"[163] and "you must love the Lord your God with all your heart, with all your soul, with your entire mind,[164] and with all your strength."[165] This is the greatest and the first commandment.[166] The second resembles it: "You must love your neighbour as yourself."[167] There is no commandment greater than these.[168] On these two commandments depend the whole Law, and the Prophets too.[169]

The Lord, by his inclusion of the Prophets along with the Law, seemed to further support the Pharisees against the Sadducees, who emphasized the Torah, although the actual argument by Jesus had come exclusively from the Torah. Yet, the Lord also supported

---

154	Mark 12:28
155	John 6:44
156	Matthew 22:36
157	Mark 12:28
158	Matthew 22:36
159	Exodus 19:2, 16, 20:18-19, 32:15-16, 34:1, 29, Deuteronomy 4:10-12, 5:1-2, 23-27, 9:8-10, 18:16-19
160	Isaiah 65:17-23
161	Isaiah 52:7, 9; Isaiah 64:1-9, 65:1-7
162	Exodus 19:16-20, 20:1
163	Mark 12:29; Deuteronomy 6:4, 5:1, 3
164	Matthew 22:37, Mark 12:30
165	Mark 12:30; Deuteronomy 6:5; Luke 10:27
166	Matthew 22:38
167	Matthew 22:39, Mark 12:31; Leviticus 19:18; 1 John 3:17-18
168	Mark 12:31
169	Matthew 22:40; Psalm 147:19-20, John 1:17

the whole of God's Law and the Prophets with these two great commandments, not just one commandment; and in the Lord's new covenant there would be a third: his very life would be the entire living Law.[170] Then, in what must have been quite a surprising move to his Pharisee colleagues, this conscripted scribe, who by his ensuing conversion was not like the others, and in the sincerity of his heart for the will of God, said to Jesus:

> Well spoken, Master; what you have said is true: "He is one and there is no other."[171] To "love him with all your heart, with all your understanding and strength, and to love your neighbour as yourself," obeying these is far more important than any burnt offering or sacrifice.[172]

Jesus, seeing how wisely this scribe of the Law had spoken, simply said to him as he also may say to some of us:

> You are not far from the kingdom of God.[173]

By the Lord's public elevation of this honest scribe, by his contrasting him to his peers, implicitly, the Lord's statement also was an overt criticism of the Pharisees. After that, in their futile attempt to deny their own hypocrisy, now the Pharisees, also like the Sadducees,[174] didn't dare to question Jesus any more.[175] But, as Jesus was teaching in the Temple,[176] while the Pharisees were still gathered around him,[177] Jesus then put a question to them, as he now asked:

> What is your opinion about the Christ? Whose son is he?[178]

---

170 John 15:12
171 Mark 12:32
172 Mark 12:33; Matthew 9:13; Hosea 6:6, Psalm 40:7-9, Hebrews 10:4-10; Matthew 12:7, Isaiah 53:11, 66:3
173 Mark 12:34; Luke 17:20-21, Matthew 4:17, 3:1-2; Isaiah 66:1-2, Exodus 20:20, Jeremiah 31:31-33
174 Luke 20:40
175 Mark 12:34; Luke 20:40, 26, Matthew 22:22, 46; Isaiah 66:4
176 Mark 12:35
177 Matthew 22:41
178 Matthew 22:42; Matthew 1:1; Galatians 3:29, 16, Genesis 12:1-2, 7,

They told him, "David's."[179] Then, in rhetorical puzzlement and pronouncement of fact, Jesus raised his voice to address the vast assembly filling the Temple:

> How can the scribes,[180] as also do the people,[181] maintain that the Christ is the son of David?[182] Why, David himself,[183] was moved by the Spirit,[184] and calls him Lord,[185] in the Book of Psalms,[186] where he says:[187]
>
> The Lord declared to my Lord:
> take your seat at my right hand,
> till I have made your enemies your footstool?[188]
>
> If here David, himself, calls him Lord, then in what way can he be his son?[189]

As the great crowd listened to Jesus with delight,[190] he was their hope, as the Messiah, the Christ;[191] and when Jesus had challenged the Pharisees and scribes, they were thrilled, for no one could think of anything to say in reply.[192]

And on that day, from that moment forward, no one else dared

Genesis 17:5-7, 15-16, Revelation 1:5, Genesis 17:21, 22:1-2; Genesis 5:1, 1:26, Colossians 3:10, Ephesians 4:22-24, 2:10, Ephesians 5:2

179 Matthew 22:42
180 Mark 12:35; Matthew 22:42
181 Luke 20:41; Matthew 21:9-11
182 Mark 12:35, Luke 20:41
183 Luke 20:42
184 Matthew 22:43, Mark 12:36
185 Matthew 22:43; Hebrews 1:3, Ephesians 1:21; Hebrews 1:13, Colossians 1:15-20, 2:15, Romans 8:38-39, 1 Peter 3:22
186 Luke 20:42
187 Matthew 22:43
188 Matthew 22:44, Mark 12:36, Luke 20:42-43; Psalm 110:1, Joshua 10:24; Acts 2:34-35, 29-33
189 Matthew 22:45, Mark 12:37, Luke 20:44; Ephesians 1:22-23, 17-21, 2 Samuel 7:10-12
190 Mark 12:37
191 Luke 1:47. 51-55
192 Matthew 22:46

to ask Jesus any further questions.[193] In fact, now, Jesus had reached the completion and pinnacle of his public debate; and he had declared that the resurrection and our life with God was at its centre: to be achieved, with the celebration of the Eucharist, by Christ's death on the cross, and to be shown, after his ensuing passion and the concurrent Passover and Sabbath rest,[194] in the revelation of God's power by the Lord's resurrection on Easter Sunday.[195] And our centre in this life—for those who would be found worthy of the resurrection to eternal life, that is, for what would be our share in God's new creation as lead by Christ as the first-born of many sons and daughters in the new Adam,[196] destined as his children of the resurrection—would remain our unreserved and total love of God, embedded in our love of neighbour and our love of self,[197] and also, as Jesus would announce shortly to his disciples, in our mastery of the new commandment that Jesus would give us soon with his Eucharist, namely, to love one another as he loved us,[198] which is the essence for anyone who hopes to be a Christian.

But the children of the world define their eternity by the relative duration and termination of their political and social dynasties,[199] by their marriages or sexual conquests,[200] by the progeny of their spouses or lovers, by the extent of their fame or material legacy, by their power over the lives and fortunes of others, and by their manipulation of the forces and actions of history; and they face life and death pragmatically, in their pleasure-seeking and through their ambitions. On the other hand, the children of the resurrection,[201] at first, for a time they also live and act in the world, but as the children

---

193   Matthew 22:46; Matthew 7:28-29
194   Genesis 2:2; John 19:14, 30-31, 42
195   John 20:1, Luke 24:1, Mark 16:1-2, Matthew 28:1; Acts 3:15, 5:30-31, Hebrews 2:10, 12:2; 1 John 1:3
196   John 1:4, Romans 5:15, Colossians 3:10, 2 Corinthians 3:18
197   John 15:10
198   John 15:12, Ephesians 5:2
199   Luke 12:13, 16-20, Acts 12:20-23; Matthew 6:19, 19:16, 21-22, Mark 8:36, Luke 9:24, Matthew 16:24; John 6:5-6, 14-15
200   Luke 20:34
201   Romans 8:24-25

of God;[202] and they shun the values and aspirations of this world,[203] as God's devoted children of the Light.[204] Some of these children of God,[205] like all children of the resurrection, even now do not marry, for already their hearts are set on the spirit of God,[206] and in this world they already are fully alive in his eternal spirit.[207] Whether unmarried or married, their progeny is the fruit of the spirit in cooperation with the power of God to transform lives and even to change the course of human history, by acting with the fortunes of God's grace. And through this legacy and call of Christ,[208] destiny's children of the resurrection will live forever with the risen Lord in the spirit of God.[209] God's children face life and, in their proper share of the passion of Christ,[210] also death, with faith and courage—for in Christ theirs is one life, and one hope, in the eternal and divine spirit of the one, only, true, and living God.[211]

Readings: Luke 20:45-47, 21:1-4, Mark 12:38-40, 41-44; Matthew 23:1-39

Throughout human history, before the coming of Christ, knowledge of God was a divine capacity of the soul,[212] nonetheless limited by our sin and by our material existence. Even so, God was manifest implicitly in his creation,[213] and also through the human knowledge of good and evil,[214] by knowledge of good as God, being synonymous with the perfection of God, the all-good, in contrast to our human knowledge of good and evil through the distinctive

---

202 1 John 3:18; Matthew 7:24, 26
203 John 15:19
204 John 12:36; Matthew 5:14-15, Mark 4:21-22, Luke 12:35, 2, 8, 12, John 13:16
205 Galatians 3:26
206 Romans 8:5, Colossians 3:1-4
207 Romans 8:9; John 5:24
208 Romans 6:3-11, John 15:16, 19-20
209 Romans 8:29-30; Matthew 17:2, 9, John 11:25-26
210 Romans 8:16-17
211 Mark 12:29-31; John 1:14, 8:31-32; Psalm 27:1
212 Genesis 2:7, 6:3, Psalm 104:30; Genesis 6:17-19, 7:15-16
213 Romans 1:20, Psalm 104
214 Genesis 2:17, 3:3-5

imperfections of sinful man.[215] In order to restore mankind to the life of God, accomplished ultimately by God's creating all things new in Christ, God revealed himself in covenant to Adam and Eve, the first humans; to Noah and his sons, when the Lord destroyed the earth in the flood, towards his purpose of restoring mankind to a new creation in his spirit;[216] and to Abraham,[217] the father of Israel and of many nations, as our father in faith,[218] whose descendants in faith are recipients of God's promises through Abraham's and David's human co-descendent, the Christ,[219] but begotten of the Father's love.[220]

The full revelation of God is accomplished in Jesus, the incarnate Word of God;[221] but first, this was preceded by God's openly established prior covenants, by the revelation of the Law through Moses, and by the word of God given to us through his prophets.[222] Christ never replaced the Law and the prophets;[223] but these imperfect covenants were replaced, by Christ,[224] who was their perfect fulfilment. They were replaced by himself, as the divine embodiment of his new, final, and everlasting covenant with the whole of mankind, which was established on the cross and confirmed by the resurrection. Anyone who rejected this covenant, by their rejection of Jesus, would be doomed by their unilateral rejection of God's covenant promises.[225] Therefore, the Scribes and Pharisees in particular, who had resisted the Christ, were not defending the prior covenants that God had made with his people, Israel. Rather, they were clinging to their own hypocrisy and sin, against obedience

---

215   Romans 7:21-23
216   Genesis 8:1, 1:2, Proverbs 8:30-31, Wisdom 10:1-4
217   Wisdom 10:5
218   Genesis 14:18-20, 15:1-6, 17:1-8, 18:1-2, 9-10, 21:1-3, 22:15-18, 25:19-28
219   Luke 1:54-55
220   John 3:6, 6:63, 57, 14:10, 15:9, 1:34, Luke 9:35, Mark 9:7, Matthew 17:5, John 20:17; 1 John 1:3, 2:23-25, 3: 23-24, 5:11
221   John 1:18, 14:7, 8-10, 21
222   Romans 9:4-5
223   Matthew 22:40, 5:17, 20
224   Ephesians 1:9-10
225   Romans 9:6-8, 2:7-8

to God's Law, which they denied that they opposed;[226] nonetheless, they manifestly were defending their own positions of worldly power and status,[227] and not the Law of God.[228]

So, at some moment late on this Wednesday afternoon, while Jesus was teaching in the Temple,[229] he specifically addressed the gathered disciples, but then with such a voice that he clearly spoke beyond them and to the listening crowds,[230] who overheard everything that Jesus now intended for everyone:[231]

> The scribes and the Pharisees occupy the chair of Moses.[232] Therefore, you must do and observe whatever they tell you; but don't be guided by their example, because they fail to practice what they preach.[233] Although they tie up heavy burdens and lay them on people's shoulders, they won't lift a finger to move them. Not they![234] Whatever they do is designed only to draw attention to themselves, like their widening their phylacteries and lengthening their tassels.[235] Be wary about the teachers of the Law![236] They love to take front seats in the synagogues and places of honour at banquets,[237] to walk about in long robes, and to be greeted with respect in market squares,[238] saluted as "Rabbi."[239] But these are men who devour the property

---

226 Luke 16:17, Matthew 6:1-2, 5, 16; Romans 2:5-6, John 9:40-41
227 Matthew 6:24, Luke 16:14-15
228 Matthew 5:19
229 Mark 12:38
230 Luke 20:45
231 Matthew 23:1
232 Matthew 23:2; John 7:19
233 Matthew 23:3
234 Matthew 23:4; Luke 11:46
235 Matthew 23:5; Deuteronomy 11:18, 6:8, 5:1, 22, Exodus 13:9, 16; Numbers 15:38-40
236 Mark 12:38, Luke 20:46
237 Mark 12:39, Luke 20:46; Matthew 23:6
238 Mark 12:38, Luke 20:46; Matthew 23:7
239 Matthew 23:7

of widows,[240] and then, for show, recite long prayers.[241] The sentence they receive will be the more severe.[242]

Then, before Jesus now continued with his public address, he may have turned towards his disciples, who were close at hand, or he may have made his remarks to them at some other time; but either way, the Lord quite definitely now continues his thoughts.[243] And very likely, Jesus may have adjusted his voice to accommodate more gently his proximity to his disciples; but while everyone was listening, clearly he instructed the disciples, in front of his public and theirs:

> However, you must not let yourselves be called Rabbi, because you have only one Master,[244] and you are all brothers.[245] You must not call anyone on earth your father, because you have only one Father,[246] and he is in heaven.[247] Nor must you let yourselves be called teachers, for you have but one Teacher, the Christ.[248] For the greatest among you must be your servant.[249] Anyone who exalts himself will be humbled, and anyone who humbles himself will be exalted.[250]

Then, without his missing a beat, Jesus exploded in scathing rhetoric against the self-righteous hypocrisy of those self-exalted princes of the Temple, the Pharisees and scribes.[251] And he warned them solemnly seven-fold, fully and finally, of their certain perdition if, against his desire and hope for them,[252] they remained rebellious

---

240 Mark 12:40, Luke 20:47; Mark 12:42-44, Luke 21:1-4
241 Mark 12:40, Luke 20:47; Matthew 6:1, 5
242 Mark 12:40, Luke 20:47
243 Matthew 23:6-7
244 Matthew 23:8; John 13:13; Colossians 3:22
245 Matthew 23:8; 1 John 3:1, 11, 10, 2:9-10
246 Matthew 23:9; Romans 8:15
247 Matthew 23:9; Matthew 6:9
248 Matthew 23:10; John 13:13-14
249 Matthew 23:11; John 13:15-16, 15:12-15; Matthew 20:25-28, Mark 10:42-45, Luke 22:24-27
250 Matthew 23:12; Luke 14:11, Matthew 23:6, Luke 14:7; Luke 11:43, Matthew 23:7; Luke 18:14, 11-12, Mark 12:41-42; Luke 1:52
251 Psalm 119:161-163
252 Exodus 25:21-22, Matthew 5:17-19, 9:13; Romans 4:20, 5:2, 5, 9-11; 1

and stiff-necked,[253] and unrepentant and blindly unbelieving in Jesus, the Christ;[254] if they continued, as they shamelessly were doing in their hearts and in their thoughts and actions,[255] with their refusal to heed his words,[256] who not only was from God in his faithful love, but even far greater than Moses and aligned with him as mediator of the Law,[257] he was the very Word of God made flesh for the light of men,[258] God's only Son,[259] and in life and in death on the cross made flesh for the life and salvation of the world:[260]

> How terrible for you, scribes and Pharisees, you hypocrites! You slam shut the kingdom of heaven and lock the door in people's faces, neither going in yourselves nor allowing entrance to others who want to go in.[261]
>
> How terrible for you, scribes and Pharisees, you hypocrites! You travel over seas and across countries to make a single convert; and when you succeed, you make him twice as much the child of Gehenna as you are.[262]
>
> How terrible for you, blind guides! You teach, "If someone swears by the Temple, it has no binding force;

John 2:1-3, John 15:10-12; Matthew 23:37; Psalm 119:145-152

253 Deuteronomy 31:24-27, Psalm 119:157-160
254 John 5:24, 44, 6:28-29, 37-40, Romans 3:22-26
255 Matthew 13:14-15, John 12:39-41, Isaiah 6:1-10
256 John 5:45-47, Deuteronomy 31:27, Luke 16:29-31; Psalm 119:25-32
257 Matthew 17:2-3, Deuteronomy 32:47, Romans 2:12-13, 3:21, 27-28, 4:14-15, Hebrews 10:26-29, 8:6-9; John 1:17, Revelation 15:2-4, Deuteronomy 32:4, 31, 43, Psalms 118:1, 119:41-48, Romans 15:9, 2 John 1:3, 6, 1 John 5:3, John 15:12, Matthew 11:29-30; Exodus 24:3-8, 1 Corinthians 11:24-27; Exodus 25:16, Deuteronomy 5:22, 1-21, 32, 6:1-6, 7:6-12, John 15:16-17, 1-2; Psalm 119:97-104
258 John 1:4, 9, 8:12, 9:5, 11:9-10; Psalm 119:129-136
259 Matthew 21:37, John 10:36, 7:28-29; Matthew 17:5, Mark 9:7-8, Luke 9:34-35; Psalm 119:105-112
260 John 1:1, 14, 10-11; John 6:45, 51, 63, John 10:10-11; Psalm 119:73-80
261 Matthew 23:13; Luke 11:52; John 10:9, Psalm 118:19-21; Luke 16:16-17; Psalm 119:169-176
262 Matthew 23:15; 1 John 3:10, 8-9; Luke 13:28; Psalm 119:89-96

but if by the gold of the Temple, then one is bound to the oath."[263] Blind fools! Which has greater value, the gold, or the Temple that makes the gold sacred?[264] And you teach, "If anyone swears by the altar, it means nothing, but if by the offering on the altar, then one is obligated."[265] Which is more important, the gift, or the altar that makes sacred the gift?[266] So then, anyone who swears by the altar is swearing by it, and by all the offerings on it.[267] And anyone who swears by the Temple is swearing by it, and by the One who dwells therein.[268] And, when someone swears by heaven, he is swearing by the throne of God, and by the One who is seated on it.[269]

How terrible for you, scribes and Pharisees, you hypocrites! You pay to God a tithe of even the most ordinary herbs,[270] mint and dill and cumin, but you have neglected the weightier matters of the Law—justice, mercy and fidelity! These you should have practiced, and not neglected the others.[271] You blind guides, who strain out gnats and swallow camels.[272]

How terrible for you, scribes and Pharisees, you hypocrites! You clean your cup and dish on the outside and leave the inside full of extortion and self-indulgence.[273] Blind Pharisee! First cleanse the inside of cup and dish, so that it and the outside may be clean.[274]

---

263 Matthew 23:16
264 Matthew 23:17; Psalm 119:69-72
265 Matthew 23:18; Mark 7:11-13, 9, Matthew 15:5-11, 14
266 Matthew 23:19; Psalm 119:65-68
267 Matthew 23:20
268 Matthew 23:21
269 Matthew 23:22
270 Deuteronomy 14:22
271 Matthew 23:23, Hosea 2:21-22; John 7:19, 5:45, Romans 9:31, 10:2-8; Psalm 119:33-40
272 Matthew 23:24; Psalm 119:137-144
273 Matthew 23:25; Luke 11:39; Psalm 119:41-48
274 Matthew 23:26; Psalm 119:117-120

How terrible for you, scribes and Pharisees, you hypocrites! You are like whitewashed tombs, which appear beautiful on the outside, but on the inside are full of dead men's bones and every kind of corruption.[275] In the same way, on the outside you appear righteous, but inside you are filled with hypocrisy and lawlessness.[276]

How terrible for you, scribes and Pharisees, you hypocrites! You build the tombs of the prophets and decorate the memorials of the upright,[277] and you say, "If we had lived in the days and time of our ancestors, we never would have joined them in shedding the blood of the prophets."[278] Thus your own evidence testifies against you, that you are the children of those who murdered the prophets![279] Very well then, finish off what your ancestors started.[280]

You snakes, and sons of snakes! How can you expect to escape the approaching condemnation to Gehenna?[281] Therefore, behold, I am sending you prophets and wise men and scribes; and some of them you will slaughter and crucify, some you will scourge in your synagogues and pursue from town to town;[282] and doing so, you will draw down upon yourselves the blood of every righteous person ever shed upon the earth, from the righteous blood of Abel to the blood of Zechariah, son of Barachiah, whom you murdered between the sanctuary and the altar.[283] Amen, I say to you: all these

---

275   Matthew 23:27; Luke 11:44; Psalm 119:113-116
276   Matthew 23:28; Psalm 119:121-128
277   Matthew 23:29; Psalm 119:17-20
278   Matthew 23:30
279   Matthew 23:31; Luke 11:47-48; Psalm 119:21-24
280   Matthew 23:32; Acts 7:52; Psalm 118:17-18, Isaiah 66:3-5; Psalm 119:145-152
281   Matthew 23:33; Genesis 3:1, Job 1:6-7, John 8:44, 38; Deuteronomy 32:5, 20, Luke 11:32, Matthew 24:50-51; Psalm 119:53-56
282   Matthew 23:34; Luke 18:31-34; Luke 11:49, Acts 5:40, 7:55-58, 8:1-3, 9:1-5, 5:38-39, 1 Corinthians 9:16-17; Psalm 119:9-16
283   Matthew 23:35; Genesis 4:8, 2 Chronicles 24:20-21; Psalm 119:81-84

things will fall upon the present generation.[284]

Jerusalem, Jerusalem, you who kill the prophets and stone those God sends to you! How many times have I yearned to gather your children together, as a hen gathers her chicks under her wings, but you were unwilling![285] Behold, your house will be deserted, desolate.[286] For, I promise you, you will not see me again until you say, "Blessed is he who comes in the name of the Lord."[287]

After this discourse of the Lord to the Pharisees and scribes, while Jesus was standing there in the Temple, he walked away from them, as then he had told them all he had to say to them, and he found a quiet spot to sit down, an unobtrusive position opposite the Temple treasury.[288] Looking up from moment to moment,[289] he casually observed the people placing money into an alms box outside the treasury chamber.[290] And although he saw many of the rich putting in a great deal,[291] Jesus also noticed a particular poverty-stricken widow putting in two small copper coins, worth about a penny.[292] Calling his dispersed disciples, for them to gather rapidly around him,[293] Jesus told them:

Truly, I tell you, this poor widow has put in more than any of the other contributors to the treasury.[294] For they have all put in money they could spare easily from their wealth; but she, from her poverty, has offered all

---

284 Matthew 23:36; Luke 11:50-51; Psalm 119:49-52
285 Matthew 23:37; Luke 13:34; Deuteronomy 32:11, Psalm 17:8, Isaiah 66:10-13, Luke 18:16-17, Isaiah 66:14; Psalm 119:85-88
286 Matthew 23:38, Isaiah 6:11-12, Romans 11:1-10; Luke 13:35, Romans 11:11, Psalm 119:1-8
287 Matthew 23:39, 2 Corinthians 3:15-16, 14; Luke 13:35; Psalm 118:26, Matthew 21:9, 24:30, 26:64; Romans 11:12, Psalm 119:57-64
288 Mark 12:41
289 Luke 21:1
290 Mark 12:41, Luke 21:1
291 Mark 12:41, Luke 21:1
292 Luke 21:2, Mark 12:42
293 Mark 12:43
294 Mark 12:43, Luke 21:3

she had, everything she had to live on.[295]

The new covenant of the Lord was not like the old covenant of the Law, written on tablets of stone and carried by Moses down the mountain, when Moses, also in his anger and with God's anger in the Law's condemnation of the Israelites, threw down those tablets before God and in their sight, when Moses then saw Israel worshiping the golden calf they had fashioned for themselves.[296] The Law could only bring death because under the Law everyone is condemned by sin;[297] and there is no power through the Law for the expiation of sin. But under the new covenant there is eternal life,[298] established in the blood of Christ,[299] who, as one with God and the God-man, is both its author and its mediator.[300] In this new covenant, now not written by God on tablets of stone, Jesus gives us himself, by example and sacrifice the embodiment of his new commandment,[301] written in our hearts by the life-giving Spirit of the living God.[302] And it is likewise only through our selfless love and service to others that we fully love the invisible God in his primacy and in his totality.[303] This now was the very love of the penniless widow,[304] and also it would be the same love as witnessed in the 20th century lives of Dietrich Bonhoeffer and Maximilian Kolbe, each of whom surrendered his own life to certain death in Nazi concentration camps, by offering all they had, their lives in exchange for others, just like Christ, who surrendered all he had to give in order to save us from death, his entire life poured out to death on the cross for us, for the forgiveness of our sins.[305]

Under the covenants of the Old Testament, there had been

---

295 Mark 12:44, Luke 21:4; Matthew 22:37-40
296 Exodus 32:7-8, 15-19
297 Romans 3:19-20, 4:15
298 John 17:3, 1 John 4:9-10
299 Romans 3:25-26
300 Hebrews 2:17, 10-16, 5-9, 5:1, 5-10, 7:6-28
301 John 15:12; 1 John 3:11, 2:6
302 2 Corinthians 3:3, 6; 1 Corinthians 12:7; 1 John 2:27-
303 Matthew 25:40; Matthew 23:11, Deuteronomy 6:5, Romans 13:8-10
304 Mark 12:42, 44, Luke 21:2, 4
305 John 10:17-18, Philippians 2:3-8

various divinely instituted laws, customs and traditions: the Decalogue,[306] the Sabbath rest,[307] male circumcision,[308] certain dietary restrictions and practices,[309] the keeping of feasts and holy days,[310] and proscriptions for the various types of sacrifices and offerings.[311] In the transitions of the early church, there had been significant controversy among Christianized Jews who thought that Jewish customs and traditions, like circumcision,[312] were to be conserved; or that Jewish customs should be adopted by Gentile converts to Christianity; or conversely, Gentile Christians often were in a quandary when they encountered Jewish traditions among Christianized Jews, or pagan customs surrounding meals with their friends, families, and relatives.[313] However, there never was an absolute value to even any of the divine institutions of the old covenant, except for the necessity or requirement to love. For us God's commandment to love never was to be put aside, especially by the misplaced substitution of, or preoccupation with, simply human traditions.[314]

Therefore, for Jews and Gentiles alike, after Christ there would be no more temple sacrifices or offerings,[315] no more annual festivals, New Moons, or Sabbaths,[316] no more circumcisions,[317] and all foods would be declared clean.[318] The new covenant, according to the Lord's own description,[319] is like a new cloth or a new wine that entirely replaces the old: the new cloth of the new covenant cannot simply be attached to the old covenant by stitching new cloth onto

---

306   Exodus 20:1-17, 35:2-3; Deuteronomy 5:6-21
307   Exodus 20:8-11, Deuteronomy 5:12-15
308   Genesis 17:10-11
309   Genesis 9:3-4, 2:9, 16-17, 3:22-24; Genesis 32:31-33; Exodus 12:1-10, 13:3-7; Leviticus 3:16-17
310   Exodus 23:14-17, Deuteronomy 16:1-17; Leviticus 23:1-44, 16:29-31
311   Leviticus Chapters 1-7
312   Galatians 6:11-16
313   1 Corinthians 10:27-32
314   Mark 7:8
315   Hebrews 10:4-10, Hosea 6:6
316   Colossians 2:16, Hosea 2:13
317   Galatians 5:6
318   Mark 7:19, 1 Corinthians 8:8-13, 10:25
319   Matthew 9:16-17

the old cloak. But, so that the tear in the cloak does not become worse, the old cloak must be discarded altogether, just as new wine is neither put into old wineskins, lest the wineskin burst. Instead, the wine of the new covenant is poured, by the blood of Christ, into fresh wineskins, so that both the wine and the skins are preserved, just as was true for the new cloth.[320] Under the new freedom of Christ's new covenant,[321] the old order of the old covenant was completely overthrown; and in this new order of the new covenant, every person is established as an entirely new creation—by our reconciliation to God in Christ.[322]

Jesus, as our visible pattern of this new covenant, as Christ had been in his example for Saint Paul,[323] simply defines for us a single law—namely, to love,[324] and also a corresponding tradition for us— to both celebrate and to live this love in the Eucharist, perpetually and in perpetuity.[325] Within this new law and tradition of Christ, every human culture is not just allowed, but is encouraged to retain its now specifically Christianized customs, languages, music, and indeed, its every form of art. So, there must no longer be any implicit or allegedly explicit cultural or ethnic imperialism in our lives, but only our respect for cultural diversity and our proactive defence of it, which is intrinsic to everyone's particular celebration of their new life in Christ,[326] as we strive to live our love of God everyday in our personal and interpersonal lives, and as we so do everywhere within the living customs and languages and developing traditions of our local liturgies, all centred in Christ.

---

320 Colossians 3:12-14
321 Romans 6:15-18, 7:6, Galatians 5:13-14
322 2 Corinthians 5:17-18, Hebrews 10:14, Galatians 6:15
323 1 Corinthians 11:1, 4:1, 9-17, 9:19-23, 2 Corinthians 5:19-21, 3:5-6
324 John 15:17, 1 John 3:11, 23, Matthew 5:43-48, I John 4:8, 16-17; Matthew 5:17, 22:37-40, 7:12; Romans 9:16-18, 22-24, 8:35-39, 1 Corinthians 1:9, 12:31-13:13
325 1 Corinthians 11:23-25, Luke 22:19-20, Matthew 26:26-29, Mark 14:22-25, John 12:24, 1 Corinthians 15:36-37
326 Romans 8:29, Colossians 3:10-11

Reflective Prayer: Psalms 140:2-14, 124:1-8, 69:2-37

Antiphon: Your ways, O Lord, are faithfulness and love
　　　for those who keep your covenant.

　　Deliver me, O Lord, from evil men;
　　　　keep me safe from the violent,[327]
　　whose hearts are bent on plotting evil,
　　　　who stir up conflicts day after day;[328]
　　their tongues are as barbed as a serpent's,
　　　　like viper's venom the words upon their lips.[329]
　　Keep me, O Lord, from the clutches of the wicked;
　　　　preserve me from violent men,
　　　　for they are determined to achieve my downfall.[330]
　　Arrogant men are setting snares along my path;
　　　　they hide pitfall and noose to trap me where I walk.[331]

　　I say to the Lord: "You are my God,"
　　　　listen, O Lord, to the cry of my prayer.[332]
　　Yahweh, my Lord, you are my saving strength,
　　　　my helmet for my head when the day for battle
　　　　　　comes.[333]
　　Lord, do not grant the wishes of the wicked;
　　　　do not let their plots succeed.[334]
　　Do not let their proud heads prevail,
　　　　but let them be overwhelmed by their own malice.[335]
　　Let God rain down red-hot coals upon them,
　　　　cast them into the mire never to rise again.[336]
　　Let the slanderer find no rest upon the earth;
　　　　instead, quickly trap the violent in their evil.[337]

327　Psalm 140:2; Luke 20:20; Proverbs 1:11
328　Psalm 140:3; Mark 12:13; Psalm 31:13
329　Psalm 140:4; Matthew 22:16-17; Genesis 3:15
330　Psalm 140:5; Mark 12:15; Jeremiah 15:21
331　Psalm 140:6; Luke 20:24; Jeremiah 15:20
332　Psalm 140:7; Mark 12:17; Psalm 31:14
333　Psalm 140:8; Luke 20:26; 1 Thessalonians 5:8
334　Psalm 140:9; Matthew 22:23; Isaiah 59:7
335　Psalm 140:10; Mark 12:19; Proverbs 1:18
336　Psalm 140:11; Luke 20:32; Psalm 31:17
337　Psalm 140:12; Matthew 22:29; Psalm 31:18

I know the Lord will secure judgement for the poor,
    and justice for the needy.[338]
Then the righteous will praise your name,
    the upright will dwell in your presence.[339]

Antiphon: Your ways, O Lord, are faithfulness and love
    for those who keep your covenant.

If the Lord had not been on our side
    —let Israel say it again—[340]
if the Lord had not been on our side
    when people attacked us,[341]
then they would have swallowed us alive
    in the fury of their anger;[342]
the waters would have engulfed us,
    the torrent running right over our heads;[343]
raging waters would have drowned us.[344]

Blessed be the Lord, who did not leave us
    to fall as prey to their fangs.[345]
Our life, like a bird, has escaped
    from the fowler's snare;
    the net was broken and we escaped.[346]
Our help is in the name of the Lord,
    who made heaven and earth.[347]

Antiphon: Your ways, O Lord, are faithfulness and love
    for those who keep your covenant.

    Save me, God, for the waters have risen up to my neck![348]

---

338   Psalm 140:13; Luke 20:34-36; Romans 3:5
339   Psalm 140:14; Mark 12:26-27; Romans 2:6-8
340   Psalm 124:1; Mark 12:28; Romans 8:31
341   Psalm 124:2; Matthew 22:34-36; Exodus 15:4
342   Psalm 124:3; Mark 12:29; Proverbs 1:12
343   Psalm 124:4; Matthew 22:37; Exodus 14:29
344   Psalm 124:5; Mark 12:31; Exodus 14:28
345   Psalm 124:6; Matthew 22:40; Romans 3:13
346   Psalm 124:7; Mark 12:32-33; Romans 6:22, 7:6
347   Psalm 124:8; Mark 12:34; Romans 8:34
348   Psalm 69:2; Matthew 22:41; Genesis 7:4

Gospel (on the Road to) Emmaus / 243

I am sinking into the muck of the deepest swamp,
   where there is no firm foothold;
   I have stepped into deep waters,
   and the waves are rushing over me.[349]
I am exhausted with my calling out,
   and my throat is hoarse;
   my eyes are strained with weariness,
   searching for my God.[350]
More numerous than the hairs on my head
  are those who hate me without cause,
  those who seek to kill me,
  my powerful and treacherous enemies.
  How can I give back what I have never stolen?[351]

God, you know the folly of my sin;
  my offences are not hidden from you.[352]
Let those who hope in you, Lord most high,
  not be made fools of because of me;
  let those who seek you, God of Israel,
  not be disgraced because of me.[353]
It is for you that I suffer insults,
  that shame covers my face.[354]
I have become an outcast to my brothers,
  a stranger to my mother's sons.[355]

Because zeal for your house consumes me,
  I am scorned by those who insult you.[356]
I have mortified myself by fasting,
  but this only brings taunts against me;[357]
when I clothe myself in sackcloth,

---

349   Psalm 69:3; Mark 12:35; Psalm 31:22
350   Psalm 69:4; Luke 20:42; Isaiah 50:2
351   Psalm 69:5; Matthew 22:44; John 15:25, Isaiah 52:3
352   Psalm 69:6; Mark 12:37; Jeremiah 15:16
353   Psalm 69:7; Matthew 23:1-3; Jeremiah 15:17
354   Psalm 69:8; Matthew 23:12; Jeremiah 15:18
355   Psalm 69:9; Matthew 23:8; Jeremiah 15:19
356   Psalm 69:10; Matthew 23:9; Matthew 27:39-40
357   Psalm 69:11; Matthew 23:4; Luke 23:35

> I become their laughing-stock,[358]
> the gossip of people sitting at the gate,
> and the topic of drunkards' songs.[359]

Antiphon: Your ways, O Lord, are faithfulness and love
  for those who keep your covenant.

> And so, I pray to you, O Lord,
>   for the time of your favour;
>   answer me in your faithful love,
>   the constancy of your saving power.[360]
> Rescue me, and do not let me sink in the mire;
>   save me from those who hate me,
>   and from the watery depths.[361]
> Do not let the waters flood over me,
>   nor the deep swallow me up,
>   nor the pit of the swamp close its mouth upon me.[362]
> Answer me, Lord, for your faithful love is generous;
>   in your tender mercy, turn your face to me.[363]
>
> Do not hide your face from your servant;
>   hasten to answer me, for I am in trouble.[364]
> Come close to my side and ransom my life;
>   redeem me, for I am pressed in by my enemies.[365]
> You know well their insults,
>   the shame and disgrace I endure;
>   all my oppressors are known to you.[366]
> Insults have broken my heart beyond my strength;
>   in vain I looked for compassion,
>   for consolers, but not one could I find.[367]

---

358 Psalm 69:12; Matthew 23:5; Luke 23:39
359 Psalm 69:13; Matthew 23:6-7; Matthew 27:39-40
360 Psalm 69:14; Matthew 23:10; Matthew 27:46, Psalm 22:1, 2 Corinthians 6:2
361 Psalm 69:15; Luke 20:46; Psalm 22:4-5
362 Psalms 69:16, 35:25; Mark 12:40; Isaiah 54:7
363 Psalm 69:17; Luke 21:3-4; Isaiah 54:8
364 Psalm 69:18; Matthew 23:11; Psalm 31:16
365 Psalm 69:19; Matthew 23:31; Psalm 22:16, Isaiah 53:5
366 Psalm 69:20; Matthew 23:32; Romans 15:3
367 Psalm 69:21; Matthew 23:25; Isaiah 51:12

Instead, they put gall in my food;
   and while I am thirsty, they give me vinegar for
      drink.[368]

Antiphon: Your ways, O Lord, are faithfulness and love
      for those who keep your covenant.

Let the abundance of their own table be their snare,
   a trap for their friends.[369]
Make their eyes so dim they cannot see;
   and keep their backs forever bent.[370]
Pour out your fury upon them;
   let your burning anger overtake them.[371]
Reduce their encampment to desolation;
   leave their tents with none to dwell in them,
   for hounding the one you already had struck,
   for redoubling the pain of the one you had wounded.[372]
Add that to their crime after crime;
   exclude them from your saving justice.[373]
Strike them from the book of life;
   do not count them among the upright.[374]

As for myself, in my affliction and pain,
   raise me up by your saving power.[375]
I will sing the praises of God's name,
   glorify him with thanksgiving,[376]
for this will please Yahweh more than oxen,
   more than sacrificial bullocks with horns and
      hooves:[377]
      "You, who are humble and poor, see and be glad;

---

368   Psalm 69:22; Matthew 23:23; Matthew 27:34, 48, Mark 15:23, Luke 23:36, John 19:28-30
369   Psalm 69:23, Romans 11:9; Matthew 23:15; Psalm 22:25-26
370   Psalm 69:24, Romans 11:10; Matthew 23:19; Ephesians 5:1-2
371   Psalm 69:25; Matthew 23:13; Genesis 6:7
372   Psalm 69:27; Matthew 23:38; Isaiah 53:10
373   Psalm 69:28; Matthew 23:29; Isaiah 53:11
374   Psalm 69:29; Matthew 23:33; Isaiah 53:12
375   Psalm 69:30; Matthew 23:27; Romans 8:35
376   Psalm 69:31; Matthew 23:35; Romans 8:38-39
377   Psalm 69:32; Matthew 23:34; Hebrews 10:5, 8-10

>   you who seek God, take courage![378]
>   For God listens to the needy,
>   and does not spurn his people in chains.[379]
>   Let the heavens and earth sing praise,
>   the seas and all that moves in them!"[380]
>
> For God will rescue Zion,
>   and rebuild the cities of Judah,
>   so that people shall dwell in the land and possess it;[381]
> the descendents of his servants shall inherit it,
>   and all who love God's name shall dwell therein.[382]

Antiphon: Your ways, O Lord, are faithfulness and love
   for those who keep your covenant.[383]

>   Glory be to the Father,
>   and to the Son,
>   and to the Holy Spirit,
>   as it was in the beginning,
>   is now,
>   and ever shall be world without end.
>   Amen.

---

378   Psalm 69:33; Mark 12:41-42; Psalm 31:24
379   Psalm 69:34; Luke 21:4; Colossians 2:14-15, Isaiah 49:8
380   Psalm 69:35; Luke 20:41; Genesis 9:7-11
381   Psalm 69:36; Matthew 23:37; Romans 11:11, Isaiah 49:17
382   Psalm 69:37; Matthew 23:38-39; Romans 11:15, 4:13, Galatians 3:16, 29
383   Mark 12:44

Chapter 34

WEDNESDAY EVENING, THE 13ᵗʰ NISAN (5ᵗʰ APRIL, 30 CE)– THE RESTORATION OF THE KINGDOM OF GOD IN CHRIST IS NEAR, AS ALSO WAS THE BASIS FOR, AND THE ORIGIN OF, THE WRITTEN GOSPEL: AND ALTHOUGH EVERYONE'S BEEN INVITED, THE JEWS FIRST, THEY'RE STILL NOT FULLY UNDERSTANDING– EXCEPT FOR THE FIRST ONE FROM AMONG THE HUNDREDS OF THOUSANDS–SHE HAD BEEN LISTENING TO THE MYSTERY IN THE LORD'S DIALOGUES AND REVELATIONS: MARY OF MAGDALA, THE SISTER OF MARTHA AND LAZARUS FROM BETHANY!

Readings: Matthew 24:1-44, Mark 13:1-37, Luke 21:5-36

It was late in the day on Wednesday, just two days before Jesus would die; and it was now immediately after Jesus had finished with his final public denunciation of the Pharisees and Scribes of the Law.[1] Many of these would not follow Jesus; and, regrettably so, he would be denouncing some of them again at his second coming.[2] So, also now, Jesus had strongly cautioned them that soon their house would be deserted; and he told them emphatically that they would not see him again until they should proclaim of him, "Blessed is he

---

[1] Matthew 23:1-7, 13-32, Mark 12:38-44, Luke 20:45-47, 21:1-4
[2] Matthew 26:64, 24:30, 25:34, 41

who comes in the name of the Lord,"[3] just as the crowds had done, only three days before, when they had welcomed Jesus into Jerusalem as the Messiah, the Son of David, in his kingly procession.[4] Yet, it was because Jesus also desired God's mercy fully for all,[5] that he had vigorously warned the Pharisees and scribes regarding their lack of faith and about their non-acceptance of his words.[6] Then, after doing so, he left the Temple,[7] abandoning them to their own eventual desolation and destruction if they so chose,[8] where they would remain in peril,[9] if they continued their refusal to heed his words, the scriptures, and the prophets; if they didn't follow him,[10] where they could not go;[11] and unless, in faith,[12] they had repented and embraced God's forgiveness and love through the cross of Christ, by following Jesus as he was leading them in his way of the cross, and beyond his cross and our own crosses, with Jesus to the resurrection and the glory we would share with him in his name,[13] together with the Father and the Spirit. Amen.[14]

But, because Jesus had critiqued the sin and hypocrisy of the Pharisees and scribes throughout his public ministry,[15] and not just that afternoon only, by now they were already quite familiar with the Lord's speech against them, and just as some of us now also may

---

3	Matthew 23:39, John 7:33-34; Psalm 118:26, Philippians 2:10-11, Revelation 15:4
4	Matthew 21:9, 22:41-45
5	Matthew 23:33-34, 9:13; Psalm 118:1, Ephesians 2:4, Romans 11:32
6	John 12:25-26
7	Matthew 24:1
8	Matthew 23:35-38; Luke 16:29-31, 24:44-47
9	John 8:21
10	John 6:63, 12:48-49, 39-40
11	John 16:28
12	John 9:39, 2 Corinthians 5:7, Ephesians 2:8, Philippians 3:9
13	Psalm 118:18, 16-17, 19-22, Matthew 21:42; Luke 9:23-24, Philippians 3:10-11, Romans 8:16-18
14	Romans 16:27
15	Luke 11:37-54, 12:1; Matthew 5:20, 6:2, 5, 16, 7:5, 26; Matthew 11:16-19, Luke 7:31-35; Matthew 12:41-42, 13:13-15, 15:1-9, 16:12, 21:33-46; Luke 14:1, 7-11, 28-33, 15:1-7, 16:14-15, 19, 23-31, 17:20-21, 18:9-10; John 2:1, 18-22, 4:1-3, 5:25, 39-40, 6:28-29, 58, 7:19-20, 8:3-7, 21, 24, 31-34, 9:39-41, 11:44-48, 12:10-11

deserve. Yet, even so, in their idolatry and slavery to the world,[16] many of them ignored the Lord's fiery criticism;[17] and they only multiplied their long-standing determination to destroy Jesus,[18] if only they could find some way then, both in their sin and in ours, to kill him.[19] And also now for the disciples, although Jesus already had told them plainly three times about his coming passion and death,[20] they still had not grasped what all along he had been telling them. Instead, what was about to happen, now in just two days time, would scatter the disciples in a fearful confusion, at first.[21] Only later, after the Lord had risen from the dead,[22] and then not until after the coming of the Spirit at Pentecost, would God's arrangements for our salvation become clearer to the spirit-emboldened disciples, then most astonishingly and profoundly so.[23]

But now, as when from the previous year close to Passover after the Lord had fed the five thousand from five barley loaves and two fish,[24] everyone would have made Jesus King prematurely, especially now;[25] indeed, even from the very beginning it was so, when Andrew first had sought out his brother, Simon Peter, telling him that he had found the Messiah, and then when, along with Andrew to Peter, John also had run to fetch his brother James.[26] In fact, all of the disciples had longed for and had believed regarding the Christ, that in fulfilment of the scriptures, Jesus would be the one, as God's King, to restore David's throne to Israel, in God's Kingdom

---

16   John 8:33-36
17   John 12:42-43
18   Matthew 12:14, John 5:18
19   John 8:37, 11:53, Mark 14:1, Matthew 26:3-4
20   Luke 9:22, 44, 18:31-34
21   Matthew 26:56, Mark 14:50; Luke 22:31-32, Matthew 26:31, Mark 14:27, John 16:32, Zechariah 13:7
22   Matthew 26:32, Mark 14:28, Luke 24:1-8
23   Luke 24:30-45, 46-49, Acts 1:4-5, 2:1-4, 14-39; John 14:15-17, 3:3, 8; 1 John 4:13; Matthew 10:26
24   John 6:8-9
25   John 6:14-15
26   John 1:41-42

to come;[27] just as Nathanael (Bartholomew)[28] had proclaimed of the Lord in the beginning;[29] and just as also very recently James and John had longed to sit, soon, with the Lord in the glory of his kingdom;[30] and just as the crowds, most recently and dramatically, had proclaimed of Jesus in Jerusalem that he was their king.[31] And, if imminently Jesus were to become King of Israel—exactly what the Pharisees and the chief priests now anticipated and feared—then surely there would be the most severe repercussions from Rome against themselves, against their temple, and against the nation.[32]

Yet, if the Pharisees and scribes were to have any hope for their place in the heavenly Kingdom of God, or indeed even hope to share in its establishment upon the earth, they would have to surrender their lifestyles, their power, and their present priestly positions, that always had been unmerited because their levitical privilege was purely a function of birth. And now, in their calling from the Lord,[33] and, in fact, for every child of Eve, all born in sin, as snakes and the offspring of snakes;[34] but as this calling was explicitly articulated by Jesus two Passover's earlier to Nicodemus, a leader among the Jews, when Nicodemus had met privately with the Lord;[35] soon now their levitical priesthood would be replaced by the imminent and superior priesthood of Christ.[36] Because, not just the physical descendents of Levi or descendents of the sons of Aaron;[37] but now,

---

27	John 1:43-49; Mark 1:15-15, Matthew 4:23, 5:17-20, Luke 4:42-44; Matthew 10:1-7, Luke 9:1-2; Matthew 6:9-10, Luke 11:2; John 18:36, Hebrews 12:2, 1 Corinthians 15:24-28; Zechariah 12:8, Malachi 3:1
28	Matthew 10:3
29	John 1:49
30	Mark 10:37, Matthew 20:20-21; Luke 17:22, Matthew 13:17
31	Matthew 21:10-11, John 12:13, Luke 19:37-40, Mark 11:9-10
32	John 11:48-49; Amos 9:8-10, 11, John 12:24
33	Matthew 23:33-34; 22:41-44, 34-40, 21-22, 1-3; 21:33, 43, 28-32, 9-17, John 2:18-22, Matthew 3:1-2, 7
34	Genesis 3:15; 1 John 5:1
35	John 3:1-5
36	Matthew 21:12, Mark 11:15, Luke 19:45, John 2:13-16; Leviticus 16:11-16, Hebrews 9:11-12, 7:15-17, 20-22, 28, 8:1-2, 6, 9:24-26; Psalm 110:4, Genesis 14:18, 1 Corinthians 11:23-25; Matthew 22:41-44, Psalm 110:1, Matthew 22:45-46, Acts 2:22-35, Hebrews 1:13, 7-8
37	Numbers 3:2-3, 6, 12, 7-9

in fact for anyone, and not just Jews but for everyone, to enter God's Kingdom—in the same and very faith of Abraham,[38] who, at the Lord's command, would have sacrificed Isaac, his only son by his wife Sara[39]— so now to enter God's Kingdom, through our faith in God, the Father, who gave us his only true Son,[40] everyone now must have faith in Abraham's descendent, the Christ,[41] and be born again.[42] Thereby, when we become God's children through baptism,[43] we also are joined with Christ, through his death and resurrection, into his royal priesthood,[44] as an entire kingdom of priests.[45] This privilege has been totally unmerited, except through our faith in Christ by the privilege of his grace;[46] for us, however, it is merited entirely and fully by the mercy and sacrifice of Christ.[47]

So, for Jesus, his focus now was on the great day of our salvation that was at hand, presently only in two days time.[48] But the disciples, in contrast, still had their heads in the clouds; or, more particularly, as they were going away from the temple with the Lord, they now were entirely preoccupied with the colossal colonnades and buildings of the temple, previously constructed in their elegant splendour under Herod the Great.[49] Like daydreaming schoolchildren, the disciples were not giving their thoughts to their Master's actual mission;[50] instead, they even tried to draw the Lord's attention away from his own thoughts, and towards the grand marble buildings and structures of the temple, particularly Herod's Royal Portico. The latter would have been a genuinely magnificent distraction: with its two side-aisles, nine

---

38	Romans 4:16
39	Genesis 22:1-3, 8-10, Hebrews 11:17-19; John 1:35-37
40	Romans 4:25, 1 Peter 1:20-21, Romans 8:3
41	Galatians 3:16, 26-27, 29, John 3:3-5
42	John 3:5, 15-16
43	Romans 8:17
44	Hebrews 5:5-6, 7:11-17
45	Romans 6:3-5, Revelation 20:6, 7:9-17, 5:1-8, 9-10, 1 Peter 2:9, Daniel 7:18
46	John 3:3, 5-7
47	John 3:14, Hebrews 10:5; Hebrews 10:19-23
48	2 Corinthians 6:2, Acts 3:26, Isaiah 49:8, John 8:33-36, 56, Galatians 4:4-6, 5:1
49	Matthew 24:1
50	John 10:18

metres wide by fifteen metres high, and its centre-aisle of twice those dimensions, with its ornately-carved wooden roof supported by 162 gleaming white-marble columns, respectively, for the side and centre aisles, rising to their height of fifteen and thirty metres, and topped by their Corinthian capitals. It was at this moment when one of the twelve disciples [probably the Iscariot][51] said to Jesus, "Master, look at the size of those stones and the size of those buildings!"[52] And also some of the other disciples chimed in about how the temple was adorned with its fine stonework and votive offerings.[53]

But then, literally and figuratively, Jesus could have dropped a bomb, as he told them:

> You see all of these great buildings and all of these things you are staring at now—in truth I tell you, the time will come when not a single stone will be left upon another; everything will be destroyed, and everything will be pulled down.[54]

That pronouncement, now from the Lord made for the second time, clearly was not rhetorical; but only now did it leave the disciples nearly speechless, as they made their way with Jesus to the Mount of Olives, an irregular walk of only about one-kilometre; but now the distance was interminable as their thoughts raced in shock psychedelically ahead of them. Foremost, the very contemplation of the coming destruction of the temple, and implicitly with it all of Jerusalem, explicitly contradicted the disciples' most deeply held messianic political expectations for the nation of Israel: for it to be a temporal regnum of everlasting peace and justice,[55] which was a basic belief and unquestioned aspiration that fervently they still would hold forty-four days later, right up to the Lord's clarification of this same issue the very moment before his ascension,[56] to be followed another ten days after that by their eventual understanding

---

51 John 6:70, Matthew 4:8-9, Luke 4:8
52 Mark 13:1; Mark 11:17-18, 12:7-12
53 Luke 21:5; Luke 4:5-8
54 Matthew 24:2, Mark 13:2, Luke 21:6; Luke 19:41-44, Jeremiah 26:18
55 Isaiah 60:17, Joel 4:18-21, Amos 9:13-15; Galatians 5:5, 2:19-20
56 Acts 1:3, 6-11

Gospel (on the Road to) Emmaus / 253

through the Lord's gift of the Holy Spirit on Pentecost.[57] Still, for now, the disciples had not yet understood the prophecy of Ezekiel, that on the day that the Lord cleansed us from all our guilt, he would be building a New Jerusalem from its ruins,[58] and the structures of that city would be the myriad indestructible temples of the Spirit in our hearts,[59] with Jesus as our King.[60]

But, in contrast, the Pharisees and scribes had believed that Jesus, as King, would bring the destructive wrath of the Romans down upon themselves, the temple, and the nation, which they actually would bring upon themselves;[61] and the disciples had believed, with the coming Kingdom of God, the great Day of Yahweh,[62] that God's power ultimately would bring Jesus to David's throne.[63] Yet now, with this present revelation from the Lord, it seemed to them that the Kingdom of God actually would bring about the very destruction of the world itself,[64] and with the world their temple, the physical centre of their religious and social world[65]—so that, with the world's destruction, there not only would be the metaphysical destruction of evil, along with Satan's spiritual powers, but there would be the full destruction of his intrinsic material powers, too.[66] Also now, the thoughts of the disciples raced back to the original destruction of the first temple, to the formerly glorious times of Solomon's temple, now having been destroyed under Nebuchadnezzar for 616 years (and four months) earlier.[67] And, at the same time, their thoughts rushed

---

57   Acts 2:1, John 16:13, Acts 2:33
58   Ezekiel 36:33-36, Revelation 21:10
59   John 4:23-24; John 2:19-21, 1 Corinthians 3:16-17
60   Revelation 5:13, 22:3
61   John 11:48-49, Matthew 23:30-36, Obadiah 15; Matthew 24:1-2
62   Joel 4:14-16, Isaiah 60:19-20, Amos 5:14-20; Matthew 27:51, 45, 28:1-2, Mark 16:2, Luke 24:1-3, John 20:1, 1 John 1:5-7, Revelation 21:23
63   Daniel 7:13-14, Matthew 26:63-65; Isaiah 60:21-22, Jeremiah 3:17-18, Joel 4:17-21, Amos 9:10-12
64   John 1:10; 1 John 2:2, 15-17; 1 Corinthians 7:29-31, 1 Peter 4:7, Revelation 20:11, 21:1-2
65   Psalm 122:1-9
66   Luke 8:26-30, 9:1-2, 49-50, 10:17-20, 11:14-18, 2, 4:33-37; Matthew 8:29, 12:28; John 12:31-32, Revelation 20:1-3, 7-10; 1 Corinthians 15:24-26, 50-53; 1 John 3:7-10, Matthew 3:1-7
67   2 Kings 25:8-9; Daniel 1:1, 2 Chronicles 36:5-21; 2 Kings 25:1-4, 8-17,

forwards: now to the same relative fate for their majestic second temple of Jerusalem. And with its devastation for the second time, their aspirations for the kingdom of Israel were incomprehensibly shaken.

So, after the disciples arrived to their place at the Mount of Olives, in what then must have seemed to them like an eternity; and then only after Jesus had sat down; at last, Peter, James, John, and Andrew, the two sets of brothers and the first disciples of the Lord,[68] found themselves quietly alone with Jesus.[69] And as these five were facing the temple from the mountain groves across the Kidron Valley,[70] these four disciples, now on behalf of the other eight, who had been talking quietly about all of this among themselves, and then also on behalf of the rest of us,[71] these four disciples put everyone's burning question to Jesus:

> Master, tell us! When will this happen? And then, what sign will there be of your coming and of the end of the world,[72] when all of this is about to take place?[73]

In reply, Jesus spoke to all of the disciples with unmistakable allusions to the language and allegories of the prophets. He began, at first, by telling them and his temporal church of the immediate generation, and of the near and distant futures:

> Watch out! See that no one fools you.[74] Many will come using my name and saying, "I am He,[75] the One,[76] the Messiah,"[77] and that, "The time is near;"[78]

　　　18-20, 25:1-7, 8-21; Jeremiah 39:1-2, 3-10; Lamentations 1:1, 10, 21
68　　Mark 1:16-20, Matthew 5:18-22; Luke 5:1-2, John 1:35-37, 40-41
69　　Matthew 24:3, Mark 13:3
70　　Mark 13:3; Zechariah 14:4
71　　Mark 13:37, John 18:19-20; Matthew 25:32, 2 Thessalonians 1:8-11
72　　Matthew 24:3; Daniel 7:12-14; Matthew 4:1, 8-12, 17, 5:2-3, 10, 18-20; 1 John 5:3-4
73　　Mark 13:4, Luke 21:7; John 12:31-32, 16:33
74　　Matthew 24:4, Mark 13:5; John 8:44; Colossians 2:8
75　　Mark 13:6; John 8:24, 9:36-37
76　　Luke 21:8; 1 John 5:19-20
77　　Matthew 24:5; John 4:25-26, Deuteronomy 18:19
78　　Luke 21:8; Revelation 1:3, 1 John 2:18

and they will deceive many.[79] Don't follow them.[80] And when you hear at hand the sounds of war and revolutions,[81] and rumours of war, see that you are not alarmed.[82] Listen, don't be terrified,[83] for this is something that must happen first;[84] but the end will not be yet,[85] for it will not come at once.[86] Nation will fight against nation, and kingdom against kingdom.[87] There will be famines and earthquakes,[88] and plagues in various places;[89] and there will be awesome events and great signs in the skies.[90] Yet, all these are just the beginning of the birth pangs.[91]

For now, however, the disciples still expected that Jesus would be their King in a temporal kingdom of Israel, even if only they had imagined this would be soon after the coming destruction of the temple. Its destruction, so then it seemed to them, would lead directly and immediately to the messianic kingdom, newly and permanently restored by Christ.[92] But, his "kingdom of heaven" would not be

---

79   Matthew 24:5, Mark 13:6, Luke 21:8; 1 John 5:21
80   Luke 21:8; 1 John 2:22, 4:1-5, 2 Peter 2:1-3, Jude 4, John 10:4-5
81   Luke 21:9
82   Matthew 24:6, Mark 13:7; Daniel 10:1, 5-6, Revelation 1:12-18, Daniel 12:2-3, Matthew 25:34, 41, 46
83   Luke 21:9; Daniel 10:19, Zephaniah 3:13
84   Matthew 24:6, Mark 13:7, Luke 21:9; Daniel 9:25-26
85   Matthew 24:6, Mark 13:7
86   Luke 21:9; Daniel 2:20-22, 23, 28-36, 44; 1 Corinthians 2:3, Daniel 2:5, 10-13; 1 Corinthians 2:4-10; Revelation 1:1, 19, 3:22-4:1, 5:11-14; Daniel 2:22, John 8:12, 1 John 1:5, Psalm 139:12
87   Luke 21:10, Matthew 24:7, Mark 13:8; Zechariah 14:3, Revelation 16:16, 19:19, 20:7-9, Ezekiel 38:1-18, 39:1-8
88   Matthew 24:7, Mark 13:8; Amos 6:11, 8:11-12, Zechariah 14:5, Ezekiel 38:19-20; Acts 11:27-30
89   Luke 21:11; Amos 6:9-10, Zechariah 14:12, Revelation 15:1, 15:8-16:1, Ezekiel 38:23
90   Luke 21:11; Matthew 16:1-4; Isaiah 60:20, 13:10, Ezekiel 32:7, Joel 4:15, Amos 8:9, 5:18, 20, Zechariah 14:6-7; Matthew 24:29-30, 25:31, 26:64, Daniel 7:13
91   Matthew 24:8, Mark 13:8; Isaiah 66:7-9; John 16:21, Revelation 12:1-2, 5; Romans 8:22-23
92   Zechariah 12:8; Colossians 1:18, Ephesians 1:9-10, 22-23; Haggai 2:6-9, Hebrews 12:28; 1 Corinthians 12:12-14, Hebrews 10:19-21, Revelation

of this world;[93] although it would be in the world,[94] like leaven in dough,[95] slowly but surely working its way towards its inevitable victory over death and sin,[96] which already is gained for those who, through faith and action,[97] are joined with Christ to his cross and resurrection.[98] True religion, however, being truly bound to God and to the mind of Christ,[99] was not to be confused with politics. And contrary to the violent aspirations of many of the political true believers of his age and of ours, the coming of the Messiah and of his kingdom was not to be confused with some political movement, or a political leader, or revolutionary warfare.[100] And neither were the true Messiah and his kingdom to be substituted for, or be replaced by, political actions or ambitions.[101]

God's kingdom would not be built upon the hypocrisies of human greed and ambitions, nor upon the foul blood of political soldiers in the strange name of God, Alla(h), or Yahweh.[102] Rather, God's kingdom was to be established truly upon the will and love of God: upon the foundation of the prophets and the apostles together with Christ, the Righteous One,[103] as our cornerstone;[104] constructed through his grace, in the righteousness and holiness of the saints,[105] by the walls of his "Salvation" for us, and by the gates of our "Praise;"[106] built with the blood of Christ along with the blood

---

	21:11, 18-24
93	John 18:36
94	John 17:15
95	Matthew 13:33, Luke 13:20-21
96	John 16:11
97	James 2:14-17, 3:13; 1 John 2:8
98	John 16:33, 12:31-32; Romans 5:10-11, 8:24-25; Daniel 12:2-3, Revelation 21:6-7
99	1 Corinthians 1:14-16, Ephesians 6:20; Romans 6:22
100	John 18:36
101	John 6:14-15, 11:47-48, Luke 23:2, John 18:33-35
102	Revelation 21:8; 1 John 3:14-15
103	Isaiah 53:11; John 8:46, Hebrews 1:9; Acts 3:14, 7:52, 22:14; 1 Peter 3:18
104	Matthew 21:42; Acts 4:11, Matthew 16:16-18, Ephesians 2:20
105	Revelation 22:14-15
106	Isaiah 60:18, 16; Ephesians 2:21-22, 1 Peter 2:4-6, Revelation 21:10-18; Isaiah 54:11-12

of his saints, the "Martyrs of Jesus."[107]   And after Christ's sacrifice from their very first blood, from the martyrdom of Stephen,[108] and unto the present, the answer to the traditional American Catholic Baltimore Catechism question, "Why did God make me?", remains for all the saints and martyrs, for all of us, the same reply: God made me to know him, to love him, and to serve him in this world;[109] and to be with him forever, both in this world and in the happiness of the next.[110] So, we are made, not for kingdoms of the earth, but for God, who is with/in us.[111]

But in every generation, period, or age, there are false Messiahs who make one fundamental, and a most critical error: they substitute their cultural or personal political aspirations and ambitions in place of true religious faith and justice, as if they were one in the same. This was no exception for the Lord's time.[112] In 66 CE, the revolutionary expression of messianism would lead to the eventual destruction of Jerusalem, its temple, and the nation of Israel itself in 70 CE. Although those events had been anticipated by the Lord, they were written down in the gospel of Mark very likely five to ten years prior to their occurrence; afterwards, they may have been reproduced, wholly or in part, by the other synoptic writers, Matthew and Luke, such that when those evangelists wrote their later versions of the gospel, they may not yet have been informed directly by any of those later events, or by any firsthand knowledge or post-hoc experience of them. Those still future events would have been anticipated in oral tradition from Our Lord and through his written gospel that he inspired. John's gospel was written later, by more than twenty-five years.[113] Yet, even in our own times, and in this same Middle-Eastern territory, messianic politics still provides seemingly intransigent conditions for finding any genuine or lasting

---

107   Revelation 1:6, 9; 2:2, 10, 13, 26-27; 3:5, 10-12, 19-21; 5:1, 9-10; 6:9-11; 7:9-10, 14; 17:6, 18:24, Matthew 23:35-36
108   Acts 7:58-60, 55-58, Hebrews 9:11
109   1 John 3:23, 4:11-12, 16-17; John 12:26; Revelation 1:5-6
110   Revelations 3:20, Luke 22:29-30, Revelation 19:9, John 2:1-5, 11; John 17:24
111   Luke 17:20-21; 1 Corinthians 12:27
112   Acts 5:36-37, 21:38
113   John 11:47-48

peace and justice between the co-existing and competing states of Palestine and Israel, with their factionalisms and nationalisms over shared territories and individual identities.

Similarly, in my present time, it seems that conflicting versions of Eastern and Western messianism account: for so-called "insurgent" bombs in the daily bloodshed of an unstable Iraq; for the nuclear ambitions of neighbouring Iran; for yesterday's bloodshed at Moscow's Lubyanka and Park Kultury metro stations, where two female suicide bombers 40-minutes apart blew themselves up killing and injuring passengers on packed metro trains; and, from just one of many sad examples: for the continuing propagation of mass starvation in the Sudan, when worldwide malnutrition contributes to the deaths of more than five million children every year,[114] now one child every twenty-four seconds, which is to name just one of the many such sins of destruction against God's temples of the Holy Spirit. This also has been the error of some violent distortions of faithful "Theologies of Christian Liberation,"[115] once much the rage in Latin America, as this error has often been celebrated in the example of the former medical doctor turned violent mercenary and revolutionary Marxist, Ernesto (Che) Guevara. Yet now, this messianic error still continues to absorb us: whenever politics, both in philosophy and action, becomes religion, as in right-wing fascism, or as in revolutionary left-wing communism, or as in the latter's opponent, unbridled capitalism—or whenever religion becomes politics, as happens in unyielding Zionism, in radicalized Islam, and even among some Christian groups or Catholic minorities, whenever they forget their centre of true justice and holiness,[116] and instead, operate in the world as political parties rather than as religion—as also happens whenever political parties or politicians hijack religion to their ends; or conversely, whenever religious devotion becomes a simple political or social manifestation, rather than any genuine adherence, or true obedience, to the will of God.[117]

---

114 Matthew 25:37, 40, 45
115 Galatians 5:1, 13-15
116 Matthew 1:23, Luke 1:32-33
117 John 6:37-38, 4:34, Matthew 4:4; Ephesians 6:6-7

Likewise, politics with a religious agenda is as much in error as is religion with some purely political agenda. Therefore, entrenching religious beliefs into political constitutions to the detriment of democratic minorities, as occurs through an advocacy of combined religious and political fundamentalism, is intrinsically wrong, as much as is the suppression of religious freedoms, or as is the autocratic policy of repressive theocratic states; as much as it would be for an alleged Christian to kill an abortionist in the name of Christ, or for alleged Christians to bomb medical clinics where the evil of abortion takes place; just as it is today for terrorists who use perceived injustice, and purportedly Islam, as a platform to justify their outrageous murders and revolutions in public places and in sacred spaces. So also it was for Jim Jones to lead his followers, first from the American heartland churches of Indianapolis to his Peoples Temple of San Francisco, and then from San Francisco to Jonestown, Guyana, where in 1978, finally in the name of his "revolutionary socialism," he directed more than 900 adults, or their infants and children, to their mass murder/suicides. Yet, the root for all of these shocking evils has been the substitution of political values for genuine religion,[118] which, in the example of the United States, is as much an error among some groups of the so-called political "religious right," as it is for any who may form some anti-religious "political left."

So, as the Lord spoke to Peter, James, John, Andrew, and the other disciples, he now needed all of them, both then and in the future, to be religious leaders—and not for any of them to loose their focus by their becoming armed revolutionaries, especially the apostles, who were critical for his future church's foundation.[119] And so, just as many persons, and some nations, now put their faith in the technologies of war, the Lord then wanted his disciples, and his kingdom of saints, instead to put their faith in him.[120] And then, just like now, he wanted politicians to be genuinely holy, or to become religious according to genuine holiness—not for his present and future religious leaders to exchange their vocational roles by becoming professional politicians or political governors of state.

---

118   James 1:27
119   John 18:10-11, 36
120   Ephesians 6:10

The Lord, therefore, warned them, firmly and clearly, against the inevitable false Messiahs, "Watch out; don't be fooled; don't follow them."[121]

Eventually, the disciples would follow the Lord's instructions, but as yet they then were not quite ready to do so;[122] also like the founder of the religious order of the Jesuits, St. Ignatius of Loyola, who eventually turned away from his military career and similarly exchanged his political sword for the cross of Christ; and also like St. Paul, the tentmaker, who would put down his figurative sword of militant persecution and take up the gospel for the sake of Christ.[123] But later, in faithfulness, St. Paul also would accept his chains and the sword that would take off his head.[124] In his letter to the Philippians, St. Paul has provided us with his final will and testament to the power of God,[125] to his faith in Christ,[126] and to his confidence in the final and universal dominion of God's kingdom,[127] superior to any cosmic forces of evil,[128] and superior to all the imperial powers of Rome.[129]

Jesus, then, continued his revelations to his disciples for the immediate and future generations, just as Jesus had warned the twelve when he had sent them out for the first time on his authority, in pairs alone to the House of Israel.[130] But now he was preparing them, for their going out soon to evangelize the world:

---

121 Luke 21:8; James 1:16, 14-15, 3:14-18; 1 John 5:21
122 John 18:3, Luke 22:49, John 18:10, Matthew 26:52
123 Galatians 1:13; Ephesians 6:11-17, 1 Corinthians 1:18
124 Galatians 6:14; Acts 25:1-2, 9-12, 13-14, 25-26, 26:1, 28-29, 28:16-20, 30-31, Philemon 1:22-25
125 Philippians 3:5-8
126 Philippians 3:9-11
127 Philippians 3:12-21, 2:10-11
128 Revelation 12:7-9, 12, 13:2
129 John 18:37, Acts 24:10-21, 25:10-12, 23:11, 20:24; Romans 8:38-39, Colossians 2:9-10, 14-15; Colossians 1:16-18; Revelation 13:7, 17:7, 9-14; Daniel 7:24-26
130 Luke 9:1-2; Luke 10:1

But,[131] watch out![132] Before all these things happen,[133] they will seize you and persecute you;[134] and hand you over to sanhedrins and to synagogues,[135] where they will beat you and scourge you.[136] They will throw you in prisons,[137] and turn you over to be tortured and put to death.[138] You will be hated by all nations because of my name,[139] and you will stand before governors and kings for my sake,[140] since first the gospel must be proclaimed to all the nations;[141] and that will be your opportunity to bear witness before them.[142] Carefully keep this in mind:[143] when they lead you away and hand you over,[144] you are not to prepare your defence in advance,[145] nor are you to worry beforehand about what you are going to say, but say whatever will be given to you when that moment comes.[146] For it won't be you who are speaking, but the Holy Spirit;[147] and I myself will give you an eloquence and a wisdom in speaking that none of your adversaries will have any power to resist, nor be able to refute.[148]

131	Luke 21:12
132	Mark 13:9, Matthew 10:16-17
133	Luke 21:12
134	Luke 21:12; John 16:2, Acts 8:1, 4; Acts 22:4-5, 9:1-2, 10-14; Acts 9:15-16, 1 Thessalonians 2:14-15, 1 Peter 4:16-17
135	Mark 13:9, Luke 21:12; Matthew 10:17; Acts 4:1-7, 5:27, 22:30
136	Mark 13:9, Matthew 10:17; Acts 5:40-41
137	Luke 21:12; Acts 5:17-18, 19-21, 25; Acts 8:3
138	Matthew 24:9; John 16:21; Romans 8:35-37; 1 John 3:16
139	Matthew 24:9; 1 John 3:1
140	Mark 13:9, Luke 21:12; Matthew 10:18; Acts 13:7, 28:7; Acts 9:15, 23:11, 27:24; Acts 24:1-2, 27, 25:1-2, 13-14, 32
141	Mark 13:10; Matthew 24:14; Luke 24:44-47
142	Luke 21:13; Luke 24:48, Acts 1:8, 23:6-11
143	Luke 21:14
144	Mark 13:11
145	Luke 21:14
146	Mark 13:11; Matthew 10:19
147	Mark 13:11; Matthew 10:20; John 15:26; Luke 24:49, John 1:32-33, Acts 5:32, 4:31, 2:1-4; 1 John 2:27
148	Luke 21:15; John 15:27; Acts 5:29-33, 7:51-54

You will be betrayed by parents and brothers, and by relatives and friends; they will put some of you to death.[149] Brother will hand over his brother to death, and a father his child; and children will come forward against their parents to have them put to death.[150] You will be hated universally on account of my name;[151] but even so, not a hair of your head will be lost.[152] Then many will give up their faith, as they will keep on betraying and hating one another.[153] Many false prophets will arise; and they will deceive many.[154] And with an increase in lawlessness, love in most people will grow cold.[155] But by your persevering to the end, you will win your lives.[156] This gospel of the kingdom will be proclaimed throughout the world as evidence to the nations,[157] and then the end will come.[158]

When the Lord spoke, he was quite explicit about what his disciples would suffer, beginning with the persecutions of Jewish Christians by the leaders of the Jews, continuing with the Roman persecutions of Jewish and Gentile Christians throughout the empire, and running through the present age, right till the end of time. Then, Jesus next unleashed a full *kaxxa infernali* [159] of biblical

---

149 Luke 21:16; Luke 8:20-21, 23:23; Matthew 10:34-37, Luke 12:52-53, Micah 7:5-7
150 Mark 13:12; Matthew 10:21; Micah 7:5-6
151 Mark 13:13, Luke 21:17; Matthew 10:21
152 Luke 21:18; Matthew 10:30; Matthew 10:29, 31, Luke 12:24, 31-32
153 Matthew 24:10; Zechariah 14:13-14, Haggai 2:7, Isaiah 60:9-10, Revelation 21:24, 26
154 Matthew 24:11; 1 John 2:18, 2 John 7; Revelations 2:15, 9:11
155 Matthew 24:12; Daniel 12:4, Romans 6:19, 1 John 4:7-8, 1 Corinthians 13:1-10
156 Mark 13:13, Luke 21:19, Matthew 24:13; 2 Corinthians 6:2-10, 2 Thessalonians 1:4-5, Romans 2:7-8; Revelation 2:10-13, 13:10
157 Matthew 24:14; Isaiah 60:3, 16, 22; Joel 3:5, Romans 10:9-13; Acts 1:6-8, Romans 10:15, 1 John 4:9-10; Matthew 13:18-19
158 Matthew 24:14; Matthew 10:23; Luke 19:43-44, 23:27-29, Matthew 23:35-36
159 "Hell Chest" [literal Maltese: *kaxxa* (box), *infernali* (of hell)]: the barrage of mixed and colourful fireworks and very loud petards that concludes a typical Maltese village *festa*, or feast.

language from the prophets,[160] which both reflected their imminent and their later prophetic fulfilments: the former in the passion, death, and resurrection of the Lord;[161] the latter by the destruction of Israel by Rome in forty years time. Most explicitly now Jesus especially quoted phrases from the prophet Daniel;[162] but the evangelist also boldly underlined the emphasis that the Lord had intended for all of his future audiences, by the evangelist's use once again of equally explicit biblical language, namely, "Let the reader understand,"[163] as Jesus then told them:

> So,[164] when you see Jerusalem surrounded by armies, know that its desolation is at hand;[165] when you see the *appalling abomination* set up in the holy place, where it ought not to be;[166] then those in Judea must escape to the mountains.[167] And those inside the city must escape from it;[168] if anyone is on the housetop, he must not come down to collect any of his belongings from the house,[169] just as a person in the field must not turn back to get his cloak,[170] and just as those in the countryside must not go to the city to take refuge in it.[171] For these days are the time of retribution,[172]

---

160   Luke 21:20; Isaiah 29:3, Jeremiah 52:4-5, Ezekiel 4:1-4, 21:27; Luke 24:44, Luke 17:25, Acts 3:18, 24
161   Malachi 3:17-18
162   Matthew 24:15
163   Mark 13:14, Matthew 24:15; Daniel 9:25
164   Matthew 24:15
165   Luke 21:20; Daniel 9:26; Isaiah 10:3, 13:9, 17:9, 24:12, 47:11, 51:19; Isaiah 25:1-2, 7-12, 60:18, 61:4, Matthew 21:42, 22:43-44
166   Mark 13:14, Matthew 24:15; Daniel 9:27, 11:31, 2 Thessalonians 2:4-5, Revelation 13:4, 8, 11-18, Habakkuk 2:18-20, Wisdom 14:7-11, Acts 5:30
167   Mark 13:14, Matthew 24:16, Luke 21:21; Genesis 19:17; Ezekiel 6:1-10, Romans 11:2-5, Obadiah 11, John 19:23-24, Obadiah 12-15; Obadiah 17, Isaiah 4:3, Ezekiel 7:7; Joel 3:5, Acts 2:20, Romans 10:13, Isaiah 4:4, John 19:25, Matthew 27:55-56, Mark 15:40-41, Luke 23:28-32, Romans 3:23-24, Isaiah 4:5-6, Joel 4:17
168   Luke 21:21; Acts 8:1
169   Mark 13:15, Matthew 24:17
170   Mark 13:16, Matthew 24:18; Luke 17:31, Matthew 24:41, 40
171   Luke 21:21; Luke 17:32, Genesis 19:26, Luke 17:33-35
172   Daniel 9:26-27; 1 Thessalonians 5:9-11, 4:13-18

when all that scripture says must be fulfilled.[173] Woe to pregnant women or to mothers with nursing babies in those days;[174] for great calamity will come upon the land and God's retribution will fall upon this people.[175] Pray that, when you make your escape, that this time not be in winter,[176] or on the Sabbath.[177] For those days will be a time of *great distress, unparalleled* since the beginning,[178] from first when God made the world to exist,[179] nor as there ever will be again.[180] If that time had not been shortened, no human being would have survived; but shortened that time will be, for the sake of those who are chosen.[181] Some will fall by the edge of the sword, while others will be led away captive to all the Gentile nations;[182] and Jerusalem will be crushed underfoot by the Gentiles, until their time is fulfilled.[183]

And if anyone says to you then, "Look, here is the Christ!" or "Over here!" or "Look, there he is!" don't believe it;[184] for false messiahs and false prophets will arise and provide (great)[185] signs and (wondrous) portents,[186] (enough)[187] to mislead and deceive (even)[188] the elect, if that were possible.[189] Therefore, you must be on your

---

173	Luke 21:22; Luke 24:25-27, 35-36, 44-47
174	Mark 13:17, Matthew 24:19, Luke 21:23
175	Luke 21:23
176	Mark 13:18, Matthew 24:20
177	Matthew 24:20
178	Matthew 24:21; Daniel 12:1
179	Mark 13:19; Revelation 16:17-18
180	Mark 13:19, Matthew 24:21; Genesis 9:11-15
181	Matthew 24:22; Mark 13:20; Romans 11:29
182	Romans 11:30-32, 11; Revelation 13:10
183	Luke 21:24; Romans 11:23-25, 12; Revelation 11:2, 13:5-7, 18, 20:1-6; Mark 1:14-15
184	Mark 13:21, Matthew 24:23; Luke 17:20-21, 21:8
185	Matthew 24:24
186	2 Thessalonians 2:2-3, 9-12, Revelation 13:11-18, 19:19-21; John 3:1-2
187	Matthew 24:24
188	Matthew 24:24
189	Mark 13:22, Matthew 24:24; Revelation 17:13-14, 19:20, 13:8, Jeremiah

guard.[190] Listen,[191] I've given you clear warning ahead of time![192]

And they will say to you,[193] in the days of the Son of Man,[194] "Look, there he is;"[195] "he is in the desert!"[196] Or, "Look, here he is;"[197] "he is in some hiding place!"[198] But don't move,[199] don't go there;[200] and don't believe it,[201] don't set off in pursuit.[202] For,[203] when the Day of the Son of Man arrives,[204] his coming then will be just like lightning striking in the east,[205] as it flashes from one part of the heavens and entirely lights up the rest,[206] far, far into the west.[207] You know the proverb, "Wherever the corpse is, there too the vultures will gather."[208] Also in those days,[209] immediately after the time of distress,[210] there will be signs in the sun, the moon, and the stars:[211] the sun will be darkened,

---

1:5, Revelation 14:1, 4, Jeremiah 2:3, Revelation 14:5, Genesis 18:17-19, Romans 4:3, 16-17, 25; 1 John 3:7-9

190	Mark 13:23; Mark 13:6, 33; Revelation 20:7-10
191	Matthew 24:25
192	Mark 13:23, Matthew 24:25; Hebrews 2:1-4, 2 Timothy 4:3-5; 1 John 2:26
193	Matthew 24:26; Luke 17:21
194	Luke 17:22
195	Luke 17:23
196	Matthew 24:26
197	Luke 17:23
198	Matthew 24:26
199	Luke 17:23
200	Matthew 24:26
201	Luke 17:23
202	Matthew 24:26; Luke 17:20-21; Matthew 24:11
203	Matthew 24:27
204	Luke 17:24, 22
205	Matthew 24:27
206	Luke 17:24
207	Matthew 24:27; Psalm 97:4, Zechariah 9:14;
208	Matthew 24:28, Luke 17:37; Luke 17:20, John 3:3; Isaiah 66:24, Revelation 19:17-21, Ezekiel 39:17-20
209	Mark 13:24; Matthew 24:29; 2 Peter 3:8-9, Matthew 3:1-2
210	Matthew 24:29, Mark 13:24; Revelation 7:14, 20:4-6
211	Luke 21:25

the moon will not give its light;[212] and the stars will fall from the sky.[213] On earth, entire nations will be in agony, bewildered by the turmoil of the ocean and its raging waves,[214] with people fainting away in terror and fear in anticipation of what menaces the world,[215] for the celestial powers in space will be shaken.[216] Then the sign of the Son of Man will appear in heaven,[217] and all the peoples of the earth will mourn;[218] and they will see the Son of Man coming on the clouds of heaven,[219] with great power, and great glory.[220] And then he will send the angels,[221] with a loud trumpet and a voice,[222] to gather his elect from the four winds,[223] from the ends of the earth to the ends of the sky,[224] from one heaven's end to the other.[225] When these signs begin to happen, stand erect and hold your heads high, because your liberation is near.[226]

---

212 Mark 13:24, Matthew 24:29; Isaiah 13:10, Joel 3:4, Revelation 6:12; Amos 8:9, 5:20, Luke 23:44-46, Acts 2:20, 14, 22-24, 32-33, 37-41
213 Mark 13:25, Matthew 24:29, Luke 21:26; Isaiah 13:10, Joel 3:3, Revelation 6:13, 20:11, 21:1; 2 Peter 3:10, Revelation 6:14, Isaiah 34:4; Matthew 27:51-53
214 Luke 21:25
215 Luke 21:26
216 Mark 13:25, Matthew 24:29, Luke 21:26
217 Matthew 24:30; John 3:13-14, 36, Matthew 3:7, Amos 5:18-19, Numbers 21:5-8, Exodus 32:11, Deuteronomy 8:14-20; John 12:46
218 Matthew 24:30; Revelation 1:7, Amos 8:10
219 Mark 13:26, Matthew 24:30, Luke 21:27; Daniel 7:13; Mark 14:61-62, Matthew 26:64, Revelation 1:7, 14:14, 20:11; Luke 22:67-68, Matthew 4:12, 17
220 Mark 13:26, Matthew 24:30, Luke 21:27; Matthew 25:31; Zechariah 14:6-9, Genesis 4:26, Philippians 2:11
221 Mark 13:27, Matthew 24:31; Hebrews 1:7, 14, Joel 4:11, 9-10
222 Matthew 24:31; Isaiah 27:13, Joel 2:1, Revelation 10:7, 11:15; 1 Corinthians 15:52, 1 Thessalonians 4:16-17, 1 Corinthians 15:53; 1 Thessalonians 4:14-15
223 Mark 13:27, Matthew 24:31
224 Mark 13:27; Deuteronomy 30:4-5
225 Matthew 24:31
226 Luke 21:28

Take the fig tree as a parable,[227] or indeed, take every tree:[228] as soon as its twigs grow tender,[229] its buds have formed,[230] and its leaves begin to sprout,[231] you know,[232] and you can see for yourselves,[233] that, now,[234] summer is near.[235] So with you, when you see these things happening,[236] know that he is here, right at the gates;[237] know that the kingdom of God is near.[238] In truth I tell you, before this generation has passed away, all these things will have taken place.[239] The sky and earth will pass away,[240] but my words will never pass away.[241]

But, as for the day and the hour, no one knows exactly when this will happen: not the angels in heaven,[242] not even the Son;[243] no one knows this, except the Father alone.[244] For, as it was in Noah's day,[245] so will it be in the days when the Son of man comes.[246] In those days

---

227   Mark 13:28, Matthew 24:32
228   Luke 21:29
229   Mark 13:28, Matthew 24:32
230   Luke 21:30
231   Mark 13:28, Matthew 24:32
232   Mark 13:28, Matthew 24:32
233   Luke 21:30
234   Luke 21:30
235   Mark 13:28, Matthew 24:32, Luke 21:30
236   Mark 13:29, Matthew 24:33, Luke 21:31
237   Mark 13:29, Matthew 24:33; Revelation 1:1-3, 3:20
238   Luke 21:31; Luke 17:21, Matthew 3:2, Malachi 3:1-3, 2:17, Revelation 3:19
239   Mark 13:30, Matthew 24:34, Luke 21:32; Mark 9:1, Matthew 16:28, Luke 9:27, John 21:22-23, 1:1, 14; 1 John 1:1-4, John 21:24-25
240   Isaiah 34:4, 51:6, 65:17, 66:22; Hebrews 1:10-12, Revelation 21:1-5; 2 Peter 3:13
241   Mark 13:31, Matthew 24:35, Luke 21:33; Psalm 119:89, Isaiah 40:8, Matthew 23:34; John 5:21, 6:63; Revelation 19:13, Isaiah 63:1, Revelation 19:16; Revelation 22:10, 12; 1 Peter 1:25
242   Hebrews 1:4; 2 Peter 2:4
243   Hebrews 1:8-9
244   Mark 13:32, Matthew 24:36; Acts 1:7; John 5:27, 10:30, 5:30, 14:20, 23; John 1:32, 14:16-17, 16:7, 15:26
245   Genesis 6:13-18, 7:11-16, 8:1-14
246   Matthew 24:37, Luke 17:26; 2 Peter 3:3-4, Acts 13:41, Jude 17-19,

before the Flood,[247] people were eating and drinking, marrying wives and taking husbands, right up to the day Noah went into the ark,[248] and they knew nothing of what was happening,[249] right until the final moment when the Flood came, swept them all away,[250] and destroyed them all.[251] It will be the same as it was in Lot's day:[252] people then were eating and drinking, buying and selling, planting crops and constructing buildings.[253] But on the day Lot left Sodom, fire and brimstone rained down from heaven and destroyed all of them.[254] And that too is how it will be on the day when the Son of Man comes to be revealed.[255]

Watch yourselves! Don't let your hearts become coarsened through debauchery and drunkenness,[256] and by the anxieties of life,[257] lest that day will catch you suddenly by surprise,[258] like a trap,[259] for that day will come down upon everyone living on the face of the earth.[260] Be on your guard, stay awake![261] For you never know when the time will come,[262] on which day

---

      Habakkuk 1:5
247   Matthew 24:38
248   Matthew 24:38, Luke 17:27
249   Matthew 24:39
250   Matthew 24:39, Luke 17:27; 2 Peter 2:5
251   Luke 17:27; 2 Peter 3:5-6
252   Luke 17:28; Luke 21:21, 23:33
253   Luke 17:28
254   Luke 17:29; 2 Peter 2:6-10, 3:7; Genesis 19:23-29, Psalm 11:6; Matthew 10:14-15, 11:20, 23-24
255   Luke 17:30; 2 Peter 3:8-9; Malachi 3:5-7
256   Luke 21:34; 2 Peter 2:17-19, 12-16, 20-22; Matthew 13:14-15, Acts 28:27; Ezekiel 36:26-27
257   Luke 21:34; Luke 12:22-23, 29-31; Matthew 13:22
258   Luke 21:34; 1 Thessalonians 5:3
259   Luke 21:35; Matthew 25:30, 8:11-12, Luke 16:22-26; Psalm 116:3, 8, Psalm 55:22; 2 Peter 3:10; 1 Thessalonians 5:4-8, Psalm 140:4, 7-8
260   Luke 21:35; 1 Thessalonians 5:9-10
261   Mark 13:33, Matthew 24:42; 1 Thessalonians 5:11
262   Mark 13:33

your master will come.²⁶³ But you may be quite sure of this: that, if the householder had known at what time [of the night]²⁶⁴ the burglar would come, he would have stayed awake,²⁶⁵ and would not have allowed anyone to break through the wall of his house.²⁶⁶ Therefore,²⁶⁷ you too must stand prepared, because the Son of Man is coming at an hour you do not expect.²⁶⁸ Stay awake,²⁶⁹ and pray at all times for the strength to survive all that is going to happen, and to be ready to hold your ground before the Son of Man.²⁷⁰

It will be like a man travelling abroad: he has gone from his home, and left his servants in charge, each with his own work to do;²⁷¹ and he has told the doorkeeper to stay awake.²⁷² So stay awake, because you do not know when the master of the house is coming: at evening, midnight, cockcrow or dawn;²⁷³ if he comes unexpectedly, he must not find you asleep.²⁷⁴ Who then is the wise and trustworthy servant whom the master placed over his household to give them their food at the proper time?²⁷⁵ Blessed is that servant if his master's arrival finds him doing exactly that.²⁷⁶ In truth I tell you, he will put him in charge of everything

---

263 Matthew 24:42; Luke 12:37; Acts 7:55-56
264 Mathew 24:43
265 Mathew 24:43
266 Matthew 24:43, Luke 12:39
267 Matthew 24:44
268 Matthew 24:44, Luke 12:40; Acts 7:57-58, John 18:3, 12-13, 28, 19:1-7, 14-16
269 Luke 21:36; Luke 12:41, 1 Peter 5:8
270 Luke 21:36; Psalms 1:5-6, 76:7-9; 1 Corinthians 1:8-9, 15:58; Acts 7:59-60; 1 John 4:17-18, 3:21-23, 2:28; Ephesians 6:10-20
271 Matthew 13:23, 23:34, Ephesians 4:11-13
272 Mark 13:34; John 10:7, 18:16-17, 21:15-17
273 Mark 13:35; Luke 12:38
274 Mark 13:36; Luke 12:35-36, Matthew 25:1, Revelation 19:7-9, 21:2
275 Matthew 24:45, Luke 12:42; John 6:51-63, 64-69; Acts 6:1-4
276 Matthew 24:46, Luke 12:43

he owns.[277] But if the servant is dishonest,[278] and says to himself, "My master is taking his time in coming,"[279] and sets about beating his fellow menservants and servant-girls, eating and drinking with drunkards, and getting drunk,[280] his master will come on a day he does not expect and at an hour he does not know;[281] and the master will cut him off and send him to the same fate as the hypocrites,[282] where there will be weeping and grinding of teeth.[283] What I am saying to you, I say to all: Stay awake![284]

With the death and resurrection of the Lord soon to be at the epicentre of the new church in Jerusalem and of the gospel to the nations,[285] persecutions against the church eventually would come. And with the death of Stephen in Jerusalem, circa 35 CE, now in about five years,[286] many followers of "The Way,"[287] or of the "brotherhood,"[288] would scatter from the city to the countryside to avoid the house to house searches by Saul, or by his henchmen, to avoid being sent to prison, or even to escape from being murdered.[289] As these disciples fled, they mainly were "Hellenists," Greek-speaking Jews from outside of Palestine, as was Stephen, who read the scriptures in the Greek, the Alexandrian Septuagint translation from the Hebrew. On the other hand, "Hebrews," who were the

---

277 Matthew 24:47, Luke 12:44; Matthew 25:14, Mark 13:34
278 Matthew 24:48
279 Matthew 24:48, Luke 12:45
280 Matthew 24:49, Luke 12:45
281 Luke 12:46
282 Matthew 24:51, Luke 12:46
283 Matthew 24:51; Matthew 25:30, 25-26
284 Mark 13:37; Hebrews 12:25, Ephesians 4:10-14, Isaiah 60:1-3; Matthew 13:24-30, 9, Acts 28:28; Mark 14:37-42, Luke 22:45-47, John 18:25-27; Matthew 25: 5, 8, 2-4
285 Isaiah 66:6-7, Matthew 24:8, Mark 13:8; Matthew 28:1-8, 11-15, Acts 1:7-8, 13:32-39; 1 Corinthians 1:18
286 Acts 6:7-12, 7:51-59
287 Acts 18:26, 24:14-16
288 Acts 15:22; 1 Peter 2:17, Acts 4:32-37, 9:23-27, 11:27-30; Mark 3:33-35, Acts 12:25, 13:2; 1 John 3:13-14
289 Acts 8:1-3, 9:4-6, 20-22; Acts 22:20, John 16:2

Christian Jews native of Palestine, spoke Aramaic in the vernacular and they read the scriptures in its original Hebrew or, as in the Book of Daniel, also with a partially vernacular Aramaic text.[290]

But as "Hellenists" and "Hebrews" both fled from the persecution in Jerusalem, they spread throughout the territories of Judea and Samaria and beyond, and they went as far away as Phoenicia, Cyprus, and Antioch on the Orontes River, the Syrian capital of the Roman province. Importantly, Antioch mediated Eastern-Western worlds and then was the third largest city of the Roman Empire. And there in Antioch, the Jewish followers of Jesus from Jerusalem proclaimed the message of the gospel, but only to the Jews.[291] However, independently of these proselytising "Hebrews," some "Hellenists" from Cyprus and from Cyrene in North Africa (today's Northeast Libya) started preaching to the Greek-speaking Gentiles in Antioch; and although these Gentiles had never first been Jews, they came to be the very first of the "chosen" to call themselves "Christians,"[292] by the name of the rising "sect" that would become known throughout the world. And Antioch also would become an independent cosmopolitan centre for the new Christian churches,[293] eventually with its unified supervision from Jerusalem.[294]

After Saul/Paul's conversion and baptism in Damascus in 35 CE,[295] initially for one or two years he went off to Arabia, regions east of Jordan and southeast of Damascus, to preach the gospel before returning to Damascus.[296] Back in Damascus, Saul's preaching in the synagogues proved to be so powerful, in his demonstrations that Jesus was the Christ, that non-believing Jews determined to kill him; but their plot was thwarted by lowering Saul at night over a wall in a basket and out of Damascus; and from there he escaped to

---

290   Daniel 2:4-7:28
291   Acts 11:19
292   Galatians 1:15, 12, John 15:16, 1-2, Acts 11:20, 26
293   Matthew 18:20, 13:31-32; Mark 4:30-31, 3, 14, 32; Luke 13:18-21, 29-30, Romans 11:16-24
294   Acts 11:22-23
295   Acts 9:3, 17-19
296   Galatians 1:16-17

Jerusalem.[297] Once in Jerusalem, Barnabas then took charge of Saul and introduced him to Peter, as leader of the universal church, and to James, the relative of the Lord, who, under the evident principles of subsidiarity and collegiality, would become leader of the church in Jerusalem.[298] Over the fortnight of Saul's stay, when he also had preached in Jerusalem, the Hellenist Jews were so provoked by this that they wanted to kill him, just as had happened in Damascus.[299] So when the Christian community got wind of their murderous intentions, the "brothers" immediately took Saul safely to the port city of Caesarea, where they shipped him home to Tarsus.[300]

And there in Cilicia, Saul, the tentmaker,[301] continued to preach until Barnabas seven years later went to Tarsus to bring Saul back to Antioch, where for a year they first preached the gospel together.[302] Then, sometime after King Herod's (Agrippa I) death in 44 CE, Barnabas and Saul, probably in 45 CE, went up to Jerusalem as delegates from Antioch with famine assistance; when they returned, Barnabas brought back his cousin, John Mark, with them to Antioch, as their assistant in the work of the gospel.[303] After a short while, with support from the Christian community at Antioch, Saul/Paul would undertake the first of his three missionary journeys with colleagues, 46-49 CE, 50-52 CE, and 53-58 CE.[304] Then, finally, after Paul's arrest in Jerusalem and his imprisonment of two years at Caesarea,[305] in 60 CE Paul would leave from there on his mission from Christ: to

---

297   Acts 9:20-25, 2 Corinthians 11:32-33, Acts 9:26
298   Acts 9:27, Galatians 1:18-20, Matthew 13:55, Mark 6:3, Galatians 2:9
299   Acts 9:27-29, Galatians 1:18
300   Acts 9:30
301   Acts 18:3
302   Galatians 1:21-24, Acts 11:25-26
303   Acts 12:24-25, Colossians 4:10; Acts 13:5
304   Acts 13:1-2, 4-6, 13-14; Acts 13:49-51, 14:1-7, 19-28, 15:1-2, 2 Timothy 3:11; Galatians 2:1, Acts 15:3-4, 22-23, 30-35; Acts 15:36-41, 16:1-12, 2 Corinthians 2:12-13, Philippians 4:15, Acts 17:1, Philippians 4:16, Acts 17:10-17, 18:1, 5-11, 18-23; Acts 18:24-28, 19:1-10, 11-20, 21-23, Ephesians 3:2-6, Acts 20:1-3, Titus 3:12, Acts 20:4, 1 Thessalonians 2:13, Acts 20:5-6, 13-18, 36-38, 21:1-8, 15-17
305   Acts 21:27-33, 37-40, 22:22-30, 23:6-35, 24:27, 25:1-6, 7-12, 13-15, 22-24, 26:30-32

Rome via Malta to bear witness before the emperor,[306] Caesar Nero, whom John provides a numerical encryption of his name as the beast, 666.[307]

During those times, not only Christians were persecuted, but hand in hand so were the Jews; and that contributed to their forced migrations to Palestine and throughout the Roman and eastern worlds as "Hellenists." After Tiberias Caesar, Caligula was emperor from 37 CE. And in 38 CE, he initiated a persecution of Jews in Alexandria; in the following year, he ordered his statue to be erected in the temple in Jerusalem, a victory custom typical of the Roman imposition of their pagan gods. In 41 CE, Claudius then became emperor, in the same year that Herod Agrippa I became king of Judea and Samaria. During Herod Agrippa's brief reign, he gained popular support in Jerusalem from Hellenist and Hebrew Jews through his persecution of Christians, most notably when he had James, the brother of John, beheaded.[308] Then he arrested Peter; and apparently in 44 CE, when King Herod put Peter in prison in the last days before Passover, he intended to have Peter tried and executed as soon as Passover had finished, and to be done with him.[309] But Peter, miraculously, was freed when an angel of the Lord intervened,[310] which is when we first meet John Mark, who would be an assistant of Paul and Barnabas together, but with them only briefly.[311]

For, when Peter had escaped from prison, straightaway he went to the household of John Mark's Hebrew mother, Mary.[312] The details of the episode, when Peter is left standing outside knocking at the door,[313] are quite comical—and quite detailed—because Mark must have been there, and Mark also had sufficient opportunities to retell his story to Luke because both of them were together

---

306   Acts 24:27; Acts 27:1-20, 27-29, 39-41, 28:1, 11-16, 30-31; Acts 23:11, 19:21
307   Revelation 13:18
308   Acts 12:1-2
309   Acts 12:3-4
310   Acts 12:5-11
311   Acts 12:25, 13:5, 13
312   Acts 12:12
313   Acts 12:13-18

sometime much later, at least as working colleagues of Paul when he was a prisoner in chains in Rome.[314] Mark also would accompany Peter later when Peter was a prisoner in Rome.[315] Peter's escape from Herod in Jerusalem had been a serious moment for the fate of the church, despite its actual comedic elements. However, in God's irony, it was most unfortunate for the guards, whom Herod then executed in substitution of Peter because of his escape.[316] Yet soon afterwards, King Herod then also met his fate of God's justice.[317]

When Barnabas and Saul, in Antioch, were set apart by the Holy Spirit for Paul's first missionary journey, their initial destination had been no accident: they had started with the homeland of Barnabas, the Hellenist Levite from Cyprus.[318] Their assistant, John Mark, the cousin of Barnabas,[319] also must have had Cypriot relatives from his father's side in relation to Barnabas. Later, when Paul proposed to Barnabas that they undertake their second missionary journey, Barnabas again suggested taking his cousin John Mark, but Paul was reluctant because of John Mark's premature termination of his earlier participation, after his going on with them only to Cyprus.[320] Barnabas disagreed with Paul's reluctance, and so, parting his company, Barnabas and Mark sailed off together to Cyprus.[321] This John Mark, or John, or Mark, is none other than Mark, the evangelist and missionary, the first to produce a written full canonical gospel, his originally Greek-language "gospel," or the "good news," prompted by their evangelization within a dominant Hellenist environment, the intellectual and cultural legacy of Alexander the Great, mediating Western and Eastern worlds.

Literally, Mark initiates this gospel with the words: "The

---

314 2 Timothy 4:11, Colossians 4:10, 14, 18, Philemon 1:24; Acts 19:29, 27:1-2
315 1 Peter 5:13
316 Acts 12:19
317 Acts 12:20-23
318 Acts 13:4, 4:36-37
319 Colossians 4:10
320 Acts 15:36-38
321 Acts 15:39

beginning of the gospel about Jesus Christ, the Son of God."[322] This is the historical beginning of the written Gospel's first literary and canonical text. Characteristically, concise and precise in his catechesis, Mark particularly intended his written gospel as an essential tool for teachers of the Word and as a fast-track primer for Gentile converts and students: so we have the first Christian textbook within the biblical tradition. Similarly, at the beginning of John's very contemplative, philosophical, poetic, and complexly integrated gospel, the last of the four canonical gospels, and also written by the apostle and evangelist in the universal Greek, John paraphrases Genesis and the opening of Mark's gospel: he shows that Jesus Christ is the gospel, literally and figuratively the living Word of God, who existed as God and with God, before the world existed and in the beginning of creation:

> In the beginning was the Word: the word was with God and the Word was God. He was with God in the beginning. Through him all things came into being, not one thing came into being except through him.[323]

Not only do we have our individual existence through the Word,[324] but as John continues his introduction to the gospel, the Word was made flesh, and was and is our life among us,[325] living in us now,[326] so that in the life of God's spirit we may be God's children unto eternal life and eternal light.[327]

Then for Matthew, when he begins his gospel, the second to be written, he chooses, like John, to emphasize the humanity of the divine Christ,[328] so that he starts with the human "genealogy of Jesus Christ," who, truly God, is also truly our flesh, our faith, and our King, the physical descendant of Adam, Abraham, and David.[329]

---

322   Mark 1:1
323   John 1:1-3, Genesis 1:1; John 1:4-5, Genesis 1:2-5; 1 John 1:5, John 8:12, Revelation 1:16, 21:23
324   1 John 3:9; Romans 9:8, 4:16-17
325   John 1:12-14
326   2 Corinthians 5:16, 1 Corinthians 13:12, 1 John 3:2, 24
327   John 17:23-26, 12:36; 1 John 1:1-7, Ephesians 5:8
328   John 1:14
329   Matthew 1:1-17

Matthew, over Mark's absent account, chooses to describe only briefly "how Jesus came to be born."[330] But then Luke, Paul's companion and colleague, when he begins his gospel, starts with a prologue, noting that previous gospel accounts already have been written; and we may infer from his naming of those sources as "eyewitnesses" and "ministers,"[331] that implicitly Luke means the accounts provided for us through "Matthew" and "Mark;" and after theirs, Luke's is the third gospel account to be finalized. But, after his initial prologue, Luke provides an expanded narrative introduction regarding the incarnation of God. Neatly, Luke provides parallel accounts for John the Baptist and for Jesus, respectively, for their annunciations and births,[332] and for their circumcisions and hidden lives.[333] But after that, all four gospel accounts take up from where the present gospel narrative also begins: it starts like the beginning of Mark's gospel narrative, with the anticipation of the Christ and the coming of John the Baptist, as the kingdom of God is at hand.[334]

But before the written word of the gospel ever existed, the Word of God existed from eternity, and then he existed in the hearts of men, by grace and by faith:[335] through God's revelations through his prophets; by their fulfilment in the incarnation of his Son through the virgin Mary by the power of the Holy Spirit; and in our hearing the proclamation of his words from those who came before us who have heard his words and followed his voice. This is precisely how Matthew, the tax collector, describes himself in his gospel account when Jesus came to him:

> As Jesus was walking on from there he saw a man named Matthew [or Levi][336] sitting at the tax office, and he said to him, "Follow me." And he got up and

---

330 Matthew 1:18-25
331 Luke 1:1-2
332 Luke 1:5-25, 57; Luke 1:26-56, 2:1-20
333 Luke 1:59-80; Luke 2:21-52
334 Mark 1:2, Matthew 3:1, Luke 3:1, John 1:6-8, 19-37; Mark 1:14-15, Matthew 3:2, 4:17, Luke 17:20-21, John 1:26-27, Revelation 4:1-2, 22:20
335 John 6:65, Romans 4:24-25
336 Mark 2:13-14, Luke 5:27-28

followed him.[337]

This account reminds us,[338] according to recent commentary by Pope Benedict XVI, that "those who seem to be the farthest from holiness can even become a model of the acceptance of God's mercy and offer a glimpse of its marvellous effects in their own lives."[339] Matthew, at first, had preached among Palestinian Jews, but ironically his gospel written down in Aramaic came into being when he decided to reach out to other peoples,[340] Greek-speaking Gentiles: "he sought to put in writing, for those whom he was leaving, what they would be losing with his departure."[341] Although Matthew had composed a first gospel in his mother tongue, only the Greek form survives as his gospel for the universal church.

Like Matthew, Mark also had been a close disciple of the Lord, although not necessarily one of the seventy-two whom the Lord had appointed.[342] Unlike Matthew's native Jewish roots, Mark, as a young man from Jerusalem, was a Jew with a "Hellenist" father, probably from Cyprus, and a "Hebrew" mother. However, like Matthew in his gospel account, Mark also seems to have described himself in an attitude of open confession before taking up his call to evangelize. In Gethsemane, like the other disciples,[343] Mark may have temporarily deserted the Lord, when the Lord was seized by armed men from the Sanhedrin:

> A young man followed with nothing on but a linen cloth. They caught hold of him, but he left the cloth in their hands and ran away naked.[344]

---

337   Matthew 9:9; John 10:27
338   Matthew 9:10-13, 11:19; 1 Corinthians 1:26-31
339   Benedict XVI. General Audience. Paul VI Audience Hall, Wednesday, 30 August 2006.
340   Matthew 2:1-2
341   Benedict XVI, Ibid., citing his source as Eusebius of Cesarea, Historica Ecclesiastica, III, 24, 6.
342   Luke 10:1-2
343   John 16:32
344   Mark 14:51-52; 2 Corinthians 5:2-3, Hebrews 4:13, Revelation 16:15

And Mark spent the rest of his life listening to the Lord's voice,[345] and spreading his word,[346] ultimately to Alexandria, Egypt, where he was martyred.

In Luke's gospel, there also are self-references, but unlike in Matthew's and Mark's accounts, they are not immediately evident. Luke, the medical doctor, had been a convert of Paul's missionary preaching to the Gentiles,[347] so he wasn't there as an original "eyewitness" or "minister" of the Lord, as Luke himself explains.[348] However, as a practicing physician, a natural student and researcher, Luke was a systematic collector and collator, a diligent organizer and chronicler, and an exuberant collaborator, but now not for natural medicine, but for the health of souls, by his narration and proclamation of the gospel, written in two books.[349] And throughout Luke's Greek-language gospel account, his personality shines through it, with its grace from the Lord; which is precisely how Luke makes reference to himself implicitly in his gospel account, through his living personal relationship with the Lord, and by his own vocation to evangelize:

> No one lights a lamp and puts it in some hidden place or under a tub; they put it on the lamp-stand so that people may see the light when they come in....If, therefore, your whole body is filled with light, and not darkened at all, it will be light entirely, as when the lamp shines on you with its rays.[350]

On the other hand, John was more the modern historian than was Luke, with his frequent topographical details, very precise chronologies, and clear depiction of motivations. And of the four evangelists, John is distinctive by his narrative structure, his emphasis on language and theological poetry, and by the particular maturity of his profound reflections; but all of the evangelists were great

---

345   John 10:27, 8:31-32, 47
346   John 10:16; 2 Corinthians 5:4-5
347   Colossians 4:10-11, 14
348   Luke 1:2
349   Acts 1:1-12
350   Luke 11:33, 36; Luke 8:16-18, 11:33-36; John 8:12, 9:5, 12:36, 46

theologians, as also was Paul as he preached the gospel; and in their common faith community, in their discipleship of Christ, they all influenced each other's theology. Although modest in self-reference, John does provide his singularly-defining, signature self-reference in his gospel, namely, "the disciple he (Jesus) loved."[351] Clearly, John, also the first bishop of Ephesus,[352] followed the Lord as well as Peter, his fishing partner,[353] together in the service of the Lord; and from the Lord, John was the definitive source for this late first-century gospel in his name. Sometimes John surely had written it in his own hand; but other times, he must have provided oral accounts to his disciples for their writing them down. But however its composition came to be constructed, ultimately it was edited in its final version by John's disciples from Ephesus,[354] where Paul, because of his earlier missionary labours there for the gospel,[355] had helped to establish Ephesus as a shining example of the church for the whole world.[356] Paul is the invisible "fifth evangelist," behind the scenes for the others, and as expressed in Luke's Acts and in Paul's letters as gospel commentary and explanation.

Readings: Matthew 25:1-46

If we are going to be Children of the Light,[357] and have enough stamina not to backslide until the Lord comes,[358] then we are going to have to carry sufficient oil in our individual lamps.[359] So there on the Mount of Olives, as Jesus was speaking to the twelve disciples as the sun went down, he continued by telling them two parables:

> The kingdom of heaven, then, will be like this: Ten virgins, who were attendants for a wedding, took their

---

351 John 13:23, 34; John 19:26, 27, 1 John 4:19; John 21:20, 21-22, 1:38, 37; 1 John 4:8-11
352 Titus 1:7-9; 2 John 1:1, 3 John 1:1
353 Luke 5:4-7, John 21:2-11
354 John 21:24
355 Acts 18:19-21, 19:1, 8-10
356 Ephesians 1:13-15, Revelations 2:1-5, Matthew 5:14-16, Ephesians 2:20
357 John 12:36, 1 John 3:1-2
358 Luke 12:35-36
359 Matthew 25:3-4, 29-30

lamps and went out to meet the bridegroom.[360] Five of them were foolish and silly, while five of them were sensible and wise.[361] The foolish ones, although they took their lamps, they took no extra oil with them.[362] On the other hand, the sensible ones brought flasks of oil with their lamps.[363] Since the bridegroom was long delayed, they began to nod off and soon fell asleep.[364] But at midnight, suddenly there was a cry, "Look, the bridegroom! Go out and meet him."[365] All those wedding attendants woke up then and trimmed their lamps;[366] and the foolish ones said to the wise, "Give us some of your oil; our lamps are going out!"[367] But the sensible ones replied, "No, there may not be enough for us and for you; you had better go to the merchants and buy some for yourselves."[368] While they had gone off to buy it, the bridegroom arrived and those who were ready went in with him to the wedding feast, and the door was locked.[369] Afterwards, the other attendants returned and said, "Lord, Lord, open the door for us!"[370] But in reply he said, "In truth, I tell you, I don't know you."[371] So stay awake, for you know neither the day nor the hour.[372]

Then without stopping, Jesus immediately told them his second parable:

It is like a man who was going abroad; so he called in

360	Matthew 25:1
361	Matthew 25:2
362	Matthew 25:3
363	Matthew 25:4
364	Matthew 25:5; Mark 13:33, 36; Matthew 24:48-49
365	Matthew 25:6; John 3:29, Matthew 9:14-15
366	Matthew 25:7
367	Matthew 25:8
368	Matthew 25:9
369	Matthew 25:10
370	Matthew 25:11; Matthew 7:21, 24
371	Matthew 25:12; Matthew 7:23
372	Matthew 25:13; Mark 13:35; Matthew 24:50

> his servants and entrusted his property to them.³⁷³ He gave to each one according to his ability: to one he gave five talents; to another, two; and to a third, he gave one talent; then he set out on his journey.³⁷⁴

In the days of Christ, a talent was a large unit of money, and valued at 720 ounces of silver, it would have been equivalent then to 6000 days of wages, more than sixteen years wages for each talent. Over a lifetime of accumulated earnings, such as for one's retirement today, one, two, and five talents would be equivalent, respectively, to more than 16-years, 32-years, and 80-years earnings. Yet, these assets were starting points, not the end points for three respective lifetime earning potentials, as provided to us by the Lord. Many persons are very conservative with their material assets, or they can be economical or shrewd with those resources, even if they were given to them in someone else's generosity. The question is: what do we do with such gifts as these from the Lord?³⁷⁵

Ultimately, the issue will not be our different starting points, or how much we have left when the property owner returns. Nor will the issue be the absolute value, or exactly how much we earn; rather, in the end, we will be judged upon our proportional gains, or upon our personal efforts, relative to whatever abilities, or talents, we have been given.³⁷⁶ So, Jesus continued with his parable:

> The one who received five talents promptly went and traded with them, and made another five.³⁷⁷ The one who received two made two more in the same way.³⁷⁸ But the man who had received one talent went off and dug a whole in the ground, and buried his master's money.³⁷⁹ After a long time had passed, the master of those servants returned and went through his accounts

---

373   Matthew 25:14; Matthew 24:45-47, Matthew 25:29; Mark 13:34; Luke 19:12; John 6:63
374   Matthew 25:15; Luke 19:13; John 14:25-26
375   Luke 16:11-12
376   Romans 12:6-13; 1 Corinthians 12:4-11
377   Matthew 25:16
378   Matthew 25:17
379   Matthew 25:18; Luke 19:14

with them.[380] The one who had received five talents came forward bringing five more. "Sir," he said, "you entrusted me with five talents. See, I have made another five."[381] His master said to him, "Well done, my good and faithful servant. Because you were trustworthy in small matters, I will give you greater responsibilities; come, share with me in your master's joy."[382] Next the one who had received two talents came forward and said, "You entrusted me with two talents; here are two more that I have made."[383] His master said to him, "Well done, my good and faithful servant. Because you were trustworthy in small matters, I will give you greater responsibilities; come, share with me in your master's joy."[384]

Then the one who had received the single talent came forward last. "Sir," he said, "I knew, from what I had heard, that you were a hard man, harvesting where you had not sown and gathering where you had not scattered;[385] I was afraid, and I went off and buried your talent in the ground; it belongs to you; so here you are, you can have it back."[386] But his master answered him, "You wicked and lazy servant! So you knew that I harvest where I had not sown and gather where I did not scatter?[387] Well then, you should have deposited my money in the bank; at least, when I returned, I would have gotten interest back with my money.[388] So now, take the talent away from him and give it to the

---

380   Matthew 25:19; Luke 19:15
381   Matthew 25:20; Luke 19:16
382   Matthew 25:21; Luke 19:17; Matthew 25:34
383   Matthew 25:22; Luke 19:18
384   Matthew 25:23; Luke 19:19
385   Matthew 25:24; Matthew 13:23; Luke 19:21; Matthew 13:23, John 15:8, 16
386   Matthew 25:25; Luke 19:20; Mark 4:18-19, John 8:47, 15:22, 12:47
387   Matthew 25:26; Luke 19:22; John 9:41, 12:48
388   Matthew 25:27; Luke 19:23; Matthew 25:42-45; 1 John 4:20-21, John 12:49

person who has ten.[389] For to everyone who has, even more will be given, and he will become more than rich; but anyone who has not, will be deprived of even what he has.[390] As for this useless servant, throw him into the darkness outside, where there will be wailing and grinding of teeth.[391]

If the word of God has found a home in us,[392] it cannot just stay with us only as words; but this living gospel demands of us our active love for all our brothers and sisters.[393] And as the word of God becomes deeply rooted within our hearts, with whatever talents God has given us, five, two, or one, we are entrusted with the responsibility to sow God's seed of the gospel in the world around us.[394] But if we should not take up this responsibility, we may loose whatever we have been given by God. God's gifts will not return to him without producing its fruit. For, if we should fail, then what we have been given will be entrusted to someone else, who will provide a fine harvest from God's property. And the inevitable victory of God's grace, from the teamwork of his saints,[395] is the thirty, sixty, hundredfold multiplication of the Lord's fruits for his harvest.[396] What a mighty return of his talents there has been to the Lord from his saints: Peter and Paul, Mark and Luke, Matthew and John, Timothy and Titus, Benedict and Augustine, Cyril and Methodius, Dominic and Catherine of Siena, Francis and Claire from Assisi, Francis Xavier and Isaac Jogues during epochs of human exploration and colonisation, Mother Teresa and the Great Pope John Paul II.

These were all missionaries of the Word. Some of them were apostles, some were evangelists, and others were colleagues or assistants of St. Paul.[397] Some established original communities for

---

389   Matthew 25:28; Luke 19:24-25; John 15:2, 12:50
390   Matthew 25:29; Luke 19:26; John 15:5, 12:35
391   Matthew 25:30; Matthew 24:51, 13:42; John 15:6, 12:36
392   1 John 4:9, John 8:31-32
393   1 John 3:16-20
394   Matthew 13:24, 18, 4-9; Mark 4:3, 13-14; Luke 8:11, 15
395   Matthew 18:20, 28:20; John 9:4
396   Mark 4:8, Luke 8:8, Matthew 13:8, Romans 7:4, 6
397   1 Thessalonians 3:1-2, 2 Timothy 4:5; 2 Corinthians 8:23; Philemon

religious life, separately for men and for women, and others were reformers and innovators for religious communities, but also with patterns of religious life built upon the same rule, the Word of God. Some were pioneering evangelizers, while many of them also were martyrs for the faith. Cyril invented the "Cyrilic" alphabet, and with Methodius translated the Gospel into the Slavonic language; and Methodius, with the assistance of a team of priests at Constantinople, later translated most of the additional Scriptures. Some, like our contemporaries, have fully exploited theatre arts and the modern world of electronic media communications for God's word. And like the Lord, with God's seed entrusted to our individual talents, we too are called to carry out God's work as Children of the Word,[398] the Word of God,[399] as Light for the world.[400] In a genuine manifestation of a recent modern gospel, Maria Valtorta, "Little John,"[401] in her visions and dictations, wrote her Gospel of Jesus Christ,[402] Poem of the Man-God, originating from Good Friday,[403] 23rd April 1943.

As for myself, personally, although I may have one or two "talents," I am not supposed to bury the Lord's gifts of mercy in the ground, as I used to do, which would be digging my own grave. In the initial moment of God's continuing and faithful grace, I began this Gospel Emmaus on 12th September 2003, approximately from the Exultation of the Holy Cross,[404] and this was preceded by my confession and prayer, in my recognition of and rededication to the cross,[405] which I still find to be a challenging daily task, depending upon the hour or the minute.[406] So, for the Lord's harvest, I am writing this book, so that wherever his word is sown and scattered through my cooperation with the grace there may be a double or

---

      1:23-24, Colossians 4:10, 14
398   Mark 4:14, John 5:24-25; 1 John 1:1, 3:9; John 14:21
399   John 1:1
400   John 8:12, 9:5; 1 John 1:7; Matthew 25:7, 3-4
401   John 21:25;
402   John 15:5
403   John 15:2; Romans 6:5, 2 Timothy 2:11, 1:9-10
404   John 15:1, Luke 13:6-9, Mark 8:38; 2 Timothy 4:1-5
405   Isaiah 53:4-7, Romans 6:10-14; 1 John 1:8-9, 3:5-6; 2 Corinthians 4:1-2, 5-6
406   2 Corinthians 12:9; Romans 9:15-18, 21, Titus 3:3-5

quadruple return to God on the Master's investment in poor me. For, each day has its own troubles and its requirements;[407] but the Lord's commission to take up his cross each day and to follow him is made easier by his grace and through our daily prayer.[408] But if, in our knowledge and without repentance,[409] we should refuse to be his Children of the Word,[410] then we also should deserve to be thrown together with the hypocrites, and completely alone without his light to shine on us;[411] indeed, with such a great fall, we would stumble into the void of darkness, with total consciousness and full knowledge of our sin and despair, forever.[412] Praise to God for the riches and "talents" that he gives us, and for the blessings God has provided to those who have preceded us, as our forefathers in Christ; and may those myriad gifts be used wisely by all of his mere servants.[413]

Against this background, and still alone with the twelve disciples on the Mount of Olives, Jesus now continued with his revelations about his final coming and judgement at the end of the world:

> When the Son of Man comes in his glory, escorted by all his angels, he will sit upon his throne of glory,[414] and all the nations will be assembled before him.[415] And he will separate people one from another, as the shepherd who separates sheep from goats.[416] He will place the sheep on his right hand and the goats on his left.[417] Then the King will say to those on his right, "Come, you whom my Father has blessed; inherit the kingdom prepared for you from the foundation of the

---

407	Matthew 6:34, Luke 14:27
408	2 Corinthians 1:2-7, 8-11, John 15:7, 1 John 5:14-15
409	Matthew 25:26, John 9:41
410	John 14:15, Mark 12:28-34, John 14:23; 1 John 2:5, 10
411	Luke 11:36; 1 John 1:5
412	Luke 20:17-18, 1 John 2:9, 11, Matthew 25:30, 46, Hebrews 6:4-8
413	Luke 17:10
414	Matthew 25:31; Revelation 22:12
415	Matthew 25:32; Mark 4:29, Daniel 7:13, Revelation 14:14, 20:11-12
416	Matthew 25:32; John 10:1, 14
417	Matthew 25:33; Matthew 13:30, Luke 6:47-49

world.[418] For I was hungry and you gave me food, I was thirsty and you gave me drink; I was a stranger and you welcomed me,[419] naked and you clothed me, sick and you cared for me, in prison and you visited me."[420] Then the upright will answer him and say, "Lord, when did we see you hungry and feed you, or thirsty and give you drink?[421] When did we see you a stranger and welcome you, or naked and clothe you?[422] When did we find you sick or in prison, and go to see you?[423] And the King will answer them, "In truth, I tell you, in so far as you did it for one of these least brothers of mine, you did it for me."[424] Then he will say to those on his left, "Depart from me, with your curse upon you, to the eternal fire prepared for the devil and his angels.[425] For I was hungry and you gave me no food, I was thirsty and you gave me no drink,[426] I was a stranger and you gave me no welcome, naked and you never clothed me, sick and in prison and you never cared for me."[427] Then it will be their turn to ask, "Lord, when did we see you hungry or thirsty or a stranger or naked or sick or in prison, and not come to help you?"[428] He will answer them, "In truth, I tell you, in so far as you did not do this for one of these least ones, you did not do it for me."[429] And they will go off to eternal punishment,[430] and the upright to eternal life.[431]

---

418 Matthew 25:34; John 17:24, Revelation 21:7, 22:13
419 Matthew 25:35; Acts 11:27-30, Philemon 1:8-10, 17-21
420 Matthew 25:36; Matthew 10:42
421 Matthew 25:37; John 13:34
422 Matthew 25:38; John 13:35
423 Matthew 25:39; Matthew 18:5, Acts 9:4-5
424 Matthew 25:40; Luke 6:20-26
425 Matthew 25:41; Revelation 20:14-15, 21:8
426 Matthew 25:42; James 5:5-6
427 Matthew 25:43; James 2:14-16
428 Matthew 25:44; Luke 6:46, 1 John 4:20
429 Matthew 25:45; 1 John 3:17
430 Matthew 25:46; Matthew 13:40-43
431 Matthew 25:46; John 6:51, 58; 1 John 5:20, John 6:54-56

Readings: Matthew 26:1-16, Mark 14:1-11, Luke 22:1-6

When Jesus had finished speaking these words, he had finished saying everything he had intended to say for his public ministry,[432] but, as oftentimes we also need to focus and also should remember,[433] he then reminded the disciples:

> As you know, in two days time it will be the Feast of Passover, and the Son of Man will be handed over to be crucified.[434]

The Passover Feast would begin from twilight on Thursday, but from the evening vigil on Thursday it was the 14th Nisan, the start of the Preparation Day (from evening to daytime), when the Passover lamb was led to its slaughter, and when the whole of Israel would start to celebrate the approaching Passover that would begin on Friday evening, on the day of the feast, immediately with the Sabbath. Tomorrow, on the day for the Lord's Passover meal, on the Thursday evening at the start of Passover celebrations, yet also in anticipation of his crucifixion on Friday, Jesus would gather the disciples for his Passover meal of the "new covenant" in his body and blood, the Eucharist, instituted in the Lord's three-day liturgical celebration of his "new covenant" Passover from death to resurrection. Those three days would be calculated from the evenings, only to be broken by the Lord's resurrection at Easter dawn. Now, however, it was calmly Wednesday evening, just two liturgical days before the Friday evening start of Passover.[435] However, in accordance with the Old Covenant promises, this time on Passover Preparation the Lord would be crucified on Friday; and after the third day, on our Sunday, on the first day of the week, he would rise again.[436] Yet, before this must happen,[437] first Jesus would be handed over to be crucified for our sins.[438]

---

432 Matthew 26:1; Matthew 20:17-19, 17:22-23, 16:20-23
433 2 Corinthians 5:14-15
434 Matthew 26:2
435 Matthew 26:2, Mark 14:1
436 John 2:19
437 Mark 8:31, Matthew 16:21, Luke 9:22, 24:26-27
438 Matthew 26:2

But on this Wednesday evening, as usual, Jesus wasn't finished quite yet with his regular working day.[439] Now, at the end of the Lord's public ministry,[440] and on the vigil of his New Passover Covenant, Simon, the former leper implicitly understood as cured by the Lord, would be hosting a dinner celebration for Jesus at Simon's home in Bethany.[441] The events in Bethany on that evening,[442] along with the total accumulation of humankind's present, past, and future sins, would lead directly and inevitably to the Lord's Passion in nearby Jerusalem.[443] Once, Simon had been a leper from the sons of Israel;[444] but, by his faith in Jesus, he had been healed.[445] And now, through the obviously visible sign of Simon's healing, Jesus also had plainly marked out Simon for everyone to see, just as his leprosy had marked him formerly as sinner and outcast,[446] that the bondages of Simon's sins had been broken through the Lord's grace,[447] as it is for all who maintain their faith and good works in Christ.[448] This anticipatory grace for Simon had been gained through the Lord's victory death and resurrection, just as the Lord's victory of grace has anticipated our own sins.[449] This grace would be maintained only in Simon's unity with the Lord through blessings from the Father, both with Christ and for Simon, and for each of us, to go and bear fruit for God.[450]

While Jesus was reclining at table at Simon's house in Bethany,[451] a woman came up to Jesus with an alabaster jar of very costly perfumed

---

439   Matthew 8:20
440   Matthew 4:23, Luke 6:18-19, Mark 1:40-42
441   Matthew 26:6, Mark 14:3, John 12:1-2
442   Matthew 26:3-5, Luke 22:1-2; Mark 14:10-11, Matthew 26:14-16, Luke 22:3-6
443   John 2:1-4, 12:23
444   Matthew 15:24
445   John 3:14
446   Leviticus 13:45-46; Mark 1:44, Matthew 8:4, Luke 5:14, Leviticus 14:10-20
447   Romans 7:6, 4
448   Matthew 25:35-36, James 2:14-17, 1 John 3:14
449   John 1:26-29; Romans 5:6, 17-21; Luke 24:46-47, Acts 10:43, Luke 5:24-26
450   Hebrews 5:5, John 6:44, 15:1-3, 12:26, 24-25
451   Matthew 26:6-7, Mark 14:3

oil, pure nard, and breaking the jar she poured the oil on his head.[452] In fact, the woman was then Mary of Magdala, the sister of Martha and Lazarus.[453] Just four days earlier,[454] on the previous Saturday evening, Mary also had anointed the Lord's feet, again in Bethany, but at the dinner celebration for Lazarus.[455] At this earlier dinner,[vii] Judas had objected to her lavish recognition of the Lord; and instead, he put forth his politically correct argument that the oil might have been sold and the money given to the poor. However, Judas was a thief and he had intended to line his own pockets with the money.[456] But now, some if not all the disciples are the ones to take up this previous argument from Judas,[457] and indignantly among themselves they also said: "What a waste! This oil could have been sold for over three hundred denarii, and the money given to the poor."[458] And then, in their dismay and hostility, the disciples became publicly abusive with their criticism of Mary.[459] The Lord knew of all that the disciples were thinking and saying,[460] and of what they were not thinking, namely of his passion and crucifixion,[461] and also of the potential malicious effect their bitter attack represented for Mary's soul;[462] and immediately, with Mary's hope in the resurrection yet to be clarified and manifested, and in her defence of her realization of his approaching death on the cross,[463] Jesus also came to her defence against the error of the disciples:

> Why are you troubling this woman, and upsetting her? Leave her alone. What she has done for me is a good work.[464] The poor, you will always have with you,[465]

---

452   Mark 14:3, Matthew 26:7
453   John 12:3, 11:1
454   John 12:1, Matthew 26:2
455   John 12:1-3
456   John 12:6
457   John 12:4-5
458   Matthew 26:8-9, Mark 14:4-5
459   Mark 14:4
460   Matthew 26:10
461   Mark 10:32-34, Matthew 20:17-19, Luke 18:31-34, John 12:23-36
462   Mark 14:6, Matthew 26:10
463   John 12:3, Mark 14:3
464   Mark 14:6, Matthew 26:10; John 12:7
465   Matthew 26:11, Mark 14:7

and you can do them good whenever you wish,[466] but you will not always have me.[467] She has done what she could:[468] in pouring this perfumed oil upon my body,[469] she has anointed my body beforehand, to prepare it for my burial.[470] In truth I tell you, whenever this gospel is proclaimed throughout the whole world, what she has done will be told in memory of her as well.[471]

The disciples still had not grasped the situation stated explicitly by the Lord that in only two days time, the Son of Man would be handed over to be crucified;[472] and although he would never leave them,[473] very soon he would not always be with them in his physical body.[474] Of course, the actual body and blood of Jesus would be given to us in his Eucharist that we eat, along with his given sacrifice on the cross.[475] Yet, Mary's good work for the Lord was all and everything she could do once she finally had understood and accepted that Jesus must die for our sins, unlike the disciples, who had not understood up to this point so far.[476] Mary of Magdala's embracing dedication, her consecration of total self to the Lord's passion and death, in fact reflects the central value of the cloistered religious life, which often seems strange, and sometimes, even is ridiculed by the world outside its convent walls. Yet, for easy example, we may compare Mary's virtuous act to the cloistered life of the Maltese Beata, the Benedictine nun Maria Adeodata Pisani.

When Terezina (Maria Adeodata) Pisani was fifteen years old, her father, a Neopolitan Baron, was involved in some uprisings and was deported to Malta; and at age nineteen, in 1825, she was brought to live at Rabat, Malta, on the outskirts of Mdina, the ancient capital

---

466 Mark 14:7
467 Matthew 26:11, Mark 14:7; John 12:8
468 Mark 14:8
469 Matthew 26:12
470 Mark 14:8, Matthew 26:12
471 Mark 14:9, Matthew 26:13; Luke 22:19
472 Matthew 26:2
473 John 14:18-20
474 Matthew 26:11, Mark 14:7; John 12:8, 16:28
475 John 6:53, Luke 19:19-20
476 Matthew 16:21-23, 17:22-23, 20:18-22

and fortified city in the central southwestern highland of the island of Malta. Throughout those years, her mother had longed for and continued to insist that her daughter should marry, but Terezina, although rich and noble and attracting many interested suitors, she renounced them all. Instead, in 1828, Terezina decided to join the Benedictine cloister of St. Peter's Monastery at Mdina, where she lived out her life for another twenty-five years. As Sister Maria Adeodata, she generously disposed of all her property, assisting her debt-ridden father; her poor mother and close relatives; men and women with religious vocations who were poor; and she also set aside a large sum of her wealth, and the best part of her belongings, for distribution to the poor. For herself, she retained only the barest minimum, including even giving away part of her own daily food. Sister Maria Deodata's dedication to the Lord, and to her fellow nuns, was a value higher than any of her riches or her potential married life, even greater than her obvious good works for the poor.[477] Like Mary of Magdala, the cloistered Maria Deodata had her priorities straight, accepting the Lord's cross and his promised resurrection; those priorities were not of this world.

But now, in contrast, with Jesus' rebuke to the disciples over Mary, one of the Twelve, namely Judas Iscariot, resolved to slip away that night so he could make an offer to the chief priests to hand Jesus, the Lamb of God, over to them,[478] according to the priorities of the world. Previously the chief priests, the elders of the people, and the high priest Caiaphas had consulted together; and already they had agreed to arrest Jesus by some deception so that they could put him to death.[479] Although they had been looking for some way to do this, as they didn't know yet how they could accomplish this, except that is, whenever they should manage it, they resolved to avoid the Passover festivities, to head off their sparking a potential riot among the people.[480] So, when Judas came to them that evening, they, indeed, were very delighted when he asked them,[481] "What are you

---

477   John 12:8, Matthew 25:40, 45
478   Matthew 26:14, Mark 14:10
479   Mark 14:1, Matthew 26:3-4; Luke 22:1-2
480   Matthew 26:6, Mark 14:2, Luke 22:2
481   Mark 14:11

prepared to pay me if I can hand him over to you?"[482]

On the spot they paid Judas only one-tenth the amount he might have made from the sale of Mary's alabaster jar of spikenard, his wages of thirty pieces of silver.[483] And from that moment onwards, in his dedication to corruption and sin and with his betrayal of the Lord,[484] Satan entered into Judas,[485] and vigorously Judas looked for some opportunity to hand Jesus over to the chief priests and scribes, in secret, of course, without people getting to know about it.[486] Judas, now, had embarked upon a surreptitious vendetta against the Lord's interferences in his ongoing embezzlements, a chosen path entirely willed by Judas, leading to his ultimate and unfortunate destruction.[487] The path to eternal life through the cross was now the narrow alternative; yet this route to holiness eluded nearly everyone's full understanding,[488] except for Mary of Magdala's profound appreciation,[489] and for Mary, the mother of Jesus, who already had surrendered her son to God.[490]

During the Lord's entire public life, from the wedding feast at Cana with his mother and the disciples, to Simon the Leper's dinner celebration at Bethany, and gradually during the Lord's prior hidden life in the Holy Family,[491] Mary, the Lord's mother and the mother of our salvation,[492] knew along with Jesus that the hour of his purpose would come one day;[493] and Mary would be there with her Son along the way and at the foot of the cross,[494] like Mary of Magdala's

---

482   Matthew 26:15
483   Matthew 26:15, Zechariah 11:12; Mark 14:5
484   Mark 7:15, 21-23; John 6:64, 70-71
485   Luke 22:3-5; John 13:27
486   Matthew 26:16, Mark 14:11, Luke 22:6; John 13:27-30
487   Matthew 7:13, John 17:12, 3:36
488   Luke 9:23, 44-45, 14:27
489   Luke 10:39, 42, John 11:2, 19, 32, 12:1-3, Mark 12:24-27, 14:3, 8, John 3:16, Psalm 115:17-18
490   John 2:1-5
491   Luke 2:33-35, 41, 51
492   Luke 1:38, 46-48
493   John 12:28
494   Luke 23:27, John 19:25

doing everything she could to assist him.[495] Now, the first day for the Lord's being lifted from the earth,[496] referring to his death, and not to his resurrection, according to the Lord's reckoning, it was in only two days;[497] but also by the reckoning of the high priest, Caiaphas, and of his colleagues, its time must not be when the people would celebrate Passover,[498] on this Friday evening; and so it would be, but still according to the rubric from God to Moses,[499] on the Preparation Day.

But first, and similar to the hundreds of dinners the Lord had celebrated with Pharisees and scribes; with lepers, tax collectors, and other social outcasts; with his dearest friends and with bitter enemies; Jesus soon would be celebrating his meal of meals, the feast of his new Passover Eucharist, the New-Covenant's new first day of unleavened bread,[500] with himself as high priest and minister of the celebration of his body and blood offered on the cross, and simultaneous with the celebration of his body risen from the dead.[501] This is the same celebration that is memorialized in the daily celebration of Mass—in our sharing of his Word and in the breaking of the bread—and it is required of everyone, at the request of Christ,[502] to take and eat the incarnate Word of God at our weekly celebrations on Sundays or on its vigil, on Saturday evening. So, let us resolve, now, to join ourselves more closely to the Lord's passion, death, and resurrection, like Mary of Magdala's anointing of the Lord, by making our celebration of the Eucharist more frequent, more vibrant and joyful, and more consciously, in the visible body of Christ,[503] which Eucharist is the absolute centre of our Christian daily lives.[504]

495	Mark 14:8
496	John 3:14, 12:32, 20:9, 17
497	Matthew 26:2
498	Matthew 26:5, John 19:42
499	Exodus 12:6, 15-18
500	Mark 14:12, Matthew 26:17, Luke 22:7, Acts 2:42
501	Hebrews 7:11, 26-27, 12-16, 20-22, 28, 8:1-2, 6-8, 12, 9:11-15, 10:11-14, 19-21
502	Luke 22:19-20; 1 Corinthians 11:23-26; John 20:19, 26, 21:1, 12-14, Acts 2:42, 46-47
503	1 Corinthians 11:27
504	Ephesians 1:22-23, 1 Corinthians 12:27, 4-6

Prayer Reflection: Colossians 1:12-20; Psalm 115:1-18; Revelation 4:11, 5:9-14

Antiphon: He is the first-born of all creation;
>in everything the primacy is his.

>Let us give thanks with joy to the Father
>>for having made you fit
>>to share the lot of God's saints
>>and with them to inherit the light.[505]

>Because, that is what he has done:
>>he rescued us from the power of darkness
>>and brought us safe to the kingdom of his beloved
>>>Son,[506]
>>in whom we enjoy our freedom,
>>the forgiveness of our sins.[507]

>He is the image of the unseen God,
>>the firstborn of all creation.[508]
>For in him were created all things
>>in heaven and on earth:
>>everything visible and invisible,
>>thrones, dominions, sovereignties, powers—
>>all things were created through him and for him.[509]

>He exists before all else that is,
>>and in him all things are held together.[510]
>He is the Head of the Body, the Church;
>>he is the beginning,
>>the first-born of the dead,
>>so that primacy might be his in everything.[511]

---

505 Colossians 1:12; Matthew 25:3-4; Revelation 21:23
506 Colossians 1:13; Matthew 25:7-10; Mark 1:14-15
507 Colossians 1:14; Mark 14:3; Galatians 1:4, John 8:35-36
508 Colossians 1:15; Matthew 24:23-24; Mark 16:15
509 Colossians 1:16; Matthew 24:11-13; Colossians 1:22-23
510 Colossians 1:17; Mark 13:19-20; John 1:3
511 Colossians 1:18; Mark 13:34; Romans 16:25, Colossians 1:26-27

It pleased God to make absolute fullness reside in
> him,[512]
and through him to reconcile everything in his person,
everything on earth and in the heavens,
making peace through his death on the cross.[513]

Antiphon: Our God is in heaven,
> and he has power to do all he wills, alleluia.

Not to us, Lord, not to us,
> but to your name give glory
> because of your faithful love and constancy.[514]

Why should the nations ask,
> "Where is their God?"[515]
Our God is in heaven;
> and he creates whatever he wills.[516]
Their idols are silver and gold,
> the work of human hands.[517]

They have mouths, but don't speak;
> eyes, but don't see;[518]
they have ears, but don't hear;
> noses, but don't smell.[519]
They have hands, but don't feel;
> feet, but don't walk;
> and no sound comes from their throats.[520]
Their makers will come to be like them,
> and so will all who trust in them.[521]

---

512 Colossians 1:19; Matthew 26:3-4; Matthew 9:35-37
513 Colossians 1:20; Matthew 26:1-2; 1 Corinthians 1:18, 21
514 Psalm 115:1; Mark 14:8-9; Galatians 1:15-16
515 Psalm 115:2; Matthew 24:38-39; 1 Corinthians 9:16-17
516 Psalm 115:3; Luke 21:5-6; Galatians 1:3-5
517 Psalm 115:4; Mark 14:10-11; Galatians 1:11
518 Psalm 115:5; Matthew 25:44; Galatians 1:12
519 Psalm 115:6; Matthew 25:42-43; Galatians 1:13
520 Psalm 115:7; Matthew 25:45-46; Ephesians 6:19-20
521 Psalm 115:8; Matthew 25:41; 2 Corinthians 4:3-4

House of Israel, trust in the Lord;
   he is your help and shield.[522]
House of Aaron, trust in the Lord;
   he is your help and shield.[523]
You who fear the Lord, trust in the Lord;
   he is your help and shield.[524]

The Lord remembers us and will bless us;
   he will bless the House of Israel,
   he will bless the House of Aaron.[525]
He will bless those who fear the Lord,
   small and great alike:[526]
May the Lord grant you increase,
   for you and all your descendants.[527]

May you be blessed by the Lord,
   the maker of heaven and earth.[528]
The heaven above the heavens belongs to the Lord,
   but the earth he has given to Adam's children.[529]
The dead do not praise the Lord,
   nor those who sink into the silence;[530]
but we, the living, bless the Lord,
   both now and forever, Alleluia![531]

Antiphon: Lord, you have made us a line
        of kings and priests for God, our Father.

Our Lord and God, you are worthy
   to receive glory and honour and power,
   for you created the whole universe;
   by your will, when it didn't exist, it was created.[532]

---

522   Psalm 115:9; Matthew 24:6-8; Galatians 2:7
523   Psalm 115:10; Mark 13:9-10; Galatians 2:8
524   Psalm 115:11; Luke 21:14-15; Galatians 2:9
525   Psalm 115:12; Matthew 24:21-22; Romans 1:16-17
526   Psalm 115:13; Matthew 25:14-15; Galatians 2:10
527   Psalm 115:14; Matthew 25:16-17; Romans 15:20
528   Psalm 115:15; Matthew 25:21, 23; Philippians 1:27
529   Psalm 115:16; Matthew 24:45-46; Mark 10:29-30
530   Psalm 115:17; Matthew 25:26-27; Proverbs 8:35-36
531   Psalm 115:18; Matthew 25:34; Acts 20:24
532   Revelation 4:11; Mark 13:24-26; Genesis 1:1-2

Gospel (on the Road to) Emmaus / 297

Worthy are you, O Lord, to take the scroll
  and to break its seals,
    because you were sacrificed, and with your blood
    you purchased people for God,
      those from every tribe, language, nation, and race.[533]
You made them a line of kings and priests for God,
  and they shall reign upon the earth.[534]

Worthy is the Lamb, that was sacrificed,
  to receive power, riches, wisdom and strength,
  honour, glory, and blessing.[535]
To the one seated on the throne and to the Lamb,
  be all praise, glory, and power,
  forever and ever.[536] Amen.[537]

Glory be to the Father,
  and to the Son,
    and to the Holy Spirit,
  as it was in the beginning,
    is now,
    and ever shall be world without end. Amen.

---

533   Revelation 5:9; Matthew 24:31; Galatians 3:8
534   Revelation 5:10; Luke 21:28; Ephesians 1:13-14
535   Revelation 5:12; Matthew 24:44; Romans 16:26
536   Revelation 5:13; Luke 21:36; Romans 16:27
537   Revelation 5:14; Mark 13:31; Revelation 22:3-7

Chapter 35

Thursday, the 13th/14th Nisan (6th April, 30 CE)—Christ in Jerusalem, the Daytime and Evening of His New Creation: The First Day of His Feast of Unleavened Bread, the New Covenant in His Body and Blood

Readings: John 12:20-50; Matthew 26:17-19, Mark 14:12-16, Luke 22:7-13

Even early in the morning on Thursday, Jerusalem was teaming with the many thousands of pilgrims who had come up to the city of the Lord's dwelling, its streets now already swollen for the Jewish Feast of Passover that would begin on Friday evening.[1] The concurrent celebration of the Feast of Unleavened Bread would last for a week;[2] but on its actual first day, starting with the evening after tomorrow's daylight on Friday,[3] various extended families would be sharing the Passover meal as they gathered together in their houses all over Jerusalem;[4] then, late into that night's Sabbath, after their Passover meals would be finished well beyond midnight, everyone would return to their individual tents, or to their temporary lodgings, or stay in their Jerusalem homes, for their Sabbath prayers and solemn

---

1 Deuteronomy 16:5-6, Exodus 12:6, 30-31; John 13:1, 29-30; 19:42
2 Exodus 13:3-10, Deuteronomy 16:3
3 Leviticus 23:5-6
4 Deuteronomy 6:20-25

reflections, like a people in flight out of the bondage of Egypt.[5]

But besides the Jews coming from everywhere to Jerusalem for the festival, from both inside and outside of Israel, it also happened that there were some Greeks, who were Gentile converts from paganism, or proselytes,[6] who had come to Jerusalem in order to join with the Jews for their celebrated worship of the one true God.[7] These particular Greeks had been searching diligently for Jesus among the crowds, albeit unsuccessfully; and when, at last, they did discover Philip, the Lord's disciple, they came to Philip and asked him, "Sir, we would like to see Jesus."[8] Philip, who had hailed from Bethsaida in Galilee,[9] in turn went to Peter's brother Andrew,[10] his companion and fellow home-townsman;[11] and Philip told Andrew about their request.[12] Then together, both Philip and Andrew went to Jesus to tell the Master what these Greeks had said.[13]

Somewhere in Jerusalem, Jesus had been indoors with his disciples, so as not to be seen by the crowds.[14] However, just at that moment when Philip and Andrew found Jesus, Jesus already had come outside the house and into the streets, where the crowds would see him.[15] So there, with Jesus out in the open and no longer hidden from sight,[16] Philip and Andrew put their request from the Greeks to Jesus. But it now was not the time, nor was it the responsibility of the Lord, to meet with any of those Gentiles.[17] However, later Jesus would send his disciples to them; and along with them, in truth, he

---

5   Deuteronomy 16:7-8, Exodus 12:33-34, 35-39; Deuteronomy 7:7-10
6   Matthew 23:15
7   John 12:20
8   John 12:21; Luke 2:41-43, 46-50; Matthew 13:16-17, Luke 10:23-24; Matthew 2:7-11; John 7:35-36, 6:26, 12:37
9   John 12:21
10   John 1:40-41
11   John 1:44, Luke 10:1
12   John 12:22
13   John 12:22; Matthew 10:5
14   John 11:57; Mark 7:24
15   John 12:23; John 18:4
16   Luke 8:16-17, John 8:12
17   Matthew 10:5-6, 15:24; Luke 13:29-30

would be sending both himself and the Spirit;[18] but he would do so only after he now had fulfilled both the law and the prophets in their entirety.[19] For, except through the imminent glory and sacrifice of Jesus on the cross in his obedience to the Father, together with God the Father's ultimate glorification of his Son by the Lord's subsequent resurrection from the dead,[20] until then, neither Jews nor Gentiles, no one could be saved from their sins and be raised to life.[21]

So, in reply to the question from the Greeks put to him by urgent proxy from Philip and Andrew, Jesus then declined their request, as with his poignant emotion and serene determination, he told both disciples:[22]

> Now the hour has come for the Son of Man to be glorified.[23] Amen, amen, in all truth I tell you: unless a grain of wheat falls into the earth and dies, it remains just a single grain of wheat; but if it dies, it yields a rich harvest.[24] Whoever loves his life loses it; and whoever despises his life in this world will keep it for eternal life.[25] Whoever serves me must follow me; and where I am, there with me my servant will be; and whoever serves me, him my Father also will honour.[26] Now, though my soul is deeply troubled, what shall I say: "Father, save me from this hour?"[27] Yet, it was for this very purpose that I have come to this hour.[28]

And then, in his strong and clear voice, Jesus proclaimed out loud for all the Jews, but also for everyone else to hear his obedience to his Father's works:

---

18 Matthew 28:19-20, John 16:7
19 Matthew 5:17-18, John 19:28-30; Ephesians 2:11, 14-17, 19
20 Ephesians 2:13, 1:11, Romans 3:21-26, 5:2, 10
21 Ephesians 2:12
22 John 12:23; John 12:30, 7:37
23 John 12:23; John 17:4-5
24 John 12:24; John 4:34-35, Matthew 13:23
25 John 12:25; Mark 8:35-36
26 John 12:26; John 8:12, 17:10; Luke 9:23, Ephesians 2:18
27 John 12:27; Mark 14:34, Matthew 26:37-39, Luke 22:44
28 John 12:27; John 18:37

Father, glorify your name![29]

Also then a voice came from heaven saying, "I have glorified it, and I will glorify it again."[30] The Jewish crowd, standing there nearby and hearing this according to their personal disposition, said that it was a thunder clap; while others in their individual grace from God openly declared, "It was an angel speaking to him."[31] But none of them had recognized properly what it was they definitely knew they had heard.[32] So Jesus, knowing the quandary of some and the amazement of the others, answered them, implicitly giving recognition to his Father's voice:

> This voice did not come for my benefit, but for yours.[33] Now judgement is being passed on this world; and now the prince of this world will be driven out.[34] And when I am lifted up from the earth, I will draw everyone to myself.[35]

In saying this, Jesus primarily indicated the kind of death he would die;[36] but implicitly as well, he also had indicated his future resurrection and ascension to the Father.[37] The crowd answered Jesus back, "Our Law has taught us that the Christ will remain forever.[38] How then can you say, "The Son of Man must be lifted up?"[39] Who is this Son of Man?[40] The Jews had been expecting a Messiah completely different to what Jesus was presenting to them in his own person: a Messiah of suffering, who will die for others.[41]

---

29 John 12:28; John 17:23, 7:39, 5:19-21; John 17:1, 4-5, Revelation 4:11, 21:10, 22:5
30 John 12:28; John 8:18, 54
31 John 12:29
32 John 12:37, 10:30, 2-5, 8:47, 42-43
33 John 12:30; John 11:42, 5:37-38; Luke 9:35
34 John 12:31; John 16:33; Luke 10:18; 1 John 3:8
35 John 12:32; John 8:28, 6:40; John 1:51, 3:13, Matthew 26:64
36 John 12:33; John 3:14-15, Numbers 21:9
37 John 20:11-12, 17
38 John 12:34; 2 Samuel 7:16-17, Jeremiah 33:14-22, Psalm 110:1-4; Mark 15:29-30, Luke 23:35
39 John 12:34; Isaiah 5:20-21; 1 Corinthians 1:18-19
40 John 12:34; John 12:23; John 5:25-27, Luke 10:22
41 Matthew 16:13, Luke 9:18, 20-22, 28, 30-31, 35-36

Again, these unbelievers were still blind, without any understanding, and completely in the dark,[42] except for the light of the world now standing right there in front of them.[43] Then, without any condemnation, and without any prejudice to his saving them,[44] Jesus said:[45]

> The light will be with you only a little while longer.[46] Walk while you have the light, or darkness will overtake you; for anybody who walks in the dark doesn't know where he's going.[47] While you still have the light, believe in the light, so that you may become children of the light.[48]

After saying this, Jesus then went off and hid himself from their sight.[49] It was now too dangerous for the Lord to be seen by daylight in public, so great was the murderous intent of the Jews from those who would not believe in him.[50]

Later that day after midnight,[51] in the darkness of the night,[52] Jesus, who was himself without sin and the light of the world, would surrender himself voluntarily to the powers of darkness,[53] in order to conquer the darkness of sin through the victory of his cross.[54] For his divine purpose was not to condemn the world or to judge it—that would come later, sure enough—but now it was to convict

---

42 John 12:40
43 John 1:9, 10:4; 1 John 2:9-11; 2 Corinthians 4:3-4, Isaiah 59:10
44 John 3:17, 12:47-48, Matthew 23:37
45 John 12:35; Deuteronomy 31:27-29, 30:19-20
46 John 12:35; John 7:33; Isaiah 9:1, Matthew 4:16, Luke 1:19, John 1:4, 10-11
47 John 12:35; John 1:5; John 9:39-41; Matthew 13:13, 16; Jeremiah 13:16-17, Isaiah 59:9
48 John 12:36; Matthew 13:43, 1 John 1:5-7; John 1:12-13, 9:5
49 John 12:36; John 10:31, 39, 8:59, 7:30, 44; 1 Corinthians 2:8; Isaiah 8:17
50 Isaiah 59:13
51 Exodus 12:29, 31-34, 39, 42, 51; Exodus 13:1, 11-16, Luke 2:7, Colossians 1:15
52 John 9:4
53 John 18:7-8, 36
54 John 14:30, 10:11, 18, Isaiah 43:11-13, Romans 13:2

the world of sin and to save it.[55] And before doing so, Jesus had tried to lead all non-believing Jews to his "Saving Justice,"[56] before hiding himself, but only temporarily, from their sight.[57] As for the Greek Gentiles now looking for Jesus,[58] they would not find salvation through Judaism, but only from Israel. Salvation and the worship of the one true God came from the Jews,[59] but grace and truth, and the gospel, came through Jesus Christ.[60] The Gentiles, also like the Jews, could not be saved by simply adopting the beliefs and practices of the Jews; nor could the Gentiles become Jews, because being Jewish was solely a condition of physical heritage; and for Jews and Gentiles alike, salvation simply wasn't a condition of physical heritage, of their being Jewish.[61] Nor, as many Jews had believed,[62] could anyone be saved through the Law,[63] by their keeping Jewish proscriptions and conventions. No, for only through faith in Jesus all are reborn in the image of Christ,[64] the New Man,[65] as the first of many brothers,[66] when we follow him through the way of his cross, in the way of the gospel, the only path to eternal life in the Lord's resurrection.[67]

Jesus had presented the Jews with so many signs right in front of their eyes,[68] vividly astonishing confirmations from the Father,[69] yet still they did not believe in him, in order that the proclamation of the prophet Isaiah was fulfilled:

55	John 3:17, 9:39, 12:47, 15:22
56	Romans 1:16-17, 10:21
57	John 12:36; John 12:32, 6:40
58	John 12:21
59	John 4:22, Romans 9:4-5
60	John 1:17, Matthew 1:1; Romans 10:16-17, 20, Isaiah 53:1, 65:1
61	John 8:33, 37, 39-40
62	John 7:49, 9:28-29, 8:41
63	John 1:16, Romans 6:23
64	Acts 10:42-43, 2 Corinthians 3:18; John 3:3-5, Ephesians 2:21-22, John 7:38-39
65	Ephesians 2:15, 10, Colossians 3:10-11, 2 Corinthians 5:17; Matthew 19:28, Revelation 21:5
66	Romans 8:28-30; 1 Corinthians 15:19-20
67	John 14:4, Romans 1:3-5, Acts 22:6, 21; Philippians 3:3-11; Ephesians 2:17, Colossians 3:16; John 10:9, Matthew 7:14
68	John 12:37
69	John 10:38, 14:10-11

"Lord, who has given credence to our preaching, and who has seen in it a revelation of the Lord's power?"[70]

Indeed, for this reason they were unable to believe, as again Isaiah says:[71]

"He blinded their eyes and hardened their heart, to prevent them from using their eyes to see, using their heart to understand, and changing their ways by being converted, for them to be healed by me."[72]

Isaiah had said this because he saw the Lord's glory,[73] and his words referred to Jesus.[74] Nonetheless, many believed in Jesus,[75] even among the religious authorities;[76] but because of the Pharisees, they did not openly admit it, fearing that they might be expelled from the synagogue:[77] because they put human glory before God's glory.[78] Yet, Jesus openly had declared for everyone:[79]

Whoever believes in me believes not in me but in the one who sent me,[80] and whoever sees me sees the one who sent me.[81] I have come into the world as light, to keep everyone who believes in me from staying anymore in darkness.[82] If anyone hears my words and does not observe them faithfully, it is not I who shall judge such a person,[83] for I did not come to judge the world, but

---

70 John 12:38; Isaiah 53:1, Romans 10:16, 1-4
71 John 12:39
72 John 12:40, Isaiah 6:10; Acts 28:25-28, Matthew 13:14-15, Mark 4:12; Isaiah 58:8
73 Isaiah 6:1-4
74 John 12:41
75 John 2:11, 13, 23, 4:45, 1-4, 39-42; John 6:4, 10-15, 51-53, 60, 64-66; John 7:37, 40, 8:30-32, 10:21, 42, 11:45, 48, 12:11
76 John 3:1-2
77 John 12:42; John 9:22, 7:13
78 John 12:43; John 5:44
79 John 12:44
80 John 12:44; John 8:42, 11:42; John 10:29
81 John 12:45; John 14:7; John 1:18
82 John 12:46; John 8:12; John 3:19-21, 1:9-11
83 Deuteronomy 31:24-27, John 5:45-47

to save the world:[84] so, anyone who rejects me and refuses my words has his judge already: the word that I have spoken itself will condemn him on the last day.[85] Yes, for I have not spoken of my own accord, but the Father who sent me has commanded me what to say and what to speak;[86] and I know that his commands are eternal life; and so, what I speak is what the Father has told me to say.[87]

After Jesus had gone into hiding,[88] on that day the Lord's disciples in the Synoptic gospel-narratives of Mark, Matthew, and Luke had called the first day of Unleavened Bread,[89] then it was actually the day before the Jewish feast, which initiated and combined with the evening feast of Passover,[90] after the Passover lamb would have been sacrificed.[91] The first day of the feast of Unleavened Bread begins from the evening of the Passover meal; but apparently it also had become customary for some to refer to the preceding day as the first day of Unleavened Bread, or perhaps two days were allowed for the feast. So, for the Synoptic evangelists, when the disciples had referred now to the first day of Unleavened Bread, in this case they actually would mean the day before its customary designation, which they meant for the Thursday, instead of on Friday. Yet, the disciples may have acted upon this potential anomaly, not on their own initiative, but also on their recognition of the Lord's desire to share with them in his celebration of the Passover meal before he suffered,[92] the Passover that everyone else would be celebrating normally on the evening of the day of the Lord's crucifixion, after Jesus had completed his sacrifice on the cross as the anointed one,[93]

84	John 12:47; John 3:17-18, 6:28-29, 8:15-16
85	John 12:48; John 5:38, 8:43b-44a, 47; John 8:24-26
86	John 12:49; John 8:26, 28-29, 42; 1 John 4:14, 5:20
87	John 12:50; John 5:24, 6:63c, 8:28, 10:30; John 8:51, Revelation 19:9-10
88	John 12:36
89	Mark 14:12, Matthew 26:17, Luke 22:7
90	Exodus 12:18; John 18:28, 19:14, 31, 42
91	Mark 14:12, Matthew 26:17, Luke 22:7
92	Mark 14:12, Matthew 26:18, Luke 22:8, 15
93	John 1:34, Matthew 3:16-17, Luke 4:18-19, 9:35-36; Isaiah 42:1, 61:1-2

as the Lamb of God.[94] Yet, on the day some called the first day of Unleavened Bread, on that Thursday evening of the 14th Nisan, the disciples were still unaware of the Lord's sacrifice yet to come the following day, on Friday 14th Nisan, even though several times Jesus had told them about its necessity, and without its facts penetrating their still cloudy and ambivalent understanding.[95]

Now, on Thursday, the fifth day of the week, it very likely was sometime late-morning or sometime mid-day. And the present location for the Lord's undesignated hideaway very likely was his usual get away place,[96] somewhere on the Mount of Olives, just outside and overlooking Jerusalem. It was the first day of Unleavened Bread,[97] when during the day the Passover Lamb was and had to be sacrificed.[98]   [There alone with the Lord,] the disciples came to Jesus and they asked him, "Where do you want us to go to make preparations for you to eat the Passover?"[99] He then sent two of his disciples,[100] Peter and John,[101] and he told them:

> The two of you go to prepare for us the Passover meal.[102]

When Peter and John asked him, "Where do you want us to prepare it?"[103] Jesus then said to them:

> Look, you will go to a certain man in the city.[104] When you go into the city, you first will meet a man carrying a pitcher of water; follow him,[105] wherever he

---

94 John 1:36; 1 Peter 1:19; Isaiah 53:6-7
95 Luke 18:34, 22:24, Matthew 20:20-24, John 18:10-11
96 Luke 22:39
97 Matthew 26:17, Mark 14:12, Luke 22:7
98 Mark 14:12, Luke 22:7; John 1:29, Leviticus 14:11-14, 21-22, Luke 2:24, Exodus 12:4-7, 43-46, John 19:36, Exodus 12:47-51, 13:1, Luke 3:21-22, Revelation 5:6, 12, Philippians 2:8-11
99 Matthew 26:17, Mark 14:12
100 Mark 14:13
101 Luke 22:8
102 Luke 22:8
103 Luke 22:9
104 Matthew 26:18
105 Mark 14:13

enters,[106] right into the house.[107] Go and say to the owner of the house he enters,[108] "The Master says this to you:[109] My time is near; it is at your house that I am keeping Passover.[110] Where is the room for me to eat the Passover with my disciples?"[111] The man then will show you a large upper room all furnished with couches; make the preparations for us there.[112]

The disciples did what Jesus told them.[113] They set out and went into the city.[114] There they found everything as he had told them.[115] And there, they prepared the Passover.[116]

The disciples, it seems, had been split into two teams. The first team, consisting of Peter and John,[117] prepared the Passover meal, and they had much to do, to reflect on, to pray over, and to talk about, as the Lord prepared them for his passion. Peter and John were obedient to the Lord then, but they may or may not have wondered about what seems to be an obvious anomaly for us: that they were celebrating Passover one day early. As for the Lord's second team, there were the other ten disciples, who remained near the Lord as companions and, unknowingly to them, so also to provide constraint to Judas.[118] Then, sometime around sundown, Peter and John would rejoin Jesus and the other apostles until it was time to begin the Pascal sacrifice and victory celebration, when Jesus himself would return

---

106 Mark 14:14
107 Luke 22:10
108 Mark 14:14, Luke 22:11
109 Matthew 26:18, Mark 14:14, Luke 22:11
110 Matthew 26:18
111 Mark 14:14, Luke 22:11
112 Mark 14:15, Luke 22:12
113 Matthew 26:19; John 2:5
114 Mark 14:16
115 Mark 14:16, Luke 22:13; 1 John 47-51, Matthew 26:64, 65-66; Mark 10:32-34, Luke 18:31-34
116 Matthew 26:19, Mark 14:16, Luke 22:13; Exodus 12:6-11, 34:18, 12:15, 18-20; 1 Corinthians 5:7-8
117 Luke 22:8; John 18:15-16, 20:3-4, 21:21-22, Acts 3:1-4, 4:1-3, 13-14, 18-20
118 Mark 14:10-11, Matthew 26:14-15, Luke 22:6, Matthew 26:16

with them, as the Good Shepherd and as the Lamb of God leading forth his flock.[119] So then, only after evening had fallen,[120] according to the true vigil for Passover,[121] as the Passover lamb was meant to be slaughtered on the 14th of Nisan "between the two evenings" or "between the two settings" [in Hebrew, "*beyn ha'arbayim,*"][122] that is, between the setting of the day on the 14th Nisan (midway between the sun's zenith and sunset) and the setting of evening (after sunset 14th Nisan, before the night began on 15th Nisan),[123] they would all enter together into the night of the darkness of our sin, as the long dark night of the Passion was about to begin.[124] But now Jesus, the Passover lamb, only when it was evening arrived at the upper room with his twelve disciples for his great Passover,[125] as Jesus would be the one to lead the way through the darkness for everyone,[126] for all humankind,[127] as the light and glory of God.[128]

Readings: John 13:1-20; Mark 14:17-25, Matthew 26:20-29, Luke 22:14-30, John 13:21-30

It was now the day before the Jewish feast of Passover.[129] And Jesus, knowing that his hour had come to pass from this world to the Father; and always having loved his own in the world, he loved them to the very end.[130] Jesus took his place at table, and with him the apostles also took their places.[131] As Jesus and his disciples

---

119 John 10:11, 27
120 Isaiah 60:2
121 Exodus 12:42
122 Exodus 12:6, 8, 15, 18, Leviticus 23:5-6, Numbers 9:2-3, Deuteronomy 16:6, Ezekiel 45:21
123 Exodus 29:38-41, Numbers 28:4; Leviticus 23:5-6, Exodus 12:6-8, John 19:14, 30-31
124 Isaiah 59:9; John 14:30, Luke 22:53
125 Mark 14:17, Matthew 26:20
126 Job 17:10-16, John 8:12, Isaiah 60:2, Revelation 21:22-25; Genesis 1:3, 2 Corinthians 4:6
127 Luke 2:31-32
128 Exodus 13:21-22, Isaiah 60:1; John 12:23, 28, 35, 46; 1 John 2:8
129 John 13:1
130 John 13:1; John 17:1, 11, 13, 15-16; John 15:9, 12, 17, 17:9, 12, 24
131 Luke 22:14

were at supper, the devil had already then put it into the mind of Judas Iscariot, the son of Simon, to betray him.[132] But even so, and more so, Jesus was fully aware that the Father had put everything into his own power;[133] that he had come from God; and that he was returning to God.[134] Then, before the meal began, Jesus got up from the table, took off his outer garments, and took a towel and tied it around his waist.[135] He poured water into a basin; and then he began to wash the disciples' feet and to dry them with the towel that he was wearing.[136] Jesus came to Simon Peter,[137] and Peter said, "Lord, are you going to wash my feet?"[138] Jesus answered him:

> At the moment you don't know what I'm doing, but later you will understand.[139]

"Never," replied Peter, "You will never wash my feet."[140] And Jesus told him:

> If I do not wash your feet, you can have no share with me.[141]

Simon Peter answered, "Well then, Lord, don't just wash my feet, but also my hands, and my head, too!"[142] Jesus said:

> No one who has had a bath needs washing, such a person is completely clean; and so, you too are clean, although not all of you.[143]

Jesus knew the one who would betray him, and that is why he

---

132 John 13:2; John 13:27, 6:70-71, 8:44; Ephesians 1:18
133 John 13:3; John 3:35, 10:28, 17:2; 1 Peter 1:3-5, Ephesians 1:19-23, 1 John 5:18
134 John 13:3; John 16:28, 17:11, 20:17
135 John 13:4; Exodus 12:11, Luke 12:37, 17:8-10
136 John 13:5; Philippians 2:7-8; 1 Peter 5:5
137 John 13:6; Matthew 16:18
138 John 13:6; Luke 5:8-11; John 12:3, 4-6; Leviticus 14:19-20, Hebrews 9:15
139 John 13:7; Luke 17:7-8, John 21:15-17; Hebrews 11:8
140 John 13:8; 1 Peter 5:6; Isaiah 59:12, 53:11
141 John 13:8; Colossians 3:24, 1:10-12, 1 Peter 2:9; Isaiah 53:12
142 John 13:8-9; John 21:18
143 John 13:10; John 15:3, 17:17, Ephesians 1:13-14; Matthew 28:19, Acts 2:38-41, 8:26-40, Romans 6:3-4

said, "but not all of you are clean."[144]

Peter may or may not have been the first of the Twelve to have his feet washed, nor was he the worst of them so washed;[145] however, in his future role as the Servant of Servants, by his copying Jesus, Peter provides an example of leadership for the universal church. But Peter, after seeing now what Jesus was about to do, either as the first one in line or by what Jesus may have been doing for others before he came to Peter, in his initial tempestuous reaction, Peter seemed horrified that the Lord should be washing his feet.[146] Perhaps he had felt it was something to be left for doing by the household servants, not by the Master of the house.[147] But there is another reality. Only five evenings before this, in Bethany, Mary of Magdala had anointed the feet of Jesus, and she wiped them with her hair.[148] The first one to object had been Judas Iscariot, with his excuse that it was a waste of money that could have benefited the poor.[149] And on another occasion, an unnamed woman performed the same deed, wiping the Lord's feet with her hair, but the Pharisees had objected to the Lord's permitting this when they referenced her as an obvious sinner, as a prostitute.[150] Washing the feet of a groom always was the exclusive prerogative of the bride; yet this is the intimacy of our wedding invitation,[151] when Christ our bridegroom has taken us to be his bride;[152] and as, in total relationship with him in binding faithfulness, he expects that we enter into the most perfect intimacy of his spousal love.[153]

And so, when Jesus came to him, Peter felt entirely free to express

---

144   John 13:11
145   John 13:5; Matthew 25:14
146   John 13:6; Luke 3:16; Luke 12:36
147   Matthew 18:3-4, 20:1; Matthew 25:15, Luke 12:37; Colossians 3:22-24, 4:1
148   John 12:3
149   John 12:4-6; John 13:27-29
150   Luke 7:37-39
151   John 2:2
152   John 3:29, Revelation 21:2
153   John 13:7; John 15:3-4, 17:21-23, Ephesians 1:6-7, 22-23, 2:4-5, 4:11-13, 5:2, 21-28

his grave reservations to the Lord, and bluntly told him so.[154] Yet, with perfect patience, Jesus also recognized Peter's present lack of understanding, and his charming forthrightness; and so, with equal bluntness to Peter's intimacy, Jesus told Peter that he would have no share in the Lord's ministry or in his inheritance if Jesus did not wash his feet.[155] For, indeed, Jesus very much needed the feet of Peter, rooted in the intimacy of the Lord, and of the feet of others so rooted for preaching his good news of the gospel,[156] before they shared their later reward with Christ in his glory.[157] And just as Peter had exclaimed, in his request now for an entire washing,[158] in the Lord's future work Peter would be using his feet, hands, and head, as well as all his heart and soul in his intimacy with God![159]

But, in this regard, Peter also provides a sharp contrast to Judas. Except for Judas Iscariot,[160] Peter and the Lord's other disciples had been cleansed already by the body and blood of the Lord, as they each had been baptized into his death and resurrection by receiving his spoken word and by believing in him.[161] Later on, others, too, would be cleansed by a baptism of blood, by their sharing in the sufferings of Christ through their martyrdom.[162] On the other hand, ordinarily but not exclusively, most of us have been cleansed through Christ at the first when we were baptized with water in his name.[163] That we, or anyone else, are his disciples is proven later after baptism by our evident baptism in the Spirit.[164] When Jesus had finished washing their feet, as a form of Confirmation, and he had put back on his outer garments, he went back to his centre place at the head of the table; and immediately, in their final initiation, he said to them:

---

154 John 13:8; Luke 12:41
155 Matthew 20:1-2; Luke 12:42
156 Mark 4:3, 14, 26-27; Isaiah 52:7, Romans 10:15; Luke 12:43, 1 Corinthians 12:12-14, 27; 1 Peter 4:10
157 Romans 8:28-30; Luke 12:44
158 John 13:9
159 Matthew 22:37
160 John 6:64, 71; Matthew 15:18-19
161 John 15:3, 17:8; John 6:51, 58, 63
162 Mark 10:38, Luke 12:50
163 Matthew 28:19, Mark 16:16, Luke 24:47, John 3:5; Acts 2:38, 41-42
164 John 13:35, 14:26, 13:34; 1 Corinthians 12:4-7, 1 John 4:13

Do you understand what I have done to you?[165] You call me "Lord" and "Master," and rightly so, because I am.[166] If I, therefore, the Master and Lord have just washed your feet, then you must wash each other's feet.[167] I have given you an example so that you will copy just what I have done for you.[168] Amen, in all truth I tell you, no slave is greater than his master, nor any messenger greater than the one who sent him.[169] Now that you know this, blessed are you if you do it.[170] I am not speaking about all of you: I know those I have chosen, but what scripture says must be fulfilled: "The companion who shares bread with me has lifted up his heel against me."[171] I am telling you this now, before it happens, so that when it does happen, you may believe that "I AM who I AM."[172] Amen, in all truth I tell you, whoever welcomes anyone I send, welcomes me; and whoever welcomes me, welcomes the one who sent me.[173]

Shortly after this, now as Jesus began the meal, he first offered them a toast and a blessing:

> I have longed eagerly to eat this Passover with you before I suffer;[174] because, I tell you, I shall not eat it [again] until it is given its fulfilment in the kingdom of God.[175]

165	John 13:12
166	John 13:13
167	John 13:14
168	John 13:15; 1 Corinthians 11:1
169	John 13:16; Matthew 10:24, Luke 6:40; Mark 3:14, Luke 10:1, Matthew 28:19-20
170	John 13:17; Matthew 24:46, Luke 12:35-37
171	John 13:18; Psalm 41:9, Genesis 3:15; John 13:26, 6:33, 35, 58, 64-71, 63
172	John 13:19; John 8:24, 28, 58, Exodus 3:14, John 18:4-6; John 14:29, 16:4; John 6:70, 68-69
173	John 13:20; John 17:25; John 7:16, 28-29, 8:26, 29, 42, 11:41-42, 12:44-45; Matthew 10:14-15, 40, Mark 9:37
174	Luke 22:15; Luke 12:49-50; Psalm 116:15-16
175	Luke 22:16; Luke 13:29, Revelation 19:9; Psalm 116:13-14

And taking a cup of wine, he gave thanks and said:

> Take this and share it among yourselves,[176] because from now on, I tell you truly, I shall never again drink wine until the kingdom of God comes.[177]

And sometime later on in the meal, when they still were eating,[178] Jesus took some bread, and said the blessing of thanksgiving, broke the bread, and gave it to his disciples, saying to them:

> Take it and eat;[179] this is my body,[180] which will be given up for you; do this in remembrance of me.[181]

Afterwards, when the meal had ended, he did the same with the cup.[182] He took a cup of wine, again offered thanks, and he offered it to them,[183] telling them:

> Drink from this, all of you.[184]

After everyone had drunk from it,[185] Jesus then told them:

> This is my blood, the blood of the covenant.[186] This cup is the new covenant in my blood poured out for you and for many for the forgiveness of sins.[187]

And again, just as he had done for the bread, he told them:

> Do this, whenever you drink it, as a memorial of me.[188]

176	Luke 22:17; Isaiah 42:6, Psalm 111:9
177	Luke 22:18; Psalm 116:17-19, 117:1-2; John 19:29-30
178	Mark 14:22, Matthew 26:26
179	Matthew 26:26, Mark 14:22
180	Mark 14:22, Matthew 26:26, Luke 22:19, 1 Corinthians 11:24
181	1 Corinthians 11:24, Luke 22:19; Psalm 111:5, Exodus 16:2-3, 9-15, 31
182	Luke 22:20, 1 Corinthians 11:25
183	Mark 14:23, Matthew 26:27
184	Matthew 26:27
185	Mark 14:23
186	Mark 14:24, Matthew 26:28; Exodus 24:8, Hebrews 9:18-23
187	1 Corinthians 11:25, Luke 22:20, Mark 14:24, Matthew 26:28; Hebrews 9:24-26
188	1 Corinthians 11:25, 10:16; Psalm 11:3-4

Then Jesus told them:

> In truth I tell you, from now on I shall never again drink wine until the day I drink the new wine with you in the kingdom of my Father.[189]

Having said this, Jesus suddenly became deeply troubled, and frankly he declared:

> In all truth, I am telling you, one of you is going to betray me,[190] one who is eating with me.[191]

In his saying this, the disciples also became deeply distressed,[192] as now they were completely puzzled and looked at each other in their alarm wondering whom Jesus had meant.[193] Then Jesus said, but again right to the point:

> Look, right here with me on the table is the hand of the one who is betraying me.[194]

But from this ambiguous truth, it seemed that Jesus could have referred to any of the disciples; or every one of them; or to anyone of us. And Jesus said:

> Yes, the Son of Man is on the path heading to his fate, as the scriptures says he will; but alas for that man by whom the Son of Man is betrayed![195] For that man it would be better if he had never been born.[196]

They were incredulous and began to ask one another which of them it could be, who would do such a thing?[197] But with clear certainty, and deliberate ambiguity, Jesus told them:

---

189 Mark 14:25, Matthew 26:29; Matthew 22:2
190 John 13:21, Matthew 26:21
191 Mark 14:18
192 Mark 14:19, Matthew 26:22
193 John 13:22
194 Luke 22:21
195 Luke 22:22, Mark 14:21, Matthew 26:24; John 17:12, 13:18; Romans 3:9-12, 21-26, 5:6-8, 6:6, 7:22-25, 8:5-6
196 Mark 14:21, Matthew 26:24
197 Luke 22:23; Hosea 4:1-2, John 11:49-53, 19:6, 14-16, Acts 3:14-15

It is one of the Twelve, one who is dipping his hand into the same dish with me.[198]

Yet, one by one they each protested, "Surely, Lord, it's not me?"[199] In his turn, Judas, who was his betrayer, also told Jesus, "Surely, Rabbi, it isn't me?" And to him Jesus truthfully answered:

You have said so.[200]

Then soon afterwards, and very momentarily, the focus of everyone's disturbance and denial suddenly switched: from debating: who the "traitor" could be? to: who among them was most the "hero"? That is: an argument erupted among all of them about which of them should be regarded as the "greatest."[201] Effortlessly, however, Jesus was quick to remind them of the very centre of Eucharist, the essence of his body and blood: where the Lamb of God within us becomes our practice of the love of God.[202] For, just as the same word in Aramaic, "*talya,*" indistinguishably means "lamb" and "servant," Jesus told them:

> Among the Gentiles, their kings lord it over them, and those in authority over them are given the title Benefactor.[203] But with you, this must not happen. No; the greatest among you must behave as if he were the youngest, the leader as if he were the servant [lamb].[204] For who is greater: the one seated at table, or the one who serves? Surely, is it not the one seated at table? Yet, here I am among you as the one who serves.[205]

During this exchange between the Lord and his disciples, John, the disciple whom Jesus loved, had been reclining next to Jesus at

---

198 Mark 14:20, Matthew 26:23; John 13:26
199 Mark 14:19, Matthew 26:22; Romans 7:14-20
200 Matthew 26:25; John 18:34, 38, 37; 1 John 1:6-10, 3:8-12; John 8:44, Genesis 3:3-7, 1 John 5:20
201 Luke 22:24; Luke 9:46, Mark 9:33-36, Matthew 20-21, 24
202 John 13:34; 1 John 3:23, 4:16, 12
203 Luke 22:25
204 Luke 22:26; Matthew 18:1-4, 23:11; Revelation 7:10, John 1:29, 35, Exodus 12:21
205 Luke 22:27; John 13:13-14, Philippians 2:9-11

supper.[206] And Simon Peter, having now regained his previous focus about the Lord's "betrayer," signalled to John across the table by motioning with his head, "Ask him who it is he means."[207] So, also, not to be noticed, John casually leaned back close to Jesus' chest, and softly asked him, "Lord, who is it?"[208] Jesus quietly answered:

> It is the one to whom I give the morsel of bread after I dip it in the dish.[209]

Even at this very moment, Jesus offered himself openly and intimately to Judas, if Judas would only reciprocate the intimacy of his sinfulness to the Lord. The bread was not yet the unleavened bread of the Passover meal, as it contained yeast; but Jesus would take the leaven of our corruption to the bread of his body, offered up to God, his Father and ours, not dipped in sauce, but soaked in his blood on the cross.[210] Take it, Jesus would say by his intimate gesture, and choose to be my intimate friend,[211] share in the bread of life,[212] and be cleansed of your sin.[213] But in his choice, Judas preferred his intimacy with sin over intimacy with God.[214] And Judas, at last, would betray the Lord's intimacy and friendship with a kiss.[215]

So, after Jesus had dipped the piece of bread, he gave it to Judas, son of Simon Iscariot.[216] At that very instant, when Judas had taken the bread, Satan entered him;[217] and then Jesus told Judas out loud:

---

206   John 13:23
207   John 13:24
208   John 13:25
209   John 13:26
210   John 19:14, Luke 12:1, Matthew 23:27-32; Galatians 5:9, 1 Corinthians 5:6-8
211   John 13:18; John 12:38, Isaiah 53:1-12
212   John 6:50-58, 63-64; Mark 14:22, Matthew 26:26, Luke 22:19, John 6:51
213   1 John 1:8-10; John 15:3, 13:10, 5:24, 6:40; Revelation 7:14, 22:14-15
214   2 Corinthians 5:10, 2-4; Matthew 27:4-5, Galatians 3:13, 1 Peter 2:24
215   Luke 22:47-48
216   John 13:26
217   John 13:27; John 6:70-71,48-60, 64-66; 1 Corinthians 11:21-22, Deuteronomy 4:24; Luke 22:3-6

What you are going to do, do quickly.[218]

But none of the others at the table understood why Jesus now had said this.[219] Because Judas had charge of the common fund, some of them thought Jesus simply was telling him, "Buy what we need for the feast," or that he was telling him to "give something to the poor."[220] However, when Judas had taken the piece of bread, he left at once; and it was the middle of the night.[221] And after Judas had gone,[222] Jesus then told his disciples:

> You are the men who have stayed with me through all of my trials;[223] and now I confer a kingdom on you, just as my Father has conferred one on me:[224] you will eat and drink at my table in my kingdom, and you will sit on thrones to judge the twelve tribes of Israel.[225]

The glory of Jesus, the Son of God, also is to the manifest glory of God the Father,[226] and together their glory is evident in us through the Spirit of God that Jesus has given to each of his faithful,[227] to those who stay with Jesus through all their life of trials.[228] Jesus not only gives us a share, or inheritance, with him in God's glory and spirit; but with Jesus in his kingdom, we also share both his passion and resurrection in ourselves; as we also do when we eat his flesh and drink his blood, and daily we live his Eucharist;[229] for then we become his true disciples; and therefore, Jesus also promises us eternal life with him, with us now, where he is: that is, he gives us our share with him in God's glorious kingdom, both here on earth with

---

218   John 13:27; Isaiah 59:7; Matthew 26:50
219   John 13:28
220   John 13:29; Isaiah 58:6-7; John 12:4-6
221   John 13:30; Luke 22:53
222   John 13:31
223   Luke 22:28
224   Luke 22:29; Luke 4:43-44, Mark 1:14-15; John 18:36, Luke 22:37-38, 23:2, John 19:12
225   Luke 22:30; Matthew 26:29, 19:27-28, 29; Revelation 3:21
226   John 5:19-21, 6:44, 65, 8:28-29, 10:30, 12:28, 17:1, 22, Colossians 3:17
227   John 16:13-15; 1 John 4:13, 5:10
228   Revelation 7:9-10
229   John 6:56, 54-55

his peace and in the world with him to come.[230]

Readings: John 13:31-38, 14:1-31, Mark 14:26, Matthew 26:30, Luke 22:31-39

With Judas on his way towards his chosen destruction and perdition,[231] as he now rushed off to the chief priests and Pharisees to initiate the Passion of the Christ,[232] Jesus was left alone in his unity with the Trinity and together with his remaining disciples;[233] and then he revealed to them:

> Now the Son of Man is glorified, and God is glorified in him.[234] If God has been glorified in him, God also will glorify him in himself, and he will do so at once.[235] My little children,[236] I will be with you only for a while longer; you will look for me, and as I told the Jews, "Where I am going, you cannot come."[237] And I give you a new commandment: love one another; you must love one another just as I have loved you.[238] If you have love for one another, then everyone will know that you are my disciples.[239]

Simon Peter, showing his rising mettle for leadership, was the first one to respond, as then, a bit perplexed, he asked Jesus, "Where are you going, Lord?" And Jesus answered:

---

230   John 13:8, 1 Peter 2:9, Exodus 19:5-6, Revelation 5:10; Luke 2:14, Ephesians 2:6
231   John 17:12, Acts 1:16, Psalm 69:22-28; John 13:2, 2 Thessalonians 2:9-12, Ephesians 2:2-5; Matthew 7:13, Deuteronomy 30:19
232   John 18:3
233   John 8:29, 16:32; John 1:32-33, Romans 8:14, John 16:7, Romans 8:15-17, John 17:26, Romans 5:5, John 16:14-15
234   John 13:31; John 8:54, 7:17-18
235   John 13:32; Luke 9:29-31, Romans 1:4
236   John 13:33; John 16:21; 1 John 2:29-3:2
237   John 13:33; John 8:21, 7:36, 34
238   John 13:34; John 15:12, 17; Matthew 22:34-40; 1 Thessalonians 1:4-6; Deuteronomy 5:26-31; 1 John 4:11-12, 21
239   John 13:35; 1 Thessalonians 1:7-9; Deuteronomy 5:32-33; 1 John 4:20

You cannot follow me now, where I am going,[240] but later on you will follow me.[241]

And Peter said to him, "Lord, why can't I follow you now? I am ready, after all, to lay down my life for you."[242] But Jesus told him:

> Simon, Simon! Look, Satan has permission to sift you all like wheat;[243] but I have prayed for you, Simon, that your faith will not fail; and when you do turn back to me, you also must strengthen your brothers.[244]

Then Peter answered, "Lord, I would be ready to go to prison with you, and even to death."[245] Jesus replied, so as to sustain his disciple beyond the dawn:

> Peter, you lay down your life for me?[246] In all truth I tell you, today, by the time the cock crows, three times you will have denied even that you know me.[247]

And although Jesus was now going to the cross, just as everyone who is a true Christian must follow when they also turn back to him, Jesus then told them all where else he now was going, where the disciples would not yet follow, although they did know the way:

> Do not let your hearts be troubled. You have faith in God, also trust in me.[248] In my Father's house, there are many dwelling places; if there were not, would I have told you that I am going now to prepare a place for you,[249] as I am doing. And after I have gone and prepared a place for you, I shall return to take you to

---

240   John 13:36; John 19:17-18
241   John 13:36; John 21:18-19
242   John 13:37; Romans 5:6-7
243   Luke 22:31; Luke 3:17; Luke 22:40, Matthew 6:13, Mark 1:12-13, John 17:15; 1 John 5:18-19
244   Luke 22:32; Matthew 16:18, John 21:14-15, Acts 1:15; Ephesians 2:8
245   Luke 22:33
246   John 13:38
247   Luke 22:34, John 13:38
248   John 14:1
249   John 14:2; Luke 13:18-19

myself, so that you may be with me where I am.[250] You know the way to the place where I am going.[251]

Thomas would be the next to reply to Jesus. Only the week before, he had misunderstood the Lord's words about the death of Lazarus, when Jesus had said, "But let us go to him,"[252] as if the Lord intended then to join Lazarus in death; and like Peter now,[253] Thomas then also had expressed, "Let us also go to die with him."[254] But now, also like Peter,[255] Thomas still had not understood the Lord's meaning; but he presumed that Jesus was intending to prepare some sort of revolutionary hideaway. So, Thomas said, "Lord, we don't know where you are going, so then how can we know the way?"[256] And Jesus answered him:

> I am the Way;[257] I am the Truth and the Life;[258] no one can come to the Father except through me.[259] If you know me, then you will also have known my Father; from this moment you know him and have seen him.[260]

Philip then, with great fervour and impatience,[261] was the next one to respond. He said, "Lord, show us the Father and so we shall be satisfied."[262] And Jesus, then with his patience and supportive criticism, answered him:

> I have been with you all this time, Philip; and still you don't know me?[263] Anyone who has seen me has seen

---

250 John 14:3
251 John 14:4; Deuteronomy 6:1, John 14:6
252 John 11:15
253 John 13:37, Luke 22:33
254 John 11:16
255 John 13:36
256 John 14:5
257 John 14:6; Deuteronomy 8:2-3, John 6:57-58, 63
258 John 14:6; Proverbs 8:35
259 John 14:6
260 John 14:7
261 John 1:43-46, 12:20-22
262 John 14:8; Exodus 24:16-18, 33:18-20, 34:6-8
263 John 14:9

the Father, so how can you say, "Show us the Father?"[264] Don't you believe that I am in the Father and the Father is in me?[265] The words I speak to you, I do not say on my own: it is the Father, living in me, doing his works.[266] Believe me when I say that I am in the Father and the Father is in me; or at least, believe it because of these works.[267] Amen, in all truth I tell you, whoever believes in me will do the same works that I do, and will perform even greater works, because I am going to the Father.[268] Whatever you ask for in my name, I will do; so that the Father may be glorified through the Son.[269] If you ask me for anything in my name, I will do it.[270]

If you love me, you will keep my commandments.[271] I shall ask the Father, and he will give you another Advocate [Paraclete] to be with you forever,[272] the Spirit of truth, which the world can never accept because the world neither sees it nor knows it; but you know it, because it remains with you and is in you.[273] I shall not leave you orphans; I will come to you.[274] In a little while the world will no longer see me; but you will see that I am living, and you also will live.[275] And on that day you will know that I am in my Father and you are in me and I am in you.[276] Whoever holds to my commandments and keeps them is the one who loves me; whoever loves me also will be loved by my Father, and I will love him and reveal myself to him.[277]

264	John 14:9
265	John 14:10
266	John 14:10
267	John 14:11
268	John 14:12; Hebrews 10:19-21, 4:14-16
269	John 14:13
270	John 14:14; John 15:7, 16, 16:23-24, 26; 1 John 5:14-15; Proverbs 8:35
271	John 14:15
272	John 14:16; John 16:7; 1 John 2:1, Hebrews 4:14-16, John 6:39
273	John 14:17
274	John 14:18
275	John 14:19; John 16:16
276	John 14:20; John 17:21
277	John 14:21; Matthew 11:25-27

At this, yet another disciple needed to question the Lord further. Judas[278] (Jude)[279] Thaddaeus,[280] son of James[281]—not Judas Iscariot,[282] the traitor[283]—recognized that the Lord had loved his disciples;[284] but also he was perplexed that Jesus now seemed to want to terminate, prematurely, his seemingly successful and aggressive political and religious campaigns:[285] "Lord, what has happened here? I don't understand how it could be that you intend to reveal yourself to us, but not to the world!"[286] Jesus replied:

> Whoever loves me will keep my word, and my Father will love him, and we shall come to him and make our dwelling with him.[287] Whoever does not love me does not keep my words; and my word that you hear is not my own: it is the word of the Father who sent me.[288] I have told these things to you while I am still with you;[289] but the Advocate [Paraclete], the Holy Spirit, that the Father will send in my name, will teach you everything and remind you of all that I have told you.[290]
>
> Peace I bequeath to you, my own peace I give to you; a peace, not as the world gives it, this is my gift to you.[291] So, don't let your hearts be troubled or afraid.[292] You heard me tell you, "I am going away and I will come back to you."[293] If you loved me, you would be glad that I am going to the Father, because [under these

---

278 John 14:22
279 Acts 1:13
280 Mark 3:18, Matthew 10:3
281 Luke 6:16, Acts 1:13
282 John 14:22
283 John 13:30, 2
284 John 14:21
285 John 6:14-15, 7:4, 12:19; Acts 1:6-8
286 John 14:22; John 7:3-8, 1:10; 3:14-16
287 John 14:23
288 John 14:24
289 John 14:25
290 John 14:26; John 15:26-27, Acts 1:8, 2:1-4, 4:31; 1 John 5:6
291 John 14:27
292 John 14:27
293 John 14:28; John 14:2-3

temporarily veiled moments][294] the Father is greater than I.[295] I have told you this now before it happens, so that when it does happen you may believe.[296] I shall not be speaking to you much longer, because the ruler of this world is approaching; he has no power over me.[297] But now the world must know that I love the Father and that I act just as the Father has commanded me.[298] Get up now, and let's go![299]

And so, the disciples got up to prepare themselves for their leaving from the upper room; but at once they seemed to be a bit unsure of what they needed to take along. Yet, without their asking, knowingly, Jesus then said to them:

When I sent you out, without a purse or a haversack or sandals,[300] were you in need of anything?[301]

"No, nothing at all," they answered.[302] However, Jesus told them:

But now, if you have a purse, take it; and the same with a haversack; if you have no sword, sell your cloak and buy one.[303] For I tell you this: these words of scripture are destined to be fulfilled in me, "He was counted as one of the rebellious."[304] For indeed, what was written about me is coming to fulfilment now.[305]

---

294   John 17:5, 1:14, Philippians 2:7; Mark 9:1-3, Matthew 17:2, 9, Mark 9:9-10, Matthew 26:63-64, 25:31, Hebrews 1:3
295   John 14:28
296   John 14:29
297   John 14:30
298   John 14:31; John 10:17-18
299   John 14:31
300   Luke 10:4
301   Luke 22:35; Deuteronomy 8:4-5
302   Luke 22:36; Psalm 34:9-10
303   Luke 22:36
304   Luke 22:37; Isaiah 53:12, Deuteronomy 9:7, Malachi 2:1-9, 23-24, Matthew 17:10-13; Luke 23:2, John 19:12, 18:39-40, Luke 23:18-19, 23-25, Isaiah 61:2
305   Luke 22:37

The disciples said, "Look, Lord, here are two swords."[306] Jesus answered them:

> That is enough.[307]

Then, in their solemn conclusion of the Passover evening prayers, they all sang the Hallel together.[308] And, as soon as the psalms had been sung, in the cover of the darkest of nights, the "Eleven" loyal revolutionaries and their leader, Jesus, left from their safe-house in Jerusalem, and they headed straight for the Mount of Olives,[309] where soon they would encounter their missing rebellious brother.[310]

Prayer Reflection: Psalms 110:1-7, 116:10-19; Psalms 113:1-9, 147:12-20; Psalms 114:1-8, 117:1-2

Antiphon: Here is a king of my own choosing
    who will rule on Mount Zion.

> The Lord revealed to you, my Lord,
>   "Take your throne at my right hand,
>   till I have made your enemies my footstool."[311]
> From Zion the Lord will stretch out
>   the sceptre of your power; the Lord says,
>   "Rule in the midst of your foes all around you."[312]
>
> A royal dignity has been yours, in holy splendour
>   from the day of your birth; from the womb,
>   like the dew before the daystar, I begot you.[313]
> The Lord Yahweh has sworn an oath he will never change,
>   "You are a priest forever, according to the order of
>   Melchizedek."[314]

---

306   Luke 22:38
307   Luke 22:38; Matthew 10:34-36, Luke 2:34, 1 Corinthians 1:22-23, Luke 2:35
308   Psalms 113-118; Ephesians 5:19
309   Mark 14:26, Matthew 26:30
310   John 18:3; John 13:27; Acts 1:23-26
311   Psalm 110:1; John 12:20-23; Mark 12:36, 1 Corinthians 15:21-22, 25-26
312   Psalm 110:2; John 12:32; John 19:19
313   Psalm 110:3; John 13:31; Matthew 2:1-2, 10-11, Revelation 12:5
314   Psalm 110:4; Luke 22:15; Hebrews 7:15-25

> At your right hand, Lord,
>> he will shatter kings on the day of his great wrath.[315]
> Robed in splendour, he judges the nations, heaping up the corpses;
>> he crushes heads over the whole wide world.[316]
> He drinks from a stream by the wayside,
>> and thus he holds high his head.[317]

Antiphon: I will take up the cup of salvation,
> and I will offer a sacrifice of praise.

> I trusted, even when I said,
>> "I am sorely afflicted!"[318]
> In my terror, I said,
>> "No human being can be trusted."[319]

> What return can I make to the Lord,
>> for all his goodness done to me?[320]
> I will take up the cup of salvation
>> and call upon the name of the Lord.[321]
> I will fulfil my vows to the Lord
>> in the presence of all his people.[322]
> Too costly in the eyes of the Lord
>> is the death of his faithful one.[323]

> Lord, I am your servant,
>> your servant, as was my mother;
>> I am the child of your maidservant;
>> you have loosened my bonds.[324]
> I will offer a sacrifice of thanksgiving:
>> I will call upon the name of the Lord.[325]

---

315 Psalm 110:5; Luke 22:25; John 19:15
316 Psalm 110:6; John 12:47-48; Isaiah 66:16, Revelation 19:11-16
317 Psalm 110:7; Luke 22:10; 1 Kings 1:38, John 18:1
318 Psalm 116:10; John 13:21; Deuteronomy 29:1-3, 31:29, John 12:37-38
319 Psalm 116:11; Luke 22:21-23; John 6:70
320 Psalm 116:12; John 14:15; Romans 12:1-2
321 Psalm 116:13; Matthew 26:27-28; Revelation 15:4
322 Psalm 116:14; Matthew 26:29; Revelation 5:9-10
323 Psalm 116:15; John 12:24; Isaiah 43:4
324 Psalm 116:16; John 12:26; Luke 1:38, 48-49
325 Psalm 116:17; John 12:23; Ephesians 5:2

> I will fulfil my vows to the Lord
>> in the presence of all his people;[326]
>> in the courts of the House of the Lord,
>> in your midst, O Jerusalem.[327]

Antiphon: He comes in splendour, the King who is our peace;
> the whole world longs to see him.

> Alleluia! Praise, you servants of the Lord,
>> praise the name of the Lord![328]
>
> Blessed be the name of the Lord
>> both now and forever.[329]
>
> From the rising of the sun to its setting,
>> let the name of the Lord be praised.[330]

> High above all nations is the Lord,
>> above the heavens is God's glory.[331]
>
> Who is like the Lord,
>> our God enthroned on high?[332]
>
> But he stoops to look down
>> upon the heavens and the earth below.[333]

> He raises up the lowly from the dust,
>> he lifts the poor from the dung heap,[334]
>
> to seat them in the company of princes,
>> yes, among the princes of the people.[335]
>
> To the childless wife he gives a home,
>> the happy mother of sons. Alleluia![336]

---

326   Psalm 116:18; John 14:31; Revelation 5:12-13
327   Psalm 116:19; John 13:33; Matthew 26:57-58
328   Psalm 113:1; Luke 22:27; Revelation 7:13
329   Psalm 113:2; Luke 22:7; Revelation 7:14
330   Psalm 113:3; Luke 22:8; Revelation 7:15
331   Psalm 113:4; John 13:3; Revelation 7:12
332   Psalm 113:5; John 14:12; Revelation 7:16
333   Psalm 113:6; John 13:20; Revelation 7:17
334   Psalm 113:7; Luke 22:35; John 6:54
335   Psalm 113:8; Luke 22:30; John 6:62
336   Psalm 113:9; John 14:2; Isaiah 54:1-8

Antiphon: The Word of God became man, and lived among us.

> Praise the Lord, Jerusalem,
>> Zion, praise your God.[337]
>
> For he strengthens the bars of your gates,
>> and blesses your children within you.[338]
>
> He brings peace to your frontiers,
>> and gives you your fill with finest wheat.[339]
>
> The Lord sends his word to the earth,
>> his command runs swiftly;[340]
>
> he spreads the snow like wool,
>> scatters the frost like ashes,[341]
>
> He sends hail like breadcrumbs,
>> before such cold the waters freeze.[342]
>
> Again when he sends his word they melt;
>> and when he unleashes his wind,
>> torrential waters flow.[343]
>
> The Lord reveals his word to Jacob,
>> his decrees and statues to Israel.[344]
>
> For no other nation has God done this,
>> of such laws they know nothing.[345]

Antiphon: The Spirit of the Lord has filled the whole world; perfect your work in us.

> When Israel came out of Egypt,
>> the House of Jacob from a people of foreign speech,[346]
>
> Judah became God's temple,
>> and Israel his kingdom.[347]

---

337 Psalm 147:12; Mark 14:26; John 6:55-56
338 Psalm 147:13; John 12:36; 1 Kings 19:7-8, John 6:57
339 Psalm 147:14; Mark 14:22; John 6:58
340 Psalm 147:15; John 13:34; Deuteronomy 30:11-14
341 Psalm 147:16; John 14:15; Deuteronomy 30:15-19
342 Psalm 147:17; John 14:21; John 1:18
343 Psalm 147:18; John 13:10, 14:23; John 6:63
344 Psalm 147:19; John 14:6; John 6:67-68, Isaiah 51:16
345 Psalm 147:20; John 13:35; Isaiah 66:8, John 12:36
346 Psalm 114:1; Mark 14:12; Exodus 13:3-5, 9-10, 1 Corinthians 11:23-26
347 Psalm 114:2; John 12:35; Romans 15:8

The sea fled at the sight;
   the Jordon turned back.[348]
 The mountains skipped like rams;
   the hills ran like sheep.[349]
Sea, what was it that made you flee?
   Jordon, why turn back?[350]
You mountains, why skip like rams?
   You hills, why run like sheep?[351]

Tremble, earth, before the Lord,
   before the God of Jacob,[352]
who turned rock into a pool of water,
   flint into a flowing fountain.[353]

Alleluia! Praise the Lord, all you nations,
   extol him, all you peoples.[354]
For the Lord's faithful love for us is strong,
   and his constancy remains forever.[355] Amen.

Glory be to the Father,
   and to the Son,
      and to the Holy Spirit,
   as it was in the beginning,
      is now,
         and ever shall be world without end.
   Amen.

---

348   Psalm 114:3; John 12:27; Isaiah 51:10, Exodus 14:21-22, Joshua 3:12-17
349   Psalm 114:4; John 12:28; Isaiah 44:23, Matthew 27:51
350   Psalm 114:5; John 12:37-38; Revelation 7:2
351   Psalm 114:6; John 12:39-40; Revelation 7:3, 12:12
352   Psalm 114:7; John 14:16; Acts 2:1-3, Revelation 12:10-11
353   Psalm 114:8; John 14:17; Exodus 17:5-6, John 7:37-39
354   Psalm 117:1; John 12:20; Romans 15:9
355   Psalm 117:2; John 13:1; John 6:69

Chapter 36

Friday, the 14th Nisan (7th April, 30 CE), Early in the Dark Morning Long Before Daybreak— Going to His Father, Jesus Now on His Way to the Mount of Olives with His Disciples, and Going to the Ambush There in the Garden

Readings: John 15:1-27, 16:1-33, Mark 14:27-31, Matthew 26:31-35, John 17:1-26, 18:1

As Jesus led the way among the rebellious,[1] the eleven disciples in their jubilant faith and revolutionary fervour followed right behind him, wherever Jesus was planning to go.[2] For sufficiently, with only their Lord and just two swords for weapons,[3] they were ready now for the overthrow of Satan,[4] who would have no power over their Master,[5] and they were eager for the eminent coming of the kingdom of God on earth.[6] In the Lord's hasty and clandestine departure for the Mount of Olives to pray,[7] there was no empty time; for indeed,

---

1 Romans 5:18-19, Luke 22:37, John 14:6
2 Hebrews 11:8-10, Matthew 26:30, 8:19, 21-22, John 14:1, Mark 11:22-24; John 13:33, 14:2, 12, 28-29; Hebrews 13:6-8; Matthew 19:27
3 Luke 22:38, Ephesians 6:14-17
4 John 12:31; Luke 22:5, Mark 10:42, Matthew 20:25; John 6:14-15, 27, Matthew 4:1-4; Isaiah 24:21, Revelation 19:20
5 John 14:30; Isaiah 24:22, Revelation 19:19; Luke 10:18-19, Matthew 16:18
6 John 12:26-27, Matthew 6:10; Luke 22:15-18, Mark 14:25, Matthew 26:29, John 19:28-30; Isaiah 24:23, Revelation 21:23, 3, 19:11-16
7 Mark 14:26, 1:35, 14:32

hardly any time was left at all; but Jesus was determined to use every minute allotted towards his fulfilment of the commission given to him by his Father.[8] In fact, on that night there would be no more sleep for the Lord.[9] And also, in union with his Father's divine purpose,[10] as soon as the disciples were away from the upper room, Jesus then began his discourse to them that, at first and until after his resurrection, they would have regarded as his general revolutionary encouragement,[11] if not also its being somewhat apocalyptic, and perhaps incendiary, as revolutionary rhetoric:

> I am the true vine, and my Father is the vinedresser.[12] He breaks off every branch in me that bears no fruit; and every branch that does produce fruit he prunes to make it bear even more.[13] Already you are pruned and are made clean by means of the word that I have spoken to you.[14] Remain in me, as I am in you: just as a branch cannot bear fruit on its own unless it remains on the vine, so neither can you bear fruit unless you remain united in me.[15] I am the vine, you are my branches; whoever remains in me, and I in him, produces plenty of fruit;[16] for apart from me, you can do nothing.[17] Anyone who does not remain in me is thrown out like a branch, and it withers; and these dry and lifeless branches will be gathered up to be thrown on the blazing fire, where they will be burned.[18]
>
> If you remain in me and my words remain in you,

---

8   John 14:31; Romans 8:3; 1 John 4:9-11
9   Matthew 8:20
10 John 14:10, 16:15
11 John 16:33, 1, 15:11
12 John 15:1; Isaiah 5:1
13 John 15:2; Hebrews 12:5-6, 11-13
14 John 15:3; John 13:10, 17:17-18; 1 Peter 1:23, Matthew 13:23
15 John 15:4; Matthew 21:33, 42-43; 1 Corinthians 3:11, John 17:2, 6:56-57
16 John 15:5; 1 Corinthians 12:12, 27, Ephesians 1:22-23; 1 John 5:11-12, Revelation 22:1-2
17 John 15:5; 1 Thessalonians 5:10, Ephesians 3:20-21; Romans 6:1-8, 23, Hebrews 6:4-8
18 John 15:6; Mark 11:12-14, Matthew 21:19-20, 3:10, 13:40-42; Ezekiel 15:6, 19:12-14; Matthew 3:10

whatever you want you may ask for and you will get it.[19] By this is my Father glorified, that you should bear much fruit and thereby proving that you are my disciples.[20] As the Father loves me, so also I love you; remain in my love.[21] If you keep my commandments, you will remain in my love, just as I have kept my Father's commandments and remain in his love.[22] I have told you this so that my very own joy may be in you and your joy may be complete.[23]

This is my commandment: love one another as I have loved you.[24] No one can have greater love than to lay down one's life for one's friends.[25] You are my friends if you do what I command you.[26] I shall no longer call you slaves, because a slave doesn't know what his master is doing; but I have called you friends because I have made known to you everything I have heard from my Father.[27] You did not choose me; no, I chose you and commissioned you to go out and to bear fruit, fruit that will endure; so that whatever you request in my name, the Father will give you.[28] This is my command to you: love one another.[29]

What if, for the sake of argument, somewhat simply Jesus only had been a rash idealist heading a failed military coup, or if he only was leading an army of his pacific soldier-followers into battle against the entrenched establishment? More, perhaps, like Mahatma Gandhi than Che Guevara. Yet, in fact, Jesus was heading and leading such

---

19	John 15:7; 1 John 3:21-22, John 14:13-14, 16:23
20	John 15:8; John 13:35; 1 John 3:18-19
21	John 15:9; John 17:26; 1 John 4:16
22	John 15:10; John 14:15; John 10:17
23	John 15:11; John 16:24; 1 John 1:4
24	John 15:12; John 13:34
25	John 15:13; 1 John 3:16; John 10:18
26	John 15:14; 1 John 3:1-2, 4:7
27	John 15:15; John 17:6, 26, 1:18; John 21:5-6
28	John 15:16; John 15:17-18, 14:13-14; John 17:18, 20:21; John 1:35-40, 42-43, 47-48, Matthew 4:18-19, 21, Luke 5:3-11, Matthew 9:9, Luke 6:12-13, Mark 3:13-19, Luke 9:1-2, 10:1; John 15:19, 16:33
29	John 15:17; John 15:12, 13:34; 1 John 3:23, Ephesians 4:15-16

a battle group.[30] With charismatic encouragement and determined leadership, he seemed to have maintained his troops psychologically as a unified fighting force, by fortifying their belief in his promises that everyone's stalwart sacrifices would bear fruit, if only everyone remained together, united and true to their purpose;[31] and if in their faith and courage, they pressed forward for the certain victory. But, as he also might have seemed to insist, if anyone should fall by the wayside, or if anyone should not remain united with him for the cause, those individuals would be cast body and soul into the bonfires.[32]

And also, as Jesus seemed then to have insisted, everyone supporting the struggle,[33] and all who remained committed to the doctrine,[34] would obtain everything they had hoped for:[35] the promise of the kingdom and their seats of privileged power,[36] even if they should make the ultimate sacrifice and lay down their lives for one another in the battle.[37] And even now, as Jesus then did insist, they were all friends and comrades with their Lord; they were not military persons of unequal rank, only like conscripted privates and corporals subservient to their commander-in-chief.[38] And furthermore, each one of them had been chosen specifically for their special assignments and commissions that, in their unity with [Jesus] the commander and with [the Father] his chief, they would be destined to bear lasting fruit.[39] Consequently, as Jesus at that time might seemingly have insisted: His Father and our forefathers will be glorified;[40] and all who believe will be justified by the glory of their progeny's victory now at hand![41] So, as Jesus seemed to say:

---

30   2 Timothy 2:3-4
31   John 15:4
32   2 Timothy 2:12b; John 15:6
33   Luke 22:28
34   2 Timothy 2:15-19, 3:1-8, 13-17, 4:3-4; 1 Timothy 6:21
35   John 15:7
36   2 Timothy 2:12a; Luke 22:29-30
37   2 Timothy 2:11
38   John 15:13-15; Matthew 20:25-26, Luke 22:27
39   John 15:16
40   John 13:31; Romans 9:4-5
41   John 6:40, 8:24; John 12:23, 13:32, Romans 8:30, Galatians 3:16

Let's remain together, and in keeping with my command,[42] love one another! For God's kingdom, let the victory now be won!

However, unlike the typical revolutionary group, the unity of the Lord and of his disciples was not simply as a unit banded together, as "with" one another; but Jesus was "in" them, and all of them were "in" him,[43] and "in" one another's life, too.[44] Instead of the solidarity of "with," the Lord now was speaking to his disciples about their relationship to him as a very specific intimacy that they all shared "in" Jesus and "in" each other; which was just as he and his Father shared "in" each other, that Jesus and his Father also shared "in" the disciples, if they kept his commandment of love;[45] for that is how the disciples would remain "in" the love of Jesus and of his Father. It is in that love of Jesus, in his dying for the forgiveness of our sins,[46] that the love of God the Father for us would be fully revealed;[47] because for Jesus, his Father was his exact model, and the veiled glory of the Father would be revealed in the glory of his Son, who was in full the image of the Father.[48] And when we show by our bearing fruit in the world that we remain in the love of God, we also give glory to God, like the Father and the Son glorify each other.[49] Likewise, everyone who shares in the love of God is a living sanctuary, the sign and seal of God's everlasting covenant,[50] for the vital and intimate presence of that one and triune God living within them: the Father, the Son, and Holy Spirit. This is the new and final covenant God establishes with his people: a visible covenant from God, created through the gift of the Father,[51] consecrated in the

---

42	John 15:17
43	John 15:4-5
44	1 John 1:6-7
45	John 15:9-10
46	2 Timothy 2:13; John 4:44, Luke 4:16-30, John 12:39-40; Isaiah 61:1-3, Luke 4:23, Isaiah 6:10, 53:5, 1 Peter 2:24
47	John 3:16; 1 John 4:9, Ephesians 2:4-6
48	John 14:10-13; Mark 9:2-3, 7-9, Exodus 24:16, 33:18-23, 34:29-35, 40:34-35, John 14:8-9, 7; Colossians 1:15; 2 Corinthians 4:3-4
49	John 15:8; 2 Corinthians 3:18
50	Exodus 25:8; Acts 3:25, Ephesians 2:21-22
51	John 10:29; John 6:44, 5:21, 6:40; John 17:21, 23, 14:16-17, 15:26; Romans 5:15, 6:23

body and blood of the Son,[52] and manifested by the Spirit.[53]

But, Jesus was not to be misunderstood, then or now, nor was his cause to be misinterpreted. He was not just some man marching off with his disciples to a religious or political war, like some misguided fundamentalist or terrorist of today,[54] although indeed there would be a great battle against the forces of evil for the souls of men.[55] No; instead of violence, killings and retribution, as one commonly observes in the conflicts of our warring worldly kingdoms of today,[56] their only weapon would be love. And because of their love of one another, as all disciples of the Lord followed his commands exactly,[57] indeed, many of them would be killed as they surrendered their lives in Christ to love for everyone,[58] accepting even death on a cross, if necessary;[59] but not just taking up their own cross, but also embracing the Lord's death on the cross for all of our sins.[60] So, Jesus spoke bluntly now to his disciples about the world that they soon, in fact, would be facing by their preaching and example of love, when they confronted all those who were hostile to the love of Christ.[61] However, if anyone stayed his enemy, and were not his friends,[62] they ultimately would be made his footstool,[63] only to be thrown later into utter and terrible confusion by his mighty power:[64]

> If the world hates you, you must realize that it hated me

---

[52] 1 Corinthians 11:25, Exodus 24:8, Hebrews 10:19-21, John 2:21-22; 1 Corinthians 6:20
[53] Acts 2:1-4, 2 Corinthians 3:6, Romans 8:11,14-17; 1 Corinthians 3:16, 6:19
[54] 1 Timothy 6:6-9; 1 John 4:3
[55] John 17:15, Ephesians 6:10-12
[56] John 17:14, 18:36
[57] 1 Timothy 6:12-14
[58] 1 Timothy 6:17-19; Philippians 1:28-30, 2:1-5, Colossians 3:12-14
[59] Philippians 2:8
[60] 1 Corinthians 2:2, 8-12
[61] Colossians 1:21, Ephesians 2:13-14, 17
[62] Colossians 1:22
[63] John 14:3, Matthew 22:41-46, Psalm 110:1, Hebrews 10:12-14; 2 Peter 3:9, 1 Timothy 1:15-16
[64] Exodus 14:23-24, 15:3-13; Philippians 3:10-11; 2 Thessalonians 1:5-12

first.⁶⁵ If you had belonged to the world, the world would love you as its own; but because you do not belong to the world, because by my choosing you I have drawn you out of the world, the world hates you.⁶⁶ Remember the words I spoke to you, when I said: "No slave is greater than his master."⁶⁷ If they persecuted me, they will also persecute you; if they kept my word, they will keep yours too.⁶⁸ But they will do all these things to you on account of my name, because they do not know the one who sent me.⁶⁹ If I had not come, and if I had not spoken to them, they would have been blameless; but as it is, they have no excuse for their sin.⁷⁰ Anyone who hates me also hates my Father.⁷¹ If I had not performed works among them as no one else ever did, they would be blameless; but as it is, they have seen and hated both me and my Father.⁷² But all this only serves to fulfil the words written in their Law: "They hated me without reason."⁷³

When the Advocate [Paraclete] comes, whom I will send to you from the Father, the Spirit of truth who comes from the Father, he will witness to me.⁷⁴ And you also will be my witnesses, because you have been with me from the beginning.⁷⁵ I have told you all these things so that you may not be tripped up and fall away.⁷⁶ They will expel you from the synagogues; indeed, the time is coming soon when anyone who kills you will think

---

65 John 15:18
66 John 15:19; John 15:16
67 John 15:20; John 13:16
68 John 15:20
69 John 15:21
70 John 15:22
71 John 15:23
72 John 15:24; Numbers 14:21-23; John 14:9, Proverbs 8:36; John 8:41-42, 44
73 John 15:25; Psalm 69:4
74 John 15:26
75 John 15:27; 1 John 1:1-3; Acts 4:20, 2:29-32; John 21:24, 20:30-31
76 John 16:1

he is offering a holy service to God.[77] They will do these things because they have never known the Father or me.[78] I have told you all these things so that when their time comes you may remember that I told you.[79] I did not tell you this from the beginning, because I was with you.[80]

Indeed, the Lord always had been with his disciples, not only from the beginning of his public ministry, when he first personally and publicly had called each of them to be his disciples;[81] but also he had been with them from eternity, when God first had imagined his children;[82] as well as from the initial moment God had made material the physical foundations of the world's creation;[83] and also from their mother's womb, when the Father had called them within his blessing of human procreation;[84] and from their baptism by virtue of the word of his Son;[85] and also, once again, when Jesus finally would call them home to the places he had prepared for them in his Father's kingdom.[86] For, from the very beginning, when God calls anyone into existence, he also calls them to perfect holiness and to their knowledge of God himself;[87] and for that purpose the Father has sent his Son, Jesus Christ, into the world as the perfect image of himself.[88]

However, the Father has not gifted everyone with the privilege of his grace to believe in his Son, so that ultimately they may know,

---

77	John 16:2; Luke 21:12, 16-19
78	John 16:3; John 8:19, 14:7
79	John 16:4
80	John 16:5; Matthew 28:20, John 7:33, 17:12
81	John 15:27, Acts 1:21-22
82	Jeremiah 1:4-5, Proverbs 8:23, Ephesians 3:11, 1:3-5, John 1:12-13; Genesis 5:1, Philippians 2:7, Romans 8:10-11
83	Genesis 1:26-28, 31; 2:1, Ephesians 3:9
84	Galatians 1:15, Isaiah 49:1, Ephesians 3:10
85	John 15:3, 16
86	John 13:36, 14:2-4, Matthew 24:42-46, 25:13; Philippians 1:21-24, Ephesians 2:19-20; John 17:24
87	1 Peter 1:16, Leviticus 11:44-45, 19:2, 20:7, Matthew 5:48; Ephesians 1:4, 4:24, Acts 2:38-39, John 17:3; 1 Corinthians 13:12
88	John 3:16, 1:14; John 14:6-7; 1 John 3:1-3

love, and serve God, and thereby share eternal life with Jesus in God's Spirit.[89] If the harvest is plentiful, but also somehow no one is sent into the harvest to labour for the Lord,[90] then it could be possible that some people might be excused in their ignorance of God's Son. But even so, and more so for us, our knowledge of Christ no longer excuses us if we should fail our personal responsibility to bring the gospel to the world: so, on the one hand, there should be no excuse for anyone's personal ignorance of Jesus Christ;[91] and on the other hand, by our efforts people can share the grace and joy of believing in God's Son,[92] and in Christ inherit their share of eternal life in God's kingdom by living "in" the life of God through Jesus, the source of life.[93] God's wish and hope is for every person who has lived, or who still is alive,[94] to believe in his Son.[95] But this grace of faith and of our justification, a gift from the Father and derived from his Son's sacrifice on the cross, depends upon the fruitfulness of the Lord's disciples,[96] if any of them are truly to be called his active disciples;[97] and this grace also depends upon our prayers to God, when we ask the Father, in the name of Jesus his Son, for God's kingdom to be established on the earth.[98]

Our prayers and actions are a necessary partnership with God to bring about his kingdom;[99] and they depend upon our use of God's grace poured into our hearts to accomplish these prayers and actions,[100] and to bear fruit. If we don't perform, and if we don't

---

89   John 3:18-19; Matthew 13:11, 13-15, John 12:39-40, 6:65
90   Luke 10:2, Matthew 9:35-37, Luke 10:1
91   John 15:22, 16:9, 8:24, 9:41
92   John 15:11; 1 John 1:4; 2 John 12; John 16:22
93   Revelation 22:1, John 15:4-5, Revelation 22:2
94   Romans 5:12-21; Genesis 3:14-15, 6:8-12, 17-18, 9:8-11, 12:1-2, 15:1-6, 17:1-8, 15-21; Romans 4:1-25, Galatians 3:6-29, 4:21-31
95   1 John 4:9-10, John 6:39
96   Romans 9:23-24
97   John 15:8, 8:31, Mark 4:20; John 13:35, James 2:24; Romans 11:13-15, 12, 16-24, John 15:5
98   John 3:18, 15:16, 14:13-14; Matthew 6:9-10; 1 Corinthians 1:9, 9:23, Revelation 1:9; Luke 5:1-2, 4-7, 9-10, John 21:5-6, 11
99   John 15:1, 4-5, 16, 1:35-39, 12-14, Revelation 21:2-5; 2 Corinthians 5:15-21, 6:1-2; 1 John 4:12-13, 19
100   John 14:12; 2 Corinthians 1:20-22, Galatians 4:6

produce, our gift of grace and faith, along with our salvation, may be passed over to someone with more abundant grace, to bear even greater fruit for God.[101] But, just as from the beginning, as Jesus always had been present to give his personal protection and guidance to his disciples,[102] so for all of us, Jesus also provides a helper to give success to our variously assigned tasks on earth, while we are alive. Therefore, because Jesus now was going to the Father, as we do when we die, he told the disciples that he would be sending the Advocate, or Paraclete, later to help them; so that, just as the Father had sent his Son, Jesus would be sending the Spirit to them, to help them in their tasks of bringing Christ to the world of sinners:[103]

> But now I am going to the one who sent me; yet, not one of you asks me, "Where are you going?"[104] And because I have told you this, your hearts are filled with grief.[105] Even so, I am telling you the truth: it is best for you that I am going, because if I don't go, the Advocate [Paraclete] will not come to you; but if I go, I will send him to you.[106] And when he comes, he will show the world how wrong it was about sin, about righteousness, and about condemnation:[107] about the world's sin, because they do not believe in me;[108] about who was in righteousness, because I am going to the Father, and you will see me no longer;[109] and about condemnation, because the prince of this world already has been judged.[110]
>
> There is much more I still want to tell you, but it would

---

101 John 15:1-2, Luke 13:9; Matthew 25:29, 13:12; Isaiah 5:1-2, Matthew 21:33-43; Genesis 1:26-28
102 John 10:14, 27-30, 6:39, 17:12
103 John 20:21-23
104 John 16:5; John 14:12
105 John 16:6
106 John 16:7; John 7:38-39
107 John 16:8
108 John 16:9; John 8:21
109 John 16:10; John 8:22-24, 46; 1 John 2:29; Hebrews 1:3; Matthew 24:27-28, 25:31-33
110 John 16:11; John 8:15-16, 26

> be too much for you to bear now.[111] However, when the Spirit of truth comes, he will guide you to the complete truth, because he will not be speaking alone, but he will say only what he has been told;[112] and he will reveal to you the things that are coming.[113] And he will glorify me, because everything he reveals to you will be taken from what is mine.[114] Everything that the Father has is mine; and that is why I told you everything the Spirit reveals to you will be taken from what is mine.[115]
>
> In a little while you will no longer see me; and a little while later you will see me again.[116]

When the disciples heard these words from Jesus, some of them began to ask one another, "What does this mean, when he says, 'In a little while you will no longer see me, and a little while later you will see me again,' and, 'I am going to the Father?'[117] What is this 'a little while'? We don't know what he means."[118]

However, Jesus knew of their reluctance to ask him about this. Even though they very much had wanted to question him, partially because of their confusion, partially out of anxiety for their ambitions, and partially in their simple denial of the truth, they did not dare to do so; but then Jesus directly told them:

> You are discussing with one another what I said, 'In a little while you will no longer see me, and a little while latter you will see me again.'[119] Amen, I tell you in all truth, you will be weeping and wailing, while the world will be rejoicing; you will be sorrowful, but your grieving will turn to joy.[120] When a woman is in labour,

---

111 John 16:12
112 John 16:13; John 8:28
113 John 16:13; Luke 18:31-34, 24:25-27, 45-49, Acts 1:4-5, 2:23-33
114 John 16:14
115 John 16:15
116 John 16:16; John 7:33; John 20:20
117 John 16:17; John 16:16, 13:33, John 16:10, 5
118 John 16:18
119 John 16:19
120 John 16:20; Isaiah 66:10

she suffers because her hour has come; but when she has given birth to a child, she forgets the suffering in her joy that a child has been born into the world.[121] And likewise with you: you are in anguish now; but I will see you again, and your hearts will be full of joy, and no one shall take that joy away from you.[122]

When that day comes, you will not question me about anything; but Amen, in all truth I tell you, anything you ask from the Father, he will give you in my name.[123] Until now you have not asked anything in my name; ask and you will receive, and so your joy will be complete.[124] I have been telling you of these things in a veiled speech; but the hour is coming when I shall no longer speak to you in such language, but tell you about the Father in plain words.[125] When that day comes, you will ask in my name; and I am not telling you that I shall pray to the Father for you.[126] For the Father himself loves you because you have loved me and have believed that I came from God.[127] I came from the Father and have come into the world, but now I am leaving the world and going back to the Father.[128]

Then the disciples answered Jesus, "Now you are speaking plainly, not using obscure language.[129] And now we see that you know everything and that you do not need to wait for anyone's questions to be put into words; because of this we believe that you came from God."[130] But Jesus answered them:

Do you believe at last?[131] Listen; the hour will come—

121	John 16:21; Isaiah 66:7-9
122	John 16:22; John 16:6; Isaiah 66:14
123	John 16:23
124	John 16:24
125	John 16:25
126	John 16:26; John 16:23
127	John 16:27
128	John 16:28; John 16:10, 13:1
129	John 16:29
130	John 16:30; John 16:19
131	John 16:31

and indeed it has come already[132]—tonight, you will all fall away from me, for the scripture says: "I shall strike the shepherd and the sheep of the flock will be scattered."[133] Each of you are going to be scattered, each going his own way to his own home and leaving me alone; but I am not alone, because the Father is with me.[134] However, after my resurrection I shall go ahead of you to Galilee.[135]

At this, Peter altogether by-passes the Lord's central statements about the shepherd's being struck and the resurrection, and he seems only to understand the Lord's issue as criticism of his own personal integrity; so Peter says to Jesus, "Even if everyone falls away, my faith will not be shaken; I will never fall away."[136] And Jesus answered him:

> In truth I tell you, this day, this very night in fact, before the cock crows twice, you will have disowned me three times.[137]

Jesus, emphatically now, had repeated his earlier prediction of Peter's denial; just as Jesus had told him only a short time ago, when they had been together in the upper room.[138] But now Peter's protest became even more vehement, as he earnestly repeated his loyalty to the Lord, "Even if I have to die with you, I will never disown you."[139] And this time, all of the disciples said the same thing.[140] And, just like all of them, all of us have said and done the same thing, even though through our weaknesses and insufficient will we have failed the Lord, sometimes greatly. But God always accepts the return of a humble sinner.[141]

---

132 John 16:32
133 Mark 14:27, Matthew 26:31; Zechariah 13:7, Ezekiel 34:5-6, 12
134 John 16:32
135 Mark 14:28, Matthew 26:32; Mark 16:7, Matthew 28:7
136 Mark 14:29, Matthew 26:33
137 Mark 14:30, Matthew 26:34
138 Luke 22:34
139 Mark 14:31, Matthew 26:35; Luke 22:33
140 Mark 14:31, Matthew 26:35; Mark 14:18, Matthew 26:22
141 Luke 18:14

Then, in his great compassion as the shepherd of the flock,[142] Jesus told them in his quiet but firm reply, as he spoke to us as well:

> I have told you all of this so that you may find peace in me; in the world you will have trouble, but be courageous: I have conquered the world.[143]

Jesus and his disciples, at that moment, were standing opposite, and now in front of the Kidron valley on the Jerusalem side.[144] As Jesus stood there outside of the fortified city walls with his disciples, he raised his eyes in prayer to his Father in heaven.[145] And with the disciples surrounding Jesus under a myriad stars of heaven, also reflecting in the late night sky their bright repose as Abraham's descendants and the Lord's apostles,[146] Jesus began to pray with them out loud:

> Father, the hour has come: glorify your son, so that your Son may glorify you;[147] so that, just as you gave him authority over all humanity, he may give eternal life to all you have entrusted to him.[148] And this is eternal life: to know you, the only true God, and Jesus Christ, whom you have sent to earth.[149] I have glorified you on earth by finishing the work that you gave me to do.[150] Now, Father, glorify me with you, with the glory that I have had with you before the world ever existed.[151]
>
> I have revealed your name to those whom you took out of the world to give them to me; they always belonged to you, and you gave them to me; and they have kept your word.[152] Now at last they know that everything

---

142   Matthew 9:36, John 10:7-9, Psalm 23:1-4
143   John 16:33; John 14:1, 27; 1 John 5:4, Romans 8:35-37
144   John 18:1, Psalm 23:4
145   John 17:1; John 11:41-42
146   Genesis 22:17, Revelation 12:1
147   John 17:1; John 12:27-28, 13:31-32, 1:14
148   John 17:2; Matthew 28:18, John 10:28-29, 3:35, 6:38-40
149   John 17:3; 1 John 2:20-25
150   John 17:4; John 19:28, 30, 4:34, 10:17-18
151   John 17:5; John 8:54, 1:1-4, 10; 1 John 1:1-2
152   John 17:6; John 13:10, 14:23-24; 1 John 3:1-3

you gave me comes from you,[153] because I have given them the words that you gave to me, and indeed they have accepted them, and they truly understand that I came from you, and they have believed that it was you who have sent me.[154]

I pray for them; I am not praying for the world, but for those you have given me, because they belong to you.[155] All I have is yours, and all you have is mine, and in them I have been glorified.[156] I will no longer be in the world, but they are in the world, and I am coming to you; holy Father, keep those you have given me true to your name, so that they may be one, just as we are.[157] While I was with them, I protected them in your name and kept them true; I watched over them, and none of them was lost except the one who was destined to be lost, the son of destruction,[158] in order that the scriptures are fulfilled.[159]

But now I am coming to you, and I speak these things in the world, so that with me they may share my joy to the full.[160] I have given your word to them, and the world hated them, because they belong to the world no more than I belong to the world.[161] I'm not asking you to remove them from the world, but I ask that you keep them safe from the Evil One.[162] They don't belong to the world any more than I belong to the world.[163] Consecrate them in the truth; your word is truth.[164] As

---

153	John 17:7; John 8:42, 7:29
154	John 17:8; John 8:28, 3:11, 32-34, 5:36, 16:30
155	John 17:9; John 10:29, 6:37
156	John 17:10; John 10:30, 16:15; 2 Corinthians 3:18
157	John 17:11; John 14:28, 10:30; Revelation 4:11, 5:12, 5:13, John 17:1
158	John 6:70, 8:44, Exodus 12:23, Revelation 12:9-12, 20:13-15, Psalm 69:28; 1 John 3:8-12
159	John 17:12; Acts 1:16, Psalm 41:9, Acts 1:20, Psalm 69:25-28
160	John 17:13; 1 John 1:4
161	John 17:14; John 15:18-19; 1 John 4:4-5
162	John 17:15; 2 Thessalonians 3:3, 1 John 5:18-19
163	John 17:16; 1 John 2:15-17
164	John 17:17; John 8:43-45, 31-32, 18:37; 1 John 1:10

you sent me into the world, I have sent them into the world;[165] and I consecrate myself for them, so that they too may be consecrated in truth.[166]

I pray not only for my disciples, but also for those who through their word will come to believe in me.[167] May they be one, just as you, Father, are in me and I am in you,[168] so that they also may be in us, and so the world may believe that you are the one who sent me.[169] I have given them the glory that you gave to me, so that they may be one, as we are one.[170] With me in them and you in me, may they be brought together in perfect unity,[171] so that the world will know that it was you who sent me, and that you have loved them just as you loved me.[172]

Father, they are your gift to me;[173] I want all those you have given me to be in my company where I am, so that they may always see my glory, which is your gift to me, because you loved me before the world was made.[174] Righteous Father,[175] the world has not known you, but I have known you; and these men have known that you sent me.[176] I have made known your name to them

---

165	John 17:18; John 15:27, 18:20, 20:21; 2 Corinthians 2:17, 2 Thessalonians 3:1-2
166	John 17:19; John 1:33, 3:8, 4:23-24, 7:37-39, 14:17, 15:26; 1 John 1:9, John 20:22-23, Genesis 2:7; Ephesians 1:13, 2 Thessalonians 2:13, 1 John 2:27
167	John 17:20; 1 John 1:2-3
168	John 17:21; John 10:38, 14:10-11
169	John 17:21; 1 John 4:15-16
170	John 17:22; John 10:30
171	John 17:23, Ephesians 4:12-13; 1 Corinthians 12:12-14, 27, Romans 12:4-5
172	John 17:23; Matthew 21:37-39, John 3:16
173	John 17:24; John 14:2, 3:35, Psalm 68:18-20; 1 John 5:1
174	John 17:24; Ephesians 1:4-5, John 10:29, 28; John 1:1-5, Proverbs 8:22-23, 30-36, John 3:36; Genesis 2:5-7, Revelation 22:1, 17
175	John 17:25; Genesis 1:26-27, 2:1-3, 8:8-9, 11:31, 12:1-10, 13:1, 18, 14: 17-23, 15:1-6, 17:1-2, 18:1-2, Exodus 3:1-6; John 1:14, 1 John 1:1-3
176	John 17:25; Exodus 19:1-25, 20:18-21, 24:1-18, Hebrews 12:18-24, 3:5-19, 4:14

and I will continue to make it known, so that the love with which you loved me may be in them,[177] and I may be in them.[178]

As soon as Jesus had finished this prayer, he crossed the Kidron valley with his disciples,[179] not by going around the valley by taking the high route to the northeast towards Bethany.[180] But instead, he went through the valley, much like the Lord's having walked uphill with the disciples from Jericho to Jerusalem, as he had done with them just the week before.[181] But now, they were just outside the city walls about 150 metres beyond the Pool of Siloam,[182] as Jesus made his way with his renegades: first along the length of the entire 600-metre floor of the deep valley, at an incline of roughly 2 cm/metre, an initial height of 12 metres; and then they walked a further 800 metres up the slopes of the Mount of Olives, climbing about 7.5 cm/metre uphill, or a further height of 60 metres towards Gethsemane, for the Lord's immediate destination.[183] Just like the Lord Jesus, King David once before had stood in this bed of the Kidron: in haste, David had brought his whole household from Jerusalem into the valley, just as Jesus now had brought his disciples; from there David had directed them into the safety of the desert; and then, while everyone had made their escape from the perilous conspiracy of Absalom, David's renegade son, David stayed behind and climbed these very slopes.[184]

However, the conspiracy now was against Jesus; and instead of Absalom, it was being directed by the chief priests and Pharisees, as the leading renegades; and under the guidance of Judas, the

---

177   John 17:26; Ephesians 2:18, John 6:46, 14:8-9, 15:9, 12, 15; Exodus 3:13-15; 1 John 4:7-12, 3:17
178   John 17:26; 1 Corinthians 1:9, Ephesians 4:1-8, Romans 8:9-11
179   John 18:1; Psalm 68:18
180   Luke 19:29
181   Luke 19:1, 28; 1 Corinthians 9:24-25, Philippians 2:16, 3:14, Hebrews 12:1-2
182   John 9:7, 13:5, 15:8, 16-17, 16:32, 17:18-19
183   Mark 14:32
184   2 Samuel 15:13-14, 23, 30; Psalm 3:1-8

conspiracy's deadly force already was in motion;[185] yet, also like King David, Jesus already had planned with the Father for God's entire household to escape from their own evil treachery.[186] This time, unlike the ill-fated death of David's son Absalom,[187] the renegades of the household of God would be saved by another renegade, Jesus crucified.[188] And by his death, it would be possible for the whole family of man to escape from the treachery of their sins,[189] if only they believed in Jesus, and lived faithful lives in his love and saving justice.[190] King David's relationship to his son Absalom reflects for us not only the relationship of God the Father with his Son, but also it shows God our Father in relationship to all of God's children, as the Father is revealed to us by his Son.[191] It is the Father who leads his children safely into the desert and who leaves them there in his loving hand, while he searches for his lost sheep;[192] it is the mournful Father who in great anticipation awaits his son's return and who weeps upon loosing his son, but whose grief also turns to rejoicing at his lost son's return;[193] it is the Father who seeks the return of all who are blind unbelievers, but also he rewards with sight those who had been blind, and those, like Lazarus, who once had been dead but now believe, he raises to life;[194] and it is the Father who entrusts his children from his own loving hand into the loving hands of his Son.[195]

And when, through and in the death of Christ, we are drawn by the Father and through the Son to believe in his Son, who died

---

185	John 18:3, 11:47-50, 13:21, 28
186	John 16:32, 14:2; John 15:1, Matthew 20:1, Ephesians 2:19-20; John 17:15
187	2 Samuel 18:9-15, 24-33; Luke 20:41-44
188	Hebrews 2:14-15, John 8:35-36, Romans 8:15, 21; Luke 22:37, 23:2, John 19:12, 16, Isaiah 53:12
189	1 John 2:2
190	1 Corinthians 15:20, James 1: 17-18, 21-25; James 1:27, John 17:14; 1 John 4:19, 3:16-23, 4:7-12
191	John 17:26
192	Exodus 2:10, 15, 23, 12:37-42, Revelation 12:5-6; 2 Samuel 15:13-14, 23, Luke 15:4, 2 Samuel 18:5, 12, Luke 15:7-10, Matthew 9:36, John 10:11
193	2 Samuel 18:24-32, 19:1-5, 6-7, Luke 15:25-30; Luke 15:31, John 17:10, Luke 15:32
194	John 9:10-11, 39-41, 11:37-44, Luke 15:32
195	John 10:29-30, 17:11-12, 6:37-40, 17:6, 2

for the forgiveness of our sins;[196] and when, through our life in the resurrection of his Son, we share with Christ in the glory that the Father gave to his Son;[197] then everyone has the power from God to become like his Son, as adopted sons of the Father, his children of God, his children of the light.[198] By our becoming God's true sons and daughters,[199] in our life shared with the Father, his Son, and the Holy Spirit,[200] we become with his Son light for the world;[201] and the Father also gives us a share in his Son's sufferings, not only in his Son's glory.[202] And as God's children,[203] but not as children of the world,[204] we glorify the Father by our love;[205] so that whatever we may ask of the Father in the name of his Son, then the Father in his love will give to us, his children,[206] especially a share of the Holy Spirit.[207]

Because the Father loves his children, just as he loves his Son,[208] the Father, in his love for his children, sent to us his Son,[209] the incarnate Word of God,[210] made flesh for the life of the world:[211] life, first of all, through his Son's death in the flesh, when his Son mediates the total remission of our sins;[212] life, secondly, through the Son's human life in the flesh among men,[213] when the divine Son

---

196   Romans 4:25, John 14:6, 6:44, Romans 8:29; John 10:30, 17:23
197   John 11:25-26, Colossians 2:12, 3:3-4, John 17:22, 24
198   Romans 8:15, 1 John 3:1-2, John 12:36; 1 John 1:5, John 8:13, James 1:17; Romans 8:19-20, 1 Corinthians 13:12, Revelation 22:4-5
199   Romans 8:14, 16
200   1 John 1:3, Galatians 4:6
201   John 9:5, Matthew 5:14-16; John 9:4, 17:1, 21-22
202   Romans 8:17-18, 1 Corinthians 15:48-53; John 17:22, 26, 15:1, 4-5
203   John 1:12-13
204   1 John 3:10, 2:15-17, John 16:33, 1 John 5:4-5
205   John 15:17, 13:34; 1 John 3:11, 4:12
206   John 15:8, 14:13, 16:24, 26-27; Luke 11:11-12, Matthew 7:9-11
207   Luke 11:13, John 14:26, 15:26, 16:14-15; 1 John 4:13, John 15:7
208   John 17:23
209   1 John 4:9
210   John 1:14; 1 John 1:1
211   1 John 1:2, John 6:51, 33
212   1 John 4:10, John 3:14-16, Hebrews 2:6-9, 16-17
213   John 3:12-13, 15:12; 1 John 4:12

is an exact reflection of God the Father and of his perfect love,[214] since God is love and comes from God;[215] life, thirdly, because the Word of God speaks God's own words, not uniquely the words of the Son, but only the Father's words and commands,[216] and his words and commands are eternal life;[217] life, fourthly, because by the Son's coming as the Word incarnate, he gives us an understanding of the Father and the Son, and to know the one true God and Jesus Christ, and to believe in him, is eternal life;[218] but, alternatively, those who hate the Father and the Son have never known God, and unless they believe in God's Son, they will die in their sins;[219] and lastly, also because of his coming as a flesh-and-blood man, there is life because Jesus gives us his body and blood in the Eucharist.[220]

The Son of God, Jesus in the flesh as the Son of Man, is the revelation of God to humankind superior to, but continuous with, God's revelations to his prior servant Moses,[221] for although Moses was the intimate friend of God,[222] Jesus comes from his Father's side to humankind, as a Son over his household,[223] but also in the form of a slave.[224] It was the Father, not Moses, who gave to the world from heaven the true bread of God.[225] When the Jews hurled their abuse at the faith of the blind man, who had regained his sight from Jesus, they claimed to put their faith in Moses.[226] But then, even many Jews did not keep the Law of Moses,[227] let alone keep their faith with

---

214 John 1:14, 12:45, 14:7, 15:13, 10:11, 14-15, 8, 10; 1 John 4:16
215 1 John 4:8, 7; 1 Corinthians 13:1-13
216 John 3:34, 7:16, 12:49, 14:24, 17:6-8
217 John 5:24-25, 6:63, 8:51, 12:50
218 1 John 5:20, John 17:3; 1 John 4:7, John 6:40; Deuteronomy 30:19
219 John 15:24, 16:3, 8:19, 21, 24
220 John 6:53-58, Luke 22:19-20; Luke 24:35, Acts 2:46
221 John 13:16
222 Exodus 33:22, 34:29-35
223 John 17:2, Hebrews 3:5-6; John 8:35-36, Exodus 2:5-10, 3:6-15, John 17:26, Hebrews 11:23-29, Exodus 32:48-52, 34:1-5, John 8:14, 16:28, 17:24; Exodus 20:1, 18-21, 34:28-35, Luke 9:26, 28-36
224 Philippians 2:7-8, John 13:12-15, Mark 10:44-45
225 John 6:32
226 John 9:28-29
227 John 7:19

God.[228] And keeping or not keeping God's word has always been an individual's absolutely free and determining choice between life and death: when God first spoke his words to Adam,[229] the father of the human race; also when he gave his words to his chosen people, the Israelites, through Moses;[230] and finally, when his Son spoke his Father's own words face-to-face for the whole of humankind.[231] But even if the Jews only had been just listening to Moses,[232] they would have known the clear truth that God had commanded them to listen to Jesus, God's Son, the prophet.[233]

And now, because Jesus was returning to his Father, he also would be sending his disciples into the world, just as his Father had sent him into the world.[234] And just as Jesus had spoken his Father's words directly to them,[235] so also his disciples would be sent to take his words of the gospel directly to others.[236] Jesus had finished his first work on earth,[237] but the matter of the unfinished work of the kingdom of God necessarily would be left to all his disciples, who remain in the vine of Christ.[238] Every disciple of the Lord is called to build the kingdom,[239] everyone with enough faith and courage to be his true disciple.[240] Whenever Jesus comes to anyone, or more properly, when in grace we come to let Jesus into our hearts,[241] he also sends that person into the world to give their testimony of Jesus in their life. And so it was that some, who had been listening to his voice, said to others, "Jesus is, indeed, the prophet."[242] And also, the Samaritan woman at Jacob's well testified to her townsmen of her

---

228	John 6:45; John 6:31, 49-51
229	Genesis 2:16-17, 3:1-5
230	Deuteronomy 30:15-20
231	John 6:63
232	John 7:19; John 1:11, 12:48
233	John 5:46, Deuteronomy 18:15-19; Acts 3:22-26
234	John 17:11, Luke 19:11-13; John 1:9-10
235	John 17:14, 17
236	John 17:18-20
237	John 17:4
238	Luke 17:20-21, John 17:23; John 15:4-5
239	Mark 4:2, 8-14, 20, John 15:8, 16, Matthew 25:14-15, 20:1-2
240	Matthew 9:37, Luke 14:26-27, Mark 10:28-30
241	John 7:37-38
242	John 10:27-28, 7:40, Deuteronomy 18:15

experience of Jesus, who would give her living water.[243] And because of her testimony of faith, many believed in Jesus, or because of her word, many then were attracted to the Lord; and from the words Jesus had spoken to them directly, many of her Samaritan townsmen came to believe that Jesus was Saviour of the world.[244] There was likewise the case of the royal official at Capernaum, who had been in Cana: he believed there what Jesus had told him about his son, that his son dying at home would live; and so, on his way home, when the official testified to this to members of his family, as they also testified to him about his son's cure at the very moment of the Lord's words, his entire household came by faith to believe in Jesus.[245]

Jesus also had cured the man at the Pool of Bethesda in Jerusalem: but then Jesus quickly had disappeared into the crowds, so that later he came to the former cripple a second time in order to remind him of the favour given to him from God.[246] It was after the man had recognized his conversion through Jesus that he went back to the temple, now for his second time, and that he proclaimed to the authorities that Jesus had cured him.[247] Previously in his illness, the man had been lying around doing nothing for thirty-eight years, although the time is relative for each of us; but wanting to be made well again, and doing exactly as Jesus had commanded him, he had picked up his mat and walked.[248] And we can be sure that he continued to walk as a disciple of Jesus, wherever God would be sending him.[249] I may have picked up my pen and walked with Christ, but we also have been commanded to love one another, just as Jesus has loved us, and although a challenge it is more a joy.[250] And, like that man born blind,[251] as once every child of God was born;[252] some of us are

---

243   John 4:19, 28-30, 39; Isaiah 35:7
244   John 4:40-42; Isaiah 65:1
245   John 4:50-53; Isaiah 35:10
246   John 5:13-14; Isaiah 35:6
247   John 5:15
248   John 5:5-9
249   John 15:9-10; 2 Corinthians 5:7
250   John 15:11-12; 1 John 1:4, 2:3-6; 1 John 3:16, 23-24
251   John 9:1; Isaiah 35:5
252   1 John 2:28-29

sent, by Jesus and to the glory of the Father,[253] to wash in the Pool of Siloam, those of us who are sent in God's mercy, when we have been made clean by our baptism,[254] and our sins are forgiven.[255] Everyone baptized, therefore, has been sent as a disciple of Jesus into the world,[256] so that before we also return with Jesus to the Father,[257] while we are alive and even after we die, the works of God might be revealed in us.[258] For any true disciple of Jesus, this is everyone's life purpose, to bring about God's kingdom.[259] All the others are disciples of the world,[260] those who define personal existence: by expanding their careers or families; by enjoying life's pleasures, or the best of the "good life," for as long as possible; by avoiding the "miseries" of poverty, aging, illness, or death for themselves or for loved ones, at any cost; and until the end comes for their earthly life, by achieving, securing, or fully exploiting their wealth, power, fame and/or sexual prowess.[261]

Readings: Matthew 26:36-46, Mark 14:32-42, Luke 22:39-46; Matthew 26:47-56, Mark 14:43-52, Luke 22:47-54, John 18:2-11

After their more strenuous crossing of the Kidron valley at night, Jesus arrived with his exhausted disciples to a place in the valley at the foot of the Mount of Olives, a small plot of land called Gethsemane, where they entered a garden.[262] As they had reached the place, Jesus told the disciples:

---

253 John 8:54-55
254 John 9:6-7; 1 Peter 3:21, Romans 6:4-6; Isaiah 35:8
255 John 9:39-41, 3:18-21
256 John 9:7, 17, 20-25, 30-38
257 John 16:28, 14:2-4, 6; 2 Corinthians 5:8-9, Philippians 1:21-24
258 John 17:1, 9:4-5, 15:5; John 17:10, Luke 8:16-18, 19:24-26, John 15:8
259 John 17:18, 25
260 1 John 5:19, Matthew 4:8, Luke 4:5, 8:11-14, 12:21-24, 29-32, 17:26-33; Mark 8:34-35; 1 John 2:15
261 John 17:15, 6:63, Romans 8:5-6, Philippians 3:18-19, Ephesians 4:17, 22-23
262 Matthew 26:36, Mark 14:32, Luke 22:39, John 18:1; 2 Samuel 22:29-30

> Stay here,[263] and pray not to be put to the test,[264] while I go over there to pray.[265]

Then, taking with him Peter and the two sons of Zebedee, James and John,[266] Jesus withdrew from the larger group of disciples, going into the garden about a stone's throw away.[267] There with the three disciples, he was suddenly overcome by a great sadness, and he began to feel terror and anguish.[268] Speaking to them, he said:

> My soul is sorrowful to the point of death. Wait here and stay awake with me.[269]

Then going on a little further,[270] he knelt down and prayed:

> Father, if you are willing, take this cup away from me; nevertheless, not my will, but let your will be done.[271]

At saying this, an angel came down from heaven and appeared to Jesus to give him strength.[272] Then Jesus threw himself face down to the ground;[273] and in his anguish, he prayed even more earnestly,[274] that, if it were possible, this hour might pass him by,[275] but now with his sweat falling to the ground like great drops of blood.[276] In his deepest intimacy with the Father,[277] Jesus prayed:

> Abba, Father![278] For you all things are possible;[279] if it

---

263   Mark 14:32, Matthew 26:36
264   Luke 22:40
265   Mark 14:32, Matthew 26:36
266   Matthew 26:37, Mark 14:33
267   Luke 22:41
268   Matthew 26:37, Mark 14:34
269   Matthew 26:38, Mark 14:34
270   Mark 14:35, Matthew 26:39; Mark 1:35, Matthew 14:23
271   Luke 22:41-42
272   Luke 22:43; Luke 1:19, 24-28
273   Mark 14:35, Matthew 26:39
274   Luke 22:44; John 6:38-40, 3:14-15
275   Mark 14:35, Matthew 26:39; John 12:27
276   Luke 22:44
277   John 17:1, 23
278   Mark 14:36; Romans 8:14-15, Galatians 4:6-7
279   Mark 14:36; Mark 10:26-27, Luke 18:27, Acts 2:23-24

Gospel (on the Road to) Emmaus / 353

is possible, let this cup pass me by;[280] and so, take this cup away from me.[281] Nevertheless, let it be as you, not I, would have it.[282]

After Jesus had been praying for a while, he came back to the disciples and found all of them sleeping,[283] just like the nodding or dreaming dozers on some Sundays in the pews at church. So now, first Jesus woke up Peter; and then Jesus roused the others, saying to them:[284]

> Simon, are you asleep?[285] So you hadn't the strength to stay awake with me, not even for one hour?[286] Stay awake, and pray not to be put to the test;[287] your spirit is willing enough, but human nature is weak.[288] And why are you all asleep? Get up now, and pray not to be put to the test.[289]

Then, a second time, Jesus went away and prayed in the same words:[290]

> My Father, if this cup cannot pass by without my drinking it, then your will be done![291]

Coming back again to the disciples, Jesus once more found them sleeping; their eyes were so heavy,[292] as they were fast asleep, that they could find no answer for him,[293] except perhaps for their few unintelligible mumbles. This time, Jesus just left them there; and

---

280   Matthew 26:39
281   Mark 14:36
282   Mark 14:36, Matthew 26:39; Matthew 6:10
283   Matthew 26:40, Mark 14:37; Ephesians 6:18
284   Matthew 26:40, Mark 14:37; Matthew 16:18
285   Mark 14:37
286   Mark 14:37, Matthew 26:40
287   Mark 14:38, Matthew 26:41; Matthew 6:13, Luke 22:31, Mark 14:30
288   Mark 14:38, Matthew 26:41; Matthew 26:33-34; 2 Corinthians 11:30, 12:7-10
289   Luke 22:46; Matthew 26:31
290   Mark 14:39
291   Matthew 26:42
292   Matthew 26:43, Mark 14:40
293   Mark 14:40

he went away again, now for the third time, to pray as he repeated the same words.[294] When eventually he came back to the disciples,[295] he still found them sleeping soundly, exhausted from sheer grief.[296] Jesus spoke to them:

> Now you can sleep on and have your rest.[297] Look,[298] it's all over;[299] the hour has come, when now the Son of man is to be betrayed into the hands of sinners.[300] Get up, let's go![301] Look,[302] my betrayer is not far away.[303]

And, while Jesus was still speaking, suddenly a large number of men appeared, and at the head of the group leading it was Judas,[304] one of the Twelve.[305]

Judas, the traitor, knew the exact place in the garden where to find Jesus because before then, Jesus, often at night, had gone there with his disciples.[306] And now with Judas, there was a cohort of Roman soldiers and also the temple guards, carrying torches and lanterns, and armed with swords and clubs; all of them had been sent by the chief priests,[307] temple lawyers,[308] the Pharisees,[309] and the elders of the people,[310] who intended, this time they thought, to

---

294　Matthew 26:44
295　Matthew 26:45
296　Luke 22:45; Matthew 17:22-23, 26:21-22, John 16:5-6, 20-22, 17:11, Mark 14:33-34
297　Matthew 26:45, Mark 14:41
298　Matthew 26:45
299　Mark 14:41
300　Matthew 26:45, Mark 14:41
301　Mark 14:42, Matthew 26:46; John 14:31
302　Matthew 26:46
303　Matthew 26:46, Mark 14:42
304　Matthew 26:47, Mark 14:43, Luke 22:47; John 17:12, Colossians 2:8-10
305　Matthew 26:47, Mark 14:43; Matthew 10:1-4, Mark 3:13-19
306　John 18:2; John 8:1-2, Luke 21:37, Mark 11:19; Mark 11:11, Matthew 21:17
307　Matthew 26:3-5
308　John 5:39-40
309　John 11:45-46, 12:11
310　Matthew 26:47, Mark 14:43, John 18:3; John 11:47, Luke 22:66, Acts 4:5-6

capture the Lord with a guaranteed force.[311] But knowing everything that was to happen to him,[312] Jesus briskly stepped forward and said to them:

> Who are you looking for?[313]

They answered, "Jesus the Nazarene." He said to them:

> I AM.[314]

Judas, his betrayer, also was standing with them.[315] When Jesus said to them, "I AM," they moved back and fell to the ground.[316] And again, Jesus asked them:

> Who are you looking for?[317]

They said, "Jesus the Nazarene."[318] Jesus answered:

> I told you that I AM. So, if it's me you're looking for, let these others go.[319]

He did this to fulfil his own words, "I have not lost any of those you have given me."[320] Then Judas approached Jesus to kiss him.[321] Jesus said to him:

> Judas, are you betraying the Son of man with a kiss?[322]

The traitor had prearranged a signal with his counterparts, having said to them, "The one I shall greet with a kiss, he is the man; arrest him,[323] and when you lead him away, make sure he is well-

---

311 John 7:6, 19-20, 25, 30, 8:59, 10:39, 11:53-54, 57; John 10:17-18
312 Luke 18:31-34
313 John 18:4; John 1:47-51, 3:13-14, 2:18-19, 22
314 John 18:5; Colossians 1:19, 2:9
315 John 18:5; Psalm 40:6-7
316 John 18:6; Exodus 3:14, 5, John 11:10
317 John 18:7
318 John 18:7
319 John 18:8; Colossians 1:20
320 John 18:9; John 6:39, 10:28, 17:12
321 Luke 22:47
322 Luke 22:48; John 13:26
323 Mark 14:44, Matthew 26:48

guarded."[324]   So, at once, Judas went up to Jesus, saying, "Rabbi!" and the traitor kissed him.[325] In response, Jesus said to him:

> My friend, do what you came here to do.[326]

Then stepping forward,[327] they seized Jesus and arrested him.[328] However, regardless of what everyone may have thought at that moment, Jesus would not actually be captured then; rather, very shortly after this, Jesus, in fact, would surrender himself to them, according to his Father's will.[329]

And suddenly, one of the followers of Jesus,[330] who up to now had been a bystander to these events,[331] grasped his sword and drew it;[332] it was Peter, who had one of their two swords,[333] and as Peter drew it, he cut off the right ear of the high priest's servant, whose name was Malchus.[334]   Jesus addressed Peter:

> That is enough.[335]   Put your sword back in its scabbard,[336] for all who draw the sword will perish by the sword.[337] Or do you think that I cannot call upon my Father, who at this moment would send more than twelve legions of angels to defend me?[338] But then, how would the scriptures be fulfilled that say that this is the way it must be?[339] Am I not to drink the cup that the

---

324   Mark 14:44
325   Matthew 26:49, Mark 14:45
326   Matthew 26:50; John 13:27
327   Matthew 26:50
328   Matthew 26:50, Mark 14:46
329   Galatians 1:4, Ephesians 5:2, 1 Timothy 2:6, Titus 2:14
330   Matthew 26:51
331   Mark 14:47; Psalm 17:9-13
332   Matthew 26:51; Matthew 16:21-22
333   John 18:10; Luke 22:38
334   Matthew 26:51, Mark 14:47, John 18:10
335   Luke 22:51; Matthew 16:23
336   Matthew 26:52, John 18:11
337   Matthew 26:52; John 18:36
338   Matthew 26:53; Matthew 16:24, 27-28, John 17:1, 21:20-23, 18-19
339   Matthew 26:54; Mark 10:45, Matthew 20:28

Father has given me?[340]

Jesus then touched the ear of Malchus, and Jesus healed him,[341] not just his ear, but all of him, also his soul; which afforded yet another parable and a sign from Jesus, his clear signal directed to the top of the Temple hierarchy, to Caiaphas the high priest, the man at that time who was spiritually responsible for the House of Israel, and who also was now in charge, surreptitiously behind the scenes, for the arrest of Jesus.[342] However, as Jesus had said, there would be a changing of the guard soon, from Caiaphas to Cephas;[343] and therefore, Peter would be the one made accountable to God for his management of Christ's new Church,[344] with its new covenant, a new priesthood, and Christ its victim and high priest.[345]

But for now, as Jesus faced the crowd,[346] he addressed the chief priests and the captains of the Temple guard and the elders who had come for him,[347] any and all of those in some position of Temple authority:

> Am I a bandit that you had to set out [to capture me][348] with swords and clubs?[349] When I was teaching among you in the temple day after day you never then [tried][350] to lay a hand on me.[351] But now these events are happening to fulfil the scriptures;[352] this is your hour, this is the reign of darkness.[353]

---

340 John 18:11; Mark 14:36, 2 Corinthians 5:21, John 19:28-30; Psalm 16:5-6, John 18:37, Isaiah 53:10, John 6:15, 14:6; Psalm 16:7-8, John 8:29, 16:28; Psalm 16:9-10, John 2:19, 5:21, 11:25; Psalm 16:11, John 3:16, 14:2-4
341 Luke 22:51; Mark 4:10-12
342 John 11:49-50, Matthew 21:42-43, 45-46
343 Luke 20:16
344 Luke 12:41-43, John 21:15-17, 10:14-16
345 Hebrews 7:11-28, 8:1-13, 9:11-28; 1 Peter 2:4-10
346 Matthew 26:55
347 Luke 22:52
348 Mark 14:48, Matthew 26:55
349 Mark 14:48, Matthew 26:55, Luke 22:52; John 10:8
350 Luke 22:53
351 Mark 14:49, Matthew 26:55, Luke 22:53
352 Mark 14:49, Matthew 26:56
353 Luke 22:53; 1 John 1:6, Galatians 5:24, 19-21; 1 John 2:17

Now, as Jesus offered himself into their hands, all of the disciples deserted him and ran away.[354] At that same time, there also had been a young man who was following Jesus; he had been wearing nothing but a linen cloth, and when they also caught hold of him,[355] he left the cloth in their hands and ran away naked.[356] But just then, the Roman cohort and its tribune and the Jewish guards seized Jesus;[357] and so, they now ignored the others, who either were fleeing or had escaped, and they bound Jesus with cords and lead him away.[358] As they took their silent prisoner directly to the house of the high priest, Peter followed them, at a distance.[359]

Prayer Reflection: Psalms 59:1-17, 68:1-35, 78:52-72

Antiphon: God is my strength and my stronghold,
    the God who loves me faithfully.

> Rescue me from my enemies, O God;
>   be my stronghold, lift me from the reach
>   of those who have come to destroy me.[360]
> Deliver me from evildoers;
>   from bloodthirsty men save me.[361]
> They have set an ambush for my life;
>   the powerful conspire against me
>   for no fault, no sin of mine, O Lord.[362]
> Despite my innocence, they hurry
>   to take up their positions to kill me;
>   wake up, come near me, and see my plight![363]
> O Lord, you are God of hosts, God of Israel;

---

354   Matthew 26:56, Mark 14:50; Matthew 26:31, Mark 14:27; Romans 5:6-15
355   Mark 14:51
356   Mark 14:52; 1 Peter 5:13, Revelation 16:15
357   Luke 22:54, John 18:12; Psalm 68:18, John 18:1, 17:24
358   John 18:12; Philippians 2:6-8, 2 Corinthians 2:14-16, Colossians 2:15
359   Luke 22:54; John 1:42, 21:21-22; Galatians 5:25
360   Psalm 59:1; 1 Samuel 19:11-12; 2 Samuel 22:1-3; Matthew 26:1-2, John 3:14; John 15:17
361   Psalm 59:2; 1 Samuel 19:18-19; 2 Samuel 22:4; John 15:23-24
362   Psalm 59:3; 1 Samuel 20:1; 2 Samuel 22:5-6; Matthew 26:3-5; John 15:18-19
363   Psalm 59:4; 1 Samuel 20:30-32; 2 Samuel 22:7; John 15:25

> arise to punish all the nations;
> show no mercy on evil traitors.[364]

> Back at nightfall they return,
> snarling like dogs, prowling through the city.[365]
> Listen to the filth their mouths pour out;
> with sharp swords on their lips,
> they say, "Who is there to hear us?"[366]
> But you, Lord, laugh at them;
> and you deride all the nations.[367]
> You are my strength,
> my eyes are fixed on you;
> for you, O God, are my stronghold;[368]
> You are the God who loves me faithfully.[369]

Antiphon: God is my strength and my stronghold,
> the God who loves me faithfully.

> > You are the One who is coming to meet me;
> > let my eyes look down in triumph upon my enemies.[370]
> > Don't annihilate them, lest my people soon forget;
> > but shake them with your power, O Lord, our shield,
> > and bring them to their knees.[371]
> > Sin is in their mouths and on their lips,
> > so let them be trapped in their pride
> > for the curses and lies they speak under oath.[372]

---

364   Psalm 59:5; 1 Samuel 21:2-3, 4-7, 9-10; Luke 22:19-20, 35-38, Matthew 26:23-24; John 16:20
365   Psalm 59:6; 1 Samuel 21:11; John 17:9, 20; John 10:11, 27; John 8:47
366   Psalm 59:7; 1 Samuel 21:12-13; John 15:3; John 10:12, 24-26; John 8:37
367   Psalm 59:8; 1 Samuel 21:14-16; John 15:8; John 10:13, 28; John 8:31
368   Psalm 59:9; 1 Samuel 22:1-4; John 15:12, 14; John 10:14, 27, Hebrews 12:2; 2 Corinthians 12:10
369   Psalm 59:10; 1 Samuel 22:5; John 17:17, 19, 26; John 10:15, 29-30; John 8:28
370   Psalm 59:10; 1 Samuel 22:9-11, 16; John 15:26-27, 16:28; John 8:21-22
371   Psalm 59:11; 1 Samuel 22:17-20; John 15:19, 16:1-2; Romans 11:2-5, Matthew 23:30-34, Mark 13:9-10
372   Psalm 59:12; 1 Samuel 23:1-2; John 16:9; John 8:23-24, 44, 1 John 3:8, 2:22

> Destroy them in your anger, destroy them till they
>   disappear;
>   and then people will know that God is Master
>   in Jacob and throughout the whole wide world.[373]
>
> Back at nightfall they return,
>   snarling like dogs, prowling through the city,[374]
> scavenging for something to eat,
>   and growling unless they are satisfied.[375]
> But I shall sing of your strength,
>   in the morning, I will extol your faithful love;
>   you have been my stronghold,
>   a refuge in my hour of distress.[376]
> O my strength, to you I will sing your praises:
>   for God is my mighty fortress,
>   the God who shows me unfailing love.[377]

Antiphon: Let God arise, let his enemies flee before him.

> Let God arise, let his enemies be scattered,
>   let those who hate God flee before him.[378]
> You disperse them like smoke blown by the wind;
>   like wax that melts in a fire's presence,
>   so the wicked will perish at the presence of God.[379]
> But the upright will rejoice in the presence of God,
>   they shall celebrate and dance with joy.[380]
>
> Sing to God, make music to his name;
>   make a highway for the Rider of the Clouds,

---

373   Psalm 59:13; 1 Samuel 23:3-5; John 17:25; Exodus 32:11-14, Philippians 3:10
374   Psalm 59:14; 1 Samuel 23:7-8; John 16:4; John 10:10, Ezekiel 34:7-8
375   Psalm 59:15; 1 Samuel 23:12-13; John 17:15; 1 Peter 5:8, Ezekiel 34:9-10
376   Psalm 59:16; 1 Samuel 23:14-15; 2 Samuel 22:49; John 17:23; 1 Peter 1:21
377   Psalm 59:17; 1 Samuel 24:10-12, 15-23; 2 Samuel 22:50-51; John 15:7, 16:23, 17:24; 1 Peter 1:20
378   Psalm 68:1; Numbers 10:35; Matthew 26:55; Exodus 25:21-22
379   Psalm 68:2; Psalm 97:5; John 15:6; 2 Peter 3:9-10
380   Psalm 68:3; Exodus 15:13, 17-18; John 16:22; Luke 15:23-25, 31-32, John 16:32, 17:10

rejoice in the Lord, exalt in his presence.[381]
Father of orphans, defender of widows,
   such is God in his holy dwelling.[382]
God gives the lonely a home to live in;
   he leads forth prisoners to freedom,
   but rebels must dwell in the parched desert.[383]

O God, when you set out at the head of your people,
   when you marched across the desert,[384]
[pause] the earth trembled, the heavens melted
   at the presence of God,
   at the presence of God, the God of Israel.[385]
O God, you rained down a shower of blessings,
   when your heritage was dry and weary you gave them
      new life.[386]
When your family settled there, they found a home,
   prepared in your generosity for the poor.[387]

Antiphon: Our God is a saving God;
   he is the Lord, who holds the keys of life and death.

The Lord announces to the bearers of good news:
   "The Almighty has defeated a countless army.[388]
The chieftains and their armies are in flight, in desperate
      flight
   while you were at rest among the sheepfolds."[389]

---

381   Psalm 68:4; 2 Samuel 22:10-11, Deuteronomy 33:26, Isaiah 19:1; John 16:28; Matthew 26:64
382   Psalm 68:5; Exodus 22:21-23, Deuteronomy 27:19; John 15:9-10; James 1:27
383   Psalm 68:6; Numbers 14:11, 26-35; John 15:22; John 14:3-4, 12:47-48
384   Psalm 68:7; Exodus 13:21-22; 2 Samuel 22:12-13; John 14:31; Luke 4:1-15
385   Psalm 68:8; Exodus 24:15-18; 2 Samuel 22:8-9; John 18:4-6, 15:15; Deuteronomy 18:16-19, Numbers 16:1-5, John 17:19, Numbers 16:28-32, Matthew 28:1-2, 5-6, Romans 10:5-7, Ephesians 4:9, Hebrews 13:20-21
386   Psalm 68:9; Exodus 16:12-15, 17:3-7, Deuteronomy 8:3, 32:1-2; John 17:8; Ephesians 1:3, 13
387   Psalm 68:10; Joshua 24:13, Deuteronomy 6:10-11; John 17:24; John 14:2
388   Psalm 68:11; Exodus 14:6, 23, 28, Deuteronomy 11:4, 2 Samuel 22:16, 19-20; John 16:33; Romans 10:15, 1 Peter 1:18
389   Psalm 68:12; 2 Samuel 22:17-18, Exodus 15:14-16; John 16:3; John 10:14-

At home the women already are sharing out the spoils:
> they are covered with silver like the wings of a dove,[390]
> its feathers with a sheen of green and gold,
> with jewels they glisten like snow on Mount Zalmon,
> > the Dark Mountain.[391]

The mountains of Bashan are mighty mountains;
> high and rugged are the mountains of Bashan.[392]

Why are you envious, you haughty mountains,
> at the mountain God has chosen for his dwelling place,
> where God will dwell forever?[393]

The chariots of God are thousands upon thousands;
> The Lord has come from Mount Sinai to his
> > sanctuary.[394]

You have climbed the heights, and taken captives,
> you have received slaves as tribute, even rebels,
> so they may have a dwelling place with God.[395]

May the Lord be blessed day after day,
> our God, our salvation, who carries us along.[396]

[pause] Our God is a God who saves;
> escape from death comes from the Lord, our God;[397]

but God will crush the skull of his enemies,
> the long-haired heads of those who prowl about in
> > sin.[398]

The Lord has said, "I will bring them back, even from

15, 1 Peter 1:19

390   Psalm 68:13; Deuteronomy 32:30; John 15:1; Ephesians 4:11, 1 Peter 4:11, 10

391   Psalm 68:14; Deuteronomy 32:10; John 15:2; Ephesians 4:12, Revelation 21:9, 14, 18-22

392   Psalm 68:15; 2 Samuel 22:28; John 17:18, Luke 22:35; Philippians 3:13-14

393   Psalm 68:16; 2 Samuel 22:29; John 17:22; Revelation 21:10-11

394   Psalm 68:17; 2 Samuel 22:30; Matthew 26:53-54; Luke 2:11-14, Hebrews 12:22-24

395   Psalm 68:18; 2 Samuel 22:31; John 18:1; John 8:34-36, Ephesians 4:7-8, 13, John 14:2-3

396   Psalm 68:19; 2 Samuel 22:32; Matthew 26:45-46; Numbers 11:10-15, 1 Peter 2:24

397   Psalm 68:20; John 18:7-9, Mark 14:28; 2 Timothy 1:9-11

398   Psalm 68:21; John 16:11; Deuteronomy 32:41-42

Bashan
I will bring them back, and from the depths of the
sea."[399]
Then you will bathe your feet in the blood of your
enemies,
and even the tongues of your dogs will lap it up.[400]

Antiphon: Kingdoms of earth, sing praise to God,
make music in honour of the Lord.

Your solemn procession, O God, can be viewed by
everyone,
your procession into the sanctuary of my God and
king.[401]
The singers are in front, the musicians behind;
and in their midst the girls beat their tambourines.[402]
In your choirs, bless God;
praise the Lord, you from Israel's foundation:[403]
Benjamin is there, the youngest in front;
the princes of Judah, a great throng in bright-coloured
robes;
and the princes of Zebulun, the princes of Naphtali.[404]

Take command, my God, summon your power,
the divine power as you have displayed for us.[405]
Show it from your temple high above Jerusalem,
so kings may come to you bearing tribute.[406]
Rebuke these enemy nations:
the wild beast dwelling in the reeds,[407]

---

[399] Psalm 68:22; Mark 14:29-30; Ezekiel 34:13, Isaiah 66:18-20; Ephesians 4:9-10, 1 Peter 3:18
[400] Psalm 68:23; Mark 14:31; Romans 8:36, 1 Peter 4:15-17
[401] Psalm 68:24; Luke 22:54; Colossians 2:14-15
[402] Psalm 68:25; Mark 14:26; 1 Chronicles 6:31-48
[403] Psalm 68:26; Matthew 26:30; Ephesians 2:20-22
[404] Psalm 68:27; Luke 22:39; Matthew 2:6, 4:12-16, Isaiah 8:23, 9:1-3
[405] Psalm 68:28; Luke 22:51; Numbers 14:1-4, 10, 18-19, John 14:8-9, Romans 1:3-4
[406] Psalm 68:29; John 18:3; Exodus 24:16, 33:19, 34:6-9, 1 Corinthians 1:18, Isaiah 52:13, John 3:14, Numbers 21:4-9; Revelation 21:24, 26, Isaiah 60:3
[407] Ezekiel 29:3

> the herd of mighty bulls,
> that people of calves,
> who shall bow down with their ingots of silver;
> scatter the nations who delight in war.[408]
> Princes will make their way from Egypt,
> and Ethiopia will stretch out its hands to God.[409]
>
> Sing to God, you kingdoms of the earth,
> > chant the praises of the Lord.[410]
>
> Play for the Lord, the Rider of the Heavens, the ancient heavens;
> > from there he thunders with a voice of power.[411]
>
> Acknowledge the power of God;
> > his glory shines over Israel,
> > his mighty strength in the heavens.[412]
>
> God is awesome in his sanctuary;
> > he is the Lord, Israel's God,
> > who gives strength and power to his people.[413]

Antiphon: I am the good shepherd, says the Lord; and with skilful hands he shepherded them.

> God brought his people out of Egypt like sheep,
> > guiding them as his flock in the desert.[414]
>
> He led them on secure and unafraid,
> > but the sea engulfed their enemies.[415]
>
> He brought them to his holy land,
> > to this land of hills won by his right hand.[416]
>
> God dispossessed the nations before them;
> > he apportioned a heritage for each of them,

---

408 Psalm 68:30; John 18:12; Isaiah 60:11, Ephesians 3:6
409 Psalm 68:31; John 17:7; Romans 5:10-11
410 Psalm 68:32; John 16:20; Matthew 11:16-19, John 16:21
411 Psalm 68:33; John 17:2; Isaiah 42:13
412 Psalm 68:34; John 17:1; Revelation 21:22-23
413 Psalm 68:35; John 17:3-4; Revelation 22:4-5
414 Psalm 78:52; Psalm 78:14, Exodus 13:21-22; Mark 14:32; John 12:34-36
415 Psalm 78:53; Exodus 14:13-14, 27-28, 29-31; Mark 14:33-34; Mark 5:37, 35-36, 41-42, 9:1-2, 5-9
416 Psalm 78:54; Exodus 15:6, Deuteronomy 33:2; Mark 14:35; 2 Peter 3:13, Revelation 21:1

and settled the tribes of Israel in their tents.[417]

But still, they challenged the Most High God, and
    against him
they rebelled, refusing to observe his decrees.[418]
They turned back and were as treacherous as their
    ancestors,
they gave way like a faulty bow without tension.[419]
They enraged him with their high places,
and roused his jealousy with their idols.[420]

When God heard them, he vented his anger
by rejecting Israel completely.[421]
He abandoned his dwelling at Shiloh,
the tent where he had lived on the earth.[422]
He surrendered his power into captivity,
his ark of splendour into enemy hands.[423]
He gave his people over to the sword,
so enraged he was against his own heritage.[424]
Fire devoured their young men;
their young girls heard no wedding songs.[425]
Their priests were slaughtered by the sword;
and their widows sang no dirge.[426]

Then the Lord arose as though waking from sleep,
like a warrior fighting-mad after the effects of wine.[427]

417	Psalm 78:55; Deuteronomy 11:31-32; Mark 14:36; Ephesians 1:11-12, Revelation 7:13-15
418	Psalm 78:56; Exodus 32:7-9; Mark 14:37; Romans 11:32
419	Psalm 78:57; Numbers 14:1-11, 13, 19, 20-24; Mark 14:38; Hebrews 3:18-19
420	Psalm 78:58; Deuteronomy 32:21; Mark 14:40; Matthew 22:7-12
421	Psalm 78:59; Exodus 32:10, Numbers 14:12; Mark 14:43; Romans 11:11-12
422	Psalm 78:60; 1 Samuel 4:11, 22; Mark 14:44; 2 Corinthians 5:1
423	Psalm 78:61; 1 Samuel 6:1; Mark 14:45-46; Matthew 21:42-43
424	Psalm 78:62; 1 Samuel 4:10; Mark 14:47-48; Matthew 10:34-36
425	Psalm 78:63; Numbers 11:1-3; Mark 14:50; Matthew 22:2, 11-14, Luke 14:24, Revelation 19:6-9
426	Psalm 78:64; 1 Samuel 22:16-20; Mark 14:49; Matthew 23:35-36, Revelation 19:11-16
427	Psalm 78:65; Deuteronomy 32:43; Mark 14:32-34; 1 Corinthians 2:7-8

> He struck his enemies on the rump,
>   he dealt them everlasting shame.[428]
> He rejected the tents of Joseph,
>   chose not the tribe of Ephraim;[429]
> God chose the tribe of Judah,
>   Mount Zion which he loved.[430]
> He built his sanctuary like the heavens,
>   like the earth he set its foundations forever.[431]
> He chose David to be his servant,
>   took him from the sheepfold.[432]
> From tending sheep God took him
>   to be the shepherd of Jacob's descendants,
>   of Israel, God's heritage.[433]
> He shepherded them with unblemished heart,
>   with skilful hands he guided them.[434]

Antiphon: I am the good shepherd, says the Lord; and with skilful hands he shepherded them.

Lord, Jesus, Son of David and Son of God, you and we, your entire household of God, are pursued constantly by your enemies, by those who hate both you and your Father. But, when we listen to your voice and follow your commands, with our hearts fixed firmly on you, you lead us steadfastly and skilfully through every danger and peril, in order to bring us finally to the safety of our eternal home with you. O Lord, our shepherd, our sanctuary dwelling within us, and our blazing light, lead us at the head of your victory procession. We are the joyful nations you have chosen, in the love of the Father, and redeemed through your sacred blood on the cross and your glorious resurrection from the dead. Let your Holy Spirit, and all your holy gifts as jewels to us, shine forth in your New Jerusalem, in us as your children of light, your temples of God and mountain-

---

[428] Psalm 78:66; 1 Samuel 5:6; Mark 14:35-36; 1 Corinthians 1:21-25
[429] Psalm 78:67; 1 Chronicles 5:2; John 15:16; Ephesians 1:4
[430] Psalm 78:68; 2 Samuel 7:12-13; John 16:7; Ephesians 2:21-22
[431] Psalm 78:69; Genesis 1:7-10; John 15:13; John 2:19
[432] Psalm 78:70; Isaiah 50:10; John 15:20; Ephesians 1:5
[433] Psalm 78:71; 1 Samuel 16:1, 10-12, Deuteronomy 32:9, Genesis 35:10-15; John 17:5; Revelation 7:17
[434] Psalm 78:72; 1 Kings 9:4-5; John 17:12; 1 Peter 2:25

top lamps to the world, all through you and for you and to your everlasting glory and honour.

> Glory be to the Father,
>   and to the Son,
>   and to the Holy Spirit,
> as it was in the beginning,
>   is now,
>   and ever shall be, world without end.
>   Amen.

Last chapter revision, 10 April 2010, vigil of the Feast of the Divine Mercy.[435]

With subsequent scriptural footnotes added, as completed on 29 August 2010.[436]

---

435 Ephesians 2:8-10, 3:20-21
436 2 Corinthians 4:5-7, Sirach 3:17, Philippians 2:3-8

Chapter 37

Friday, the 14th Nisan (7th April, 30 CE)– The Long Eve of Darkness and Our Day of Shame: Our Lord's Day of Glory and of God's Retribution: The Conviction, Passion, Death, and Burial of Jesus Christ

Readings: Mark 14:53-54, Matthew 26:57-58, Luke 22:54-55, John 18:12-24; John 18:25-27, Mark 14:66-71, Matthew 26:69-74, Luke 22:56-61, Mark 14:72, Matthew 26:75, Luke 22:62; Luke 22:63-65, Matthew 26:67-68, Mark 14:65; Luke 22:66-71, Mark 14:55-64, Matthew 26:59-66, Luke 23:1, Mark 15:1, John 18:28

With Jesus, at last, a captive prisoner of the Roman cohort and temple priests and guards,[1] at the moment he now had surrendered himself into their hands on behalf of his flock,[2] the Lord's holy sacrifice on the cross already had begun. Also, at the same time as Jesus was taken, the disciples made their quickest of escapes into the hillsides of the Mount of Olives,[3] where all of them had scattered like sheep, as if under some sudden attack by a pack of ravaging wolves.[4] Peter, however, while keeping at a safe distance under the cover of darkness, easily trailed the torches and lanterns of the

---

[1] John 18:3, 12; Matthew 17:22, Luke 9:44
[2] John 18:8, 10:11
[3] Mark 14:50; Ezekiel 34:6
[4] Mark 14:27, Matthew 26:31; John 10:12; Ezekiel 34:5

soldiers, guards, and priests surrounding Jesus.[5] And also now, Peter was no longer alone; for soon another disciple was there right at his side with him as he followed the Lord;[6] it was Peter's close friend John, the disciple whom the Lord loved and whom Jesus would continue to love most especially.[7] Despite the chaos and confusion in their flight from capture, John somehow had managed to single out and keep up with Peter, the slower runner; and also now, Peter seems to have abandoned his sword and scabbard, while he had fled from danger, but was following the Lord.[8]

This planned attack by temple henchmen and Roman soldiers, as if against some treacherous bandit,[9] had been directed strategically, by the temple high priests and the chief priests and Pharisees,[10] against the Lord only.[11] As hypocrites and blind guides,[12] these religious leaders were the real thieves and bandits,[13] although the Lord would be crucified as one.[14] And these murderers and sons of snakes did fear the followers of Jesus;[15] for now, in their selective focus against Jesus, they had regarded the disciples as entirely secondary to their primary agenda. However, in just a few short weeks, like the Lord himself now, Peter and John also would be facing these same priests and temple elders in their temple Law court.[16] But now, only a short time after their sudden and swift attack, the armed guards marched with the Lord along the southeastern outside wall of the fortified city of Jerusalem, where Peter and John saw them pass single-file through the narrow Dung Gate. Just outside that gate, mounds of rubbish from the city had been

5	Luke 22:54
6	John 18:15
7	John 13:23, 19:26; 1 John 4:10, 3:16; John 21:22, 15:9
8	John 18:11
9	Mark 14:47-48
10	John 11:47-48, 49-53
11	Wisdom 2:12-20
12	Matthew 23:1-32
13	John 10:8, 10; Luke 21:1, 2 Kings 12:17
14	Matthew 27:44
15	Matthew 23:33-36; Mark 14:2, Matthew 26:5; Luke 22:2; John 11:48, 12:19
16	Acts 4:1-22, 5:12-42

deposited along the walls for its removal. But Peter and John stayed close behind Jesus, and yet they were out of sight, as they followed the group right through the gate and into the city. Once inside, Peter and John then knew where the entire posse was heading with its silent prisoner, straight for the palatial house of the high priest Annas.[17]

Caiaphas was now, and had been high priest for twelve years. But his sixty-one-year-old father-in-law, Annas, had held tenure in that highest priestly office for nine years: initially from the time that Mary and Joseph had found Jesus among the priests in the temple teaching in his Father's house, when their son had been twelve years old,[18] the age ordinarily, after rabbinic instruction, when male Jews publicly declared their religious manhood before God and their teachers. However, the Lord's instruction came directly from his Father in heaven, not from any doctors of the Law, who then, as now, had been completely astounded at the Lord's intelligence and his replies to their questions.[19] And then, as now many years later, the high priest Annas was the real power behind Caiaphas, currently installed as high priest. The high priest Annas, with his vast financial, political, and social capital, had arranged for his son-in-law to assume the office and authority of high priest, just as he also had arranged previously for four of his sons. So, although Annas was the *ex officio* high priest, and under Mosaic Law that office would have been kept for life; together with Caiaphas, his Roman appointed high-priest son-in-law, they were effectively co-chief liaison officers with Rome over religious matters for the Jewish people. Furthermore, the patriarchal Annas, with his twenty-four years of continuous senior religious and political authority, was the currently elected president of the seventy-one-member Sanhedrin, Israel's supreme religious council in the chair of Moses.[20]

In the arrangements Annas had forged for his local empire, he was now free to augment and to execute his political power

---

17   John 18:13
18   Luke 2:41-42, 46
19   Luke 2:47; John 7:15, 28-30, 8:48-49, 9:39-41, 10:20-21
20   Matthew 23:2, John 7:19, 5:45-46, 1:17

Gospel (on the Road to) Emmaus / 371

through his religious authority; on the other hand Caiaphas was left to tend to the official and ordinary religious responsibilities of high priest.[21] It was Caiaphas, also in his specific capacity as high priest, who had counselled the Jews, "it is better for one man to die for the people."[22] And so, in the imagery of the old covenant and in its total fulfilment, Christ was coming now, to Annas and to Caiaphas both, because Jesus Christ would be high priest of the new covenant; and as the Lamb of God, unlike all other generations of high priests before him, he alone had the power to mediate between covenants and between God and the people for the actual forgiveness of their sins, and of ours and everyone's sins.[23] Jesus was coming to the high priests, now on our great Day of Atonement and the Lord's great Day of Wrath,[24] in order to present himself, according to the custom of the Law of Moses,[25] for his slaughter in the afternoon before the twilight celebration of the Passover feast.[26] Today, then, before daylight would fade into Passover, it would be the great day for our Lord's "saving justice."[27] But also, on some other day the Lord would come again:[28] not only for everyone's personal day of judgment upon their moment of death,[29] but Jesus would come, too, at the end of time for humanity's World Day of the Last Judgment,[30] whenever its hour would be determined by the will of the Father,[31] so unto God's glory and for the glorification of his elect.[32]

When Peter and John arrived at the house of Annas, because

---

21 Leviticus 21:10-15, 1-9, 16-24, Hebrews 7:26-28, Exodus 12:5-11; Exodus 30:10, Leviticus 16:1-25, 23:26-32, Numbers 29:7-11; Hebrews 9:6-7, 2-5
22 John 18:14; John 11:49-52
23 Hebrews 10:1-10, 9:11-12, 15-17; Exodus 24:3-8, Hebrews 9:18-23, 24-26, 10:11-18
24 Exodus 12:23, Romans 9:28, John 8:24, 28; Romans 9:31-33, 10:1-3
25 Matthew 5:17-18, Hebrews 10:5-7, John 6:38, Hebrews 10:10, 14, John 6:39-40; Romans 10:4
26 Exodus 12:6
27 Romans 3:3-4, 8:33-37
28 Revelation 1:5-8
29 Matthew 24:42-44, 25:13-14, Revelation 22:12-15
30 Matthew 24:3, 14, 29-31, Isaiah 27:13, Matthew 25:31-32; Amos 5:18-20, Acts 3:19-21, Romans 2:5-8, 3:5-8, 10:22-24
31 Matthew 24:36, Acts 1:7;
32 John 17:9-10, 24; Revelation 21:6, Romans 9:15-18, Revelation 21:7-8

John was well known to the high priest, John was allowed to go in with Jesus as the entire entourage went together into the high priest's palace.[33] Peter, however, had remained outside the door; so John, as he was known to the high priest, came out of the palace and spoke to the doorkeeper; and then John brought Peter inside to the courtyard.[34] But, the girl on duty at the door not only knew John to be one of the Lord's disciples, immediately she also recognized Peter when he entered. So, she said to him, "Aren't you another of that man's disciples?"[35] Although Peter must have understood that the doorkeeper already had known John as a disciple of Jesus, nevertheless Peter curtly answered her, "I am not."[36] And because it was cold, the servants and guards had lit a charcoal fire in the middle of the courtyard;[37] and as they were standing warming themselves there, Peter also went to stand by the fire, warming himself along with the others.[38]

From his central position in the courtyard, Peter could hear and see much of the ongoing palace activity; and so, as he stood by the fire, he hoped to learn what the end results would be.[39] But soon afterwards, as the time seemed to drag on for Peter's already tired feet and legs, he decided that it would be more comfortable if he would just sit down. So he did; but then another servant-girl of the high priest, not the previous doorkeeper, went over to Peter.[40] After she looked at Peter closely,[41] now obviously peering at him,[42] she asked, "Aren't you another of his disciples?"[43] Again, Peter simply denied it, saying, "I am not."[44] Yet, with a relentless confidence the servant-girl doggedly replied, "I'm sure; of course; you, too, were

---

33	John 18:15
34	John 18:16
35	John 18:17
36	John 18:17
37	John 18:18, Luke 22:55
38	John 18:18
39	Matthew 26:58
40	Mark 14:66, Matthew 26:69, Luke 22:56
41	Mark 14:67
42	Luke 22:56
43	John 18:25
44	John 18:25

with Jesus the Galilean,"[45] "you know, the man from Nazareth."[46] But now with a rising disdain in his voice, in front of them all Peter denied it,[47] as he said, "Woman, I don't know him."[48] Peter also said, hoping to close this subject with her for good, "I don't know what you're talking about."[49]

The servant-girl may not have been at Gethsemane to see Peter; but she likely had been a reliable and keen observer of Jesus and his disciples, perhaps from the early public ministry. But now Peter was claiming that he never even had been a disciple.[50] Yet, perhaps in defence of the earlier servant girls, after a while someone else, a third witness, saw Peter at the fire and insisted with him, "You are too one of them."[51] But again Peter denied that he had been a disciple of Jesus, "No, my friend, I'm not."[52] Peter was feeling the heat of his questioners, which unlike the charcoal fire, was too hot for his comfort. So, Peter decided to move towards the gate into the forecourt;[53] and from there, although for Peter it may have been considerably chillier, it seemed far more comfortable to him than their searing line of fire. And as Peter moved away from them, a cock crowed.[54]

Meanwhile, the high priest Annas had been firing his own questions at Jesus, interrogating him extensively about his disciples and about his teaching.[55] But the only explanation Jesus then was prepared to give them was his sacrifice on the cross. So, after a lot of badgering from the high priest, only eventually did Jesus answer them:

> I have always spoken openly for the whole world to hear;

45	Matthew 26:29
46	Mark 14:67
47	Matthew 26:70
48	Luke 22:57
49	Matthew 26:70
50	Mark 3:14, Matthew 4:18-20, Luke 5:8-11, 22:31-34
51	Luke 22:58
52	Luke 22:58
53	Mark 14:68
54	Mark 14:68
55	John 18:19

I have always taught in the synagogue or in the Temple, where all Jews come together; and I have said nothing in secret.[56] Why ask me? Ask those who heard me about what I taught; they know what I said.[57]

Persons, supposedly, were not allowed to testify against themselves; but instead, witnesses were needed to bring charges against the accused, so it was that Jesus had said, "Why ask me? But ask those who heard me." As Jesus had said this, one of the temple guards standing there slapped him in the face, saying to him, "Is this the way you answer the high priest?"[58] And so as not to accuse himself, but only to elicit testimony from his accusers, Jesus answered the guard:

If I have said something wrong, point it out to everyone;
but if not, why do you strike me?[59]

About an hour after this, another man, with a group of colleagues, came up to Peter.[60] He was one of the high priest's servants; in fact, he was a relative of Malchus,[61] the man whose ear Peter had cut off; and this person told Peter, "Didn't I see you in the garden with him?"[62] The man and his bystanders all insisted, "You are certainly one of them! Why, even your accent gives you away; you are a Galilean."[63] But Peter replied, "My friends, I don't know what you're talking about."[64] And then Peter started cursing and swearing like a fisherman, "If I am not telling the truth, may God punish me! I don't even know the man you are talking about."[65] At that instant, while Peter was still saying these words, "I don't even

---

56	John 18:20
57	John 18:21
58	John 18:22
59	John 18:23
60	Luke 22:59
61	John 18:10
62	John 18:26
63	Luke 22:59, Mark 14:70, Matthew 26:73
64	Luke 22:60
65	Mark 14:71, Matthew 26:74

know the man," the cock crowed,[66] and now for the second time.[67] And, at that very moment, also as Peter finished saying, "the man you are talking about," the Lord turned from inside the house and looked straight at Peter.[68] As their eyes met, Peter remembered the words Jesus had spoken to him that night, "Before the cock crows today,[69] twice,[70] you will have denied me three times."[71] Peter then rushed outside, and away from the compound and past the gate; and immediately, bursting into uncontrollable tears,[72] he wept long and bitterly.[73]

After this, Annas ordered that Jesus should be sent, bound, to the high priest Caiaphas.[74] That meeting, however, would have to wait until the morning, because by Mosaic Law a formal trial before the Sanhedrin was not allowed at night. So, for the remaining hours until dawn, the guards took Jesus to a holding cell, just a small one-person-sized hole dug in the ground, where they continued to amuse themselves by abusing Jesus with their mocking and by beating him,[75] in imitation of his captors and the esteemed high priest, Annas, when Jesus had stood before him.[76] So, the guards blindfolded Jesus, and then they questioned him, saying, "Prophecy![77] Prophecy to us Christ![78] Go, play the prophet;[79] tell us, then, who it was that struck you."[80] And besides hitting him with their fists, some also were even spitting in his face.[81] The men who guarded Jesus, while his hands were tied and he was in his

66	Matthew 26:74, Luke 22:60, John 18:27
67	Mark 14:72
68	Luke 22:61
69	Luke 22:61, Matthew 26:75
70	Mark 14:72
71	Luke 22:61, Matthew 26:75; Matthew 18:21-25
72	Mark 14:72
73	Luke 22:62, Matthew 26:75; Matthew 18:26-27
74	John 18:24
75	Luke 22:67
76	John 10:24; John 18:22
77	Luke 22:64
78	Matthew 26:68
79	Mark 14:65; Deuteronomy 18:18, John 4:25
80	Luke 22:64, Matthew 26:68
81	Mark 14:65, Matthew 26:67; Isaiah 50:6-10

prison hole, also heaped many other insults on him,[82] not unlike the human degradation and unspeakable abuse of tortured prisoners sometimes reported in our own times, perhaps even at the hands of our own governments or local police. And then, collectively against Jesus,[83] even the attendants to the high priest joined right in and struck him too.[84] Yet, throughout the night Jesus remained absolutely silent, never resisting, despite the pain and insults he suffered;[85] as Jesus also was fully absorbed in prayer.[86]

A few hours ago, Peter had told Jesus that he was willing to go to prison, even to die for the Lord.[87] But now, after denying his discipleship and even his knowing of the Lord, Peter had fled in his shame and remorse; although John remained with the Lord, as close as distance and circumstances would permit. At Peter's last denial, when the Lord's eyes had met with Peter's,[88] who was the Lord's designated leader,[89] Peter knew with a bone-penetrating numbness that he had stumbled, as we all do when we disown the Lord if we sin, or if we fail to witness to his calling for us, or if we should disavow God's love for us, by failing to keep his commands to love.[90] But, after Peter had stumbled, he had not hardened his heart against grace, as many are doing who abandon God and true faith.[91] Even before Peter had stumbled, the Lord also had told him two things: first, that he would deny the Lord,[92] as we all also have done; and second, that when he returned, he should provide support to his brothers;[93] and in both cases, Jesus had told this to him, and to us, ahead of time, so

---

82 Luke 22:65
83 Psalm 22:16
84 Mark 14:65
85 Matthew 5:38, Exodus 21:24-25, Leviticus 24:20, Deuteronomy 19:21, Matthew 5:39; Luke 18:32; Isaiah 53:3-4
86 Luke 6:27-29; Isaiah 25:1-12, 26:1-6
87 Luke 22:33
88 Luke 22:61
89 Matthew 16:18
90 John 15:10, 13:34
91 John 12:40, Matthew 13:15, Isaiah 6:9-10
92 Luke 22:34
93 Luke 22:32

that he, and we, and the others would not fall away.[94] And Peter would recover;[95] for in his and in our repentance, when we confess our sins and acknowledge through faith and action that Christ is our Lord and Saviour, Jesus already has forgiven our sins in all its violence, through his suffering and death on the cross, a forgiveness witnessed to us by the power of his resurrection from the dead, and which we witness for others by the power of our love in Christ. More than once, like Peter, I too have stumbled and recovered through the Lord's mercy;[96] and if our life is a constant prayer, as the Lord's was for us, then, at last, we also will persevere in God's grace.[97] In that grace, like Peter's in his grace after the Lord prayed for him,[98] we also give support to our brothers and sisters through our active love and prayer.

But, do we really have the courage to witness to the love of God in our lives, even if we, like the Lord, should have to go to prison, or even be killed? On 14 August 2006, a veteran news journalist, 60-year-old Steve Centanni, and his 36-year-old cameraman, Olaf Wiig, were kidnapped from their car at gunpoint in Gaza. During their captivity by Islamic militants, images of hostage situations in Iraq, where victims were being executed or beheaded, passed vividly through their minds when they were interrogated by their captors about their knowledge of Islam, and who they thought Jesus was, and who Mohammed was. Their captors had believed that the problems between the Muslim world and the West would be solved only if the West converted to Islam; and so they thought that it would be a good idea for the journalists themselves to convert to Islam, if they also wanted to live and to go free. After thirteen days captivity, the journalist and his cameraman were released, just two days after their simulated conversion to Islam on videotape was shown to the world. But, once Centanni no longer was held hostage, immediately, at a news conference, he asserted that his publicly sworn to "conversion" had been made at gunpoint; yet even so, indeed, despite their experience,

---

94 John 16:1
95 John 21:17; Acts 1:15-22, 2:14, 22-23, 36-38, 3:12-20
96 Isaiah 59:9-20, 61:10-11, Romans 11:32-36
97 2 Timothy 2:11-13
98 Luke 22:32-34

he and his cameraman still shared a great respect for Islam, and they worried for the plight and aspirations of the Palestinian people.

Then, just sixteen days later, on 12 September 2006, Pope Benedict XVI delivered a university lecture at Regensburg, where once he had been professor. And in that lecture, the Holy Father engaged as essential the relationship of reason to the nature of God. By taking as his starting point a text written in 1391 by the Byzantine emperor Manuel II Paleologus on the subject of Christianity and Islam, and by combining it with Saint John's paraphrase of the opening verse of Genesis in verse one of his written gospel,[99] John's profound bridge between the Old and New Testaments, the Pope articulated his fundamental theme: not to act reasonably, in accordance with reason, with *logos*, is contrary to the nature of God; for it also was God, who divinely revealed himself as *logos*, as the incarnate Word of God, and who acted and continues to act on our behalf with love.

As the Pope then presented his argument: it was the synthesis of Greek philosophical inquiry with Biblical faith, even present in the late wisdom literature of the Old Testament, but culminating in the Septuagint, the Greek translation from the Hebrew, and integral to the New Testament in its Greek language and early Gentile Christian culture, that enabled emperor Manuel II to articulate his very specific and abrupt statement pertaining to Mohammed's command in Islam, as inhuman and evil, to spread by the sword the faith he preached; the emperor's conclusion was that violence in religion and violent conversion is incompatible with the nature of God and the nature of the soul. But unfortunately, shortly after these papal remarks, in a post-modern world of instant communication and media sound bites, the Pope found himself under fire by a worldwide Muslim backlash; and, like Peter, the Pope himself was being pilloried by questions of discipleship around the fire in the middle of the high priest's courtyard. However, in this case, to the Pope's dismay, the furies of some and of the many produced enough noise to obscure the profound truths that the Holy Father had sought to express: namely, violence is against God, and against reason, because reason, and God's implicit command to act with reason, is essential to the

---

[99] Genesis 1:1, John 1:1

nature of God.

The Holy Father, originally, had intended to engage a church dialogue with Christians, and with Islam and other religions, so as to include reason in our understanding of God's nature, and in our religious faiths and moral actions; and dialogue with science and theology, so as for the natural sciences to include God and a broader rationality beyond its limited rational methods, and for theology to express and explore in its inquiry the true rationality of faith; and dialogue with human sciences and institutions, so as to counterbalance the contemporary subjective construction of morality and of our interpersonal and social worlds, and so as to confront the fear of reason apparent in modern attempts to dehellenize the West; when, in fact, Greek thought and its expressions of enlightenment and reason have always been an intrinsic part of Christianity, and also have been fundamental to the foundation of Europe itself. But in the Moslem teaching of God's transcendence, and in various other religious expressions of the belief in God's total otherness, God is rendered as unbounded by any human categories, including reason. And these views make the mystery of God's incarnation, as the Word, even more remote and inaccessible. Yet, as the Holy Father then writes, the faith of the church has always insisted that there is an analogy between God's eternal Creator Spirit and our created reason: for God, in fact, "unlikeness remains infinitely greater than likeness, yet not to the point of abolishing analogy and its language." And so it was that the Holy Father concluded the theme of his university lecture: "It is to this great *logos*, to this breadth of reason, that we invite our partners in the dialogue of cultures."

The day after the Pope's Regensburg lecture, on 13 September 2006, Sister Leonella (nee Rosa) Sgorbati returned to Mogadishu, Somalia, from Uganda, where she had been scouting for hospitals to train her nursing students, from the school she had set up in a hospital run by the SOS Village organization in Somalia. The Islamic courts that controlled the region had made it difficult for this Consolata Missionary Sister to obtain her own re-entry visa to Mogadishu, but finally she managed to come back, in time for her to celebrate the feast of the Exultation of the Holy Cross on the following day. She had served in various hospitals in Kenya from 1970-1993, until she was elected as the Regional superior of the Consolata Missionary Sisters in Kenya, a post she had served for six years. It was in 2001, after a sabbatical, that she first had spent several months in Mogadishu attempting to set up a nursing school, which ultimately she did in 2002, and its first students had graduated only in 2006.

But on 17 September 2006, on Sunday, the day of the Lord's resurrection, after working in the Mother and Child Ward she had established, Sister Leonella left the SOS hospital to have noontime lunch with three other sisters at home, only 30 feet from the hospital. But then, hiding behind bushes, a lone gunman attacked her and her bodyguard, killing them both. Only a short time before this attack, Somalia jihadist Shiek Abubukar Hassan Malin had stoked so-called "Pope Rage" regarding Benedict XVI and his Regensburg address by declaring: "Whoever offends our Prophet Mohammed should be killed on the spot by the nearest Muslim." However, despite such potential direct incitement, although the good sister, and others, may have been victims of the recently growing Islamic radicalism in Somalia, also in Somalia disgruntled Somali warlords also abound. Nonetheless, undeniably marked for Christ by the nun's habit she always wore, as the 65-year-old Sister Leonella lay in hospital dying from bullet wounds, she gave her final words of discipleship in her native Italian, "I forgive; I forgive."[100]

After these crucial events it would be another two years before senior Vatican and Islamic scholars would launch their first bi-annual Catholic-Muslim Forum, lasting for three days beginning just yesterday on 4 November 2008, as I now provide this observation, in dialogue between their respective delegations of twenty-eight members and advisors. But exactly one week before this gathering in Rome, inclusive of its meeting with Pope Benedict XVI, thirteen-year-old Aisha Ibrahim Duhulow was buried to her neck in a hole in the ground at a stadium in the port city of Kismayu, Somalia, where she was stoned to death by fifty men in front of nearly 1,000 spectators,[101] after she had been accused of adultery and found

---

100 Luke 23:34, Acts 7:59-60; Matthew 18:28-35
101 Luke 23:23

"guilty" under sharia law.[102] In fact, the young girl had been raped by three men while she had been travelling on foot to visit her grandmother in Mogadishu. Such is the real nature of satanic violence disguised as giving honour to God;[103] just as Jesus himself would be suffering at the hands of his murderers;[104] just as today in Iran (6 September 2010) Sakineh Mohammadi-Ashtiani is facing death by stoning for her "conviction" of "adultery," while the world seeks clemency for her; and also just as Johann Ludwig Klemmer and his wife Anna Maria Elizabeth, my direct ancestors, had suffered in Christ,[105] at the hands of their murderers.[106]

And, at the very moment two years ago, as I first was writing this chapter and paragraph, in Iraq fifty Muslims are being slaughtered every day, as targeted victims are rounded up, executed, and their bodies dumped around Baghdad. In a month of such violence, the number of victims nearly matches those killed in the single day of the 11 September 2001 attacks against the World Trade Center in New York, and against other American targets in Washington, by disciples of an infamous Evil, an Antichrist.[107] And only yesterday (on 2 October 2006, as I then wrote) a 32-year-old gunman entered a single-room Amish school house in Paradise, Pennsylvania, in rural Lancaster County, which is very close to the American home of my original immigrant ancestor, Johann Ludwig Klemmer. Like many other immigrants of his time, he had sought the religious and political freedoms found in the New World of Pioneer America. Yet, religious freedom is more than a Christian value; it also has been a true value in Islam, supported by the verse from the Qur'an (Sūrah 2:256),[108] that there should be "no compulsion in religion." The same values for non-violence in religion, likewise, defend against the violent imposition of political beliefs, and against all forms of

---

102 John 8:4-5
103 John 8:7
104 John 19:15-16
105 Matthew 23:35, Philippians 3:10; Revelation 5:9, 7:9,13-14
106 Philippians 3:18
107 1 John 5:19, 4:2-3, 2:18, 4, 9
108 The Holy Qur'an. (2000). [Translated by Abdullah Yusuf Ali]. Ware, Hertfordshire: Wordsworth Editions Limited, p. 33.

violence whatsoever, as also these are directed against the love of God.[109]

My ancestral protagonist, Johann Ludwig Klemmer, was born in Friedelsheim, Rheinland-Pfalz, Germany on 24 January 1720. Following the marriage of his parents on 16 September 1710, Ludwig was born their second child, after an elder brother, the nine-year-old Johan Andreas, born in Alsheim (30 August 1711), where their father, Johann Henrich Klemmer (born 13 June 1688), had married their mother, Anna Catharina Daughnier (the widow of Michael Daughnier, and daughter of Heinrich Sinn). It was Johann Henrich's father, Hans Jacob, who had immigrated from Affoltern, Canton of Zurich, Switzerland, to Ludwigshaffen in the Palatinate, where about 20 km west of Ludwigshaffen, in the village of Friedelsheim, Hans Jacob Klemmer (born 16 August 1652) had married Anna Catherine Pfaffman on 17 September 1678.

But before Hans Jacob Klemmer, and three generations before Johann Ludwig; in April 1635, Johann Henrich's grandparents, Henrich Frantz "Tommi" Klemmer (born 20 August 1615) and his wife Barbara Urmer (or Urmi) Klemmer, were married in Affoltern Am Albis, Zurich, Switzerland, where all of their eight children (including Hans Jacob's twin brother, Felix) were born (1639-1655), and also where, before the children, their father, Henrich Frantz "Klimmer," had been born (1615), who was the fourth child of Hans Jacob Klymmer (born 1573) and wife Anna Hediger Klymmer. Before them, Henrich Frantz's grandfather had been Frantz Klymmer. Apparently, Frantz Klymmer was born in France (circa 1536), where it seems the family once may have lived in or near Montbeliard,[110] which is on the border of the Alsace near Switzerland. However, no later than 1566, Frantz and his wife were living their family life in the district of Affoltern, Zurich, Switzerland, because early that year a daughter, Elsbeth, was born to them there (29 January 1566). Already this was six years before the infamous Paris St. Bartholomew's Day Massacre (24 August 1572), with its subsequent

---

109   1 John 4:20, Revelation 22:14-15
110   An oral family tradition from about 1840, written in 1900 by Joseph Neal Clemmer.

violent hysteria between Roman Catholics and Huguenots spreading throughout France. So their departure from France was not sparked by this later specific event; but perhaps it was influenced by cultural precursors before the hysteria reached its infamous flash point. And in the year following this horrible slaughter, born to Frantz and his wife, was their second child, likewise in Affoltern, Zurich: Hans Jacob Klymmer (1573).[111]

Hans Jacob's son, the Henrich Frantz Klemmer family, with their eight children born in Affoltern, Zurich, also had secured the family's religious and social culture and their safety and security in Switzerland throughout the brutal "Thirty Years War," which was ended only after Catholic "France" had regained the Alsace region from Germany under the Treaty of Westphalia in 1648. Their grandson, Johann Ludwig's father Johann Henrich Klemmer, was an only child, and he was baptized into the Reformed church in Friedelsheim, after his father, the second "Hans Jacob," had resettled there. During that protracted period of Catholic-Protestant violence throughout Europe, the Amish (Mennonites) also had fled to and from Zurich, and also to Germany, and elsewhere; and indeed, there were Mennonites present with a church in Friedelsheim, too; but, there in Friedelsheim, the Klemmer families were Reformed, not Mennonite. But also, later in America, Johann Henrich Klemmer and his wife, Johann Ludwig's parents, eventually became active in the Lutheran church in Philadelphia.

In fact, along with the Reformed, the Anabaptists, and the Lutherans from Germany and elsewhere, various religious denominations and sects made their way to William Penn's political experiment in religious tolerance in America, known as Pennsylvania: and so it was that, in 1730 on the Ship Alexander & Anne, captained by one William Clymer, Johann Henrich Klemmer, Johann Ludwig's father, was my first ancestor to land in America: in Philadelphia from Rotterdam, by way of Deal, England; together with his wife, Catherina, and his eldest son, the 19-year-old Johan Andreas, on 5 September 1730. Andreas died later in 1737. Ten years later, in November 1747, Johann Henrich and his wife are listed together as

---

111   Genesis 28:20-21

witnesses for a marriage at St. Michaelis and Zion Lutheran Church in Philadelphia. And seventeen years after Andreas' death; after their surviving second son Johann Ludwig Klemmer; their third and last child was born a son of the New World: Joseph Klemmer (born 16 September 1754); and he was baptized "Joseph" in Philadelphia,[112] also at St. Michaelis and Zion Lutheran church, on 21 September 1754. Later, Joseph Klemmer would fight as a soldier in America's Revolutionary War for Independence, in 1776.

However, in 1730, when Johann Henrich Klemmer came to America, he also had left his ten-year-old son, Johann Ludwig, my direct ancestor, back in Germany, in Friedelsheim. Why this should have been so is cause for interesting speculation, whether by personal choice or because of family circumstances. If Ludwig was only ten, the decision may have been his own; although, incorrectly, some historical sources have over-estimated his age as seventeen. But, when Johann Henrich Klemmer had made the journey to America, it would be another seventeen years before the 27-year-old Ludwig "Klemer," like his father, older brother, and his mother before him, also would arrive to Philadelphia in 1747.[113] This was twenty-nine years before the future Philadelphia Congress of the United States would declare American Independence (4 July 1776). And incidentally, among the original signers of that declaration, was one George Clymer, native born (1739) of Philadelphia; orphaned at age seven, he was the son of Christian Clymer and nephew of John Clymer, two Mennonite brothers, who had come to Philadelphia in 1695 from Bristol, England, seeking religious freedom.

But, after his family's earlier departure from Friedelsheim, Johann Ludwig Klemmer had stayed on with relatives for eleven more years before he took a wife: on 24 January 1742, on his 22nd birthday, Ludwig had married 23-year-old Anna Maria Elizabeth Boeckel (born 26 June 1718), in Alsheim-Gronau, Rheinland-Pfalz, Germany. Ludwig's bride was his first cousin, the daughter of his father's sister-in-law: she was the daughter of Johan Adam Boeckel

---

112   Genesis 37:3
113   One "m" in the <u>Palatine Index</u> by Charles M. Hall (2001), lists of immigrants.

and Sabine Sinn Boeckel, daughter of Henrich Sinn. Anna Maria may have been pregnant (unlikely), or she became so soon after she and Ludwig were married (most likely). Their first son, Caspar "Jaspar" Klemmer, was born in Friedelsheim (about 1741/1742), where also, their second son, Jacob Klemmer, was born three years later (1745). But, only after toddler Jacob was old enough to travel, Johann Ludwig Klemmer's family finally made their voyage to America: it seems that they came down the Rhine from Gronau, Germany, to Rotterdam, taking six weeks, passing through twenty-six customs houses; then most likely, Ludwig left from Rotterdam to immigrate to the New World with his wife, who was pregnant once again; with two young sons, their journey took another ten or twelve weeks.

But, their *in utero* son, George Valentine Klemmer, was born in America, 16 km southeast of Gettysburg, one-hundred sixteen years before that area became the great battlefield and sacred cemetery of the American Civil War: where more than 7,500 men died in that three-day battle (1-3 July 1863); and where four months later President Lincoln also commemorated the living and the dead who had struggled there, in his famous address on 19 November 1863. George Valentine Klemmer was born nearby to there, in Conewago, Littlestown, Pennsylvania, which was then York County, on 10 February 1747, shortly after Ludwig and Anna Maria Elizabeth had arrived in America, apparently to her brother's place of residence, with their five-year-old and two-year-old sons. And there in Littlestown, George Valentine "Felty" Klemmer was baptized at Christ Reformed Church on 6 May 1747 by Reverend Michael Slatter; the child was named after the witness, the mother's childless brother, (Georg Velte) Boeckel, as George Valentine. Later on in America, three more Klemmer children would be born to Ludwig, the blacksmith, and to Anna Maria Elizabeth: in Littlestown, Lorentz Clemmer (about 1751) and George Ludwig Klemmer (Feb 1752), and in Salisbury, Frederick, Maryland there was born their daughter, Anna Maria Clemmer (1756). George Ludwig Klemmer would be my direct ancestor through his son David Fishburn Clemmer, also born in Littlestown (11 September 1780).

Like many European immigrants of that period, Johann Ludwig

Klemmer, his wife, and his father and mother, fervently sought and advocated the religious and political freedoms that they had found in a New World of opportunities, especially without compulsion in religion. However, in 1754, the family of Johann Ludwig Klemmer had moved about 80 km southwest from Littlestown to an area of rugged and unmarked wilderness on the Potomac River, to what now is Williamsport, Maryland. There, their infant daughter, Anna Maria, accidentally had drowned, perhaps while the mother was tending to the family laundry.[114] As the 36-year-old Johann Ludwig Klemmer and his 38-year-old wife, Anna Maria Elizabeth, my great-great-great-great-great grandparents, were returning home from the funeral on horseback, their funeral train was attacked near Huyets Crossing, on 20 August 1756, by fifteen Delaware Indians. Similarly today, and tragically, funeral trains also are being attacked by Muslim sectarian-political "insurgents" in Iraq. And like the many innocents who now are victims of violence, two-hundred and fifty years ago, in the attack at Conococheague Settlement, Baker's Ridge, Frederick, Maryland, Ludwig and the second man with them, George Hicks, were killed immediately; but, on the following day, Anna Maria Elizabeth was ruthlessly murdered, when she attempted to escape her captivity by the Indians: and consequently, their five children were orphaned.

Easily, one can imagine the fragile vulnerability of Anna Maria before she attempted to escape: a daughter buried, a husband dead, a young child and two older boys at home, two of her children held captive, and herself an unprotected woman. The two sons, nine-year-old George Valentine and his brother, seven-year-old Lorentz, however, remained captive at Wills Mountain Indian village, just slightly west of Cumberland, Maryland, until the conclusion of the French and Indian War in 1763; in Europe, that conflict between France and England was known as the "Seven Years War" (1756-1763). It was ironic that Ludwig was killed in another French conflict, and on the same day as his great-grandfather's birthday: Henrich Frantz Klemmer (born 20 August 1615), whose grandfather, Huguenot

---

[114] Oral explanation from Louise Heiny Clemmer, my paternal grandmother, to myself circa 1960-1962.

Frantz Klymmer, had fled from 16th century persecutions of Catholic "France" for Affoltern, Zurich. On that fateful day in 1756, Ludwig and Anna Maria Elizabeth's fifth child, my direct ancestor, George Ludwig Klemmer, was only four years old; and Ludwig's 68-year-old father, Johann Henrich Klemmer, would live yet for another thirty-five years, before he died in Pennsylvania.

In 1763, after their seven-year captivity, George Valentine Klemmer and Lorentz Clemmer were reunited with the other brothers in Pennsylvania. It seems that the two older brothers, Caspar and Jacob, had been looked after by the relatives. But in 1756, the youngest brother, George Ludwig Klemmer, was the baby of the family; and he was raised then by Jacob Froneback, after the four-year-old orphan had been delivered to him by his mother's brother, uncle George Valentine Boeckel, who had sponsored George Valentine Klemmer's baptism in 1747. Then, at age twelve, George Ludwig was appointed another guardian by the court, one Casper Cline; and still another at age fourteen, one Thomas Fisher. Later George Ludwig Clemmer, the shoemaker, married his wife Modlena about 1773/1774; all eight of their children were born in Littlestown; and George Ludwig died in Rockbridge, Virginia, at the age of seventy-six.

George Ludwig and Modlena's third son, David Clemmer, married Martha "Mattie" Wilson, daughter of Robert Wilson, on 11 May 1806 in Rockingham County, Virginia, and David died in Montgomery County, Ohio on 19 December 1848, and was buried in Preble County, Ohio;[115] their son George Clemmer married Elizabeth Repetau in 1836 in Cincinnati, Ohio;[viii] their ninth child Benjamin Rakestraw Clemmer married Ellen Flood, an Irish Catholic, in 1886 in Fort Wayne, Indiana;[ix] where their son Edward George Clemmer married Louise

---

115   David Fishborn Clemmer was born in Littlestown, Pennsylvania on 11 September 1780; and his younger brother John (born 14 March 1786) also died in Preble County, eighteen years after his brother, on 2 May 1867. Older brother Andrew also had gone with David to Montgomery County, Ohio, in 1815, after the entire family had gone to Virginia in 1803. The eldest brother and four sisters stayed in Virginia, although all the siblings had taken spouses from Virginia. David's wife, Martha, preceded David in death by four years, at sixty-three years of age, on 3 November 1844.

Esther Heiny in 1915;[x] their sixth child, Benjamin Othmar Clemmer,[xi] married my mother, Rita Cecelia Weaver,[xii] eldest daughter of Martin Anthony Weaver[xiii] and Marcella May Bobay,[xiv] on 17 May 1947; and I was their firstborn (28 June 1948) of three surviving sons and three daughters. And after me, (and also before me through the Father of us all),[116] each of my four sons were born of their mother Kathleen Ann Herber:[xv] Kenneth Benjamin Clemmer (27 February 1974), James Anthony (Clemmer) Dearlove (8 October 1975),[117] Andrew John Clemmer (14 February 1978), and Stephen Joseph Clemmer (20 March 1980).[118]

In the uncle's responsibilities for the orphaned Klemmer family, George Valentine Boeckel provided for Ludwig and Anna Maria Elizabeth's four youngest Klemmer sons in his will in 1768; the eldest brother, Casper, not mentioned in the will, already had married in 1766. While in Littlestown, three of the Klemmer brothers each seem to have named a child after their father or mother: John Ludwig Clemmer (27 December 1778) was born to George Valentine and his first wife Margaretha Elizabeth Dettero; Anna Maria Clemmer (20 February 1782) was born to Lorentz and his wife Anna Maria Dentlinger; and also Anna Maria Clemmer (11 June 1782) was born to George Ludwig and his wife Modlena. But Anna Maria not only was the name of the brothers' mother and the wife of Lorentz, but it also was the name for George Valentine Boeckel's wife, the childless aunt Anna Maria Rheinhardin. And thereafter, avoiding the French and the Indians, all five of the brothers anglicized their surname to "Clemmer."[119]

But yesterday in America, in Paradise, Pennsylvania, after the gunman systematically bound eleven Amish school girls, aged six to thirteen, he shot each of them in the head with an automatic pistol, irrationally killing many, three instantly, and putting any of

---

116   Matthew 23:9, Ephesians 3:14-15, Matthew 6:9; Psalm 22:27-31
117   And my first grandchild, Quincy James Dearlove, was born to Jim and Jenni in Denver, Colorado, on 8 July 2009, at 3:45 p.m. in good health and with a calm spirit (1 John 4:7).
118   John 3:3-6, 13-14; Romans 14:7-9; Galatians 4:4-6, Romans 8:14-17, 28-29, Colossians 1:17-19, John 14:9-11
119   Matthew 12:46-50; John 20:17, Matthew 28:19-20

the initial survivors on life-support, apparently over a twenty-year-old obsession he had with his having molested two small girls, aged three and five, when he was twelve; and then he turned the gun on himself, like Judas in his final act of denial of God's forgiveness.[120] But the Amish, in their Christian witness to the nature of God, are pacifists;[121] and they shun the world for a simpler rural community life.[122] After the tragedy, the families of the victims declared that they would be praying at their funerals not only for themselves and the victims, but also for the killer and his family, too, because "healing comes through forgiveness."[123] Some people kill the body, or with Satan even attempt to kill the soul. But all who murder and kill deny God by their violence: this is the singular truth expressed by Pope Benedict XVI in his Regensburg address, that to act unreasonably, without reason, without *logos*, opposes and denies the very nature of God.[124] God with his eternal life in us is reason and love, not hatred and violence.[125]

When morning light came to Jerusalem,[126] there was a meeting of the elders of the people, the chief priests, and scribes.[127] Then, those who had arrested Jesus brought him before their council,[128] to Caiaphas the high priest and to the chief priests and the entire Sanhedrin already assembled there.[129] They were looking for evidence against Jesus,[130] however false,[131] or trumped up the charges might be, just so they could have Jesus executed.[132] Yet, they still could not find any evidence;[133] and although several witnesses

---

120 Matthew 27:4-5, Acts 1:18
121 Matthew 5:9, 39
122 Matthew 5:3-4
123 Luke 6:28, Matthew 18:21-22; 1 John 2:2, 4:10
124 Matthew 23:34-35, Acts 2:36, 25-28, Psalm 16:11; 1 John 4:9
125 1 John 3:11-16
126 Luke 22:66
127 Luke 22:66, Mark 14:53
128 Luke 22:66, Matthew 26:57
129 Matthew 26:57, Mark 14:53, 55; Deuteronomy 17:8-13
130 Mark 14:55, Matthew 26:59
131 Matthew 26:59
132 Matthew 26:59, Mark 14:55
133 Mark 14:55, Matthew 26:60

came forward to give false testimony against him,[134] their evidence was conflicting.[135] Eventually two more witnesses came forward,[136] and they made their statement of evidence against Jesus.[137] The first witness stated:

> This man said, "I have power to destroy the Temple of God and in three days build it up."[138]

Then the second witness, attempting to corroborate this first evidence, testified:

> We heard him say, "I am going to destroy this Temple made by human hands, and in three days build another, not made by human hands."[139]

If these charges were true statements, and they were, but not in the way they had misunderstood them, as an attack against the house of God,[140] and as an assault against their centre of religious and political power in Jerusalem; yet, even on their point of evidence, they did not agree.[141] On the face value of the evidence, did Jesus seem to say that he was going to destroy the Temple, or did he seem to claim only to have the power to destroy it? And if the Temple were to be destroyed, did Jesus seem to claim only that he had the power to rebuild it in three days, or that when it would be built, it simply would not be built by human hands? However, regarding both the Temple of his body and the power of God to raise him from the dead, all of these statements above were true.[142] Then, the high priest Caiaphas rose and said to Jesus, "Have you no answer to that; do you have anything to say for yourself? What is this evidence that these men are bringing against you?"[143] But Jesus always remained

---

134   Matthew 26:60, Mark 14:56
135   Mark 14:56
136   Matthew 26:60
137   Matthew 26:60-61, Mark 14:56
138   Matthew 26:61; John 2:19, 10:17
139   Mark 14:58; Acts 6:8, 1:8, 6:9-14; Ephesians 2:13, 16, 15, 14, 17-18, 21-22
140   Acts 7:48-50, Isaiah 66:1-2
141   Mark 14:59
142   John 2:20, 10:18, 11:25, 12:28-30; Acts 2:24
143   Matthew 26:62

silent;[144] he made no answer,[145] not to any of the charges levelled against him.

The Sanhedrin had failed to produce any clear or substantive evidence against Jesus for a single charge from two witnesses, as had been required under the Law.[146] Nor did they succeed to obtain from Jesus self-incriminating depositions, which of themselves would have been against the Law, because no one was obliged to testify against himself, and evidence from witnesses were always required in a fair trial. So, no longer relying upon human witnesses, but in fact only upon God,[147] to obtain according to God's sworn promises the Son of God's conviction for our sins,[148] the high priest then put his second question to Jesus.[149] Caiaphas said:

> I put you on oath by the living God to tell us if you are the Christ, the Son of God?[150] Are you the Christ, the Son of the Blessed One?[151] If you are the Christ, tell us,[152] now.

And Jesus, at first presenting his preliminary evidence against them, answered:

> If I tell you, you will not believe;[153] and if I question you, you will not answer.[154]

Then, with barely a pause in his voice, Jesus continued:

> But I tell you this,[155] from now on,[156] this you will

---

144 Matthew 26:63, Mark 14:61
145 Mark 14:61
146 Deuteronomy 17:6
147 Deuteronomy 1:17
148 Genesis 12:7, Galatians 3:16, Genesis 15:4-6, Romans 4:16, 20-25, Genesis 17:4-7, 19, 22:9-18, 28:10-15; 2 Samuel 7:8-11, 18-29
149 Mark 14:61
150 Matthew 26:63; Matthew 23:16-22, Hebrews 10:30-31; Hebrews 7:20-25
151 Mark 14:61
152 Luke 22:67; John 10:24
153 Luke 22:67; John 5:39-44, 6:28-30, 12:37-40, 44; Hebrews 10:28
154 Luke 22:68; Matthew 21:24-27, Isaiah 66:4; Hebrews 10:29
155 Matthew 26:64
156 Luke 22:69, Matthew 26:64

see:[157] "the Son of man will be seated at the right hand of the Power of God,"[158] and "coming on the clouds of heaven."[159]

At this first statement from Jesus, all of the Sanhedrin rose to their feet, and together they all asked him, "So, then you are the Son of God?"[160] And Jesus replied with his final statement:

It is you who say I am.[161] It is you who say it;[162] and I am.[163]

With this last word of Jesus, "I am," for the revealed name of God,[164] the high priest tore his robes,[165] saying, "He has blasphemed."[166] Caiaphas thought that he had torn the vestments of his office only as an expression of his outrage, but the act would have been in violation of the Law;[167] yet in God's reality of that moment, the act of the high priest also represented the termination of his office, for the Law was coming to an end through its actual fulfilment:[168] for now, Jesus would be our eternal high priest in the new covenant;[169] and for the remission of our sins, Jesus soon would be ascending to his Father on high.[170] There no longer would be a need for the inferior priesthood of Aaron, just an imperfect reflection of the promised Redeemer, rather than the only perfect high priest.

---

157   Mark 14:62, Matthew 26:64
158   Luke 22:69, Mark 14:62, Matthew 26:64; Psalm 110:1-2; Hebrews 4:14-15, 8:1-2
159   Mark 14:62, Matthew 26:64, Daniel 7:13; Psalm 68:4, 33-35; Luke 21:27, Mark 13:26, Matthew 24:30, Hebrews 9:28
160   Luke 22:70
161   Luke 22:70
162   Matthew 26:64
163   Mark 14:62; Exodus 3:14; John 18:4-6
164   Matthew 22:32, Exodus 3:6, 14; John 10:30, 36
165   Mark 14:63, Matthew 26:65; Exodus 28:4, 31-32, 35, Exodus 39:1-31
166   Matthew 26:65
167   Exodus 28:32, 39:23
168   Mark 15:37-38, Luke 23:45, Matthew 27:51-53; Romans 7:1, 4, 6; Hebrews 10:8
169   Hebrews 9:11, 7:15-17
170   John 16:28, 10, 17

And so, by the sacrifice of the body of Christ,[171] the Temple also was being torn down;[172] and it was being replaced by the temple of the Son of God,[173] not built by human hands; but his temple of God's spirit would be rebuilt in our lives by the living spirit of God,[174] and as our own bodies would be nourished by the body and blood of Christ in the Eucharist.[175]

Caiaphas then proclaimed, "What need do we have now for testimony from witnesses? There, just now, you have heard the blasphemy."[176] And they replied, "What further need do we have for evidence? We ourselves have heard it from out of his mouth."[177] Now, they all had become witnesses according to the Law; but also now they were subject to the Law's condemnation,[178] unless they would believe in the Son of God.[179] Then, asking for their legal opinion as required by Law, Caiaphas said, "What do you find?"[180] And their verdict was unanimous:[181] he deserved to die.[182] At once, in a furious eruption they started spitting at Jesus and striking him with their fists,[183] according to the Law's command.[184] Then the whole assembly rose;[185] they had Jesus bound; and they brought him before Pilate, the governor.[186] As an entire body, all according to their plan,[187] they led Jesus from the house of Caiaphas to the Praetorium,[188] the former residence of King Herod the Great,

---

171   Hebrews 10:5, 9-10
172   Mark 14:58; Matthew 27:51
173   Matthew 26:61; 2 Samuel 7:12-13
174   John 7:38-39; 1 Corinthians 6:19
175   John 6:53-56, Luke 22:19-20
176   Matthew 26:65, Mark 14:63-64
177   Luke 22:71
178   Deuteronomy 19:16-21
179   John 8:24
180   Mark 14:64, Matthew 26:66; Deuteronomy 17:9
181   Mark 14:64
182   Mark 14:64, Matthew 26:66; Jeremiah 26:11-15, Matthew 23:35-36
183   Mark 14:65, Matthew 26:67
184   Deuteronomy 17:7
185   Luke 23:1
186   Mark 15:1, Matthew 27:2
187   Mark 15:1, Matthew 27:1; Matthew 26:3-5, John 11:49-53
188   John 18:28

where Pilate had been staying while he was in Jerusalem now for the Passover feast. Pontius Pilate, who then had been governor for four years, otherwise would have been at his normal residence in the Roman provincial city of coastal Caesarea.

Readings: Matthew 27:1-10; Luke 23:1-7, Mark 15:1-5, Matthew 27:11-14, John 18:28-38; Luke 23:8-12; Luke 23:13-19, John 18:39-40, Mark 15:6-11, Matthew 27:15-18; Matthew 27:19; Mark 15:11-14, Matthew 27:20-25, Luke 23:20-23; John 19:1, Mark 15:15, Matthew 27:26, Luke 23:16; John 19:2-3, Matthew 27:27-30, Mark 15:16-19; John 19:4-15, Luke 23:24; Mark 15:20, Matthew 27:31; John 19:16, Luke 23:25, Mark 15:15, Matthew 27:26

Previously, the chief priests and the elders of the people had met very early in the morning, while it still had been dark, to discuss every last detail for bringing about the death of Jesus.[189] So, when the Sanhedrin had sentenced Jesus to die, they already had prepared meticulously all of their arguments for persuading Rome to execute the death sentence.[190] However, what they hadn't planned for was to have opposition from Judas Iscariot, who had betrayed the Lord into their hands.[191] Nonetheless, that particular opposition is what they got. When Judas found out that Jesus had been condemned by the Sanhedrin, he deeply regretted what he had done; and in his great remorse he went back to the chief priest and elders with the money that they had given him, the thirty silver pieces in his hands.[192] Judas told them, "I have sinned by betraying innocent blood, an upright man."[193] But they replied, "Of what concern is that to us? It's your problem, so you look to it."[194] Then, flinging down the silver pieces to the floor of the temple sanctuary,[195] Judas left and went off and

---

[189] Matthew 27:1
[190] Matthew 27:2
[191] Mark 14:10-11, Luke 22:47, John 18:2-3; Matthew 27:3
[192] Matthew 27:3; Matthew 26:15
[193] Matthew 27:4
[194] Matthew 27:4; Zechariah 11:9-11
[195] Matthew 27:5; John 2:14-15

hanged himself.[196]

Judas had returned the money to the priests, although he knew that by such a repayment he could not expiate his sins, or theirs; yet, with his action, he had forcefully made public his confession of guilt to the priests. But the chief priests only dismissed Judas, like the ritual goat led out to Azazel in the desert,[197] where Judas, led by the spirit of Satan, would find him.[198] And at the same time, they denied their own priestly involvement in any expiation of his sin, or of theirs, although implicitly they also acknowledged their own guilt: when gathering up the money from the floor, they said, "It is against the Law to put this money in the treasury; for it is blood money."[199] Yet, by Judas taking his own life, he could not find any justice, human or divine, to expiate his sin—for only the life of the Lord could expiate sins;[200] and Jesus was that man waiting ready and alone to carry away the guilt of all the sins of the whole world.[201] And precisely, this is where Judas had failed God; Judas had not accepted by faith that there could be the forgiveness of his sins,[202] through the blood of Christ,[203] even if those were the most horrendous of sins.

The difference between Judas and Christ, when Jesus like Judas had gone into the desert and had confronted Satan there, was that Jesus was led by the Spirit of God;[204] and Jesus also had faith and he prayed, just as the Lord repeatedly had encouraged his disciples to have faith and to pray.[205] However, like Judas, the chief priests and elders also were misled by the spirit of their father, Satan;[206] and in their hypocrisy they too had failed because, falsely, they believed that they could be saved simply by minding the details of the Law,[207]

---

196 Matthew 27:5; Zechariah 11:13, 2 Kings 12:17
197 Leviticus 16:8, 10, 20-22
198 John 6:70, 13:27
199 Matthew 27:6
200 Romans 3:25-26
201 Isaiah 53:5-6, Leviticus 16:21-22
202 Romans 3:22
203 Romans 3:23-24
204 Luke 4:1-2, Matthew 4:1
205 Matthew 7:11, 21:22, Mark 11:21-25, 14:37-38, 1 Peter 5:7-10
206 John 8:44, Matthew 23:33, John 8:38
207 John 5:45, Romans 3:21; Romans 7:6

as they ritually obeyed its letter, but then entirely ignored its spirit. As the Lord had said of them, they were like white-washed tombs: on the outside, in their public illusions and private delusions, they presented themselves as upright before God and men;[208] but on the inside,[209] both in the secret desires of their hearts,[210] and in the public hypocrisy of their sins,[211] they were full of corruption and evil.

So, acting as if they would not be contaminated by the guilt of their crimes, if only, within the letter of the Law, they carefully dissociated themselves from the money involved, the priests and elders discussed what they should do with the blood money; and, in the end, they decided to buy the potter's field as a burial place for foreigners.[212] That is the reason, today, the field is still called "Field of Blood,"[213] or "Hakeldama" in Aramaic.[214] Others also have said that the field's name is derived from the circumstances of Judas' death at this place; that is, consistent with local folklore for the death of the wicked, the belief that Judas had fallen headlong to the ground, and there he had burst open from the middle, with all of his entrails pouring out.[215] However, irrespective of the actual nature of the death of Judas, either by his hanging himself or by being crushed on the rocks and disembowelled, and whichever oral tradition gives the potter's field its name; by this transaction the chief priests and elders fulfilled what had been spoken through the prophet Jeremiah:[216]

> And they took the thirty pieces of silver,[217] the value for a man with a price on his head, the pittance for the precious One,[218] set by the children of Israel;[219] and for

---

208	Matthew 3:7; Luke 3:7-9
209	Matthew 23:27; Luke 11:44, John 7:19
210	Mark 7:20-23
211	Matthew 23:28, Luke 12:1-5
212	Matthew 27:7
213	Matthew 27:8
214	Acts 1:19
215	Acts 1:18; Wisdom 4:19
216	Matthew 27:9
217	Zechariah 11:12; Jeremiah 32:9
218	1 Corinthians 6:20; 1 Peter 2:6, Isaiah 28:16, Acts 1:18, Luke 20:18-19
219	Matthew 27:9; Jeremiah 32:6, 13-15, 44

this sum they gave them the potter's field, just as the Lord had commanded me."[220]

When the chief priests and elders had brought Jesus from the house of Caiphas, the high priest, to Pilate, the governor, it was then very early in the morning's first light, while many people still would have been in bed.[221] But the priest and elders did not enter the Praetorium; instead, because it was a Gentile dwelling, they remained outside in order to avoid becoming defiled, so that they could eat the Passover.[222] Pilate, understanding this, and the apparently urgent nature of this early rousing given to him from the chief priests and elders, came to them outside; and as he saw Jesus before him, he asked them, "What charge do you bring against this man?"[223] They replied by throwing their responsibility onto Pilate, "If he were not a criminal, we would not have handed him over to you."[224] But Pilate, not wanting to become involved in their religious disputes, told them, "Take him yourselves, and try him by your own Law."[225] This would be Pilate's first effort to wash his hands of the matter, and perhaps, even now to go back to bed. But the Jews, implying that they were seeking Rome's jurisdiction and the death penalty, answered him, "We are not allowed to put a man to death."[226] This was to fulfil the words Jesus had spoken indicating the manner of death he was going to die.[227] Then they began making very specific accusations about Jesus, saying to the governor, "We found this man inciting our people to revolt;[228] he opposes the payment of taxes to Caesar;[229] and he claims to be the Christ, a king."[230]

So, having heard these initial charges, Pilate went back into the

---

220 Matthew 27:10; Jeremiah 18:1-12, 19:1-4
221 John 18:28
222 John 18:28
223 John 18:29
224 John 18:30
225 John 18:31
226 John 18:31
227 John 18:32; John 12:32, 3:14, Matthew 20:19
228 Luke 22:37, John 6:15
229 Luke 20:20-25
230 Luke 23:2; Luke 22:67, Matthew 26:63-64

Praetorium, and from his seclusion inside the palace he called Jesus to him.[231] Jesus, then, was brought before the governor, and as he stood before him, the governor put this question to Jesus,[232] "Are you the king of the Jews?" Now, originally, Pilate had intended a total detachment regarding this matter of Jesus; but Jesus would not let him off, no less than the Sanhedrin, as he also does insist for us, and for every person on the earth, that Pilate should, like the rest of us, take a personal position on the question he had asked,[233] namely, "Who is Jesus, king of the Jews?" So Jesus replied:

> Do you ask this on your own, or have others said this to you about me?[234]

Pilate answered, "I am not a Jew."[235] The implication that Pilate intended by this reply was, "Of what concern is this to me," which also was the equivalent answer the chief priests and elders had given to Judas, when Judas in his regret had protested to them that he had betrayed innocent blood.[236] However, Pilate, for now, continued to dissociate himself from the matter, saying, "It was your own people and the chief priests who have handed you over to me: So why? What have you done?"[237] Jesus replied:

> My kingdom is not of this world; if my kingdom did belong to this world, my attendants would have fought to prevent me from being handed over to the Jews. But, as it is, my kingdom is not here.[238]

Pilate said to him, "So, then, you are a king?"[239] And Jesus answered,

---

231	John 18:33
232	Matthew 27:11
233	Matthew 16:13-15
234	John 18:34; Luke 9:18-20
235	John 18:35; John 4:22
236	Matthew 27:4
237	John 18:35
238	John 18:36
239	John 18:37

It is you who say it,[240] that I am a king.[241] I was born for this, and for this I came into the world, to testify to the truth;[242] and whoever is on the side of truth listens to my voice.[243]

Pilate, in his political and life experience, and in a world of falsehood, deceit, deception, and of manipulative power games, was a cynic. "Truth?" said Pilate, "What is that?"[244]

And after saying this, the governor went out again to the Jews, and there he told the chief priests and the crowd, "I find no case against him."[245] But then, they resumed accusing Jesus of many crimes.[246] Yet, as the chief priests and elders did so, Jesus still made no answer at all.[247] So, again Pilate questioned Jesus, "Don't you hear how many charges they have made against you?"[248] "Aren't you going to make a reply?"[249] But to the governor's amazement, Jesus again did not answer him one word.[250] As the chief priests persisted in their accusations, they also added, "He is inciting the people with his teaching throughout the whole of Judea: all the way from Galilee, where he started, and down to here."[251] When Pilate heard this, suddenly he thought he had found a possible way out; and he asked, "Is this man a Galilean?"[252] And finding that Jesus, indeed, came under Herod's jurisdiction,[253] Pilate was much relieved to shuttle his responsibility for the case. And, immediately, he sent Jesus off to Herod, the tetrarch of Galilee,[254] who also was in Jerusalem at that

---

240   Mark 15:2, Matthew 27:11, Luke 23:3; Matthew 26:64
241   John 18:37
242   John 18:37; John 12:27; John 14:6
243   John 18:37; John 8:45-47
244   John 18:38; John 4:23-24
245   John 18:38, Luke 23:4
246   Mark 15:3; John 8:46
247   Matthew 27:12
248   Matthew 27:13; Mark 15:4
249   Mark 15:4
250   Matthew 27:14, Mark 15:5
251   Luke 23:5
252   Luke 23:6
253   Matthew 2:23, 4:13
254   Luke 3:1

time.[255]

Herod Antipas, at first, was delighted when he saw Jesus; now for a long time he had wanted to see Jesus: for he had heard about him,[256] but most of all he had been hoping to see Jesus perform some miracle.[257] So, Herod Antipas questioned Jesus at length, but Jesus gave him no reply.[258] At the same time, the chief priests and scribes were vigorously pressing their accusations.[259] In the end, however, Herod and the priests and scribes were disappointed in their meeting. For both, their respective objectives had gone unsatisfied: for Herod, royal entertainment; and for the priests, support for a Roman death sentence against Jesus. Herod, however, in order to console himself, created his own sporting fun: and together with his soldiers, he treated Jesus with contempt and mocked him; then afterwards, after mockingly dressing Jesus in a resplendent cloak, as "king," Herod sent him back to Pilate.[260] Although Herod and Pilate had been former enemies, on that very day they became good friends.[261]

Then, when Jesus had returned to Pilate, Pilate had what he wanted: a solid political agreement with Herod enabling the release of Jesus, or so he had thought. So, Pilate summoned the chief priests, leading men, and all the people to a public meeting.[262] Although Jesus would remain perfectly silent, according to the will and power of God,[263] Pilate, now the Lord's very determined defence advocate as the Roman governor, was confident that he would obtain the release of Jesus. There, in front of the Praetorium, Pilate addressed them all:

> You brought this man before me and accused him of being a popular agitator; and now I have examined the matter myself in your presence, and I have found

---

255 Luke 23:7
256 Luke 23:8; Luke 9:7-9
257 Luke 23:8
258 Luke 23:9
259 Luke 23:10
260 Luke 23:11
261 Luke 23:12
262 Luke 23:13
263 Luke 3:21-22, 12:50; John 18:11, 19:11

no basis in the man for the charges you have brought against him.[264] Nor has Herod found any grounds, for he has sent him back to us; so, as you can see, there is nothing the man has done to deserve the death penalty.[265] Therefore, I shall have him flogged and then I will release him.[266]

Now at festival time, according to the governor's practice,[267] Pilate used to release a prisoner for them, anyone the people would choose.[268] And at that time there was a notorious bandit and murderer,[269] whose name was Barabbas, who was in prison along with other rebels who had committed murder during a popular revolt in the city.[270] When the crowd had assembled at first, already it had begun to ask Pilate for this customary favour.[271] So, in answer to their prior request, Pilate then said:

> According to your custom, I should release one prisoner for you at the Passover.[272] So, would you like for me to release for you the king of the Jews?[273]

Pilate truly desired to set Jesus free.[274] He had realized that it was out of jealousy that the chief priests had handed Jesus over to him.[275] However, the chief priests had incited the crowd to demand that he should release Barabbas for them, instead of Jesus.[276] So the crowd shouted down Pilate's proposal, "Not this man, but Barabbas!"[277] And they howled as if one voice, "Away with him!

---

264 Luke 23:14, John 18:38
265 Luke 23:15
266 Luke 23:16; Acts 3:13
267 Matthew 27:15
268 Mark 15:6, Matthew 27:15
269 John 18:40, Luke 23:19
270 Mark 15:7, Matthew 27:16, Luke 23:19
271 Mark 15:8
272 John 18:39
273 John 18:39, Mark 15:9
274 Luke 23:20
275 Mark 15:10, Matthew 27:18
276 Mark 15:11
277 John 18:40

Give us Barabbas!"[278] Pilate, still wanting to free Jesus, was surprised by the unity and strength of their opposition. So, once again, Pilate asked the crowd:

> Which one do you want me to release to you: (Jesus) Bar-abbas [Son of- the-Father],[279] or Jesus, who is called the Christ?[280]

Just at that moment, as Pilate was seated in the chair of judgment, Pilate's wife sent him a message, which read, "Have nothing to do with that righteous man; for I have suffered greatly because of a dream about him that I had today."[281] But then, seemingly even louder, they thundered back, "Crucify him! Crucify him!"[282] And for the third time, Pilate spoke to the crowd:

> What crime has this man committed? I have not found him guilty of any capital offence, so I shall have him flogged and then let him go.[283]

Then Pilate had Jesus taken away to the inner part of the palace,[284] led off by the governor's soldiers into the Praetorium,[285] where he was scourged.[286] After this, with the entire cohort gathered round Jesus,[287] the soldiers twisted some thorns into a crown and put it on his head,[288] and they stripped him of his clothes and dressed him up in a scarlet robe,[289] as if to simulate a royal purple.[290] And placing a reed in his right hand,[291] they made fun of him by kneeling down

---

278 Luke 23:18
279 Romans 8:14-15, Mark 14:36, 10:38, Romans 8:16-17; 1 John 5:1-2, John 12:36, Romans 8:29-34, John 8:35-36
280 Matthew 27:17; Hebrews 5:5, Psalm 2:6-7, Luke 3:21-22
281 Matthew 27:19
282 Luke 23:21
283 Luke 23:22
284 John 19:1; Mark 15:16
285 Matthew 27:27, Mark 15:16
286 John 19:1; Mark 15:15, Matthew 27:26
287 Matthew 27:27, Mark 15:16
288 John 19:2, Mark 15:17, Matthew 27:29
289 Matthew 27:28
290 Mark 15:17, John 19:2
291 Matthew 27:29

in mock homage, and they saluted him, saying, "Hail, king of the Jews,"[292] as they slapped him in the face.[293] And they also struck his head with a reed and spat on him,[294] as they mockingly went down on their knees before him.[295] Then, Pilate came outside once more, and he said to them:

> Look, I am going to bring him out to you, so that you may see that I find no case against him.[296]

As Jesus came out, then wearing the crown of thorns and the purple robe, Pilate said to them:

> Here is the man.[297]

When they saw him, the chief priests and the guards shouted, "Crucify him! Crucify him!"[298] And the crowd joined in, as they kept on shouting at the top of their voices, demanding that Jesus should be crucified; and their shouts kept growing louder and louder.[299] The chief priest and elders, in their planned arrangements, had persuaded the crowds to demand that Barabbas be set free, and that Jesus be executed.[300] When the governor spoke out and asked them:

> Which of the two do you want me to release to you?

They said, "Barabbas."[301] Pilate said:

> But, in that case, what am I to do with Jesus, who is called Christ?[302]

---

292 Matthew 27:29, Mark 15:18, John 19:3
293 John 19:3
294 Mark 15:19, Matthew 27:30
295 Mark 15:19
296 John 19:4
297 John 19:5
298 John 19:6
299 Luke 23:23
300 Matthew 27:20
301 Matthew 27:21
302 Matthew 27:22

And they all said, "Let him be crucified."[303] Pilate asked:

> But what harm has he done?[304]

Yet they only shouted all the louder, "Let him be crucified."[305] Pilate, in his most reluctant, but spineless exasperation, replied:

> Take him yourselves and crucify him: I find no guilt in him.[306]

The Jews answered, "We have a Law, and according to that Law, he should be put to death, because he has claimed to be Son of God."[307] Although Jesus was convicted for our sins under the curse of the Law,[308] clearly and emphatically they wanted his blood and they wanted ignominy: for Jesus in his innocence, in opposition to our guilt, for Jesus they wanted and absolutely insisted upon the cruellest of all imaginable deaths, crucifixion according to Roman law.

Now when Pilate heard them say this, that "he claimed to be Son of God," he became even more afraid.[309] So, taking Jesus with him, he went back into the Praetorium, and he asked him, "Where do you come from?"[310] But Jesus did not answer him.[311] So Pilate said to him, "Are you refusing to speak to me? Don't you realize that I have the power to set you free and the power to crucify you?"[312] Then Jesus replied:

> You would have no power over me whatsoever if it had not been given to you from above; for that reason,

---

303 Matthew 27:22
304 Matthew 27:23
305 Matthew 27:23
306 John 19:6
307 John 19:7, Leviticus 24:16; John 8:57-59, 10:29-31, Luke 22:69-71
308 Isaiah 53:10-11; John 7:19, Galatians 3:13, 10-12, 22-24, Romans 7:5-6, 4:15-16, 21-25; John 8:32-36
309 John 19:8; Matthew 27:19, John 18:36
310 John 19:19; John 18:37, 8:14, 28, 7:27-28, 6:51
311 John 19:9; Mark 15:3-5, 14:61, Matthew 27:12-14, 63, Luke 23:9-10; Isaiah 53:7
312 John 19:10

the one who handed me over to you has the greater guilt.[313]

Pilate, now, was very anxious to set Jesus free.[314] Pilate, at first, went back outside the Praetorium, while he left Jesus inside under guard, away from the crowd. But when Pilate came out, the Jewish leaders shouted, "If you release him, you are no friend of Caesar's; anyone who makes himself a king is Caesar's enemy."[315] Hearing these words, then Pilate himself brought out Jesus, and seated him on the chair of judgment in the place called the Stone Pavement, or in Hebrew, "Gabbatha."[316] It was the Day of Preparation for Passover, about the sixth hour, that is, late morning nearly noon: then, Pilate said to the Jews:

> Here is your king.[317]

> In reply they shouted, "Away with him, away with him, crucify him!" But Pilate shouted back over the roar of the crowd:

> Shall I crucify your king?

> And the chief priests answered, "We have no king but Caesar."[318]

Pilate saw that he was not succeeding, but that, in fact, a riot seemed imminent; so he took some water and washed his hands in front of the crowd,[319] and he said:

> I am innocent of this man's blood: it is your concern, now.[320]

And everyone, the whole people, shouted back as one, "Let

---

313 John 19:11; John 10:17-18; Philippians 2:6-8; John 3:18-21
314 John 19:12; Colossians 2:9-10
315 John 19:12
316 John 19:13; Matthew 27:19
317 John 19:14; John 12:13-15, Luke 19:38-40
318 John 19:15; John 11:49-50
319 Matthew 27:24; Deuteronomy 21:6, Psalm 26:4-6, 9-12; Galatians 3:22, Romans 3:23-26
320 Matthew 27:24; Matthew 27:3-4

his blood be upon us and upon our children!"[321] Then Pilate gave his verdict: their demand was to be granted.[322] First, he released Barabbas,[323] who had been imprisoned because of rioting and murder,[324] and now through Christ redeemed from the Law and an adopted son of the Father.[325] And then he handed Jesus over to them, to deal with as they pleased,[326] and to be crucified.[327] The soldiers, after making further fun of Jesus, removed his purple robe and redressed him in his own clothes;[328] and then they led him out from the Praesidium for his crucifixion.[329] To the great and delirious roar of the crowd, from then onwards, the Roman soldiers took into their hands complete charge of Jesus.[330]

Readings: John 19:17, Mark 15:21-22, Matthew 27:32-33, Luke 23:26-32; John 19:18, 23-24, 19-22, Mark 15:23-26, Matthew 27:34-37, Luke 23:33-34, 38, 44; Mark 15:29-33, Matthew 27:39-45, Luke 23:35-37, 39-43; John 19:25-27; Mark 15:40-41, Matthew 27:55-56, Luke 23:40; Mark 15:34-37, Matthew 27:46-50, John 19:28-30, Luke 23:46; Luke 23:45, Mark 15:38, Matthew 27:51-52, 53; Mark 15:39, Matthew 27:54, Luke 23:47, 48; John 19:31-37; Mark 15:42-47, Matthew 27:57-61, John 19:38-42, Luke 23:50-56; Matthew 27:62-66

On their way out,[331] as the soldiers now were leading Jesus away,[332] they came across a man who, just then, was passing by, having come into the city from the countryside: he was Simon from

---

321 Matthew 27:25; Matthew 23:34-36, 24:15-21; Isaiah 59:3-8, Romans 11:25-31
322 Luke 23:24; Acts 3:13, Luke 23:14-16
323 Matthew 27:26; Acts 3:14
324 Luke 23:25; Acts 3:15
325 Galatians 4:4-9; Luke 4:18-19, Leviticus 25:54, John 8:34-36, Luke 4:21
326 Luke 23:25
327 Mark 15:15, Matthew 27:26, John 19:16; Luke 9:22, 18:33; Acts 3:15
328 Matthew 27:31, Mark 15:20
329 Mark 15:21
330 John 19:16; Luke 9:44, 18:32
331 Matthew 27:32
332 Luke 23:26

Cyrene, who was the father of Rufus and Alexander.[333] They pressed him into service to carry the cross, which then Simon shouldered, as he followed behind Jesus,[334] who carried his own cross while Simon also carried the second section of the Lord's cross alone upon his own shoulders.[335] Tradition suggests that Jesus also encountered his mother, Mary, along the way, as she followed her son to the cross;[336] and that Veronica also wiped the Lord's face, with his blood and sweat leaving behind an indelible image of his face on the cloth of her veil. But, there also were several of his friends, the men and women who had followed Jesus: if some are not specifically mentioned by name, we may infer Lazarus and his sisters Martha and Mary, from Bethany, nearby;[337] all the disciples as witnesses both of his death and of his resurrection,[338] very notably so John and Thomas;[339] and especially, there were the many women from Galilee who had accompanied Jesus throughout his ministry: Mary of Magdala (the sister of Lazarus);[340] Joanna the wife of Chuza, Herod's steward;[341] Mary the mother of James and Joset (or Joseph),[342] cousins of the Lord;[343] Salome,[344] who was the mother of Zebedee's fisherman sons (the two disciples James and John); Mary the wife of Clopas;[345] Susanna,[346] together with many other women disciples,[347] as then everyone faced God's sentence.[348]

Behind Jesus, in his triumphal victory procession towards the

---

333 Matthew 27:32, Mark 15:21, Luke 23:26; Romans 16:13, Acts 11:19-21
334 Luke 23:26; Matthew 10:38, Mark 8:34, Luke 14:27, 9:23, 62
335 John 19:17
336 John 19:25
337 John 11:1, 12:1-3
338 John 11:1, 5, 12:1-3; John 15:15, 13-14; Luke 24:40-41, Acts 1:22, 2:23-24, 32, 36
339 John 19:26, 20:25
340 Mark 15:40, John 19:25
341 Luke 8:3, 24:10
342 Mark 15:40
343 Mark 3:31, 6:3; John 19:25
344 Mark 15:40; Matthew 20:20
345 John 19:25, Luke 24:18
346 Luke 8:3
347 Luke 23:40; Luke 8:2-3, 24:10, Mark 15:40-41, 16:1, Matthew 27:56
348 Hebrews 10:30-31, 9:14

cross,[349] as large numbers of people followed him, there were among them several leading women of Jerusalem, who were weeping and lamenting for Jesus,[350] as if in a funeral, like the chaotic scenes we witness today after various bloody massacres in the Middle East, in conflicts between Palestine and Israel. Suddenly, along his *via crucis*, Jesus turned around to them and said:

> Daughters of Jerusalem, don't cry for me, but weep for yourselves and for your children.[351] Behold, the days are coming when people will say, "Blessed are the childless, the wombs that have never borne children, and the breasts that have never nursed!"[352] At that time people will say to the mountains, "Fall on us!" and to the hills, "Cover over us!"[353] For, if these things are done when the wood is green, what will be done when the wood is dry?"[354]

With Jesus, two other men, both of them criminals, also were being led away to be executed,[355] both as guilty of their sin as all the rest of us are guilty of our own sins.[356] When, together, they all reached the place called Skull Hill, in Hebrew "Golgotha,"[357] all three were crucified there, outside of the city walls,[358] with Jesus in the middle and both of the criminals on either side, one to his right and the other to his left.[359] The soldiers offered Jesus wine drugged with myrrh,[360] or with gall,[361] which he tasted, but then he refused

---

349	Colossians 2:14-15; John 12:12-18, 23
350	Luke 23:27
351	Luke 23:28; Lamentations 2:21-22, 5:15-22
352	Luke 23:29; Hosea 9:14, Isaiah 54:1, 49:14-15
353	Luke 23:30; Hosea 10:8; Isaiah 2:19, Revelation 6:16-17
354	Luke 23:31; Psalm 52:8-9, Luke 3:16-17, 9; Isaiah 54:7-10
355	Luke 23:32
356	Luke 23:41; Ephesians 5:6-8
357	John 19:17, Mark 15:22, Matthew 27:33, Luke 23:33
358	Leviticus 14:8
359	Luke 23:33, John 19:18; Mark 15:27, Matthew 27:38
360	Mark 15:23
361	Matthew 27:34; Psalm 69:21

to drink it;³⁶² and finally they nailed him to the cross.³⁶³ There, suspended somewhere between heaven and earth, impaled on the structure of the cross,³⁶⁴ by his suffering and approaching death, Jesus would mediate his atonement for our sins,³⁶⁵ if only in God's mercy we also would accept his grace,³⁶⁶ and like Jesus, we would take up our individual crosses and follow him as disciples with the same faithful love as was his, according to the pattern that Jesus has shown to us.³⁶⁷ As they crucified him, Jesus said:

> Father, forgive them; they don't know what they are doing.³⁶⁸

Immediately afterwards, when they had finished crucifying Jesus, they shared out his outermost clothing by dividing it into four shares, one for each of the soldiers; and then they cast lots to decide who should get his tunic.³⁶⁹ This undergarment was seamless, woven in a single piece from the neck to the hem;³⁷⁰ so they said to one another, "Let's not tear it, but instead let's throw dice to decide whose it will be."³⁷¹ In this way the words of scripture were fulfilled: "They divided my garments among them, and for my vesture they cast lots."³⁷² And that is what the soldiers did.³⁷³ And then, they sat down, keeping guard over him as they stayed there looking on.³⁷⁴ It was still not quite the third hour, but almost the sixth hour at midday, when they had crucified Our Lord.³⁷⁵ His relatively short-distanced and torturous late-morning journey from the Praesidum to Golgatha had been effectively swift.

---

362   Mark 15:23, Matthew 27:34; Matthew 26:29
363   Mark 15:24; Psalm 22:16
364   John 8:28-30, 5:36, Hebrews 5:4-6
365   Isaiah 54:4-5, 53:10-11, Colossians 2:14, Hebrews 5:7-10
366   Romans 7:18, 6:14; 2 Timothy 1:8-9
367   Luke 14:27, 1 Peter 2:21, Philippians 3:8-11, John 6:38-39, Isaiah 54:7-8
368   Luke 23:34;
369   Mark 15:25, Matthew 27:35, Luke 23:34, John 19:23
370   John 19:23
371   John 19:24
372   John 19:24, Psalm 22:18
373   John 19:24
374   Matthew 27:36
375   Mark 15:26, John 19:14

On the cross above his head, there was an inscription written out by Pilate giving the charge against him; it read: "Jesus the Nazarene, King of the Jews."[376] Because the place where Jesus was crucified was near to the city, just outside its western walls, this notice was read by many of the Jews as they passed by, and the writing was posted in Hebrew, Latin, and Greek.[377] So the chief priests of the Jews said to Pilate: "You should not write 'King of the Jews,' but that he said, 'I am King of the Jews.'"[378] But Pilate answered:

What I have written, I have written.[379]

Also, from the sixth hour, around noon, when the Lord had been crucified, the sun's light failed; and from then until the ninth hour, even though it was the height of mid-afternoon, a great darkness, like night, overshadowed and covered the whole land.[380] At last, as had been foretold by all the prophets, the Great Day of Yahweh had come: for sinners it would be their day of eternal retribution;[381] but for those who would be saved, it is the day of God's mercy and faithful love, a day of everlasting glory![382]

Throughout, as people would pass him by,[383] they stood there watching and staring;[384] or they shook their heads at him,[385] and said, "Aha! So you would destroy the Temple and, in three days, rebuilt it![386] Then, if you are God's Son,[387] save yourself, and come down

---

376 Mark 15:26, Matthew 27:37, Luke 23:38, John 19:19
377 John 19:20
378 John 19:21
379 John 19:22, Colossians 2:15
380 Mark 15:33, Matthew 27:45, Luke 23:44; John 12:35-36
381 Matthew 3:7
382 Malachi 3:17-18, Zechariah 14:6, 9-11, Haggai 2:6-9, Zephaniah 1:14-15, Habakkuk 3:11-12, 16, Nahum 1:8, Micah 3:6, Jonah 3:10, Obadiah 15, 17-18, Amos 5:18-20, 8:9, Joel 2:2, 10, 3:4-5, 4:15, Hosea 4:5-7, Daniel 3:71-72, 9:26-27, Ezekiel 30:1-3, 34:12, Baruch 3:33, Lamentations 2:13, Jeremiah 31:35-36, 38-40, Isaiah 59:14-20, 61:1-3; Luke 4:16-21
383 Mark 15:29, Matthew 27:39
384 Luke 23:35
385 Matthew 27:39, Mark 15:29
386 Mark 15:29, Matthew 27:40; John 2:19-22, Matthew 16:4, 12:40
387 Matthew 27:40

from the cross!"[388] As for the leaders,[389] the chief priests and scribes mocked him with the same words;[390] grouped among themselves they jeered, "He saved others, but he cannot save himself.[391] If he is the Anointed One of God, the Chosen One, let him save himself![392] Let the Christ, the king of Israel;[393] he is the king of Israel![394] If so,[395] let him come down from the cross now,[396] for us to see it,[397] so we will believe in him.[398] He trusted in God; now let God rescue him, if he wants him; for he did say, "I am the Son of God."[399] Likewise, the soldiers also mocked him: they would approach him, offering him sour wine and saying to him, "If you are king of the Jews, save yourself."[400] Even the two bandit-revolutionaries, who were crucified with Jesus, taunted him in the same way.[401]

More specifically, there was just one of the two criminals, hanging there on his cross, who reviled Jesus, saying, "Aren't you the Christ? Then, save yourself; and save us as well."[402] The Father of Lies had prompted the Lord's many critics.[403] But the other criminal, whose name according to the apocryphal Gospel of Nicodemus was Dismas, spoke out against his companion; he rebuked the first criminal, saying, "Don't you have any fear of God? You received the same condemnation as he did.[404] But in our case, our sentences are deserved, and they correspond to our crimes; as for this man, he has

---

388 Mark 15:30, Matthew 27:40
389 Luke 23:35
390 Matthew 27:41
391 Mark 15:31, Matthew 27:42
392 Luke 23:35
393 Mark 15:32
394 Matthew 27:42
395 Luke 4:9
396 Mark 15:32, Matthew 27:42
397 Mark 15:32
398 Matthew 27:42, Mark 15:32
399 Matthew 27:43; Psalm 22:8
400 Luke 23:36
401 Mark 15:32, Matthew 27:44
402 Luke 23:39
403 Luke 4:13, John 8:44
404 Luke 23:40

done nothing wrong."[405] Then, to Jesus he said, "Jesus, remember me when you come into your kingdom."[406] And to him Jesus answered:

> Amen, in truth I tell you, today you will be with me in paradise.[407]

Also standing near the cross with Jesus were his mother and his mother's sister, Mary the wife of Clopas, and Mary of Magdela;[408] and there was John.[409] However, these may be five persons, and not four, with the Lord. When John refers to Our Lord's mother's sister, he may mean, of course, Mary the wife of Clopas, in which case, then John names only four persons near the cross of the Lord. But, just as John, humbly and truthfully, in his gospel refers to himself not by name, but as the disciple whom Jesus loved,[410] it is very possible that John also, here discreetly, means Salome, John's own mother, not as a relative of the Lord's mother, as was Mary the wife of Clopas, but more simply he may mean a dear disciple of Jesus, as a sister in Christ;[411] and as a sister in the Lord, also a dear friend and sister of Our Lord's mother, as are all of us, who are dear friends, and brothers and sisters of Christ.[412] If, therefore, by "his mother's sister," John does mean, in his characteristic discretion, Salome, John's own mother; then there would have been five close disciples, or friends and brothers and sisters of the crucified Lord, standing at the foot of his cross: first and foremost, there was Mary, the mother of Jesus;[413] then second, there also was Salome, the mother of James and John;[414] third, would be Mary, the wife of Clopas, and the mother of James (the younger) and Joset (Joseph);[415] fourth, would be Mary of Magdela;[416] and fifth,

---

405	Luke 23:41
406	Luke 23:42
407	Luke 23:43; Ephesians 2:1-6
408	John 19:25
409	John 19:26
410	John 19:26; John 13:23; 1 John 4:9-10, 3:16, John 15:12-13
411	Matthew 13:54-56; Mark 3:33-35, Matthew 12:49-50, Luke 8:19-21
412	John 15:14-15; 1 John 4:7-8; Romans 12:5, Galatians 3:26-29, Colossians 1:2
413	John 19:25
414	John 19:25, Mark 15:40, Matthew 27:56
415	John 19:25; Mark 15:40, Matthew 27:56, 13:55
416	John 19:25, Mark 15:40, Matthew 27:56, Luke 23:49, 8:23

last of all, there was John himself.[417]

Just as Mary, the mother of Jesus, had done at the beginning of his public life at the wedding feast of Cana,[418] there, now at the fulfilment of his life, she stands next to the cross of her son, just as Mary always had stood with him throughout his private life: from his conception,[419] through his birth,[420] and his childhood,[421] and into his manhood; and finally, now at his death, as Mary stood beneath her son's cross, now as the mother of the church.[422] As for Salome, the mother of Zebedee's sons, and for James and John, each of them would have their own particular share in the sufferings of Christ.[423] Not even two weeks earlier, Salome did not know the true meaning of her request for her sons to sit at the right and left hand of Jesus in his kingdom:[424] she had not intended the kingdom of heaven then, but David's kingdom on earth that she had imagined Jesus would be restoring to Israel.[425] Now, however, Salome, still not yet understanding the full meaning of the cross in the absence of the resurrection, was facing directly the contradiction of the cross in our personal lives.[426] As Salome stood there waiting with Jesus for his nearly three endless hours of incomprehensible agony, throughout this trauma, emotionally she must have been entirely shattered, very confused, and full of tremendous sorrow.[427]

In the gospel of Mark and Matthew, Salome is placed at Calvary, but as watching from a "distance,"[428] together with a group of women including Mary of Magdala and Mary the mother of James and Joseph, both clearly placed by John beneath the cross, and not at a "distance." John also names this latter Mary, the wife of Clopas,

---

417	John 19:26
418	John 2:1-5
419	Luke 1:26-38
420	Luke 2:7, 22-24, 33-35
421	Luke 2:51-52
422	John 19:25; Revelation 12:1-2, 5-6, 13-14, 17, John 16:21
423	Matthew 20:22, 27-28; 1 John 3:16; Philippians 3:10-12
424	Matthew 20:20-21
425	Matthew 20:23
426	1 Corinthians 1:18
427	John 16:20, 22; Mark 16:1-2
428	Mark 15:40, Matthew 27:55-56

at the foot of the cross because her son James, the brother of the Lord,[429] who until then was still a skeptic,[430] would become later a fervent believer and the future Bishop of Jerusalem. Indeed, this Mary was a relative of Our Lord's mother, "his mother's sister;"[431] and this Mary could not be the mother of the apostle James, the son of Alpheus;[432] nor can her husband, "Clopas," with absolute certainty, although with high probability, be identified with "Cloepas," who most likely was one of the seventy-two,[433] who encounters the Lord on the road to Emmaus after the Lord's resurrection.[434] Luke does not specifically mention by name those persons who stood on at a distance from the cross, or those who may have been near; but he only mentions that they were among the women who had accompanied Jesus from Galilee;[435] and therefore, implicitly, they are identified as Mary Magdalene, from whom seven demons had gone out; and notably Joanna, as another of three named persons; and then there are many unnamed others.[436] Luke, in his resurrection narrative, also names Mary Magdalene, Joanna, and Mary the mother of James as being at the tomb of Christ at dawn on Easter morning.[437] Mary of Magdala is given prominence at the cross of Jesus by each of the evangelists, because she will be the first person of record to witness the Lord's resurrection,[438] which was her special privilege through the grace of Christ, and in accord with her most exemplary devotion, and example for us to following Jesus in her, and in his, way of the cross.[439]

When Jesus saw his mother and the disciple whom he loved,

---

429 Mark 6:3, Matthew 12:46, 13:55; Galatians 1:19, 2:9; Acts 12:17, 21:18; James 1:1, Acts 15:13-35
430 John 7:3-5
431 John 19:26
432 Matthew 10:3
433 Luke 10:1
434 Luke 24:18
435 Luke 23:49
436 Luke 8:2-3
437 Luke 24:10
438 Mark 16:9, John 20:11-18, Matthew 28:9-10
439 Mark 8:31-35, 36-37, Matthew 16:21-25, 26-28, Luke 9:23, 14:27; Romans 6:5-6, Acts 26:22-23

John, standing near to her, Jesus said to his mother:

> "Woman, behold, this is your son."[440] Then to the disciple he said: "Behold, this is your mother."[441]

And from that hour the disciple took "her into his home".[442] However, the phrase in Greek from John's gospel is that the disciple took "her into the own" [αὐτήν εἰς τά ἴδια], or "her from that point as his own."[443] John took the mother of Jesus, not by her unmentioned name, but according to her functional roles as both "woman" and "mother." Previously, although Mary had begotten her only Son of God,[444] with the Wedding Feast at Cana, she could not have anything to do with Jesus as "woman," because his "hour had not come yet."[445] Jesus alone had to do only and exclusively the will of the Father for our salvation. But now, because "the hour had come,"[446] the "woman" becomes mother of all the disciples, mother for all the "children of God,"[447] as from that moment, she also had begotten John,[448] as he then took Mary completely as his own into his value system and life.[449] Mary would continue in her spiritual and physical role as the mother of Jesus, but now as the "begetter of Jesus," not only in John as her "son", but then as she became mother of the whole church,[450] and of Jesus in us.

---

440   John 19:26; John 2:4, Genesis 3:15, Revelation 12:13; 1 John 3:1, Revelation 21:7
441   John 19:27; Genesis 3:20, Revelation 12:1-2, Genesis 3:16, Revelation 21:2, John 2:1-3, Matthew 26:27-29, Luke 13:29, Mark 9:1, John 19:26, 21:23, 20-22
442   John 19:27; John 2:4-5; 1 John 4:21
443   Object of the verb phrase, took: "autēn," personal/possessive pronoun, accusative singular feminine "her"; followed by the prepositional phrase: "eis," the preposition "into," with its object "ta idia," article and adjective, both quite specifically in the accusative plural neuter "the own."
444   Luke 1:35
445   John 2:4
446   John 17:1, 19:27
447   John 1:12-13, Revelation 12:17
448   John 19:26
449   John 19:27
450   Revelation 12:1; Genesis 37:9, Luke 6:13, Matthew 19:28, Revelation 21:14, Ephesians 2:19-22

From a slight distance further away from Jesus, Mary, and John, there were also the other women who had been watching: among them there was Mary of Magdala; Mary who was the mother of James and Joset; and Salome, the mother of Zebedee's sons.[451] These women had followed Jesus and had looked after him when he was in Galilee; and there were many other women who had come up to Jerusalem with him for the feast.[452] In fact, the rest of his closest friends, all of them, men and women, stood on at a distance.[453]

Then at the ninth hour, about 3:00 o'clock in the afternoon, the darkness that had covered the land throughout the entire crucifixion became even blacker and more ominous;[454] and Jesus cried out in a loud voice:

Eloi, eloi, lama sabachthani?

That is, "My God, my God, why have you forsaken me?"[455] As Jesus then for us continued to pray silently the rest of Psalm 22 that he had started, some of the bystanders, who had heard him saying this, said to one another, "Listen, the man is calling on Elijah."[456] But Jesus, knowing then that everything was now completed, and so that the words of scripture might be completely fulfilled, said:

I am thirsty.[457]

And someone, one of the four soldiers,[458] quickly ran to get a sponge, which he fully soaked in sour wine from a jar that stood there; and putting the sponge on a sturdy reed, on a spear of hyssop stick,[459] he held the sponge to his mouth and offered it to Jesus to

---

451	Mark 15:40, Matthew 27:56
452	Mark 15:41, Matthew 27:55
453	Luke 23:28, Psalm 38:11; Luke 8:2-3, 24:10
454	Mark 15:33, Matthew 27:45, Luke 23:44; John 12:31, Matthew 16:18, Revelation 3:7-11, Hebrews 9:11-12, 12:1-4
455	Mark 15:34, Matthew 27:46; Psalm 22:1
456	Mark 15:35, Matthew 27:47
457	John 19:28; Psalm 22:15; Luke 12:50, John 4:34
458	John 19:23
459	John 19:29; Psalm 51:7

drink.[460] But the rest of them, including the leaders of the Jews,[461] said, "Wait! Let's see if Elijah will come to save him,[462] and to take him down."[463] After Jesus, now, had taken the wine,[464] Jesus gave out a loud cry,[465] and then, he calmly said:

It is fulfilled.[466]

At that moment the veil of the Temple Sanctuary was torn right down the middle;[467] and again, speaking his last, Jesus cried out in a loud voice, saying:

Father, into your hands I commend my spirit.[468]

With these words, he bowed his head;[469] and with his body's very last breath, he gave up his spirit.[470] And thus was concluded the first celebration of the eternal Eucharist, and of God's eternal love for us. And with these words,[471] suddenly,[472] as the veil of the Sanctuary was torn in two from top to bottom,[473] there was an earthquake and the rocks were split;[474] and as tombs were opened, the bodies of many holy people, who had fallen asleep, rose from the dead;[475] and these, after his resurrection, came forth from their tombs, entered the holy city, and appeared to large numbers of people.[476] The centurion, who now was standing guard in front of

---

460   Mark 15:36, Matthew 27:48, John 19:29
461   Luke 23:35
462   Matthew 27:49
463   Mark 15:36
464   John 19:30; Luke 22:18
465   Mark 15:37, Matthew 27:50
466   John 19:30; Psalm 22:27-31
467   Luke 23:45; Hebrews 9:24; Matthew 26:63-66
468   Luke 23:46, Matthew 27:50; Psalm 31:5
469   Luke 23:46, John 19:30
470   Luke 23:46, John 19:30; Mark 15:37, Matthew 27:50
471   Luke 23:46
472   Matthew 27:51
473   Matthew 27:51, Mark 15:38
474   Matthew 27:51; Amos 8:8, 9:1-5
475   Matthew 27:52
476   Matthew 27:53

Jesus,[477] and together with the others guarding Jesus,[478] when they all saw how he had died,[479] with the earth quaking and all that was happening, they were terrified.[480] But the centurion who witnessed this gave praise to God, and he said, "Without any doubt, this was an innocent man."[481] Then, the centurion and the other soldiers with him, also said, "In truth this man was the Son of God."[482] And when the crowds, all those passers-by and chief priests and scribes who had gathered for the spectacle,[483] saw what had happened, they quietly and quickly returned home beating their breasts.[484] But all of his friends remained standing there at a distance, including the many women who had accompanied him from Galilee;[485] among them were Mary of Magdala; Mary the mother of James and Joseph; and Salome, the mother of James and John,[486] who witnessed all of these events.[487] Only then, at last, the sun broke through; the grave darkness that had covered the land was lifted.[488]

Now, because it was the Day of Preparation, and to avoid that the bodies should remain on the cross during the Sabbath, for the Sabbath day of that week was a special solemnity, the feast of Passover; the Jews had asked Pilate that their legs be broken and their bodies taken away.[489] So the soldiers came and broke the legs of the first man who had been crucified with him, and then the legs of the other one.[490] But when they came to Jesus, they saw that he was already dead; so, instead of breaking his legs,[491] one of the soldiers pierced his side with his lance; and from the wound immediately there flowed out

---

477	Mark 15:39
478	Matthew 27:54
479	Mark 15:39
480	Matthew 27:54
481	Luke 23:47; Hebrews 7:26-27
482	Mark 15:39, Matthew 27:54; Hebrews 7:28, 25
483	Luke 23:35; Matthew 27:39-41, Mark 15:29-31
484	Luke 23:48; Psalm 51:1-3
485	Luke 23:49
486	Mark 15:40, Matthew 27:56
487	Luke 23:49
488	Mark 15:33, Matthew 27:45, Luke 23:44; John 1:4-5
489	John 19:31
490	John 19:32
491	John 19:33

blood and water, reflected in the image of the Divine Mercy.[492] With blood and water, in the graphic image of the moments after birth,[493] the body of Jesus after death now reflects the birth of the church, with Mary as its mother and Christ as its head.[494] For now there were two witnesses, blood and water, both of them principles of "life," his blood shed for us and the fountain of his grace,[495] and is inclusive of the third witness,[496] which the water also anticipates, that Christ would send the Holy Spirit upon his church at Pentecost.[497] This is the evidence of John, one who is an eyewitness—it is true evidence, and he knows that he is speaking the truth; he gives his testimony so that you also may believe.[498] And all these events happened in order to fulfil the words of scripture:

Not one bone of his will be broken;[499]

and again, in another passage, where scripture says:

They will look upon the one whom they have pierced.[500]

After this,[501] when it was now evening,[502] and because it was Preparation Day for Passover—that is, the day before the Sabbath,[503] a prominent member of the Jewish Council arrived to the crucifixion site at Golgatha,[504] a virtuous and upright man named Joseph,[505] himself a rich man from Arimathaea,[506] a Jewish town;[507] going towards

---

492 John 19:34; 1 John 5:7-8
493 Revelation 12:5
494 Ephesians 4:7-16
495 Romans 5:8, 10; Revelation 5:6-10, 7:17, 22:1, 21:4
496 1 John 5:6
497 John 7:37-39, Acts 1:8, 12-14, 2:1-4, 31-33, Ephesians 2:13-22
498 John 19:35; 1 John 5:9-13
499 John 19:36; Exodus 12:46, Psalm 34:20
500 John 19:37; Zachariah 12:10; John 3:14, Numbers 21:7-9, John 12:32, John 3:15-16; Revelation 1:7, Philippians 3:10-12
501 John 19:38
502 Matthew 27:57, Mark 15:42
503 Mark 15:42
504 Luke 23:50, Mark 15:43
505 Luke 23:50
506 Matthew 27:57, Mark 15:43, Luke 23:51
507 Luke 23:51

Caesarea, it was some thirty-five kilometres northwest of Jerusalem. Joseph of Arimathaea was a disciple of Jesus,[508] although a secret one because he was afraid of the Jews.[509] He had not consented to what the others had planned and carried out;[510] and he himself lived in the hope of seeing the kingdom of God.[511] This man boldly had gone to Pilate asking for the body of Jesus,[512] asking Pilate for his permission to remove the body.[513] Pilate was astonished that Jesus should be dead already, so he summoned the centurion and asked him if Jesus had been dead for some time.[514] Having been reassured of this by the centurion, Pilate then granted the corpse to Joseph,[515] ordering that it should be handed over.[516] So with Pilate's permission, they came to take away the body of Jesus;[517] Nicodemus, the one who had come to Jesus at night,[518] had come as well, and he brought along a mixture of myrrh and aloes weighing around a hundred pounds;[519] and Joseph had brought with him a shroud.[520]

Joseph took the body of Jesus down from the cross,[521] and together they wrapped it in clean linen cloths along with the spices,[522] following the Jewish burial custom.[523] At the place where Jesus had been crucified, there was a garden, and in this garden a new tomb,[524] in which no one had yet been buried,[525] that originally Joseph had intend for himself and

---

508	Matthew 27:57, John 19:38
509	John 19:38
510	Luke 23:51
511	Mark 15:43, Luke 23:51
512	Mark 15:43, Matthew 27:58, Luke 23:52
513	John 19:38
514	Mark 15:44
515	Mark 15:45
516	Matthew 27:58
517	John 19:38
518	John 3:1-2, 7:50-52
519	John 19:39
520	Mark 15:46
521	Mark 15:46
522	John 19:40, Mark 15:46, Matthew 27:59
523	John 19:40; John 11:44
524	John 19:41
525	John 19:41, Luke 23:53

that he had hewn in stone out of the rock.[526] Because it was the Jewish Preparation Day,[527] and the Sabbath lamplight was nearly shining,[528] and because the tomb was nearby, they laid Jesus there.[529] Then Joseph rolled a large stone across the entrance of the tomb and went away.[530] Meanwhile, Mary of Magdala and Mary the mother of Joset were there sitting opposite the sepulchre;[531] they took careful note of the tomb and how and where the body had been laid.[532] Then having done so, they returned to their dwelling where they prepared spices and ointments; and on the Sabbath day they rested, as the Law commanded.[533]

The next day, that is, the one following the Preparation Day,[534] and now on the Sabbath and in violation of the Sabbath rest,[535] the chief priests and Pharisees went as a group to Pilate.[536] They said to him:

> Your Excellency, we recall that, when this impostor was still alive, he had said, "After three days I shall be raised up."[537] Therefore, give the order that the sepulchre be kept secure until the third day; lest his disciples come and steal him away and tell the people, "He has risen from the dead."[538] This last bit of fraud would be worse than his first.[539]

Pilate said to them, "You may use your guard; go and make everything secure, as well as you know how."[540] So they went and

---

526   Mark 15:46, Matthew 27:60, Luke 23:53
527   John 19:42, Luke 23:54
528   Luke 23:54
529   John 19:42
530   Mark 15:46, Matthew 27:60
531   Matthew 27:61, Mark 15:47
532   Mark 15:47, Luke 23:55
533   Luke 23:56; Exodus 16:29, Deuteronomy 5:12
534   Matthew 27:62
535   Luke 23:56; John 5:16-18, Matthew 12:5-8, 8:20, Genesis 2:2-3, Exodus 20:11, Deuteronomy 5:12-15; 2 Corinthians 5:17-18, Luke 13:31-33
536   Matthew 27:62
537   Matthew 27:63; John 2:19-22, Matthew 22:59-61, 16:21
538   Matthew 27:64; Acts 2:22-32
539   Matthew 27:64; Matthew 26:63-64, 16:13, 20, 17:23, 20:18-19, John 4:7-10, 25-26, 27-30
540   Matthew 27:65

secured the sepulchre, first by fixing seals to the stone and then by setting the guard.[541]

Reflective Prayer: Psalm 22:1-31

Antiphon: Look! There is the Lamb of God
    who takes away the sin of the world.[542]

    My God, my God, why have you forsaken me?
      Why should your saving help remain so distant
      from my groans and cries of anguish?[543]
    My God, every day I call to you, but you do not answer;
      every night, you hear my voice, but I find no relief.[544]

Yet, you are enthroned as the Holy One,
    the Most High God to the praises of Israel![545]
Our ancestors trusted in you,
    they trusted and you rescued them.[546]
They cried out to you for help,
    and you delivered them;
    in you they trusted,
    and they were not disappointed.[547]

But I am a maggot and not a man,
    the scorn of mankind, despised by all.[548]
Everyone who sees me mocks me;
    they sneer at me and curl their tongues;
    they shake their heads at me, saying:[549]
"He trusted himself to God, let Yahweh deliver him;
    if the Lord loves him, let the Lord save him."[550]

---

541   Matthew 27:66; Daniel 6:18
542   John 1:29; Mark 9:9-13
543   Psalm 22:1; Matthew 27:46; Isaiah 6:8, 59:1
544   Psalm 22:2; Mark 14:60; Isaiah 6:11-13, 59:2
545   Psalm 22:3; Mark 14:61-62; Isaiah 6:1-3
546   Psalm 22:4; Matthew 27:20-23; Luke 1:73-74
547   Psalm 22:5; Matthew 27:24-26; Isaiah 7:13-14, Luke 1:57, 76
548   Psalm 22:6; Luke 22:63-65, Mark 14:65; Numbers 11:1-17
549   Psalm 22:7; Matthew 27:39-42; Exodus 17:3-7
550   Psalm 22:8; Matthew 27:43; Exodus 14:10-14

Yet, you are the one who drew me from the womb,
    and comforted me at my mother's breast;[551]
I was thrust upon you from the womb,
    from my birth I belonged to you.[552]
Do not stay far from me,
    for trouble is close by;
    and there is no one else to help me.[553]

Antiphon: You must keep the animal till the fourteenth day of the first month;
    then the whole assembly of the community of Israel
    will slaughter it at twilight.[554]

Many bulls surround me;
    like the wild bulls of Bashon, they hem me in.[555]
They open their jaws against me,
    like roaring lions ravaging their prey.[556]

My life is poured out like water,
    all my bones are disjointed;
    my heart is turned like wax,
    melting away within me.[557]
My mouth is as dry as a clay pot;
    my tongue sticks to the roof of my mouth;
    you lay me down in the dust of death.[558]

---

551   Psalm 22:9; Luke 23:27-31, 11:27-28; Isaiah 43:7
552   Psalm 22:10; Mark 15:21-22, John 18:37; Isaiah 43:1
553   Psalm 22:11; Mark 14:43; Isaiah 43:2-6; Daniel 9:20-27, 10:5-7, Revelation 1:12-17
554   Exodus 12:6; Luke 9:29-31
555   Psalm 22:12; John 19:1-3; Daniel 14:23-30, Revelation 20:1-3, 7, 10
556   Psalm 22:13; John 19:4-8; Daniel 14:31-42
557   Psalm 22:14; John 19:33-34, Ezekiel 47:1, Revelation 22:1; Job 7:11-18
558   Psalm 22:15; John 19:28; Job 7:19-21

A pack of dogs surrounds me;
  a gang of evildoers closes in on me,
  as if to hack off my hands and feet.[559]
I can count every one of my bones,
  while they look at me and gloat.[560]
They divide my clothing among themselves;
  and for my garments they cast lots.[561]

O Lord, do not stay away from me;
  you, my strength, come quickly to help me.[562]
Rescue my life from the sword,
  the precious life I have from the clenched jaws of
      dogs;[563]
save me from the lions mouth,
  my poor life from the horns of wild bulls![564]

Antiphon: And now I have seen and I testify
  that he is the Chosen One, the Son of God.[565]

Then I will proclaim your name to my brothers and sisters;
  in the assembled community I will praise you:[566]
"All you who fear the Lord, praise him!
  All you descendants of Jacob, honour him!
  All you descendants of Israel, reverence him![567]

For God has not despised
  nor disregarded the suffering of the poor,
  has not turned his face away from me,
  but has heard me when I cried for help.[568]

---

559 Psalm 22:16; Luke 23:33; Psalm 59:6
560 Psalm 22:17; Mark 15:29-32; Psalm 59:7
561 Psalm 22:18; John 19:23-24; Philippians 2:5-8
562 Psalm 22:19; Matthew 27:47-50; Job 1:6-22, 2:1-10
563 Psalm 22:20; Luke 22:52-53; Job 7:1-10; Job 38:1-4, Isaiah 45:9-10, Job 42:1-6, 10-17
564 Psalm 22:21; John 18:19-23; Job 16:6-11; Job 1:8, Job 2:4, Isaiah 53:3-5, Matthew 27:3-4, 19, Luke 23:47
565 John 1:34; Matthew 17:5
566 Psalm 22:22; Luke 22:66-71; Luke 1:46-47
567 Psalm 22:23; Mark 15:40-41; Luke 1:55
568 Psalm 22:24; Luke 23:44-46; Luke 1:48, 54

> I will praise you in the thronged assembly,
> > I will fulfil my vows before all who fear him.[569]
> The poor will eat and be satisfied;
> > those who seek the Lord will praise him;
> > may your hearts enjoy life forever!"[570]

All the ends of the earth will remember the Lord and
> > return to him,
> all the families of nations will bow down before him.[571]
For the Lord is king,
> the ruler of the nations.[572]
All who prosper on earth will bow down before him;
> all those who are mortal, who go down to the dust,
> will kneel in homage.[573]
Their descendants will serve him,
> will proclaim his name to future generations.[574]
For those still to come, they will hear of the Lord;
> and these will proclaim his saving justice to a people
> > yet unborn;
> he has fulfilled it.[575]

Antiphon: Your father Abraham rejoiced to think
> > that he would see my Day;
> > he saw it and was glad.[576]

> Glory be to the Father,
> > and to the Son, and to the Holy Spirit,
> > > as it was in the beginning, is now,
> > > > and ever shall be world without end. Amen.

---

569 Psalm 22:25; Luke 23:47-49; Luke 1:49, Exodus 32:7-14
570 Psalm 22:26; Luke 23:39-43; Luke 1:53
571 Psalm 22:27; John 18:33-36; Luke 1:51; Isaiah 60:1-3, 19-22
572 Psalm 22:28; John 19:19; Luke 1:52; Philippians 2:9, Colossians 1:15-18a
573 Psalm 22:29; John 19:38-40; Luke 1:68-71; Philippians 2:10, Colossians 1:18b-20
574 Psalm 22:30; John 19:26-27, Luke 23:54-56; Luke 1:73-75; Galatians 6:14-15
575 Psalm 22:31; John 19:30; Luke 1:50, Luke 1:72, 77-79; Hebrews 9:27-28
576 John 8:56; John 8:57-58

Let us pray:

Lord, send down your abundant blessing upon your people who have devoutly recalled the death of your Son in the sure hope of the resurrection. Grant them pardon; and give them comfort. May their faith grow stronger and their eternal salvation be assured. We ask this through Christ our Lord.

Amen.

Chapter 38

Easter Sunday, the 16ᵗʰ/17ᵗʰ Nisan (9ᵗʰ April, 30 CE)—After the Friday Preparation Day for Passover and the Sabbath Rest, from Early Easter Morning unto That Late Evening: On the Third Day, We All Are Now Sent into the New Creation of the Lord from Its First Day

Readings: John 20:1, Matthew 28:1, Mark 16:1-2, Luke 24:1, Matthew 28:2-4, John 20:2; John 20:3-10; John 20:11a, Mark 16:3-4, Luke 24:2-4, Mark 16:5-7, Matthew 28:5-7, Luke 24:5-8, Mark 16:8, John 20:11b-13; John 20:14-18, Mark 16:9-11, Matthew 28:9-10, 8, Luke 24:9-12; 1 Corinthians 15:5; Matthew 28:11-15; Mark 16:12-13, Luke 24:13-35; Mark 16:14, Luke 24:36-43, John 20:19-25, Acts 10:40-41

After the Sabbath day was over,[1] very early in the morning on the first day of the week,[2] and while it was still dark,[3] in purely pragmatic terms Jesus would have been dead for perhaps about 38 hours,[4] as Mary of Magdala left her house and set out for the

---

1   Mark 16:1, Matthew 28:1; Exodus 20:11, Genesis 2:1-3
2   Luke 24:1, John 20:1
3   John 20:1
4   Luke 23:44-46, 24:1; 1 Corinthians 15:4, Luke 24:46, Hosea 6:12, Acts 2:29-31, 2 Samuel 7:12, Psalm 16:10, 49:7-9

tomb;[5] and together with her was the other Mary,[6] the mother of James and Joset.[7] Mary Magdalene, still haunted by her traumatic experience of the Lord's crucifixion,[8] had sensed a deep restlessness within herself, as an impatient and demanding preoccupation. She was disturbed repeatedly by her memories of their hasty burial of the Lord's body,[9] when she would re-imagine the body's place in the tomb, and when she recalled the reverent expertise of Joseph of Arimathaea, as he had engineered the large stone to cover the tomb's entrance,[10] while she had given comfort to the grieving mother of Jesus, and as Joseph and the others had raced to finish their labours of sorrow before the swiftly approaching darkness would announce the Sabbath eve.[11] But, only constrained by the interminably long night after the Sabbath Passover,[12] she could no longer bear being away from her Lord;[13] so, moved by deep personal grief and by the creative spirit of God,[14] when it was still the dark of night, and the stars were brightly shining,[15] Mary of Magdala the sister of Lazarus, with her constant companion Mary the Lord's relative, quickly and quietly walked to the tomb,[16] anticipating a corpse. She also knew that shortly, as soon as dawn would break, the other women would be coming with their burial spices and ointments to join up with them at the tomb.[17]

But then while Mary Magdalene and the other Mary were on their way to the sepulchre, at the tomb the temple guards suddenly were disturbed by what seemed to them to be a violent earthquake:

5	John 20:1
6	Matthew 28:1
7	Mark 16:1, 15:47, Matthew 13:55
8	John 19:25, Mark 15:40
9	Acts 13:29-30
10	Mark 15:43-47, Matthew 27:60; Matthew 27:61, Luke 23:55
11	Luke 23:54
12	Psalm 63:6; Exodus 16:29; Exodus 20:8-10, Deuteronomy 5:12-15; Exodus 13:20-22, Luke 12:49-50
13	1 Corinthians 6:17, Ephesians 4:4, Romans 7:4
14	John 16:20; Romans 8:9-11, 1 Corinthians 3:16, 6:19-20, Romans 8:11; Mark 16:9, Matthew 12:28, Ephesians 2:18, 2 Corinthians 3:18
15	Isaiah 60:19-20
16	John 20:1; Matthew 12:7-8, Mark 12:7-8, Luke 12:7-8, John 12:7-8
17	Mark 16:1-2, Luke 24:1

for an angel of the Lord, having descended from heaven, came, in an instant like a bolt of light; he rolled away the stone as it roared, and sat upon it.[18] At this truly thunderous and stupefying moment, while the guards were vigilantly maintaining their post, the angel's incandescent face resembled lightening, and his clothes were as white and pure as snow.[19] However, the guards were so shaken with fear of him that they became like dead men:[20] they were ashen, faint-hearted, and speechless; yet, almost immediately, they gathered themselves up; and, instinctively now, they scattered in terror. Some would flee to their homes; but a few of them, dreading the implications and the consequences of their present failure for their lives and careers, but also for their souls, they went straightaway to the temple elders.[21]

After the guards had fled, then, in that finite moment before the absolute moment when the dark of night first begins to change to the imperceptible light of day,[22] through the spirit of the One God,[23] life returned to the same physical body of the Lord, the singly incarnate God-Man,[24] the second person of the Holy Trinity begotten of the Father's love, conceived of the virgin Mary, but never created.[25] Now through his Father, the perishable material body of his and her son, Jesus, was restored in the imperishable substance of his Father's new creation;[26] and in the glory of God's eternal spirit,[27] the risen Jesus Christ and Son of God was now, as always and forever, completely

---

18 Matthew 28:2; Romans 13:11-12
19 Matthew 28:3, Psalm 51:7, 1; Luke 2:9, Revelation 10:1
20 Matthew 28:4; Matthew 23:27-31
21 Matthew 28:11; Matthew 23:33-35, Romans 9:22-24, 30-33, Matthew 21:42-43
22 Genesis 1:2-5, John 1:1-5, Luke 1:78-79, Isaiah 60:1-2; 1 John 2:8, 1:5-7, Romans 6:8-11
23 Genesis 1:2, Luke 1:34-35, 3:21-22, Psalm 2:7-9; John 10:17-18, 12:28, 16:7;
24 Colossians 2:9-10; 1 John 1:1, John 1:14, Luke 1:38
25 Mark 1:9-11, 9:7; 1 Peter 1:20-21
26 2 Corinthians 5:17, Philippians 3:21, Matthew 13:43; 1 Corinthians 15:35-57
27 Matthew 17:2, 5, Exodus 33:18-23, 3:6; Acts 9:3, 22:6, 26:12-13, Revelation 21:23, 22:5, 1:16-18

sovereign,[28] the first-born of all the living,[29] of all who are the sons and daughters of God.[30] And shortly thereafter, when initially Mary of Magdala arrived at the sepulchre, she saw that the stone had been moved away from the tomb;[31] and she also noticed the still burning embers of the campfires, now obviously freshly deserted.[32] Then, within the eternity of a barely fleeting moment, Mary ran away from the tomb in a great panic; she came to Simon Peter and the other disciple whom Jesus loved, that is, to John; and quite visibly out of breath, she told the pair of disciples her only plausible explanation for the open tomb, as breathlessly, for herself and the other Mary who was absent, she blurted out her dreadful conclusion, "They have taken the Lord out of the tomb, and we don't know where they have put him!"[33]

Actually, Mary of Magdala hadn't even looked in the tomb, not yet anyway; but clearly the tomb had been breached and the guards were no longer there. And indeed, Jesus was not there; for he had risen, and now he was gone soon to his mother, Mary: she was the first person actually to see the risen Christ.[34] The gospel only implies this, it is not explicitly stated; just as also there is no explicit human witness to the actual moment of the Lord's resurrection—but only explicit human references and witnesses to the moments before the resurrection and to the time afterwards. Both the Lord's resurrection and his first appearance to his mother are implicit truths of the gospel, explicitly demonstrated by both the Lord's and his

---

28 Luke 23:46, Mark 12:35-37, Ephesians 1:17-23, Philippians 2:10-11, Colossians 2:15
29 John 5:25-26, Romans 10:9; Romans 5:10, 1 Corinthians 15:20-26, Colossians 1:15-18, John 16:21-22, 3:5, Romans 8:28-30, Galatians 4:4-7, Acts 13:32-34, Luke 3:22; Revelation 1:5
30 1 John 2:29, 3:1-2
31 John 20:1
32 Maria Valtorta, Ibid., Chapter 613, "The Resurrection."
33 John 20:2; Matthew 28:1
34 St. Ignatius of Loyola, "The Resurrection of Christ Our Lord and His First Apparition," in The Spiritual Exercises of St. Ignatius; and Maria Valtorta, Ibid., Chapter 614, "Jesus Appears to His Mother."

mother's fruits.[35] As the new Eve,[36] Mary has become the mother of all the living, just as her son is the first-born of all the living; the joy of experiencing the risen Lord by his mother, her risen Lord and ours, was hers the first in the whole of God's creation, just as she was also the first human ever to experience the Lord, within the life-giving tomb of her womb;[37] and by giving birth to her son, at the Lord's resurrection she also gave birth to all of God's children of the light.[38]

It made no sense, as at first the two Maries had believed, for the guards to have stolen the body of the Lord; for that supposition would have contradicted the very reason the Lord's enemies had arranged with Pilate to post their own guards as a sound control for securing the tomb against trickery or deception.[39] Nonetheless, while the risen Lord, in fact, was with his mother, Peter and John now had set out for the tomb;[40] and Mary Magdalene, but more slowly, followed behind them as she returned to the tomb for her second visit that morning. Peter and John, as men, outpaced Mary Magdalene; and although Peter and John ran together, the other disciple was younger and he ran faster than Peter, and so John reached the tomb first;[41] he bent down and saw the burial cloths lying on the ground, but did not go in,[42] in his deference to the role of Peter.[43] When Simon Peter arrived after John, Peter went into the tomb, and he saw the burial cloths lying there,[44] and also the cloth that had covered the head of Jesus; it was not with the burial cloths on the ground, but it was rolled up in a place by itself.[45] Then the other disciple, who had arrived to

---

35   Luke 1:42, John 12:24, Matthew 13:23; John 15:1-5, 8, 16, Matthew 7:15-20
36   Genesis 3:20, Revelation 12:2, 5
37   Luke 1:26-35, 38-45
38   John 16:20-21, Luke 2:7; John 12:36, 1 John 3:2
39   Matthew 27:62-66
40   John 20:3
41   John 20:4
42   John 20:5
43   Matthew 16:18, John 1:42
44   John 20:6
45   John 20:7

the tomb first, also went in; and when John saw, he believed,[46] as he became the first of the Lord's immediate disciples to believe.[47] But until that moment, neither disciple had understood the scripture: that he had to rise from the dead.[48] And from that moment, John now believed although Peter did not yet have sufficient faith.[49] But then both of the disciples returned home together,[50] while Mary Magdalene remained there in the garden, standing alone outside and near the tomb, weeping.[51]

Meanwhile, at the first sign of the light of dawn,[52] the other Mary, the mother of James and Joset,[53] whose sons at this time were still among the sceptical relatives of the Lord,[54] was returning to the tomb for her second visit that chaotic morning, together with Salome, the mother of John and James,[55] with Joanna of Chuza, and with several other of their women companions;[56] and just as the sun was rising,[57] they arrived to the tomb with the spices they had prepared.[58] Also, the Lord would have been with his mother at John's house,[59] during this time while John's mother Salome was out of the house and on her way to the tomb. Mary, the Lord's relative, who was the mother of James and the wife of Clopas,[60] had been with the Lord near his cross, and she had been with Mary Magdalene earlier that morning when together they had seen the

---

46	John 20:8
47	John 1:12-14; John 6:62, 20:17, 6:63; 1 John 1:1-3, 2:24-25, 3:2-3, 5:20; Revelation 1:5, 22:5, John 4:10, 14, 23-24, Romans 8:6-11
48	John 20:9; Luke 18:31-34, 11:29, John 6:30, 39-40
49	Mark 16:14
50	John 20:10
51	John 20:11
52	Luke 24:1
53	Matthew 28:1, John 19:25
54	Matthew 13:55-58, Mark 3:20-21, 22, 30-35, 6:3, Matthew 10:34-36, Mark 6:4
55	Mark 16:1
56	Luke 24:10
57	Mark 16:2
58	Mark 16:1, Luke 24:1
59	John 19:27
60	Luke 24:10, John 19:25

open tomb;[61] but the other women hadn't believed this story from Mary, the Lord's relative, when she had returned from her first trip to the tomb. In fact, even now as the women were coming to the tomb accompanying Mary the Lord's relative, Mary alone remained silent against their general denial and disbelief for her original story, as the other women in their ongoing convictions had been saying to each other, "Who will roll away the stone for us at the entrance of the tomb?"[62]

However, when they arrived, they found that the stone which was very large, indeed, had been rolled away from the tomb;[63] and already there, outside the tomb, they found Mary Magdalene standing there, weeping.[64] Just as the women arrived, Mary Magdalene then had stooped to look inside the tomb;[65] and when the others followed after her, upon entering the tomb, they could not find the body of the Lord Jesus.[66] As they all stood there puzzling over this event,[67] suddenly at their side,[68] they saw a young man in a white robe;[69] in fact, there were two men: both of them in brilliant clothes,[70] angels in white, who were standing right there at their side.[71] Struck with amazement,[72] and terrified as well,[73] the women bowed their heads to the ground.[74] And then, both of the angels, as true eye-witnesses of the Lord's actual moment of his resurrection,[75] spoke together; and they said to the women:[76]

61	Matthew 28:1, John 20:1
62	Mark 16:3
63	Luke 24:2, Mark 16:4
64	John 20:11
65	John 20:11
66	Luke 24:3
67	Luke 24:4
68	Luke 24:4
69	Mark 16:5
70	Luke 24:4
71	John 20:12, Luke 24:4
72	Mark 16:5
73	Luke 24:5
74	Luke 24:5
75	Matthew 28:2
76	Matthew 28:5, Luke 24:5

There is no need for you to be so amazed and afraid.[77] We know that you are looking for Jesus of Nazareth, who was crucified:[78] So, why look here among the dead for someone who is alive?[79] He's not here; for he has risen,[80] just as he said he would;[81] come and see, here is the place where they laid him.[82] Remember what he told you when he still was in Galilee:[83] that the Son of Man must be handed over into the power of sinners and be crucified, and rise on the third day.[84] So then, [and they remembered his words[85]] you must go quickly and tell his disciples,[86] and Peter,[87] "He has risen from the dead;[88] and now he is going ahead of you to Galilee; that is where you will see him."[89] Behold, I have told you.[90]

The women hurried out from the tomb; and all of them, including Mary Magdalene, ran away from the tomb, as they were shaking and trembling with fear, frightened out of their wits; and also because they were so scared, they said nothing to anyone,[91] not even to each other. But, although they had been afraid, they now began to be filled with awe and a genuine great joy; and so, coming away from the tomb quickly, the women ran straightaway to tell the disciples.[92] The women who returned from the tomb included Mary of Magdala; Joanna, wife of Chuza; Mary, the mother of James; and many others,[93] and when they came to the disciples, they told the

---

77	Mark 16:6, Matthew 28:5
78	Mark 16:6, Matthew 28:5
79	Luke 24:5
80	Matthew 28:6, Luke 24:6, Mark 16:6
81	Matthew 28:6; Mark 16:7
82	Matthew 28:6, Mark 16:6
83	Luke 24:6
84	Luke 24:7; Luke 9:22
85	Luke 24:8
86	Mark 16:7, Matthew 28:7
87	Mark 16:7; John 20:9
88	Matthew 28:7
89	Matthew 28:7, Mark 16:7
90	Matthew 28:7; Mark 16:7, Luke 24:6
91	Mark 16:8
92	Matthew 28:8; Psalm 16:11
93	Luke 24:10

Eleven, and also all of the others, everything that had happened.[94] But this story of theirs seemed to be so far fetched, to be such pure nonsense, that the disciples didn't believe them.[95] Peter, however, decided to check out Mary Magdalene's and the other women's story: and so now for his second time he headed back to the tomb,[96] but he went alone; and now once again, he also was running.[97] At the tomb, when Peter bent down, he looked into the tomb, but all he could see were the linen cloths, and there was nothing else.[98] This time, however, Peter carefully gathered up these burial cloths, taking with him all that he had found, and he came out of the tomb; but only now for the first time was Peter no longer set mentally looking backwards for the Lord in the tomb. Then, like the now fearless women earlier before him, he also went back home,[99] but still not comprehending, utterly amazed at what had happened.[100]

Meanwhile, earlier on, when Mary Magdalene had been on her way to tell Peter and John at the first time,[101] and simultaneously splitting up, when Mary the mother of James had gone back initially to tell her women companions of the tomb's disturbance,[102] some of the temple guards at the tomb had gone off into the city to tell the chief priests, including Caiaphas and Annas,[103] all that had happened.[104] These, then, called a meeting with the elders; and after discussing the matter, they decided to bribe the guards, as if everyone, or anyone, could blindly ignore God and keep him quiet;[105] but nonetheless, resorting to typically corrupt worldly standards, they seductively gave

---

94 Luke 24:9; Luke 24:22-23
95 Luke 24:11
96 John 20:4-5
97 Luke 24:12
98 Luke 24:12
99 John 20:19, Acts 1:13
100 Luke 24:12
101 John 20:2
102 Mark 16:1, Luke 24:10
103 Matthew 26:57, John 18:12-13
104 Matthew 28:11; Matthew 28:2-3
105 Luke 13:32, Matthew 28:14; Hebrews 4:13, Revelation 1:8, 22:13, John 1:51, Matthew 5:18

the guards a considerable sum of money,[106] with these instructions, "This is what you must say, 'His disciples came during the night and stole him while we were asleep.'"[107] And then, also having calculated clearly the human likelihood of this knowledge making rounds, they said, "If any of this should ever come to the governor's ears,[108] we ourselves will satisfy him (Pontius Pilate) and ensure that you don't get into trouble."[109]

So, the guards took the money and carried out their instructions from the temple elders and chief priests; to this day, this has been the story circulating among the Jews.[110] Also, variations of this same false story are expressed even after nearly two millennia, in the 21st century, by today's atheists and non-believers.[111] As artefacts of Jesus' death, there is the cross recovered by St. Helen, and the "Shroud of Turin,"[112] defended by its believers against its critics as a relic of the cross and the resurrection. But, as scientific evidence, there would be no dead body of Christ to be found as some alleged myth-busting archaeological artefact, replicating the initial error of Peter and Mary Magdala. But, with the Spirit of God, there is only the evidence of the living Christ in our churches and in our souls, in our faith and action among the living; in his living word; in the living body and blood of Christ at the centre of our lives in the sacrament of the Eucharist; and Christ, very-much-alive-in-us, through the gifts of his other sacraments. And also, undeniably, to be witnessed by the whole of humankind, then in the fullness of time at the end of the world, the living Christ will return to earth arrayed in the majesty and power of his risen glory.[113]

But, after Mary Magdalene had spoken with the disciples, she

106	Matthew 28:12
107	Matthew 28:13; John 20:1-2
108	Matthew 28:14; Matthew 27:11, Mark 15:1, Matthew 27:62-64
109	Matthew 28:14
110	Matthew 28:15
111	Mark 16:16
112	Four days ago, 10 April 2010, the shroud has been placed on display in the Milan cathedral for the first time in a decade; and on 2nd May, Pope Benedict XVI will be making a spiritual visit during its exposition.
113	Revelation 1:13-18, 22:12-15

returned to the tomb alone; and now for her, for the third time that morning, she stood outside of the tomb, weeping.[114] Then, peeking once more into the tomb, she again saw two angels in white, now sitting there, one at the head and one at the feet, where the body of Jesus had been.[115] And this time, when the two angels spoke, they said to her, "Woman, why are you weeping?"[116] And Mary, still facing the tomb and still believing that the guards had stolen the Lord's body,[117] replied to them, "They have taken away my Lord, and I don't know where they have put him."[118] But as she said this, she turned around; and she saw that Jesus was standing there, although she didn't yet recognize that it was Jesus,[119] who was facing the tomb. Then, just as the angels had spoken to her, Jesus casually said to her:

> Woman, why are you weeping?[120] Who are you looking for?[121]

Mary, believing him to be the gardener, said to him, "Sir, if you are the one who carried him away, tell me where you have put him, and I will go and take him."[122] Mary wanted him to tell her where he had taken the body, so that she could bring the corpse back to return him to the tomb, obviously dead. She never imagined that Jesus could rise from the dead, no more than she could imagine earlier for her brother Lazarus, who had died, that he would be raised to life again in front of her eyes.[123] Then in that moment, simply, Jesus said to her only one word:

> Mary![124]

Suddenly, all the thoughts in her head turned around; and initially

---

114 John 20:11
115 John 20:12
116 John 20:13
117 John 20:2
118 John 20:13; John 11:33-34
119 John 20:14; John 1:31; John 14:21
120 John 20:15
121 John 20:15; John 1:35-41
122 John 20:15; John 20:13, 11:34
123 John 11:32, 44
124 John 20:16; 1 John 4:9, Ephesians 3:16-21

understanding she exclaimed to him in Hebrew, "Rabbuni!"—which means, "Teacher."[125] When the Lord had called her "Mary," who was "dead for fear," by her name, Jesus had called her into existence again, as dead people do not have names. And at that moment of new life in her, she in turn called Jesus by the name she knew so well for him, "Rabbuni," as if to say to him, "Come back to life so that you can continue teaching me how to be yours and yours alone."[126] And falling to her knees, she attached herself and embraced him.[127] Jesus said to her:

> Don't hold on to me, because I have not yet ascended to the Father; but go and find my brothers, and tell them, "I am ascending to my Father and your Father, to my God and your God."[128]

Jesus was telling her, "Don't continue holding on to me," because "if I don't go to the Father, I cannot send you the Holy Spirit, who will remind you all that I have taught you."[129] Jesus implied that by her holding on to him, "You want me to come back to life as your Master and Teacher, but you won't let me send you the one who will remind you of how I was a teacher to you." So, Mary did leave go of Jesus, and once again, now for her third time, she went to tell his companions, who all were in mourning and in tears.[130] Mary Magdalene told them, "I have seen the Lord," and she also told them all the other things Jesus had said to her.[131] Even so, still the disciples would not believe her when they heard her say that he was alive, and that she had seen him.[132]

Later on, after the other women from Galilee had left the disciples, also telling them of their encounter with angels at the tomb, these women were all together on the road heading home.

---

125 John 20:16; John 11:28, 43; John 1:48-51; Genesis 28:12
126 Luke 10:39
127 Romans 8:38-39
128 John 20:17; Exodus 3:13-16
129 John 14:16, 26, 15:26, 16:7
130 Mark 16:10
131 John 20:18
132 Mark 16:11

Suddenly,[133] coming on towards them, there was Jesus coming to meet them; and he greeted them, by only saying,

>Hello.[134]

Then, at first, slowly in a moment of amazement, and then more quickly, they approached him, and they embraced his feet, and did him homage.[135] At this time, Jesus already had ascended to God the Father,[136] and now, in fact, he had returned. Jesus told them a new second message:

>Don't be afraid; but go and tell my brothers that they must go to Galilee, and there they will see me.[137]

Then these women, too, went and told the disciples that they had seen the Lord.

But at some later point, after this encounter on the road, Jesus then also appeared to Peter.[138] And only after this was Peter, now comprehending, fully amazed at what had happened:[139] that the Lord is alive and risen from the dead. Then, humbly, respectfully, and without any aspect of superiority or coercion,[140] Peter obediently, joyfully, and faithfully went back to tell his brothers what happened and to encourage them, gently and determinedly, in their faith.[141] Nonetheless, like many of the people around us everyday, all of the disciples continued to have their serious doubts,[142] except now for the two apostles, for Peter and for John,[143] and except for Mary Magdalene and for her other women companions,[144] as these persons continued to spread the word that the Lord is risen. Likewise,

---

133	Matthew 28:9; Matthew 18:20
134	Matthew 28:9; John 20:16, 19
135	Matthew 28:9; John 20:17
136	John 1:51, Genesis 28:12, Hebrews 4:14, 9:11-12
137	Matthew 28:10
138	1 Corinthians 15:5; Luke 24:34
139	Luke 24:12; John 20:18, Matthew 28:10
140	Matthew 7:4-6
141	Luke 22:31-32; John 21:15, Matthew 20:25-28, 24:45-51, Luke 12:41-42
142	Luke 24:38, Mark 16:14, Matthew 28:17
143	Acts 3:10-15, 4:10-13
144	Luke 24:9-10, 34

when the later persecutions would come to the early Christians, their dispersal among the Gentiles, like these same first believing disciples of Easter morning, would help spread this word of the risen Christ throughout the world. These core events of Easter morning paralleled and modelled the future of evangelization in its core: the interaction of our emergent faith with another's Christian witness; and one's personal, spiritual encounter with the risen Christ.[145]

Now, later that very same day, two disciples were going to a village called Emmaus about sixty furlongs, or twelve kilometres, northwest from Jerusalem.[146]   And as they walked along the road, they were talking together about all that had happened.[147]   And, as the two were talking together and debating it, it happened that Jesus himself drew near to them and he walked by their side;[148] but their eyes were prevented from recognizing him.[149]   Obviously overhearing their conversation, but also having known their thoughts, Jesus politely said to them:

> What are these things that you are discussing as you walk along?[150]

Then the two disciples stopped in their tracks, completely motionless; they looked at each other, their faces downcast;[151] and then one of them, named Cleopas,[152] replied to him, "You must be the only visitor to Jerusalem who doesn't know the things that have happened there these last few days."[153] And Jesus asked them:

> What things?[154]

And they answered:

145	1 Peter 4:10
146	Luke 24:13
147	Luke 24:14
148	Luke 24:15; Matthew 18:20
149	Luke 24:16; Mark 16:12; John 20:14
150	Luke 24:17
151	Luke 24:17
152	Luke 24:18; John 19:25
153	Luke 24:18
154	Luke 24:19

Gospel (on the Road to) Emmaus /441

The things that happened to Jesus of Nazareth, who was a powerful prophet in deeds and speech, and highly regarded by God and by all the people;[155] and how our chief priests and our religious leaders handed him over to be sentenced to death, and crucified him.[156] It was our hope that he would be the one to set Israel free;[157] and that's not all: two whole days have passed since all these things have taken place;[158] then some women from our group of followers have astounded us: they were [today] at his tomb early in the morning,[159] and when they did not find his body,[160] they came back and told us that they had seen a vision of angels who declared that, indeed, he was alive.[161] And some of the men who are with us then went to the tomb and found everything just as the women had said, but of him they saw nothing.[162]

Then still not recognizing Jesus, he said to them:

Oh, you foolish men! So slow to believe all that the prophets have said![163] Wasn't it necessary that the Christ should suffer these things before entering into his glory?[164]

Then, beginning with Moses and going through all of the prophets, he interpreted for them the passages in all the scriptures that referred to himself,[165] that is, to the Christ. Eventually, when they approached Emmaus, the village where they were going, he gave them the impression that he was going further on;[166] but they

---

155   Luke 24:19
156   Luke 24:20
157   Luke 24:21; Luke 1:71
158   Luke 24:21
159   Luke 24:22; Luke 24:1, Matthew 28:1, Mark 16:2
160   Luke 24:23; Luke 24:3
161   Luke 24:23; Luke 24:4, 6-7, Matthew 28:1, 5-8
162   Luke 24:24; Luke 24:12, John 20:3-7, 10
163   Luke 24:25
164   Luke 24:26
165   Luke 24:27; John 1:45, 46-51
166   Luke 24:28; John 20:19, Luke 24:36, 47

urged him, this seemingly wise gentleman, to stay with them, saying, "But it's nearly the evening, and the day is almost over."[167] So, at their invitation and insistence, he went inside to stay with them.[168] Now, while he was with them at table, it happened that he took the bread, said the blessing, broke it, and then gave it to them.[169] And with that, their eyes were opened and they recognized him; but at that same moment, he vanished from their sight.[170]

Then they said to each other, "Didn't our hearts burn within us as he spoke to us on the road and explained the scriptures to us?"[171] And at that very instant they set out and returned to Jerusalem, where after a two-hour's walk and now at night, they found the Eleven gathered together with their companions,[172] including Mary Magdalene and the others who had seen the risen Lord.[173] These women told the two disciples from Emmaus, "The Lord has indeed risen, and he has appeared to Simon."[174] Not withstanding Friedrich Nietzsche, Jean-Paul Sartre, and other modern Sadducees to the contrary,[175] God was not dead: instead, he is both the living God, and God of the living.[176] And then, in response to the companions, the two disciples told their story of what had happened on the road and how they had recognized him at the breaking of the bread;[177] but even so, except now for Peter and John, rendered silent in their presently suffering faith,[178] the Eleven didn't believe them either.[179]

Then, at last, Jesus showed himself to the Eleven, also while they were at table,[180] in the evening of that first day of the week, when

---

167	Luke 24:29
168	Luke 24:29
169	Luke 24:30; 1 Corinthians 11:23-24, Acts 2:42, 46
170	Luke 24:31
171	Luke 24:32; 1 Corinthians 15:3-4
172	Luke 24:33
173	John 20:8, Matthew 28:10, Luke 24:10, Mark 16:1
174	Luke 24:34; 1 Corinthians 15:5
175	Matthew 22:23, 29, Acts 23:8
176	Matthew 22:31-32; Matthew 16:16, 26:63
177	Luke 24:35
178	1 Peter 3:15-17; 1 John 5:9-11
179	Mark 16:13
180	Mark 16:14; Luke 24:30, 35

the doors were locked, in the room where the disciples were, for fear of the Jews.[181] Except for Thomas who was absent,[182] the Eleven were now alone by themselves and they were still talking about all of this when Jesus himself came and stood in their midst.[183] In a state of alarm, they were terrified; they thought that they were seeing a ghost.[184] And he said to them:

>Peace be with you.[185]

And as Jesus said this, he showed them his hands and his side; and the disciples were filled with joy at seeing the Lord.[186] Then he said to them:

>Why are you so troubled? And why do doubts and questions arise in your hearts?[187] Look, by my hands and my feet, you can see that it is I myself; touch me and see for yourselves; a ghost does not have flesh and bones, as you can see that I have.[188]

Then he showed them his hands and his feet.[189] He reproached them for their unbelief and obstinacy, because they had not believed those who had seen him after he had risen.[190] Yet, seeing him truly alive, their joy was so great that they still could not believe it, because they were dumbfounded; so he asked them:

>Do you have anything here to eat?[191]

And they gave him a piece of grilled fish,[192] which he took and

---

181	John 20:19
182	John 20:24
183	Luke 24:36, John 20:19; Matthew 18:20
184	Luke 24:37; Matthew 14:26, John 6:19; John 6:55, 51, 14:10-11, 6:57, 63
185	Luke 24:36, John 20:19; Matthew 14:27
186	John 20:20; John 16:20, 16-19; John 14:1-7
187	Luke 24:38
188	Luke 24:39; John 6:20
189	Luke 24:40
190	Mark 16:14; 1 Peter 1:8
191	Luke 24:41
192	Luke 24:42; John 21:9

ate in front of their eyes.[193] Then, he said to them again:

> Peace be with you.[194] As the Father has sent me, so I am sending you.[195]

After saying this, he breathed on them and said:

> Receive the Holy Spirit.[196] When you forgive anyone's sins, they are forgiven; if you refuse to forgive anyone's sins, they are retained.[197]

Then, in the same manner as he had come, Jesus vanished from their sight, leaving his disciples and the rest of us to do whatever must be concluded.

The experience of the disciples, just now in that second liturgy of the first Easter evening,[198] had been, and is, a synopsis, model, and rationale for the entire Eucharist, that we celebrate weekly on Sundays (or at Sunday vigil on Saturday evening), or at our daily Mass: from the Lord's dramatic entrance rite to the blessing at the rite of dismissal, there was the continuous presence of the Word, a critical homily, and the sharing of a meal. From the opening greeting of Peace, everyone experienced the joy of the risen Christ, as, hopefully, we may experience in our liturgical celebrations through our music and our religious art, in our reading and hearing the word of God, in the homilies we receive from our priests, and in the Eucharist we share; or if our liturgy is not this experience of the risen Lord, then something in our celebrations, or in us, needs fixing. And at the concluding dismissal we are sent with the Holy Spirit into the world, where in our daily lives, with the ministering Christ now living in us, we are duty bound to forgive one another's sins; and if we should need by circumstances to refuse to administer his forgiveness to others, unfortunately because of their intransigence in some sin, then those

---

193 Luke 24:43; Acts 10:40-41
194 John 20:21, 19
195 John 20:21
196 John 20:22; Matthew 14:28-30; John 6:21, 1 Peter 1:9
197 John 20:23; Matthew 18:21-22, 5:23-24
198 Luke 24:30, 41; Acts 2:42

sins are retained. We have been sent into the world.[199]

If the risen Lord lives in us, our sins have been forgiven;[200] and there should be no dread of sin or its preoccupation in us, but only our genuine and active love for one another, as God's love eventually achieves its perfection in us.[201] But if we have sinned against anyone, and in them we have offended our Lord, then we must make reparations with our brothers and sisters, preferably before we share in the following Eucharist with our risen Lord:[202] where at Eucharist we celebrate his forgiveness of our sins through his death on the cross;[203] and, as his disciples, we truly celebrate the promise of our glorious share in Christ's resurrection:[204] for those who have joined themselves to the Lord, for those who become one with him in his body and blood: in the Eucharist and through the visible body of Christ, with the whole church, the risen Christ in the world.[205] In the risen Lord, we have been doubly privileged: with the eternal existence of our body and soul,[206] and by his saving grace.[207] How can the world ever come to know the risen Christ, and to believe in his salvific action,[208] if we don't allow the Holy Spirit to mould our individual lives in the world, to the pattern[209] and substance[210] of Christ's life in our lives in the world?[211] And for this mission, fortunately, we do have the aid of Christ: in the scriptures,[212] in the

---

199   John 17:18, 20:21; Luke 10:1-2, 5-6, 10-12
200   1 John 1:6-8
201   1 John 3:18-20, 2:4-6, 4:12
202   1 Corinthians 11:26-29
203   1 Peter 2:24; Romans 3:25-26
204   1 Peter 2:9; Ephesians 1:18-23, Colossians 3:1-4
205   Ephesians 4:4-6
206   1 Corinthians 15:44-45, Matthew 22:30, 25:46; Luke 9:27, Revelation 1:9-15, John 21:23, Mark 14:61-62, Luke 12:40
207   Matthew 25:34, Luke 12:32, Matthew 20:20-23, John 14:2, Matthew 19:29, Ephesians 2:19-22; 1 Peter 5:10-11, Revelation 7:9-12
208   Revelation 15:4
209   Colossians 2:12, Romans 6:3-6
210   Luke 9:23; 1 Peter 2:21, Romans 8:18, Philippians 3:10-11
211   Luke 9:24, Ephesians 4:7-8, 11-13
212   Luke 24:32, 44-45

Eucharist,[213] in his Church,[214] and in our regular daily prayers:[215] to assist our weaknesses of faith and action.[216] So now, let us pray.

Reflective Prayer: Psalms 42-43:1-11, 1-5; 63:1-11; 46:1-11

> God, come to my assistance.
> Lord, make haste to help me.
>
> Glory be to the Father, and to the Son, and to the Holy Spirit.
>
> As it was in the beginning, is now, and ever shall be world
>   without end.
> Amen. Alleluia.

Antiphon: As a deer yearns for flowing streams,
   so my soul longs for you, my God, alleluia.

> As a deer that yearns for streams of water,
>   so my soul is yearning for you, my God.[217]
> My being thirsts for God, the living God;
>   when can I go to see the face of God?[218]
> My tears have become my food, day and night,
>   as I am taunted all day long,
>   "Where is your God?"[219]
>
> Those times I remember as I pour out my heart:
>   how I would lead the rejoicing crowd
>   under the roof of the Most High,
>   how I went in procession with them
>   into the house of God,
>   amid cries of gladness and praise,
>   the multitude wild with joy.[220]

---

213   Luke 22:19-20
214   Luke 22:32
215   John 16:24
216   Matthew 14:31-32, Ephesians 4:1-3
217   Psalm 42:1; Matthew 28:1; John 7:38, Revelation 22:17
218   Psalm 42:2; John 20:1; Luke 12:49-50, 23:46
219   Psalm 42:3; John 20:2; Joel 2:17
220   Psalm 42:4; John 20:3-4, 8; John 12:1-2, 9-13, Isaiah 51:11

Why, my soul, are you so downcast;
  why do you groan within me?
  Hope in God! I will praise him still,
  my Saviour,[221] and my God.[222]

When my soul is downcast within me,
  I think of you:
  from the countryside of the Jordan and Mount
      Hermon,
  from the land of the Hill of Mizar, the humble
      mountain.[223]
Here, deep calls to deep in the roar of your waters;
  your torrents and all your waves sweep over me.[224]

At dawn God sends his faithful love,
  and even through the night;
  the song it inspires in me
  is a prayer of praise to my living God.[225]

I will say to God, my rock:
  "Why have you forgotten me?
  Why must I go around in mourning
  with the enemy harassing me?"[226]
With death in my bones,
  when my enemies taunt me,
  the whole day long they say to me,
  "Where is your God?"[227]
Why, my soul, are you so downcast,
  why all these sighs within me?
  Hope in God! I will praise him still,
  my Saviour and my God.[228]

---

221 Psalm 42:5
222 Psalm 42:6; John 20:9-10; Isaiah 51:14-15
223 Psalm 42:6; Matthew 28:2-3; Matthew 16:13
224 Psalm 42:7; Matthew 28:4-6; John 19:33-34, Genesis 1:1-2
225 Psalm 42:8; John 20:16, 19; Luke 1:78
226 Psalm 42:9; John 20:3-7; Luke 1:71
227 Psalm 42:10; Luke 24:10-12; Luke 2:25-29
228 Psalm 42:11; Luke 24:34; Matthew 16:16-18, 21-23, 17:1-2, Mark 9:9-10

Antiphon: You have come to Mount Zion
            and to the city of the living God, alleluia.

    Grant me justice, God;
      defend my cause against a faithless people;
      from the treacherous and the unjust, rescue me.[229]
    For you, O God, are my strength:
      Why have you abandoned me?
      Why must I go about in mourning,
      harassed by the enemy?[230]

    Send forth your light and your truth;
      let these be my guide,
      to bring me to your holy mountain,
      to the place where you dwell.[231]
    Then I shall come to the altar of God,
      to the God of my joy.
      I will praise you on the harp,
      O God, my God.[232]

    Why are you downcast, my soul,
      why do you groan within me?
      Hope in God! I will praise him still,
      my Saviour and my God.[233]

Antiphon: Whoever thirsts will drink freely
            of life-giving water, alleluia.

    O God, you are my God, for you I pine;
      for you my soul is thirsting,
      my body longs for you,
      like a parched land, lifeless and without water.[234]
    So I gaze upon you in the sanctuary,
      to see your power and your glory.[235]

---

229   Psalm 43:1; Matthew 28:12-13; Revelation 14:1, 4-5
230   Psalm 43:2; Matthew 28:9; Revelation 14:6-11
231   Psalm 43:3; Mark 16:12, Luke 24:33; Luke 2:30-32
232   Psalm 43:4; Luke 24:30-31; John 20:21, Revelation 7:9-11
233   Psalm 43:5; Mark 16:13; 1 Corinthians 15:19
234   Psalm 63:1; John 20:19; Luke 22:15, 19
235   Psalm 63:2; John 20:20; Acts 7:55-56

For your faithful love is better than life itself;
   my lips will speak your praise.[236]
Thus I will bless you all my life,
   in your name I will lift up my hands.[237]
My soul shall be filled as with a banquet,
   a song of joy on my lips and praise in my mouth.[238]

On my bed when I think of you,
    reflecting and meditating about you
    through the watches of the night,[239]
I recall that you have always been my help,
    and in the shadow of your wings I rejoice;[240]
My heart clings to you,
    and your right hand upholds me.[241]

But those who are hounding me to death,
    may they go down to the depths of the earth;[242]
be given over to the blade of the sword,
    and left as food for jackals.[243]
Then the king shall rejoice in God;
    all who put their trust in the Lord shall gain
       recognition,
    for the mouths of liars will be silenced.[244]

---

236   Psalm 63:3; John 20:18; Isaiah 6:5-7
237   Psalm 63:4; Luke 24:30; Matthew 14:16-19
238   Psalm 63:5; Luke 24:35; Matthew 22:2
239   Psalm 63:6; Luke 23:55-56, 24:1
240   Psalm 63:7; Luke 24:2-5; Isaiah 51:16
241   Psalm 63:8; John 20:16-18
242   Psalm 63:9; Luke 24:22-23; 1 Samuel 23:14
243   Psalm 63:10; Luke 24:24; John 20:1-2
244   Psalm 63:11; Luke 24:25; John 20:24-25

Antiphon: The streams of the river gladden the city of God, alleluia.

> God for us is both refuge and strength,
> > an ever-present help in time of distress:[245]
> so we shall not be afraid, though the earth should quake
> > and mountains tumble into the depths of the sea;[246]
> though its waters rage and foam,
> > and the mountains totter at its surging waves;[247]
> for the Lord of hosts is with us,
> > our citadel is the God of Jacob.[248]
>
> Streams of the river gladden the city of God;
> > it sanctifies the dwelling of the Most High.[249]
> God is within the city, it cannot be shaken;
> > God comes to its rescue at the break of day.[250]
> Nations are in uproar, and kingdoms are shaken:
> > as he raises his voice, the earth crumbles away.[251]
> The Lord of hosts is with us,
> > our citadel is the God of Jacob.[252]

---

245 Psalm 46:1; John 20:11-13, 16; Isaiah 63:9
246 Psalm 46:2; Matthew 28:2, 5-6; Isaiah 63:19b, 64:1-3; 1 Corinthians 2:9, Matthew 27:50-53
247 Psalm 46:3; Luke 24:37-38; Romans 8:37-39
248 Psalm 46:7, 11; Luke 24:39-40; Luke 20:37-40, Jeremiah 23:6
249 Psalm 46:4; John 19:34, 20:20, Luke 24:41-43, John 20:21-23; Ezekiel 47:1, Revelation 22:1
250 Psalm 46:5; Mark 16:1-2; Revelation 22:3-5
251 Psalm 46:6; Matthew 28:11-14; Revelation 21:1-4
252 Psalm 46:7; John 20:19; Genesis 2:4b-10, 22-24, Revelation 22:14

Come, consider the works of the Lord,
> the astounding deeds he has done on the earth.[253]

He puts an end to wars throughout all of the earth,
> he breaks the bow, the spear he snaps,
> and he burns the shields with fire.[254]

He says: "Be still and know that I am God,
> supreme among the nations, supreme on the earth."[255]

The Lord of hosts is with us,
> our citadel is the God of Jacob.[256]

Antiphon: The Lord is risen as he said, alleluia.

> Glory be to the Father,
>> and to the Son,
>>> and to the Holy Spirit,
>> as it was in the beginning,
>>> is now,
>>>> and ever shall be world without end. Amen.

> God our Father, creator of all,
>> today is the day of Easter joy.
> This is the morning on which the Lord appeared to men
>> who had begun to lose hope;
>>> and he opened their eyes to what the scriptures foretold:
>>> that first he must die, and then he would rise
>>> and ascend into his Father's glorious presence.
> May the risen Lord
>> breathe on our minds and open our eyes
>> that we may know him in the breaking of bread,
>> and follow him in his risen life.
> Grant this through Christ our Lord.

> Go in peace, alleluia, alleluia.
> Thanks be to God, alleluia, alleluia.

---

253 Psalm 46:8; Luke 24:24-27; 1 Corinthians 15:3-8
254 Psalm 46:9; Luke 24:36; Jeremiah 23:20, Isaiah 55:1-2
255 Psalm 46:10; John 20:17; Isaiah 60:16
256 Psalm 46:11; Matthew 28:1, 5-8, John 20:21; Jeremiah 31:31-34, 38-40

Chapter 39

The First Fifty Days in the Lord's New Creation: From Easter Sunday to Pentecost (9ᵀᴴ April to 28ᵀᴴ May, 30 CE)—Days after the Resurrection of the Lord to the Coming of the Holy Spirit; and Both Resurrection and Pentecost Are Concurrent with Our Baptism into Christ's Death and in the Birth of the Church

Readings: Matthew 27:50-53, Acts 10:40-41, Mark 16:14, 1 Corinthians 15:3-5; John 20:24-31, 21:1-25; Matthew 28:16-20, Mark 16:15-20; 1 Corinthians 15:6-7; Luke 24:44-53, Acts 1:1-14; 1 Corinthians 15:8, Acts 9:1-9, 22:6-21, 26:2-6, 23:6-7, 26:7-18, 19-32; Galatians 3:23-29, Ephesians 4:7-8, 3:1-3, 2:11-22, 3:5-11, Philemon 1-25

At the very moment Jesus had yielded up his spirit to the Father, with his death on the cross, the earth quaked;[1] and the earth quaked again at the very instant when his eternal spirit returned to his lifeless body cold in the tomb on Easter morning.[2] The death and resurrection of Christ, in his full humanity and divinity, are two elements in one unified salvation event, as was signified by the adjoining earthquakes; and as the simultaneous fulfilment and conclusion of the covenant and its replacement were indicated by

---

[1] Matthew 27:50-51
[2] Matthew 28:2

the Temple curtain torn from top to bottom upon his death,[3] as also the rocks of tombs were split open upon his death,[4] and the rock covering his own tomb was opened upon his resurrection from the dead; and as then holy people also rose from the dead, like the Lord, and appeared to others,[5] along with the resurrection of the Lord, as an integral consequence of the Lord's death upon the cross. These two elements, death and resurrection—both for the Lord and for ourselves—are as unified as three persons in one Triune God; just as when we were baptized,[6] the Father, the Son, and the Holy Spirit are as integral to us for our lives, for our death, and for our future resurrection as they were to the life,[7] death,[8] and resurrection of the Lord.[9]

There are sceptics who declare that the resurrection of Christ is a myth;[10] but for anyone to deny the resurrection of Jesus is also to deny that Christ died on the cross for the forgiveness of our sins.[11] Such modern scepticism is to be found today within secular humanism and within so called eupraxophy, as "good conduct and wisdom in living," or simply, its living in the world and for the world without God or religion or Christ.[12] Such secular beliefs and values give primacy to corporeal humans as temporary and soulless beings; and such rationalist philosophies build barriers between persons and the spirit of God,[13] and they entomb individuals within their self-made idol of living man:[14] with faith in man, but not in the Creator who gives him life;[15] with full trust in the power of each

---

3	Hebrews 6:19-20
4	Matthew 27:52
5	Matthew 27:53
6	Romans 6:5-6
7	Luke 1:35; John 16:28, 17:25, 18:36, 20:21; Matthew 28:19
8	John 1:32-33, Luke 12:50; Luke 9:30, 35, 15:23; Romans 6:3
9	John 7:39; John 12:28; Romans 6:4
10	Mark 12:18, 24-27, Acts 4:1-2, 33; Acts 17:16-18, 29-34; 1 Peter 1:3, 2 Timothy 2:8-13
11	1 Corinthians 15:12-22, 29
12	Romans 12:2
13	1 Corinthians 2:14-15, 10-13
14	Psalm 115:4-8
15	Psalm 115:3, 96:4-7

individual person, but without trust in the power of God and the person of Jesus Christ;[16] and finally, they place one's human destiny purely in a sarcophagus, ultimately full of irrelevant fleshless bones after spiritually empty lives, without the life of God in them,[17] in a fleeting and imperfect world;[18] but without God, without religion, without Christ, without a trust in God—and without any hope in the only existential salvation, which is through God's Son, our gate unto eternal life in the resurrection.[19] But, contrary to this false ideology and idol of men and women, as our being only temporary living flesh and bone,[20] God has made Christ alone supreme over all;[21] and it is only in Christ that all men and women, who believe,[22] will be brought to eternal life, body and soul, in the shared spirit of God.[23]

On Easter day and evening, the risen Lord was seen, not by the whole people, but only by those witnesses God had chosen beforehand.[24] Before Jesus had ascended to his Father as the risen Christ, to his God and to our God and Father,[25] he was seen first of all by his mother, Mary, in whose participation with her son and in her redemption through him,[26] she herself was conceived immaculately; and, in her son's conception within her womb, she was entirely pure and virginal; and therefore, for her in most particular of God's graces to humankind, Mary always had been completely without sin. After Mary, Jesus then showed himself to Mary of Magdala,[27] who, like the Lord's mother, was now also entirely pure, because through the Lord's death and resurrection her many sins

---

16	1 Corinthians 2:16
17	Ephesians 4:18
18	1 Corinthians 15:33, Matthew 5:18, 24:35-36
19	John 1:51, 10:9, 11:21-27; Acts 2:26-27, 23:6-8, Romans 8:19-25
20	Acts 24:15
21	Colossians 1:18-19
22	John 11:25-26
23	1 Corinthians 15:23-28; Galatians 3:29
24	Acts 10:40-41
25	John 20:17
26	Luke 2:35
27	John 20:14

had been completely forgiven;[28] for with her faith in Jesus and in her faithful discipleship to follow the Lord in her reformed life, after the Lord's mother, she was the one person most distinguished by her love,[29] by her complete dedication to follow in the footsteps of the Lord, right to his cross and to the resurrection.[30] Her repentant and spiritually-focused life is an ideal metaphor and true model for every aspirant Christian.

Then, after the risen Lord had returned from his heavenly Father, he also appeared on Easter to the many women of Galilee: to those who had followed Jesus wholly, like Mary of Magdala, and who had served with him throughout his public ministry, providing for the Lord and for the Twelve out of their personal wealth and every disposable resource:[31] so the risen Christ appeared: to Mary, the wife of Clopas and mother of James, the relative of the Lord;[32] to Salome, "his mother's sister,"[33] the mother of the sons of Zebedee, the apostles James and John, whom the Lord had called his "Sons of Thunder" when he first had appointed the Twelve from among his disciples;[34] to Joanna, the wife of Chuza, Herod's steward, who also had endured many persecutions in order to follow Christ, including those initially directed at her from her husband;[35] to Susanna and several other unnamed women, also like Susanna, who were cured by the Lord from their evil spirits and ailments.[36] After these, the risen Christ then appeared to Peter alone; and afterwards to the two disciples, Cleopas and Simon,[37] on their way on the road to Emmaus,

---

28   Mark 16:9, Luke 7:47-48, 37-46, 8:1-2
29   Mark 14:9; 1 John 3:16, Romans 6:6
30   Mark 8:34-35
31   Luke 8:3, 16:9; Mark 10:29-30, Matthew 6:31-33; Matthew 6:21, 13:44-46, 19:21
32   Matthew 28:1, 9, Mark 16:1, Luke 24:10; Mark 6:3, Luke 4:16-30
33   John 19:25
34   Mark 16:1, 3:17
35   Luke 24:10, 8:3; Luke 9:7-9, Mark 6:14-16, Matthew 14:1-2; Matthew 10:36, Luke 14:26, 2:34, Mark 10:29-30, 8:37, 34-36
36   Luke 24:10, 8:2-3
37   The only disciple specifically named by Luke is Cleopas; the other disciple may be "anonymous" for Luke's intended theology. However, a name for the second disciple is suggested by Eusebius of Caesarea, the father of Church history, citing Hegesippus as his source: Paul L. Maier's

and with his staying on with them there at their invitation;[38] and last of all on that Easter evening, when the risen Lord revealed himself to the Eleven, but without the absent Thomas.[39]

But, in the first few days after the Lord's resurrection, during the first week of Easter, the risen bodies of many holy persons also had come out of their tombs, at first broken by the earthquake at the sacrifice of the Lord by his death on the cross; like the risen Lord, many of these holy persons entered Jerusalem; and like the risen Lord, now reunited with him in their bodies and souls, they also appeared to a large number of people.[40] However, from the current viewpoint of psychological science, the modern sceptic might assert that these phenomena are evidence for some kind of mass hysteria among his faithful followers, and that these so-called apparitions of the dead were only projections of imaginative minds under the stress of events surrounding the Lord's very public execution; just as some positivists also might regard the many such appearances of Christ to his closest disciples to be only some collective mental construction, and not a fact of material reality. Also, such analytical assertions have been used by some non-believers to explain away, for example,

---

(2007) <u>Eusebius: The Church History</u>. Grand Rapids, Michigan: Kregel Publications, pp. 92, 106, 139. Eusebius (3:11, 32; 4:22) provides that Clopas was the Lord's relative, the brother of Joseph, and that the son of Clopas was Symeon (Simon), who was selected by the Apostles to succeed James as the second Bishop of Jerusalem, after the martyrdom of James; and Simon too was subsequently martyred. The inferential supposition is that the unnamed disciple had been the son of Cleopas. Maria Valtorta's account of the Lord with the disciples at Emmaus (Chapter 621) also provides Cleopas and Simon as names for the two disciples; however, in Maria Valtorta's account, Simon seems to have a different relationship to Cleopas than the father-son relationship and relatives of the Lord specified by Eusebius: "I am Cleopas, the son of Cleopas, and he is Simon, both from Emmaus, and relatives [to each other], because I am the husband of his oldest daughter [son-in-law and father-in-law], and we were disciples of the Prophet." In both accounts, the names for both disciples may be reconciled, but not their relationships. Luke's "anonymous" disciple is theologically preferred.

38 1 Corinthians 15:5; Mark 16:12, Luke 24:13-15, 33-34
39 John 20:19, 24, Luke 24:36-37, 42-43, Acts 10:41
40 Matthew 27:51-53, Revelation 20:5-6, 11-15

the 20th Century series of apparitions of Our Lady involving three shepherd children at Fatima, Portugal, initially on 13th May in 1917, with its related 13th October report of a so-called spinning "solar phenomena" observed by the crowds, all within the collective and experiential context of World War I, but which dried their rain-soaked clothes in ten minutes.

And such materialistic rationalism might be applied, as well, by sceptics to other alleged supernatural events within the traumatic context of human wars: to the earlier apparitions of Our Lady at Lourdes, France, to Bernadette Soubirous in 1858, at a time of war and social turbulence between France and Germany; and starting from 1981, to the apparitions of the Madonna to six children at Medjugorje, Yugoslavia, preceding and during its civil war. Also, sceptics may be inclined by similar logic to reject the multiple apparitions of the Lord to Saint Paul,[41] and they may attribute his famous conversion experience, as Saul, to the self-induced psychological stresses of Saul's pro-Pharisee and anti-Christian persecutions. Likewise, too, sceptics may want to reject the truth of the Lord's apparition as the Divine Mercy to Sister Maria Faustina Kowalska,[42] and rather than as authentic, they also may prefer to reject her Diary, explained as given over to imagination within the emotionally turbulent context of 1931-1938 pre-World-War-II Poland. Or, once again, sceptics similarly may disregard the manifestation and revelation of the Gospel in the "visions" and "dictations" of the bed-ridden shut-in, Maria Valtorta,[43] which Maria first began to write from her home in Viareggio, Italy, on Good Friday, 23rd April 1943, also under conditions of war; and her masterwork from Our Lord was concluded then only on the 8th December 1951,[44] on Mary's great feast of her Immaculate Conception, ninety-seven years after its solemn papal declaration. As I am writing this at 60 years of age, it now seems likely to me [but it would be only a temporary conclusion] that the conclusion of this manuscript also will fall on 8th December 2008, simultaneous with the date of my wedding to Joan Zammit at St.

---

41   Acts 26:12-18, 9:3, 16, 23:6, 11; 2 Corinthians 12:1-10
42   John 20:19-21, 14:1
43   John 21:24-25
44   John 10:4, 27, Matthew 25:20

Barbara's Church, Valletta, after our first fifteen years together, the Lord's gift to us.[45]

Truly, a number of human experiences are well explained by the mental combinations of imagination and desire in the human psyche, and these have been described properly, that is, adequately and scientifically, as hallucinations, an explanation readily available, even to classical psychiatry, in 1853.[46] However, some persons even may find any concept of a supernatural or divine intervention in human affairs, whether to Adam and Eve,[47] Noah,[48] Abraham,[49] Isaac,[50] Jacob,[51] or to Moses,[52] before the Age of Christ, or to anyone during the time of Christ, or to anyone today in the Last Age,[53] to be beyond their primary belief in the existence of only a natural world.[54] But, to actively and utterly maintain such a belief requires the denial of any and every possible personal experience of God in one's life, a personal God who loves us;[55] precludes any recognition of the Creator in nature;[56] dismisses anyone's need of, or desire for, or actual experience of, God in prayer;[57] refuses the use

---

45   Genesis 1:27; Ephesians 4:7-8, John 15:12, 17
46   Brierre de Boismont, Alexandre-Jacques-Francois (1853/1976). Hallucinations, or The Rational History of Apparitions, Visions, Dreams, Ecstasy, Magnetism, and Somnambulism. Philadelphia: Lindsay and Blakiston [Reprinted New York: Arno Press].
47   Genesis 3:14-15, Revelation 12:1-9
48   Genesis 6:8-18, 9:8-17
49   Genesis 12:1, 15:1-6, 18:1-2, 22:1-2, 11-18
50   Genesis 26:1-5, 23-25
51   Genesis 28:10-18, 31:3, 32:2-4, 23-31, 33:18-20, 35:1-15
52   Exodus 3:1-6, 11-12, 19:1-6, 20, 24:3-4, 14-18; Exodus 32:15-19, 30, 33:1, 7-11, 12-23, 34:1-2, 6-10, 28-35; Deuteronomy 4:10-20, 9:7-29, 18:13-19; Exodus 34:19, Luke 9:28-31, Exodus 33:19-23, Luke 9:34-35, Deuteronomy 18:19, Luke 9:36, John 5:45-47, 14:10, 24, Luke 9:26, 24:44, John 6:67-69
53   Hebrews 9:26-28, 1 Thessalonians 5:1-3, Matthew 24:42-44, 1 Corinthians 1:4-8, Galatians 4:4, Ephesians 1:10, Matthew 28:20
54   1 John 2:15-17; 1 Corinthians 15:19; 1 Timothy 4:8-10
55   1 John 4:9-10
56   Romans 1:18-20
57   1 Thessalonians 5:17; Luke 6:12, 9:28, 11:1-2, 18:1, 5-8; Philippians 4:6-7, Ephesians 6:18-20, Colossians 4:2-4, 1 Thessalonians 5:25; 1 Peter 4:7-10, Romans 12:11-13

and grace of any of the Lord's institutional sacraments;[58] excludes any reading of, listening to, or active living of the scriptures;[59] and also, in a world that either substitutes God for faith in man, or in disillusionment with man altogether, it fails to trust in God; this belief, whether in a so-called distant, or absent, or non-existent God, by its own pernicious bias, undermines any sincere, but fragile faith,[60] while also it seeks to eliminate any conscientious effort by searching souls to discern the active Spirit of God in our noisy, everyday lives.[61]

Yet, for the Lord's closest disciples, especially among his earliest and specifically chosen apostles, just as the Lord also continues to choose us today to be his disciples and "little" apostles,[62] they often were the most critical and pragmatic of rational sceptics: like the two apostles and saints, Thomas and Paul. Thomas, who was called "Didymus" (the Twin), and who was one of the Twelve, was not with the remaining disciples when Jesus had come to them on Easter evening.[63] So, when the other ten disciples told Thomas, "We have seen the Lord," he refused to believe them and said, "Unless I can see the holes that the nails made in his hands and I can put my finger into the nail marks; and unless I can put my hand into his side; I will not believe."[64] And then, as for Paul, his threats to slaughter the Lord's disciples, and with them the Body of Christ, was so extreme that, as Saul, he even pursued so-called "Followers of the Way" out of Israel and into foreign cities.[65] However, apart from their rational and critical scepticism, the first disciples of the Lord also shared in the heritage of their vital faith: belief in God's true revelation of his covenants with his chosen people, revealed to Abraham and through Moses and all the prophets,[66] and demonstrated through the signs

---

58 Mathew 28:19-20; Luke 22:19-20, John 6:54-55; John 20:21-23; John 16:7, Luke 24:49, Acts 2:1-4
59 Hebrews 4:12
60 Mark 4:14-20
61 John 3:5, 1 Corinthians 12:4-7; John 6:64-65; Mark 4:14-20
62 John 15:16, 1-2; Acts 10:42-43
63 John 20:24
64 John 20:25
65 Acts 7:51, 55-60, 8:1-3, 9:1-4, 26:9-11; 1 Corinthians 12:27-30, 12-14
66 Matthew 5:17; Luke 16:29-31, 18:31, 24:25-27; John 1:45; Acts 26:22,

of his power and glory,[67] that God would establish an everlasting covenant of peace with Israel through King David's descendant,[68] the Messiah, the Christ.[69]

Many of the disciples were fishermen, and they too were rational men who well understood the nature of the sea,[70] the necessary skills of seamanship, and the practical judgments of fishing;[71] and yet, along with their rational judgment, their faith seemed always to need constant encouragement from the Lord.[72] And after the Lord, their anticipated Messiah, had been crucified, they also, rationally so, hid in fear for their own lives;[73] and they never imagined, not even once, the quite unthinkable and that which they were afraid to ask from Jesus, although some of them had quietly discussed what it might mean,[74] that he would be raised from the dead,[75] even though they had witnessed such miracles, raising the dead to life,[76] and although, but only afterwards, they remembered that Jesus precisely had said this.[77] And as rational men, when once before the Lord had walked to them upon the Sea of Galilee in the dark of night,[78] and now after the resurrection of the Lord, when Jesus had appeared to the Eleven, less Thomas; at first, on both of these

---

28:23
67   Exodus 3:3-6, 6:2-5, 11:1, 4-7, 12:1, 14, 12-13, 42, Ephesians 2:13-18, Hebrews 9:14-15, 24-28; Exodus 13:21-22, 14:19-27, John 14:6; Exodus 16:4-8, John 6:30-31, 48-51; Exodus 17:1-7, John 7:37-39; Exodus 19:9-11, John 1:6-8, 29-34; Exodus 19:16-25, 20:1, 18-22, Luke 9:22, 28-36; Exodus 24:1-11, Luke 24:36-43, Acts 10:39-43, Revelation 21:2-3, 10-22, Hebrews 12:18-25, 9:11-14
68   Acts 1:6
69   Deuteronomy 34:10, 18:13-19, Galatians 3:16, 19-29, Genesis 12:7, 17:19, 26:1-6, Romans 4:2-3, 13-17; 2 Samuel 7:5, 8-13, 27-29, 1 Kings 6:1, 12-14, 8:24-27, John 2:17-22, Luke 20:41-44, Mark 11:8-11, Matthew 21:9
70   Luke 8:22-25
71   Luke 5:4-5, John 21:3-6
72   Luke 17:5-6
73   John 20:19, 16:32
74   Mark 9:30-32, Luke 9:44-45
75   Luke 9:22, 18:33-34, John 20:9
76   Mark 5:38-43; Luke 7:11-15; John 11:32-44
77   Luke 9:22, 43-45, 24:6-8
78   John 6:19, Mark 6:49, Matthew 14:28

occasions, they thought that they were seeing a ghost.[79]

Now, however, they actually were seeing a new kind of body in the risen Lord: it was unbounded by the normal and usual natural rules of materiality—a risen body not restricted by closed doors, nor by stony unbelieving hearts;[80] not restricted by limitations of space and distance, nor by any estrangement from God through sin or by the absence of faith; not restricted by the constraints of time, for the eternal God is always present, ever present to the hearts of those who seek him; and nearly always, at first, Jesus was not recognized as the Lord;[81] but he was noticed in the signs of his wounds, or in the breaking of the bread, or in a spoken word; whom also we find in Christ, as we share in the suffering, and hunger, and discourse of our loving relationships for all of our brothers and sisters of this world,[82] and which we also find in our loving relationships with those departed who already dwell with God in the next world. The body of the risen Lord also was a spiritual body—sometimes it was displayed in its greater or lesser glory of the resurrection, which even then in the Lord's transfiguration before Peter, James, and John on the mountain had been only a partial manifestation of his coming glory[83]—a spiritual body totally united with a renewed material body, never more like our frail bodies to die, or to grow old, or to be sick; never again a weary or tired body, nevermore a body with its need for sleep.[84] The risen body of Christ, united with its soul, breathed; its thoughts were conscious, not brain-dead; it spoke; it ate real food;[85] and it was fully alive and awake, anywhere and simultaneously in the present world;[86] and yet, it was also a material and spiritual body, fully informed and infused by the spirit of God in the kingdom of heaven;[87] and also, the risen Christ was, and is,

---

79 Luke 24:37
80 John 20:19, Luke 24:38, Mark 16:14
81 John 20:6; Luke 24:15-16, Mark 16:2, John 21:8
82 Matthew 25:37-40, 1 Corinthians 13:3, Romans 12:5
83 Matthew 17:2, Luke 9:32, Revelation 1:12-18, 1 Corinthians 13:12, Revelation 21:22-23
84 1 Corinthians 15:42-44, 1 John 3:2
85 Luke 24:42-43, John 21:9
86 1 Corinthians 15:6
87 1 John 1:3

in full communion with all the saints, both in heaven and alive in us, on the earth.[88]

On Easter Sunday, on the first day of the Lord's resurrection, the risen Christ, at first, had shown himself on six distinct occasions to various disciples. There would be no other more immediate manifestations of the risen Lord; that is, not until exactly one week had passed, when again on our Sunday, according to the day of the Lord's new creation on the first day of the week, and now the eighth day of Easter: the disciples were in the house again, and this time Thomas was with them.[89] Although the doors were closed once more, nonetheless Jesus came into the room and he stood among them, and he said, "Peace be with you."[90] And there, in front of Thomas, once again Jesus showed them the wounds of his hands and in his side. And then Jesus spoke to Thomas, as the Shepherd who speaks to one of his bewildered lambs:[91]

> Put your finger here and see my hands. Give me your hand and put it into my side. Do not be unbelieving anymore, but believe.[92]

Ten days earlier, in the same room of the Last Supper,[93] Thomas had said to Jesus, "Lord, we do not know where you are going; so how can we know the way?"[94] Now, the Lord's earlier answer to that question from Thomas stood before his eyes, "I am the Way; I am Truth and Life."[95] And now, Thomas replied in his confession of faith, "My Lord and my God!"[96] Then Jesus told Thomas:

> You have come to believe because you can see me. Blessed are those who have not seen, and yet have

---

88	Ephesians 4:13, 15-16, Matthew 25:21, 23, Revelation 5:13, 7:9-10, 15-17, 22:3-5
89	John 20:26; Acts 1:13; Mark 14:15, Luke 22:12
90	John 20:26; John 20:19
91	John 10:14-15, Matthew 18:12, Luke 15:4; Ezekiel 34:11-12
92	John 20:27
93	Luke 22:11
94	John 14:5
95	John 14:6; John 11:25
96	John 20:28

believed.[97]

For believers and for sceptics alike, the risen Christ is not to be found by looking backwards into the tomb, like some archaeologist;[98] nor is he to be found by dwelling in the sad personal experience of our occasional, and inevitable, life-tragedies.[99] For, the risen person of Christ is seated in heaven in his power and glory at the right hand of the Father,[100] where now Christ hears our prayers.[101] Yet, also, the risen person of Christ is with us now,[102] just as truly as he stood among his disciples and gave them his post-resurrection blessing of peace.[103] For the living and risen Christ also is to be found on earth: within his church,[104] in our faith,[105] and in our direct and personal experience of the power of the Lord's death and resurrection in our personal lives,[106] and in our experience of the risen Lord through our fellowship and communion within the community of believers.[107]

Implicitly one week later on, on the fifteenth day of Easter, Jesus again revealed himself to his disciples.[108] This was now the third time, after rising from the dead, that Jesus would reveal himself to the disciples.[109] And according to the risen Lord's instructions, they had gone on, then, to Galilee.[110] So, it was by the Sea of Tiberias (the Sea of Galilee, or the Lake of Gennesaret); and it happened

---

97   John 20:29; Luke 10:23-24; 2 Corinthians 5:7
98   John 20:6-7, 11
99   Job 3:1, 11-16, 7:6-10; John 11:21, Job 23:8-10; Matthew 8:20, Luke 11:9-13, 6:47-49
100 Matthew 26:63-64
101 Hebrews 2:18, 7:25
102 Revelation 1:17, 21:5-6, 22:1; John 4:10-14, 7:37-38, Ezekiel 47:1, 48:35
103 John 20:19, 26; Isaiah 7:14, Matthew 1:23, Luke 2:10-14, Revelation 21:3, Ephesians 2:17, John 14:27
104 Mark 13:21-23, John 1:35-42, Matthew 16:16-18; Acts 9:36-40, Mark 5:41, Luke 8:40-42, 49-56, Matthew 9:25-26, Acts 9:41-42, John 11:41-48; Romans 8:9-11, 12:3-9, 14:7-9
105 Philippians 3:9
106 Philippians 3:10-11; 1 Timothy 1:14-16
107 1 Corinthians 10:16-17; 1 Thessalonians 2:13, Ephesians 1:19-20
108 John 21:1
109 John 21:14
110 Matthew 28:7, 10

like this.[111] Seven of the disciples were together by the sea: Simon Peter,[112] Thomas called the Twin,[113] Nathanael (or Bartolomew) from Cana in Galilee,[114] the sons of Zebedee (James and John),[115] and also together with them there were two more of his disciples.[116] Preceding this early morning appearance, on the night before, Simon Peter had decided and said, "I'm going fishing;" and the others, agreeing with him, replied, "We'll also come with you."[117] However, when they went out and got into the boat, as sometimes may happen according to my own experience when my grandfather and I have gone fishing, they had caught nothing that night.[118]

In the morning, when already it was becoming light, Jesus was standing there on the shore, although the disciples did not realize that it was Jesus.[119] Jesus called out to them:

> Friends,[120] haven't you caught anything yet?[121]

And they answered him, "No."[122] Then, as they were offshore in the boat coming in from their night of useless fishing, Jesus told them:

> Throw the net out to starboard, over the right side of the boat, and you'll find something.[123]

So, they cast the net out and they could not pull it in because of the quantity of fish.[124] At this moment, the disciple whom Jesus

---

111   John 21:1
112   John 21:2; John 1:42, 13:36, Luke 24:34
113   John 21:2; John 20:27-28
114   John 21:2; John 1:47-51
115   John 21:2; Mark 3:17, 5:37, 9:2, 13:3, 14:33
116   John 21:2
117   John 21:3
118   John 21:3; Luke 5:1-5
119   John 21:4; Luke 24:15-16
120   John 15:15; 1 John 3:1-2
121   John 21:5
122   John 21:5
123   John 21:6; Luke 5:4-5
124   John 21:6; Luke 5:6

loved [John] said to Peter, "It is the Lord."[125]   At these words, "It is the Lord," Peter quickly tied his outer garment around himself (for he was completely naked), and he jumped into the sea.[126]

Then, the other disciples came on in their second boat; and they assisted in towing the net with the fish to shore, as the first boat was only about 200 cubits [90 metres or 100 yards] from land.[127] And as soon as they came ashore, they saw that a charcoal fire was there with some fish cooking on it, and that also there was some bread.[128] Jesus said to them:

> Bring over some of the fish you have just caught.[129]

So Simon Peter went aboard the boat and dragged the net ashore, full of large fish, one hundred and fifty-three of them; and even though there were so many, the net was not broken.[130] Then Jesus told them:

> Come, and have some breakfast.[131]

Even in the Lord's transformed appearance, none of the disciples dared to ask him, "Who are you?" for they knew quite well that he was the Lord.[132] Jesus then stepped forward; he took the bread and gave it to them, and likewise the fish.[133] When they had finished breakfast, Jesus then said to Simon Peter:

> Simon, son of John, do you love me more than these others?[134]

And Peter answered, "Yes, Lord, you know that I love you."[135]

---

125   John 21:7
126   John 21:7; Luke 5:8, Matthew 14:28-32, Mark 4:38-39, Luke 8:22, 24:46-47, Acts 1:8
127   John 21:8; Luke 5:7
128   John 21:9; John 6:9-13, Mark 6:44; Luke 24:30
129   John 21:10; Matthew 14:15-18
130   John 21:11; Luke 5:9-10
131   John 21:12; John 6:27-35
132   John 21:12; John 20:19-21
133   John 21:13; Luke 22:19, 24:41-43
134   John 21:15; John 18:17
135   John 21:15; John 14:15

And he said to him:

> Feed my lambs.[136]

A second time Jesus said to him:

> Simon, son of John, do you love me?[137]

And he replied, "Yes, Lord, you know that I love you."[138] Jesus said to him:

> Look after my sheep.[139]

Then for a third time he said to him:

> Simon, son of John, do you love me?[140]

Peter was hurt that Jesus asked him a third time, "Do you love me?" and he said, "Lord, you know everything; you know that I love you."[141] Jesus said to him:

> Feed my sheep.[142]

Then Jesus said to Peter:

> Amen, in all truth I tell you, when you were young, you put on your own belt and walked where you liked; but when you grow old, you will stretch out your hands; and someone else will put a belt around you and lead you where you would rather not go.[143]

In these words he signified the kind of death by which Peter would glorify God; and after this Jesus said:

> Follow me.[144]

---

136 John 21:15; John 10:7, 2-5, 6:48-51
137 John 21:16; John 18:25
138 John 21:16; John 14:21
139 John 21:16; John 10:12-13, Luke 15:4, John 10:14-15
140 John 21:17; John 18:26-27
141 John 21:17; John 14:22-23
142 John 21:17; John 10:16
143 John 21:18; Luke 9:24-26
144 John 21:19; John 12:32, 13:36-38, 6:57-58, 12:26, Luke 5:11, 9:23

With Jesus in the lead along the shore, Peter turned and saw the disciple following whom Jesus loved—the one [John] who had leaned back close to his chest at the supper and had said to him, "Master, who is the one who will betray you?"[145] Seeing him, Peter said to Jesus, "What about him Lord?"[146] Jesus answered:

> If I want him to remain until I come, what does that matter to you? You are to follow me.[147]

The rumour then went out among the brothers that this disciple would not die.[148] But Jesus had not said to Peter, "He will not die," but rather, "If I want him to stay until I come."[149] The Lord clearly intended more than John's "staying around" until the Lord appeared. The present active infinitive "to stay" in John's Greek text is μένειν [menein],[150] the same verb μείνατε [meinate], aorist active imperative second-person plural used earlier by the Lord,[151] meaning you "abide, remain, stay," also conveyed by the sense of the Lord's statement, "On that day, you will know that I am in my Father, and you in me, and I in you,"[152] whereby mutually we "abide" in God's love, and he "abides" in us.[153] Jesus wanted the disciple John to "remain" as he had been at the Last Supper, pressed against the breast of Jesus,[154] in that very position: close to him, so as to listen to the heart of Jesus and to his will.[155] Then, Jesus says, "we [the persons of God] will come and abode [μονήν monēn] with him."[156] The concept of "abide" and "abode" are derived from the same root verb, μένω [meno], which also has been applied by those called

---

145 John 21:20; John 13:23-25
146 John 21:21
147 John 21:22; Matthew 8:19-22, Luke 9:57-62; Matthew 19:21-22, 27-29, Luke 18:22-23, 28-30
148 John 21:23; Mark 9:1, Matthew 16:28, Luke 9:27
149 John 21:23; Revelation 22:20, 12-15
150 John 21:22-23
151 John 15:4, 9; John 21:15-17
152 John 14:20
153 John 15:9-10, 14:21; Ephesians 3:19
154 John 13:23, 21:20
155 John 15:12, 14:23
156 John 14:23

"Mennonites,"[xvi] by all who "abide in the Lord" until he comes.[157]

Later on, while the eleven disciples were still in Galilee, they also set out to the mountain where Jesus had arranged to meet them.[158] When they saw him [there on Mount Tabor, most likely on a Sunday, on the 36th day of Easter], they fell down in worship, although some of them, in their struggling comprehension and lingering incredulity, still hesitated.[159] But then, Jesus approached near to them and, with an intimately tender and deeply felt love, he wholeheartedly and fervently spoke to them,[160] saying:

> All power in heaven and earth has been given to me.[161] Go, therefore,[162] go out to the whole world and proclaim the gospel to all creation;[163] and make disciples of all nations; baptizing them in the name of the Father and of the Son and of the Holy Spirit,[164] and teaching them to observe all of the commands I gave you.[165] Whoever believes and is baptized will be saved; whoever does not believe will be condemned.[166] These signs will accompany those who believe: in my name they will cast out devils;[167] they will have the gift of tongues;[168] they will pick up snakes in their hands and be unharmed if they should drink deadly poison;[169] they will lay their hands on the sick, and they shall recover.[170] And behold, I am with you always; yes, to the end of time.[171]

---

157 John 21:22
158 Matthew 28:16
159 Matthew 28:17
160 Matthew 9:36-37
161 Matthew 28:18; Ephesians 1:10
162 Matthew 28:19
163 Mark 16:15
164 Matthew 28:19
165 Matthew 28:20
166 Mark 16:16; Luke 10:10-12
167 Mark 16;17; Luke 6:12-13, Mark 3:13-15, Luke 9:1-2, Mark 6:12-13
168 Mark 16:17; 1 Corinthians 14:1-5, 13-19
169 Mark 16:18; Acts 28:3-6
170 Mark 16:18; Luke 9:1-2, 10:1, 9, Mark 6:12-13, James 5:14-15
171 Matthew 28:20

Then Jesus also told them:

> Look, this is what I meant when I spoke to you when I was still with you, that everything written about me in the Law of Moses, in the Prophets and in the Psalms, was destined to be fulfilled.[172]

And then he opened their minds to understand the scriptures,[173] saying to them:

> Thus it is written that the Christ would suffer and on the third day rise from the dead,[174] and that in his name, repentance for the forgiveness of sins would be preached to all the nations, beginning from Jerusalem.[175] You are witnesses to these things.[176] And now I am sending upon you what the Father has promised; so stay in the city until you are clothed with the power from on high.[177]

And with those spoken words, which are the central core of the gospel message,[178] Jesus temporarily left them; and immediately, the eleven disciples returned to Jerusalem. After they had returned there, again to the upper room,[179] they heard of how the risen Lord had appeared to more than five hundred brothers at a single moment;[180] and how afterwards, the Lord also had appeared to James,[181] the sceptical relative of the Lord,[182] who later would become the primary elder and first bishop of Jerusalem.[183] Saint Paul also indicates that after the Lord's appearance to James, the risen Christ then had

---

172   Luke 24:44; Luke 24:27, 9:22, 4:14-22; Acts 24:14
173   Luke 24:45
174   Luke 24:46
175   Luke 24:47
176   Luke 24:48
177   Luke 24:49; John 14:26, 15:26, 16:13
178   Ephesians 1:3-7; Mark 1:14-15
179   Luke 22:11-12
180   1 Corinthians 15:6
181   1 Corinthians 15:7
182   Mark 6:3, 3:21, John 7:5
183   Acts 15:13, 21:19, James 1:1

appeared to "all of the apostles,"[184] beyond the Twelve, Paul in this case meaning many of the others who were, or who would become pillars of the early Christian community. Also among those who were favoured to see the risen Lord, there was Joseph of Arimathaea: for, as Saint Ignatius of Loyola notes in the Spiritual Exercises, this event is read in the Lives of the Saints and may be piously believed. After the Ascension of the Lord, and last of all, the risen Lord appeared to Saint Paul, as if to one born abnormally;[185] and even if Paul, by his admission, was the least of the apostles because of his initial persecution of the church,[186] nonetheless, also through God's grace, he would become the great apostle of the Lord to the Gentiles;[187] moreover, later on, even to the most passionate centre of his soul, Paul would long for, and fervently he would pray for, the Christian conversion of all his Jewish brothers and sisters.[188]

In the 20th Century gospel of Maria Valtorta ("Little John"), Maria also portrays other specific Easter apparitions of the Risen Christ. Accordingly, on Easter Day, Jesus appears individually to Lazarus[189] and to Joanna, wife of Chuza;[190] the risen Christ appears to the collective of Joseph of Arimathaea,[191] with Nicodemus[192] (and Manaen[193]); then, the Lord makes another appearance to the group of shepherds from Christmas Day;[194] and then, individually, the Lord appears to Martha the sister of Lazarus,[195] and also he appears in special "gifts" to the various Gentile acquaintances of Martha and of the women from Galilee, who had accompanied the Lord throughout, where the concluding "gift" from the Lord's appearance to Martha was the peaceful and joyful knowledge of her death and

---

184   1 Corinthians 15:7, 1:9
185   1 Corinthians 15:8; John 3:3-8
186   1 Corinthians 15:9
187   Romans 1:1-5; Mark 9:35, Luke 22:24-27, Matthew 23:1, 8-12
188   Romans 9:1-5
189   John 11:1-5, Luke 10:38-39, John 11:43-44, 12:1, 9-11
190   Luke 8:2-3, 23:49, 24:9-10, 33-34
191   Luke 23:50-51, John 19:38, Mark 15:43, Matthew 27:59-60
192   John 3:1-2, 7:50-52, 19:39-40
193   Luke 10:1-2
194   Luke 2:7-16, 20, 19:37-38, 24:36
195   Luke 10:38-42, John 11:1, 17-28, 39-40

of her eventual wedding nuptials. These special favours of the risen Lord are plausible for all of these individuals.

But these suggested appearances may be confirmed as fact only if Maria's gospel is a revelation from the Lord,[xvii] as it truly seems to be.[196] Her post-resurrection accounts, those provided in my present annotation, seem to be consistent with the truth of the gospel. Then, besides those above "gifts," also in Maria Valtorta's "visions and dictations," Maria provides yet another twenty-one specific accounts of the risen Christ, apparently drawn from among the several hundreds of the Lord's post-resurrection appearances.[197] According to Valtorta's editors, these appearances of the risen Christ had taken place in the week after the Lord's second appearance to the disciples with Thomas present,[198] but before the Lord's third appearance to the seven disciples on the lake shore in Galilee,[199] that is, during the specific time-frame when the eleven disciples had been in Galilee and away from Jerusalem.

However, from the mountain in Galilee,[200] those disciples had returned immediately to Jerusalem, such that on the 40th day of Easter,[201] that was, on the Thursday, the Lord then rejoins with them during that day, there in the upper room. While the risen Christ was at table with them, he also was present with them, implicitly, as he celebrated Eucharist; and he told them not to leave Jerusalem, but to wait there for what the Father had promised: he had said:

> It is what you have heard me speaking about:[202] for John baptized with water, but in a few days from now, you are going to be baptized with the Holy Spirit.[203]

Then, after Jesus had spoken to them,[204] he took them out of

---

196	Ephesians 4:11-13
197	1 Corinthians 15:6
198	John 20:26
199	John 21:1
200	Matthew 28:16
201	Acts 1:3
202	Acts 1:4; Luke 24:49, John 15:26
203	Acts 1:5; John 1:33
204	Mark 16:19

the city to the Mount of Olives, as far as the nearby outskirts of Bethany.[205] After they had gathered together, they then asked him, "Lord, has the time come now for you to restore the kingdom to Israel?"[206] And Jesus answered them:

> It is not for you to know times or dates that the Father has established by his own authority,[207] but you will receive the power when the Holy Spirit comes upon you, and then you will be my witnesses not only in Jerusalem but throughout Judea and Samaria, and indeed, to the remotest ends of the earth.[208]

As he said this,[209] he raised his hands and blessed them;[210] and as he blessed them, he was taken up to heaven while they looked on,[211] and a cloud took him from their sight;[212] and there in heaven at the right hand of God he took his place.[213] They were still staring into the sky as he was going, when suddenly two men in white were standing beside them.[214] They said:

> Men of Galilee: why are you standing there looking up into the sky? This Jesus who has been taken up from you into heaven will return in the same way as you have seen him going to heaven.[215]

Then walking from the Mount of Olives, as it is called, only a short distance away, no more than a Sabbath walk,[216] they went back

---

205　Luke 24:50; John 11:18, Acts 1:12
206　Acts 1:6; John 1:41, 47-49, 6:15, 26, 11:47-50, 12:12-13, Mark 11:9-10, John 18:33-36, Luke 22:37-38, 1:68-75
207　Acts 1:7; Matthew 24:36
208　Acts 1:8; Matthew 24:14
209　Acts 1:9
210　Luke 24:50
211　Luke 24:51, Mark 16:19, Acts 1:9; John 6:62, 56-62
212　Acts 1:9; Luke 9:34
213　Mark 16:19
214　Acts 1:10; Luke 24:2-4;
215　Acts 1:11; Luke 24:5-7; John 1:51, Genesis 28:10-12, 20-22, Ephesians 1:8-13; Matthew 24:30-31, 1 Thessalonians 4:16-18, Matthew 28:19-20
216　Acts 1:12

to Jerusalem as the Lord had instructed them;[217] when they reached the city, straightaway they went to the upper room where they had been staying.[218]

Therefore, there now were Peter and John, James and Andrew, Philip and Thomas, Bartholomew (Nathanael) and Matthew, James son of Alphaeus and Simon the Zealot, and Jude son of James.[219] And all of these devoted themselves with one heart in prayer;[220] and together with them after the Lord's Ascension at the centre of this pre-nascent church, at its heart there was Mary the mother of Jesus whom they embraced, as she also embraced them, and as she continues to embrace the church of her Son today, that include the various signs of her manifestations in the world;[221] and together with the Eleven, soon to be made Twelve again, in the essential integrity of the future church, there also were the women companions from Galilee;[222] also there were a number of the Lord's relatives;[223] most notably for the soon to emerge Christian community in Jerusalem, there was James.[224] All of them in this initial core group had been privileged to experience the risen Christ directly; just as, equally, all had known Christ intimately in the power of his forgiveness of their sins:[225] and of all forgiven sinners, like those of us who serve the Lord in the experience of his forgiveness of our sins through Christ's death and resurrection, perhaps the most well known forgiven sinners to us, excluding our own self-knowledge, are three of its saints and

---

217	Luke 24:49; John 16:7
218	Acts 1:13; Luke 22:10-12
219	Acts 1:13; Luke 6:13-16
220	Acts 1:14; Luke 6:12
221	Acts 1:14
222	Acts 1:14; Luke 8:1-3, John 19:25, Matthew 28:9-10, Luke 24:9-11, 33-34, Matthew 16:18;
223	Acts 1:14
224	1 Corinthians 15:7
225	Ephesians 2:4-6, Luke 24:46-48, Acts 2:32-36, 37-39, John 15:27; Romans 3:23-24

"apostles:"[226] Mary of Magdala,[227] Simon Peter,[228] and Paul.[229]

But Mary, the mother of the Lord, and now as she also was the mother of the entire church among its group of founding apostles,[230] with her Son as its mystical head,[231] she was the most privileged person of all humanity: by her immaculate conception, first, she was conceived without sin through the grace of her Son and her God;[232] the child was conceived in her by the power of the Holy Spirit,[233] in what was, for her alone, the very first Pentecost from the Father;[234] then, she gave birth to the Lord;[235] and afterwards, Jesus, her Lord and her God, dwelled with her face to face in her private life at home for nearly thirty-three years;[236] yet, also from the beginning of her Son's public ministry, she always had been there on the prayerful sidelines and in the pragmatic background;[237] knowingly throughout her life, she shared intimately in the entire passion and death of her Son;[238] and lastly, she also had experienced her Son in his full risen glory on Easter Morning.[239] And now, as these founding apostles had gathered together, both the little "apostles" and the great ones, each one of them chosen by the Lord himself as his friends for their particular tasks of service,[240] as the pre-nascent church, they waited and prayed for the coming of the Holy Spirit that soon would come upon them: that now would be just ten days later, on the Day of

---

226 1 Corinthians 15:7; Mark 3:16; 1 Corinthians 15:8-9, Galatians 2:8, 1:11-12, Ephesians 3:3-8
227 Luke 7:36-38, John 19:25, 20:11-14
228 Luke 22:60-62, 32-34, 24:34
229 Acts 9:1-6, 1 Corinthians 15:3-4, 8, Acts 9:17-20
230 Revelation 21:14, 1 Corinthians 15:5, 7, 12:27-30, 4-7; John 19:26-27, 2 Corinthians 5:6, 8-9
231 1 Colossians 1:18
232 Luke 1:26-28
233 Luke 1:35
234 Acts 1:4, Luke 3:21-22, 1:30-33
235 Luke 2:4-7
236 Luke 2:39-40, 51-52, 1:46-49
237 John 2:5, Mark 3:31-32
238 Luke 2:34-35, John 19:25
239 John 20:30-31
240 John 15:15-16; Galatians 1:15-16

Pentecost, the 50th day of Easter.[241]

Readings: Acts 1:15-26, 2:1-13; Proverbs 8:1-36, Genesis 1:1-2, Ephesians 3:14-21; 1 Corinthians 12:4-11

Between Ascension Thursday and the Sunday morning of Pentecost, this ten-day period defines an essential and parallel contrast between Simon Peter and Judas Iscariot in their personal choices of service to God, or of respective disservice by abandonment: Peter, the rock and shepherd, would lead the church of Christ ably and wisely.[242] Accordingly, after some initial days of prayer, on one of the early days, perhaps on the Lord's Day one week before Pentecost, Peter stood up in the midst of the brethren—there were about one hundred and twenty persons [twelve (founding "apostles,"[243] or twelve new tribes of Israel) by ten = 120; Saint John, later on, also would describe the future product of the saints by tribes as 12 by 12000 = 144,000, plus a number of saints, impossible to count, from all the nations[244]] in the congregation,[245] and Peter said:

> Brothers, it was necessary for the passage in scripture to be fulfilled, which the Holy Spirit spoke beforehand through the mouth of David concerning the fate of Judas, who had guided those men who arrested Jesus.[246] He was numbered among us and shared in our ministry.[247] And as you know, he bought a plot of land with the money he received for his treachery, and there falling headlong, his insides burst open and were poured all over the ground.[248] This became widely known to everybody in Jerusalem, and so the plot of land came to be called in their language, "Hakeldama,"

---

241 Luke 24:49, Acts 2:1-3; John 16:13, 17:26, 14:12-17
242 Matthew 16:18, 21:42-43, John 21:15-16, Matthew 24:45
243 Revelation 21:14, 19
244 Revelation 7:5-9
245 Acts 1:15; Luke 10:1-2, 9:1-2, Revelation 21:14, 16-17
246 Acts 1:16; Luke 22:47; John 17:12, 8:44
247 Acts 1:17; Luke 6:12-14, 16, 9:1-2
248 Acts 1:18; Matthew 27:5

or "Field of Blood."[249] This was predicted in the Book of Psalms where it says: "Reduce his encampment to desolation, with no one left to dwell in it."[250] And again it says, "[May his life be cut short,] let someone else take his office."[251] So now, out of the men who had been with us that whole time that the Lord Jesus was with us,[252] from the time he was baptized by John until the day when he was taken up from us,[253] one person must be chosen,[254] along with the other Eleven,[255] to become a witness with us to his resurrection.[256]

And so, they nominated two candidates: Joseph, known as Barsabbas, who was also surnamed Justus; and Matthias.[257] And then they prayed:

> Lord, you know everyone's heart;[258] show us, therefore, which of these two you have chosen,[259] to take over the place in this apostolic ministry, which Judas abandoned to go to his own place.[260]

Next, when they had given lots to them, as the lot fell to Matthias, he then was counted as an apostle along with the other eleven;[261] so now there were twelve.

---

249   Acts 1:19; Matthew 27:6-8
250   Acts 1:20, Psalm 69:25
251   Acts 1:20; Psalm 109:8
252   Acts 1:21
253   Acts 1:22; Acts 10:36-38, Luke 3:21-22, 24:50-51
254   Acts 1:22
255   Acts 1:26
256   Acts 1:22; Luke 24:48, Acts 1:8, 2:32, 3:15, 5:32, 10:39-43, Luke 1:1-4; Acts 3:14, Mark 14:63, Matthew 26:65-66, Luke 11:48, 49-54; Acts 6:13-14, 7:51-54, 57-58
257   Acts 1:23
258   Acts 1:24; Mark 2:8, Matthew 9:4, Luke 5:22; Luke 16:15; John 4:29, 6:15, 64, 21:17; Hebrews 3:15, 4:7, Psalm 95:8-11; 1 Corinthians 4:5, 1 Thessalonians 3:13; 2 Corinthians 3:3, Romans 8:27, Philippians 4:6-7, Colossians 3:15; 1 Thessalonians 2:4
259   Acts 1:24
260   Acts 1:25; Mark 14:20-21, John 13:18, 12-20, 6-11
261   Acts 1:26

The initial group of disciples, who had gathered in the upper room,[262] and which only now also included Matthias, eventually would spend a full nine days together in prayer;[263] historically, this was the origin for the church's practice of a novena of prayers. Then afterwards, on the morning of the tenth day, after this select group of men and women "apostles" chosen by God would be gathered together for their morning prayers,[264] it soon would become Pentecost day.[265] Under Mosaic Law, the original Pentecost corresponded to the Harvest Feast, or the Festival of Weeks, that started on the fiftieth day: seven weeks after the time when one first began to put the sickle into the standing grains of wheat;[266] when, on the first day of the feast, on the day after the Sabbath, namely on the first day of the week, or on our Sunday, one celebrated the feast by presenting to Yahweh the first sheaf of the harvest,[267] which was a voluntary offering proportionate to the degree of God's blessings;[268] and also on the feast, one would rejoice in the presence of God, in the place that God had chosen as the dwelling place of his name.[269] This temple place now was Jerusalem, but soon God's dwelling place would be anywhere throughout the world, wherever the Spirit willed to go.[270]

But now, as Pentecost, the new Harvest Feast of the Lord, bringing in the grain for eternal life,[271] was about to begin, ultimately it would end only when the work of the harvest would be finished upon the earth.[272] And this feast would begin, not with the sound of trumpet blasts,[273] but now with the roar and fire of the divine

---

262   Acts 1:13-14
263   Acts 1:13-14
264   1 Corinthians 15:5-6
265   Acts 2:1; John 4:23-24, Acts 2:4-6
266   Exodus 23:16, Leviticus 23:15-16, Deuteronomy 16:9; John 4:35
267   Leviticus 23:9-11
268   Deuteronomy 16:10; Matthew 9:37, Luke 10:1-2, John 4:36-38
269   Deuteronomy 16:11; Romans 8:9, 1 Corinthians 3:16, 6:19, 16-17, John 14:23; Acts 7:44-50, Hebrews 8:10
270   John 3:8; 1 Corinthians 3:16
271   John 4:36; John 12:24
272   Revelation 14:14-16
273   Numbers 10:10

wind of the Holy Spirit;[274] and this work of the Spirit in our lives would not be over until the harvested wheat and the grapes of the vineyards of the earth were ripe at the end of time.[275] Then, for those souls harvested in God, there would be the final and eternal celebration of the Lord's Eucharist with him, for those who have been destined in their holiness from God to be in communion with him for all eternity.[276] And so now, with the coming of the Holy Spirit at Pentecost, the Lord, then, would be sending his labourers into the harvest.[277]

Suddenly, there came from heaven the noise as of a violent wind which filled the entire house where they were meeting;[278] and there appeared to them tongues of fire; these separated and came to rest on the head of each one of them.[279] And everyone present was filled with the Holy Spirit and they began to speak in different languages, as the Spirit gave them this power to express themselves.[280] Now, at that time, there were devout Jews living in Jerusalem from every nation under heaven.[281] At this mixture of sound, they all assembled in a large crowd, but each one of them was bewildered to hear these men only speaking in his own language.[282] They were astounded and amazed; and said:

> Surely, all of these men speaking are Galileans, aren't they?[283] So how is it that each of us hears him in his own native language?[284] We are Parthians, Medes, and Elamites; people from Mesopotamia, Judea and

---

274 Acts 2:2-4
275 Revelation 14:16-20
276 Luke 22:19-20, John 6:53-54; Matthew 22:2, 25:1-6, John 3:27-28, Ephesians 5:27, John 3:29-30, Galatians 2:20, Revelation 19:5-7, 21:2, 9-14, John 9:4; John 6:27-29, 35-40, 14:2, 6:65, Luke 2:14, John 12:26, 1 Corinthians 6:20, 14, 2 Thessalonians 2:13-14
277 Matthew 9:37-(38), Luke 10:2-3
278 Acts 2:2
279 Acts 2:3
280 Acts 2:4
281 Acts 2:5
282 Acts 2:6
283 Acts 2:7
284 Acts 2:8

Cappadocia, Pontus and Asia,[285] Phrygia and Pamphylia, Egypt and the parts of Libya around Cyrene; residents of Rome,[286] both Jews and Gentile converts to Judaism, Cretans and Arabs; and yet, we all hear them preaching in our language about the marvels of God.[287]

These continued to be astonished and perplexed as they asked one another, "What does this mean?"[288] But also, there were others who just simply laughed it off, saying, "They've drunk too much new wine."[289] Although everyone then had heard the twelve apostles preaching to them in his own language, only some of these men, perplexed as they now were, were seeking honest answers; the others simply scoffed in their disbelief. However, momentarily, Peter would be stepping forward alone, as the recognized leader of the church, just as the Pope also does today; and through the actions of the Spirit, anyone who obeyed God and listened in good faith would be hearing, with the gift of understanding from the Spirit, Peter addressing each of them in his own native tongue.[290] These, then, were men of the entire known world of that time.

They were Latin and Greek speaking, and also with the Holy Spirit's full respect to individual persons and the local cultures of nations,[291] they were vernacular speaking from the western Greco-Roman world of the currently vast empire of Rome and the former empire of Greece. And they were men from the East, the ancient centres of modern civilization: from Mesopotamia and the land of Eden,[292] and from as far away as the ancestral home of our righteous father in faith, of Abraham from Ur of the Chaldaeans, Elam;[293] and the Elamites were descendants of Shem, the son of Noah,[294] and after

---

285   Acts 2:9
286   Acts 2:10
287   Acts 2:11
288   Acts 2:12; Acts 1:8
289   Acts 2:13
290   Acts 5:32
291   Acts 2:8
292   Acts 2:9; Genesis 2:10-14
293   Acts 2:9; Genesis 11:26-31, Romans 4:1-3
294   Genesis 10:1, 22, 6:6-14; Luke 8:22

the Great Flood, Abraham was the first-born descendant of all the first-born descendants of Noah;[295] just as like Noah and Abraham, Christ now in his sole righteousness, as we are made righteous through his death, he is the first-born from the dead and, also in his resurrection from the dead and in the first fruits of the Spirit, for our sakes he is first-born of all the living;[296] so that now, forever and ever, Jesus is Lord of both the dead and of the living.[297]

They were men from the south: they were Arabs and North Africans from Egypt and Libya around Cyrene, home to the future disciples to the ancient seat of the church in Antioch, Syria: Simon, Rufus and Alexander, and Lucius.[298] And they were men from the north, today's Turkey, from its Mediterranean coastlands to the coasts of the Black Sea: home to Saint Paul of Tarsus in Cilicia,[299] and the other lands he evangelized,[300] including Asia Minor and their seven churches,[301] the seven golden lamp-stands for the Lord,[302] starting from the great church centred at Ephesus.[303] Today, that same evangelization of the world starts with us, if we are filled with the Holy Spirit.[304] Saint Paul constantly depended upon the Holy Spirit to tell him where to go in his missionary journeys;[305] and so also he rushed to Jerusalem, hoping to be there in time for the celebration of the great feast of Pentecost,[306] before the Holy Spirit guided him, at last, on to Rome in his chains.[307] And to this same purpose, both for evangelization and for guidance from the Holy Spirit, we now must turn to prayer.[308]

---

295   Genesis 11:10-26, Luke 3:34-36; Romans 4:16-17
296   Colossians 1:18, 1 Corinthians 15:20, 23
297   Romans 14:7-9; Luke 7:11-17, Mark 5:35-43, Acts 9:36-42, 20:7-12
298   Mark 15:21; Acts 11:20, Romans 16:13, Acts 13:1
299   Acts 9:28-30, 11:25-26, 21:39; Acts 15:36, 41
300   Acts 14:1, 6, 16:1, 6-7, 12, 17:1, 10, 16-18, 18:1
301   Revelation 2:1, 8, 12, 18, 3:1, 7, 14
302   Revelation 1:20, Matthew 5:14-16
303   Ephesians 1:13-14
304   1 John 2:27, 3:18-20, 24, 4:1-6
305   Acts 16:6-12
306   Acts 19:21-22, 20:16
307   Acts 21:33, 23:11, 24:20-23, 25:12, 26:6-8, 24-32; Ephesians 6:18-20
308   Acts 1:14, 2:1; Acts 4:29-31, 10:44-48, 19:1-7, 2:14-18; Luke 3:16, Matthew 28:19; 1 John 4:13

Reflective Prayer: Psalms 103:1-22; 47:1-9; 104:1-35

Antiphon: Bless the Lord, my soul;
>> never forget all he has done for you, alleluia.

> Bless the Lord, my soul;
>> from the depths of my being, bless his holy name.[309]
>
> Bless the Lord, my soul;
>> and never forget all his blessings.[310]
>
> He forgives all your guilt,
>> heals all your ills;[311]
>
> he redeems your life from the grave,
>> crowns you with faithful love and tenderness;[312]
>
> he fills you with good things all your life,
>> and renews your youth like an eagle's.[313]
>
> The Lord does deeds of righteousness,
>> brings justice to all the oppressed;[314]
>
> he revealed his ways to Moses,
>> his mighty deeds to the people of Israel.[315]
>
> The Lord is compassion and love,
>> slow to anger and rich in mercy;[316]
>
> his indignation does not last forever,
>> nor his resentment remain for all time;[317]
>
> he does not treat us according to our sins,
>> nor repay us as our deeds deserve.[318]

---

[309] Psalm 103:1; John 20:21
[310] Psalm 103:2; John 20:22
[311] Psalm 103:3; John 20:23-24
[312] Psalm 103:4; John 20:25
[313] Psalm 103:5; John 20:26; Deuteronomy 32:11
[314] Psalm 103:6; John 20:27
[315] Psalm 103:7; John 20:28-29
[316] Psalm 103:8; John 21:12
[317] Psalm 103:9; John 21:15
[318] Psalm 103:10; John 21:16

For as the heavens tower over the earth,
  so strong is his faithful love for those who fear him;[319]
As far as the east is from the west,
  such is the distance from us that he puts our faults.[320]
As tenderly as a father treats his children,
  so the Lord has compassion on those who fear him.[321]

For he knows of what we are made,
  he remembers that we are dust.[322]
As for man, his days are like the grass;
  he blooms like the flowers of the field;[323]
as soon as the wind blows, he is gone,
  never to be seen there again.[324]

But the Lord's faithful love is forever,
    for those who are faithful from age to age;
    his saving justice reaches out to their children's
       children;[325]
as long as they keep his covenant in truth,
    and carefully obey his commands.[326]

The Lord has fixed his throne in heaven;
  his sovereign power rules over all.[327]
Bless the Lord, all his angels,
   mighty warriors who fulfil his commands,
   attentive to his voice, and obedient to his words.[328]
Bless the Lord, all his armies,
   servants who do God's will.[329]

---

319 Psalm 103:11; John 21:17, Luke 24:44
320 Psalm 103:12; Luke 24:45-46
321 Psalm 103:13; Luke 24:47-48
322 Psalm 103:14; John 21:19
323 Psalm 103:15; John 21:20-21
324 Psalm 103:16; John 21:22
325 Psalm 103:17; Matthew 28:19
326 Psalm 103:18; Matthew 28:20
327 Psalm 103:19; Matthew 28:18
328 Psalm 103:20; Luke 24:49; Luke 24:4-8
329 Psalm 103:21; John 21:5-6; Matthew 28:2

Bless the Lord, all his creatures,
> every place where his dominion rests.
Bless the Lord, my soul!³³⁰

Antiphon: God ascends to shouts of joy,
> the Lord to trumpet blasts, alleluia.

All you peoples, clap your hands;
> cry to God with shouts of joy.³³¹
For the Lord, the Most High, is glorious,
> the great king over all the earth.³³²
He subdues peoples under us,
> brought nations under our feet.³³³
He chose a land for our inheritance,
> the glory of Jacob whom he loves.³³⁴

God mounts his throne amid shouts of joy;
> the Lord goes up to trumpet blasts.³³⁵
Sing praise to God, sing praise;
> sing praise to our king, sing praise.³³⁶
God is king of the whole world;
> learn the hymns, sing praise to God.³³⁷
God reigns over the nations;
> God sits upon his holy throne.³³⁸

The princes of the nations assemble
> with the people of the God of Abraham;
> for the rulers of the earth belong to God,
> who is enthroned on high.³³⁹

---

330   Psalm 103:22; Mark 16:15
331   Psalm 47:1; Acts 1:3; Revelation 7:9, Deuteronomy 32:43
332   Psalm 47:2; Luke 24:50-51; Revelation 7:10, Deuteronomy 32:40
333   Psalm 47:3; Acts 1:6, Hebrews 2:8-9; Revelation 7:11-12, Deuteronomy 32:41-42, Revelation 19:11-18
334   Psalm 47:4; Acts 1:7-8; Revelation 7:13-14, Deuteronomy 32:8-9
335   Psalm 47:5; Acts 1:9; Revelation 5:7-8, Numbers 10:1-4, 10
336   Psalm 47:6; Luke 24:52-53; Revelation 5:9-10, Deuteronomy 10:8; Exodus 19:6, 1 Peter 2:5, 9
337   Psalm 47:7; Acts 1:10; Revelation 5:11-12, Deuteronomy 10:12-13
338   Psalm 47:8; Acts 1:11; Revelation 5:13, Deuteronomy 10:14-19
339   Psalm 47:9; Acts 1:4-5; Revelation 5:14, Deuteronomy 10:20-22, Genesis

Antiphon: Alleluia, come Holy Spirit, fill the hearts of your faithful;
    and kindle in them the fire of your love, alleluia.

> Bless the Lord, my soul!
>   Lord God, how great you are,
>   clothed in majesty and splendour.[340]
> Wearing light as a robe,
>   you stretch out the heavens like a tent.[341]
>
> Above the rains you build your palace;
>   you make the clouds your chariot,
>   gliding on the wings of the wind.[342]
> You make the winds your messengers;
>   flames of fire, your servants.[343]
>
> You fixed the earth on its foundation,
>   to stand firm for ever and ever.[344]
> You covered it with the ocean like a garment,
>   the waters standing above the mountains.[345]
>
> At your command the waters fled,
>   at the sound of your thunder they took flight;[346]
> they flowed over the mountains and down the valleys,
>   to the place you had fixed for them;[347]
> you set a limit they were not to cross,
>   never more to return to cover the earth.[348]

    15:5-6
340   Psalm 104:1; Acts 1:13-14; Genesis 1:1-2
341   Psalm 104:2; Proverbs 8:27, John 1:2; Genesis 1:3-5
342   Psalm 104:3; Acts 2:1, John 1:1; Genesis 1:6-8
343   Psalm 104:4; Acts 2:2-3, Proverbs 8:30-31
344   Psalm 104:5; Matthew 28:20, Proverbs 8:25-26; Genesis 1:9-10, 6:17-18
345   Psalm 104:6; Proverbs 8:23-24; Genesis 6:19-20
346   Psalm 104:7; Proverbs 9:1, Isaiah 11:1-2; Genesis 8:1
347   Psalm 104:8; Proverbs 8:28; Genesis 8:2-5
348   Psalm 104:9; Proverbs 8:29; Genesis 9:8-11

You opened up springs that flow into the ravines
> that wind among the mountains;[349]
they provide water for all the beasts of the field,
> for the wild asses to quench their thirst;[350]
besides their flowing banks, the birds of the air make their nests;
> from among the leaves of the trees, they sing their songs.[351]

From your palace you water the mountains,
> satisfying the earth with the fruit of your works:[352]
you make the grass grow for the cattle;
> and for people the plants they need,
> to bring forth bread from the earth,[353]
and wine to cheer people's hearts,
> oil to gladden their faces,
> and food to build their strength.[354]

The trees of the Lord drink their fill,
> the cedars of Lebanon that you planted.[355]
There the birds build their nests,
> on the tree-tops the stork makes its home.[356]
On the mountains wild goats find a home;
> and in the crags of the rocks, badgers and coneys find refuge.[357]

Antiphon: Alleluia, the Spirit of the Lord has filled the whole world; send forth your Spirit and renew the face of the earth, alleluia.

---

[349] Psalm 104:10; John 7:37
[350] Psalm 104:11; John 7:38
[351] Psalm 104:12; John 7:39
[352] Psalm 104:13; Ephesians 4:10, Proverbs 8:22; Deuteronomy 32:1
[353] Psalm 104:14; Matthew 5:44-45, Hebrews 6:7-8; Deuteronomy 32:2, Luke 22:19, John 6:32-35, 57-58
[354] Psalm 104:15; Proverbs 8:35; Deuteronomy 32:13-14, Luke 22:20, John 6:53-56
[355] Psalm 104:16; John 4:9-10
[356] Psalm 104:17; John 4:23
[357] Psalm 104:18; John 4:21, 24

You made the moon to count the seasons;
> the sun knows its time for setting.[358]

You bring on darkness, and then night falls,
> when all the beasts of the forest roam about;[359]

young lions roar for their prey,
> and seek their food from God.[360]

At the rising of the sun, they steal away
> and go back to their dens to rest.[361]

Then man goes out to work,
> to labour until the evening falls.[362]

How varied are your works, O Lord!
> In wisdom you have made them all;
> the earth is full of your creatures.[363]

There is the sea, vast and wide!
> It teams with countless creatures,
> living things both great and small.[364]

There the ships ply their course;
> and Leviathan, your creature, is there to sport with.[365]

All of these depend on you
> to give them their food in due season.[366]

You give it to them, and they gather it up;
> your open hand insures that they are well fed.[367]

You turn away your face, and they panic;
> you take back your spirit, and they die
> and return to the dust from which they came.[368]

You send forth your spirit, and they are created
> and you renew the face of the earth.[369]

---

358 Psalm 104:19; Ecclesiastes 3:1-2; Genesis 1:14-19
359 Psalm 104:20; 1 Peter 5:8
360 Psalm 104:21; Matthew 6:32-33
361 Psalm 104:22; Matthew 6:27
362 Psalm 104:23; Matthew 6:34
363 Psalm 104:24; 1 Corinthians 12:7-11; Genesis 1:24-25
364 Psalm 104:25; John 3:5; Genesis 1:20-23
365 Psalm 104:26; John 3:7-8; Genesis 1:26, 28
366 Psalm 104:27; Acts 2:5-6; Genesis 1:11-13, John 6:10-11
367 Psalm 104:28; Acts 2:7-8; Deuteronomy 32:6, John 6:12-15
368 Psalm 104:29; Acts 2:13; Deuteronomy 32:20,Genesis 2:7
369 Psalm 104:30; John 3:6, Acts 2:11-12; Genesis 1:27, 2:7

May the glory of the Lord endure forever;
> may the Lord find joy in his works.[370]

God glares at the earth, and it trembles;
> God touches the mountains, and they smoke.[371]

I will sing to the Lord all my life,
> make music for my God while I live.[372]

May my musings be pleasing to him,
> for the Lord gives me joy.[373]

Let sinners vanish from the earth,
> and the wicked be no more.
> Bless the Lord, my soul, alleluia.[374]

Glory be to the Father, and to the Son, and to the Holy Spirit,
> as it was in the beginning, is now, and ever shall be world without end. Amen.

Sequence of Pentecost:

Come, Holy Spirit, come!
And from your celestial home
shed a ray of light divine!
Come, Father of the poor!
Come, source of all our store!
Come, within our bosoms shine!

You of comforters the best;
you, the soul's most welcome guest;
sweet refreshment here below;
in our labour, rest most sweet;
grateful coolness in the heat;
solace in the midst of woe.

---

370 Psalm 104:31; Colossians 3:1, 12-15; Revelation 19:5-7, 15:3-4
371 Psalm 104:32; Acts 4:31; Revelation 15:1, 8, 16:1; Deuteronomy 32:22, Exodus 24:16-18, Deuteronomy 5:23-26, 18:15-19
372 Psalm 104:33; 1 Corinthians 12:4-6; Revelation 19:8-9
373 Psalm 104:34; Hebrews 2:4; Revelation 20:6, 21:1-5
374 Psalm 104:35; Hebrews 6:4-6; Revelation 19:19-21, 20:10; Deuteronomy 32:35

O most blessed Light divine,
shine within these hearts of yours,
and our inmost being fill!
Where you are not, man has naught,
nothing good in deed or thought,
nothing free from taint of ill.

Heal our wounds, our strength renew;
on our dryness pour your dew;
wash the stains of guilt away:
bend the stubborn heart and will;
melt the frozen, warm the chill;
guide the steps that go astray.

On the faithful, who adore
and confess you, evermore
in your sevenfold gift descend;
give them virtue's sure reward;
give them your salvation, Lord;
give them joys that never end. Amen. Alleluia.

Chapter 40

From the Nativity of Our Lord Jesus Christ (Winter Solstice 8 BCE) to the Birth of the Church (The Spring of 30 CE)—the Christian Family and Christian Ecumenism: the Born, the Unborn, and the Reborn

Readings: Luke 2:1-21, 22-40; Matthew 1:18-25, 2:1-23

Just as Jesus Christ, the Lord of Lords and King of Kings,[1] had gone up to heaven, so also, he first came down to earth,[2] the only beloved Son of his Father in heaven.[3] And when he would ascend from the earth to the throne of God,[4] it would have been some thirty-six years and five months before that, by the power of the Holy Spirit,[5] that the infant King was born a man,[6] uncreated,[7] the only son of the Virgin Mary,[8] in Bethlehem, in David's royal city:[9] the son of Abraham and the root of Jesse,[10] in the lineage

---

1   1 Timothy 6:15, Revelation 17:14
2   Ephesians 4:9-10
3   Luke 20:13, Matthew 3:17, 17:5, 2 Peter 1:16-18; John 1:1
4   Luke 24:51, Acts 1:9, Mark 16:19
5   Matthew 1:18, Luke 1:35
6   John 1:14
7   John 1:2-3
8   Isaiah 7:10-14
9   John 7:42, Micah 5:1-2, Matthew 2:6
10   Matthew 1:1, 6; Genesis 15:1-6, Romans 4:18-25; Ruth 4:13-22, 1 Samuel 16:7, 10-13, 17:12-15, Isaiah 11:1-5, 10

of King David through Joseph, the husband of Mary.[11] This, then, is how Jesus, the Christ and infant King, came to be born.[12] And it happened, in God's ironic and intentional opposition,[13] during the reign of the great human and deified emperor Caesar Augustus, at the time when he had issued a decree that a census should be taken throughout the whole western world: that is, throughout the vast domain of his entire Roman Empire,[14] which included the territory of Israel, then by God's will under the protection of Rome,[15] the land provided to God's chosen race.[16] However, God's domain is the whole of creation: for he is Lord of the Universe and Lord of the Sabbath,[17] Ruler over all the nations:[18] Lord of the entire People of God,[19] Lord both of those living and of the dead;[20] the one God of Israel is the true fulfilment of every human heart.[21]

Joseph was engaged to the Virgin Mary, when before they lived together, by the power of the Holy Spirit she conceived a child, who is our Emmanuel,[22] the Son of God and the Son of Man.[23] And Mary informed Joseph, her fiancée, of her pregnancy; and he was shocked, just as any future husband might be if he had found his betrothed to be with child, and that she was not made so by his own hand because he had been faithful to his bride to be and to his own

---

11	Matthew 1:6-16, Luke 1:27
12	Matthew 1:18
13	Revelation 17:1-3, 8-14, 21:5-7
14	Luke 2:1, Revelation 18:3, 9-24, Matthew 23:33-36
15	Romans 3:24-25, 5:18, 13:1
16	Romans 9:4-16
17	Genesis 2:1-3, Exodus 20:8-11; Matthew 12:8, Luke 6:5
18	Revelation 1:4-8, 2:26-27, 19:15-16
19	1 Peter 2:10, Matthew 12:7, Hosea 6:6, 1:6-9, 2:1-3, 25
20	1 Peter 4:5-6, 2 Timothy 4:1-5, Acts 10:42; Mark 12:26-27, Matthew 22:31-32, Luke 20:37-38; Romans 6:3-14, 8:1-11; 1 Corinthians 15:35-57, Revelation 21:5-8, 22-24, John 8:12, Romans 13:12, 1 John 2:8-11, 3:2, 1 Corinthians 13:12-13; Revelation 22:1-5, 21:1-5, Hebrews 12:22-23, John 4:13-14, 3:5-8
21	Luke 2:32, John 4:22; Acts 2:8-11, Ephesians 2:19-22; Genesis 11:27-31, Chapters 12-15, Exodus 3:1-15
22	Isaiah 7:14, Revelation 21:2-4, Luke 1:79, Isaiah 8:23, 9:1, Matthew 4:12-16, John 8:12, Revelation 21:22-26
23	Matthew 1:18

virginity. Yet, Joseph was an upright and honourable man: and not wanting to expose Mary to any public disgrace,[24] neither by any future claims from the child's actual father, nor also by his marrying her despite knowing that the child she carried in her womb was not his own, Joseph, therefore, decided to divorce her privately.[25] In fact, Joseph already had made up his mind to do so; not understanding the mystery, he only had not yet been able to carry out his intention, when suddenly, while Joseph was sleeping, the angel of the Lord appeared to him in a dream, and told him:

> Joseph, son of David,[26] do not be afraid to take Mary into your home as your wife, because it is through the Holy Spirit that this child has been conceived in her.[27] She will give birth to a son and you are to name him Jesus, because he is the one who will save his people from their sins.[28]

Now all of this took place to fulfil what the Lord had said through the prophet:[29]

> Behold! The virgin is with child and will give birth to a son, and they shall name him "Emmanuel."

Which name means: "God-is-with-us."[30] After the angel spoke, Joseph woke up startled in the middle of the night, and he did just as the angel of the Lord had said: from that moment, and just as the future disciple John also would later take Mary into his home as his mother,[31] Joseph now took Mary as his wife into his home;[32] and just as every Christian family should take the Lord's mother into their home.[33] Joseph had not had intercourse with Mary when she gave

---

24 Matthew 1:19
25 Matthew 1:19
26 Matthew 1:20; Luke 1:32-33
27 Matthew 1:20; Luke 1:30, 34-35
28 Matthew 1:21; Luke 1:31, 77-78; Philippians 2:10
29 Matthew 1:22
30 Matthew 1:23; Isaiah 7:10-14; Revelation 21:2-3, John 15:12
31 John 19:27; Revelation 12:1-2, 5, 20:9-10, 21:2, 19:7-9, John 2:1-2
32 Matthew 1:24
33 Mark 3:31-35, Matthew 12:46-50, Luke 8:19-21; John 2:12, Acts 1:12-14,

birth to a son; and Joseph would name him Jesus,[34] just as the angel had commanded; namely, just as the same angel Gabriel also had given Mary the child's name, Jesus;[35] and just as five months before, Gabriel also had commanded Zechariah to give the name of John to his son;[36] and as John's mother, Elizabeth, had declared "John" to be her son's name,[37] to the great astonishment of the relatives, who had expected that the child would be named after his father; and as from that moment when Zechariah had written his child's name on a tablet, and simultaneously, also to everyone's great astonishment and in God's signature, Zechariah then had recovered his ability to speak, after his period of seemingly stroke-induced penance.[38]

Joseph now, in his vocation and in his relationship with Mary, prefigured the relationship between Christ and his church: so, he took Mary into his home and he cared for her as his wife;[39] but also, he had no intercourse with her, to keep her pure and holy perpetually for God.[40] And now, Joseph would care for Mary's unborn son, as if Jesus had been his own son,[41] but now knowing in the revelation from the angel of the Lord that this child, in fact, had been conceived by the Spirit of God as God's Son; and knowing that God's spirit was made flesh so that our sins might be forgiven.[42] So, instead of a quiet divorce as Joseph had imagined at first to be necessary,[43] Joseph and Mary, now in their marriage as husband and wife, committed themselves together to life in the spirit,[44] apart from the flesh except in their union with Christ;[45] and they made their perpetual vows to

---

        Ephesians 4:22-24, Revelation 12:17, 7:13-17, 21:3-4
34   Matthew 1:25
35   Luke 1:32
36   Luke 1:13
37   Luke 1:60
38   Luke 1:59, 63-64, 22, 65
39   Ephesians 5:25
40   Ephesians 5:27; Ephesians 5:21, Matthew 1:25, John 6:63; Luke 1:46
41   Luke 3:23, Matthew 2:16; Luke 4:22
42   Matthew 1:20-21; Isaiah 1:18, Psalm 51:7; John 1:14
43   Matthew 1:19-20
44   John 6:63, 3:6, Matthew 1:18, Luke 1:34-35, John 1:10-13, Romans 7:5-6, 8:3-4, 12-14, Ephesians 1:4-6
45   Ephesians 5:30-32

God by their chastity and fidelity to one another; and in another nine months, but also throughout Mary's sheltered pregnancy even when she would be away from Joseph, they would be living this mutual commitment vividly every moment and every day in the physical and spiritual presence of the living Word of God.[46]

Immediately after Joseph took Mary into his home, Mary went alone to her cousin Elizabeth, who lived in the hill country of Judah.[47] And there for about three months,[48] she assisted Elizabeth with her pregnancy with John, who would be a herald for Mary's son as the Baptist; and with both infants in association *in utero*, Mary would assist Elizabeth like a mid-wife so as to prepare John's way for her son.[49] But then, shortly after John's birth, and now in her fourth month of pregnancy, Mary returned to her home at Nazareth to be with her husband.[50] Then after nearly five months had passed from John's birth, it happened that the decree was issued from Caesar Augustus that the whole world should be enrolled in a census,[51] for the purposes of Roman taxation. This census first began while Quirinius [Publius Sulpicius Quirinius] was governor of Syria [between 12-6 BCE], when both Quirinius and Sentius Saturnius [between 9-6 BCE] were legati of Syria; but Luke only mentions Quirinius, and not Saturnius for this "first registration."[52] Although most scholars place this census of Quirinius in 6 CE,[53] the actual process may have begun earlier, from 8-6 BCE. Accordingly, everyone went to be registered, each to his own town.[54] So Joseph set out for the difficult journey to Judea with Mary his then very pregnant wife, from Nazareth in Galilee where they were living to David's city called Bethlehem, since Joseph was of that house and the family lineage of David,[55] in order to be registered together with

---

46   John 1:14, 1 John 1:1; John 1:1-5, 9
47   Luke 1:39
48   Luke 1:26, 56
49   Luke 1:76, 3:1-6, 1:80
50   Luke 1:56; Luke 2:4
51   Luke 2:1
52   Luke 2:2
53   Acts 5:37
54   Luke 2:3
55   Luke 2:4

Mary, his betrothed, who was with child.[56]

However, one modern proposition that we will be considering is that the trip would have been springtime, in the month of April, but it did occur according to our conventional [and also true] expectations for a December journey; and after a rugged and mountainous trek of more than 120 kilometres, when they had come to the town of Bethlehem, the time came for Mary to have her child.[57] And although the journey itself may have been labour-inducing, there in difficult circumstances Mary gave birth to a son conceived not coincidently around the Spring equinox, our new life in Christ beginning mid-way between our darkness and his light,[58] her first-born;[59] and she wrapped him snugly in bands of cloth and laid him there in a manger, because there had been no room available with sufficient privacy for them to stay in the ordinary living-space.[60] There, where he was born, in the solitude of the shepherd's cave that was a winter shelter for livestock, with the newborn Christ child and his mother and Joseph, who had respected Mary's virginity with her delivery,[61] there also were an ox and a donkey looking on, as representatives for an obdurate Israel, as foretold by the prophet:

> The ox knows its owner and the donkey its master's manger; but Israel doesn't know, and my people do not understand.[62]

Now in the countryside close by, there were simple and humble shepherds living in the fields and guarding over their sheep during the watches of the night.[63] As they looked on, an angel of the Lord appeared directly over them and the glory of the Lord shone around them; and they were terrified.[64] But the angel said:

---

56 Luke 2:5
57 Luke 2:6
58 Luke 1:79, John 8:12; 1 John 1:5-7, John 1:19-21
59 Exodus 13:2
60 Luke 2:7
61 Matthew 1:25
62 Isaiah 1:3; Romans 10:21, 11:8, Isaiah 29:10-14; John 1:11, 12:34-36
63 Luke 2:8; 1 Samuel 16:10-12, Luke 1:68-69, 52, 20:42-43, John 10:7-11
64 Luke 2:9; Ezekiel 1:27-28, 43:2

Don't be afraid; look, I proclaim to you good news of great joy that will be shared by all of the people.[65] For today in the city of David, a Saviour has been born to you; he is the Anointed One, the Lord.[66] And by this sign you will recognize him: you will find a baby wrapped in swaddling clothes and lying in a manger.[67]

And suddenly, with the angel there was a multitude of the heavenly hosts singing and praising God, and saying:[68]

Glory to God in the highest heaven! And on earth peace to those whom God favours![69]

When the angels straightaway had gone from them into heaven, the shepherds said to one another, "Let's go, now, to Bethlehem to see this marvellous thing that has happened, which the Lord has made known to us."[70] So, in haste, the shepherds went to the familiar place, and there they found Mary and Joseph, and the baby lying in the manger.[71] When they saw the child, they repeated the angel's message that they had been told about the child;[72] and everyone who heard it was amazed by what the shepherds said to them.[73] However, quietly, Mary treasured all these things in her heart, and henceforth she reflected about them often.[74] And the shepherds then returned to their flocks, glorifying and praising God for all that they had been privileged to hear and to see that Christmas Day: just as the angel of the Lord had told them they would find the Messiah.[75]

And then one week later, on the eighth day of the birth of Christ, when according to the Law for that day only Mary would not

---

65   Luke 2:10
66   Luke 2:11; 1 Samuel 16:13, Mark 1:11, Matthew 3:17, Luke 3:22, John 1:34
67   Luke 2:12; Luke 2:7
68   Luke 2:13; Revelation 7:11
69   Luke 2:14; Exodus 33:19; Revelation 7:12, 9-10
70   Luke 2:15
71   Luke 2:16
72   Luke 2:17
73   Luke 2:18
74   Luke 2:19; Luke 2:51
75   Luke 2:20

be regarded as unclean,[76] Mary and Joseph first took their infant child to the Temple in nearby Jerusalem, where according to God's covenant with Abraham,[77] the father of us all,[78] the infant sovereign King of the promise was circumcised into that covenant;[79] and then Mary and Joseph also gave him the name of Jesus,[80] the name that the angel had given him before his conception.[81] Then thirty-three days after this,[82] when the day came for both of them, Mary and her son, to be purified according to the Law of Moses, once again they took Jesus to the temple in Jerusalem to present him to the Lord.[83] The Law of the Lord says, "Every first-born male shall be consecrated to the Lord."[84] So, they also offered the sacrifice, in anticipation of his future cross, in accordance with what is required in the law of the Lord, "a pair of turtledoves or two young pigeons."[85]

Now there was in Jerusalem a man whose name was Simeon: he was an upright and devout man, awaiting the restoration of Israel; and the Holy Spirit rested upon him.[86] The Holy Spirit had revealed to him that he would not see death until he had seen the Christ, the Anointed of the Lord.[87] Prompted by the Spirit, he came into the Temple; and when the parents brought in the infant Jesus to perform the custom required by the Law,[88] he took Jesus into his arms and blessed God, saying:[89]

Now, Master, you are letting your servant go in peace;

76	Leviticus 12:2-3
77	Genesis 17:1-16
78	Genesis 17:4-6, 15-16; Romans 4:10-13, 16-17, Genesis 17:17, 21:1-7; Luke 1:54-55
79	Genesis 3:15, 17:10-14; Acts 15:1-2, Galatians 2:1-21, Colossians 2:9-15
80	Luke 1:30-33, Matthew 1:21
81	Luke 2:21
82	Leviticus 12:4
83	Luke 2:22
84	Luke 2:23; Exodus 13:2, 12
85	Luke 2:24; Leviticus 12:8, 5:7; Mark 11:15, 27-28, Colossians 1:15-20
86	Luke 2:25
87	Luke 2:26
88	Luke 2:27
89	Luke 2:28

your word to me has been fulfilled:[90] for my own eyes have seen your salvation,[91] which you have prepared in the sight of every people:[92] a light of revelation to the Gentiles, and the glory of your people Israel.[93]

The child's father and mother were amazed at the things that were being said about him;[94] and Simeon blessed them and said to Mary his mother:

> Look, this child is destined for the destruction and salvation of many in Israel, to be a sign that is opposed[95]—and a sword will pierce your very soul too[96]—so that the secret thoughts of many hearts may be laid open.[97]

Also in the Temple, there was a prophetess named Anna, the daughter of Phanuel, of the tribe of Asher; she was quite old; she had been married for seven years in her days of girlhood,[98] before becoming a widow; but already now she was eighty-four years old, and even in her old age she never left the Temple, night and day, worshiping God with fasting and prayer.[99] At that very moment, when Simeon had been speaking to Mary, she came up and she began to praise God; and she spoke continuously then about the child to all who were awaiting the deliverance of Jerusalem.[100] After the parents had completed all that the Law of the Lord had required of them, it would have appeared from text, taking Luke's gospel in isolation from Matthew's, that they had returned to Galilee, to "Nasrat," to their own humble and simple country town of rurally

---

90   Luke 2:29; Luke 1:70, 55
91   Luke 2:30; Luke 1:69, 71
92   Luke 2:31
93   Luke 2:32
94   Luke 2:33
95   Luke 2:34; 1 Corinthians 1:22-24
96   Luke 2:35; John 19:25-27, 2:1, 4, 11-12
97   Luke 2:35; Mark 4:22, Matthew 10:26, Luke 8:17; 1 Timothy 5:24-25, Matthew 25:31-32; John 9:41, 8:47, 42-43
98   Luke 2:36
99   Luke 2:37
100 Luke 2:38

isolated Nazareth.[101] But it is Matthew's gospel that provides the link between Bethlehem and Nazareth.

After Jesus had been born at Bethlehem in Judea during the reign of King Herod [it would, in fact, be nearly two years later], there suddenly appeared in Jerusalem some magi, royal astrologers, from the east;[102] and they were going around the city and asking everyone, "Where is the infant king of the Jews? We saw his star at the rising and have come to do him homage."[103] When King Herod heard of this, he was greatly troubled, and with him so was the whole of Jerusalem.[104] Herod then assembled all the chief priests and the scribes of the people, and he enquired of them where the Christ was to be born.[105] They told him, "In Bethlehem in Judea, for this is what the prophet wrote:[106]

> And you Bethlehem, land of Judah, you are by no means
> the least among the rulers of Judah, for from you will
> come a ruler who will shepherd my people Israel."[107]

Then Herod summoned the magi to see him secretly; and he asked these royal astrologers the exact date of the star's appearance.[108] Afterwards, he sent them on to Bethlehem, telling them, "Go and search diligently for the child, and when you have found him, let me know, so that I too may go and do him homage."[109] And having listened to what the king had to say, the magi went on their way.[110]

Before the arrival of the magi to Jerusalem [in December 6 BCE], in 7 BCE, during the year following the birth of Christ [in December 8 BCE], Herod already had arranged a handy kangaroo court, a trial in Beruit, against his two sons by his second wife and

---

101 Luke 2:39; John 6:41-42, 8:18-19, 7:25-27, 40-52
102 Matthew 2:1
103 Matthew 2:2
104 Matthew 2:3
105 Matthew 2:4
106 Matthew 2:5
107 Matthew 2:6; Micah 5:2, 2 Samuel 5:2
108 Matthew 2:7
109 Matthew 2:8
110 Matthew 2:9

queen Mariamme I, Alexander and Aristobulus, while his reliable, old friend Saturnius was still governor of Syria (9-6 BCE); and then so followed the execution of Alexander and Aristobulus in Sebaste, Samaria. Irrationally, Herod had believed, with his suspicious nature and the mental deterioration of his arterio-sclerosis that aggravated his violent dispositions, that the two princes had been plotting his death. Herod's covert meeting now with the magi was consistent with his earlier ruthless handling of family intrigues; the meeting was not officially recorded: first of all, so as not to arouse any public suspicion of his antipathy towards the child Messiah; and secondly, not to suggest or give too much importance to the public rumours of the usurping child's birth, with the hope that such rumours would fade away.

Also, in another reason for his secrecy, Herod may have attempted to hide from the magi the ancient prophecy of Balaam, spoken by Balaam the son of Beor as the spirit of God had come upon him,[111] which, of course, would have been well-known to the chief priests and scribes when they had come at Herod's request to tell him where the Messiah was to be born. The prophecy is recorded in the Law of Moses:

> I see him—but not in the present time. I perceive him—but not in the near future: a star is rising from Jacob, and a sceptre will emerge from Israel, to crush the brows of Moab, and the skulls of all the children of Seth.[112]

This prophecy raised a double threat to King Herod: first of all, because the star that is rising was a direct challenge to his throne; but secondly, because, although Herod's name was Greek and his religion was Judaism, by race he was Arab; and although Herod may have thought of himself as Jewish, by natural and political force he was an hereditary enemy of the Jews: his father, Antipater, was Idumaean; his mother, "Kufra" in Arabic and "Cypros" in Greek, was Nabataean. So, it also seems that King Herod was feeling the anti-

---

111 Numbers 24:3-9
112 Numbers 24:17; Numbers 15-16, 18-19; Genesis 5:7-8, 19:36-37, Exodus 15:15, Deuteronomy 2:9

Arab heat of this particular prophecy of a future king in Israel.

What was this fateful "star" of the magi that Herod so feared? The clues from Matthew's gospel that marked the "star" for the birth of Christ seem to be best explained by the astronomical-astrological hypothesis that Michael Molnar, the American astronomer, put forward in 1999 regarding the lunar eclipse of Jupiter that had occurred four times in 6 BCE.[113] With the birth of Christ, there were three most probable candidate celestial events for the "Star of Bethlehem," including our third and final consideration as the best natural explanation. The first major candidate has been the triple conjunction of Jupiter and Saturn, the massive gas-planet and the famously ringed-planet, in 7 BCE in the constellation of Pisces: 29 May, 29 September, and 4 December. This type of event occurs frequently; but for it to occur three times in one year is unusual. Jupiter (the royal planet) with Saturn (an evil omen) in Pisces (the constellation associated with the Jews) may have been thought-provoking as a triple conjunction in one year, but it would not have sent the magi on their mission.[114] In February 6 BCE, once again in the constellation of Pisces, there was the massing together of three planets: Jupiter and Saturn slipped toward the horizon in the evening sky, while Mars (the blood-red planet of conquest) entered Pisces and approached Jupiter and Saturn until they were separated by only 8 degrees—not spectacular visually—but the event would have carried potential astrological significance. Yet again, however thought-provoking this particular celestial conjunction might have been, this also was not the magi's "star."[115]

What exactly did the magi tell King Herod when he asked them for the precise date given by the appearance of the infant king's star? The vital clues to the celestial signs are provided in the rest of Saint Matthew's telling of the story. As the magi left Herod and set out, suddenly the star that they had seen at its rising[116]—and

---

113   Molnar, Michael R. (1999). *The Star of Bethlehem: The Legacy of the Magi.* New Brunswick: Rutgers University Press.
114   Molnar, Ibid., pp. 29-30.
115   Molnar, Ibid., 25-29.
116   Matthew 2:9

they were overjoyed at the sight of the "star"[117]—preceded them,[118] and it seemed to be leading them forward, until it halted over the place where the child was.[119] In a paraphrase of what an astrologer may have said, as reported by Matthew,[120] Molnar provides this technical description: "And behold the planet which they had seen at its helical rising went retrograde and became stationary above in the sky (which showed) where the child was."[121] Molnar's arguments provide the most plausible rationale for the Bethlehem "star," and for correctly dating the magi's presence in Jerusalem. He argues for 17 April 6 BCE as Christmas Day, but later I will argue the date of the Winter Solstice of 8 BCE.

This is what the Magi had reported to Herod: on 17 April 6 BCE, there had been a weakly visible occultation (eclipse) of the planet Jupiter by the moon in the constellation of Aries, the Ram, the second occultation that year; the earlier one [on 20 March] was irrelevant because it had not been visible; it was the date of this second occultation that was provided to Herod by the magi for the infant King's birth, when Jupiter was "in the east."[122] On 23 August of that year, Jupiter became stationary and then "went before" through Aries, visible for a week, before Jupiter became stationary again, or as it "stood over,"[123] its respective retrograde motion and stationing that occurred once more on 19 December in Aries. It is this fourth occultation, near to our Christmas Day, that marks when the magi found the Christ child. The prior event of 17 April 6 BCE has a regular period of 60 years, which astronomically is not very spectacular; nonetheless, for the human observers, such an event would have occurred only once in a lifetime.

---

117 Matthew 2:10
118 Matthew 2:9
119 Matthew 2:9
120 Molnar (Ibid., p. 92) states, "The passage in Matthew has strong astrological meanings, which the evangelist described in simplified literal terms." Accordingly, Molnar provides (pp. 89-96) how the Greek of Matthew's gospel corresponds to those astrological meanings for the observed astronomical events.
121 Molnar, Ibid., p. 96.
122 Matthew 2:2, 9
123 Matthew 2:9

However, more importantly, as Molnar has shown, this event would have been given great importance astrologically. According to Greek astrology, which was the Roman astrology of the day, Aries, not Pisces, was the zodiac sign that represented the territories of King Herod's kingdom (and ancestry): "Judea, Idumea, Samaria, Palestine, and Coele Syria" according to the *Tetrabiblios* of Claudius Ptolemy. According to Molnar's comparison case findings for C. Suetonius Tranquillus, the Roman historian, astrologers (*praedictum a mathematicis*) looked to Aries the Ram in their prediction that Nero (54-68 CE) would be repudiated (*destitueretur*) in Rome, only then to rise up again in the East (*Orientis dominationem*), in Jerusalem (*regnum Hierosolymorum*) more specifically.[124] Molnar also provides numismatic evidence from antiquity, the original inspiration for his inquiries as an astronomer about the "star" when he purchased a Roman coin from Antioch, Syria: the coin he found shows Aries the Ram (the sign of the Jews) looking back at an overhead star, proving from astrological sources that Judea was represented by Aries, the Ram.[125]

On 17 April 6 BCE,[126] what had happened was this: Jupiter emerged in the east as a morning star (the most powerful time to confer kingships) in the constellation of Aries the Ram (the sign of the Jews); and furthermore, the Sun was in Aries where it is exalted, and the Moon was in close conjunction with Jupiter in Aries; and Saturn was also present in Aries. Therefore, the three rulers of Aries' trine (Sun, Jupiter, Saturn) were present in Aries; and Saturn and Jupiter were said to be attendants on the rising sun. These specific conditions were described by the Roman Firmicus Maternus,[127] an astrologer who had converted to Christianity in the time of Constantine: and accordingly, he demonstrates for us that these conditions would have been interpreted by various astrologers of that period to herald the birth of a divine, immortal, and omnipotent person born under the sign of the Jews: and now, as it seems, this same interpretation could have been applied as a specific celestial

---

124   Revelation 13:18
125   Molnar, Ibid., pp. 109-116, 119-123.
126   Molnar, Ibid., pp. 96-101.
127   Molnar, Ibid., pp. 104-109, 119

reference to Christ, theoretically born on 17 April 6 BCE;[128] however, such an interpretation could be applied to anyone born on that date, or a few days after Jupiter's heliacal rising.[129]

The magi were Zoroastrian priests, possibly from Babylon (Mesopotamia), but more likely from Persia (Parthia), and both nations were represented among the visitors to Jerusalem on Pentecost.[130] These magi realized the significance of the 17 April 6 BCE occultation in Aries;[131] but it also seems that they may not have set out on their journey to the kingdom of the Jews until they had been prompted by their second sighting, the occultation of 23 August 6 BCE; and lastly, as the "star" that went before them, and then stood over the place, there was their third and final sighting for the same occultation on 19 December 6 BCE.[132] These later retrograde and stationing conditions were important secondary regal conditions. Therefore, the journey of the magi from Persia to Jerusalem may have been done in less than 118 days. When they entered the house, they saw the child,[133] with its mother Mary, and falling to their knees, they did him homage.[134] Then opening their treasures,[135] they offered him gifts of gold,[136] frankincense,[137] and myrrh.[138] And it was in this same context, before Christmas in 1967, at age nineteen when no longer in seminary, and in 2008 exactly forty-one years ago, that I wrote this sonnet, not based upon Molnar's hypothesis which then was unknown to me, but upon the alternatives Molnar had considered: the triple conjunction of 7 BCE, or the conjunction of three planets (Saturn, Jupiter, and Mars) in February 6 BCE:

---

128 Molnar, Ibid., pp. 104-109.
129 Molnar, Ibid., pp. 119, 123.
130 Acts 2:9
131 Matthew 2:2
132 Matthew 2:9
133 Hebrews 1:1-3
134 Matthew 2:11; John 1:4, 9, 14; Philippians 2:10-11, Acts 2:5-6, 9; Isaiah 52:7
135 Isaiah 60:6, Revelation 21:26
136 Hebrews 1:4-8
137 Hebrews 7:15-17
138 Matthew 2:11; Hebrews 10:7, 10

A Son is Given[139]

On Christmas Day three spheres conjoined to praise
their cosmic Lord, the Light of Light, his birth;
a brilliant sign to tell the darkened earth
that matter, space, and time had reached new days.
Round David's town angelic choirs voiced
their hymn to David's Son and King in tones
no mortal harmonies for earthly thrones
could ever match—ten thousand hosts rejoiced!

So for the Swaddled Babe the shepherds deign
their purest lamb and loyal homage paid;
the Magi at His feet their offerings laid
of royalty, divinity, and pain.
To Him, my Lord and God, what shall I give?
O every second all the days I live!

Herod had directed the magi to search for the infant King in Bethlehem,[140] about 10 kilometres due south of Jerusalem; and according to Molnar's specific hypotheses, the Christ child would have been almost eight months old—sitting, crawling, and standing with the support of his mother or some handy piece of Joseph's furniture. Perhaps in God's providence the Christ child would not have been found in Bethlehem. For we may be reminded that Saint Luke tells us the child was up north in Galilee, at home with his parents in Nazareth.[141] And then there also is Matthew, as he indicates in his quote of Isaiah:

> Land of Zebulun and land of Naphtali! The way to the sea beyond the Jordan! Galilee of the Gentiles![142] The people that lived in darkness have seen a great light; on those who have lived in a country overshadowed as dark as death a light has arisen.[143]

---

139 Isaiah 9:6; John 1:18
140 Matthew 2:8
141 Luke 2:39; Matthew 2:9
142 Matthew 4:15; Isaiah 8:23-9:1
143 Matthew 4:16; Matthew 2:9

This rising light may have been not just the true light of the world,[144] the light of Christ; but this light implicitly also may have been the rising "star" of the magi.[145] And, if so, besides in Bethlehem, it also would have shown in Nazareth, where the child Jesus grew to manhood, and where first the adult Jesus would declare that he was in himself the fulfilment of the prophets.[146] But it seems that the magi, indeed, did go to Bethlehem, as Matthew implies.[147] Maria Valtorta provides that the Holy Family stayed in Bethlehem until the later arrival and exit of the magi, for a Christ child of "around a year old;" and she also provides, by her spiritual description, an alternative account for the "Star of Bethlehem."[148] Nonetheless, having been warned in a dream not to go back to Herod, the magi returned to their own country by another way.[149] On Christmas Day, the Christ child is God the Father's gift of his Son to humanity; but also the Christmas gift of the magi for us would seem to be their initial celebration of Christmas Day on its anniversary, according to the magi's belated arrival in December 6 BCE.

However, even if the astronomical facts and astrological interpretations for Molnar's "Star of Bethlehem" are historically and scientifically correct, as I believe they are, his evidence does not confirm 17 April 6 BCE as the actual date of our Lord's birth. The Spring date he provides for the birth of Jesus would provide a proximate context, either on that date or prior to it; but, most clearly, it only establishes the time for the sudden appearance and later departure of the magi in Jerusalem, as inclusive of 19 December 6 BCE. The actual Christmas Day ranges from eight months to two years before the arrival of the magi. We know this from Herod's decree for the slaughter of infants of two years old or less.[150] Astrology, which is a matter of belief, also would expect or demand the hour rather than the April date, plus or minus a few days,

---

144   John 1:4-5
145   Matthew 2:2, 16:1-4
146   Luke 4:17-21; Isaiah 61:1-2; Jeremiah 23:5-6, Isaiah 1:26-27, 10, Matthew 28:2-6; Luke 24:44
147   Matthew 2:1, 5, 8
148   Valtorta, Maria (Chapter 35).
149   Matthew 2:12
150   Matthew 2:16

for Christmas; but for scientific validity, an astrologically non-congruent birth date for Jesus would not alter the historical consequences for the astrological suppositions of the magi in their search for the Christ child and for the alarm their visitation provoked.[151]

There are other issues related to the apparent and actual chronologies of the infancy narratives and my first interpretations with respect to the separate or unified gospels of Luke and Matthew. Like my Christmas sonnet, our prototypic and integrative cultural conceptions of Christmas Day cause us to link together two distinct visitation events: Luke's Christmas Day shepherds and Matthew's sometime-later magi.[152] Scripture, the church calendar of feasts, and Michael Molnar all appropriately separate these respective visitations: but how great is their separation in historical time? In Luke, after the birth of Jesus, the Holy Family remains close to Jerusalem for a few weeks;[153] and without the necessary context of Matthew, the family seems to return to Nazareth from Bethlehem.[154] But from Matthew, we know that the magi are directed to Bethlehem in their search for the Christ child,[155] an event that follows the birth of Christ, not immediately but by several months, and perhaps by a year or more. When the magi find the child with Mary,[156] they are now, it seems, in a proper house—not in a manger;[157] and that house is in Bethlehem, not in Nazareth.[158] Luke's reference to the family's settlement in Nazareth is a marker equivalent to Matthew's reference for the family's return to Nazareth after their having lived in Egypt.[159] Considering Luke's gospel in isolation, no less than two years [more likely four years] of the Lord's infancy would be omitted;[160] Matthew's narrative allows

---

151 Matthew 2:3
152 Luke 2:6-8, 11-12; Matthew 2:1
153 Luke 2:21-22
154 Luke 2:39
155 Matthew 2:5-8
156 Matthew 2:11
157 Luke 2:12
158 Luke 2:39
159 Matthew 2:23
160 Maria Valtorta's gospel narrative (Vol. 1, Chapters 30-35) provides the chronology of events: soon after the visitation of the shepherds, the Holy Family are provided the hospitality of a house in Bethlehem; they

for the Christ child's longer duration of living in David's royal city; followed by the family's flight into Egypt; and after some hidden time later in Egypt, they return to Nazareth.

There is, however, a faithful resolution for the actual date of the Christ Child's birth. Given the historical determination of the magi's visitation in 6 BCE, in 6 CE Jesus also was already twelve years old when his parents went with him up to Jerusalem for the feast of Passover.[161] For that year, the first day of the month of Nisan began with the evening after its new moon [Rosh Chodesh] on 18th March (according to Gregorian calendar dating), so that the twilight initiation for the Preparation Day of Passover on 14th Nisan occurred on 31st March, with the 14th Nisan continuing into the daytime of April 1st (which then by the secular Julian calendar was April 3rd). The dates I have previously cited for Holy Week in 30 CE also are according to the Julian calendar, when in that year the Passover also coincided with the Sabbath.[162] But, during the day of 1st April in year 6 CE, before that evening's Passover, which anticipates the Lord's ultimate Passover sacrifice on the cross,[163] Jesus was brought explicitly to the temple authorities for the confirmation of his Jewish manhood, and implicitly, for confirmation of his vocation.[164] And afterwards, as Jesus then went missing from his parents, he returned alone to the temple for another three days of discussions and his manifestations before the authorities.[165] In Maria Valtorta's narrative and her transcription of gospel visions for these events, she records the words of Joseph, who then attests before the authorities that Jesus was "of age" according to the Law, his having attained his twelve years of age earlier, precisely by "three months and twelve days,"[166] which are Jewish calendar lunar months and days.

---

stay until the departure of the magi, when the family afterwards takes flight into Egypt with the Child Jesus, who is "about one year old." My argument will be that Jesus then actually was "two years old."

161 Luke 2:41-42
162 Luke 23:54
163 Deuteronomy 6:20-25, Philippians 2:5-8
164 Luke 2:49-50
165 Luke 2:46-47
166 Maria Valtorta (Vol. 1, Chapter 40, p. 209), in her vision and narrative dated 21st December 1944.

By simple subtraction, twelve days from 14th Nisan yields 2nd Nisan (19th March); and the three prior lunar months, according to evening determinations after new moons, are Adar (29 days) beginning 17th February, Shevat (30 days) beginning 18th January, and Tevet (29 days) beginning 20th December; counting backwards by ninety days (2+29+30+28 = 90), provides the 2nd day of the month of Tevet in 5 CE. But the actual date for the birth of Jesus would be determined according to our solar year calendar,[167] as 21st December 5 CE minus twelve years. Therefore, the birth of Jesus would have occurred on the winter solstice of 8 BCE [remember, in this subtraction of five plus seven equals twelve years, there is no year zero], when the sun is at its lowest declination in the northern hemisphere. As such, this coordination of his birth, during the watches of the night with our year's longest darkness of night,[168] is a forceful divine reminder that Jesus Christ, our Emmanuel,[169] is the true light of the world.[170] When the Church celebrates the Annunciation on 25th March, it allows nine months of maternal gestation before we celebrate his birth on the 25th December; by this it also reminds us to respect the unified role of Mary through her Son to effect the mystery of our salvation from God: the incarnation also had depended upon the freely given "yes" of the Lord's immaculate and virgin mother to God's will.[171] The celestial coordination of the actual date of Christmas Day with the winter solstice emphasizes the divine will to our salvation.[172] But, in order for us to receive salvation, we must be obedient to God's will,[173] like Mary and her Son.[174]

---

167   Twelve years earlier by the Hebrew calendar would identify 2nd Tevet as 2nd December (Gregorian date) for 8 BCE because the year is embolismic deficient (383 days) and provides an extra month, Adar II. But the Julian calendar, a solar calendar, operated as Israel's secular calendar for the specification of the period of twelve years since the Lord's birth before his Passover rite of manhood, still 21st December (Gregorian).
168   Luke 2:8, Matthew 4:16, 14
169   Matthew 2:23, 22, John 1:9
170   John 8:12, 1:4-5
171   Luke 1:28, 38
172   Colossians 2:16-17; 2 Corinthians 4:6, 3:18
173   John 1:12-13; 1 John 1:5-7
174   Luke 2:51-52, Philippians 2:7-8

After the magi had left, suddenly, the angel of the Lord appeared to Joseph in a dream and said, "Get up, take the child and its mother, and flee into Egypt; and stay there until I tell you, because Herod intends to search for the child and to destroy him."[175] So Joseph arose from his bed that instant, and taking the child and his mother by night, they left for Egypt.[176] They would stay there until Herod was dead; and by this, the word of the Lord spoken through the prophet would be fulfilled: "I called my Son out of Egypt."[177] And when Herod eventually had realized that he had been fooled by the magi, he was furious;[178] and possessed by one of his many characteristic and bloody outrages, he so ordered the massacre of all the male children in Bethlehem and in its surrounding district, who were two years old or less according to the child King's "star," whose timing of its appearance Herod had been careful to ascertain from the magi.[179] The two-year age range was accurate and precise enough, or so Herod had thought, to be certain to eliminate his rival King. However, the prophecy of the Lord's and the king's destinies would be fulfilled; and by Herod's slaughter of the martyred Holy Innocents the words spoken through the prophet Jeremiah were fulfilled:[180]

> A voice is heard in Ramah,
> sounds of lamentation and bitter sobbing:
> Rachel is weeping for her children,
> refusing to be comforted
> because they are no more.[181]

Just as the spirit of God had led the magi to the Christ child and would lead the Holy Family into Egypt and guide them back again to Israel; so also the spirit of Satan had led Herod and his men to the slaughter of the Holy Innocents at Bethlehem, just as the same Father of Lies would lead others to the slaughter of Christ on the cross—and his murderers "would draw down upon themselves the blood of every upright person

---

175 Matthew 2:13; Exodus 1:15-22, 2:1-10; Hebrews 3:1-6
176 Matthew 2:14
177 Matthew 2:15; Hosea 11:1; Exodus 3:7-15, John 14:6
178 Matthew 2:16
179 Matthew 2:16
180 Matthew 2:17
181 Matthew 2:18; Jeremiah 31:15

that has been shed on the earth."[182] Today, those innocents include over 50 million abortions per year worldwide; the holocaust of genocide and civil war in the Sudan and Eritrea; and victims of terrorists around the world, along with innocents sacrificed to the carnage in Iraq and Afghanistan, potentially the original lands of the magi.

That is why Christ would say later, "Look—I am sending you prophets [both of the old and new testaments] and wise men [including the magi] and scribes [including this book among the other gospel texts this book records], some you will slaughter and crucify, some you will scourge in your synagogues [and also in mosques and churches while Jews, Muslims, and Christians at prayer are made to be martyrs] and hunt from town to town [not only in the early Christian persecutions,[183] but also today in the various forms of persecution that always attends the Word of God,[184] such as in Africa, the Middle East, Asia, and also in China's underground church loyal to the Vicar of Christ].[185]

But, for all those who fail to seek God, who is their true "Glory," for those who follow gods of "Futility" and the "Useless One," this also, in their choice, has been to fulfil the Lord's words spoken through the prophet Jeremiah:[186]

> What did your ancestors find wrong in me
> for them to have deserted me so far
> as to follow Futility
> and to become futile themselves?[187]
> Does a nation change its gods?
> —and these are not gods at all!
> Yet my people have exchanged their Glory
> for the Useless One.[188]

Approximately fifteen months after Herod's slaughter of the Holy Innocents in his madness to save his throne, he would be dead.

---

182   Matthew 23:35
183   Acts 8:1
184   Matthew 10:34
185   Matthew 23:34
186   Matthew 2:17; Jeremiah 2:5-11
187   Jeremiah 2:5
188   Jeremiah 2:11

Herod died either in late March 4 BCE, sometime after the 13 March lunar eclipse of 4 BCE reported by Josephus, or he died in the first few days of April in 4 BCE, allowing for the week duration of his state funeral that most certainly would have been completed before Passover, which occurred that year, in 4 BCE, on 10 April. Just thirty-three years after his death, Herod, finally, would have his and the horde's satanic desire: the Passover slaughter of Jesus, the Wholly Innocent, on a Roman cross.

Suddenly after Herod's death, the angel of the Lord appeared in a dream to Joseph in Egypt.[189] The angel said to him, "Get up, take the child and his mother with you and go back to the land of Israel, for those who sought the child's life are dead."[190] So Joseph immediately got up, and taking the child and his mother with him, went back to the land of Israel.[191] But, according to Herod's fourth and final will after he had ordered the death of his son and designated heir, Antipater, only four days before Herod died, Archelaus (4 BCE-6 CE), Herod's son by the Samaritan Malthace, had succeeded his father as ruler of Judea; when Joseph heard of this, he now was afraid to go there; and so, being warned of this in a dream, he departed for the region of Galilee.[192]

It seems that Joseph, Mary, and Jesus made their exodus from Egypt on Passover of 4 BCE, as Jesus was between his third and fourth birthday, just as the nation of Israel had done 1246 years before them, after Israel's exile of 430 years in Egypt.[193] According to the timing of events provided by the "star" of the magi, and allowing for forty-seven days of round-trip travel to and from Egypt [about three weeks for each direction], the Holy Family may have lived in exile in Egypt for exactly 430 days [one day for each Israel exile-year] or longer,[xviii] perhaps in one of the Jewish communities that modern archaeologists have found in the Nile delta,[xix] or near to Alexandria. There the child Jesus had evangelized Coptic Egypt

---

189 Matthew 2:19
190 Matthew 2:20; Matthew 2:13
191 Matthew 2:21
192 Matthew 2:22
193 Genesis 50:14, 18-26; Exodus 3:7-12, 12:37-42

first, a few decades before the arrival of Saint Mark. And after the Holy Family returned to Galilee, they then settled in a town called Nazareth; in this way the words spoken through the prophets were fulfilled: "He shall be called a Nazarene."[194] When the child grew to maturity,[195] he was filled with wisdom; and the favour of God was upon him.[196]

Readings: Acts 2:14-36, 37-47; Acts 10:1-43, 44-48, 11:15-26

On Pentecost morning,[197] God's favour of the Holy Spirit was upon Peter as he stood forward of the other eleven apostles, that also included the new-comer Matthias,[198] and in a loud voice, as the Vicar of Christ, Peter began to address the crowds,[199] all the nations of the world who were living in Jerusalem and who had gathered together at that moment,[200] as through the Holy Spirit they each had heard all of the apostles speaking to them in their own languages.[201] As the crowd began to hush to the sound of Peter's voice, they listened to his proclamation, and also any of us who are listening,[xx] if we are ready to understand the favour of God and, in proportion to the Lord's favour upon us;[202] if like him, we are ready to return his favour by the complete offering of ourselves to him, just as he offered himself in his love completely for you and me.

Peter said, "You who are Jews—indeed, all of you who live in Jerusalem—make no mistake about this; but listen carefully to what I am going to say."[203] Then, as the murmuring and commotion of the crowd settled and grew silent, Peter said, "These men are not drunk

---

194	Matthew 2:23; Judges 13:5, 7, Luke 1:31, Matthew 2:21
195	Luke 2:41-43, 46-47, 20:39-40
196	Luke 2:40; Mark 1:8-11
197	Acts 2:1-4
198	Acts 1:26
199	Acts 2:14
200	Acts 2:5, 9-11
201	Acts 2:4-6
202	Deuteronomy 16:9-10, Luke 23:33, 46, 24:1-3; Ephesians 4:7-8, 2:18, 22; 1 Corinthians 12:4, Galatians 5:5, Romans 8:14-17
203	Acts 2:14

as you imagine."[204] Suddenly the voices of the crowd rose again; and then once more they quickly descended into silence as Peter shouted out, "Why it is only the third hour of the day" [about nine o'clock in the morning].[205] "On the contrary," Peter proclaimed, "this is what the prophet Joel meant when he said:[206]

> In the last days[207]—the Lord declares—
> I shall pour out my Spirit upon all humanity:
> Your sons and daughters shall prophecy,
> your young men shall see visions,
> your old men shall dream dreams.[208]
> Even upon the slaves, men and women,
> shall I pour out my Spirit.[209]
> I will show portents in the heavens above
> and signs on the earth below.[210]
> The sun will be turned into darkness,
> and the moon into blood,
> before the coming of the Lord
> on that great and terrible Day.[211]
> And anyone who calls on the name of the Lord
> > will be saved.[212]

"Men of Israel," Peter continued, "listen to what I am about to say: Jesus the Nazarene was a man commended to you by God by the miracles, portents, and signs that God worked through him in your midst, as you yourselves know.[213] This man was put into your power by the deliberate plan and foreknowledge of God; you took him and had him crucified, killed by Gentiles, by men outside the Law.[214] But God raised him to life, releasing him from the pangs of

---

204   Acts 2:15, 13
205   Acts 2:15
206   Acts 2:16
207   Acts 2:17; Joel 2:1
208   Acts 2:17; Joel 3:1
209   Acts 2:18; Joel 3:2; Ephesians 4:1, 30
210   Acts 2:19; Joel 3:3
211   Acts 2:20; Joel 3:4
212   Acts 2:21; Joel 3:5; Acts 4:12, Romans 10:13
213   Acts 2:22; Acts 13:17; John 7:31, 2:11
214   Acts 2:23; Acts 13:27-29

Hades; for it was impossible for him to be held in death's grip,[215] as David says of him:

> I kept the Lord always before my sight,
> for with him at my right hand, I will not be shaken.[216]
> Therefore, my heart rejoiced and my tongue exulted;
> my body, too, will rest secure,[217]
> for you will not abandon my soul to Hades,
> nor will you allow your holy one to see corruption.[218]
> You have taught me the paths of life;
> you will fill me with joy in your presence."[219]

There now was a profound but palpably electric silence, as the crowd listened intently and Peter continued to speak, "My dear brothers, no one can deny that the patriarch David is dead and buried; for his tomb is with us to this day.[220] But because he is a prophet, and he knew that God had sworn an oath to him 'to make one of his descendants succeed him on the throne,'[221] he spoke with foreknowledge of the resurrection of the Christ: he is the one who was 'not abandoned to Hades,' and whose body did not 'see corruption.'[222] God raised this man Jesus to life; and of this we are all his witnesses.[223] So, now exalted at the right hand of God, he has received from the Father the Holy Spirit, who was promised;[224] and what you see and hear now is this outpouring of that Spirit.[225] For David did not himself go up to heaven, but yet he had said:

---

215 Acts 2:24; Acts 13:37
216 Acts 2:25; Psalm 16:8; Romans 9:33, 10:3-4
217 Acts 2:26; Psalm 16:9; Romans 10:10-13
218 Acts 2:27; Psalm 16:10; Acts 13:34, Romans 6:8
219 Acts 2:28; Psalm 16:11; Romans 6:9-14
220 Acts 2:29; Acts 13:36
221 Acts 2:30; 2 Samuel 7:12; Acts 13:23-25
222 Acts 2:31; Acts 13:35
223 Acts 2:32; Acts 13:30-31
224 Joel 3:1-3; John 16:5-7, 15:26, Luke 24:49; Romans 8:14-16
225 Acts 2:33; Ezekiel 36:26-38; Romans 8:10-11

The Lord said to my Lord,
'Take your seat at my right hand,[226]
until I have made your enemies your footstool.'"[227]

For this reason, the whole house of Israel can be certain that God has made him the Lord and Christ, this Jesus whom you crucified."[228]

Upon hearing this, they were cut to the heart, and they said to Peter and the other apostles, "My brothers, what are we to do?"[229] Then Peter answered for all of the apostles, "You must repent and be baptized, every one of you, in the name of Jesus Christ for the forgiveness of your sins; and you will receive the gift of the Holy Spirit.[230] The promise that was made is for you and for your children,[231] and for all 'those who are far away,' and for whomever the Lord our God 'is calling to himself.'[232] Peter then spoke to them for a long time, also using many other arguments; and he urged them, "Save yourselves from this perverse and corrupt generation!"[233] Those who accepted this message were baptized; and on that day about three thousand souls were added to their number.[234]

These believers remained faithful to the teaching of the apostles, to the brotherhood,[235] to the breaking of bread, and to the prayers.[236] And everyone was filled with a sense of awe, as the apostles also worked many signs and miracles.[237] All who shared the faith

---

226 Acts 2:34; Acts 13:21-22, 5:31; Romans 10:6-9
227 Acts 2:35; Psalm 110:1; Mark 12:36-37, Matthew 22:43-45, Luke 20:41-44; Romans 8:12-13
228 Acts 2:36; Acts 5:30, 42
229 Acts 2:37; Acts 2:29; Romans 9:1-3, 4-18; John 6:28-29
230 Acts 2:38; John 3:5-8, Ephesians 1:13; Romans 8:7-9
231 Acts 2:39; Genesis 15:4-6, Romans 4:13, Galatians 3:26-29
232 Acts 2:39; Ephesians 2:17, Isaiah 57:19, Ephesians 2:13-16; Acts 13:26, 32-33, 38-39
233 Acts 2:40; Matthew 12:39-42, Luke 11:32, John 6:30, 40; Acts 13:40-41, Habakkuk 1:5
234 Acts 2:41; Acts 13:42-47; John 15:8, 17:18-21
235 Acts 2:42; Acts 2:44-45, 4:32, 34-37, 5:1-11
236 Acts 2:42; Acts 2:46; 1 Corinthians 11:26-34
237 Acts 2:43; Acts 2:19, 5:12-16; Acts 13:3

owned everything in common;[238] so they sold their property and possessions and distributed the proceeds among all according to each one's needs.[239] Every day, as they were united in one heart and soul,[240] they would meet together at the Temple; and afterwards they would go to their homes for the breaking of bread, where they ate their meals in joy and shared their food with generosity.[241] They all praised God and together they were favoured by the admiration of all the people; so that steadily, day by day, the Lord added to their community all those who were destined to be saved.[242]

The essential teaching of the church, whether from Peter and the apostles, or later from Saint Paul, whether the gospel was proclaimed to the Jews, or later to the Gentiles, was the same: the living hope for our salvation, the fulfilment of God's promises to the patriarchs, to Abraham and to King David, comes through Jesus Christ, in the death and resurrection of our Lord for the forgiveness of our sins. In one faith, and as members of the Lord's church in one baptism, we are all brothers and sisters in Christ's universal family: both faith and community is essential to the origin of the church, whose genesis begins with the Holy Family, the first model of the living Christian community. Our faith community would not have been possible without the Lord's birth into the family of humankind on Christmas Day.

And as children of God, for that is what we now are,[243] we have been called in joy to live and share what we possess—our faith and our material possessions—so that even the most basic needs of everyone, what they can eat and where they may live, may be secured for all.[244] This was the same for the Holy family, both as refugees in Egypt and as unobtrusive residents of Nazareth for more than thirty uninterrupted years after they had returned to Israel, as Joseph, while he lived, secured the essential needs of the Holy Family, for

---

238   Acts 2:44
239   Acts 2:45
240   Acts 2:46; Acts 4:32; 1 Corinthians 11:17-22
241   Acts 2:46
242   Acts 2:47; Acts 13:48-51, 14:1-2; Romans 6:9-14
243   1 John 3:1, Luke 8:21
244   Acts 2:45-46

Mary, Jesus, and himself; as Jesus also had secured his family's needs through Joseph's trade as a carpenter after Joseph had died; and as the Holy Family also always must have been generous in its compassion and charity to others.

In Jerusalem, the earliest Christian community divested themselves of their personal property and lived a communal life of common prayer and Eucharist; and they faithfully lived the teachings of the apostles according to the gospel of Christ, as they also committed themselves to the larger brotherhood of the community of believers.[245] Even today there are those among us who have done the same: from my Malta, 70-year-old Monica Tonna Barthet sold all of her worldly possessions in uptown Sliema, Malta, to build a home in Addis Ababa for about twenty-five sick street children, ages six to sixteen years.[246] Now, in her retirement years as a lay missionary, Monica's new home has become Ethiopa; and the street children cared for at her Angels Children's Home, under the umbrella of the Kebena Kidane Mihret Catholic Church, have become her family.

Similarly, there are other courageous men and women who have joined themselves to various religious orders and communities, where in shared prayer and Eucharist, they have devoted their life's work to preaching and living the gospel.[247] Not all of us may be able, or courageous enough, to leave behind the security blanket of our possessions and go off to Africa,[248] or to other places, although some of us can. Yet, we can generously support those who do, through our support of religious communities such as Mother Teresa's Missionaries of Charity, who do go off to Africa and elsewhere, or even to our own communities; or we can give to charitable foundations that support such international, as well as local, needs for others. Everyone who is born into the world is a child of God, if they are enabled by grace and desire to know, to love, and to serve him. At Christmas time, there often are appropriately charitable campaigns conducted in the places where we live, so that God's love comes to them through us;

245	Acts 2:42
246	Luke 14:33
247	Acts 2:42; Acts 6:1-7
248	Matthew 19:21-22

and our charity should be all year round, not just at Christmas; and also, we should not give only from our material surplus, but also from our needed resources and our very lives, as may be necessary from all our love.

And likewise, we also gather together in our churches for the Liturgy of the Word and the Liturgy of the Eucharist, at least on Sundays—and some persons do so daily—and if we should want, we also can join ourselves in unity with the entire Church in praying the Liturgy of the Hours. But our living faith, Christ's life within us as his grace and living gospel within us, cannot remain encapsulated within ourselves; it also must be shared with others, initially within our local church communities, before we reach also to the ends of the earth. Then, as also now [2010] I first did for twelve months some twenty-six years ago, we can join together weekly in small communal groups with our brothers, just as the women in our community also had met with their sisters:[249] we twelve men had prepared for six months for a live-in weekend, Friday night to Sunday afternoon, that consisted of our laymen's "team," plus spiritual director, and twenty men parishioners for Christ's renewal of his church at St. Charles Borromeo Parish, Fort Wayne, Indiana: to share with one another our experiences of repentance, and of Christ's forgiveness, and of his resurrection in our lives, and of his gifts of the Spirit; and to begin, once again, to take up the scriptures, and the practice of prayer, and the brotherhood of Christ in our daily lives; and to give ourselves back to Christ and to his larger Church by our ever greater participation and involvement in our local parish community of faith: as the leaven of Christ to our families, to our parish churches, to our neighbourhoods, and to the world.[250]

At home, we also have our own families, cradles of the church, where we may be called to care for our children, for our spouses, for our parents, and sometimes even for extended family members: grandparents or grandchildren, brothers and sisters, aunts and uncles, nieces and nephews—who may be living with us, or apart from us. Sometimes, and often enough it is the case, people may

---

249 1 Corinthians 14:26-31
250 Matthew 13:33, Luke 13:20-21

have no surviving family members: perhaps they are a widow or widower, the childless or neglected elder, or a never-married or divorced or homeless person without family or relatives; or they may be the victims of some war, as a soldier or as a civilian, or victims of some disease, like cancer or AIDS; or they may be long-term or short-term patients in hospitals, or victims of some natural disaster or tragic accident, or they may be a refugee. Nonetheless, these persons may be family members of the church, and if so, we must help them particularly in the solidarity of our faith; and even if they are not baptized Christians, nonetheless we are still obliged to assist anyone, no matter his or her race or creed or politics, who may be in need of us to help them.[251]

We are specifically called by Christ for whatever tasks he has chosen for us to do.[252] And whatever they are, it is through our prayer and by our listening to the Holy Spirit, who helps us even if we don't know why or how or what to pray,[253] so that we may ascertain our long-term vocation to holiness,[254] as well as our short-term assignments, from day to day, or week to week, or month to month, but by engaging each day one at a time, minute by minute, second by remaining second. Eventually, post-Pentecost, the Holy Spirit led Peter and Paul to recognize that God had no favourites, but that Jews and Gentiles alike were each called to his salvation.[255] And likewise, the Holy Spirit will lead each one of us in his way of our repentance,[256] along his path to our eventual holiness.[257] After Jerusalem, from its centre as the city of God, and after the establishment of the early church at Antioch,[258] now the gospel of the Lord is preached and the Lord is served throughout the world, as the Lord has shown us to do, by our own hands, and feet, and hearts,[259] when we keep our heart close to his heart as the Lord supports us by his love, which is beyond

---

251 Matthew 25:40; Luke 10:25-28
252 John 15:16-17
253 Romans 8:26-27
254 John 14:4-6
255 Acts 10:34-35, Romans 2:10-11, Acts 10:44-48
256 Acts 11:15-18
257 Philippians 3:12; Luke 2:40, 1 Corinthians 13:8-13, Luke 21:33
258 Acts 11:19-26
259 Acts 1:8; 1 Corinthians 12:27, 12-26

our imagination.[260]

So now, just as this <u>Gospel Emmaus</u> is in partial fulfilment of my own calling from the Lord,[261] may you also go and bear fruit for God.[262] And accordingly, it is that my own prayer for you is joined now with Saint Paul's prayer for the Ephesians:

> This, then, is what I pray, as I kneel before the Father,[263] from whom every fatherhood and family, in heaven or on earth, takes its name.[264] In the unlimited riches of his glory, I pray that, through his Spirit, he may enable you to be strengthened with power regarding your inner spiritual self,[265] so that Christ may more and more live in your hearts through faith; so that, then, rooted in love and grounded in love,[266] you will have the strength to comprehend, with all of God's holy people, the breadth and the length, the height and the depth;[267] and so that, in knowing the love of Christ which surpasses every knowledge, you may be filled with the utter fullness of God.[268] Glory be to God! For he is able to accomplish far more than any one of us can ask or imagine by his power working in us;[269] to him be glory in the Church and in Christ Jesus, from generation to generation, forever and ever. Amen.[270]

Reflective Prayer: Psalms 2:1-12, 72:1-20, 87:1-7

Antiphon: Here is a king of my own choosing who will rule on Mount

---

260 John 14:1-2, 1 Corinthians 2:9-13
261 John 8:10-11
262 John 15:5
263 Ephesians 3:14; John 16:23-24
264 Ephesians 3:15; Genesis 1:1; Luke 1:30-31, Matthew 1:19-21, Luke 2:39-40, 51-52, 8:19-21
265 Ephesians 3:16; Philippians 4:12-13, 19-20
266 Ephesians 3:17; Colossians 2:6-7; 1 Corinthians 12:31, 13:1-13
267 Ephesians 3:18; Revelation 21:12-23
268 Ephesians 3:19; Colossians 2:10, 1:18-19
269 Ephesians 3:20; Philippians 3:8-12
270 Ephesians 3:21; Romans 16:25-27

Zion.

Why this tumult among the nations,
   this futile grumbling of the peoples?[271]
The kings of the earth take up their positions,
   princes plot together against the Lord and his Annointed.[272]
They say, "Come, let us break their shackles!
   Now, let us throw off their chains!"[273]

He who is enthroned in the heavens laughs;
   The Lord makes a mockery of them.[274]
Then in his anger he rebukes them,
   in his rage he strikes them with terror.[275]
He says, "I myself have anointed my king
   on Zion, my holy mountain."[276]

I will proclaim the decree of the Lord:
   He said to me, "You are my son;
   today I have fathered you."[277]
Ask of me, and I shall give you the nations as your inheritance,
   the whole wide world as your possession.[278]
With an iron rod you will break them,
   shatter them like so many clay pots.[279]

---

[271] Psalm 2:1; Matthew 2:3; Acts 2:12
[272] Psalm 2:2; Matthew 2:4; Acts 2:13
[273] Psalm 2:3; Matthew 2:17-18; Acts 2:14-15, Luke 8:27-33, Ephesians 6:19-20
[274] Psalm 2:4; Matthew 2:19-20; Exodus 14:23-28
[275] Psalm 2:5; Matthew 2:21-22; Acts 2:40
[276] Psalm 2:6; Matthew 2:6; Acts 2:23-24, 2 Samuel 23:5, John 6:38, Hebrews 8:5-6
[277] Psalm 2:7; Luke 1:31; Luke 3:21-22, Ephesians 3:15
[278] Psalm 2:8; Acts 2:30; Acts 2:44-45
[279] Psalm 2:9; Acts 2:31-32; Acts 2:46

So now, you kings, understand;
>   take warning, you earthly rulers![280]
Be submissive to the Lord with fear;[281]
With trembling kiss his feet,
>   lest God be angry and you perish on your way,
>   for suddenly his anger will blaze:
>   how blessed are those who take refuge in him![282]

Antiphon: I have made you the light of all the nations,
>   to carry my salvation to the ends of the earth.

O God, give your judgment to the king,
>   your saving justice to the son of the king,[283]
so that he may govern your people with justice,
>   and treat your poor with fair judgment.[284]
May the mountains bring peace for the people,
>   and the hills their great justice.[285]
He will defend the poor of the people,
>   save the children of the needy,
>   and crush their oppressors.[286]

He will live as long as the sun and moon endure,
>   in the sight of the generations, age after age.[287]
He will come down like rain on the meadow,
>   like showers moistening the earth.[288]
In his days uprightness shall flourish,
>   and peace abound till the moon be no more.[289]

---

280   Psalm 2:10; Matthew 2:7; Acts 2:37
281   Psalm 2:11; Acts 2:21; Acts 2:38
282   Psalm 2:12; Matthew 2:8; Acts 2:26-27
283   Psalm 72:1; Matthew 2:1; Numbers 24:7
284   Psalm 72:2; Matthew 2:2; Numbers 24:5
285   Psalm 72:3; Matthew 2:16; Numbers 24:6
286   Psalm 72:4; Acts 2:19; Numbers 24:8
287   Psalm 72:5; Acts 2:20; Numbers 24:17-19
288   Psalm 72:6; Matthew 2:5, Acts 2:17; John 7:42, 1 Samuel 16:10-13, 2 Samuel 7:12, 23:4, Acts 2:39
289   Psalm 72:7; Matthew 2:13-14; 2 Samuel 23:3

> His rule shall stretch from sea to sea,
>> from the Great River to the ends of the earth.[290]
> The beasts of the desert shall cower before him,
>> his enemies lick the dust;[291]
> the western kings of Tarshish and the islands
>> shall pay him tribute,
> the eastern kings of Sheba and Saba
>> shall bring him gifts;[292]
> all the kings will do him homage,
>> all nations become his servants.[293]

Antiphon: All the peoples of the earth will be blessed in him.

> For he saves the poor when they call out to him,
>> the oppressed who have no one to help.[294]
> He has pity on the weak and needy,
>> and saves the lives of the poor.[295]
> From oppression and violence he redeems their lives,
>> for their blood is precious in his sight.[296]

> Long may he live! May the gold of Sheba be given him;
>> let them pray for him without ceasing,
>> and bless him all the day.[297]
> May wheat abound in the land,
>> flourish even to the heights of the mountains,
>> like Lebanon with its fruits and flowers at its best,
>> sprouting up like the grasses of the earth.[298]
> May his name be blessed for ever,
>> and endure as the sight of the sun;
>> in his name every race in the world shall be blessed,
>> and all the nations shall bless his name.[299]

---

290   Psalm 72:8; Acts 2:1-3, 1:8; Genesis 15:18, 2 Samuel 3:10, 2 Kings 24:7
291   Psalm 72:9; Acts 2:35; Isaiah 13:19-22, 27:1, Daniel 7:2-3, Revelation 13:1
292   Psalm 72:10; Matthew 2:11b; Isaiah 60:5
293   Psalm 72:11; Matthew 2:11a, Acts 2:4-6; Isaiah 60:3
294   Psalm 72:12; Matthew 1:18; Isaiah 60:1
295   Psalm 72:13; Matthew 1:19-20; Isaiah 60:2
296   Psalm 72:14; Matthew 1:21; Isaiah 60:4
297   Psalm 72:15; Luke 2:6-7; Isaiah 60:6
298   Psalm 72:16; Matthew 2:23; John 12:24, Revelation 21:10, 14
299   Psalm 72:17; Matthew 2:10; Revelation 21:23-26

> Blessed be the Lord, the God of Israel,
>> who alone does wonderful deeds;[300]
> for ever blessed be his glorious name;
>> may all the earth be filled with his glory.
>> Amen! Amen![301]
> This ends the psalms [book two] of David, son of Jesse.[302]

Antiphon: Glorious things are said of you, O city of God.

> With its foundation on the holy mountain;[303]
> the Lord loves his city,
>> he prefers the gates of Zion
>> to any dwelling-place in Jacob.[304]
> He speaks of glory for you,
>> O city of God![305]
> "Babylon and Egypt I will count
>> among those who know me;
>> Philistia, Tyre, and Ethiopia,
>> these will be her children."[306]
>
> But of Zion it will be said,
>> "Everyone was born there,"
>> her guarantee is the Lord Most High.[307]
> The Lord, in his register of peoples,
>> will note for each one's place, "Born there."[308]
> Princes no less than native-born,
>> all will find their home in you.[309]

---

300   Psalm 72:18; Matthew 1:22-23; Luke 1:46
301   Psalm 72:19; Luke 2:13-14; Revelation 22:12-15
302   Psalm 72:20; Acts 2:41-42; 2 Samuel 23:1-2
303   Psalm 87:1; Acts 2:36; John 19:17
304   Psalm 87:2; Acts 2:34; Revelation 22:1-3
305   Psalm 87:3; Acts 2:33; Revelation 22:4-5
306   Psalm 87:4; Acts 2:8-11; Revelation 21:27
307   Psalm 87:5; Acts 2:25; John 3:5, Matthew 28:19, Luke 24:49, Acts 1:5
308   Psalm 87:6; Luke 2:1; Revelation 21:10-11
309   Psalm 87:7; Acts 2:28; Colossians 3:10-11, 1 Peter 1:3-5

Glory be to the Father,
    and to the Son,
        and to the Holy Spirit,
as it was in the beginning,
    is now,
        and ever shall be world without end. Amen.

First Full Draft of Book Finished, 2 January 2007
First Edited Revisions Completed, 24 December 2007
Second Edited Revisions Completed, 8 December 2008
Subsequent Preliminary Revision of Chapter 40, 28 February 2009
Final Edited Revisions of Chapters 1-40 Completed, 6 May 2010

Part Four

Sin, Faith, and Salvation through Jesus Christ; with Our True Repentance, Mutual Faithfulness, and God's Grace

Chapter 41

The Gospel (on the Road to) Emmaus: Epilogue Our Personal Journey of Faith with Jesus in Our Time of Grace Cared for by an Intimate and Loving God: Father, Son, and Holy Spirit

Readings: Genesis 1:1—3:24; John 1:1-18; Revelation 21:1—22:21

This last chapter was started on the Feast of the Epiphany in 2010, three years after I had completed the initial full draft of the preceding forty chapters written in the forty months from 12th September 2003; and then, three years ago in January 2007, I actually imagined I had finished. But since then there have been three additional layers of year-long revisions—for myself as much as for the book. Also, when I began this final chapter, the eleven previous chapters were still under their third revision, subject to the continuing processes of our collective spiritual journey: at that moment, as should be for everyone's gospel journey, the Lord's final week in Jerusalem was the central focus for the gospel narrative. As I started then to re-engage Chapter 30, I noticed that my previous review of that chapter had been concluded earlier by one year and a day, on the 2nd of January 2009; so that now that same chapter was taken up on its very next day: on the 3rd of January, but in 2010. What might appear to be just some imposition of my constructed meaning, or just nominal coincidence, is the actual providential, real-time continuation of our Emmaus pilgrimage as we approached its destination.

Although the precise course and God's intentions for this written work are always unknown to me, I have always awaited Wisdom's unfolding from the Lord with joy.[1] Just as with the eternal God in real time, we humans only have our past and present to go by: the future doesn't exist yet, except from the seeds of its past and present.[2] But despite our temporal limitations for understanding God's future,[3] we do have his eternal promise, and often we do get glimpses of that implicit future.[4] But, as someone has reminded me in a recent bit of wisdom from God, and as I believe should be our daily motto, "The past must be abandoned to God's mercy; the present to our fidelity; and the future to divine providence." So, whatever the future and eternal may be for us and for others, partially because of what we may do or fail to do, everything depends upon God's ongoing work and upon what has gone before us in God's loving hand,[5] as our personal histories unfold over time and we choose, or not, to cooperate with God's great intentions and his all-powerful grace. God provides us with his creative life and spirit;[6] he always acts in our present; and he is the context of our future: God is the source and end of history—of all our social and personal histories throughout the ages.[7]

When I started this chapter, although I did have my personal hypotheses about what some of its contents might include, as I am writing now I don't know how this work concludes, or where it concludes with you,[8] on our spiritual journey together on the road to Emmaus with the Lord, as he provides his explanations for us while we walk together with him post-resurrection towards Emmaus.[9] This journey had begun with our thirsting and our searching for God, and with our repentance that had proceeded not from ourselves, but from God's grace within us, when also we had made firm our resolution of repentance in accordance with God's eternal spirit in

---

1   John 1:1-3, Proverbs 8:1, 22-23, 34-36
2   Genesis 1:29, John 1:14, Revelation 22:2
3   John 7:37-39
4   Romans 8:22-25
5   Isaiah 46:10
6   Proverbs 8:30-31
7   Luke 19:16-26, 20:34-35, Revelation 22:12-13
8   John 4:36-38
9   Luke 24:13-15

our souls, just as the word of God through John the Baptist had at first demanded this renewal from each of us.[10]   But now, how can there be for me or for you a conclusion, let alone this book's final chapter? How can there ever be for any of us a known conclusion, when every day of our life presents its new beginnings—and each day not necessarily entirely anew? We must live and act out each day to peal away the mystery: until at last we close our eyes only to open them again in eternity, in God's own time: which had begun with God in his conception of us and with our human parents,[11] and endures forever without end.

What I do know is that my gospel journey and yours, as they must be for each of us, are not concluded in this life until we die. Everyone has his or her own journey in God, or apart from God, his or her own pilgrimage of the soul. While each journey is unique and particular for each soul, everyone also shares his or her own "common" story in God.[12] But, as the Lord has reminded me, again through my friend who has provided for us another bit of his wisdom from God: "Life is either a pilgrimage or a foretaste of death: love of self till God is forgotten, or love of God till self is forgotten." My pilgrimage and yours are incomplete journeys towards God, although mine has contained its detours, sometimes with its foretaste of death. Even now, as I daily strive to cooperate with God's grace, it seems the only variable in God's equation is my will, which is greatly challenged from time to time; however, in God's mercies, what remains a constant is his grace, which not only is sufficient—but it is even abundant—as God wants for each of us,[13] unless we should refuse his grace with our deliberate disobedience, or if we should become so inflated with ourselves that we become selfishly inattentive to God's will.[14] But Jesus, the Son of God, has made his choice for "love of God till self is forgotten," and he had completely emptied himself for each of us;[15]

---

10   Luke 3:3-9, 16
11   Genesis 1:27, 4:1, Galatians 1:15; Romans 9:8-18, 21-26
12   Matthew 9:13
13   Philippians 2:13
14   James 4:1-10
15   Philippians 2:5-6

and in his total love of God for us, he gave his own life on a cross,[16] in exchange for our acquired foretaste of death.[17] And so, just as John the Baptist at one time had reminded us previously about ourselves when we were on pilgrimage: "He must grow greater, and I must decrease."[18]

That is how it must be for us, as very soon we part our ways, as we each continue on with the Lord on our particular life's pilgrimage: Jesus must increase, as now I am forgotten.[19] But our God, who provides his increase in us, has not forgotten any of us.[20] I do know that, if our final destination should be with the Lord, as God so wishes for us, it is beyond our human imagination,[21] and yet it is always within our hope;[22] and our path to God is always illuminated for us from the Lord,[23] but only if we place our faith and trust in him:[24] for as St. Paul has reminded us, we "walk by faith, not yet by sight."[25] For this limited moment now, we only are allowed to see the means for that walk, which is Jesus,[26] not yet our final destination, except for the occasional glimpses of himself that the eternal God may provide for us.[27] Only if we become love, just as Christ loved us, will we come to share in his eternal glory, already partially revealed to us through the Spirit—if also we humbly allow ourselves to be purified in the blood of Our Lord's passion and death on the cross, as inevitably we are going to share with him, if we are joined in body, mind, and spirit to the living person of the risen Christ.[28]

However, if we are not yet love according to God's intentions for us (and by definition, if we are still alive, then we are yet so imperfect

---

16	Philippians 2:7-8
17	Mark 8:34-36; Mark 8:37, 31, 10:45
18	John 3:30
19	Galatians 2:20, Colossians 3:3-4, Romans 8:19; 1 John 3:2
20	Isaiah 49:15-16; Psalm 139:23-24
21	1 Corinthians 2:9
22	Romans 8:24-25
23	John 14:4-7
24	Romans 1:16-17, John 8:12; 1 John 4:9, 16
25	2 Corinthians 5:7
26	John 14:6
27	2 Corinthians 3:16-18
28	Philippians 2:1-5, John 14:19-20

until God calls us home), it is only by his grace that we will become fully alive: so as to be love like God; and about this only God can judge us, as indeed the Christ will judge our life according to his words when he comes again.[29] But, if for some reason we should choose to stand apart from the victim of our salvation,[30] as everyone is humanly free to do, then we will have freely chosen our own terrible and eternal folly.[31] Yet, it also continues to be the passionate and personal will of God for each of us that all of our sins be never remembered anymore,[32] and for us ultimately to be remade in the divine image of the eternal perfection of God,[33] because of God's eternal love.[34] And because this has been God's intention for us, if we do unite ourselves to his intention, we also are saved through the gift of God's mercy,[35] but only if we allow ourselves to become perfected in God's love with his grace,[36] which is a divine process only eventually completed in us by God's free hand, as we also provide our consent.[37] As long as I live, I can stake no special claim to perfection, or any merit for God's gifts, although I do profess my effort through grace to be a dedicated disciple of Jesus Christ.[38] In the end, as it always has been, as God's wisdom from a friend again has advised me for the benefit of all of us, "This is and has been the Father's work from the beginning—to bring us into the home of his heart."[39] So, whatever may have been my numerous false starts, and although no one fully appreciates God's graces, now it would be pure hypocrisy for me to insult that grace by sin.[40]

Regarding this "Gospel Emmaus," however it is that you may have come to the journey, initially from this last chapter or in its

---

29   1 Corinthians 4:5; John 12:48
30   Hebrews 9:27-28; Matthew 25:32, 44-46
31   John 6:63-64, 10:27-30
32   1 Timothy 1:15-17; John 8:10-11
33   John 12:36; 1 John 1:5; Genesis 1:1-5, Revelation 21:22-27
34   Romans 5:16
35   Romans 9:18
36   1 Timothy 1:14
37   John 6:65; 1 Timothy 1:12
38   John 8:31-32
39   John 14:10, 1-3
40   Revelation 22:14-17, John 7:37-38, Revelation 22:1

conclusion after reading the book, there may be one fundamental antithesis to the Spirit of God that may arise, a potentially intransigent position: "From my own study I do not agree with your outcome; and I am settled on what I believe."[41] As I once was shocked to discover on one real occasion, not everyone will take up the journey. Although such rejections are not always so direct, total, and absolute, as this case shows, it does happen.[42] What I have written down has been my duty and a privilege;[43] and along with its newest insights and amendments, it has been a sharing of my Christian faith through my experience of God's grace along our gospel journey.[44] If what I have written is as God intends it, it should not and cannot be a matter of simply "my personal opinions and conclusions,"[45] as if what has been put into words is only just whatever I may have "settled" upon to believe. I may have expressed my beliefs, but we have only one teacher.[46] As the Lord so provides, sometimes opposition to the gospel has been as instructive as the unexpected support that I have found from other "disciples" with me on the road to Emmaus.

Some others might claim that my motivation for this work is based upon an existential survivalist fabrication; for example, André Malraux once proposed: "The greatest mystery is not that we have been flung at random among the profusion of the earth and the galaxy of stars, but that in this prison we can fashion images of ourselves sufficiently powerful to deny our nothingness."[47] His atheistic claims would decry not only idiosyncratic or non-consensual theologies to be baseless but also all theologies for mainstream religions, whether Christian or otherwise. However, the only definitive standard, and its absolute reality, should be "God's truth." Therefore, there is no place for individual relativism apart from God, where I or anyone else might seek some privileged entitlement to his or her

---

41   2 Timothy 3:16-17, 4:3-5; 1 Corinthians 2:12-14
42   Luke 10:16
43   Luke 17:10; 2 Corinthians 4:5-6
44   1 John 1:1-4
45   John 7:17-18
46   Matthew 23:1, 8-12
47   Malraux, André (1948/1992). *The Walnut Trees of Altenburg*. Translated from the French by A. W. Fielding. Chicago: University of Chicago Press (Phoenix Fiction).

own philosophies, beliefs, or even to one's illusions or delusions, especially if, according to those convictions and values, one remains securely "settled" and unconvinced of the Gospel Emmaus journey, which you and I have been invited to take up and share,[48] by the Word and in the Eucharist,[49] with the person of the unrecognized or recognized Lord.[50]

According to false but keenly held convictions and values, today terrorists still kill and maim; atheists still reject God's existence; Christian fundamentalists may proclaim their privileged superiority over other Christians; whole civilizations may invoke their allegiance to the same "God," while they perpetrate protracted animosities; just as throughout the millennia, personal and cultural histories have given rise to various "genuine" world religions and a pluralism of their antagonists and pseudo-religious expressions. The real Spirit of God unites individuals and cultures throughout history, and draws every humble soul to the heart of the One God, who is love and truth.[51] Three years ago, a short time before I began the first revisions of the chapters, one scripture scholar kindly advised me against redaction of the gospels, and cordially informed me of previous scholarly efforts to do so. Yes, there is a unique perspective provided for us by the gospel from each evangelist. But then, there also is our own gospel pilgrimage. After our Emmaus journey on the road with the Lord, I respect and value Mark, Matthew, Luke, and John (and Paul among others) more in their integrity and not any less than before. And now, after our spiritual journey in the singular gospel of Jesus Christ, as I also re-evaluate each evangelist separately, I more keenly discern the various colors, textures, and blessings for their own gospel journeys. As for this, I was reminded once again by more of God's wisdom: "whatever it is that one understands by what one has heard, he must hasten to put it into practice."

My starting point for this Gospel Emmaus was and continues to be my still incomplete, but profound process of personal transformation

---

48 Luke 14:15-24
49 John 6:48-51; Matthew 16:5-10
50 Luke 24:13-16, 31-32
51 1 John 1:5-7

in Christ.[52] It began with God's grace and with my initial repentance, at that very personal moment when I had experienced the emptiness of my sin and I had resolved to submit myself to God's fullness.[53] My position has never been a comfortable or "settled" one when I began this work, and not even now as a private person, when I have accepted to expose myself as a person who is loved by God, before the world and before Christ,[54] against the clear reality of my former sins and imperfections, or whatever might be construed as my current faults or failures.[55] From the beginning I have relied only upon God for my continuing transformation.[56] I am indebted to God's singular love and mercy, which in God's generosity to me had been particularized with such an immediate direction, provided so graciously to me as I had experienced it, as if I had been God's only child.[57] Yet, because God in truth is our Father,[58] we are each his children.[59] I have been under obligation to God by the price of God's Son and by my renewed promise of commitment to God. God was never obligated to me except, as I discovered, by the commitment of his love.[60] After entering into this mystery, throughout gentle humbling reforms, I have been in God's peace, and on this daily pilgrimage I am always completely amazed by God's grace. And, as for God's processes in me, I have tried to follow God's implicit rules that may be summarized as this one rule: pray, strive to listen to God's Spirit, embrace it, and follow it wherever it goes.[61]

It is hard to imagine that there are those who may choose first to read this book from its end, starting from this Chapter 41, instead of engaging it from our Chapter 1, the beginning of its journey toward Emmaus, where we all must begin our walk with the Lord:

52	2 Corinthians 5:17, Galatians 3:1-4, 4:3-7, Romans 8:14-17, 24-25, 28, 35-39
53	John 1:16
54	John 3:20-21
55	Galatians 1:10
56	Ephesians 4:21-24
57	1 John 2:29-3:1; Matthew 11:25, Luke 10:21; 1 John 3:2, Luke 18:15-17
58	John 8:42-44
59	John 20:17
60	Luke 15:4
61	John 3:8; Romans 7:6, 8:14-17

necessarily, at the point of our call to repentance with God's grace. There is no other route. The first condition for us is to break with sin; and as St. John rightly has reminded us, if we say we have no sin, we are deceiving ourselves.[62] Then, as it had been in my particular case after the advocacy of Jesus Christ,[63] I accepted and committed myself to the task of this Gospel Emmaus, which for me also has been a disciplined, refined, and divinely-gifted instrument towards my keeping of God's commandments, and from God's heart, towards my hearing, understanding, and loving his word in the scriptures, and striving to put it into practice;[64] for, as it is for all of us, if anyone does keep God's word, then in such a person God's love truly reaches its perfection.[65]

The actual practice of this love, however, becomes central to everyone's specific and daily challenge for keeping God's commands. And in this, St. John has outlined two other conditions for walking in the Spirit of God's truth and love: namely, we also must be detached from the world, along with all of its disordered desires.[66] And for each of us, the specific application of that principle is known in the private interiors of our own heart and in our open heart-to-heart with God.[67] Detachment from the world does not mean being uninvolved in the world; far from it, for more and more we are required to engage the world, so that God's will may be accomplished by Christ in us. And as a final condition, St. John also warns us to be on guard against Antichrists; these are provided in the plural. Quite apart from so-called "liars," who claim that Jesus is not the Christ,[68] and the generic "Antichrist," who denies both the Father and the Son,[69] these two are contrasted by those faithful who have been anointed by the Holy Spirit.[70] It is the Spirit who enlightens and inflames his Church as

---

62   1 John 1:8-10
63   1 John 2:2
64   Luke 8:21; Ephesians 1:13
65   1 John 2:5
66   1 John 2:15-17, Galatians 5:24-25
67   Matthew 15:19, Mark 7:21-23, Galatians 5:17-24
68   1 John 2:22; 1 Corinthians 12:3
69   1 John 2:22-23
70   Mark 1:8, Matthew 3:11, Luke 3:16, John 1:32-33; Acts 2:38, 1 Corinthians 12:4-7

well as individual souls,[71] and who teaches whomever he wills what is true.[72]

Through the Holy Spirit, everyone eventually can be brought to complete truth,[73] regardless of our different starting points: particularly so if we have been privileged to come from either Jewish or Christian (Catholic or Protestant) traditions; but also if we may profess any religious principles at all, whether according to another faith or according to some individual non-religious perspective; or even if we hold to some collective position as a secularist or humanist, or as a skeptic or atheist, or as a rationalist or empiricist, or even as a nihilist; or as a pagan. God's ecumenism is very broad. Yet I am acutely aware by profession, both as a social psychologist and as a scientist, how persons also may attempt to promote their own particular religious experience as some form of universal truth. Apart from its relative subjectivity or potential solipsism, and in defense of normal standards of objectivity, both psychology and science as human activities have appealed to necessary socially-shared inter-subjective processes for verification regarding the validity of anyone's personal experience.

But any "scientific" theology and the varieties of religious experience are not just human activities and products—not if the actual manifestation of a real personal God, or some genuine "theophany," exists within human history most generally, and in the personal experience of individuals and collective groups more specifically. In the Judeo-Christian tradition, such divine revelation comes through their prophets; in the "word of God" provided by Old Testament scriptures; and also for Christians: from Jesus Christ himself, through oral tradition and the apostolic church he instituted, and in the scriptures of the New Testament. But also, divine revelation continues through the Holy Spirit, according to God's will quite creatively and unpredictably:[74] as God teaches the institutional church and its individual members, speaks universally

---

71   1 Corinthians 13:1-10
72   1 John 2:20, 27
73   John 16:13-15, 3:34, 14:7, 26; 1 John 5:9-12
74   John 3:8

to human hearts, and as God may provide certain mystical traditions from age to age.[75]

Various religious traditions also may uphold other valid sources of divine revelation, as may be confirmed by the one Spirit. But within Judeo-Christian tradition, the scriptures hold an indispensable place: their inspiration is regarded as divine, even if those biblical texts arise in specific historical human contexts and involve the mediation of human beings and the use of human languages, in both their original Semitic and Greek languages and in translation. Although I also have had access to primary Greek texts (Septuagint Old Testament and New Testament), and also to Latin, Spanish, and even Maltese bible translations, because my primary language is English, I have specifically regarded various biblical translations in English: amongst them, but in no particular order, I have used Catholic editions of the Revised Standard Version (RSV), the New Revised Standard Version (NRSV), the New Living Translation (NL), Today's English Version (TEV), the New American Bible (NAB), the New Jerusalem Bible (NJB), and even the Anderson Translation of the Codex Sinaiticus (CS), that is based upon the most ancient of surviving gospel texts. You may prefer any of these recent translations or some other bible translations; I have left that choice to you. This is not to ignore occasional acute differences in some rendered meanings between translations for some verses; Greek texts provide a standard reference.

The scriptures are not just words and documents etched on paper, like lifeless linguistic texts, indelibly fixed, to be studied as remote and immutable histories. Behind the surface, as the words penetrate mind, heart, and soul, a discerning listener may find the mind, heart, and spirit of the living God—but not only in scripture. For the word of God exists, or fails to exist, in human hearts, where every human soul meets the divine Spirit of God: the scriptures are the living word of God for our dialogue with the divine presence within us.[76] God is not derived from scriptures as a human product, although the pseudo-experience of God can be produced by any

---

75 John 16:12-15
76 Hebrews 4:12-13

man: from one's dispositions and intuitions, by his or her privileged beliefs, perhaps even by taking a drug, or according to the bias of someone's undiscerning, egotistical, and fallacious reading of scriptures. To "experience God in truth"[77] is essentially a spiritual task, a journey through the gospel,[78] and the gospel cannot be just some academic task. The experience of the divine in us requires that other one beyond ourselves: namely God, who as a free person also must wish to enter into our experience;[79] when that happens, that grace is a mercy and a mystery. Therefore, God either reveals himself, or he remains hidden to us; and Jesus reveals himself to whomever he chooses,[80] and also to whoever approaches him with some element of faith.[81] God reveals himself to all who hold his commandments, who keep the word of God and love God's Son.[82] Our own mistakes and errors have been the products of our own sins; God's true revelations are products of his love. As essential as our prayer, humility, and love of God and neighbor is for God to be with us, Christ is the cornerstone,[83] the only source and essential foundation for everything from God.

God's revelation of himself through God's Son is conditional; and it is not confined to scripture texts.[84] God is found in love and in the sharing of human hearts: when I offer my heart to God, or to my wife, or to others, or when others make God present to me from the generosity of their hearts; or even when we are alone, we each can find God in the divine heart of Jesus.[85] Like a child,[86] we must hold on to God's hand and trust the sacred heart of Jesus, as he leads us as the light, gradually step by step, while we walk otherwise through the dark in the mystery of our lives with other souls into

---

77 John 3:33-34, 18:37-38; 1 John 5:10-11; 2 John 1-6; 3 John 3-8
78 John 10:9
79 2 Timothy 1:7-10
80 John 15:16
81 Mark 4:30-32, Luke 13:18-19, 17:5-6
82 John 14:21-26
83 Mark 12:10, Luke 20:17, Acts 4:11, Ephesians 2:20-22, 1 Peter 2:4-10; Matthew 21:42, Psalm 118:22-23
84 John 5:39-47
85 Luke 12:49
86 Matthew 18:3, 19:14, Luke 18:17

the loving mystery of God,[87] until at last God will be revealed fully.[88] But for some persons, because of their specific indisposition, that experience might never come; although such a pitiful state truly requires a heart of stone. Although grace comes only from God, we also must be ready for that grace. Before God can fill our hearts, we must abandon our heart to God, who wishes to come to us. So, just let go; and let God prepare his way in us to come: the gospel is not only a written document to be understood; the gospel truly exists by the practice of God's love in us,[89] as our personal lives testify about God who lives and works in us, which originates from the Word.[90]

For every person, how God comes to us is unique, for each case of God's grace reflects the particular glory of God, which ultimately will be revealed when Christ comes in his glory at the last judgment.[91] On the last day before Jesus died, except for his revelations to his disciples,[92] for a while he had left everyone and was hidden from their sight,[93] until he displayed the public revelation of his love for us through his passion and death on the cross.[94] So it is also along our way to the glory of God: until we come to terms with the death of Jesus on the cross for our own personal sins, Jesus remains hidden for us until the moment of our grace from him. The personal origin of that grace for each of us is universally specific: Jesus died for us on the cross, which for me, two days before the Feast of the Exultation of the Holy Cross in 2003, had been the September context for the beginning of this book. Exactly sixteen months earlier, my wife Jane's only son, thirty-four-year-old Ralph, had slammed into a centre-strip utility pole, where he and his pillion rider were killed instantly in his motorbike accident. Now, as I am writing this, it is exactly eight years later.[95] For Jane and for Ralph, there is their own path to

---

87   John 8:12, 12:35
88   1 Corinthians 13:12-13; 1 John 4:8, Romans 5:4-5
89   1 Corinthians 14:36
90   John 1:1
91   Matthew 25:31-32
92   John 14:22
93   John 12:50
94   Mark 15:37-38, Matthew 27:50-53, Luke 23:47-48, John 19:33-37, 8:28
95   Today, as Ralph's mother, Jane writes, "The anniversary date is not important. I think of you, love you, and miss you, with every single

the Lord's glory, which has been a forceful reminder for me of the Sorrowful Mother as she had laid her lifeless son in the tomb. Jane's sorrow also reflects the relationship of my own sins to the death of the Lord. But if we accept the Lord's grace and our reconciliation by his death, all our sins are past; and his glory is ahead of us, perhaps still out of sight, but not if we walk in faith.[96]

As for my path to the Lord, it began from conception; and it also included almost twenty-one years in a failed marriage. Certainly, eighteen years ago, before I came to Malta, I was in serious difficulty: my first marriage had entered its terminal phases; employment was uncertain; my emotional attachments from a recent affair were still an obsession; and I also had four sons, then from ages twelve to eighteen, to love and support. My coming to Malta on the 12th October of 1992 was a painful blessing. The separation from my children, along with its financial crucifixion as I maintained child support, was extremely stressful. If I suffered much, my sons suffered more; and an angry ex-wife had her own pains and confusions. As I found myself shipwrecked on the Island of St. Paul,[97] eight-and-a-half months later the Lord provided me with Jane, at our first meeting on 25th June 1993 near the Msida Church. By October of 1993, by phone and mail I would terminate my ongoing long-distance affair, and Jane and I began our life together. We were married three years later on 3rd September 1996, but it would be another twelve years before we were gifted with the option to marry in the church, provided for us on the Feast of the Immaculate Conception 8th December 2008. For the seventeen years that we have known each other, throughout the duration we have been stretched and pulled by many difficult events; but also with the help of this Emmaus journey, my love and commitment to Jane has matured. The Lord made "our journey

---

breath, every day since you are gone. You are one of the few genuinely good persons. May you rest in peace." I believe Mary Magdalene also had felt the same way about Jesus before she recognized the risen Lord on Easter morning (John 20:11-15). As for Jane, sorrow and physical pain are her constant companions. But regarding the cross she shares, St. Paul offers Ralph, Jane, and all of us, those whom God has called, our confidence and our ultimate solace in this life (Romans 8:28-39).

96   2 Corinthians 5:7, 15-21
97   Acts 27:18-26, Luke 8:22-25

in the gospel" possible with his mercy and love, also when he had provided Jane and me to each other for our married life. We were called then by that grace to be love for each other and for others. In this calling, it always would be best for us to follow the advice of the Lord's mother at the celebrated wedding feast at Cana, "Do whatever he tells you."[98]

After my first year of chapter revisions, just before Christmas of 2007, my former oratory coach in seminary, Father Francis Kelly (Bud) Sheets, OSC, provided me with an observation: "What are you writing? I am curious. You seem to be on the verge of producing the Clemmer Life of Jesus Christ as Viewed from Malta—in multi-volumes." I was startled by the question: "Clemmer" Life of Jesus Christ. For certainly, from my original point of view, I only had sought to understand the mind of Christ,[99] whose gospel was my priority; and when the path of my gospel narrative demanded its inclusion of my personal experience, it disturbed me greatly, at first. But two months later, 24th February 2008, the Lord provided me with the reason via the Samaritan woman at the well.[100] Like her in several ways, I am just another character in the Lord's gospel story.[101] Likewise, I find other similarities between myself and the Lord's relationship with Mary of Magdala.[102] Essentially, for the Lord's purposes, you and I also are called as disciples on the road to Emmaus with Christ after the Lord's resurrection.[103] But only towards the conclusion of this work have I come to understand more clearly the context for this gospel's biographical and autobiographical narratives: what the Lord gives to each of us includes its historical contexts: the Old and New Testaments certainly, but also the blessings God has provided us in the natural settings of our families and in our specific personal histories—a truly profound mystery. God's blessings to us

---

98   John 2:5; Revelation 19:9; Ephesians 5:21; Matthew 22:1-2; Revelation 21:6, 22:17, John 4:7-10
99   1 Corinthians 2:12-16
100 John 4:7-10, 39-42
101 John 4:23-29, 39-41
102 John 12:3, 20:11-16
103 Luke 24:25-32

are intrinsic to his creation,[104] but also to our gradual, and in his hands certain, re-creation in the image of God's Son, Jesus Christ.[105]

Some of the disciples who have contributed in some way to this "Gospel (on the Road to) Emmaus" are anonymous,[106] or wish to remain so: I have never been able to identify the priest who first told me about Maria Valtorta, when I was two-thirds of the way through my initial draft of this book; and Harry, my former classmate and roommate in seminary, when I discovered his Christmas card after ten years, he became my invaluable proof-reader through all three grand revisions of the manuscript. Others by their suggestions or pointed observations have left their indirect or direct contributions after the initial manuscript: Rev. Anthony Abela (Malta), Rev. Martin Micallef (Malta), Rev. Daniel C. O'Connell, S.J. (Saint Louis, Missouri), and Rev. Peter Serracino Inglott (Malta). Others also engaged my questions and/or afforded my direct sharing and discussion of the work in progress: Rev. Francis Kelly Sheets, O.S.C. (Phoenix, Arizona) and Father Mario Attard, OFM Cap (Malta). Somehow, so very generous in his time and effort, Father Paul Sciberras (University of Malta) read the penultimate manuscript and provided me with his always relevant observations and indicative suggestions regarding the chapters. Then there also have been informal contributions through my discussions with various interested friends (Dino Stilon, Roger Davies-Barrett, and Charles Bartolo) and with family (my four sons and three sisters, quite dynamically and individually; my two brothers and their families with their discipleship; and my mother and my mother's sister).[107] My mother's passion for genealogy has supported my own research. My wife, Jane, in the background and my foreground, has supported me for years, not only by facilitating my physical existence, but by sharing her life and family with mine, and by raising me up with her endless patience, her generous heart, her criticisms and misgivings, her compassion, and her constant example of love.

---

104 Genesis 1:27-31
105 Romans 8:22-23, Colossians 1:15-23
106 Luke 24:13-18
107 Mark 3:32-35

In real time, as I am now nearing the end of this particular journey to Emmaus, it is the 16th May 2010, the final Sunday of Easter, between Ascension Thursday and Pentecost. Although the Lord ascended to heaven at the right hand of the Father on the Ascension, Christ did not leave us; as St. Matthew reminds us in his final gospel verse, Jesus had told the eleven disciples, "And remember, I am with you always, to the end of the age. Amen."[108] Then at the opening of Acts, in St. Luke's second book after his gospel regarding all that Jesus did and had taught from the beginning, Jesus ordered the apostles he had chosen not to leave Jerusalem, but to wait there for "the promise" of the Father:

> This is what you have heard from me; for John baptized with water, but you will be baptized with the Holy Spirit not many days from now.[109]

Even now, although I am waiting another week for Pentecost liturgically, the gift of the Holy Spirit already has been given to us from the Father: first upon the church;[110] and then as St. Paul reminds us, in Christ, also upon believers:

> Blessed be the God and Father of our Lord Jesus Christ, who has blessed us in Christ with every spiritual blessing in the heavenly places,[111] just as he chose us in Christ before the foundation of the world to be holy and blameless before him in love.[112] He destined us for adoption as his children through Jesus Christ, according to the good pleasure of his will,[113] to the praise of his glorious grace that he freely bestowed on us in the Beloved.[114] In him we have redemption through his blood, the forgiveness of our trespasses, according to the riches of his grace[115] that he lavished on us. With

---

108 Matthew 28:20
109 Acts 1:4-5; John 14:16-18, 26-28
110 Acts 2:1-4, 16-21, 41-47
111 Ephesians 1:3
112 Ephesians 1:4
113 Ephesians 1:5
114 Ephesians 1:6
115 Ephesians 1:7

> all wisdom and insight,[116] he has made known to us the mystery of his will, according to his good pleasure that he set forth in Christ,[117] as a plan for the fullness of time, to gather up all things in him, things in heaven and things on earth.[118] In Christ we have also obtained an inheritance, having been destined according to the purpose of him who accomplishes all things according to his counsel and will,[119] so that we, who were the first to set our hope on Christ, might live for the praise of his glory.[120] In him you also, when you had heard the word of truth, the gospel of your salvation, and had believed in him, were marked with the seal of the promised Holy Spirit;[121] this is the pledge of our inheritance toward redemption as God's own people, to the praise of his glory.[122]

Perhaps the Lord's intentions for this book are best described according to St. Paul's prayer, continued on from his letter to the Ephesians above, and as is provided for us now from the liturgy for Ascension Thursday. And whether you may have begun this chapter before or after taking up the forty chapter journey of this "Gospel (on the Road to) Emmaus," Paul's prayer also is my prayer for you:

> May the God of our Lord Jesus Christ, the Father of glory, grant you a spirit of wisdom and insight to know him clearly.[123] May he enlighten your innermost vision that you may know the great hope to which he has called you, the wealth of his glorious heritage to be distributed among the saints, the members of the church;[124] and the immeasurable scope of his power in us who believe.

---

116   Ephesians 1:8
117   Ephesians 1:9
118   Ephesians 1:10
119   Ephesians 1:11
120   Ephesians 1:12
121   Ephesians 1:13
122   Ephesians 1:14
123   Ephesians 1:17; John 14:19-21
124   Ephesians 1:18; John 14:23

It is like the strength he showed,[125] in raising Christ from the dead and seating him at his right hand in heaven,[126] high above every principality, power, virtue, domination, and every name that can be given in this age or the age to come.[127]

He has put all things under Christ's feet and has made him thus exalted, head of the church,[128] which is his body: the fullness of him who fills the universe in all its parts.[129]

Through the Holy Spirit, our Lord Jesus Christ reveals himself to us as he dwells in our heart,[130] together with the Father and the Spirit, the three persons in one God.[131] Our hope, and our heritage, is destined in God; we are not made for the earth except for the duration of a temporary garment to be discarded for what is imperishable.[132] Heaven is our true home.[133] First of all, God's revelation is not just for those who love him, but also for those whom God loves.[134] God does reveal himself to us in this life, to whomever God wishes, especially to those who become like little children,[135] especially for those who may be desperate for God, who are suffering or in trouble, or find themselves in vulnerable or intractable situations. Religious faith, however, is not childish, or a rejection of critical thinking. Even some scripture scholars are atheists, but they are unable to partake of the Spirit of God.[136] We don't have to be scripture scholars to receive God's Spirit,[137] or for God to reveal himself to us, but we do

---

125 Ephesians 1:19; Acts 2:24-28
126 Ephesians 1:20; Colossians 1:15-23
127 Ephesians 1:21; Hebrews 3:7-19
128 Ephesians 1:22; Ephesians 5:32, 22-30
129 Ephesians 1:23; Revelation 21:2
130 John 14:7, 10-12
131 John 16:13-15
132 2 Corinthians 5:2; 1 Corinthians 15:42-50
133 John 14:2-6; Philippians 3:20-21
134 Psalm 107:1-16, Luke 4:17-20
135 Luke 10:21-22, 18:16-17
136 1 John 5:5-13
137 1 John 2:20

have to love,[138] as we approach God with an open heart, even if our mind should be dull.[139]

While Pope Benedict XVI was in Malta a month ago, my wife and I were blessed with the opportunity to enjoy her eight-year-old granddaughter in the Netherlands. Jane and I had purchased tickets for the direct flight nearly three months earlier as we landed at Amsterdam's Schiphol Airport on 15th April 2010, completely unaware that our flight would be the last to arrive before 313 airports across Europe would close down stranding ten-million passengers because of the ash cloud from Iceland's Eyjafjallajökull volcano. After a very relaxing visit with Kylie and her mother for several days and an opportunity also to visit friends in Den Haag for two days, we managed a return flight to Malta on 22nd April with our originally booked tickets, on the very first Amsterdam-Malta flight to resume operations after the week of total flight shutdown. My eldest son Ken was not so fortunate, as he continued to be stranded in London for several more days before he could return to San Francisco. Six months earlier I had been in the United States, thanks to Ken's generosity and the Lord's mercy, when I could be with my father before he died. While I was in Indiana, after my son Jim and his wife both arrived for the funeral, I then had my first opportunity to hold my only grandchild, Quincy James, who now is ten months old. Although Jane could not be with me then, it was a rare opportunity for me to visit with my entire family and friends.

It is difficult for Jane and me to be so far physically removed from our only two grandchildren, just as it is difficult for me and for my four sons for us to be displaced from each other by 6,000 to 10,000 miles, or six to ten time zones. But it is far worse for Jane, for her to have lost her only son, Ralph, to the accident eight years ago. For the time being, now we have only each other and her only sister as family in Malta, her parents are deceased; because of the internet and telephone, contacts and conversations are possible, although intermittently, with my large family in America. Even so, while we

---

138   1 John 2:9-11
139   Ephesians 1:18; John 4:24-26; 1 John 3:2, 1 Corinthians 13:12-13; Luke 18:31-34

live and are away from family, we also are away from the Lord,[140] very much in the same way and with similar feelings, as being away from family. God is our Father and we are his children away from him, and sometimes dead.[141] However, in the Spirit and through the scriptures, our immediacy with the Lord is made intimate, but not so vibrant as the glory of being with the Lord face to face,[142] which for now is just as elusive as it is for Jane and I to be with our family: for those who have died before us, it is exactly so; for all of our family who are alive still, it is possible, although not so probable for us to be with each other face to face. But, because the Lord is risen from the dead and all who have died are alive to him,[143] and he is in all who are alive in him,[144] we have hope not only to be with the Lord when he finally calls us to himself,[145] but we also hope to be with each other and with the Lord in the communion of saints in heaven,[146] even if now we should be separated from each other in this life, either temporarily by circumstances or by death.[147]

And although this "Gospel (on the Road to) Emmaus" is for my children, it is intended, according to the Lord's purposes, for all of God's children.[148] It is for anyone with any impulse or element of desire from God to take up the gospel of Jesus Christ through the scriptures. Your original purpose may have been spiritual-devotional, critical, or hostile. You may be a believer or non-believer; everyone is welcomed; no one is banned. For me this has been a journey of discovery in the revelation of God: as a humble friend and as companion with the loving and merciful Lord.[149] If somehow, you may have read this book without reading its footnotes, then I would kindly suggest that you re-read the book with its footnotes, as you take them up. It is essential that you take up your bible with the

---

140   2 Corinthians 5:6-9
141   Luke 15:31-32
142   Matthew 25:31; Revelation 21:22, 22:3-5
143   Luke 20:38
144   Romans 8:11
145   Philippians 3:14
146   Romans 8:24-27
147   Romans 8:38-39
148   1 John 3:1-2
149   John 15:15, 17:25-26

book and listen to the Lord while he stays with us. For me, it always will be a time to re-read the book, to pray, to reflect, and to teach. And always, it is time for me to pick up (or return to) the primary sources: the living God within my heart, and the living scriptures (word of God) in multiple translations. I look forward to even greater knowledge of the Lord for whatever purposes are his,[150] and to that knowledge of the Lord through others who reflect God's glory.

I have started to read in Maltese Annabelle Vassallo's book, "I Want to Live."[151] I had known the 39-year-old former secretary to Rev. Professor Peter Serracino Inglott years ago when Father Peter was Rector of the University of Malta, and recently when doing this project; but now Annabelle is dying of cancer with its untreatable cerebral metastases; very publicly she has embraced and witnessed her foreshortened path to God.[152] I also am looking forward to better appreciating Myriam England's art and Father Peter's meditative commentaries and philosophical essays in a new book to be made available only next week after Pentecost;[153] as one artist-reviewer has commented about the book to our purpose, "I also love the way that the gospels and all that go with it are interpreted as a continual manifestation of the Divine; something that has been in a state of bountiful flux for the last 2,000 years."[154] Perhaps, finally, I can also take up and try to read the first book of Pope Benedict XVI's planned two-volume work, his "Jesus of Nazareth;"[155] the second volume was finished just recently, but is not yet available. In his foreward to volume one, the Holy Father identifies its central point, "It sees Jesus in the light of his communion with the Father, which is the

---

150   John 14:4-10, 16-17, 6:16-21, 8:12, 12:35-36, 49-50, 15:8-9, 16:25-28, 17:24, 3:1-16, 6:56-63, 11:25-26, 44, 5:25, 21; Ephesians 1:18-20, 2:17-22
151   Vassallo, Annabelle. (2010). *Irrid Nghix*. Gudja, Malta: Gutenberg Press. Sensiela Klabb Kotba Maltin, Numru: 234.
152   Psalm 118:17
153   Serracino Inglott, Peter. (2010). *Ikebana: Liturgy of Love—the Art of Myriam England*. Malta: MRSM Ltd.
154   Zammit Tabona, Kenneth. Art is God's grandchild [Dante Alighieri, "L'Arte al Iddionipote"]. *The Times*, Tuesday 18 May 2010, Issue 9,800, p. 20 [www.timesofmalta.com]
155   Ratzinger, Joseph [Pope Benedict XVI] (2007). *Jesus of Nazareth*. Translated from the German by Adrian J. Walker. London: Doubleday.

true center of his personality; without it, we cannot understand him at all, and it is from this center that he makes himself present to us still today."[156] Although I am an academic [by training and profession in cognitive and social psychology],[xxi] I confess that the able scholarship of the Pontiff is not always so easy for me to comprehend. On the other hand, I very much have enjoyed being with you on our spiritual journey in the company of the Lord in this "Gospel (on the Road to) Emmaus." It has been a revelation of the Lord through his gospel and within the intimate friendship that we continue to have with the Lord. The only way I know how to witness and proclaim this intimate friendship that Jesus has with us,[157] most simply and directly, is to follow the roadmap of the Gospel that this book provides, with its gift of the Lord as our own personal guide for our life's journey through the scriptures to Emmaus and beyond.[158]

Conclusion

Instead of Cleopas and the other disciple explaining these things to the eleven apostles and their companions gathered together, it is you and I who now have been witnesses of the risen Lord on the road near Emmaus. And suddenly, as we have been talking about all of this, Jesus himself, as the keystone of the corner of his church,[159] now stands in our midst, its foundation on Christ together with Peter and the apostles.[160] As Jesus spoke to them, he now speaks to us:

> Peace be with you.[161]

They were startled and terrified, and thought that they were seeing a ghost. He said to them:

> Why are you frightened, and why do doubts arise in your hearts? Look at my hands and my feet; see that it is I myself. Touch me and see; for a ghost does not have

---

156 Ibid., p. xiv.
157 John 15:15-17
158 Luke 24:32-36; John 8:30-31, 18:37, 21:25
159 Luke 20:17, Acts 4:11, Ephesians 2:20
160 John 1:42, Matthew 16:17-19, John 21:15-17, Acts 2:14, Revelation 21:14
161 Luke 24:36

flesh and bones as you see that I have.[162]

And when he had said this, he showed them his hands and his feet. While in their joy they were disbelieving and still wondering, he said to them:

Have you anything here to eat?[163]

They gave him a piece of boiled fish, and he took it and ate it in their presence. Then he said to them:

> These are my words that I spoke to you while I was still with you—that everything written about me in the Law of Moses, the prophets, and the psalms must be fulfilled.[164]

Then he opened their minds to understand the scriptures, and he said to them:

> Thus it is written, that the Messiah is to suffer and to rise from the dead on the third day, and that repentance and forgiveness of sins is to be proclaimed in his name to all nations, beginning from Jerusalem. You are witnesses of these things. And see, I am sending upon you what my Father promised; so stay here in the city until you have been clothed with power from on high.[165]

And from that first Easter Day until the Ascension of the Lord, it would be just forty days that he would remain with them, physically coming and going, but also living in their hearts. Israel first had spent their forty years in the desert before entering the Promised Land,[166] just as the Lord spent forty days in the desert before taking up his public ministry.[167] It would take me also some forty months to write the first draft of the Gospel Emmaus; then there still would be another necessary round of forty more months

---

162   Luke 24:38-39
163   Luke 24:41
164   Luke 24:44
165   Luke 24:46-49
166   Exodus 16:35
167   Luke 4:1-2

to revise it: approximately from the Exultation of the Holy Cross, 14th September 2003, until the Ascension of Our Lord, 13th May 2010, plus a few days. And now, together you and I, we are waiting for Pentecost, liturgically and spiritually: my further Pentecost and your Pentecost, and the Lord's continuation of his Pentecost for the whole church,[168] for which Christ already has sent his Advocate to us from the Father.[169] And so, the Lord has entrusted many of us with his very heart for his re-creation in us, "I came to bring fire to the earth, and how I wish it were already kindled!"[170] May the Lord God, our Father, the Son, and the Holy Spirit be with you all. Come, Holy Spirit, fill the hearts of your faithful; and kindle in them the fire of your love. Amen. Let us pray or sing:

Final Prayer: the Divine Praises

>Blessed be God.[171]
>Blessed be His Holy Name![172]
>Blessed be Jesus Christ, true God and true man![173]
>Blessed be the name of Jesus![174]
>Blessed be His most Sacred Heart![175]
>Blessed be his most precious Blood.[176]
>Blessed be Jesus in the most Holy Sacrament of the Altar![177]
>Blessed be the great Mother of God, Mary most holy![178]
>Blessed be her holy and immaculate Conception![179]
>Blessed be her glorious Assumption.[180]

---

168 Acts 1:12-14, 24-26, 2:1-4; John 10:16
169 John 14:15-20
170 Luke 12:49; John 2:23-25, 21:20-22; Romans 8:19, 26-27
171 Genesis 1:26-31
172 Exodus 3:13-15
173 John 1:14; 1 John 5:20
174 Philippians 2:9-11
175 Mark 6:30-34, 35-44; Luke 24:30-32
176 Hebrews 9:11-22
177 1 Corinthians 11:23-26
178 Luke 1:26-31
179 Genesis 3:20, Luke 1:46-49, Ephesians 5:26-27, Romans 8:14-16, Revelation 22:17
180 Revelation 12:5-6, 17

Blessed be the name of Mary, Virgin and Mother![181]
Blessed be Saint Joseph, her most chaste spouse![182]
Blessed be God in His Angels and in His Saints![183]

Manuscript and its final revisions completed on 22nd May 2010, Vigil of Pentecost

And revisions to three sentences, footnote added, made on 11th September 2010

---

[181] Matthew 1:18-23
[182] Matthew 1:16, 24-25, Luke 4:16-22
[183] Acts 2:39, Revelation 22:1-5

Chapter 42

Faith Post-Pentecost: Lead Us Not into Temptation, but Deliver Us from Presumption and Doubt

Readings: Proverbs 3:1-12, Hebrews 12:1-29, John 7:2-18

I never expected this post-epilogue chapter. But between the previous chapter's Pentecost and now, as I start to write this chapter (10th September 2010), eighty days have passed, with some final days to go before I conclude. First, let me state what didn't happen during this period of time. None of the activities that I thought I might be taking up occurred; none of those imagined books on my reading list were read, as I had presumed they would be in my concluding "Epilogue." Instead, according to a publisher's project-summary requirements, I devoted myself to writing summaries, nearly one every other day, for the forty-one previous chapters of this <u>Gospel Emmaus</u>. Of course, that also entailed re-reading each of the chapters, and in some necessary instances my making manuscript corrections or amendments, or providing more sufficient scriptural annotations for several of the chapters, as may have been required. For many chapters no modifications were required, evidently. Of course, there still may be plenty of necessary work ahead, such as format for the manuscript, or any other pre-publication preparations as the eventual publisher may insist.

However necessary those chapter summaries will be for the

publisher or for other readers (and I am thankful for the given opportunity to provide them), yet, as far as contributions go, there still is a necessary coda for me to add for all of us regarding our Emmaus gospel journey with Jesus. If we are his disciples, then we are always being taught his way, which is so for us only if we are open to the instruction of the "one Teacher," Our Lord Jesus Christ.[1] I am grateful for his discipline for me,[2] as much as I am humbled by these experiences from the Lord. And because my journey in Christ also has been supported by other disciples, there are now specific contributions from those other disciples on this journey, who, also inspired by the Spirit of truth, provide us with instruction from Christ.[3]

As today quickly became tomorrow (now 11th September 2010), I was made aware that yesterday, when I had started to write this chapter, had marked the end of the month of Ramadan daytime fasting for Moslems. And yesterday also had been the final day for the Jewish three-day feast of Rosh Hashanah: its first day (on Tishri 1) marks the start of the Jewish New Year;[4] and counting from the 25th of the month of Elul, that date of Tishri 1 also celebrates the sixth day of creation, when Adam and Eve were created the first humans.[5] Man, according to the divine plan, is meant to be involved in God's actions of his creation. For, without man in creation, the physical universe would be only a mere machine; and it would be operating simply according to the general and very specific laws of physics, or by the essential law of gravity if Stephen Hawking's proposed vision of a godless universe were absolute and true.[6] However, the three days of the feast of Rosh Hashanah also celebrate that special interdependence which exists between God and man: while man wholly depends upon God, as our Creator and sustainer, God also depends partially and collaboratively upon man to make his presence

---

1	Matthew 23:8
2	Hebrews 12:6, Proverbs 3:11-12
3	John 16:12-15
4	Leviticus 23:23-25
5	Genesis 1:26-31
6	Hawking, Stephen & Mlodinow, Leonard. (2010). The grand design. London: Bantam Press.

in the world known and felt. Human beings further reflect the glory of their Creator in that humans possess free choice; but unlike the Creator, who is completely love, man because of his freedom also possesses the possibility to sin, which is inevitable for us because of Adam's Original Sin.[7] So, beginning with the three days of Rosh Hashanah, there are ten Jewish days of atonement, which culminates on the last day with the great feast of Yom Kippur, or the Day of Atonement.[8] And fundamentally for the Jewish feast, the three days of Rosh Hashanah also proclaim that God is "King of the Universe."

Later, during this same Hebrew month of Tishri, there will be yet another period of Jewish religious meditation, the eight days of Sukkot,[9] which, now in 2010, will be from sunset 22nd September to sunset 29th September. In addition to its celebrating blessings received from the Lord,[10] Sukkot is a reminder of God's presence among his people when the "Clouds of Glory" had accompanied Israel on her forty years of wandering the desert before coming to the Promised Land.[11] Sometimes today we also may wander through life in a desert, without the water of life from Jesus who quenches our thirst for eternal life.[12] Yet, as Christians, in truth today we can celebrate the "Glory of Christ" with us now as the Risen Lord,[13] because for the sake of our future glory with him he joyfully "endured the cross, disregarding its shame, and has taken his seat at the right hand of the throne of God."[14]

On Sunday 12th September 2010, I was reminded once again of the "Glory of Christ in his Cross" as I attended Mass on the 24th Sunday of Ordinary Time in Year C, that was the seventh anniversary date for the beginning of this <u>Gospel Emmaus</u>; the occasion also presented me, as before, with the opportunity to be with Christ in the Sacrament of Reconciliation, and now, also Christ with me in the

---

7   Genesis 2:16-18, 3:6-7, 22-24, Revelation 22:1-5
8   Leviticus 23:26-32, Numbers 29:7-11; Hebrews 10:1-10
9   Leviticus 23:33-43, Deuteronomy 16:13-16; John 7:2-23, 5:2-9, 7:24
10 Proverbs 3:9-10
11 Exodus 13:21-22
12 John 7:37-39
13 Matthew 28:19-20; Acts 9:3-8, 17-19, 22:6-16; 1 Corinthians 15:1-23
14 Hebrews 12:2;

Holy Eucharist. The gospel from Luke for that day's Liturgy of the Word described three parables: the greater joy in heaven over one sinner, one lost sheep, who repents than over ninety-nine righteous persons who need no repentance;[15] the second parable described God as a woman, seeking to find the one silver coin that was lost from the ten she had, who rejoices upon finding it, as also God's angels rejoiced in God's presence over even one repentant sinner;[16] and to further demonstrate God's reasons for a celebration with a feast by God's heavenly household, Jesus described for us the parable of the prodigal son who had returned to his Father.[17] In this third parable presented by the gospel of the day, the righteous son complained to the Father, "When this son of yours came back, who has devoured your property with prostitutes; you killed the fatted calf for him."[18] But the Father replied, "Son, you are always with me, and all that is mine is yours,"[19] which also describes the relationship Jesus has with his Father, as well as our relationship to the Father that we have in Christ. Then, for the sake of the grumbling righteous son, the Father also restates what he already had made clear earlier to the rest of his household and to his son who had returned, "But we had to celebrate and rejoice, because this brother of yours was dead and has come to life; he was lost and has been found."[20]

In my lifetime, for whatever reasons and circumstances, I have committed serious sins of the deadly kind.[21] Such sins either kill the divine life in our souls, and/or kill the divine life in the souls of others, which is Satan's jealous objective in contrast to the Lord's purpose to save us from our sins:[22] whatever those sins may be, we will be judged by all of our works, by whether or not we love one another.[23] However, sometime around the middle of July 2010, I began to experience a period of spiritual trial. Seemingly unrelated

---

15	Luke 15:1-7
16	Luke 15:8-10
17	Luke 15:11-32
18	Luke 15:30
19	Luke 15:31; John 17:10, 16:14-15
20	Luke 15:32, 23
21	1 John 1:8-10
22	Revelation 12:7-9, 1 Peter 5:8; John 8:46-51
23	1 John 3:14-16; Revelation 21:5-8, 1 John 3:10

to this, on the morning of 4th August, I sent a mobile text message to a mutual friend of my wife's: we had visited the evening before, and based upon a conversation between my wife Jane and myself, I congratulated our friend on being such a fine mother of an obviously happy four-month-old daughter. However, I only signed my name rather than for the two of us, by mistake as I quickly realized, and I thought Jane would be offended by my omission. That evening, when the chance presented itself, I cowardly chose not to tell Jane about my mistake. And the next morning I received an SMS thank you from our friend: "Thanks a lot. We enjoyed your company." She implied thanks and enjoyment of Jane and me. The following day, however, our friend met Jane as a colleague, while they worked as tourist guides: and our friend thanked Jane in person, for a message Jane new nothing about, sent to a wife and young mother whose husband was working abroad. I had not been thinking how such a message from me could be misconstrued for what was not intended. I was guilty of the stupidity, much worse for not telling my wife everything. I was deeply humbled, and profusely sorry for provoking even the slightest mistrust of our confidence and fidelity. Jane is impeccable.

However, at that very moment I was not entirely innocent because of my ongoing spiritual trials; for then I was struggling with temptations to infidelity. It was entirely irrational for me to give such temptations the slightest attention;[24] but I had, and the reasons and the solutions for this would soon be made clearer to me. But with this first incident, I now was shaken to the core of my being by any possibility of my injuring or harming my wife in the slightest way, let alone by some possible adultery, when only I should love her. Then, one or two weeks later, driving by in my car on normal business, I noticed an unusually explicit gesture by a prostitute standing in her doorway. Eventually, on another day in our neighborhood, as I was walking by, I saw her again, and walked away; and then I walked back as I was being tempted to block God's will. When I arrived across the street from her corner, at that moment a man got out of his parked car and walked to her door, and they disappeared within

---

24   1 Corinthians 6:16-20; Hebrews 6:4-6

as I kept on walking. But because of my own weakness, I had been so close to such a traumatic failure. Yet at that same time, God saved me from myself, as he does with his gifts. In that moment before I walked away, the feeling I had experienced was of cold antipathy to the presence of God—as if I were thrown into the total emptiness of the Spirit, the real potential that could have existed for God's total absence from me because of any unfaithfulness to my wife that I might have harbored by my foolishness. The torture, the pain, the grief, the utter humiliation and revulsion that followed was insufferable.[25] Yet, potential sin and such calamitous destruction was lurking only inches or seconds beyond the illusions of my desires. Through my actual intention or possible action, the actual sin would have been infinitely worse.[26]

Shortly (three days) before this, in the midst of my conflicts between Satan and my soul, Father Mario Attard, OFM (Cap) had e-mailed me (20th August) this particular wisdom from God:

> Love is sufficient of itself; it gives pleasure by itself and because of itself. It is its own merit, its own reward. Love looks for no cause outside itself, no effect beyond itself. Its profit lies in the practice. Of all the movements, sensations and feelings of the soul, love is the only one in which the creature can respond to the Creator and make some sort of similar return, however unequal though it be. For when God loves, all he desires is to be loved in return. The sole purpose of his love is to be loved, in the knowledge that those who love him are made happy by their love of him.

On the next day (21st August), Father Mario again provided me with another e-mail spot of wisdom from God:

> My hope is in Christ, who strengthens the weakest by His Divine help. I can do all in Him who strengthens me. His Power is infinite; and if I lean on him, it will be mine. His Wisdom is infinite; and if I look to Him

---

25   Psalm 119:1-176
26   1 John 1:15-17

for counsel, I shall not be deceived. His Goodness is infinite; and if my trust is stayed in Him, I shall not be abandoned.

Then, on the particular day of this traumatic episode of my temptations (23rd August), but AFTER it had occurred, I received an unusually long and specifically appropriate prayer from Father Mario. And with "God's Wisdom," I prayed:

> Stay with me Lord, for it is necessary to have You present so that I do not forget You. You know how easily I abandon You.
>
> Stay with me, Lord, because I am weak and I need Your strength, that I may not fall so often.
>
> Stay with me, Lord, for You are my life, and without You, I am without fervor.
>
> Stay with me, Lord, for You are my life, and without You, I am in darkness.
>
> Stay with me, Lord, to show me Your will.
>
> Stay with me, Lord, so that I hear Your voice and follow You.
>
> Stay with me, Lord, for I desire to love You very much, and always be in Your company.
>
> Stay with me, Lord, if You wish me to be faithful to You.
>
> Stay with me, Lord, for as poor as my soul is, I wish it to be a place of consolation for You, a nest of Love.
>
> Stay with me, Jesus, for it is getting late and the day is coming to a close; and life passes; death, judgment, eternity approaches. It is necessary to renew my strength, so that I will not stop along the way, and for that I need You. It is getting late and death approaches. I fear the darkness; the temptations, the dryness, the cross, the sorrows. O how I need You, my Jesus, in this night of exile!

Stay with me tonight, Jesus; in life with all its dangers, I need You. Let me recognize You as Your disciples did at the breaking of bread, so that the Eucharistic Communion be the light which disperses the darkness, the force which sustains me, the unique joy of my heart.

Stay with me, Lord, because at the hour of my death, I want to remain united to You, if not by Communion, at least by grace and love.

Stay with me, Jesus. I do not ask for divine consolation, because I do not merit it, but, the gift of Your Presence, oh yes, I ask this of You!

Stay with me, Lord, for it is You alone I look for. Your Love, Your Grace, Your Will, Your heart, Your Spirit, because I love You and ask no other reward but to love You more and more.

With a firm love, I will love You with all my heart while on earth and continue to love You perfectly during all eternity. Amen.

May God Almighty bless you in the Name of the Father, the Son, and the Holy Spirit. AMEN.

After praying Father Mario's "Stay with me, Lord" prayer, that afternoon at 14:13, I also sent Fr. Mario this e-mail letter:

Dear Fr. Mario,

Thank you, again, for this prayer from the Lord through his Spirit. It is so appropriate for me, for each of us, and as it had been for the disciples: "Satan has permission (has demanded) to sift you all like wheat."[27] But with the Father and the Son, we also have "another" Advocate, the Holy Spirit.[28] If God, the Trinity of three

---

27   Luke 22:31
28   John 14:16

Persons, is for us, who can be against?[29] Because of God's mercy,[30] there is nothing in all of creation to separate us from the love of God.[31] We only have to surrender ourselves to God's will, to "love one another," as the Father's love is for his Son, "so that the love with which you (the Father) have loved me (Jesus) may be in them (us), and I in them (us)."[32] In ourselves, we are absolutely weak, as my trials reveal and as the Lord disciplines.[33] But (it is) only in the power of God (that) we are made invincibly strong,[34] again as my trials and God's love reveal. Praise be God, who alone saves us from ourselves,[35] and protects us from the Evil One.[36] Amen.

Ed Clemmer

The next day (24th August), I also received an e-mail attachment from my sister Teresa, the youngest of my mother's six children; and because I am the eldest child and she was my youngest sibling, I have always been her "big brother," and she my "little sister," and we have been close to each other still, through our many childhood separations and adult reunions. Teresa put into writing the experience she had shared with me in October 2009, as she drove me to Chicago for me to catch a plane back to Malta after my father's funeral. In her letter now, she also gave permission for me to use this "sharing" of hers, "if you ever see fit." And this is what Teresa has provided for each of us from God:

Foreward. This is the story of a supernatural event in my life, one that literally stopped me in my tracks. So now either your interest is piqued; or maybe you've placed a barrier of skepticism

---

29 Romans 8:31
30 Romans 9:15-16
31 Romans 8:38-39
32 John 17:26
33 Hebrews 12:6
34 2 Corinthians 12:9
35 Psalm 68:19-20
36 1 John 5:18, John 17:15

between yourself and what I am about to share. That's perfectly understandable; and if it hadn't actually been *me* who had the experience, I might find it a little hard to believe too. But, since it happened to me, doubting is not an option. Oddly, I have never really questioned, "*What* happened?" However, even three decades later, the mystery that remains for me is, "*Why* did this happen?" Finally, I've decided that the mystery itself is actually part of the gift, sustaining lifelong contemplation.

I have never tried to hide or deny what happened. In fact, the first thing I did was tell my roommate all about it. Persons close to me, my husband and my parents, have heard it from me before. But by the very nature of it, or should I say "super-nature" of it, it simply does not "come up in conversation" very often. Yet I know that this extraordinary event is a gift that was given to me, and even if I cannot fully explain why, I do know that truth needs to be told and that God's gifts are *meant to be shared*. Therefore, I'd like to share with you now the experience of my visit from the Holy Spirit.

Prelude. It was a day in the early fall of 1979 and I was walking from the chapel back to my dorm room at Saint Joseph's College [Rensselaer, Indiana]. I took a familiar path through a wooded area called "the grotto," with overgrown brush that kept any statuary hidden. A few minutes earlier at the chapel I had received the Sacrament of Reconciliation, and perhaps for the first time as a young adult, I tried to make the sacrament more meaningful than the routine "Confessions" I had learned to make in grade school. I really wanted a fresh start.

Over the previous few months I had spent a lot of time rebuilding my faith. Initially, it was in dialogue with a friend who was studying to become a Lutheran minister that I began to question and clarify my own beliefs. We had many long conversations in which he would argue his own rejections and outright disdain for Catholicism, yet we both were determined to claim the foundation of our convictions to be Christ and Bible Christianity. The arguments he would pose forced me to rethink Catholicism and its alignment with my personal beliefs. With an open mind and prayerfully asking for guidance, I looked for answers. I needed to investigate and accept only what I could unequivocally defend. And so began my personal search for universal Truth.

Compelled by a unique friendship and some very anti-Catholic Lutheran criticisms, I took a closer look at protestant "reformations." I re-read excerpts from the Bible, sometimes at random, and various inspirational books or articles from theologians and religious scholars. I was a little surprised to discover that so much of what made perfect sense had been right in front of me all my life. And although my friend and I shared strong Christian family backgrounds, we also had irreconcilable differences, particularly in his rejection of Christ's true presence in the Eucharist. As I took a fresh new look at Catholicism, I found myself truly falling in love with the Church Christ founded. I attended noontime Masses at the chapel on weekdays, sometimes with as few as two or three others present. More than once, I was struck by the content of that day's Gospel reading which seemed to directly speak to a question I would have had on my mind. I believe God was affirming and guiding my search for answers. Every turn seemed to lead me in the same direction, and eventually, I was replanted more firmly than ever right back into the faith of my upbringing. So with a new resolve, I wanted to make a good confession.

The gift. Returning from the chapel along the grotto pathway, I was feeling forgiven, ready for a new beginning. I was looking forward to whatever would be God's plan for my life. Then it occurred to me: *Complete* forgiveness meant not only my *own* sins, but also that I forgive others. I wanted to be freed of begrudging anyone who might have ever hurt me in any way. With a sincere desire to make things right, I silently prayed, "Please God, I know we are all only human and I know how easy it is to sin. If anyone has ever sinned against me, I understand that weakness. We all make mistakes. You are our *Father*. We are all brothers and sisters on earth. I know you love each of us, all of us as your children. If anyone has ever hurt me, I forgive them. Please God, forgive them too." It happened a few seconds later.

As I was walking, I began to feel the warmth of a radiant fire to my left, and I sensed the presence of another person. The fire "burned" without smoke, pure and warm, but not hot. I could feel it near me, moving toward me, about the size of a person's head. I was unmistakably aware that I was in the company of another living being. *Someone* was there. I stood still. The fire slowly approached me, closer and closer, until it touched me. Then it moved right through my side and into me. It continued to radiate and "burn" inside of me. I was stunned, but somehow I also knew I should not be afraid. I must emphasize that this was *another being*. It was *not* me. This was *not* simply a "nice, warm" *feeling* of my own. I had no control over its arrival or movements. And I knew this was a *living Holy Presence*, distinct from my own existence. I felt it enter my torso from *outside* of me, *apart* from me, then radiate through my flesh, and slowly come to rest within the center of my chest. There it continued to burn, and seemed to make my whole heart burn too. "Fire" is the best description I can give, but it was painless, actually very comforting as it "burned" inside of me.

I had stopped walking and tried to grasp what was happening. I was amazed, but instead of being frightened, I was comforted. This Holy Presence made me feel completely at peace. I thought this must be a little of what Heaven is like, to be perfectly at peace in God's company. How wonderful! Standing still, it kept burning inside of me. After a minute or so, I decided to continue walking along the path.

Slowly, I took a single step, then a few more. The fire moved with me. Each step I took, it moved too, staying in my heart. Apparently, I was going to be able to carry this torch with me! As the fire burned in me, I assumed this must literally be what it means to "carry the fire of God's love" in your heart. I thought how great it will be to have this radiant fire and to be able to share this miracle and heavenly peace with others throughout my life right here on earth! I walked another five or ten feet along the path. But then, after just a few steps, it began to fade. I slowed down. I still felt it burning, but more faintly. It resonated, weakening, seeming more and more dim. I was afraid that my movement was extinguishing it. I stopped. But it continued to fade, pulsating and weakening, until it was gone. "Oh, no. I killed it!" was my initial thought. I must have done something wrong! I thought somehow I drove it away or smothered the flame, and maybe I shouldn't have tried to walk at all. I waited a moment, hoping it would return. It didn't. So I backed up a few steps. I walked back to our initial meeting place on the path and stopped, standing still, hoping it would find me again. It didn't return. Stunned, and now a little sad that the encounter was so brief and seemingly ended, I finished the walk back to my dorm. My roommate was there and I told her all about what had just happened.

The mystery. Why me? Why then? Why not forever? I can't be certain about those answers, but I do have over thirty years of reflection now, and I will assert that much can be learned from a single experience. Most obvious, it has been my own personal proof of the existence of the Supernatural, Life beyond what we can ordinarily experience, and I am certain that I was visited by the Holy Spirit of a loving God.

I believe the visit affirms the purification brought about through Reconciliation. I did not deserve or *earn* the visit by going to confession. It was a gift. But the visit was made *possible* by the sanctification gained through God's forgiveness. The sacrament "worked." The purification was real. Without it, I believe God's Spirit would not have rested in me. His Holy Spirit did not visit me until *after* I had made my confession. And perhaps equally important, the visit came only *after* I forgave others. Forgiveness is key. Denying our own sinfulness or harboring resentment keeps the graces of God away.

For me, it not only affirmed the graces gained by Reconciliation, but perhaps more importantly, it is also an example of the *real presence of God* in the Church's Sacraments. The very essence of the Sacraments is supernatural, those times in our life when Heaven and earth come together for a purpose, a Baptism, a Marriage, the Eucharist, etc. In retrospect, I wonder why my Lutheran friend insisted on placing earthly limitations on an all-powerful God, refusing to accept that God's Presence can truly exist wherever God chooses and in whatever form God chooses, particularly in the Eucharist. This story of one encounter with Holiness pales in the light of the miracle with which we can become a part of in every

Sacrament of the Eucharist.

Again, I believe the visit was a gift, not something I had earned. Extraordinary as it was, I am certain that it does *not* mean that I have been "saved," once and for all time; that I have somehow secured my salvation forever, the way many Protestant faithful claim to be "saved." Since that day I have done plenty to lose and regain my soul, and I expect I will have to fight for my salvation every day of my life. No, the visit was not a statement of my holiness, but perhaps an indication of my weakness. In His infinite wisdom and generous love for me, perhaps God gave me the gift of those few seconds with Him to strengthen me for the trials of my life, knowing what a weak person I can be. It was an experience to guide and strengthen me.

There is no such thing as coincidence. All things happen for a reason and nothing is insignificant. In just those few seconds a lifetime of contemplation has been given to me. I may forget many things, but never that brief encounter with Holiness. Although the Fire seemed to fade away and leave me, I still have the memory of the experience, and the knowledge of what happened. My faith has been blessed with the *certainty* gained by that experience. A tiny seed of Truth has been revealed to me in an incredible way, and it is mine to reflect upon, to nurture, and to share. Each of us will individually grow to understand God in our life, creating our own path to salvation through our private relationship with Him. God completely knows each of us and calls us to Him in very individual ways. Whoever you are, as you are reading this now, may it be an addition to your own revelations of God. It has taken me more than a year to carefully write the few pages of this testimonial. It is my gift to you and to anyone who may ever read it.

Finally, I also now *know* that God is loving, peaceful, powerful, living, and good. I have known no earthly comfort such as being so close in His presence for those few seconds, and if that is what Heaven will be, then it is to be sought after by all souls.

Dedication. This testimonial is dedicated to my mom and dad, my first and lasting spiritual guides by their words and lifelong example; and to my husband, my heaven-sent companion through this life and into the next.

After this sharing from Teresa, now as she has done with me for her second time, I also told her then explicitly about the seeming culmination of my most recent spiritual trials. In telling Teresa of this, I readily offered any of the potential sacrifice of her esteem for me to be my genuine offering of myself in my humility before God. In my embarrassment, I also wanted to be strong regarding my weakness for having followed such temptations; I knew that humility was one part of the indication of my repentance, because my insufficient humility before God had been the context for my pursuit of them. I didn't trust myself alone from the jolting experience of my weakness; but as I humbled myself I did fully trust in God to provide his always sufficient strength for me, and his wisdom for love. In my letter to Teresa, I also provided her with some of my theological observations supporting her experience of the Holy Spirit. There also are a number of shared elements between her experience of her "gift" from God and my own moment of experienced "grace" for this "Gospel Emmaus." Our mutual experience of such gifts each occurred in the context of the Sacrament of Reconciliation: hers was after confession, and mine began beforehand, only as I intended my confession and as I was on my way to the priest. Although both of us received God's particular grace with certainty and humility, it is the fickleness of our human condition that casts uncertainty. But the power of God's salvation for us is sustained from God by our submission to God's will in utter humility, but not in ultimate humiliation, except through sin: rather by the power of God's love in us, we are sustained by his love.[37] As Teresa notes, the mystery of gifts is intended to sustain lifelong contemplation, and the gifts are meant to be shared.

My writing of the above sections for this chapter was simultaneous with the feast of the Exultation of the Holy Cross (14th September), which was a fitting meditation for the day. That day had begun for me with an early 6:30 rising with my wife as she prepared for work. After she left the house at 8:00, I realized only at 8:10 (as I was focused working on this manuscript) that I had intended to go to Mass at

---

37   Hebrews 2:6-13

8:30 in Valletta. So, I grabbed my "Gospel Emmaus" work bag, and I ran for the bus. I arrived at St. John's Co-Cathedral in Valletta just as Mass was about to start. Afterwards I went to work for the morning, from 9:00-12:00. Because I had no clients that day, there was another opportunity for me to work on the book. The plumber also phoned me to transfer his appointment from that afternoon to tomorrow, so that gave me more time to work on the book at home. When my wife Jane phoned me around 15:45, she needed transportation in an hour, which I provided: I drove her from San Anton Gardens to her fishing spot where I left the car. After visiting with her as she settled into her hobby, I walked the ten minutes to home, and I worked on the book for another two hours. Then I returned to Jane for 19:30, as we spent the rest of our evening together: outside for a bit longer in the cool evening breezes at the Msida Marina; and later inside the house after we drove home for a ready meal and relaxation with each other.

Now it is the afternoon of 15th September. Originally, I had thought for some time that yesterday's feast day very likely would be the finishing point for this Gospel Emmaus. Actually, and as the Lord clearly intends it to be, his death on the cross is our starting point, which should be our only backwards focus: not by our wallowing in the history of our former sins, but by our reflecting on the act of love that cancelled our entire debt of cruel sin.[38] So, as we daily look upon the cross, we have been freed to look forward to our new life in the "love of Christ," Jesus our crucified and risen Savior. Today Father Mario has sent the following from God's Wisdom: "Yes, I love the cross, the cross alone; I love it because I always see it behind Jesus' shoulders." And truly, if we keep our vision upon his cross and embrace it, Jesus is the one bearing our cross for us, who makes the yoke easy and the burden light.[39] As St. Paul has written, "the sufferings of this present time are not worth comparing to the glory about to be revealed to us."[40] For, as we look to his cross,[41] we also discover our hidden life with Jesus, which through our union with

---

38 Colossians 2:14
39 Matthew 11:29-30
40 Romans 8:18
41 1 Corinthians 2:2-5

Christ reveals now veiled for us that in his life we will be raised to eternal life with him in his glory.[42]

At some particular point of my Emmaus journey with the Lord, I invited Father Mario to come along. My initial knowledge of him was from his writing, and I recognized that the spirit of God clearly was in him. So, I adopted Father Mario for implicit spiritual direction and as a mutual friend; and we would meet occasionally at the hospital where he is one of the chaplains. For mid-July 2010, Father Mario had been away for a week, but when he returned, so also did his daily doses of "God's Wisdom." During the last week of July and the first week of August, as I worked whole-heartedly [less my unspiritual distractions] on God's book project for me, actually I was God's Gospel project on this road to Emmaus, when Satan also was busy working on me. So, in those two weeks, these also were the Lord's words from Father Mario's pen to my computer by e-mail through the Spirit of God we share, as God intended them for others, particularly for me:

25th July: "All our religion is but a false religion; and all our virtues are mere illusions; and we ourselves are only hypocrites in the sight of God, if we have not that universal charity for everyone— for the good, and for the bad, for the poor and for the rich, and for all those who do us harm as much as those who do us good." 26th July: "Humility is the virtue that requires the greatest amount of effort." 27th July: "Our true worth does not consist in what human beings think of us. What we really are consists in what God knows us to be." 28th July: "Do not lose your inward peace for anything whatsoever, even if your whole world seems upset." 29th July: "Your life consists in drawing nearer to God. To do this you must endeavor to detach yourself from visible things and remember that in a short time they will be taken from you." 30th July: "To repent is to know that there is a lie in our heart." 31st July: "He who trusts himself is lost. He who trusts in God can do all things."

1st August: "Lord, teach me to give, and not to count the cost." 2nd August: "Remember, never to fear the power of evil more than

---

42 Colossians 3:3-5; 1 Corinthians 2:9

your trust in the power and love of God." 3rd August: "I tell you that you have less to suffer in following the Cross than in serving the world and its pleasures. 4th August: "The way of humility is this: self-control, prayer, and thinking yourself inferior to all creatures." 5th August: "The poor and the sick are our owners and they represent the very person of Jesus Christ." 6th August: "Do not be surprised that you fall every day; do not give up, but stand your ground courageously. And assuredly, the angel who guards you will honor your patience." 7th August: "The person who surrenders absolutely to God, with no reservations, is absolutely safe. From this safe hiding-place he can see the devil, but the devil cannot see him."

Because Satan is such an expert in spiritual warfare, he is fully capable of attacking individual souls quite specifically. He provokes us by his temptations to one or both of two types of sins of pride: either through presumption or doubt. The first temptation to pride, by presumption, occurs either when we take hold of Satan's overt pitch to our own strengths and devices; or it may come through the seduction of a softer lie, by our taking God's munificence for granted. We are directed towards the other potential sin of pride by doubt: either through our low regard for God's salvation, as a very questionable or nil possibility for ourselves, which in the extreme becomes despair or lack of hope; or through cynicism if we presume salvation is just impossible for "the whole miserable lot of humankind."[43]

There are different degrees of presumption: in the first instance it depends upon our conviction in, and use of (or abuse of) our own powers; in the second instance, it depends upon the extent to which we may presume that God's gifts are ours, benefits that belong to us, as if they were the necessary by-products of God's good qualities. Sometimes we may take God for granted, because it is true that God is always faithful;[44] but frequently we are not, as sometimes we may abandon God. But, in God's mercy, we also may repent and return to

---

43   1 John 2:1-2
44   Hebrews 10:23

Him.[45] And doubt, or lack of faith,[46] also exists in different degrees: from a natural and rational skepticism, to an equally resolute atheism. Faith is itself also a divine gift. Even when the spirit is willing, our flesh is weak; but then, we must pray.[47] While it is true that through the flesh there is no power to save;[48] but also, in the body or out of the body, there is God's spirit to dwell in us.[49]

In opposition to God's forgiveness, the spirit of the Evil One, Satan, also would wish for us to cling to the lengthy guilty list of our former sins: and, if each one of us is honest, we all know generally, or quite specifically, what those past recent or even ancient sins have been (but we never know them entirely, for that knowledge is subject only to God's judgment and his mercy). Oftentimes, either a true or false evaluation provided to us by others suggests what may be (or may not be) our present imperfections in love. The Evil One uses all such thoughts as weapons against us: for with sufficient discouragement, humiliation, or fear, he would hope to wear us down by the degradation or suggestion, and to incite our repetition or capitulation to sin. God knows of all our individual weaknesses, of our reservations, of the limits of our hope.[50] But it is a deception, even if the sin is real, if we focus only upon our human limitations, or on the "evil" we may find in ourselves or in others. Instead, we ought to be focusing on the real power of God's love.[51] The power of God's love in us is found through the death of Jesus, for his love for us on the cross, which Christ allows us to share with him. When I began this paragraph (16th September), Father Mario had provided

---

45   On 8th October 2010, as I was correcting this finished chapter, in another "God's Wisdom," Father Mario would summarize the essence of what repentance is for all of us: "Repentance means that I am accepted by God and what is asked of me is to accept the fact that I am accepted." Therefore, repentance is rooted in faith, in that I accept God's justification of me; and accordingly, I fully accept to be bound to loving God.
46   Hebrews 11:1; 2 Corinthians 5:7
47   Romans 7:26-27
48   John 6:63, 3:6, 4:23-24
49   John 3:7-8, 7:38-39
50   Hebrews 4:15-16
51   John 3:16

today's "God's Wisdom" for us: "The proof of love is to suffer for the one you love." By God's love, God also provides sufficient courage for us to practice his love.

On Thursday 4th August, I wrote to Harry, my former classmate and my current proofreading and editing partner on our Gospel Emmaus journey through each of the versions of the manuscript: "I am attaching two documents. The first is my revised Chapter 27, most recently, as I also have been preparing a project summary for the publishers, also attached. I have written chapter summaries for the first thirty chapters. I have ten more chapters to go. Perhaps you have some impressions or feedback regarding those summaries." On Sunday 15th August, Harry replied, "Thanks for the update. I am sorry I did not respond sooner, but my computer motherboard crashed and I had to get another computer." That evening, with my heart and soul still reeling from God's wake-up call through my wife Jane on 6th August [also Feast of the Transfiguration], I wrote back to Harry:

> Hello Harry,
>
> Thanks for your suggestions [regarding chapter summaries]. The project summary is still being written; I'm on Chapter 34. And I have been making [chapter] revisions along the way—always something.
>
> Also along the way, the Lord keeps revising me. In a friendlier reminder from Father Mario with today's "God's Wisdom," he writes: "How happy I am to see myself imperfect and to be in need of God's mercy. May God Almighty bless you in the Name of the Father, the Son, and the Holy Spirit. AMEN."
>
> Well, seeing those imperfections in the way God sees me is more than quite a humbling revelation; what is greater is seeing that it has been and is God's mercy alone that saves me from those imperfections. Although my own will is required, it is insufficient without God's mercy to me—which directs me toward what I must do.

It is good to see ourselves as imperfect as we are; it is happiness to know that God is so merciful to us. Then the mystery becomes incomprehensible; but peace and happiness return in [our] acceptance of that mercy. And I am happy to move with God's will secure in his mercy and my goodwill, despite my imperfections, as they are brought to my attention with a blessing and a whack.

I will keep you updated on the project summary when it is completed, perhaps in a month.

    Ed

Then, late in the evening of 18th August, from Ohio, USA at Harry's hour of 23:06, Harry threw at me some "thought provoking questions." Indeed, they are:

Hi Ed,

If you have time I have some thought provoking questions. What kind of relationship do you have with God the Father? Do you picture Him up on this great throne and you down on a low step looking up at Him (like I do)? Or do you think of Him as a loving Father who you put your arms around and you give Him a big hug? Secondly, what will we be doing in heaven? Do you picture us praising God 24/7? Or do you think we will be on some paradise island enjoying ourselves doing whatever we want similar to Adam and Eve? Thirdly, do you picture God as a more merciful God who will let us into heaven easily as long as we are reasonably sorry for our sins, or do you picture Him as a just God who will only let those into heaven who are really good? If the latter is true, I am in big trouble.

    Have a great day!
    Harry

I found Harry's questions as I went to my computer as daylight was breaking on 19th August. It was around 6:15; and I wrote back immediately:

> Good morning Harry,
>
> Your "thought provoking questions" are sure tough to wake up to, like my non-existent alarm clock this morning (while Jane sleeps in a bit since her workday starts late morning), and I'm out of the house around 8:30.
>
> Let's do these in order: (1) What kind of relationship do you have with God the Father? The short answer is: Answer B [a loving Father who you put your arms around and you give Him a big hug].
>
> But the longer answer is: I only gradually and developmentally came to this realization. When Philip asked the Lord to show the disciples the Father (on Holy Thursday after they had eaten), the Lord explained, again patiently and plainly, that if we've seen Jesus, we also have seen the Father.[52] The Lord has revealed the Father to us, and the parable of the prodigal sons [sic] contains a great description of the "Father."[53]
>
> The essence of God is Trinity: and there are three distinctive Persons, but each is wholly LOVE. I am wholly amazed by the generosity and mercy of the Father, who continues to love us, even when we have sinned.[54] But (what is) more amazing are the gifts the Father provides for us: no one can come to Jesus unless the Father draws him.[55] And there is no explanation of "why," because it is God's free gift [to draw us to Christ]. As St. Paul reminds us, it would not be a gift if we earned

---

[52] John 14:8-14
[53] Luke 15:20-24
[54] Deuteronomy 4:31, Hebrews 13:4-5; Ephesians 2:4-5
[55] John 6:44, 10:29-30, 5:19-21, 3:16-17, 5:26-28, 10:3, 5:36-38, 14:10

it.[56] And we have never earned it.[57] God's Son earned it for us on the cross.[58]

I have been amazed, in times of trial, how the Father even intervenes to provide direct reflective and tangible means for me to avoid and reject "sin," when I have been so dangerously inclined. At the same time, I am reminded of my particular deficiencies to love God with "whole heart, mind, and soul—without the slightest, tiniest of reservations,"[59] and then "love of neighbor as thy self"[60] also kicks in. For, if we do not love our neighbor whom we see, how can we love God whom we don't see?[61] Believe me, our love of God is revealed in our love of neighbor.[62] And if God loves me so much, as to draw me to his own Son,[63] and to be generous with his mercies with me,[64] I also have to love myself, and give my Father a hug as he surrounds me with his love.[65]

Question 2: Answer, already we are suppose to be praising God 24/7, now and in the hereafter.[66] Our lives need to be one large hymn of praise to God.[67] Sometimes, there are momentary lapses or gaps or distractions, if our attention is turned elsewhere, as we may learn to remove the "distraction" and get on with our praise of God. But at the Wedding Banquet in heaven,[68] I think we will be able to enjoy whatever we normally might

---

56	Romans 5:15-18
57	Romans 4:3-8; 1 Corinthians 6:19-20; Ephesians 2:7-9
58	Colossians 2:13-14
59	Mark 12:30; Deuteronomy 11:13-16, 18-21
60	Mark 12:31; Mark 12:32-34
61	1 John 4:20
62	1 John 3:16-18
63	John 5:19
64	Hebrews 12:9-10
65	Romans 8:15, Galatians 4:6; Luke 15:20, John 14:21, 20:17, Hebrews 2:11
66	Ephesians 5:15-20, Revelation 19:7-8
67	Colossians 3:16
68	Luke 14:13, 16, 21-23, Matthew 22:2; John 2:1-2, 11, Revelation 21:2, 22:17

do at such celebrations.[69] They are not solemn, grim affairs.[70] We will be in relationship with each other and (with) all the saints as well as in communion with the Trinity, but not as an abstraction:[71] rather, as God fully revealed, and we sharing in the glory of God, as we also give glory to God.[72] Maybe we can even have a good Pinochle tournament.

Question 3: No, God is not an easy God, but he also is merciful.[73] We are being transformed into a "New Creation," unlike the old sinner we have been.[74] After his forgiveness—and it is total forgiveness—Jesus so many times tells the man or woman of faith, "Your faith has saved you," but "don't sin anymore."[75] And, in fact, as "Children of God" (as John reminds us in his first letter), we don't sin, because God's seed is in us.[76] We are called to perfection.[77] But we are [were] not born that way. God makes us perfect, and we just have to trust [God] and let him do it. When we accept God's mercies to us, we are on our way to perfection. "Be holy, for I am holy," says God.[78]

Catch you later, Buddy. We always keep learning in this life, and it's not over until the Lord calls us,[79] whenever it may be that the Father decides: he is the one who provides us [with] our time and his mercy.[80] Jesus is our loving salvation, and we must trust him who shows

---

69 John 14:2-4, 2:9-10, Luke 22:28-30
70 2 Corinthians 5:5
71 Hebrews 12:18-24; John 15:9, 17:26, 14:22-23, 15:12-13
72 1 Corinthians 13:12, Revelation 7:9-17; Ephesians 2:6, Colossians 3:1-4
73 Hebrews 8:12
74 Ephesians 2:10
75 John 5:14, 8:11
76 Romans 8:19; 1 John 3:6, 9
77 John 15:16
78 Leviticus 11:45, 19:2; Matthew 5:8, Colossians 3:5-10; 2 Corinthians 13:5, 1 Corinthians 15:34, 1 John 3:2-3
79 Matthew 24:50
80 Acts 1:7, Luke 13:6-9

us the way.[81] And the Holy Spirit is our boundless life and unity with the eternal God, which goes where God wills.

>Have another Good Day,
>Ed

>P.S. We are never really good. As Jesus reminded the scribe who asked him, "Good Teacher, what good must I do?"[82] Only God is "Good."[83] In God's mercy, he makes us "Good" in our unity with his Son.[84]

It is now the feast of Yom Kippur (Saturday afternoon, 18th September). After my initial drafting of the new text from 16th September, yesterday and today were spent entirely with revising and providing the scriptural annotations regarding my letter to Harry. Earlier, on 1st September, Father Mario had sent me another note of "Wisdom" from God: "The more you are in suffering and difficulties and are 'desperate' for God, the more He is going to come to your aid, reveal Who He is and show you the way out." I had not started this chapter yet, but I was wondering then precisely how God would enable it. I knew this chapter would be necessary, but I needed humility and guidance from God; I was still perplexed. Then, when God was ready for me to start writing (10th September), Father Mario also provided me with another particularized "Wisdom" from God:

>God is fire which warms and inflames the heart and womb. And so, if we feel in our hearts coldness, which is from the devil, for he is cold, then let us pray to the Lord for he came to warm our hearts with perfect love, not only of him but of our neighbor too. And in the face of his warmth, the cold of the hater-of-good will flee away.

This brings us back to the 23rd and 24th of August, when on the

---

81   John 14:5-11, 10:25-28
82   Mark 10:17, Matthew 19:16, Luke 18:18; Mark 12:28
83   Mark 10:18-19, Matthew 19:17-19, Luke 18:19-20; Mark 12:29-31
84   2 Philippians 2:5-9; 1 Corinthians 13:4-8, 13

23rd I had felt my desire for sin as a deep cold, along with my greater need for humility before God; and then immediately afterwards on the 24th, Teresa unexpectedly provided me with her experience of the comforting "fire" of the Holy Spirit within her. The Holy Spirit is the absolute antithesis of sin, as the theology of St. John reflects, as God protects those who are born of God,[85] and as God perfects his love in us.[86]

The connection between the Holy Spirit and the forgiveness of sins is made by the Risen Lord on Easter Sunday in the upper room with the disciples, as Jesus breathes on them and says, "Receive the Holy Spirit. If you forgive the sins of any, they are forgiven them; if you retain the sins of any, they are retained."[87] The Holy Spirit is given to the disciples first on Easter, fifty days before the eventful coming of the Spirit upon the church at Pentecost.[88] And that "Paraclete" [paraklētos, παράκλητος], whom Jesus had described at the Last Supper also with the meaning of "Advocate" and "Comforter," Jesus now also sends to us from the Father: "the Spirit of truth who comes from the Father, he will testify on my behalf."[89] Teresa, in her experience, received the comforting "fire," while for me on the other hand, between the icy coldness of potential sin and the fire of purification for God's will, after my recent errors in judgment I had experienced his consuming "fire,"[90] and for both of us, each experience testifies to Christ's central mission: "to bring fire to the earth," both by our purification of all our sins by his death on the cross,[91] and by his sending of the Holy Spirit to us according to the desire of his sacred heart, as "fire" in our hearts,[92] which is the divine source for our great peace and joy,[93] but is more profoundly so the source of every gift of the Holy Spirit, most particularly the divine

---

85   John 3:5; 1 John 5:18
86   John 3:7-8; 1 John 4:9-12
87   John 20:22-23
88   Acts 2:1-5, 38-39
89   John 15:26
90   Hebrews 13:29, 26-28
91   Luke 12:49-50
92   Acts 2:3
93   John 20:19-22

power in us to love.⁹⁴

And so, the above section was finished as Yom Kippur ended as evening fell on the 18th September; our Day of Atonement was achieved for us in Christ. It is now the following day, Sunday (19th September), and one week after my last Sacrament of Reconciliation, and after my morning's celebration of the Eucharist. There had been two other notable events from yesterday; and from the intentions of God both events continue our narrative. The first event came with the morning newspaper when I was at work: yesterday's headline from Gordon P. Vassallo's commentary read, "Love is goal of our earthly pilgrimage."⁹⁵ The writer was commenting upon Cardinal John Henry Newman's sermon on love, as the Holy Father Benedict XVI was in England, which included his historic visits to Lambeth Palace and Westminster Abbey, which no Pontiff had done since the foundation of the Church of England, when King Henry VIII broke with Rome in 1534; and where today, as I write, the Pope is celebrating Mass in Cofton Park, Birmingham for the occasion of Cardinal John Henry Newman's beatification. What struck me was the Cardinal's citation in his sermon of two verses from the letter of St. Paul:

> If I had the gift of being able to speak in other languages without learning them, and could speak in every language there is in all of heaven and earth, but didn't love others, I would only be making noise.⁹⁶ If I had the gift of prophecy and knew everything about everything, but didn't love others, what good would it do? Even [if] I had the gift of faith so that I could speak to a mountain and make it move, I would still be worth nothing at all without love.⁹⁷

And the second of yesterday's key events came to me from Father Mario, who had provided yesterday's "God's Wisdom" with these

---

[94] Romans 8:12-17, 36-39; 1 Corinthians 13:4-7, 1 John 3:16-24, 4:7-12
[95] www.timesofmalta.com/articles/view/20100918/opinion/love-is-goal-of-our-earthly-pilgrimage
[96] 1 Corinthians 13:1
[97] 1 Corinthians 13:2

words: "Humility and charity go hand in hand. The one glorifies, the other sanctifies.[98] May God Almighty bless you in the Name of the Father, the Son and the Holy Spirit. AMEN."

Initially, I was struck by these familiar verses from Saint Paul, not only because they were verses keenly known to me from my scientific research of more than thirty years ago with Father Dan O'Connell, S.J., when we had used that scripture in a study of rhetorical reading; but for me in this time, I saw those verses now in a way that I had never understood before. They specifically were God's words to me very personally, now. In my former academic profession as a psychologist, I had focused mainly on language and communication; and I am familiar with several languages besides my native English (notably with Maltese, Spanish, Italian, French, Latin, and elemental German); even more so, my wife Jane speaks those first five languages fluently, and she understands Portuguese and attempts to learn Dutch. As central to our shared lives as these interests and facility with languages are, if I am without love—they are nothing. And even if there may be some gift of prophecy and knowledge in this <u>Gospel Emmaus</u>, (admittedly through whatever is God's will, and this work is his), if I failed in love by my not loving others (although through this work I am loving my God and others too), then without love in me there would be no good in whatever I may do. Undoubtedly, although I do have the gift of faith (but not so much as to move mountains, as my temptations revealed), if I should have the greatest possible faith (and faith is only possible from God), my true faith would be nothing if I am without love. So, the first two essential ingredients for our life-pilgrimage on the road to God are humility and love, described by "God's Wisdom" and St. Paul.[99]

Then today, less than an hour ago, as Pope Benedict delivered his sermon on Cardinal John Henry Newman,[100] the Holy Father has recognized the holiness of this saintly "confessor," who bore such eloquent witness to the Lord by his "priestly ministry," and especially

---

98   Philippians 1:19-20
99   Philippians 2:1-13
100   www.vatican.va/holy_father/benedict_xvi/homilies/2010/documents/hf_ben-xvi_hom_20100919_beatif-newman_en.html

by his "preaching, teaching, and writing":

> In Blessed John Henry, that tradition of gentle scholarship, deep human wisdom and profound love for the Lord has borne rich fruit, as a sign of the abiding presence of the Holy Spirit deep within the heart of God's people, bringing forth abundant gifts of holiness. Cardinal Newman's motto, *Cor ad cor loquitur,* or "Heart speaks unto heart," gives us an insight into his understanding of the Christian life as a call to holiness, experienced as the profound desire of the human heart to enter into intimate communion with the Heart of God. He reminds us that faithfulness to prayer gradually transforms us into the divine likeness.

So, the model of Blessed John Henry provides a rationale for us, as Christ has led us on his Emmaus journey, as God speaks to us in our hearts, and as God leads us towards our ultimate intimacy and union with the Trinity: so for our life's Gospel journey, only three elements then are required: humility, love, and prayer.

Hope and faith are derived from love: the greatest of these is love.[101] All three require courage, but love is primary. Without love, there is nothing. With love, even if hope and faith are weak, love maintains our hope and supports our faith; love is the cornerstone and the engine of life. Love is the essence of God. Present sins, if we listen to the Spirit of God,[102] may provide us with shame, guilt, and possibly fear.[103] But, as Father Mario provides in today's "God's Wisdom," we are reminded, "His door is always open, unlike man's. We can always say to Him in our hearts, 'Lord, have mercy.'" This prayer and every prayer (especially our prayers of love and gratitude to God) is our first resource that we have with our God who is always there for us. Christ already has taken our individual guilt and shame upon himself through the cross; he already has exchanged our own death from sin, to our resurrection from the dead by his life in us.[104]

---

101   1 Corinthians 13:13
102   1 John 3:20-24
103   1 John 4:17-21
104   John 5:25, 6:51; John 5:21, 6:65

If there is humility in us, we can make the prayer. Then it is with God's mercy and grace that Jesus breathes his Holy Spirit upon us, and so leads us to his perfect love.

Another day has come and gone; and this new day (20th September) is almost gone itself. But the perfect beginning has come to me at 18:30, when I collected today's "God's Wisdom" from Father Mario: "The Lord is passing meek, and merciful, and good; and when the soul knows Him, she marvels greatly, and exclaims: 'O what a Lord is ours.' May God Almighty bless you in the Name of the Father, the Son and Holy Spirit. AMEN." The description, of course, refers to Christ, the Lord. But, in this case, my soul also recognizes this description as belonging to my wife, Jane, through whom I love Christ. And because of her as God's gift to me, I can also exclaim, "Oh what a Lord is ours!"

Jane is a sacred sacramental "sign" of God's love for me; and she is my vocation to love, in the same "sign" of God's covenant of love that God provides for both of us. Jane is meek: she does not assume airs, or presume status, or privilege, but she only affirms her own personal dignity and self-respect, which I affirm in her. She is merciful: never is she vengeful, spiteful, or continuously complaining for the many wrongs committed against her, or when she is angry because of injustices she sees perpetrated against others, or as she suffers when she learns of the sorrows or pain of others and she wants to comfort them. And Jane is good: she is honest, astute, and selfless for nearly anyone she meets, as she gives of her patience, of her time, and of her increasingly more limited physical energy; she always provides the sincerity and reflection of her unique and complex character, while she manages to hide the trauma and sorrows of her personal crosses. It has been a blessing from God for me to have Jane as my wife. She is thoughtful and generous, even as she humbly shares the woes of her day with me. Most importantly, she allows me to love her, to share her world, and to assist to all her needs. She is unquestionably generous in allowing me such complete freedom to pursue my passions and projects, while I provide the daily necessities for household management and everyday living.

Jane has provided me with a home, with a new country, with an income-producing job, with my connection to and integration with humanity, allowing me to live again after so much oppression. She has been a comforter and a sympathetic advisor to all my personal circumstances. She has allowed me to share my family with her, even as her own family has been reduced, either by death, or by distance, or by their peculiar separations. She has shared her family with me: her father had been such a generous and admirable man, more the age of my mother's father, but still a gracious father-in-law to me. Jane's son Ralph was her great joy and sorrow, as together we all struggled with his demons; but Ralph also made us all better persons, although we suffered too. His great patience, gargantuan determination, and perpetual respect for individuals, including social outcasts, were most remarkable; he displayed so much of his mother's character, and the courageous effect of his mother's love on him. We missed Ralph so very much, as Jane's soul still suffers from his death as a mother's worst nightmare come true. She and I may have shared the joys and the sorrows and the anguish together; but there is nothing to remove her pain. It is my privilege from God to love Jane, as much as it is for her to love me; and so often she seems to do a better job of it. She is like a wife and a mother; because she is a wife and she has been a mother. I am glad to be her husband, for us to be exclusive and intimate friends. Although we have so many acquaintances and associates and there is family, our devotion to each other is reserved for us.

Jane, my mother, and my mother's sister, are the three most exclusive women of my life; and I don't seek any such relationship with any other persons, man or woman. There are, however, special relationships with my four sons and with family. Yet, by far, the most intimate relationship I have with anyone is my relationship with God. In part, this book also shares that intimacy with you. The intimacy of God with us in our soul is more profound than every possible human relationship, even the relationship I have with my wife; yet, that very relationship I have with Jane reflects the intimacy God has with me. There is love; there is mystery; there is trust; there is comfort; and there is hope. Now, as my writing of the above has slipped into today (21st September, my mother's birthday),[105] Father Mario has sent us another piece of "God's Wisdom" for the day: "And every day, when your heart especially feels the loneliness of life, pray. Pray to the Lord, because even God needs our prayers." This is true, just as there should never be loneliness between spouses. Imagine the loneliness God would feel when we are espoused to him, as we are, but we also fail to talk to him. Our prayer to God should be as natural as the fluid intimacy between a husband and wife together.

It is so tragic when the experience of marriage goes wrong or a marriage is destroyed. It may be difficult to believe in marriage again; or perhaps, it may be even more difficult to believe in a God again, when human love in its most intimate character has been shattered, just as when we loose someone in death: like our spouse, or even a child. My wife Jane had suffered both: a first marriage that failed just as it started; and a grown son who died unexpectedly a few days after her unique "night terror" of visiting "death," his leaving behind an infant child. For me, my first marriage also had failed, in a relationship lasting twenty-one years; and as I had to leave that relationship behind, I was separated from the only element that made that failed relationship worthwhile, my four sons; more importantly, we were separated from each other, long before the advent of e-mail. But, unlike Jane, for me, all of my sons are alive. They each now have their own lives, of course; and we keep in touch; but the geographical distances are prohibitive. Jane and I each have a grandchild, her granddaughter and my grandson, but circumstances limit opportunities for the grandchildren to connect to their Maltese grandparents. But now, in God's providence, Jane and I have each other and, in God's most visible blessing to us, we have recently remarried in the Church. For marriage is the model for God's divine love for us. Marriage also is the model for Christ's description of heaven: we are espoused to God.[106] Indeed, "Oh, what a Lord is ours!" God, who is perfect love,[107] is espoused to us.

---

105 Actually, as my mother would remind me on 5th October 2010, her birthday was 13th September (1926); for I had confused the date (21st) with the birthday of my mother's sister, Aunt Mary Ann, 21st May (1943).
106 John 2:1-11, Revelation 21:2
107 John 13:34-35, 17:20-26; 1 John 3:23, 4:7-12

In my real time, it is now the early morning (23rd September) of Sukkot which began last night. Yesterday, a Wednesday, had been a full day: in the morning, Jane and I went to work, she to her half-day of tourist guiding and I went to work in Valletta, which included some sales and my review and writing for this chapter. We arrived back home simultaneously at 13:00. Jane began to tackle pan-grilling the fish she had caught recently taken from our freezer; she already had cleaned them that morning as I assisted in the cleanup after her, now preparing the fish with capers and olives and mint, just as her mother used to do in the Mediterranean style. I began preparing another Mediterranean dish: a salad of green, red, and yellow bell-peppers, so that they would be ready for cooking with their garlic and olives after lunch; we only ate fish for lunch. Afterwards, about 14:45, we enjoyed some minutes of computer-time together; then Jane assembled her fishing gear, as I carried it and her folding chair to the car, and drove her to her fishing spot. From there I drove off to Valletta for an appointment with a client. By 16:00, I had returned to Msida, but Jane needed more bait (frozen shrimp) and we needed some few groceries: so I drove off to buy both; then returned to Jane as she fished. Because I had bought gross salt, I could add it then to the shrimps she had been using for that day.

Leaving the car with her, and unlocked because of the threat of rain, I walked home carrying the bread, salt, balsamic vinegar, and the new container of frozen shrimp in my arms. Once home, I immediately lit the gas stove to boil our fish soup, for which Jane had cleaned the fish mid-day, while I had peeled and cut the potatoes and garlic, and she had added a fresh tomato, after frying the garlic in oil. With the soup on, I edited this chapter for more than two hours until 19:00; then I walked to fetch Jane and the car. As I found her, she had just lost part of her fishing pole to the sea; but she had saved her bobber, one of the floats I had brought for her from America. We arrived home about 19:45, in time for listening to the local news as I boiled Maltese sausages and prepared myself a cucumber/tomato salad, while Jane prepared the pepper salad with garlic, olive oil, and vinegar. We were both exhausted as I cleared the table and stacked the dishes for today's washing up of dishes and pans, which I had rinsed and stacked for the task. We attempted to find some light television to relax; and at 22:00, I found some walnut ice cream for dessert, which Jane loves but her diabetes doesn't; by 23:00, our medications were consumed, lights out.

After my chronicle above regarding yesterday, written this morning, the rest of today runs along: it is approximately 16:30; Jane has another 90 minutes or so of work; I returned home about 13:30, with morning business finished and with a replacement computer-mouse in hand. After grabbing a salad for lunch, I completed some business and tackled the dishes, finishing in time for me to run again to Valletta by car to meet a client at 15:30. This morning as I caught the bus to work, poor Jane was still trying to figure out her transportation to the Port, where she started her workday late morning. After returning home around 16:00, I addressed some needs for order in the house, so that when Jane returned home, the usual clutter would not disturb her required peace. More frequently, I miss this priority as I rush to "higher-order" activities; however, I believe that I may be still trainable for keeping focus on Jane, as I try to learn. There is a fine difference between balancing and ignoring, and the daily issue is always never ignore; do remember; be genuinely sorry when I can improve; always think a little bit more about her than I do for me; and make evident that I love her, especially by the ordinary things I sometimes forget or take for granted. Hopefully, after I retrieve Jane from the Port, we will be OK about visiting a neighbor in hospital: we've only managed one visit already, as these weeks have piled up. Jane is trying to balance her end-of-day fatigue, her need to rest, her neighbor's needs, and her own desire to make a charitable visit as a friend. It isn't always so easy.

Now from the perspective of Friday morning (24th September), we did get to the hospital yesterday evening. Out of respect for Olga's privacy, I remained in the hospital lobby while Jane bought Olga a small item from the gift shop and proceeded to Olga's room on WS1 (Women's Surgery First Floor), yellow ward. Olga now had moved to a private room, as Jane meets Olga's husband going out of the room as he leaves for home after spending the day with his wife. Her daughters are looking on, as Olga seems to be barely more than skin and bones surrounded by various bags of bodily fluids. Jane, frankly, doesn't know what to say during her 15-minute visit, which Jane concludes by telling Olga, "We'll throw a party when you come home." As we drive home, Jane with obviously pressing anguish tells me what had happened; at the same time, I point out a pleasant distraction: on the horizon above the highway, the moon reveals itself as a full, sharp, white-orange disc, stamped against the cloudless light-blue sky of the remaining light of day. At home, although I would like to write, we spend the rest of the evening together as Jane's sadness and shock are barely contained. She shows me her vulnerable insecurities. I know that she appreciates our evening relaxing together. When we decide to sleep, my wrist watch chimes midnight.

At 4:45 this morning (24th September), Jane thinks that it is an hour later as we both get up for our bathroom visits (my first visit was two hours before). The Msida bells of St. Joseph's Church then ring out five o'clock. I roll over on my back. Fifteen minutes later, Jane holds me and says, "Whenever I see pain and suffering, I realize how much we need each other." A few minutes later, a horse and carriage passes beneath our open balcony window. When the church bells chime 5:30, I get up and leave Jane in bed to her snoring, as I climb the stairs in the dark without the lights, so as not to disturb her sleep. Outside my library window, there are thick dark clouds partially illuminated by the western moon, which is not in sight obstructed by buildings: it's like an Édouard Manet painting. I try to write; but I'm unsuccessful as Jane's mobile alarm rings out 7:00. When her phone sounds again, I go downstairs to help turn off her alarm, and I set her phone to charge. Again I try to write, but I manage only some revisions. At Jane's request, from the stairwell I pitch her some necessary clothes from the upstairs bedroom. Then I get dressed; put out the rubbish; pack my things including breakfast, close and lock the balcony, comb my hair, and wait for Jane; there was no time today for a shower or shave. Jane barely remembers to take her pill for diabetes, almost forgets her phone, but on the way to the car she has forgotten her lipstick and umbrella—she'll be making do with her pre-packed plastic rain cape. This morning I should have provided her with greater assistance. I drive her to work and return home to park the car, as I take the bus to Valletta just on time for work. There I write the two paragraphs above; now as I finish typing, it is time for me to gather together Jane's fishing gear; pick her up at 17:00 from a hotel; and deliver her to the Msida Marina for her hobby.

A week ago, on the evening Yom Kippur began, which this year was on Friday on the day Jesus died for our sins, Jane and I saw a film together at St. Paul's Bay, which we combined afterwards with a Chinese Buffet. The film, "Agora," was from the Chilean-born Spanish director Alejandro Amenábar, and it had been shot entirely in Malta. Hundreds of Maltese were involved in the film's production, including several of Malta's leading actors whom Jane and I have often enjoyed in our local theatre productions. The protagonist of this film was Hypatia, the late 4th-century CE Egyptian mathematician, astronomer, and philosopher. Although none of her academic works have survived, she was at the heart of promoting advances of knowledge in Alexandria, where her father was librarian for the famous library in the city Alexander the Great had founded. In the film, Hypatia espouses religious tolerance and the brotherhood of all men and women—a very modern woman, indeed—against the backdrop of initial political violence by the Pagans to preserve their culture against the Christians, which was followed by violent Christian retaliation, which in turn forces the Pagans to share political power with Christians.

Eventually, the Christians also set out to eliminate or expel the Jewish population from Alexandria. When this Christian violence is directed towards the library of Alexandria, most of its manuscripts are destroyed. Hypatia removes her household and her remaining "mini-library" to safer quarters; and the buildings housing the former library are expropriated by the Christians for their religious purposes. As the Christians persecute and displace the Jewish population, Hypatia by her opposition also is singled out to die: in actual fact, her pulverized and naked body was dragged through the streets of "Christian" Alexandria, in public display of the "witch," a "woman" who had dared her freedom in the truth, for the common brotherhood of man, and for the pursuit of knowledge. To remain free, she had the courage never to wed, and courage to resist her forcible "baptism and conversion" into Christianity, which she had properly recognized would be an unjust cooperation with the political oppression.

In slightly more than two centuries, Islam would rise to take Arabia by storm in its eventual political ascendancy over North Africa. Islam would also advance throughout Africa to the Middle and Far East, and into parts of Europe, perhaps most notably as a political threat for "Christian" Europe into Spain and Turkey. Much of Renaissance European scholarship finds its scientific and Western heritage in cultural contributions from the Arabic world. But eventually, the last Moorish bastion in Spain, Granada, fell in 1492; and the Ottoman Turks in their European ambitions were crushed by the failed Great Siege of Malta, which campaign over several months in 1565 was concluded on 8th September. Christianity would be extended throughout the world by the colonial expansion of European powers, sometimes jeopardizing indigenous cultures and populations.

Only two weeks ago, Terry Jones from Gainesville, Florida, a so-called "Christian" Pastor with a proclaimed 50-member congregation, proposed his aborted stunt to burn the Qur'an on the 9th anniversary of the 11th September 2001 terrorist attack. Controversy also raged in the United States over plans to place an Islamic cultural center and mosque a few blocks from the site of New York's "ground zero." The attack was blamed on reactive political and religious fundamentalism derived from Islamic cultures. More than 3,000 had perished in the holocaust, which includes the many lives lost at the Washington, DC site and in the crash of Flight 93 in Pennsylvania, where the fourth and final plane of the attack was thwarted by its passengers and crew. The imposition of religious or political goals through violent methods violates the divine dignity God provides for humans by our freedom and reason, not unbridled freedom, but only our dignity of freedom based in truth. Hypatia was closer to God than were many religious and political fundamentalists of her time and ours; for God does not impose his will on anyone. However, God does insist that we freely love him (and consequently our neighbor as ourselves) in spirit and truth.

As I now am writing, it has become Saturday (25th September). In one week, on 2nd October, my youngest son Stephen and his bride

Danielle Wyck will be married (God bless them!) after the conclusion of the three Jewish feasts of Sukkot, Shemini Atzeret, and Simhat Torah. Stephen has not converted to Judaism, as much as Danielle's relatives may have wanted him to do so; and she herself also insists to be independent from her traditional religious upbringing. While Stephen is very much interested in philosophy and religion, he also claims to be an atheist, just like my eldest son Kenneth, who also values his freedom to pursue the truth. On the other hand, my artistic and gay son Andrew replied to me sixteen days ago (9th September), just before I started this chapter, with his first encouragement of this nature for me, "Dad, I don't yet grasp the nature of your spiritual challenges, but know that I'm available for your confidence." His words melted my heart. My son Jim and his wife, Jenni, don't speak about religion, but Catholicism runs in their families. Among my brothers and sisters, there is a 4/2 Catholic/Protestant split. My historical Christian family heritage runs both ways: from both sides of the Catholic/Protestant Reformation divide. In our individual lives, however, God speaks to us through the heart; and that is where spiritual and unspiritual forces of the world are in universal conflict for our souls. But, "if we only have love," just as in all of the words for the Jacques Brel song,[108] which concludes:

> Then with nothing at all
> But the little we are
> We'll have conquered all time
> All space, the sun, and the stars.

Then, "if we only have love," we also have the ultimate freedom to learn of God, who is love; and then somehow, in ways God makes plain to those who seek him, we love God back; and as God chooses, he leads us to eternal life with him.

---

[108] www.stlyrics.com/lyrics/jacquesbrelisaliveandwellandlivinginparis/ifweonlyhavelove.htm

Last Tuesday (21st September), I wrote my mother, Rita, a short e-mail on her birthday,[109] around 20:00 hours:

> Hi Mom,
>
> I thought of you throughout the day; happy 84th birthday! Jane worked all day, and I was home writing [on the national holiday in Malta].
>
> Soon, I will get you a decent letter. Hope you are OK. I have had recent communications from Ken and Andrew.
>
> Love you,
> Ed & Jane

Less than three hours later, Mom had replied, but I didn't read the letter until the morning of 22nd September:

> Thanks Ed and Jane. I had a peaceful happy day. I am grateful that I feel as good as I do for 84 years of age.
>
> Received a two-page handwritten invitation for a Memorial outdoor Mass and Hog Roast on October 9th on QofA [Queen of Angels] playground. The memorial is for all who have died this past year. Since the family was invited, I e-mailed an invitation to Martin, Carol, M.B. [Mary Beth] and Teresa. This is something like the Bible Story where it was necessary to go into the highways and byways to find guests for the celebration.[110] Joe and Anne Clemmer are flying to Virginia that weekend to visit Martin and Bert. Martin said he would have wanted to attend. Carol said she did not like pig or the kind of food they would serve. M.B. said they are going to Kate's soccer [football] game. Teresa said, "I am coming, Mom, and Darryl will too if he feels his back can tolerate the trip that day." Joel and Edie had

---

109 This Tuesday already was eight days after Mom's birthday (13th September), when I had forgotten her birthday because I was engrossed in writing this chapter. But there was Providence, given Mom's reply.

110 Matthew 22:1-10, Luke 14:15-24, Matthew 22:11-14

> planned for several weeks to fly to [Washington] D.C. to be with Amanda and Don to celebrate Edie and Don's shared birthday. Joel said they never go anywhere and then the event has to be on that weekend.
>
> I'm almost through Volume 2 of "The Poem of the Man-God' [Valtorta's Gospel visions and dictations]. Hope you and Jane are doing all right.
>
> Love and prayers,
> Mom

I thought it was a good idea for QofA to celebrate, with a "Memorial Mass" and "Hog Roast," those who had died in the past year. And so, this celebration also would include prayers for my father, who had gone to the Lord last October. After all, if Luke's gospel provides the "fatted calf" to celebrate the return of the "Prodigal Son,"[111] then a "Hog Roast" ought to be just fine, and lots of fun and good company, for everyone to celebrate all the "Children of God" who had gone home to their "Father."[112] The 9th October date for the celebratory "Mass and Roast" was an especially interesting congruence: that day will be the "feast date" for Blessed John Henry Newman. At the beatification of John Henry by the Pope himself just last Sunday in England, the Church had recognized the date of his conversion in 1845 as Blessed Cardinal Newman's "feast," when the adult John Henry Newman had been received into the Church; it would not be the traditional date of the saint's death and entry into heaven. This unique emphasis from the Church directs us to the essential importance for our ultimate conversion in faith (yes, mine and yours, too). I also was pleased to note Mom's progress towards reading Maria Valtorta's Gospel journey with Christ, my Christmas gift to Mom.

Unfortunately, my sister Carol's excuse for not attending the "Hog Roast," if not certainly the Mass, pertains to her taking exception to anything Roman Catholic. She has sent me several anti-Catholic biblical tracts, both printed and in video, in her sincere

---

111 Luke 15:23-24
112 Romans 8:14-25, John 14:1-2

interest to convince me regarding her bizarre, sectarian "Christian" beliefs. Whenever I have responded to those beliefs, she always has replied with cut-and-paste arguments from her sect. When I shared intermediate drafts of the Gospel Emmaus with her, she was petrified and scandalized that I would ever "interpret" or seek to "change" the Word of God. I kindly asked her to point out to me specifically anywhere she thought there was a problem, so we could discuss it. Carol would not say much; so there was nothing much I could say. No dialogue seemed possible. But when my father died, I offered Carol my condolences, which seemed not to comfort: she thought that my father could not be saved, as she once had explained to me according to her concepts of "heaven" and the "non-existence of hell." Perhaps she thinks and dreads the same about me: that presumably, after death, my unjust "soul" will be destroyed; and that "no one justified goes to heaven when they die, not until after the Last Judgment"; and that heaven will be formed as "a new material earth," after the end-time cataclysm. I felt sorry for Carol in her particular beliefs, which also lead her to withdraw defensively from most of her family, as she clings to her cultish church-friends. Her concepts about heaven and God seemed so enslaving and restrictive, so unrecognizable from my understanding of our God in the Gospel.

The gift of faith, and of God's mercies to us, are in God's hands, except for the fact that we all are free to pray for even greater faith and also for God's mercy, both for ourselves and for others. Our honesty and humility are essential, along with our natural curiosity and our critical thinking, as we journey along our individual paths to God in our hearts. In God's love for us, while we are making the trip of our lives, the Lord also provides his Church, shepherded by Christ under Peter (now Benedict XVI), who feeds and tends to us, if we are alert and listening sheep.[113] My wife Jane was formed in the Catholic faith in the ambient of "Catholic" Malta, the constitutional religion and traditional culture. Like others, Jane has been skeptical while she struggles honestly with her faith. From her experience of personal sorrow and from the injustices she witnesses in the world around her, both at home in Malta and throughout the world, Jane challenges the

---

113 John 21:15-19; John 10:1-10, 16, 27-30

existence of a righteous "God." She sees too little immediate divine justice and compassion for there to be so much suffering and misery in the world. God, of course, calls for us to exercise our capable measure of justice and compassion for others. Jane is also afraid: she is afraid of her own death and of the likely pain to suffer it. She already experiences much physical and psychological pain for her 66 years. It was in empathy and need that Jane told me yesterday in bed, "Whenever I see pain and suffering, I realize how much we need each other."

And we do need each other. For actually, when we look upon Jesus on the cross, we should realize how much we are needed for loving each other, as we look back on the God who loves us.[114] Yes, Jane, "God loves you," even as the world is cruel and often senseless. In truth, I am yours from God to bring you God's love with my love as I give my life for you. And I thank you for loving me and all the others, as God also reveals himself to me through you. God is love, and God calls everyone to their destiny with him in love.[115] And when I look at Jesus on the cross, I know my past and my future: both the passion of God's love for us by Jesus dying for our sins, and the passion of my own life and death and death to sin in Christ. Also, my future (and yours) rests in the passion of God's love for us, who desires our eternal life with him. And it is my life in the Spirit of God that enflames the passion of my love for God. Humility, love, and prayer are the keys to our discovery and recognition of God along our Gospel journey with Christ on the road to Emmaus: if we dialogue with the Risen Christ.[116]

It already has become the Lord's Day, Sunday (26th September), as I track down God's thoughts and aspirations for us. Together, Jane and I began the day late around 7:45, and by 8:30 our day's master plan was set, as we set about the chronic affairs of putting order in the house around us. In seventy-five minutes we removed the clutter, cleaned the bathroom, arranged the bedroom, swept and mopped some floors, I hung out laundry on the roof and threw another

---

114 Romans 8:31-37
115 Romans 8:28-30
116 Luke 24:32

load in the machine to wash, and I showered, shaved, and dressed for church. Then we drove to 10:00 Mass at St. John of the Cross (Ta'Xbiex) for the English-language Mass. We stopped beforehand to say hello from the car to some friends who had returned recently from two weeks in America. Just as we were passing by their house, they were going in their door. And after exchanging a few words, we snatched the morning's newspapers from a convenience shop. Returning home after Mass, we tackled more chores as I prepared the mid-day meal and read parts of the newspaper aloud to Jane. After eating, I hung out more laundry on the roof to dry; put away the clean dishes to make way for the new accumulation of dishes and pans I washed up; and Jane carefully prepared her fishing tackle. Then, as usual, I delivered Jane to her fishing spot and left the car; walked home; finished mopping and cleaning; and then I sat down to continue this chapter.[117]

From Father Mario, I downloaded his "God's Wisdom" for the day: "Faith has three enemies: reliance on natural reason, fear, and skepticism. May God Almighty bless you in the Name of the Father, the Son and the Holy Spirit. AMEN." It seems that the Holy Spirit had been with Father Mario as part of God's concerns for Jane. In the morning, Jane had continued to tell me, with tears in her eyes, how she suffers with the pains of others, as she also thought of Olga in hospital. Jane also was concerned about how some people might have been disturbed by the day's gospel and homily,[118] if they were given to believe that some of their "self-centered" relatives were suffering in hell. After we arrived home from Mass, Jane phoned a friend, another tourist guide, who had comforted Jane when Jane had had her heart by-pass surgery three-and-three-quarter years ago. Now her friend was going through the same operation and was not looking well afterwards. That morning Jane also had noticed the emaciated man on the church steps as we left from church after Mass. Jane had grown up with him when they had been children

---

117 When I finished around 18:15, as I put on the cabbage to boil, I would be thirty minutes late for Jane at 18:30, as we spent another hour of fishing until darkness fell. I hope not to be late for Jane again, as she also needed my help and caught a few more fish.

118 Luke 16:19-31

together living in Valletta. While now on the phone, Jane told her friend about the Healing Service that would be held on Friday at church, thinking that this service could be some comfort for her. Jane had admired the layman giving the announcements at the end of Mass who had so elegantly articulated the mission and rationale for the Healing Service. Jane regretted that the persons involved in such healing ministries seemed not to address those in hospital who, like Olga, were not able physically to attend. But I pointed out to Jane that those in hospital were not ignored, and that the healing ministry benefited many of the individuals it targeted and hoped to reach.

The Liturgy of the Word of this morning also seemed to be directed towards me specifically, and not only for the universal Church. In the second reading,[119] from Paul's letter to Timothy, I heard:

> But as for you, man of God, shun all this; pursue righteousness, godliness, faith, love, endurance, gentleness; fight the good fight of the faith; take hold of the eternal life, to which you were called and for which you made the good confession in the presence of many witnesses.[120]

Yes, the confession of faith of this <u>Gospel Emmaus</u> must be continued for the rest of my life. And yes, there will always be tribulations and trials, and even temptations to sin. But if we cooperate with grace (and not with the temptations) there will be no sin,[121] as there had been sin before the grace for this gospel had been given to me in God's love, for my benefit and for the benefit of others. In the moment before this grace, when I had prayed to God, my prayer in faith had been answered immediately. And seven years later, as this particular part of my work for God is finishing, I also know that God continues to answer that original prayer as I ran to him:[122] my passions are only for God, for his love of us all, and for

---

119   2 Timothy 6:11-16
120   2 Timothy 6:11-12
121   1 John 3:1-11
122   Luke 15:20

the whole of his creation. And I now realize that because God is my ultimate passion, I also share within my heart God's passionate love for my wife, Jane.[123]

In my real-time as I now write, we are in the middle of the Jewish week of Sukkot, just as it had been when Jesus had made his way to the festival,[124] after his relatives had suggested to him that he show himself to the world, although they did not believe in him.[125] But in the gospel of today's Sunday liturgy, we read of Abraham's reply to the rich man who was in his place of eternal torment, and who now begged for the beggar Lazarus, who was near to the bosom of Abraham in heaven, to be sent from beyond death to warn his five living brothers, so that they will repent. This is what Abraham said to the rich man:

> If they do not listen to Moses and the prophets,[126] neither will they be convinced even if someone rises from the dead.[127]

And so today many still do not listen to the Gospel. Jesus would rise from the dead, in accordance with Moses and the prophets,[128] and as the Church today performs the prophetic and teaching mission given to it. This is in fulfillment of the promise Jesus had made that he would send the Holy Spirit upon the Church and into hearts of believers, as Jesus had proclaimed on the final day of Sukkot:

> Let anyone who is thirsty come to me, and let the one who believes in me drink. As the scripture has said, out of the believer's heart shall flow rivers of living water.[129]

I can only encourage those seeking the truth of God, to pray, to take up the scriptures, and to come to know Jesus Christ through the resources of the Church, from which Christ provides his sacraments

---

123 Ephesians 5:25-33
124 John 7:14
125 John 7:4-5
126 Luke 16:29
127 Luke 16:31
128 Luke 24:44-49, 18-27, 32
129 John 7:37-38

and his teachings, as the Father and Son also send the Holy Spirit to the Church and into our hearts. This "Gospel (on the Road to) Emmaus" is just one tool for you. May the Lord kindly lead you into the passion of his heart,[130] which God shares with everyone who loves him; he has mercy on others. For Jesus Christ is our Sovereign light:[131]

> In the presence of God, who gives life to all things, and of Christ Jesus, who in his testimony before Pontius Pilate made the good confession, I charge you to keep the commandment without spot or blame until the manifestation of our Lord Jesus Christ, which he will bring about at the right time—he who is the blessed and only Sovereign, the King of kings and Lord of lords. It is he alone who has immortality and dwells in unapproachable light, whom no one has ever seen or can see; to him be honor and eternal dominion. Amen.[132]

After Sunday, work for this chapter was spent on Monday and Tuesday wholly with revisions and certain additions. This morning is Wednesday (29th September) the last day of Sukkot, which ends this evening at sunset. Initially, before breakfast, I found this "wisdom" from God from Father Mario, intended for yesterday: "The intellect is made blind by these three passions: avarice, self-esteem, and sensual pleasure. May Almighty God bless you in the Name of the Father, the Son and the Holy Spirit. AMEN." If our sight has been restored by grace, then God is our passion and love becomes our action in the world. Our passion for God is supported by the virtue of poverty, the practice of detachment, and charity towards the poor. Passion for God is found in our constant humility before God and in our humble service for others. And passion for God is lived in the unity of our life with the Spirit of God within us, and is fostered in us by our ready and conscious attention to God's presence and will through prayer and reflection, without any divisions from God or

---

130   Luke 12:49
131   1 John 1:5, John 1:1-10; John 7:2-4, 14-18; Exodus 13:20-22, John 8:12
132   1 Timothy 6:13-16; John 18:36-37

neighbor because of sin in us.

Then after my morning's work and afternoon lunch, and my bringing home another ream of A4 paper and replacing the cartridge for my printer, I found our final "God's Wisdom" for us from Father Mario: "When it's God speaking....the proper way to behave is to imitate someone who has an irresistible curiosity and who listens at keyholes. You must listen to everything that God says at the keyhole of your heart. May God Almighty bless you, in the Name of the Father, the Son and the Holy Spirit. AMEN." That pretty well sums up our journey with the Lord in his Gospel for us. For my sake and yours, I pray that God's words have found their way into our hearts. Let us pray for God to lead us, by his light and the sound of his voice, so that one day we may enter face to face with God into his unapproachable light.

Concluding Prayer

Heavenly Father, all holiness and glory are yours. You are Creator of the Universe and you are the Father Creator of all your human children. Each one of us is necessary; and each one of us is loved by you. Most particularly, in your unique choice, you created me and all the persons known and unknown to me, whom you love. Thank you for your blessing of life and of my family with its history, as a particular patrimony of courage and faith. Lead us kindly into your unfathomable light. Discipline us in your love; caress us with your embrace; and hold us in your hand; so that we may be surrounded always by your tangible presence, and we may be directed to your will by your love running through us.

Thank you for the heritage of your revelation and covenants of love made known to your people Israel. Thank you for the knowledge of you revealed to us through your Son. Thank you for the gifts of the Spirit which you send to us. Bring your kingdom to its fruition in fullness; and bless the work of your creation. You instill in me sufficient curiosity to love what you have made and to want to know all about it, and to enjoy it, and to praise you in your work, especially as you intend for me to be fruitful for my God, as

I love you by my labor and as I enjoy your blessings. You are the owner and vinedresser who cultivates the vine, our life through your Son in us; and you prune us as his branches, to become the more perfect likeness of your first-born Son. Continue to bless us.

As your children, forgive us our wrong-doing, as we forgive those who injure us, even if others should not forgive us or they make seek to harm us. Father, forgive them, and also lead them into your light. Lead us not into temptation, but keep us safe from the Evil One. As our Father, where we are weak, give us courage; where we lack faith, provide us to have confidence in you; where we are slow to love, provide us with a sufficient measure of your love.

Jesus Christ, our Lord, have mercy on us. You are the Lamb of God, the light that shines in our darkness, who takes away the sins of the world. Lead us into the light of your love. Take my heart, since you know it, and place your heart in mine. You call us "friends," for that is who you are. Let me never let go of your hand. You so loved your friends as to lay down your life for us on the cross. Now that you, our closest friend, have died, we must live for you upon the earth: because we want your love to live in us not only for ourselves, but we want your life to live in all others, and especially for our families. For you have eternal life; and our life in God comes completely through you, as the Father draws us to you. The glory of your cross and resurrection is your heritage for us. Show us the way to the Father, where we will dwell with God and see you as you are.

Come Holy Spirit, enlighten our minds and enflame our hearts. Lead us by your holy light. Provide comfort to our woes; peace to our thoughts; tranquility to our hearts; direction to our wills; and love to all our actions. Guide the Church, in the mystery which is the Body of Christ, to complete unity in the truth. We thank you for all your blessings; for your revelation through the prophets; for your gift of the inspired gospel through the evangelists from Jesus Christ. Lead all of God's children to a greater knowledge of God. Grant us wisdom to abide in God's spirit. Fortify us with your strength and love. Increase our devotion and submission to God. Let the fire of your love reign in our souls. Renew the whole of creation through the conversion of hearts, especially my own. Amen

I am off to fetch Jane from work,[133] and to see a film together, "Eat, Pray, Love." An admirable ambition, but we also must work and work for God. Amen.

Shortly after the film, around 21:00, Olga died.[134]

So, just as Sukkot had ended, Olga now was finally "home." We should celebrate for her with a "party," as Jane had proposed to Olga in hospital.[135] May the Lord welcome her now, and all of us, into his eternal light. Amen. Instead of Sukkot's "Pillars of Glory by Cloud or Flame" to lead us through the desert and wastelands of our lives, now to lead us, if only we come to Christ to quench our thirst and drink from him, we have "rivers of living water" flowing from the hearts of believers, the gift of the Holy Spirit sent from Jesus Christ and the Father, and provided to us from Pentecost.[136] Lord, grant that all your children remain in your light. Amen. Bring to repentance those who still are in darkness; and by their acceptance of your mercy and love, lead them and all God's household, full of their praise and gratitude to you, into your glorious and eternal light.[137] Amen.

Completed 29th September 2010
Last day of Sukkot 2010

Edited post-hoc amendments or footnotes,
From 30th September to Sunday 10th October 2010

---

133 It is 16:45, 29th September 2010.
134 We learned of Olga's death, 30th September, around 7:15 when Jane phoned me in the morning on her way to work. And so, after I had concluded, the Lord now presented us with his own continuing narrative.
135 During Jane's last visit (23rd September) with Olga, six days before Olga died, one week ago.
136 Exodus 13:20-22, John 7:2, 14, 37-39, 14:16-17, Acts 2:1-3, 38-39; Romans 8:9, 1 Corinthians 12:3-7; Revelation 22:1, 20-21
137 The Lord's concluding commentary is provided to us from the readings of the liturgy for today, 10th October 2010, 28th Sunday in Ordinary Time, Year C: 2 Kings 5:14-17; 2 Timothy 2:8-13; Luke 17:11-19

Endnotes:

i. [p. 57] According to national (NSO) statistics for the year 2008, there were 35 church annulments versus 153 positive civil cases involving Maltese citizens; and 31 divorces were obtained by Maltese from abroad. There also were 519 separations filed, of which couples 464 were both Maltese, while another 50 couples involved one Maltese spouse. In the same year, in Malta there were 2,482 registered marriages: 840 (or 34%) were civil marriages, and of these 300 involved at least one Maltese spouse, while of these over a third, 107 couples, were both Maltese; the remainder of 1,642 were religious marriages, the substantial portion of which 1,564 were Catholic marriages, including 67 couples previously married by the State who chose to validate their marriage in the Church; and 44 individuals had remarried after their previous vows had been annulled by the Church. Also, in Malta between 2006 and 2008, there were 1,028 new or introduced church and civil annulment cases; 844 pending cases; and about 3,500 sworn separation applications submitted or mediations introduced, with more than 1,000 separation cases pending—or a total of 6,360 couples, or up to 12,720 individuals (excluding the affected children of those relationships) in dysfunctional or broken marriages (or for the three-year period, 3% of the total 2008 Maltese population).

ii. [p. 63] Marriage is regulated according to Book IV, Part 1, Title VII of Canon Law (Canon 1055-1165). There are various conditions for the validation of sacramental marriage, inclusive of baptism, conformity to the essential properties of marriage (its unity and indissolubility), and matrimonial consent; and likewise there are numerous impediments that may invalidate a marriage. Certain diriment impediments are qualities that intrinsically render a person unqualified to contract a valid marriage (Canon 1073), and these conditions may be either general, or very specific: for example, regarding the specific minimum age for marriage (Canon 1083). Typically, the likely grounds for nullity of a marriage involve issues of matrimonial consent (Canon 1095-1105). These may include: incapacities of reason or defects of judgment or psychological reasons (Canon 1095); ignorance regarding the basic nature of marriage (Canon 1096); error about an intended quality of a person, of such importance, that without it the person would not have married the other (Canon 1097); if a person should enter marriage deceived by some fraud, which deception by its very nature disturbs the essential spousal relationship (Canon 1098); an error concerning the unity of marriage that also determines the will for marriage (Canon 1099): such as, for example, the belief that there must be an "open" marriage or multiple spouses or sexual partners; if one or both parties totally simulate marriage, essentially excluding marriage itself, or if marriage is just partially simulated (Canon 1101.2): by excluding some essential element of marriage, for example, by intending to exclude the conjugal act, or by excluding the effect of this act, namely, its resultant children, for example by always using artificial contraception or abortion, or there may be other conditions of simulation: excluding sexual fidelity or a partner's right (with responsibility) to sexual relations, or by excluding the good of spouses: by violating a person's fundamental physical, moral, spiritual, sexual, or psychological integrity; entering marriage with some conditional consent (Canon 1102.1), which is to require a future contingent condition which does not yet exist, whether or not it later materializes; or also, if an individual enters into marriage because of force or fear (Canon 1103), which is a serious and objective influence, resulting from an outside source, and which causes the person to marry in order to be free of that force or fear.

iii. [p. 125] Actually, this hypothetical imagery of my original presentation introduces the problem of determining the actual historiography of this event, while nonetheless it amplifies the intentions of Luke the evangelist. The real-time logic of this sequence, for our theological journey to Jerusalem as near to the Lord's passion, would at first suggest that this encounter of Zacchaeus, the tax-collector, with Jesus had occurred in the Spring (being late March or not later than 1st April of 30CE). In fact, another chronology is presented in Maria Valtorta's gospel account, as directed by Jesus at the outset of her chapter 416: placement of "the beggar on the road to Jericho" (chapter 414) is followed by "the conversion of Zacchaeus" (chapter 415); the dates of those respective visions were 17th May 1944 and 17th July 1944, with the Lord's commentary regarding chapter 415 provided on 18th July 1944, my wife Joan's birthdate, and continued on 19th July 1944; the instruction itself to the notebooks' chapter-placement occurred later, on 13th April 1946. The conversion of Zacchaeus (chapter 415) then precedes a clear period of "summer drought" (chapter 416); followed by eventual chapters demarcating later late-autumn weather (chapter 479, "a gloomy persistent drizzle") and the autumn feast (possibly in October) of tabernacles (chapter 483). The actual spring chronology of Jesus at Jericho is provided much later by Valtorta: in chapter 576, where "hawthorns bend their new shoots;" chapter 577, where "the hay is drying in the sun;" and chapter 578, where daybreak is broken by "the trills of the awakened birds," "the limpid notes of blackcaps," and "the flute-like song of blackbirds"), which is preceded by the initial events of our present Chapter 29, given by Valtorta as "the rich young man" (chapter 574, "April morning" and "springtime") and "The third prophecy of the Passion; the request of Zebedee's sons" (chapter 575, "the country is pleasantly fresh after the dew"). Luke includes this narrative of Zacchaeus, as we have followed for this gospel, within the chronology of the Lord's final journey to Jerusalem, as an example of what it means for a Christian to make this journey to the cross with Jesus. In the actual final spring journey through Jericho, in Valtorta's gospel presentation, we have the opportunity to see the enduring Christian qualities of Zacchaeus who accompanies the Lord to Jerusalem.

iv. [p. 139] In the beginning when I first wrote this chapter, I had attempted to deduce the chronology from whatever temporal and historical cues the scriptures provided; but my original assumptions, as much theological as historical, were only confirmed for me with the chapter's final revisions in January 2010. Previously, I had ascertained the year as 30 CE; and I also had understood the date for the Lord's crucifixion as 7th April, but I had not been aware of its determination and recognition by such renowned scripture scholars as believer Henri Daniel-Rops (Jesus and His Times, 1954) and unbeliever Geza Vermes (The Resurrection, 2008). However rational had been my original "best" approximations for gospel chronologies, until more recently I had not yet understood the precise liturgical chronologies for the month of Nisan; and, if we also allow the authenticity of Maria Valtorta's "Poem of the Man-God," she provides seemingly even more accurate, and otherwise precise chronologies for the Lord's arrival to Bethany from Jericho: namely, in the early morning, "the last drops of dew are evaporating on leaves and stems in meadows and the sun is still rising in the vault of heaven" (chapter 579), but then either on the Thursday or, more likely, on the Friday before the Sabbath, as the farmers are working the fields and "drop their tools" to greet Jesus upon his arrival (chapter 579); by Maria Valtorta's written account, the supper at Bethany occurs on the Sabbath (chapter 584); and the entry into Jerusalem is presented by her transcriptions as occurring on the first day of the week (chapter 588, in a vision dated Palm Sunday, 30th March 1947), after the Lord, upon his arrival to Bethany, tells Lazarus that he intends to go to town, "The morning after the Sabbath," which, together with the resurrection and dinner celebration of Lazarus, truly anticipates the Lord's death and Easter triumph.

v. [p. 140] This follows John Walker's Fourmilab Calendar Converter (www.fourmilab.ch/documents/calendar/). However, separate allegedly scientific determinations from two sources have provided discrepant astronomical dates for the new moon for Nisan of 30 CE: Wade Cox of the Christian Churches of God (www.ccg.org) provides Wednesday 22nd March at Jerusalem civil time 20:22; while Kenneth F. Doig (New Testament Chronology, Lewiston, NY: Edwin Mellen Press, 1990) provides a more congruent date of Thursday 23rd March at 19:54; the former also argues incorrectly on behalf of a Wednesday crucifixion and Saturday resurrection, while the latter incorrectly specifies 30 days for the month of Adar, preceding Nisan in 30 CE. Walker's astronomical calculations provide for 29 days for Adar, and 30 days for Nisan.

vi. [p. 217] My original source for historical information was provided throughout Stewart Perowne's (1956, 2003) The Life and times of Herod the Great. Gloucestershire: Sutton Publishing Limited. Another alternative, more recent, and clearly very authoritative source has included Samuel Rocca's (2008) Herod's Judaea: A Mediterranean State in the Classical World. Tübingen: Mohr Siebeck, pp. 76-77. Among other useful sources is the book by Aryeh Kasher and Eliezer Witztum (2006), King Herod: A Persecuted Persecutor. A Case Study in Psychohistory and Psychobiography. Berlin: Walter de Gruyter & Co., pp. 175-180.

vii. [p. 289] Although similar in their characteristics, suggesting that the two dinners may be reformulations of one and the same tradition, the argument from scripture provides strong indications for separate events. First of all there is chronology: John 12:1 places the first dinner at an unnamed location in Bethany six days before Passover, and before the Lord's procession to Jerusalem (John 12:12-13); while the dinner in Bethany at the house of Simon, shared in common between the accounts of Mark and Matthew here, provide an event after the conclusion of four days intervening between the Lord's procession and Wednesday evening. Secondly, this is not the first time that John presents a distinctive chronology for similar appearing events: John revealed a Temple cleansing from two years before, but ignores the event described by the Synoptic evangelists for Holy Week; now once again John provides for the earlier dinner for Lazarus, apart from the present account in the house of Simon the Leper. Maria Valtorta only provides for the Sabbath dinner in Bethany (Chapter 584), and leaves the Wednesday evening of Holy Week (Chapter 595) open for the Lord to be with the disciples alone in prayer, and not at dinner; but the former does not exclude the later. There is however a unity implied by the second dinner event at Simon's house. (And in Valtorta's Chapter 584, she does imply Simon's house is nearby, "I do not see the women disciples. Not even Mary. Perhaps they preferred to remain in Simon's house with the distressed Mother.") The unity is provided by the mercies obtained by Lazarus, who had died, by Mary, who had been a renown sinner, and by Simon, likewise a sinner formerly by virtue of his leprosy, but each now restored and wholly grateful. They are contrasted to the disciples, especially to the Iscariot, now with emphatic focus as culmination before the Lord's Passion.

viii. [p. 387] George Clemmer was born in Perry Township, Montgomery County, Ohio, on 13 June 1816; after fifteen years on the farm, he served an apprenticeship to carpentering at Dayton, Ohio; then he worked two years in Cincinnati, where he married Elizabeth, of Albemarle County, Pennsylvania. Two years later, in September 1838, they came to Hicksville, Ohio, where he assisted to build the first grist mills in the county, and he worked at his trade steadily until, on 28 August 1862, he enlisted in Company D, One Hundredth Regiment Ohio Volunteer Infantry, to serve three years: whereupon he was sent to check General Kirby Smith in Tennessee; was in the Knoxville siege (November 1863); then, for four months bridge-building, he ruptured himself and was sent to hospital; came home on furlough for three months; then he rejoined his regiment at Nashville; but being unable to do duty he was put in a field hospital, later discharged from the hospital at Wilmington, North Carolina on 24 September 1864, with the assistance of a letter from the respected Hicksville doctor B. M. Rakestraw; but was not discharged from the Union Army until 5 March 1865, when he finally returned home and followed his trade. He built many homes in Hicksville, including the Boon-Bevinton Company Building with its original woodwork, counters, and circular staircase of solid walnut. Both George and Elizabeth were members of the Disciples Church; however, after the German Reformed Church was organized about 1850, George Clemmer donated the ground (Lot 14) for building their first church in 1852, a one-story brick building with shingle roof and cupola, replaced by a new church in 1879.

ix. [p. 387] My paternal great-grandfather, Benjamin Rakestraw Clemmer, was born at Hicksville, Ohio on 1 December 1852; he was nine-years-old when his 46-year-old father had joined the Union Army, and twelve-years-old when his father returned to Hicksville for good after his military discharge. The young Benjamin obviously learned and mastered the skills of his eventual trade in carpentry under his father. My paternal great-grandmother, Ellen Flood, was born on 19 November 1865 in Fort Wayne, where she lived on Rockhill Street. Her father, Michael Flood, son of William Flood and Anna Lannon Flood, was born 1820 in Kilkenny, Ireland; he had married Ellen Wall Flood (from Limerick, Ireland), and they lived at 124 Chicago Street, Fort Wayne. Ellen Wall's mother was Nora Dillon (also from Limerick, Ireland), and her grandmother, Nora Connors, was from County Down, Ireland. Although Ellen Flood Clemmer was the last of seven children and was named after her mother, her older sister, Nora Flood Quinn, was named after her grandmother and great-grandmother. Various tragedies beset the family: in November 1862, three years before Ellen was born, in a twelve day period, a sister, Ann, and two brothers, John and James, died in the (cholera) plague: their ages, respectively, six years and six months; five years and ten days; and eight days old. An older brother, also named John, drowned in the Mississippi River, whose surviving son, John, was reared by Aunt Nora Quinn, whose only daughter, Mary, died of tuberculosis. Ellen's other brother, Jerry, remained a bachelor. Benjamin Rakestraw Clemmer was 33-years-old when he married the 20-year-old Ellen Flood; and he was baptized on 6 May 1886 at the Immaculate Conception Cathedral in Fort Wayne, also when they were married. As a skilled carpenter, Benjamin at some time constructed wooden doors for the Cathedral. But, ten years before this marriage, in 1876, he also had married 24-year-old Clara Holmes Clemmer, the single mother of a two-year-old daughter, Eva McNab, in Cass County, Dowagiac, Michigan, where his older brother by thirteen years, David Clemmer, was a prominent resident and a gallant veteran of the civil war; but Benjamin Rakestraw Clemmer and Clara Clemmer were divorced sometime prior to 1880, when Clara then was living with her mother. After Benjamin married his second-wife Ellen Flood, they returned to his birthplace to live, in Hicksville, Ohio, Defiance County, where all five of their children were born, and where Benjamin and Ellen managed a hotel and tavern together, the "Baltimore Hotel."

x. [p. 387] My paternal grandfather Edward George Clemmer was born 20 February 1889; and he first met my grandmother, Louise E. Heiny, younger by two years, at her father's grocer's picnic; the neighbourhood Heiny grocery had been located on Creighton Avenue in Fort Wayne. They married at St. Mary's Catholic Church, Fort Wayne, on 22 June 1915. When they married, Edward's father (Benjamin) already had been dead for two years; Benjamin had died in Defiance, Ohio, and he was buried in Hicksville; but Edward's father had abandoned the family, it seems in 1901, when Edward then left school after the 6th grade, and his thirty-five-year-old now single-parent mother, with five children ranging in ages from two to fourteen years, moved their residence to Fort Wayne, where the family lived in an apartment on Brackenbridge Street. After Edward and Louise married, they lived sixteen blocks due south of Edward's mother, at 3020 South Harrison Street until 1953, when they moved to 5620 Standish Drive, where they lived as a retired couple until Louise died at home on 11 December 1976 of a heart attack; and Edward, depressed by the loss of his wife, died on 2 October 1977, after six months of residence at St. Anne's Home. When Edward and Louise occupied their first marital home, his mother Ellen had been working for several years at Ruhlroads Department Store, which she did until, after illness, she came to live with Ed and Louise and their family for about five years, when my father was born, until Ellen died on 18 February 1929. In fact, from 1901, Edward had been a helpful provider for his mother and his two younger sisters, Elizabeth and Stella, until the sisters married. Both of Edward's brothers were dead: David, the eldest son, was nearly 20-years-old when he died of appendicitis on 2 August 1907; and two years later, the baby of the family, twelve-year-old Benjamin Joseph Clemmer, drowned on 27 August 1909. When Benjamin drowned, the 20-year-old Edward was with his brother Benjamin in the boat; but because Edward couldn't swim, he was helpless to save his brother. My grandfather seems never to have forgiven himself the accident; but fifteen years after his brother had died, Edward named my father, also the baby of his family, "Benjamin." It seems that grandfather also had named his eldest daughter, "Mary Ellen" (born 22 November 1917) after his mother, "Ellen." When Edward had left school at about age twelve, in order to help his mother and older brother David support the family, he worked numerous part-time and full-time jobs in Fort Wayne, simultaneously and consecutively: Edward began by working for C. O. Lepper (West Jefferson) Drug Store seven days a week, for $1.50 per week; then he took up the Max Campion News Stand (Calhoun and Williams Streets) from 6:00 a.m., before returning to the drug store for the full day's work; then he also carried a Journal newspaper route at 3:30 a.m. (from 2300 Calhoun Street south to Creighton Street); then in 1904, he worked for Meadows Dairy, where his brother David worked before he died, but Edward left that employment twice; for one year Edward also worked at a rolling mill; then he began as stable boy for the horses of another dairy, Schlosser Company (eventually, after they went out of business, the same premises were occupied by Eskay Dairy, at 1501 Fairfield Avenue). Thus had begun his future career as a dairyman: in 1917, he went to Fort Wayne Dairy (now Meadow Gold Dairy) for one-third stock as assistant manager, and after the dairy sold out in 1920, he went to Pleasant Hill Dairy until Thanksgiving Eve 1920, when he was laid off; but as their accountant eventually he would make himself indispensable, leaving them for nearly five years, when he then worked for Scholsser Brothers (Fulton and Main Streets, in the subsequent News Sentinel Building) in ice cream sales, until he returned to Pleasant Hill Dairy in October 1925 on his condition of acquiring one-half interest; eventually under his majority ownership, Pleasant Hill Dairy was incorporated in 1927 with two business partners: Ralph Urbine (a relative, Louise's brother-in-law, who had married her nearest-older sister, Marie) and Carl Neiter; then Edward successfully managed the business accommodating clients throughout the Great Depression and the war years, until he retired from Allen Dairy in 1953, having sold the operations to Allen Dairy in 1948 for his net-worth share of $150,000. At the dairy, my grandfather also provided my Dad (and his brother Don) with their initial post-war employment (while their eldest brother Uncle John, exempted from military service, collected milk from the farms before and after the war); and after Mom and Dad were married, they rented from Grandpa the top floor (2226 ½ Holton Avenue) of a two-storey apartment, where we lived until 1957, along with relatives living downstairs and next door (Uncle Don's family) on the adjoining former properties of the dairy, that Edward had repurchased after selling. When I was a young boy, around 1958, Grandpa gave me two coins: an 1886 silver dollar and an 1852 large cent: the former the year that his father and mother had married, the latter the year when his father was born; along with the partial set of Indian Head pennies he also gave me (1880-1909), they were a sentimental legacy to me as his namesake and fourth grandchild. Also every Christmas Eve, for all of his grandchildren, Grandpa (Ed) provided ample clothes, purchased for all of us by his daughters Aunt Mary Ellen and Aunt Rita, and cash as gifts, while for this annual event with extended family, Grandma (Louise) amply provided us her delicious sourcream sugar cookies and Christmas cookies of various shapes and colours with vanilla icing. Uniquely, Grandpa also gave a $1000 to my father in 1961, for the first two years of my secondary education in seminary, until I was old enough to work my way through high school and college, inclusive of my later educational bank loans to be repaid.

xi. [p. 387] My father, in fact, had been named after two of his uncles: "Benjamin," after his father Edward George Clemmer's deceased youngest brother; and after "Othmar," his mother Louise's older brother by eight-years; Othmar would die at forty-nine years of age, when my father was eight-years-old. Othmar had been the third child of the mother Othmar and Louise shared by their father's second marriage. Louise Esther Heiny was born 13 April 1891; she was the youngest of the nine children of Nicholas Heiny borne to him by his second wife Margaret Weisbrod, after her parents were married in 1879 at St. Mary's Church, Fort Wayne, where thirty-six years later Louise Heiny and Edward George Clemmer would be married. There also had been three surviving children by Nicholas Heiny's first marriage with Elizabeth Schele, who had died in 1877;

four children were born in Fort Wayne to Nicholas and his first wife Elizabeth: Clemence, born in 1867, who had died when Louise was fourteen-years-old; although Catharine was born in 1869, the infant died the next year; then Louise also had two older half-sisters, by twenty and sixteen years, Elizabeth and Margaret, who both married. Louise's father Nicholas Heiny had been born in 1842 in New York City, the de facto eldest child after his infant sister, Catherine, did not survive birth in 1837. His father, Clemence Gottlick Heiny (born in Baden, Germany, 1806) and his French-born mother, Barbara Richet Heiny, came to America from Strasbourg, France, in 1836, sailing the ship "Europe." The family ultimately moved from New York to Allen County, Indiana, in 1857: along with fifteen-year-old Nicholas, there were his seven-year-old brother and sister, twins Ehrhart and Elizabeth, who also had been born in New York, in 1850. Ironically, after 62 years, both twins died the same year in 1912; and three years later, when Nicholas died (1915), the family business where Louise's father had employed her before she married, the Heiny Grocery, continued on.

xii. [p. 388] My mother was born 13 September 1926 at the home of her father's parents, Joseph Isidore Weaver and Mary Catherine (daughter of William Meyer) Weaver: on Hathaway Road, about seven miles from the Fort Wayne city limits; and Mom was baptized Rita "Cecelia," after her maternal grandmother, "Cecelia" White (Blanc) Bobay, at St. Vincent de Paul Catholic Church on Auburn Road. Across the road from the church, she began her first and second grade at Sacred Heart Academy, which she completed at seven-years of age, a few weeks after Mom's first communion on April 30th, when the school closed in 1934. [For Mom and I, the closure of the academy, owned and operated by the Holy Cross Sisters of South Bend, Indiana, was profoundly crucial for both of our lives. In the wake of the Great Depression, the sisters had sought to consolidate their operations and to strengthen their college in South Bend. In March 1936, the pastor of St. Vincent's, Father Charles Keyzer, informed the Prior of the Crosier Fathers at Onamia, Minnesota, about the academy; but thanking the pastor, the Prior suggested that the pastor write again in two years, as there was no chance then for them to buy it. In March 1938, the pastor wrote the Prior again, and interviews were scheduled with Bishop Noll. Later that year, the academy, with its accompanying 160-acre farm on Wallen Road, was purchased for $45,000 from the Holy Cross Sisters by the Crosier Fathers, who then established a seminary, opening for 22 students on 12 September 1939, shortly after Hitler invaded Poland, and France and England then declared war on Germany. In 1942, with the seminary's first graduates, the religious house of the Crosiers was elevated to a Priorate; and, at Bishop Noll's suggestion, the old Sacred Heart Academy was renamed Sacred Heart Seminary, owned and operated by the Crosier Fathers, but exclusively in the interest of the Fort Wayne diocese, with 63 students enrolled in September 1942; that year, the Berghoff family also provided a 31st December $48,000 contribution to the Crosier Fathers towards their building fund. Eventually, in 1947, the Order transferred their faculty of philosophy and the novitiate for Brothers from Hastings, Nebraska, to the Sacred Heart Seminary at Fort Wayne; and ten years after the Spink Wawasee Hotel had closed its doors as the leading resort in Indiana, on 15 August 1948, the Crosier Fathers had acquired that property and transferred Bishop Noll's seminary from Fort Wayne to Lake Wawasee, where I attended the diocesan seminary between 1961-1966, with 198 students in 1966.] Mom attended Cathedral Grade School in Fort Wayne for third grade, which was near to her father's central-city employment, riding with him in his car each morning when he went to work. Because Rita's parents wanted her to attend a Catholic school, they sold their home on Coldwater Road near Pine Valley, and the family moved into the parish of St. John the Baptist Catholic Church in Fort Wayne, living in various rented houses, while for the next five years she attended the parish's grade school. Mom graduated in 1940, with the highest grade of the girls and an award of a year's tuition to Central Catholic High School; and three months later, the family moved, now for the last time, into their new home. Then during her third year of high school, on 21 May 1943, Mom's sister was born, my Aunt Mary Ann, which Mom described one year later in her senior diary, "the happiest moment of my life." She then wrote, "I feel as if I have lived two lives, the second one commencing the day my sister was born." In 1944, when Mom graduated from Central Catholic, she was among seven classmates with high honors for all four years; also with a medal for high grade in four years of Latin. After she had placed second in a senior speech contest, she was asked to deliver the speech for her graduation ceremony, which was effective and short. Mom also had studied piano during her school years from first grade through freshman year of high school; and she also had successfully played piano for her grade-school graduation ceremony, unexpectedly from memory after her sheet music fell to the floor. She not only introduced me to the piano at home, she has always continued to play piano and organ, and has given music lessons to some of her grandchildren, too. Later, her sister Mary Ann also took up the piano and teaching of music, where now "in retirement" Mary Ann still directs choirs and plays the organ for multiple Catholic liturgies; yet each summer, she and her social-worker farm-reared husband, Paul, also lead youth groups to Kentucky to build houses for poor families. Also from Mom, I have taken her love of music throughout my life, and my choral performances into seminary and decades of church choirs. Mom also assisted me with her Latin skills, as she introduced me to the language in the year before I started my seminary training. It seems, like Mom, we both have always been disciplined and accomplished students. Mom also had attended two classes, psychology and music theory, at Saint Francis College (now University) during its first year of existence (also my undergraduate Alma Mater for three years, 1967-1970, in psychology and social work). Mom worked for the Company Secretary where her father had held executive employment, at Lincoln (National) Life Insurance Company; she worked part-time while attending high school, while she juggled both her job and homework; and full-time thereafter, until she took a position at Tokheim Corporation (now the international producer of metered fuel pumps) where she worked until she married Dad in 1947. Mom had first met Dad on a blind date arranged by their two lifelong friends, Delores Jehl and Richard Berghoff [their future Best Man; the Berghoff family not only contributed to the Crosier Fathers, they also provided Mom with a husband], when Dad showed up by himself at Mom's home (4429 South Wayne Avenue) in his Navy uniform on 15 December 1945, while he was home on furlough, having driven to Fort Wayne from San Francisco with his brother, Don, also a sailor on leave at the end of the war. Nine months later, on Mom's 20th birthday, Dad gave Mom her engagement ring; and eight months later they were married at the Catholic church of St. John the Baptist, with the wedding reception held at the nearby home of the bride's parents (only three short city-blocks away, walking). Mom's four-year-old sister Mary Ann was the flower-girl, who also then muddied her dress wandering away from home that day; but she was the reason Dad and Mom made our weekly Sunday afternoon-evening Weaver family visits thereafter: which commitment always included dinner, afterwards my three-handed Pinochle with Grandpa and Dad after

Grandpa napped (and sometimes a four-handed card game with great-grandma Mary Weaver), and television. Thus I gained my life-long second primary-home; and Aunt Mary Ann became my de facto and spiritual five-years-older sister.

xiii. [p. 388] Grandpa and Grandma, Mart and Marcella, were my godparents, and also my surrogate parents along with Mom and Dad; they also provided the central familial context for the primary development of my religious identity and faith: quiet, meditative, prayerful, without compulsion, and open to the Spirit, where God comes to us in our hearts through reflection and in the personal relationships and social communities (and institutional church) God provides for us. Martin A. Weaver was born (25 June 1903) in Pulaski County, Indiana, where his great-great-grandfather Henry Weaver (born 1790) had settled in America, after immigrating from Germany with his wife Barbara (born 1791) and their three sons: Frederick (born 1818), George (born 1820), and John (born 1825); Henry and Barbara's fourth son, Jacob, was born (1834) in New York. In 1840, the Henry Weaver family is found in Lancaster County, Pennsylvania; and afterwards, from 1844-1845, in Ohio (Scipio Township, Seneca County); Henry and Barbara Weaver both died in Pulaski: Henry on 7 June 1862, and Barbara on 2 November 1863. Frederick (Martin's great-grandfather) and his first German-born wife Lydia Ruch (born October 1820), were married at St. Mary's Church in Tiffin, Ohio (22 November 1842); and their two children, Henry Weaver (Martin's grandfather) and Levi Weaver were also born in Tiffin, Seneca County, Clinton Township: Henry Weaver (on 7 July 1844) and Levi (1845); but Frederick was deeded property of 40 acres in Pulaski County on Christmas Day 1845. But in February 1847 his wife Lydia died, after giving birth to Susannah (born 5 January 1847), who in turn died seven months later (14 August 1847). Frederick Weaver then took a second German-born wife, Mary Anne Hoover (born in Meckenberg, 1828): Mary Anne was ten years his junior, and she and Fredrick were married on 4 January 1848 in Pulaski, where five more children were born to the couple: Jacob (1848), John (1849), Mary (1852), Susannah (1853), and Catherine (1856); then Frederick Weaver died the following year (13 October 1857), at 39-years of age, with the eldest of the seven children, Henry, then only 13-years-old. Prior to Frederick's arrival in Indiana, Frederick's immigrant father, Henry Weaver, with Fredrick's other three brothers, George, John, and Jacob, also had settled in Indian Creek Township of Pulaski County, where the lands adjacent to the Indian Creek tributary to the Tippecanoe River had often continued to be favorite camping grounds for the Potawatomi Indians who had separated from their tribes deported earlier to Kansas during the November 1838 "trail of death." And on 3 December 1849, Henry Weaver deeded another 40 acres to his son Frederick. Henry Weaver also would deed the ground for the first Catholic church founded in Pulaski County; while Frederick then built the church, in 1851: it was a 15x24 foot frame building, with two windows and a door: at first it was called "St. Anne's," but later "St. Francis of Assisi." Frederick's firstborn son, Martin's grandfather Henry Weaver, married Magdalene Haas (born 31 July 1851 in Pulaski) on 1 September 1867; they had ten children. Henry and Magdalene Weaver's fourth child was Martin's father, Joseph Isidore Weaver (born 8 November 1874), who at Pulaski on 5 February 1895 would marry Mary Catherine Meyer (born 13 April 1877); they had eight children: three boys (Adrian, Theodore, Julius); my grandfather (Martin) was the fourth child; then there was another boy (Ralph), a girl (Ruth), a boy (Otto); and lastly a girl (Irene), who at six months died of typhoid fever. Although I knew Ted and Ralph, I remember well only Grandpa's younger siblings, particularly Ruth and Otto. Aunt Ruth by profession was a butcher; she was a colorful extrovert: smoked cigars; cussed, drank beer, and played cards viciously with the men; Ruth and her equally extrovert husband, Pete Peden, loved to fish, and Pete's gentle graciousness and perpetual laughter and sense of humor were contagious; Ruth and Pete had five children, except for the second child, all girls. Uncle Otto had married Rowena Greenwalt; but they were childless, so they adopted an infant son; unfortunately, the hyperactive child, who was slightly younger than me, was mentally disturbed: sometimes Eddie Joe (he also shared my name) would experiment with inflicting pain on people or pets using matches and pencils; and after Otto and Rowena moved to California, their troubled son eventually found terminal residence in a California prison. Except for future felon Eddie Joe and for Ruth and Pete's youngest daughters (Nancy, Sharon, and Suzanne), all of Grandpa Weaver's nieces and nephews were of my mother's generation: like Adrian's daughter Olive, or Ruth and Pete's eldest daughter Vivian: and although I knew some of them, most of the Weaver cousins belonged to my more distant world of adults. Grandpa lived in Pulaski for eight years; while a young boy, he weeded and topped onions for five cents an hour, about $3.00 a week. There he also learned how to fish from his mother Mary: to help put food on the table, she used to line up all her children along the river bank with cane poles. Then in 1910, Grandpa's family lived in Ege, Indiana, where now his parents, Joseph and Mary, are buried in the cemetery next to the Immaculate Conception Church; Joseph died (26 September 1938) ten years before I was born, so I never knew him; Mary, however, often would stay with Grandpa and Grandma for periods of time, until she died of cancer when I was seventeen (17 July 1965) at 88-years of age, and a few weeks after complications from surgery for a broken hip. Both parents of Grandpa's mother, Mary, had died in Pulaski County: Mary's father William Meyer (25 August 1915) was 69-years-old when he died, having been born in Baden, Germany (on 13 May 1846); and her mother Barbara (Sattig) Meyer (16 April 1940) was 89-years-old when she died, having been born in Milan, Ohio (on 4 August 1851). William Meyer's father, Xavier Meyer, also had been born in Baden (3 October 1812; died 19 December 1887), and with William's mother Maria (Schmidt) Meyer (born 25 March 1817; died 30 December 1898), the whole family had immigrated to the United States in 1849, when William Meyer was just three-years-old, the sixth-born of Xavier and Maria's eight children; their fourth and fifth children were both named Mary, the first Mary had died at age five. After their immigration, they came to Milan, Ohio, near Sandusky, where Xavier Meyer had been a shipbuilder and his children tended to the farm, and where his third of five sons, William Meyer, eventually found his local Milan-born wife Barbara Sattig; Barbara's father, Martin Sattig (Martin Weaver's namesake; Barbara also had a brother named Martin), had been a construction engineer on the Erie Canal and was born in Alsace, Germany (1811); her father had immigrated to America in 1824, and died in Norwalk, Ohio (15 June 1903); while Barbara's mother, Mary Magdalene (Humm) Sattig, was French born. In Milan, Ohio, the schoolgirl Barbara Sattig in her rural one-room-schoolhouse had been four years older than her famous classmate, Thomas Alva Edison, the great American inventor and scientist, who left Milan at age seven and had seemed to Barbara to be rather disinterested in his schoolwork. After William and Barbara were married, the newlyweds journeyed to Missouri by covered wagon, where their first child, Charles Meyer, was born near Jefferson City in 1871, and Charles would later marry a Pulaski Weaver relative, Mary Weaver, before his sister Mary C. (Meyer) Weaver married Martin Weaver's father Joseph; William and Barbara Meyer are found in Pulaski, Indiana, probably earlier and not later than 1874, where there was already a second child, Louise, and when the third child, Martha, was born in Beaver Township (20 September 1874); in 1877, Grandpa Martin Weaver's mother Mary was the fourth-born of William and Barbara's nine children, while the youngest five children were boys except for number eight, a girl; the last born, Phillip, died at age fifteen. In 1911, when Martin Weaver then was about eight-years-old, his family (parents Joseph and Mary and their seven children) lived in Monterey, Indiana (Tippecanoe Township, Pulaski County); then from 1912-1916, they were in Swan, Indiana (about six miles north of Huntertown); from 1916-1926 Grandpa Weaver then lived in Huntertown, Indiana (about nine miles north of Fort Wayne on Route 3, Lima Road). Grandpa had said to my mother, while living on "Nanny West's place," he hauled logs and gravel, worked on highways, and broke horses. Then during two summers, while yet in high school, he worked on the B & O (Baltimore & Ohio) Railroad on maintenance and way; he also cooked for the men on the railroad one summer, on the condition that he would do no dishes. He attended International Business College (Fort Wayne); then worked at Wells Truck and Axle Company in Auburn, Indiana. One summer he also worked at hanging steel and putting in towers around Mishawaka, Indiana; then, still in his late teens, he worked two years for Bowser Company of Fort Wayne; and, in 1923, he worked just six months for Studebaker Company of South Bend. After this respectable history of manual labor, he found his final employment from 13 November 1924, when he began work at Lincoln (National) Life Insurance Company, Fort Wayne, until he would retire in 1967; it would be his idea to introduce "National" to the company's original name of Lincoln Life. Grandpa's brother Ralph also was a LNL employee until Ralph retired in 1970. After Mart and Marcella were married (26 November 1925), at first they moved their home to the rural outskirts of Fort Wayne in 1926; then they moved to the city proper from 1935, but only into their new home when it was completed in 1940. Grandpa had designed their final home on 4429 South Wayne Avenue; and he had built it himself, together with the contractor, Fred Roth; then in 1957, the last house Fred constructed before he would retire was the home of my parents, his son-in-law and eldest daughter, Ben and Rita Clemmer, which Grandpa also helped build with Dad, although I also pounded in a few nails for "2427." Later on, soon after his other daughter, Mary Ann, was married to Paul and living in Chicago, Grandpa laid out the design and finished the upstairs bedroom and attic storage under their roof. Grandpa also designed and custom-built his boat that we used for fishing at Ridinger Lake (Kosciusco County, Indiana), where we stayed every August at the "Crisalena," our rented four-week summer cottage on the 136-acre glacial lake; except when Grandpa preferred to be alone, usually trolling for bass, I nearly always was Grandpa's fishing partner, when we set anchor and quietly fished for bluegill, finding time for serious reflection, delightfully interrupted by our catch; and at night, from the early evening, we took our regular spot anchored around the incandescent light off shore, while Grandpa, Dad, and I fished for crappie. Grandpa had invented his surefire method for catching forty or fifty of the ten-or-twelve-inch fish every night: we caught and preserved the skipjack minnows from the lake overnight for bait, then with a fly-fishing rod, the thick line was greased to float on the water, with about a ten-foot nylon fishing line attached; at the line's end the tiny hook was gently put through the minnow's gill and out its mouth, which bait was eagerly devoured by the fish we caught after we had gently lowered the nylon line into the water and the heavier line ran and pulled beneath the water; we were finished only when the fish stopped biting, as we outwitted the fish and the other fisherman around the permanent lamp posted 100 feet off shore from our cottage, under the night skies wonderfully full of galaxies of stars, and sometimes streaking Perseids, as I saw God in his universe and with us in our boat.

xiv. [p. 388] If Grandpa Weaver brought with him to marriage his German-Catholic side of the family, as his wife Grandma Weaver also brought her deep Catholic-French heritage, along with the many relatives and first cousins of her primary family. She was born Marcella May Bobay on 1 May 1905, the middle of seven children born to Edward Ferdinand Bobay and Cecelia Augusta White (Blanc) Bobay, born in Fort Wayne: Edward on 9 June 1869, and Cecelia on 11 February 1874). Great-grandpa "Edward" Bobay (also my namesake with Grandpa "Edward" Clemmer) and his wife Cecelia were both descendants of the earliest French settlers of Allen County, Indiana: his grandfather Germain Bobay and her grandfather Lawrence White (Blanc). Edward and Cecelia Bobay were married in St. Vincent's Church on 25 January 1898, and they lived the first few years of their marriage south of Fort Wayne, at the rural community of Hessen Cassel, where their first two sons were born; then they moved to Fort Wayne, where Edward worked as a teamster, and they lived on Weisser Park Avenue, where three more children were born to them, including Marcella Bobay (Grandma Weaver); sometime later, not before 1907 and after Edward's father, "John," had died (17 August 1902), the family moved back to the Bobay farm (Highway 27 North) so Edward could help his mother, where then the last two children were born. Marcella's father, Edward Bobay, had been the second child of the eleven children born to Jean "John" August Bobay (born in Perry Township, Allen County, on 3 August 1843) and Julie Celina (Tournier) Bobay (who had been born in Etroitefontaine, France on 16 January 1845, one hour after midnight, at home; to Julie Celina Tournier's 23-year-old father, Gabriel Tournier (a locksmith), and her 25-year-old mother, Josephine Tournier, both born in France (in 1820 and 1818); Julie's grandfather, Aimable Tournier (born in France, Etroitefontaine, Canton of Villersel, in Haute Saone, on 15 November 1797) had arrived in the United States with his family on 9 January 1852. Likewise, Edward Bobay's grandfather, Germain Bobay, arrived to the United States via New York Harbour (Ellis Island) on 6 May 1840; Germain was born on 24 February 1807, to Andre Bobay and his second wife Elizabeth Cordier, who resided at Saint Germain-Le-Chatelet, Canton of Fontaine, District of Belfort, Department of Haut Rhin. Germain Bobay died an early casualty of the 1850-1860 cholera epidemic: he died while the children were away at school; Edward Bobay's father John, then was the fifth-born but third-eldest of the eleven children born to Germain and Pauline (Perrey) Bobay (who was born 1805 in France): third-born Pauline (born February 1838) died at six years of age (31 August 1844); fourth-born Pierre Francois Xavior (born July 1841) died at three months (29 October 1841); the last child, Francis, was born in 1849 and died in 1860; while Edward F. Bobay's middle name was derived from Germain and Pauline's last surviving child, Ferdinand, who was born in 1848 and was twenty-one-years-old, and still a bachelor for four more years, when Edward was born; and before the children arrived home from school, Germain already was buried in an unmarked trench on the north side of St. Vincent's Church. Marcella's mother, Cecelia (White) Bobay, was the eighth of eleven children born to Briss White; Briss White and his wife, Mary Celeste Roussey, were married in Fort Wayne at St. Mary's Church on 21 May 1855; and both of them had been born in France: Briss Blanc (2 May 1828; died

1914) and Mary Celeste Roussey (20 January 1835; died 1881); they both had immigrated with their parents from France: for Briss White, the eldest child, his father Lawrence Blanc (born 1795) and mother Mary Frances Perriquey (born 1784) arrived in the United States with their three children (Briss, Marie, and Lawrence) on 1 May 1842; for Mary Celeste (White) Roussey, the seventh of nine children born in France, her father Pierre Roussey (born 24 August 1792) and mother Francoise Narbet (born 1798) arrived in the United States with their children on 1 August 1847. For my Grandma, Marcella (Bobay) Weaver, there were two older brothers and a sister (Raymond, Oscar, and Erma), followed by two younger brothers and a sister (Harley, Virgil, and Velma). Grandma's brother Virgil Bobay married Geneva Meyer Bobay, whose father was Charles Meyer, the eldest brother of husband Martin Weaver's mother, Mary C. (Meyer) Weaver. The families of Grandma's two sisters provided the usual focus for our family gatherings, although there were frequently entertaining encounters with the younger brothers, too; Harley and Velma were Grandma's favorites, both had a terrific sense of humor, like Grandma who at times could become hysterical with her spontaneous laughter over simple everyday absurdities. Grandma's sister Erma had married John Brothers and they lived on their family farm (Washington Township, now part of the Pine Valley Golf Course, Fort Wayne), not far from the Bobay farm; they had one son, Larry, who determinedly would marry his sweetheart, an endearing Amish girl Laura German, in a double wedding with her sister. On the other hand, Grandma's sister Velma had married Martin Scherschel; eventually Velma and Mart had eleven children, which he supported by employment at a meat packing company. Apart from reunions with the extended family, and with the two Martins, Mart Weaver and Mart Scherschel, as brothers-in-law, the families of the two Bobay sisters, Marcella and Velma, were constantly intertwined: for birthdays, holidays, or simple weekends, and my family with theirs, when our families would blend together at their respective households: either at the Scherschels in New Haven, a small town east of Fort Wayne, on the Maumee River with its railroad and trucking industry, where their large country-style frame house also enjoyed surrounding open spaces; or at Grandma and Grandpa Weaver's, where their basement afforded ample recreational space, with a pool table that also could be covered to become a second dining table (my brother Joel now has Grandpa's pool table) and there was an electric train set (which my son Jim Dearlove now retains, after my former father-in-law, Norbert Herber, saved it from the auction block). This was the nexus of my experience of family, in its collaboration and normal chaos, with its relational conflicts and resolutions, and also for Aunt Mary Ann, our life shared with the Scherschel cousins: Roseanne, two years older than Mary Ann, was a parallel mother for her ten brothers and sisters, until she married Bernard Spieth; Thomas, ring-bearer at my parent's wedding, one year older than Mary Ann, was an excellent diesel mechanic, after he got out of the Navy and married Joan Stirnkorb; there were three Scherschel cousins younger than Mary Ann, but older than me, a girl and two boys: Marita, Robert, and Stephen; I often went with Stephen when we paired up, and assisted with his newspaper route; but also I found his sister Patricia very compatible, less than a year younger than I; then there were five other cousins who ranged in parallel to the ages of my other brothers and sisters: Richard, Edward, Catherine, Mary Jo, and Kevin. The youngest, Kevin, also was the last to be married, only a month before his father Martin Scherschel died on 7 July 1984. Then eight years later, on 15 February 1992, my grandfather, Martin Weaver died; I also presented the eulogy with his daughter Aunt Mary Ann and her husband Paul after the funeral Mass, at St. John the Baptist Church. Later that summer, I saw Marcella for the last time at St. Anne's Home, as she lay sleeping, emaciated, slowly dying with Alzheimer's; she then died, after Mom's attentive care, on 5 November 1993. A short time afterwards, only one to three weeks later, early one morning Mom experienced a wide-awake vision of her father, Martin Weaver, either a lucid dream or something more supernatural: Rita, my mother, described it as follows: "He appeared suddenly like the flash of a TV screen; but unlike looking at a picture, it was as if Dad were sitting across the table from me in person. He was dressed in a white suit and had a youthful appearance (about forty-years-old), the way he looked in the picture in my bedroom. He was smiling broadly." Then, as Mom recounted the event, she said, "Dad, you're smiling. Is Mom in heaven?" He responded to Mom, "She has her arms." Mom states, sometime after putting her experience to paper, "Then he left as quickly as he had appeared." After some contemplation, Mom offered a possible explanation for her father's response: "Mom has a Franciscan symbol on her tombstone, of a cross with arms around the cross. The reality of this experience never fades. I think about it every day. Wherever Dad is, he is very happy. Must be heaven." I will not attempt to explain the full depth of this symbolism in my mother's experience, except as one key to say, like St. Francis with his arms around the Lord from the cross in the apparition of Jesus to him, Grandma Marcella May Weaver had endured her final years of suffering in her spiritual unity with the Lord on his cross of sorrow for our sins; and both Marcella and Martin Weaver had been Third Order Secular Franciscans. It would be another ten years before Grandma's sister Velma died: on Christmas Eve 2004, as the rest of us celebrated the Lord's first coming, as I am also preparing now to do with today's readings on the Fourth Sunday of Advent 2009, exactly two months after my father's death (Luke 1:45, Micah 5:1, Hebrews 10:5-10); by conformity with God's will, Jesus came to be born amongst us (Hebrews 1:1-6, John 1:9-13), in order to save all of us from our sins, so that joint-heirs with Christ we may be gathered together with him for eternity, provided that we share his suffering, so as to share his glory (2 Peter 3:9; 2 Thessalonians 2:1, 1 Thessalonians 5:9-11, Romans 8:17, Galatians 4:4-5).

xv. [p. 388] Kathleen (born 21 November 1948) was the eldest of five children by her parents, Norbert and Mary Herber; as a grade-school classmate of my sister Carol, I knew her one year behind me by her reputation as an outstanding student, and also through secondary-school as an aspirant to convent for the Sisters of the Precious Blood (Dayton, Ohio), until the convent school closed, leaving her a classmate of my sister's in their final year at Central Catholic High School in Fort Wayne. Except for church on occasion, we first met again at a birthday party for Carol, before we all started studies at St. Francis College, after I had returned home from seminary after one year at Loras College (Dubuque, Iowa). We began to date only four months later, New Year's Eve 1967; and four years later we were married in Fort Wayne, Indiana, at Queen of Angels Church on 29 December 1971, while we lived in St. Louis, Missouri, for nine years, where our children were born. We were one year in Oswego, New York, 1980-1981, before returning to Fort Wayne, 1981-1986. Then we lived together five years in Methuen, Massachusetts, thirty miles north of Boston on the New Hampshire border while I taught at Emerson College (Boston), until my ultimate separation from the family during my last year in the States, when I taught at the Benedictine college of St. Anselm in Manchester, New Hampshire, 1991-1992, and I would arrive in Malta on 12 October 1992.

xvi. [p. 468] The Anabaptist Christian (Mennonite) sect originated from the Netherlands, and its name is taken from its reformation leader Menno Simons (zoon) [Meno Simonis], Menno son of Simon (circa 1496-1561). While Mennonites (Amish) have co-mingled with my family history both in Europe and America, I have been influenced by their Christian witness through their Indiana communities located in Grabill and Harlan (near Fort Wayne) and in Shipshewana (nearer to Lake Wawasee). Their prominent Christian values are tolerance (Colossians 3:8-13), charity (Colossians 3:14), communal life (Colossians 3:15-17), obedience (Colossians 3:18-21), hospitality (Colossians 4:5-6), and simplicity of life style (1 Thessalonians 4:11-12).

xvii. [p. 471] My general opinion, now (in November 2008) that I am at the point of reading "The Passion," after beginning to read her five-volume "Poem of the Man-God" in January 2008, only when I first had completed the forty chapters of this book, and while throughout this year I had tackled the lengthy process of my "final" editing of this work, is that her gospel is a genuine revelation. Primarily, I found the spirituality of the work profoundly consistent with the entire gospel, a guiding light for conversion in Christ; as a psychologist, I also noted her many interesting and defining details regarding the process of her visions, where she is entirely conscious and active in her writing environment, while simultaneously Maria is actively living and experiencing every possible sensory dimension within the vision as an observer, in real or suspended time. Also, from moment to moment, I was aware of her integrated gospel sources, without my trying to annotate them; she herself, at times, frequently uses her own bible to identify the Lord's narration during her visions and dictations. Lastly, the Lord's "gift" to Maria is such a well-crafted and poetic construction, and her personal and interpretative commentary is such a humble and dedicated work of a suffering servant, that even with her interpretive variations on certain historical issues where I would choose to differ, the truth of its whole comes from the Spirit of God. Quite often I found her narration of the gospel compelling and essential to my own spiritual journey, and it was a parallel to my own task of living and constructing the gospel in my own life. Her gift to us from the Lord is unique. My only help for constructing the Gospel Emmaus has been the gospel texts, which are openly available to everyone, my experience and analysis, and the Spirit of God, who is the only and true source for all of his gifts.

xviii. [p. 511] Maria Valtorta provides, in her transcription of dictated commentary from Jesus, that it was "after about four years" before his Mother went back to Nazareth and entered her house (Vol. 1, Chapter 35, p. 184). It is not clear whether those years refer to her absence from Nazareth or to their departure from Bethlehem; the former seems most likely: after three years of age but before the child Jesus turned four. This timing is consistent with a Winter Solstice 8 BCE date of birth in Bethlehem, the magi's arrival to Jerusalem later in December 6 BCE, and a final return of the Holy Family to Nazareth sometime in (mid-Spring of) 4 BCE.

xix. [p. 511] It was only after my original speculation that I took up my first reading of Maria Valtorta. Towards the end of Volume One, she provides us with a letter to Our Lord from his mother, who cites Matarea (Vol. 1, Chapter 133, p. 723; also again as Our Lady teaches the Magdalene, in Vol. 2, end of Chapter 246, p. 581); only gradually did I come to understand the significance of this location. Matarea (today's Al Matariyyah) is one of three parts of the ancient city of Heliopolis, part of today's El Cairo district called Al-Zeitoun, east of the Nile and north of the apex of the Delta. Heliopolis was the center of the Egyptian Sun-cult to Rē and its various personifications of the Sun-god including Horus, which seems an appropriate residence for the exiled Christ child, Son of God, Light of the World, born as Man-God on the Winter solstice, and finally rising from the dead in his Easter glory. As part of Egyptian creation beliefs and their synchronous relationships between gods and men, land appears from the chaotic waters, but an egg appears, hatches, and yields the Sun, and as it rises into the heavens, the creation of all living matter follows. Another tradition describes the same creation as a lotus bud that floated on the surface of the waters, and from the open petals there emerges the Sun-god Horus. Our Christian "New Creation" begins with the death of Jesus and his resurrection from the dead just before the break of Easter day [which we also celebrate with Easter eggs]. On the night of 2 April in 1968 [Tuesday of Holy Week], the first of several apparitions of Our Lady above the St. Mary Coptic Orthodox Church at Zeitoun (in Matarea, Egypt) was reported and witnessed by many thousands and is described by its historian Pearl Zaki; and beginning on 11 December 2009, another similar transfiguration of the Holy Virgin was reported, this time on the domes of the Virgin Mary and Archangel Michael Coptic Orthodox Church in Warraq al-Hadar, Giza, Cairo, which also was witnessed by hundreds of thousands of Christians and Muslims, by both believers and non-believers, and posted as a video on You-Tube. It now seems that Mary [Settana Mariam, Our Lady Mary], in her vocation as God-bearer, Theotokos, had carried her son to Matarea, and from there she also continues to carry Christ to the world.

xx. [p. 512] Not only listening to Peter as he then speaks to us, but also to the present Vicar of Christ (John 10:2-4, 16, 27-28), now Benedict XVI. In his recent apostolic journey to Malta, in his homily on the Floriana Granaries (Third Sunday of Easter, 18 April 2010), the centre of the Pope's message, as it also reflects my own motivations for this task, would have been immeasurably consistent with Peter's first preaching on Pentecost: "It is our love for the Lord that moves us to love those whom he loves, and to accept gladly the task of communicating his love to those we serve." So I strive to maintain that focus. "In every area of our lives we need the help of God's grace. With him, we can do all things: without him we can do nothing."

xxi. [p. 551] See O'Connell, Daniel C., & Kowal, Sabine (2008). *Communicating with One Another: Toward a Psychology of Spontaneous Spoken Discourse*. New York: Springer, p. 107; Clemmer, Edward. J., O'Connell, Daniel C., & Loui, Wayne. (1979). Rhetorical pauses in oral reading. *Language and Speech*, 22, 89-99; Clemmer, Edward J., & Carrocci, Noreen M. (1984). Effects of experience on radio language performance. *Communication Monographs*, 51, 116-139; Clemmer, Edward J., & Payne, J. Gregory (1991). Affective images of the public political mind: Semantic differential reference frames for an experience of the 1988 presidential campaign. *Political Communication and Persuasion*, 8(1), 29-41; and Clemmer, Edward J. (2000). *Alfred Sant Explained: In-Novella ta' Malta fil-Mediterran*. Malta: PIN (Pubblikazzjonijiet Independenza). Father Dan, my Jesuit mentor and colleague is now 82-years-old, and twenty years my senior. It was the Lord's destiny that brought me to Saint Louis University in 1971, when I first met Dan and Sabine in Statistics class, Father Dan as the instructor and Sabine as a fellow student; and it also was the Lord's destiny that through Father Dan events would bring me to the University of Malta in 1992. When I told

Father Dan about Jane's and my wedding in the church on 8th December 2008, I confided, "God's mysterious ways are getting less mysterious, but I'm still astonished at his blessings." And Dan, with his blessings and his love, wryly responded, "You're right, Ed; He becomes less mysterious as He goes, but He's still a couple of eternities ahead of us." I can also thank God for the blessing of Father Dan's friendship of nearly thirty years and the spiritual relationship we have shared mutually in the Lord.

Appendix

Synopses of the Forty-two Chapters

Volume One:

Part One (Chapters 1-20): From the Coming of John to the Lord's Transfiguration

1. John the Baptist—The Desert Messenger

Like Mark's 1:1-5 beginning, regarding our contemporary lives, our gospel narrative begins with our call to repentance by John the Baptist, as the Precursor for the Christ.

> Readings: Luke 3:1-9; Mark 1:1-5; Matthew 3:1-10; John 1:19-23

> Readings: Luke 3:10-17; John 1:24-28; Mark 1:7-8; Matthew 3:11-12

> Prayer Reflection: Psalm 1:1-6

2. Zechariah, Elizabeth and Mary—The Presence of God

At first, as disciples of John the Bapist, we are unaware of this chapter's retrospective preamble to the Incarnation and the parallel narrative for John the Baptist. Our attention is focused upon Mary, who, by providing her assent to the will of God, makes present God-with-us in the flesh by the power of the Holy Spirit.

>Readings: Luke 1:5-25, 39-45, 56-66

>Readings: Luke 1:26-38

>Prayer Reflection: Psalm 113:1-9

3. Christ—A Mighty Servant is Come to Build a House

In this next retrospective chapter, for the time being the birth of Christ and the Flight to Egypt are bypassed (presented in the first part of Chapter 40 as a final retrospective). Here we focus on the presentation of Christ to the Temple, twice: first as an infant soon after his birth, and upon his Jewish manhood when the child Jesus comes of age.

>Readings: Luke 1:39-45, 56-66; Luke 2:22-38

>Prayers: Magnificat (Luke 1:46-55), Benedictus (Luke 1:68-79), Nunc Dimittis (Luke 2:29-32), Psalm 84:2-4, 11

>Reflective Prayer: Psalm 34:1-22

4. John and Jesus, the Christ—By Whose Authority?

As if we are original disciples, we resume our journey in the context of John, who is questioned by the Pharisees; and Jesus is baptized (by someone) at Bethany. By God's authority, Christ is the cornerstone of our salvation.

>Readings: Luke 3:15-21; Mark 1:7-11; John 1:19-32; Matthew 3:11-17

>Prayer: Psalm 118:19-29

5. Jesus and the Devil—The Kingdom of God in the Desert of Sin

Jesus, in prayer with his Father, prepares himself for his public mission by fasting for forty days and nights, while like us Jesus also experiences his temptations with Satan in the desert.

> Readings: Luke 7:24-33; Mark 1:12-13; Luke 4:1-13; Matthew 4:1-11
>
> Reflective Prayer: Psalm 91:1-16

6. Discipleship and Cana—Invitation to a King's Wedding Feast

This is the figurative "week of Creation" before the coming of the "time of the Lord": first, the initial few disciples are chosen; and a wedding feast occurs on the "sixth day," before the implied concluding seventh sabbath day of rest, before the Lord begins his appointed time of re-creation.

> Readings: John 1:35-51; Revelation 19:6-8
>
> Prayer: Psalm 15
>
> Readings: John 2:1-12; Matthew 22:1-14; Luke 14:15-24
>
> Prayer Reflection: Psalm 24:1-10

7. A Passover Journey—Return to Cana from Judea through Samaria

After a period of time in Judea with his disciples, the Baptist is arrested and Jesus returns to Galilee, heading through Samaria, where he stops at Jacob's well and meets a Samaritan woman.

> Readings: John 3:22-30, 4:1-4; John 4:5-41
>
> Prayer: Psalm 80:2-20

8. The Prophet Comes to Galilee—Prophecy and Faith at Home

Jesus finds an absence of faith at Cana and in his home town of Nazareth among his own people, but greater faith is found in a Roman citizen who is a government official at Capernaum.

> Readings: Matthew 4:12-17, Mark 1:14-15, Luke 4:14-15, John 4:43-45
>
> Readings: John 4:46-54; Luke 7:1-10; Matthew 8:5-13
>
> Readings: Luke 4:16-28; Matthew 13:51-58; Mark 6:1-6
>
> Reflective Prayer: Psalms 111:1-10, 19:1-14

9. Catching Men and Facing Demons—Be Not Afraid

The four fisherman and pairs of brothers, Peter and Andrew, James and John, are called to be "fishers of men." In Capernaum, where Jesus lives, at the synagogue Jesus confronts a demon who has possessed a man; later Jesus heals Simon's mother-in-law; but after preaching and driving out demons, Jesus always returns to prayer; and despite the plea of the crowds to remain with them, he cannot stay in one place. Yet, we are each called by Jesus to follow him wherever he goes despite our sinfulness, and also because of our demons or illnesses.

> Readings: Matthew 4:18-22, Mark 1:16-28, Luke 4:31-37
>
> Readings: Mark 1:29-34, Luke 4:38-41, Matthew 8:14-17
>
> Readings: Mark 1:35-39, Luke 4:42-44
>
> Readings: Luke 5:1-11
>
> Reflective Prayer: Psalms 51:1-19, 32:1-11

10. The Divine Mercy among Outcasts and the Respectable Priests, Lawyers, and Politicians—Sin, Forgiveness, and Our Call to Repentance

Jesus cures a leper who comes to him, and Jesus sends him to the priests. Then Jesus forgives the sins of a paralized man; and to show his power to forgive the sins of a paralized humanity, Jesus cures him. Later, Jesus calls Matthew the tax collector, who leaves everything to follow Jesus. When the Pharisees object to these mercies, Jesus indicates the purpose of his mission.

> Readings: Hosea 5:15, 6:1-3; Mark 1:40-45, Luke 5:12-16, Matthew 8:1-4
>
> Readings: Hosea 5:1-7; Mark 2:1-12, Luke 5:17-26, Matthew 9:1-8
>
> Readings: Hosea 6:4-11; Mark 2:13-17, Luke 5:27-32, Matthew 9:9-13
>
> Prayer and Scripture Meditation: Psalm 50:7-13, Psalm 40:2-14, 17-18

11. The Widow of Nain and a Sinful Woman at Dinner— Empathy and Love in the Footsteps of the Prophets

Jesus raises back to life the dead son of the widow of Nain, not only in sympathy for her loss, but as a sign of our future life in the Lord's resurrection because of his death to come. And a sinful woman shows her great love for Jesus because her great sins have been forgiven her. At this time, yet unknown to the reader, these respective gospel episodes, as the widow of Nain and the sinful woman, bear remarkable applications as respective prototypes regarding my wife and myself, which I have recognized, but for now these parallels to our lives from the gospel events are barely intimated by myself, or not at all; but later on these will become evident as gracious instructions for all from the Lord, who is our paradigm for eternal life and everyone's salvation.

> Readings: Luke 7:11-17
>
> Readings: Luke 7:36-50
>
> Reflective Prayer: Psalm 103:1-22

12. Pharisees and Teachers of the Law versus the Lord of the Sabbath—Counter Accusations, Refutations, and Death Plots

Jesus is Lord of his "New Creation," as the disciples pluck and eat grains of wheat from the fields on the Sabbath. To prove his point, Jesus cures a man with a crippled right hand on the Sabbath, as Temple lawyers looked on. Then in Jerusalem for the feast of Pentecost, on the Sabbath by the pool of the five porticoes, Jesus heals a crippled man, whom Jesus instructs to take up his mat and walk. Although the authorities are making plans to kill Jesus, Jesus proffers the refutation of his Father's testimony: his works and himself to whom the scriptures testify.

>Readings: Mark 2:23-28, Luke 6:1-5, Matthew 12:1-8

>Readings: Mark 3:1-6, Luke 6:6-11, Matthew 12:9-14

>Readings: John 5:1-18; John 5:19-29; John 5:30-47

>Reflective Prayer: Psalm 41:2-14

13. Jesus Sends Them Apostles of the New Covenant—A Retreat to the Hills and Crowds along the Lake

The twelve "apostles" are chosen so that Jesus may "send them out" to preach, and then later there would be Paul. As the "Word," the foundation of the New Covenant, Jesus preaches its summary on the hills of Capernaum: by the eight beatitudes, each now taken separately, and contextualized by scripture and by their modern context. With the sixth beatitude, my own story is only initially unveiled. Afterwards, some would and others would not follow Jesus, but many did, including some women who had been cured of evil spirits and diseases, who provided for the Lord's proclamation of the "Good News of the kingdom of God" out of their resources.

>Readings: Luke 6:11-12, Matthew 12:14-16, 9:36-37, 10:1, Mark 3:6-13; John 5:17-18, 6:1-2

>Readings: Luke 6:12-16, Mark 3:13-19, Matthew 10:1-4

>Readings: Exodus 19:1-8; Matthew 4:25, 5:1-12; Luke 6:17-26; Matthew 23:10, Luke 11:43, Mark 12:39-44

>Readings: 1 Samuel 1:1-28; Luke 11:43, Matthew 23:5-12

>Readings: Matthew 23:13-22; Luke 12:13-21

Readings: Luke 11:42, Matthew 23:23; Leviticus 11:41-45, Matthew 23:24

Readings: Mark 7:1-5, Luke 11:39-41, Matthew 23:25-28

Readings: Matthew 7:7-8, Luke 11:9-10, Mark 11:24-25

Readings: Matthew 27:33-44, 23:15; Philippians 3:10

Readings: Matthew 8:18-22, Luke 9:57-62; Luke 8:1-3

Prayer Reflection: Psalms 5:1-12, 4:1-8; Canticle of Hannah: 1 Samuel 2:1-10

14. The Word of God, the Kingdom of Heaven, and the Church are God's Eternal Love

The Word of God is compared to a sower who went out to sow his seed, and to other parables. Then away from the crowds, Jesus explains these parables to the "Twelve." That same day, when evening approached, Jesus told his disciples to cross to the other side of the lake. When they are caught in a violent squall, the disciples emplore the sleeping "Teacher" to save them from drowning. The winds and sea obey the Lord's command; and when they come ashore, their journey reflects the history and later fate of Gamala on the Golan Heights: they encounter a fearsome man possessed by Legion, whom the Lord sends out of the man into the herd of pigs, who plunge from a narrow clift into the lake and drown. The citizens of the community notice that the man is no longer possessed, and they want Jesus to leave; but the man wants to come with Jesus. Jesus tells the man to remain with his family and people, so to speak of the Lord's mercy.

Readings: Matthew 13:1-9, 24-33, 44-49, Mark 4:1-9, 26-31, Luke 8:4-8, 13:18-21

Readings: Matthew 13:10-17, 18-23, 36-43; Mark 4:11-12, 13-20; Luke8:9-10, 11-15

Readings: Matthew 8:23-27, 28-33, Mark 4:35-41, 5:1-20, Luke 8:22-25, 26-39; Psalm 107:23-32, 1-22 (Prayer Reflection of a Gadarene (or Gergesene) [or Gamalean]

Disciple)

15. Jesus Urgently Wanted, Men and Women of Faith and Revolutionary Spirituality Needed, and Good Shepherds Required—Apply Within

When Jesus and the disciples return home, Jesus is questioned by some disciples of John the Baptist about why his disciples did not fast. Various men and women of faith urgently approach Jesus: Jarius is interupted by the incident of a woman with a hemorrhage; the daughter of Jarius dies and is raised to life, in front of limited witnesses; two blind men follow Jesus right into his house; and someone brings a mute demonic to Jesus, who cures him. After going round to villages and towns and curing every disease and illness, at the sight of the crowds Jesus felt greatly sorry for them, who were like abandoned sheep without a shepherd. Jesus summons the Twelve disciples for their apostolic mission and sends them out. The nature of Holy Orders is explained accordingly in our contemporary context, especially at its highest level, fully for the Pope and bishops, as good shepherds. Those with a vocation may apply to the Lord, within us.

> Readings: Matthew 9:1, 14-17, 18-26, Mark 2:18-22, 5:21-43, Luke 5:33-39, 8:40-46; Matthew 9:27-34, 35-36

> Readings: Matthew 9:37, 10:1-16, Mark 6:7-13, Luke 9:1-6

> Reflective Prayer for Repentance (Amplified Text): Psalm 10:1-18

16. Violence against the Kingdom of Heaven from King Herod and the Political and Religious Elite—and Revolutionary Monarchists in Opposition to the Bread of Life: Who, then, is the Baptist and Jesus?

In this chapter, the political context of the Herodian dynasty is made explicit for the conjoined missions of John the Baptist and Jesus, the Christ. From prison, John sends two of his disciples to Jesus with a question, in parallel to the testimony John had given earlier when the Pharisees had sent priests and Levites from Jerusalem to ask John who he was. Jesus provides his answer to John's disciples; and accordingly, he addresses the crowds revealingly. Then, two events occur near Tiberias, the palacial residence of Herod in Galilee: the birthday dinner for Herod and how John the Baptist came to be killed; and the event near Passover, how from five loaves and two fish, Jesus provides food for the multititudes, who then want to make him king.

> Readings: Luke 3:1-2, 19-20, Matthew 14:1-2, Mark 6:14-16; Matthew 11:2-6, Luke 7:18-23; Matthew 14:3-12, Mark 6:17-29
>
> Readings: Matthew 14:13-23, Mark 6:30-46, Luke 9:10-17, John 6:1-15
>
> Reflective Prayer: Psalm 78: 1-4, 8-11; 12-20; 21-33, 38-39; 52-58; 65-72

17. The Aftermath: the Repercussions of Bread and Fish, and the Ramifications of Food for Eternal Life—So, Do You Also Want to Leave?

As evening approaches, after Jesus fails to show up, the disciples set out for Bethsaida by a single boat. During a fierce gale on the Lake Gennasaret, Jesus comes towards the disciples by walking across the waters. Peter is the only one to join the Lord upon the waters; but when his faith also fails, he is supported by Jesus who saves him, as the disciples take Jesus into their boat. Mysteriously they arrive at Gennasaret; when searchers from Tiberias find Jesus in the synagogue at Capernaum, they question him. In our contemporary terms, Jesus seems to hold a "Press Conference," which proves to be a political disaster. Many decide to leave Jesus and return to their former ways because they find his words unacceptable. Jesus asks the disciples if they also would like to leave him. The "twelve" stay on, but Jesus indicates that one of them is a "devil."

> Readings: Matthew 14:24-26, Mark 6:48-56, John 6:16-21, 22-25

Readings: John 6:25-71

Prayer Reflection: Psalm 139:1-24

18. Lost Sheep Preoccupied with Traditions about Ordinary Food versus the Faith of House-Dogs Begging for Scraps of Real Food—Pharisees and Scribes as Children from the House of Israel versus a Syrian-Phoenician-Born Woman of Greek Origin Fighting for Her Child

We are introduced to God's divine time according to the created earth's luni-solar Hebrew calendar. The Pharisees are shocked and question Jesus because the disciples do not observe certain human traditions; but Jesus shocks the Pharisees because they disregard God's laws. Immorality does not consist of breaking traditions, but it truly comes from "within" human hearts. We consider our use of God's time that he provides for us, both for work and for rest. Jesus takes the disciples "on holiday" to the Mediterranean coast near Tyre and Sidon, which would be the future portals of evangelization to the Gentiles. Upon their arrival, Jesus and the disciples are disturbed by a woman of persistent faith, a Gentile not of the House of Israel, who is rewarded.

Readings: John 7:1, Matthew 15:1-20, Mark 7:1-23

Readings: Matthew 15:21-28, Mark 7:24-30

Reflective Prayer: Psalm 90:1-17

19. The Disciples' Mission Journey is a Perilous Exodus, Not a Holiday—But Don't Forget to Laugh in Ministry to the Ragtag Church

Jesus continues to set his example for the present and future missionary church, as he set about on foot and by boat in a clockwise journey around the regions of the Lake of Galilee, healing physical illnesses and restoring victims of spiritual traumas. In the region of the Decapolis, Jesus heals a deaf man with a speech impediment. In a deserted place, Jesus feeds the four thousand from the assistance of the disciples with their seven loaves of bread and a few fish, just as through Christ we evangelize our faith communities today. After Jesus and the disciples return to Capernaum, their point of origin, the Pharisees and Sadducees demand a "sign" from Jesus. Recognizing their poisonous calumnies, Jesus immediately departs with his disciples for "the other side of the lake"; and in their haste the disciples forgot to take bread. The lack of perception and close-mindedness of the disciples leads Jesus to review with them his twice feeding of the multitudes, and his meaning regarding the "yeast" of the Pharisees and Sadducees. From the "other shore," Jesus returns with the disciples back across the lake to Bethsaida, where trouble had continued brewing due to the Pharisees and Sadducees. There Jesus leads a blind man out of the village, cures him, and warns him to go home without going back into the village; and likewise, sometimes when the Lord has cured us, destructive environments must be shunned.

> Readings: Mark 7:31, Matthew 15:29-31, Mark 7:32-37; Mark 8:1-10, Matthew 15:32-39

> Readings: Matthew 16:1-4, 5-12, Mark 8:11-13, 14-21; Mark 8:22-26

> Reflective Prayer: Psalms 90:1-17, 146:1-10

20. A Messiah of Suffering and Glory—and for his Disciples Too: An Interpenetration of the Human and the Divine

Jesus leaves Bethsaida with the disciples, heading north on foot to the region of Caesarea Philippi. Peter professes Jesus to be the Messiah, revealed to Peter by God the Father. Shortly thereafter, Jesus openly proclaims to them, without their understanding of it, that he must suffer greatly, be rejected and killed, and on the third day be raised. Peter attempts to rebuke the Lord, but Jesus provides that anyone who wants to be his follower must renounce himself, take up his cross, and follow him. Then Jesus leads Peter, James, and John up a mountain, when the Lord is transfigured in majesty, accompanied by Moses and Elijah who discuss the Lord's mission to Jerusalem, and the voice of the Father proclaims Jesus his beloved Son, "with whom I am well pleased; listen to him." There is no revelation of

God superior to the revelation from Christ: not from the Buddha, or Moses and Elijah, or Mohammed, or Mary Baker Eddy, or Joseph Smith, or from any other honoured religious prophet, philosopher, or poet: theologians and various persons of God are all welcomed to their debate of this point. The experience of the transfiguration by the disciples is discussed, as we also are led to consider our own personal transfiguration in Christ.

>Readings: Matthew 16:13-20, 21-23, 24-28; Mark 8:27-30, 31-33, 34-38; Luke 9:18-21, 22, 23-27

>Readings: Matthew 17:1-13, Mark 9:2-13, Luke 9:28-36; Matthew 17:14-23, Mark 9:14-32, Luke 9:37-45

>Prayer Reflection: Psalm 16:1-11

Part Two (Chapters 21-30): Anticipated Life in the Resurrection, from Galilee to Bethany

21. Please, Do Not Disturb the Church in Training: Jesus is Giving Private Lessons to his Disciples

The nature of faith in Christ, our insufficient faith, and the state of faithlessness are compared and contrasted by their examples and counter-examples: by the father of an epileptic child, by the poverty of faith among the disciples themselves, and by the scribes and the crowds, potentially ourselves, as a "faithless generation." Faithlessness occurs because of our sin, our misplaced beliefs and values, our politics of self-reliance, and our reluctance to love and to forgive. Faith comes from God and is supported by God against our natural limitations to accept God's munificence in the cross. Crises of faith occur because of the inevitable scandals of evil, the horrors of human suffering, our own personal injuries or psychological traumas, the grief of broken or terminated relationships, and perceived challenges to our often human concepts of religion. Faith is supported by our prayer, by our repentance and acceptance of the cross, and by surrendering our life to God's love in the service of others. Faith requires that we seek the well-being of others according to God's will; that we change and become humble like little children; that we become the compassionate eyes, hands, and feet of Christ; and that we repair and forgive each other our many mutual injuries and transgressions. Everyone will be "salted with fire": as is illustrated by the specific case of my wife, by her and our holocaust with the sacrifice of Christ.

> Readings: Matthew 17:14-27, 18:1-5, Mark 9:14-41, Luke 9:37-50
>
> Readings: Mark 9:42-48, 49-50, Matthew 5:13, Luke 14:34-35;
>
> Matthew 18:6-9, 10-14, Luke 15:1-7; Luke 17: 1-2, 3-4, Matthew
>
> 18:15-35
>
> Reflective Prayer: Psalm 96:1-13

22. The Autumn Feast of Tabernacles, the Festival of Water and Light—Jesus, Nicodemus, an Adulteress, and Those Who Would Kill a King

When Jesus decides not to go down to the Jerusalem feast, his unbelieving relatives insist that Jesus should go; and not only, but that he also should show himself to the world. Secretly, Jesus does make his way to Jerusalem and he appears in public half-way through the feast, although the authorities wanted to kill him. In the course of his teaching in the Temple, Jesus presents himself as the Son of the Father; and he invites listeners to come to him and drink of his life-giving waters and in the coming life of the Spirit. In retrospective, the earlier secret meeting of Jesus with Nicodemus near Passover is recalled: there, in the Garden of Olives, Jesus explains his saving mission to Nicodemus, and that no one can enter the Kingdom of God without being "born from above," through water and spirit. In actual time, after a night in the Garden of Olives, Jesus returns to the festival early in the morning, when the Pharisees and scribes bring to Jesus a woman who had been caught in adultery, as we each have been caught in our sins, as we could admit. But through her, Jesus reveals his saving ministry to the world: although everyone is condemned by the Law, by her faith in Jesus she is saved; and as Jesus forgives the woman her sins, he warns her not to sin again. Jesus describes himself as the light of the world, and he warns the Pharisees that if they don't believe that "I am who I am," then they would die in their sins. They would only know him, as Jesus would reveal himself to the world, when finally he would be "lifted up" on the cross for our sins and for the sins of the world.

Readings: John 7:2-53; Psalms 31:2-16, 55:2-15

Readings: John 3:3-21, 31-36; Psalm 45:2-18

Readings: John 8:1-11, 12-30; Psalms 42:2-12, 43:1-5, 31:17-25, 119:153-160, 116:1-9

Prayer Reflection: Psalm 55:16-24

23. Faith in Action—Divine Justice and Christ our Justification, Descendants of Abraham, Disciples of Moses, and Various Blind Men

When Jesus continued his discourse in the Temple, he told those who were listening and who believed in him, "If you continue in my word, you are truly my disciples; and you will know the truth, and the truth will make you free." Those who objected claimed to be slaves of no one, and descendants of Abraham. But whoever sins is a slave; and no one is justified before God as a physical descendant of Abraham, as was Israel; but we are made righteous only by our faith in Abraham's descendant, namely, to Jesus Christ. Abraham was found righteous because of his faith in God's promise; and those who are justified are spiritual descendants of Abraham by faith. If we do not allow the word of God to penetrate into us, it is because we are not children of God, but children of the Devil, whose desires, by our sin, we prefer to carry out. Our blessings from God do not proclaim our justification; just as also our misfortunes from God do not indicate our sinfulness. To the glory of God, Jesus restores the sight of a man born blind, just as he restores spiritual insight to all who have faith in him. Even though we too may have been blind from birth, this man now sees; and those alleged disciples of Moses claiming sight, in their sin, remain blind.

>Readings: John 8:31-59

>Readings: John 9:1-41

>Reflective Prayer: Psalm 40:2-18

24. To All Pharisees—An Invitation for Our Purification: from Candlemas to Chanukah to Calvary, Because I am the Gate of the Sheepfold and the Good Shepherd—Sincerely yours, Jesus, the Lamb of God and Lord of the Sabbath, I AM Who AM, the Son of God, Who is My Father, and We are One

By his ritual purification after his birth according to the Law of Moses, Jesus was first brought to the Temple to acknowledge his vocation to purify us from our sins. To this end, Jesus is the Lamb of God, and also the Good Shepherd, who lays down his life for his sheep. On the other hand, the Pharisees of the Temple are like "hired men," who only plunder, rob, and steal. Once again, Jesus later presents himself to the Temple for the Chanukah feast, himself the "Temple of God," as a sign that he has come to purify us from our sins. Mid-way through the feast is the Winter Solstice, when on the last day, on Sunday, Jesus appears in the earliest hours of the morning to the Temple, as the "light" of our purification, exactly 100 days before his Good Friday holocaust. Under the colonnades of Solomon's Portico, Jesus is challenged by his scoffers and detractors. Jesus intimates that no one will ever snatch his sheep out of his hand--or out of his Father's hand--that he and the Father are One. Jesus defends himself as the "Son of God," and he slips away from the Temple out of their hands. In our share of God's divinity, we are all "sons of God," and its meaning for us is explored, including the dark side of various human claims to divinity made in the 20th century by such political or religious ideologues as Vladimir Lenin, Mao Zedong, and James Warren (Jim) Jones of People's Temple infamy; and there also have been representative counterclaims to God's existence and his "divinity" in Man, by Friedrich Nietzsche and Jean-Paul Sartre. The holocausts of millions speaks to the need for our purification from sin.

>Readings: Psalm 69:2-13, John 2:17-19, John 10:1-21

>Readings: John 10: 22-39; Wisdom 2:12-24

>Prayer Reflection: Proverbs 8:22-36, Psalms 82:1-8 and 23:1-6

25. Keeping the Lord's Focus—Towards Jerusalem from Galilee via Samaria: Always Giving Thanks to God, and Praying Constantly

While passing through a Samaritan village, Jesus is rejected and the disciples James and John ask the Lord if they should call down fire from heaven to burn them up; Jesus scolds them throughly. Following Jesus in his mercy includes our journey with him towards the cross in Jerusalem, and like Jesus, without a place to lay our head and rest. Following the Lord is our exclusive task, and it permits no loss of focus throughout the journey; we are not allowed to look back to the former life we have left behind by our renounciation of sin and of self for the sake of the gospel, who is the Lord. For various reasons, many potential disciples do not take up their vocation to follow Jesus; but the Lord sends out the seventy-(two); and he asks those disciples to pray for "the master of the harvest" to send out "workers" to gather it in. Along the border between Samaria and Galilee, ten lepers encounter Jesus, who sends them to the priests, and while they are on their way, they realize that they are healed. Like the Samaritan leper who returns to Jesus to give praise to God: this event is the prototype for my personal experience of Jesus as I was healed on my way to the priest. Jesus arrives (in Bethany) to the home of Martha, sister of Mary Magdala and Lazarus: like many of us, Martha was preoccupied with many things for serving her guests; Mary, however, was selectively at the feet of Jesus attentive to all his words, as we may be privileged to hear. Jesus then departs for Bethany (across the Jordan), where he remains with the disciples. When they ask Jesus to teach them how to pray, he provides for us the Lord's Prayer, the essential communal prayer of Christians; and with a number of parables, Jesus describes "Our Father in heaven" as loving Providence and Divine Justice.

> Readings: John 10:39-40, Matthew 19:1-2, Mark 10:1, Luke 9:51
>
> Readings: Luke 9:52-56; Luke 9:57-62, 10:1-3; Luke 10:16-20, 17:11-19
>
> Readings: Luke 10:38-42; Luke 11:1, John 1:28, Luke 11:2-4, Matthew 6:9-13, 14-15, Mark 11:25
>
> Readings: Matthew 6:5-8, Luke 11:5-13, Matthew 7:7-11, Luke 18:1-8
>
> Prayers of Faith and Reflection: Psalm 26:1-3, 27:1-14

26. Lenten Sermons near Bethany across the Jordan—Faith in the Light of Fruitful Works and True Repentance: Followers versus Pharisees

As Jesus was nearing the end of his mission, he reminds us now about our own journeys in our given vocations moving towards their end when we may least expect it: and we either must choose to be true followers of Jesus or, like the Pharisees, we can be hypocrites: that choice, with its radical consequences, is entirely and freely ours to make. But we must be careful, and not careless or presumptuous: if our spiritual house has been swept clean and tidily put in order after an unclean spirit had occupied us, it may bring back seven other spirits more evil than itself to move in and set up house, making us worse off than before. And if Mary, the Lord's mother, was blessed to have suckled her son, more so are truly blessed those who "hear the word of God and keep it." Christ is our Light, greater than Solomon or Jonah or even the shining lamp of John the Baptist, urging us to true repentance and faith in him. But we must be careful that the light inside us does not become darkness. Jesus, our Divine Mercy, urges us to fasten tight our clothes at the waist and to light our lamps, as his children of the Light: and "blessed our those servants whom the master finds watchful when he arrives." We see this in the example of the holy Pontiff John Paul II, called to the Lord at 21:37 on the Vigil of the Feast of the Divine Mercy, on 2 April 2005. In similar mercies and gifts from the Lord, in footnote I also now recount the death of my father, Benjamin, at 21:37 on 20 October 2009, according to the precise time of the Lord's chronologies, not only for the death of my father, but also according to my own personal time allotted within my own calling in the gospel by God, as also is your own time. Peter also asks the Lord, "Is this parable meant just for us, or for everyone?" Jesus provides us his answers: for, when a person has been entrusted with much, a great deal will be required; and when we have done what we have been commanded to do, like the newly elected Pope Benedict XVI has done, we should say of ourselves, "We are just ordinary servants"; for whatever we have done in the Lord, "we were obliged to do." In the second part of this chapter, on another day of the Lord's private preaching, Jesus warns the twelve disciples (and implicitly Judas Iscariot specifically) of the hypocrisy of the Pharisees: "There is nothing covered up that will not be revealed, nor hidden as secret that will not be known," which is true also for us. He also tells them not to be afraid of those who kill the body and after that can do no more; but rather, be afraid of the one "who, after he has killed, has the power to cast (body and soul) into Gehenna; yes I tell you, fear that one!" But, because we are precious in God's sight, we also have reason not to be afraid: for God even knows the count for the hairs of our head, and he assigns us far greater worth than even his care for just a few or even hundreds of sparrows. Moreover, everyone who acknowledges Jesus in the presence of men, "the Son of Man will declare himself for him before the angels of God." And everyone [and there are many by their prejudice or prejudgment] who speaks (even) a word against the Son of Man, "will be forgiven." However, anyone who "blasphemes against the Holy Spirit" [which is an entirely fatal sin] will not be forgiven. And when they may kill or persecute you after they take you before synagogues and governors and kings, "the Holy Spirit will teach you when the time comes what you must say at that moment." The manner of our death neither implies our guilt, nor our innocence; but if we do not turn from our sins, then we will perish catastrophically as we die. We are like "a fig tree" which is cultivated by the Lord, with the Father, the planter of the vineyard, looking for "fruit" on it; Jesus, as the gardener, may be given some short time by the planter to work with us, but if no fruit is produced, Jesus tells the planter, "You can cut it down."

>   Readings: John 10:41; Luke 11:24-36, 12:35-48, 17:7-10

>   Readings: John 10:42; Luke 12:1-12, Matthew 10: 26-33, Mark 4:22; Luke 13:1-9, [10-17], 18-19, [Luke 13:22-24, Matthew 7:13-14, Luke 13:25-30], Luke 13:31-33

>   Reflective Prayer: Psalm 107: 1-9, 17-22, 33-43

Volume Two:

27. More Sermons at the River Jordan: The Virtue of Poverty and the Use of Possessions—Renunciation, Simplicity of Life, and Reliance on God

As ordinary experience often shows, like the two brothers arguing over inheritance, we may be preoccupied with property and wealth, even for "ordinary" possessions, to the point of greed. So, the Lord clearly warns us against any kind of greed, contrary to our pragmatic concerns and anxieties, "Our life is not made secure by possessions." Jesus, accordingly, provides us with the parable of the Rich Man who had far more possessions than he ever could possibly need or use. And through various commands, instructions, exhortations and explanations, combined with empathy, encouragement, vivid illustrations, and forceful conclusions, Jesus urges us to have faith and to rely on God's providence, for us to seek our real treasure, which is the kingdom of heaven (Jesus) provided to us by his Father, which nothing can destroy and no one can steal from us. Then, in a synagogue on a Sabbath, where Jesus teaches, he calls a crippled woman over to him and cures her infirmity; but the synagogue leader objects to the healing, which Jesus describes as her liberation from Satan. Then, to make his point again on another Sabbath, in front of the Pharisees at a dinner party, Jesus heals a man who is suffering from edema; noticing how the dinner guests had picked places of honor at the table, Jesus also tells them a series of parables: inclusive of his admonition for them to invite "the poor, the crippled, the lame, and the blind," not just those who could pay them back; as the Lord, as the servant of God, also has invited them to the heavenly banquet;

and as another servant of the Lamb of God, Mother Teresa of Calcutta, has focused her work on the poorest of the poor and the dying. On the morning after this Sabbath, Jesus confronts the crowd following behind him on the road with their possessions: no one could be his disciples without taking up his own cross and following Jesus: above his father and mother, his wife and children, his brothers and sisters, and yes, even his own life; and providing them with short strategic parables, he plainly tells them, "none of you, unless he renounces all of his possessions, can be my disciple." And so, as God sometimes very directly leads us, we have been called to the virtue of poverty: in my personal experience, after first leaving all of my possessions behind, the Father then provided the opportunity for me to write this book; but even more so, this virtue has been illustrated to me by the faith and trust in God's providence by the Poor Friars or Poor Nuns (without money), when most recently one of their brothers and two of their sisters (v.v.) of Jesus and Mary were visiting in Malta from Sicily. When Jesus returns to the far side of the Jordan, he returns to a parable about two sons, of which the younger son asked his Father to divide his property and provide him with his share of the estate. Through this parable we learn of God the Father's compassion and care for us, who is genuinely a Father and not a Master, and who wants for us to be his sons (and daughters), not his servants. In another parable, although as disciples we may be proper stewards of money, we must be faithful stewards of true wealth: for we cannot be slaves of both God and money. Jesus then also was targeting the Pharisees for their love of money, but implicitly he also was aiming at the heart of Judas Iscariot. Although the Pharisees just sneered at Jesus, he told them another parable as a warning: about a Rich Man and a beggar named Lazarus, both who died: Lazarus went to the bosom of Abraham, while the rich man went to his place of torment. The rich man's experience of the abyss that separates the soul from God is also described for us in Saint Maria Faustina Kowalska's diary as the "Terror of the Soul." This provides an answer to the rich man's request to send Lazarus from the dead to warn his brothers: but as Abraham responds, "If they do not listen to Moses and the prophets, they will not be persuaded even if someone [Jesus Christ] were to rise from the dead." However, through God's constant mercy, we may take up the grace to repent.

> Readings: Luke 12:13-21; Luke 12:22-31, Matthew 6:25-33, Luke 12:32-34, Matthew 6:19-21; Luke 14:1-24, 25-33
>
> Readings: Luke 13:10-17, 14:1-6; Luke 14:7-24; Luke 14:25-33
>
> Readings: Luke 15:11-32, Luke 16:1-15; Matthew 6:1-4, Luke 16:19-31
>
> Prayer Reflection: Psalm 118:1-29

28. Marriage and Celibacy are Permanent Vows: Two Paths for the Contemplation of God's Promises of His Eternal Life and Eternal Love

The Pharisees and scribes engage their strategy to provoke divisions and they attempt to weaken Jesus among the crowds, and among his disciples, by posing the most central religious question for husbands and wives in the most fundamental human anthropology of personal lives: "Does our law provide any justification whatsoever for a man to divorce his wife?" The astonishing answer that the Lord provides is the New Covenant explanation for the permanence of marriage, which also provides for celibacy as a parallel vocation, after we are sealed with Christ by baptism into his death and resurrection, and we are bound with Jesus in God's eternal love: both by our suffering with Jesus in his cross and by living our covenant commitment in the promise of his eternal life. The context for marriage and celibacy as permanent vows is explained: according to the book of Genesis and the Old Testament provisions from Moses; according to the expanded teaching of Jesus, the writings of Saint Paul, and the provisions of Canon Law for valid sacramental marriage; according to the personal experience of my own marriage vocation, which included a divorce and church annulment and eventual remarriage in the church; according to the ongoing context of the divorce and marriage debate in Malta in my contemporary experience; and according to the evaluative biographical history within my personal experience of significant selected persons in religious life, or who like myself once may have approached religious life, or who may have left it. When Jesus receives word from Martha and Mary that Lazarus is sick, he first waits two days before concluding his preaching mission at Bethany beyond the Jordan. The delay at first seems inexplicable, but even more so is Jesus' sudden decision to return to Judea, where the Jews had tried to stone him. Curiously, after Jesus tells them plainly that Lazarus was dead and "Let's go to him," Thomas believes that the Lord also intended to die with Lazarus; so, Thomas suggests, as they do, that they all follow the Lord to die with him in Judea. But the sickness of Lazarus would not end in the death of Lazarus, but in his resurrection from death and in the glory of God, so that all disciples may believe in Jesus, who is our resurrection and eternal life. In Bethany of Judea, Jesus meets with Martha and Mary, who with their brother portrayed an ideal Christian community, and he addresses their faith in the resurrection; and then, Jesus glorifies the Father, who glorifies the Son, by raising Lazarus to life after his four days of death. Because of this many believed in Jesus, but others went to the Pharisees and told them what Jesus had done. While the Sanhedrin consequently plot the death of Jesus, Jesus leaves with his disciples for the town of Ephraim, safely and quietly near the desert, but which also is close enough to reach Jerusalem. Just as the Lord had called Lazarus out of the tomb (and he calls us), Saint Faustina on the day of her profession of religious vows was called like Lazarus by the priest, "Rise, you who are dead to the world, and Jesus Christ will enlighten you." And so also it is now for us, whether by our marriage or by our celibacy, we are each called through the eternal love of God to be the Lord's New Covenant "Children of the Light."

>Readings: Matthew 19:3-12, 13-15, Mark 10:2-12, 13-16, Luke 16:18, 18:15-17; 1 Corinthians 7:1-16, 17, 24, 25-40

>Readings: John 11:1-54

>Prayer Reflection: Isaiah 54:1-10, Psalms 65:2-6, 22:23-32

29. The Final Journey to Jerusalem: On the Road to the Revolution, and to the Cross and the Glory

On the road again, now heading for Jerusalem, Jesus is pursued by a rich young man, who asks, "Good Master, what good deed must I do to inherit eternal life?" Jesus replies with a series of questions about "good," and provides him with his stock answers, until the young man asks in the end, "What do I still lack?" The answer from the Lord is simple and direct, "If you wish to be perfect, there is still one thing for you to do: go and sell everything you own and give the money to the poor, and you will have a treasure in heaven. Then come, follow me." The answer proves to be disturbing for the young man, and for the disciples as well, when the Lord tells his disciples twice, "Yes, it is easier for a camel to pass through the eye of a needle than for a rich man to enter the kingdom of heaven." In the context of their ongoing political and religious expectations, the disciples ask Jesus, "In that case, who then can be saved?" Jesus explains, "Everything is possible with God." Pursuing the matter further, on behalf of everyone, Peter asks, "So then, what are we to have?" Jesus tells him there will be "thrones," and whatever they may have left behind for the sake of the gospel, they will be repaid "a hundred times over," both in the present age and in the world to come--not without its accompanying "persecutions," but also with the inheritance of "eternal life." And Jesus adds, "Many who are now first, will be last; and the last will be first." Patiently Jesus provides them with a parable, "The kingdom of heaven is like the owner of an estate who went out early in the morning to hire day-laborers for his vineyard." In the Lord's generosity, whenever we heed his call, he provides the same wage: the Lord entrusts us with his property, and in exchange for our sins through the redemption of Christ, he provides us with heavenly treasures. While still north of Jericho, Jesus takes the disciples aside and tells them exactly why they are going to Jerusalem and what will happen there; but they could not understand and they also were afraid to ask. Soon after, the mother of Zebedee's sons approaches Jesus together with her sons James and John, and they ask Jesus to grant their request, unconditionally. The Lord responds first, as he also has responded to me on 12th September 2003 when this Gospel Emmaus began, "What is it that you want me to do for you?" Jesus grants what is his to give to them (as he has done for me); but he could not give them what is reserved for his Father, namely, "seats at my right or at my left" in the kingdom. In fact, there are no positions of rank in heaven among the saints who have been perfected in God; however, there is an order of entry into heaven depending upon the requirements of God for our ultimate perfection. The other disciples are furious at this political maneuver by James and John, and Jesus immediately calls all of them together and reveals to them the centerpeice of his revolution: "whoever wants to be first among you must be your slave; just so, the Son of Man did not come to be served but to serve, and to give his life as a ransom for many." But, given their presently insufficient faith, the truly amazing story of our ransom by the Lord was for now completely beyond their comprehension. But, at or near Jericho, Jesus finds examples of absolute faith in two blind men begging along the road. Again, as Jesus asks us, he asked each of them, "What do you want me to do for you?" Indeed, both men regain their sight, as Jesus tells them, "Your faith has saved you." For we walk by faith, not by sight. In a final case illustration from Jericho, we are provided the example of Zacchaeus, the tax collector for the Romans, who was a true descendant of Abraham in faith. The gospel account of Maria Valtorta directs us to the actual historiography of the event, which in Luke is presented for us according to the theological intention of the evangelist. Also, as the Lord was a guest in his house, I recount how my father once received the Lord to our home in the person of a Dominican priest. At the time, some of our judgments of my father were harsh, like some of the murmurings against Zacchaeus; but only decades later did I come to understand my father's rationale for giving glory to God: for, by the Lord's mysterious mercy to my father, he had survived the inferno of war on the island of Roi-Namur, in February of 1944. Afterwards, in front of Zacchaeus and his guests, Jesus also tells us a parable about what he expects of us, when as a nobleman he goes off to a "distant land" to be made King, before he would return again to deal with his servants and with those who did not want him as King: the Lord is superabundantly generous with us, but for those who do not want him as King, he will dispense his appropriate justice, familiar to us in the brutal example of rulers among the pagans (Gentiles), who make their authority over them felt, "bring them right here before me and execute them in my presence."

> Readings: John 11:55-57; Matthew 19:16-30, Mark 10:17-31, Luke 18:18-30; Matthew 20:1-16
>
> Readings: Matthew 20:17-19, 20-28, Mark 10:32-34, 35-45, Luke 18:31-34; Luke 18:35-43, Mark 10:46-52, Matthew 20:29-34; Luke 19:1-10, 11-28
>
> Reflective Prayer: Psalm 2: 1-11

30. Saturday Evening, 9th Nisan (1st April, 30 CE): A Resurrection Dinner Party

From Jericho, Jesus leaves with his core disciples, probably under the cover of darkness, without the crowds and without being noticed, and arrives to the home of Lazarus, Martha, and Mary in Bethany outside of Jerusalem. The Lord's timing according to the Hebrew liturgical calendar is exact and intentional, as they arrive sometime before the Sabbath. But on Saturday evening, after the Sabbath, the Lord now begins to celebrate the Grand Liturgy of his week-long New Creation, in parallel to the creation of Genesis and, at the end of his purpose, a parallel to Saint John's theological week of creation that had preceded the Lord's mission. The evening of the first day begins with the supper celebration: like Lazarus raised from the dead, Jesus was now anticipating his own death and resurrection; and at the end of the week, as dawn broke on Easter morning of the seventh day of the New Creation, Jesus the life and resurrection would be raised from the dead. Yet, before the Lord would arrive to the Resurrection, already there was evidence for the transformations of Lazarus, Martha, and Mary in Christ; yet their understanding of the Lord, as also for the disciples, was still in formation, awaiting the Lord's revelations for the week ahead. Judas Iscariot also had changed; but he was hardened by the corruption of his sin and his lack of faith. Likewise, with the crowds, we fall somewhere within this same range of believers or unbelievers, between Judas and Lazarus: either transformed by our sin into hearts of stone, or transformed by the power of Christ into heirs of eternal life. The choice is ours, whether or not we join our will to the grace and will of God. God's grace is more powerful than our insufficient faith: we need to pray and to trust the one, Jesus, who loves us so completely, with a pure heart.

>Readings: John 12:1-8, 9-11; Psalms 26:1-12, 18:1-51, 57:1-12

>Prayer Reflection: Psalm 78: 5-7, 34-37; 40-47; 48-55; 56-61; 62-69, 72

>Concluding Prayer

Part Three (Chapters 31-40): Grand Liturgy of the Lord in God's New and Eternal Creation

31. Sunday Afternoon, 9th Nisan (2nd April, 30 CE): Jesus Humbly Enters Jerusalem as King on the Colt of an Ass—He Makes His Way Straight for the Temple, to His Father's House, in Triumph and in Peace

On the first day of the week, on Sunday morning after the initial post-Sabbath evening celebrations, the Lord's morning in prayer or in community with his Twelve disciples is not recorded for us. But mid-day, setting out from the Mount of Olives near Bethany, Jesus sends two disciples into the village of Bethphage to fetch a colt of a donkey. Mounting the colt, Jesus sets out for Jerusalem in humble submission to his destiny and mission. The crowds converged coming down from Bethphage and up from Jerusalem, cutting palm branches and spreading them with their cloaks on the road before him, and singing praise. It seems that Jesus follows the route of Solomon, when King David had annointed his son King, approaching the city from a southern gate, entering from the gate near the spring of Gihon. The Pharisees are particularly alarmed, as Jerusalem is in an uproar. Jesus makes his way straight for the interior of the Temple; where he surveys his Father's house, and immediately leaves. It was very late in the day, as the first day in the liturgy of the Lord's New

Creation was concluding, and Jesus quickly exits with his disciples, apparently by the eastern gate along Solomon's Portico, returning to the Mount of Olives.

> Readings: John 12:12-19, Matthew 21:1-11, Luke 19:28-44, Mark 11:1-11
>
> Reflective Prayer: Psalms 135:8-14, 118:19-29, 122:1-9

32. The Next Day, on Monday, 10th Nisan (3rd April, 30 CE), Jesus Works Tirelessly in His Father's House, to God's Great Honour and Glory—But at the Beginning Early in the Morning, Jesus Openly Declares God's War Against the Chief Priests and Religious Authorities by Assaulting the Moneychangers in the Temple, and at the End of the Workday He Leaves—Then, on Tuesday Morning and Afternoon, the 11th Nisan (4th April, 30 CE), He Returns for the Ongoing Revolution

On Monday morning, the second day of the liturgical week of New Creation, Jesus was hungry; implicitly, he had prayed and fasted throughout the night, but he was hungry for more than just food. As Jesus and the disciples were on their way to Jerusalem from the Mount of Olives, Jesus is overheard cursing a fig tree for its lack of fruit although it was not the time for figs. Immediately, the fig tree withered, but this was not yet noticed by the disciples. For now that action parable formed a kind of Penitential Rite, reminding us of our needs for repentance and to bear fruit; for Jesus was hungry for the fruit of his mission: which was to be derived from his approaching death on the cross and from his preaching and teaching, from his Body in the Eucharist and by his living Word, which are his food for the world. The Lord's only food now was doing the work of his Father on our behalf, a labour that the disciples also would be sharing with the Lord, when they would later fast and, in their union with Christ, be fruitful. The withered fig tree also was a warning for everyone, both for the disciples and for the Pharisees; but that event would also provide the occasion for strengthening the faith of disciples in prayer. Once in Jerusalem, however, Jesus made straight away for the temple, where he overturned the stalls and tables of the money changers, where all sorts of cattle, sheep, and pigeons were being sold. At first, our narrative account of the temple cleansing is a redaction from the four evangelists, but as will be shown (in the next chapter) John's account involves an earlier cleansing of the Temple around Passover of two years earlier. For the rest of the day, while Jesus teaches in the temple, we are not provided information about what Jesus specifically taught; instead, we are permitted to experience briefly what our lack of faith would be like if we, too, were without our intimacy with the living Word of God. But we are witnesses to the effects of Jesus' teaching: the chief priest and scribes wanted to kill him. And when they ask Jesus to justify himself, he responds, "Destroy this temple, and in three days I will raise it up." As Jesus continued to teach, the blind and the lame came to him, and he cured them, as he cures all those who admit their sinfulness and go to him. Then even the children began to shout, like yesterday's adults, "Hosanna to the son of David." When evening came, Jesus left them and went out of the city back to Bethany, where he spent the night. Then on the third liturgical day, on Tuesday morning, Jesus returns to Jerusalem by yesterday's route, when Peter is the first to notice that the fig tree has withered away, and together the disciples ask, "How did the fig tree dry up so quickly?" They get their answer in a lesson on faith, prayer, and forgiveness. Likewise, we are given the example of Saint Mother Teresa of Calcutta: silence, prayer, faith, and love are fruits of each other. Our forgiveness and mercy to others should become the centre of our fidelity to God and of our faith in him. Once again, straight away, the priest, elders, and scribes confront Jesus in the temple, as they ask him, "Tell us: what right do you have for doing these things? And who gave you this authority to do them?" Because they are unwilling to answer the Lord's question, "Where did John's baptism come from? Was it from heaven or from man?," Jesus does not tell them "my authority for doing these things." But Jesus does provide them with a parable about two sons: "Which of the two sons, in your opinion, did the father's will?" They answered, "The one who didn't want to go and work in the vineyard, but later, thinking better of it, changed his mind and went." Then Jesus replied to them, "Tax collectors and prostitutes are entering the kingdom of God ahead of you." In contrast to themselves, those "public sinners" recognized their sin and asked for God's mercy, and in their penitence, they had acted in faith: by breaking with sin, and through their acts of love. These authorities, however, still rejected God's grace surrounding them despite its manifestation among allegedly "obvious" sinners. Likewise our potential transformation by righteousness (Christ) is described by Saint Therese of Lisieux, "Love has so worked within me." But for the unrighteous, Jesus provided another parable for the chief priests and Pharisees: "There was a man, a landowner, who planted a vineyard." Because they knew Jesus was speaking about them, they would have arrested him on the spot, but because they also feared the crowds, who regarded Jesus as a prophet, they left him and went away. Jesus, by his one sacrifice in the one faith we share with the prophets, would not only make righteous the blood of the prophets, he also would sanctify all righteous blood shed upon the earth throughout the whole of human history. For the crowds who remained, including some of the Pharisees acting as spies, Jesus tells us another parable as a warning, "The kingdom of heaven may be compared to a king who gave a feast for his son's wedding. But when the king came in to meet the guests, he noticed a man there who wasn't dressed in his wedding clothes." That man is thrown into the darkness outside. Jesus concludes, "Although many are invited, not all are chosen." Yet, our prayer with Jesus concludes, "Everyone whom the Father gives me will come to me; I certainly will not reject anyone who comes to me." In my ending prayer, I conclude with St. Teresa of Avila, "Blessed and praised be the Lord, from Whom comes all the good that we speak and think and do. Amen."

> Readings: Mark 11:12-14, Matthew 21:18-19; Matthew 21:12-13, Mark 11:15-18, Luke 19:45-46, John 2:13-17; Luke 19:47-48, 21:37-38; John 2:18-22, 23-25, Matthew 21:12-17, Mark 11:19

> Readings: Mark 11:20-21, Matthew 21:20-22, Mark 11:22-25; Matthew 21:23-27, Mark 11:27-33, Luke 20:1-8; Matthew 21:28-32; Matthew 21:33-46, Mark 12:1-12, Luke 20:9-19; Matthew 22:1-15

> Reflective Prayer: Psalm 31:1-24

33. Wednesday Morning and Afternoon, the 12th Nisan (5th April, 30CE)—Christ in the Temple among the Pharisees and Scribes, Those Scholar-Hypocrites of the Law, Snakes and Sons of Snakes, and Opponents to the True Devotees of God's Law to Love: Jesus and His Children of the Resurrection

Early in the morning of the fourth liturgical day, on Wednesday, Jesus is sitting in the Temple among the techers, listening to them, and asking them questions, which is a parallel to twenty-four Passovers ago, when Jesus had been twelve years old. The previous two Passovers that Jesus had spent with his disciples is linked to this third and final Passover: the first, in 28 CE, is according to John's gospel the first Temple cleansing by the Lord, a manifestation of the glory of the Lord who dwells among us; the second, in 29 CE, includes a series of events (the feeding of the five thousand near Tiberias; and the Bread of Life discourse at Capernaum, where the "bread" of a future Eucharist and the "flesh" of his Passover passion and sacrfice is unified, "the bread that I will give is my flesh, for the life of the world"); and the third, in 30 CE, presents the Lord's "Passover of Glory." The challenges by the Pharisees and the Temple scribes from six months earlier are now continued, as these now send their disciples with some Herodians to Jesus. The context of the Herodians from Herod the Great is summarized before we take up their question which is addressed by Jesus, "Is it permissable to pay taxes to Caesar or not?" The Lord's answer silences them. Then, in the afternoon, the Sadducees, who deny any resurrection of the body, take up another line of attack, "Now at the resurrection, when they all rise again, whose wife among the seven will she be, since the woman had been married to all the brothers?" The Lord's answer, applauded by the Pharisees against the Sadducees, also silenced them. But the Pharisees, in order to justify themselves, put together another plan as they dupe a dedicated and sincere scribe to ask the Lord, "Which of the commandments is the greatest of the Law?" The scribe of the Law agrees with the Lord's answer; and the Lord silences the hypocrisy of the others, telling him, "You are not far from the kingdom of God." Jesus then pins the Pharisees with a question of his own, "What is your opinion about the Christ? Whose son is he?" And the crowd listens to Jesus with delight. To be found worthy of the resurrection to eternal life depends upon our unreserved love of God, embedded in our love of neighbour and our love of self, and mastery of the Lord's new commandment, "Love one another as I have loved you." The children of the world are visibly contrasted with God's children, children of the Light and of the resurrection. Throughout human history, knowledge of God has always been a divine capacity of the soul; but also God revealed his covenants with humankind directly, and ultimately through the incarnate Word of God, Jesus Christ. The Pharisees and scribes, however, carried a most grave responsibility as the authorized interpreters of God's revelation through the Law of Moses and the Prophets. So, the Lord's final discourse to the Pharisees and scribes in the temple recognizes their authority, but also unequivocally condemns their hypocrisy, while explicitly providing the disciples with the example of the one Teacher, the Christ. Jesus warns the hypocrites of their condemnation and approaching desolation, and he walks away from them, leaving them to their final choice: how terrible it would be for them or us to be forsaken by God. But Jesus provides a final lesson on the day for his disciples when he sees a poverty-stricken widow, who offers everything she had to live on, two small copper coins, to the temple treasury. Her act was like the Lord's, who surrendered all he had to give, his life poured out to death on the cross for the forgiveness of our sins: a selfless act of love also repeated in the 20th century lives of Dietrich Bonhoeffer and Maximilian Kolbe. Soon the old covenant would be fulfilled and be overthrown by the new covenant of our reconciliation in Jesus as a new creation: for the old Law would be replaced by the new covenant law of love, according to the visible pattern of Christ.

> Readings: Luke 20:20-26, 27-40, Matthew 22:15-22, 23-33, Mark 12:13-17, 18-27; Matthew 22:34-40, Mark 12:28-34; Luke 20:41-44, Matthew 22:41-46, Mark 12:35-37

> Readings: Luke 20:45-47, 21:1-4, Mark 12:38-40, 41-44; Matthew 23:1-39

> Reflective Prayer: Psalms 140:2-14, 124:1-8, 69:2-37

34. Wednesday Evening, the 13th Nisan (5th April, 30 CE)—The Restoration of the Kingdom of God in Christ is Near, as Also Was the Basis for, and the Origin of, the Written Gospel: And Although Everyone's Been Invited, the Jews First, They're Still Not Fully Understanding—Except for the First One from among the Hundreds of Thousands—She Had Been Listening to the Mystery in the Lord's Dialogues and Revelations: Mary of Magdala, the Sister of Martha and Lazarus from Bethany!

The Kingdom of God would not be an earthly kingdom, as the disciples imagined it also would be. And one's entry into God's heavenly kingdom would depend upon our faith in Christ, by the privilege of his grace merited for us exclusively by his mercy and sacrifice, and by our being reborn in Him by both water and Spirit. The Lord's focus now was on that "great day" for our salvation just in two days time; but the disciples, more or less, as they were going away from the temple, still had their heads in the clouds. One of them remarked about the temple, "Master, look at the size of those stones and the size of those buildings!" Jesus replied, "Not a single stone will be left upon another; everything will be destroyed; everything will be torn down." Still dazed and amazed by the prospect of such a catastrophe, after arriving to the Mount of Olives, some of the disciples put their burning question to Jesus, "Master tell us! When will this happen? And then, what sign will there be of your coming and of the end of the world, when all of this is about to take place?" The Lord gave his answer in the language and allegories of the prophets: there would be war, or rumors of war, revolution, famines, earthquakes, plagues, and signs in the skies, but this would not be the end, but only the beginning of the birth pangs. Jesus also warned them against being deceived: the only true Messiah and his kingdom were not to be mistaken for political actions or ambitions. Yet, in 66 CE, the Jewish revolutionary expression of messianism would lead to the eventual destruction of Jerusalem, its temple, and the nation of Israel itself in 70 CE. Even today, still among factions in Israel and elsewhere, Messianic politics subverts genuine religion and adherence, or true obedience, to the will of God. Instead, the Lord had wanted his disciples, like the future saints Paul and Ignatius of Loyola, to put their faith in Him--not like many today who put their faith in the technologies of war; rather, the disciples would be sent out to evangelize the world. But there would be betrayals and death, and an increase in lawlessness, as love in most people would grow cold; and only by persevering to the end would they win their lives. When Jerusalem was surrounded by armies and the temple defiled in the coming retribution, those inside the city, or in Judea, must escape: some would suffer violent deaths; others would be led away as captives to all the Gentile nations; and Jerusalem would be crushed. Regarding his coming, the Lord once again warned of false messiahs. And after a period of distress, the nations would be in agony; there would be cosmic signs in the heavens; on earth, the turmoil of oceans and raging waves would induce terror and fear; then the "sign of the Son of Man" would appear in heaven. He would come in glory on the clouds of heaven, as his elect also would be gathered throughout the earth beyond the skies. From those signs, we would know that "the kingdom of God is near." Although the sky and earth will pass away, never the Lord's words. Yet only the Father knows the exact day and hour; so watch yourselves and stay awake: "pray at all times for the strength to survive all that is going to happen," and "be ready to hold your ground before the Son of Man," when before the Christ we each must account personally for our entire life: you do not know when the master of the house is coming. "Who then is the wise and trustworthy servant whom the master placed over his household to give them their food at the proper time?" That servant is blessed "if his master's arrival finds him doing exactly that," providing spiritual "food" for his household. He must not find you asleep: for if the servant should be dishonest, he will suffer the same fate as the hypocrites. With the "Day of the Lord" certain to come upon us all, Jesus also had ennunciated his program of evangelization. It would include the death in Jerusalem of the first Christian martyr, Stephen, around 35 CE, very notably with the blessing of Saul/Paul, who before his conversion in Damascus had been hellbent on persecuting the "Body of Christ." Under the local and Roman persecutions to come, both Christians and Jews spread throughout Judea, Samaria, and beyond, particularly to Antioch, the third largest city of the Roman Empire. There Jewish followers of

Jesus from Jerusalem, or "Hebrews," proclaimed the gospel among other Jews, while Greek-speaking Jewish Christians, "Hellenists," began preaching the gospel to Gentiles living in Antioch. Meanwhile, soon after Stephen's death and after Paul's conversion, Paul went off to Arabia to preach the gospel for a year or two on his own before he returned to Damascus, where Paul's preaching was so effective that his life was in danger. So the Christian community shipped him home from the port city of Caesarea to Tarsus in Cilicia for seven years, until Barnabas brought Paul back to Antioch. In Jerusalem, after James (John's brother) had been killed, Peter was imprisoned by Herod Agrippa I shortly before Passover in 44 CE, but miraculously Peter escaped, and later that year, Herod Agrippa was struck dead. Then, most likely in 45 CE, Barnabas and Paul brought famine assistance to Jerusalem from Antioch; and returning to Antioch with them, Barnabas brought his cousin, John Mark, as their assistant in the work of the gospel. But on Paul's first missionary journey (46-49 CE), John Mark went with them only as far as Cyprus. Later, when Paul proposed making his second missionary journey (50-52 CE) with Barnabas, Barnabas suggested taking his cousin again; but Paul was reluctant. When Barnabas disagreed with Paul, Barnabas and John Mark went off together to Cyprus, leaving Paul who went off with others. This John Mark is the future evangelist Mark, who later also would evangelize Egypt. Paul also would undertake his third missionary journey (53-58 CE). Then, after Paul's arrest and two years imprisonment at Caesarea, in 60 CE Paul would leave on his great journey for Christ: his appeal to Rome to bear witness before the emperor. About this same time, Mark's Greek gospel was the first canonical gospel to be written. Matthew's Greek gospel for the universal church was the second of the canonical gospels to be written, although his original Aramaic gospel has not survived. Luke, Paul's companion, provides us with the third canonical gospel, also in Greek, with its second volume Acts of the Apostles. Mark, Luke, and Paul remained working colleagues through Paul's initial period of imprisonment in Rome and later, until eventually back in prison he was beheaded mid-decade (67 CE) under Nero. John was the source of the fourth canonical gospel compiled at last by his disciples at Ephesus, where Paul originally had evangelized. John also provides his three epistles; and his book of Revelation is the biblical omega to the alpha book of Genesis: after the first-century period of duress, the "Kingdom of God was near" and the canonical gospels are written. Paul's activities and letters, in his theology and contributions towards the others, is a "fifth evangelist," central to the gospel mystery and revelation of Christ. With the disciples on the Mount of Olives, Jesus continues with the substance of Matthew's Chapter 25, that provides the parable of the "Ten Virgins" and the parable of the "One, Two, or Five Talents." If we are going to be God's "Children of Light," we are going to need sufficient "oil" with our "lamps," and we must be ready when the "bridegroom" appears. As for any riches entrusted to us by the Lord, those "talents" must be returned to him with their proportionate increase, for he harvests his bounty from where he had not sown, and he gathers crops from where he had not scattered seed. And so the evangelists and all the saints have provided their thirty, sixty, or hundredfold increase. Of special notice are all missionaries of the Word, and also the founders or reformers for religious communities, which are established according to the rule of the Word of God. The pioneering Slavonic translations of the Gospel by Saints Cyril and Methodius anticipate our contemporary methods for communication of God's Word. Maria Valtorta's modern gospel, Poem of the Man-God, as visions and dictations from the Lord, is acknowledged. I also humbly acknowledge the Lord's mercy and grace in his having provided me with the responsibility for this journey for us through this Gospel Emmaus. Against this background, Jesus continues with his discourse to the disciples on the Mount of Olives regarding "when the Son of Man comes in his glory," when he will separate people like sheep from goats: our love of God, or lack of it, is ultimately linked to our love of Christ in our neighbor: the hungry, the thirsty, the stranger, the naked, prisoners. With these words, Jesus then had finished everything he intended to say for his public ministry. But, as evening now approaches, Jesus reminds the disciples, "As you know, in two [liturgical] days time, it will be the Feast of the Passover, and the Son of Man will be handed over to be crucified." This chronology is explained in its relation to the Preparation Day (14th Nisan) and the Day of the Feast (15th Nisan). On this Wednesday evening, Jesus goes to the house of Simon the Leper for his final dinner celebration before the Preparation Day would come. But it is only Mary of Magdala who recognizes that Jesus is going to his death. And unlike her annointing and wiping of the feet of Jesus four evenings earlier, she now pours her perfumed oil on his head. The disciples object to this as a waste and offense against the poor, but the Lord comes to Mary's defense. Mary's virtuous act may be compared to the priorities of the cloistered life and service to the poor exercised by the Maltese Beata, Benedictine Maria Adeodata Pisani. However, when Judas objects to the Lord's defense of Mary, it is soon after that Satan enters Judas and Judas sets out that evening to betray the Lord. Yet, long before this, willingly, Mary, the mother of Jesus, already had surrendered her son to God. We are invited to share in the death and resurrection of the Lord more closely by our celebration of Eucharist--the center of our Christian lives--in the sharing of his Word and the breaking of the Bread. Our final prayers exalt the sacrifice of Christ.

> Readings: Matthew 24:1-44, Mark 13:1-37, Luke 21:5-36
>
> Readings: Matthew 25:1-46
>
> Readings: Matthew 26:1-16, Mark 14:1-11, Luke 22:1-6
>
> Prayer Reflection: Colossians 1:12-20; Psalm 115:1-18; Revelation 4:11, 5:9-14

35. Thursday, the 13th/14th Nisan (6th April, 30 CE)—Christ in Jerusalem at Passover, the Daytime and Evening of His New Creation: The First Day of His Feast of Unleavened Bread, the New Covenant in His Body and Blood

On Thursday morning, some Greeks, who were Gentle converts from paganism, request to see Jesus, but the hour for the Son of Man to be glorified had come. Later, when Jesus was "lifted up from the earth, " he would draw everyone to himself, Gentiles too. A "voice" is heard from heaven, and Jesus admonishes, "while you still have the light, believe in the light, so that you may become children of the light." Then Jesus hid himself from their sight. Some still did not believe, although the Father had sent Jesus and had commanded him what to say and what to speak; whoever believes in Jesus also believes in the Father and sees the Father, "the one who sent me." The day is called the first day of Unleavened Bread, although it is one day in advance of its celebration with the evening Passover meal on Friday. Yet, during the day Peter and John are directed to prepare the "Passover meal" that would begin for them on Thursday evening, on the 14th Nisan that would continue into Friday, when the Passover lamb (and the Lamb of God) would be slaughtered according to Mosaic convention "between the two evenings" or "between the two settings," actually from near to the ninth hour, or "between three o'clock in the afternoon and sunset" on Friday. Leading the way, just as it was evening on Thursday (the beginning of 14th Nisan), Jesus arrives at the upper room with his twelve disciples. At the first, Jesus washes the feet of each of the disciples: Peter and ten other disciples provide a contrast to Judas Iscariot: the former received the spoken word of Jesus and believed in him; Judas already was intent on his betrayal. After toasts and blessings, sometime during the meal Jesus institutes his Eucharist; and when Jesus suddenly became deeply troubled, he announces that "one of you is going to betray me, one who is eating with me." Each of them protest, "Surely, Lord, it's not me?" Soon, instead of debating who among them the "traitor" could be, the disciples argue about which of them should be regarded as the "greatest." Jesus as "lamb" and "servant" provides himself for their example of how to be "greatest." Peter and John coordinate with each other to have the Lord indicate his betrayer; and with intimacy towards Judas, Jesus offers Judas a piece of bread that Jesus had dipped in the sauce. At that instant, Satan enters Judas, and Jesus tells him, "What you are going to do, do quickly." Judas leaves at once, and it was the middle of the night. After Judas had gone, Jesus tells his disciples, "You are the men who have stayed with me through all of my trials; and now I confer a kingdom on you, just as my Father has conferred one on me." As Jesus explains, he also provides them with a new commandment: "Love one another; you must love one another just as I have loved you." Then four of the disciples, each in their turn in their dialogue with Jesus, asks questions of him during his discourse: Peter is first, followed by Thomas, then Philip, and lastly Judas Thaddaeus, son of James. Simon Peter asks, "Where are you going, Lord?" and "Lord, why can't I follow you now?" Jesus indicates that Peter will follow him, yet Satan has permission to sift them all; but the Lord himself has prayed for Peter's faith not to fail, and that when he does "turn back to me," Jesus tells Simon to strengthen his brothers; and Jesus informs Peter that even that very day, three times Peter will have denied "even that you know me." Jesus tells them: don't be troubled, have faith in God, trust in me; and in my Father's house, there are many dwelling places; I am going now to prepare a place for you, "as I am doing." After he has gone and prepared a place "for you," Jesus tells them, "I shall return to take you to myself, so you may be with me where I am." The Lord states, "You know the way to the place where I am going." Then Thomas interjects, "Lord, we don't know where you are going, so then how can we know the way?" Jesus states he is the Way, the Truth, and the Life: "No one can come to the Father except through me." If you know me, then you will have known my Father; from "this moment," you "know him and have seen him." Philip responds, "Lord, show us the Father and so we shall be satisfied." Patiently Jesus explains, "I am in the Father and the Father is in me." And Jesus encourages their "belief in him," their "even greater works," their prayer "in my name," and, finally, "if you love me, you will keep my commandments." Jesus himself will ask the Father to give them "another" Advocate, the "Spirit of truth," which the world can never accept, which it neither sees nor knows; but you know it, "because it remains with you and is in you." Jesus continues, in a little while, the world will no longer see me; but "you will see that I am living, and you also will live" and on that day "you will know that I am in my Father and you are in me and I am in you." Jesus says, "Whoever holds to my commandments and keeps them is the one who loves me; whoever loves me also will be loved by my Father; and I will love him and reveal myself to him." Then Judas Thaddaeus asks, "Lord, what's happened here? I don't understand how it could be that you intend to reveal yourself to us, but not to the world!" Later the disciples would make Jesus known: "Whoever loves me will keep my word, and my Father will love him, and we shall come to him and make our dwelling with him," and "the Advocate, the Holy Spirit, that the Father will send in my name, will teach you everything and remind you of all that I have told you."

Jesus also tells them, "my own peace" I bequeath to you, "not as the world gives it." Although the ruler of this world was approaching, Jesus told them, "he has no power over me." But, by the Lord's great revelations to come (with his passion, death, and resurrection), the world must know that "I love the Father" and that "I act just as the Father has commanded me." Jesus tells them, "Get up now, and let's go." The revolution for our salvation from our sins seems to begin, as the Lord urges them to swords, and he tells them, these words of scripture are destined to be fulfilled in me, "He was counted as one of the rebellious." Saying that "two swords are enough," Jesus leads the "Eleven" loyal revolutionaries out of Jerusalem and towards the Mount of Olives, where they would soon encounter their missing "rebellious" brother, Judas Iscariot: as Jesus soon would take the rebellion of everyone's sin upon himself. The psalms (with scriptural reflections) are mostly taken from the Hallel, prayers that solemnly conclude Passover evening.

> Readings: John 12:20-50; Matthew 26:17-19, Mark 14:12-16, Luke 22:7-13

> Readings: John 13:1-20; Mark 14:17-25, Matthew 26:20-29, Luke 22:14-30, John 13:21-30

> Readings: John 13:31-38, 14:1-31, Mark 14:26, Matthew 26:30, Luke 22:31-39

> Prayer Reflection: Psalms 110:1-7, 116:10-19; Psalms 113:1-9, 147:12-20; Psalms 114:1-8, 117:1-2

36. Friday, the 14th Nisan (7th April, 30 CE), Early in the Dark Morning Long Before Daybreak—Going to His Father, Jesus Now on His Way to the Mount of Olives with His Disciples, and Going to the Ambush There in the Garden

We now follow Jesus from the Jerusalem safe-house of the Last Supper to the moment he willingly surrenders himself unto the hands of "Darkness" on the Mount of Olives. The initial discourse of Jesus is "I am the true vine, and my Father is the vinedresser" (John 15:1-17), at first considered as if it only had been some sort of idealistic and ill-fated revolutionary rhetoric. But that simple hypothesis begins to fail when we consider the most crucial element of the discourse, the extraordinary intimacy of vine and vinedesser and of our being "in" the vine of Christ: "whoever remains in me, and I in him, produces plenty of fruit; for apart from me, you can do nothing." "If you keep my commandments, you will remain in my love, just as I have kept my Father's commandments and remain in his love." And "this is my command to you: love one another." And, if we remain "in" the vine of Christ, we also can expect to be pruned by the Father, so that we may bear more fruit; but if we do not remain "in" the vine, without his life in us we will dry up and wither, destined only for the fire. Then the second part of the Lord's discourse (John 15:18-16:5) addresses the consequences of "because by my choosing you, I have drawn you out of the world." Namely, you will be hated, persecuted, expelled from synagogues, killed; but even so there will be many witnesses for Christ: first, "the Holy Spirit," and "you also will be my witnesses." Jesus had not told them earlier about these future things, because he had been with them personally protecting them, as even God had been with them in His love and intentions for them even before creation. However, not everyone has been gifted by God's grace of faith. That is why persons are chosen in their faithful partnership with God (vine and vinedresser): to bear fruit in Christ for his work of our salvation and for the world's. In the third part of the Lord's discourse (John 16:5-15), Jesus gives emphasis to "the Advocate," whom he would send to them from the Father: "it is best for you that I am going, because if I don't go, the Advocate will not come to you; but if I go, I will send him to you." And when the "Spirit of Truth" comes, he will "show the world how wrong it was about sin and righteousness and judgement," "he will guide you to complete truth," and "he will glorify me, because everything he reveals to you will be taken from what is mine" (and from what is the Father's because "all that the Father has is mine"). When Jesus also told them, "In a little while you will no longer see me, and a little while later you will see me again," the disciples were confused. But Jesus understands their confusion, and he explains what he means in an analogy to childbirth: their sorrow will turn to joy, and they will be able to ask for and to obtain anything from the Father "in my name," for "the Father himself loves you." He is the Father of

God's children: the New Creation, reborn in Christ and gifted with the Spirit. Then Jesus plainly tells them, "I came from the Father and have come into the world, but now I am leaving the world and going back to the Father." The disciples affirm with Jesus their belief that he came from God. But, even so, Jesus replies, "tonight you will all fall away from me," leaving me alone, although he explains, "I am not alone because my Father is with me." Then the disciples overlook the Lord's next statement entirely, "However, after my resurrection I shall go ahead of you to Galilee." Peter takes issue with the Lord's claims regarding their desertion, "Even if everyone falls away, my faith will never be shaken; I will never fall away." Jesus now informs Simon Peter quite specifically, "This day, this night in fact, before the cock crows twice, you will have disowned me three times." And oftentimes, sometimes very greatly, we likewise have failed the Lord; yet, reassuringly for Peter, for all of the disciples, and for us, God always accepts the return of a truly humble sinner. Jesus told them these things, as he tells us, so that we all may find peace in him: "In the world you will have trouble, but be courageous: I have conquered the world." Then, standing with the disciples outside Jerusalem's city walls and in front of the Kidron Valley, Jesus prays to his Father under the stars of heaven (John 17:1-26). This prayer is an intimate summary of the relationship between God the Father and the Son, providing for their mutual glorification and revelation because of the finished work of the Son for our salvation, according to the love of the Father for the Son, which God provides for us as his children. Jesus also prays for the disciples and for those who will come to believe in the Son, who is sent to us by the Father. Because God's love for us has pre-existed the world from eternity, the Father entrusts to the Son's care those the Father had given to the Son to share the Son's company and to see the Son's glory with the glory of the Father: for them to know the Father and the Son and be sanctified in the Spirit, which is love. Jesus then crosses the Kidron valley with his disciples, according to the route of King David. But now, instead of David to save his household from the conspiracy of Absalom, Jesus is saving the househld of God. Jesus is the revelation of God to humankind, superior to and continuous with God's revelations to Moses and the Prophets. And now, because Jesus was returning to his Father (and ours), he would be sending his disciples into the world, just as his Father had sent him: confirmed in truth by the Spirit. Along with the Holy Spirit, they too would be his witnesses: as had been the Samaritan woman at Jacob's well; as the royal official, with a sick son at Capernaum, and his household had testified to their faith in Jesus; as the man cured at the Pool of Bethsaida in Jerusalem also had testified to the religious authorities about Jesus; and as Jesus then sends others into the world to give their witness: perhaps, God willing, even myself. After crossing the Kidron Valley, Jesus arrives with his exhausted disciples to the garden on the Mount of Olives, where they sleep but he continues to pray, not only for himself and the Father's will, but also that the disciples not be put to "the test." Judas arrives with a Roman cohort and its tribune and Jewish guards, as Judas betrays the Son of Man with a kiss. Jesus protects his flock by handing himself over to the "reign of darkness." The disciples all flee, but Peter follows the prisoner Jesus at a distance.

>Readings: John 15:1-27, 16:1-33, Mark 14:27-31, Matthew 26:31-35, John 17:1-26, 18:1

>Readings: Matthew 26:36-46, Mark 14:32-42, Luke 22:39-46; Matthew 26:47-56, Mark 14:43-52, Luke 22:47-54, John 18:2-12

>Prayer Reflection: Psalms 59:1-17, 68:1-35, 78:52-72

37. Friday, the 14th Nisan (7th April, 30 CE)—The Long Eve of Darkness and Our Day of Shame: Our Lord's Day of Glory and of God's Retribution: The Conviction, Passion, Death, and Burial of Jesus Christ

This is the longest chapter of the book. In general, it exposes the violence of sin, as violence of any kind is against the essential nature of God, who is reason and love. The chapter begins where the former chapter had left off: John now has found Peter, who has discarded his sword, as they follow Jesus from outside the Jerusalem walls through the Dung Gate, and straight to the palacial house of the high priest Annas, the ex-officio high priest under Mosaic Law and the highest religious political authority as president of the Sanhedrin. His son-in-law Caiaphas, who was appointed by Rome also as high priest, is in charge of official and ordinary religious responsibilities of high priest. John, who was known to the high priest, was allowed to go in with Jesus, while Peter waited outside until John brought Peter inside after speaking to the doorkeeper. From his very entrance, Peter begins to deny that he is a disciple of Jesus; and events lead to Peter's further denials while Jesus is questioned by Annas, until the cock crows for the second time and the eyes of Jesus and Peter meet, when Peter rushes away in tears. Annas orders that Jesus should be sent to Caiaphas, but that meeting is postponed until daylight, as Jesus is restrained and abused throughout the night, while he is absorbed in prayer. Although Peter had professed that he would never fall away, he did; just as I have done; and we all do. Yet, with the Lord's love and mercy, Peter returned; and in Christ we each are able to return and persevere in God's grace. But, do we have the courage to witness to the love of God in our lives, even if we should be imprisoned or killed? Contemporary examples for such situations are presented: the kidnapping of journalist Steve Centanni and cameraman Olaf Wiig by Islamic militants in August 2006; the distortions of Pope Benedict XVI's lecture at Regensburg in September 2006, as the Pope found his message against violence and for acting according to reason, as the essence of the nature of God, pilloried in its public condemnation by segments of the Muslim world, followed five days later by the violence-stoked murder of Sister Leonella (nee Rosa) Sgorbati in Somalia; just as two years later, thireen-year-old Muslim Aisha Ibrahim Duhulow was stoned to death, an innocent victim of further violence against God; just as there are many other examples of further violence against the crucified Christ: the slaughter of innocents, and Muslims, by terrorists in New York or in Iraq, or the violence in October 2006 perpetrated by a lone gunman against Amish school children in Pennsylvania, just as near to there my direct ancestral protagonists, Johann Ludwig Klemmer and his wife Anna Maria, were murdered in America in August of 1756. Their original story is traced back to two centuries earlier, to the murderous Catholic-Huguenot conflicts of the 16th century, 17th-century conflicts between France and Germany, through various migrations from France to Switzerland and Germany and immigrations to America, and through the 18th-century conflict of the "Seven Years War" between England and France, when Ludwig and Anna Maria Klemmer were the initial casualties of that war waged as the "French and Indian War" in America. The direct line from Ludwig and Anna Maria's family is traced through their orphaned four-year-old son, my direct ancestor George Ludwig Clemmer, through subsequent generations in war and peace, to my present moment. That heritage is traced and described in footnotes for both my paternal and maternal sides of the family, that includes their Protestant and Catholic Christian heritage and my spiritual heritage in faith derived through Christ from them: for Christ's victory upon the cross for our sins is made evident, through them as well as for me, by those five centuries of my personal history, as has been realized for all of us by these events being described for Jesus now, in the year 30 CE. The direct narrative link has been provided in my real-time experience by the irrational violence against the Paradise Pennsylvania Amish children near to my ancestral home, and by the Pope's Regensburg address: God is reason and love, not hatred and violence. After this historical and genealogical interlude, our gospel narrative is brought back to Jesus now in the morning light, when he is brought before Caiaphas and the entire Sanhedrin, as they are looking for evidence to inflict their ultimate violence, which today is reflected by sin in the world: the passion and death of Jesus Christ, as also experienced by others as mutual violence (or the absence of love) directed against others. But, if by faith and grace we are joined to the death and resurrection of Christ, sin in us already has been defeated and Christ's victory, through his love now in us, is won for our salvation. When the Sanhedrin fails to obtain collaborative testimony from two witnesses, as required under the Law, they attempt to solicit from Jesus himself self-incriminating testimony, also against the Law. The Lord's final statements are interpreted by the entire Sanhedrin as blasphemy, as Caiphas tears the vestments of his office. Soon, the testimony of the initial two witnesses would be fulfilled, as the inferior priesthood of Aaron was being replaced by the only perfect high priest of the New Testament, by Jesus himself who would rebuild our lives by his death and resurrection: not by human hands, but also by the temple of the spirit of God living in us. The assembly was unanamous in its verdict: "He deserved to die." And for this purpose, they lead Jesus to Pilate, who was in Jerusalem for the feast. In the meantime, Judas Iscariot objects to their conviction and regrets his betrayal of Jesus. Because of his lack of faith in Jesus for the expiation of our guilt and the forgiveness of our sins, Judas takes his own life; on the other hand, the chief priest and elders acknowledged their own guilt by refusing to return the blood money to the temple treasury, who falsely believed they could be saved through the details of the Law, despite their hypocrisy and corruption: and they buy the potter's field according to the prophecy of Jeremiah, as a burial place for foreigners. When Jesus is brought before Pilate, he did not want to be involved in their Jewish religious disputes. But forced by the initial charges, Pilate puts questions to Jesus about his "kingship," as a means of defending Jesus against their charges of incitment and opposition to Caesar; and as an advocate and judge for Jesus the defendant, Pilate finds "no case" against him. But the chief priests and the elders insist upon their case against Jesus. When Pilate understands that Jesus is a Galilean, from Herod's jurisdiction, Pilate shuttles the case off to Herod Antipas, who also was in Jerusalem for the feast. Herod's meeting with Jesus the "miracle worker" is a disappointment. He treats the silent Jesus with contempt, and sends him back to Pilate. Again, as was corroborated by Herod, Pilate finds "no basis" for their claims that Jesus is a popular agitator; so, Pilate asserts that he will have Jesus flogged and released. Yet, hoping to free Jesus, Pilate invokes the custom to release a prisoner, and offered them a choice: a notorious bandit and murderer, (Jesus) Barabbas [Son-of-the-Father], or Jesus called the Christ. In God's irony, the crowd shouted for the release of Barabas, as every child of God would be released by God's Son, for those who would believe in him. As Pilate was seated in the chair of judgment, his wife sends him an urgent message: as dreams were regarded as having divine sources, she admitted to a disturbing dream about the righteous Jesus. As the crowds roar for the Lord's crucifixion, Pilate again finds Jesus "not guilty," and he still intends to release Jesus after having him flogged. Jesus is led into the Praetorium, where the Roman cohort scourage him, crown his head with thorns, mock him as "king," slap his face, strike his head, and spit on him. Pilate brings Jesus out to show the crowd that he finds "no case" against him; and he presents the "man," wearing the crown of thorns and the purple robe. As the crowds shout for his crucifixion, Pilate again presents them with their choice for release, either "Barabbas" or "Jesus, the Christ." They demand the release of Barabbas as they continue to call for the Lord to be crucified. Pilate tries to absolve himself from his responsibility, when he tells them, "Take him yourselves and crucify him: I find no guilt in him." But the Jewish authorities reply that Jesus should be put to death according to their Law because he has claimed to be "Son of God." Alarmed by this newest revelation, Pilate takes Jesus back into the Praetorium and attempts to question him, but Jesus remains silent. Only when Pilate describes his own "power" for life and death does Jesus respond, "You would have no power over me whatsoever if it had not been given to you from above." But there is no absolution from his guilt, as Jesus also tells him, "For that reason, the one who handed me over to you has the greater guilt." Leaving Jesus inside the Praetorium, Pilate returns to the crowd, who play their political trump card, "If you release him, you are no friend of Caesar's; anyone who makes himself a king is Caesar's enemy." Then Pilate himself brings Jesus out and places him on the chair of judgment and proclaims, "Here is your king." The crowds roar for his crucifixion, "We have no king but Caesar." In fact, a riot seemed imminent, so Pilate washed his hands in front of the crowd, "I am innocent of this man's blood; it is your concern, now." In fact, we are made innocent only by the blood of Christ, as the whole people shouted back as one, "Let his blood be upon us and upon our children." Pilate then gave his verdict: their demand was to be granted. Barabbas then was released, and Jesus was handed over to them to be crucified, controlled by the Roman soldiers who took complete charge of Jesus. The soldiers also requisitioned Simon from Cyrene to assist Jesus in carrying his cross, as we all must be willing to do by choice as disciples of Jesus. Various men and women disciples follow Jesus to the cross, while others are more distant witnesses. On route to Golgotha, Jesus encounters several leading women of Jerusalem who are weeping for him, but in the Lord's loving concern for the present generation and in his anticipation of Jerusalem's later destruction, he advises them to weep for themselves and for their children. As Jesus is crucified between two criminals, he refuses a drugged wine as a sedative before they nail him to the cross; and as they crucify him, he asks his Father to forgive them, "they don't know what they are doing." The soldiers divide his garments and cast lots for his tunic; on the cross above his head, an inscription written out by Pilate in Hebrew, Latin, and Greek provided the charge against him, "Jesus the Nazarene, King of the Jews." From noon to mid-afternoon, the sun's light failed as a great darkness covered the whole land. Throughout, passers-by, the leaders, priests, scribes, the soldiers, and even the bandit-revolutionaries crucified with Jesus challenged and taunted him to save himself. Yet, Jesus provided the Christian model: he who would save himself would be lost, but "whoever loses himself for the sake of the Gospel" would be saved. But one of the criminals crucified with Jesus objected to the other criminal's abuse, as he admits his own guilt and the Lord's innocence; and he asks in Jesus name, "Jesus, remember me when you come into your kingdom." The Lord's reply to this one, as to all who wanted Jesus for his King, was forgiveness of his sins and his salvation that very day, "Amen, in truth I tell you, today you will be with me in paradise." Standing with Jesus near the cross were his mother, the apostle John, the two Maries (of Magdela and the wife of Clopas), and possibly John's mother, Salome; others, who would be witnesses also to the Lord's resurrection, were witnesses to his death a distance: but prominence is given to Mary of Magdala, the first-named witness of the Lord after his resurrection; and under the cross, Jesus defines the birth of the church when Jesus gives his mother (as the new "Eve") and John to each other, "Woman, behold, this is your son." And to the disciple, and to all disciples, "Behold, this is your mother." And from that moment, John took his mother, Mary, completely "as his own," into his value system and life, as we should take Mary into our life with her Son. Near mid-afternoon, when the Passover lamb was to be sacrificed, Jesus cried out the beginning of Psalm 22 in prayer, "My God, my God, why have you forsaken me?" Bystanders thought Jesus was calling on Elijah to save him, but Jesus then declared, "I am thirsty" (also Psalm 22:15). One of the soldiers offered Jesus a drink of sour wine from a soaked sponge on a hyssop stick, which indicated by his drinking that the kingdom had come, as Jesus gave out a loud cry, and calmly said, "It is fulfilled." At that moment the veil of the Temple Sanctuary was torn from top to bottom, and as he cried out, "Father, into your hands, I commend my spirit," the earth quaked and he bowed his head and gave up his last breath. Many who had gathered for the spectacle returned home beating their breasts. Other disciples stayed on as witnesses, as then the darkness that had covered the land was lifted as the sun broke through. Because the Passover feast was fast approaching, the soldiers hastened the death of the two criminals by breaking their legs; but because Jesus already was dead, one soldier pierced his side with a lance, and blood and water flowed from the wound: both as an image of the Divine Mercy and as a graphic image of the moments after birth: in this case the birth of the church with its elemental principles of life, his "blood" shed for us and the "fountain" of his grace, and the anticipation of "life in the Spirit" that would come upon the church at Pentecost. After asking permission from Pilate to remove the body, Joseph of Arimathaea provides the tomb for the Lord, and a shroud, while Nicodemus provided a mixture of myrrh and aloes. As Joseph rolled the stone across the entrance of the tomb, Mary of Magdala and Mary the mother of Joset carefully note the tomb and where and how the body of Jesus had been laid. At the recommendation of the chief priests and pharisees, Pilate orders the tomb to be secured by fixing seals to the stone and by setting the guard. Our reflective prayer is the Lord's final prayer, Psalm 22:1-31, with its prophetic and scriptural annotation.

> Readings: Mark 14:53-54, Matthew 26:57-58, Luke 22:54-55, John 18:12-24; John 18:25-27, Mark 14:66-71, Matthew 26:69-74, Luke 22:56-61, Mark 14:72, Matthew 26:75, Luke 22:62; Luke 22:63-65, Matthew 26:67-68, Mark 14:65; Luke 22:66-71, Mark 14:55-64, Matthew 26:59-66, Luke 23:1, Mark 15:1, John 18:28

> Readings: Matthew 27:1-10; Luke 23:1-7, Mark 15:1-5, Matthew 27:11-14, John 18:28-38; Luke 23:8-12; Luke 23:13-19, John 18:39-40, Mark 15:6-11, Matthew 27:15-18; Matthew 27:19; Mark 15:11-14, Matthew 27:20-25, Luke 23:20-23; John 19:1, Mark 15:15, Matthew 27:26, Luke 23:16; John 19:2-3, Matthew 27:27-30, Mark 15:16-

19; John 19:4-15, Luke 23:24; Mark 15:20, Matthew 27:31; John 19:16, Luke 23:25, Mark 15:15, Matthew 27:26

Readings: John 19:17, Mark 15:21-22, Matthew 27:32-33, Luke 23:26-32; John 19:18, 23-24, 19-22, Mark 15:23-26, Matthew 27:34-37, Luke 23:33-34, 38, 44; Mark 15:29-33, Matthew 27:39-45, Luke 23:35-37, 39-43; John 19:25-27; Mark 15:40-41, Matthew 27:55-56, Luke 23:40; Mark 15:34-37, Matthew 27:46-50, John 19:28-30, Luke 23:46; Luke 23:45, Mark 15:38, Matthew 27:51-52, 53; Mark 15:39, Matthew 27:54, Luke 23:47, 48; John 19:31-37; Mark 15:42-47, Matthew 27:57-61, John 19:38-42, Luke 23:50-56; Matthew 27:62-66

Reflective Prayer: Psalm 22:1-31

38. Easter Sunday, the 16th/17th Nisan (9th April, 30 CE)—After the Friday Preparation Day for Passover and the Sabbath Rest, from Early Easter Morning unto That Late Evening: On the Third Day, We All Are Now Sent into the New Creation of the Lord from Its First Day

The New Creation of the Lord originates with his death and resurrection, as its first day on Easter Sunday morning begins with astonishing chaos and initial disbelief. Before sunrise, while it was still dark, Mary Magdalene and the other Mary (the mother of James) set out for the tomb. Very shortly before they arrive, the guards are disturbed by what seems for them to be an earthquake, as an angel descended from heaven and rolled away the stone as it roared, and sat upon it. They flee in terror, without witnessing the resurrection, some of them going to the temple elders straightaway. When Mary of Magdala arrives at the sepulchre, the first light of day had been chasing the darkness away and she notices that the stone had been rolled from the tomb and that the guards were gone. In a panic, Mary runs to Peter and John and informs them of her inference, "They (the guards) have taken the Lord out of the tomb, and we (the two Maries) don't know where they have put him (the corpse)." Peter and John outpace Mary Magdalene as the three race to the tomb; at the same time, implicitly, the risen Lord appears first to his mother. John and Peter are the first to actually peer into the tomb, while Peter is the first to enter it, as they observe the burial cloths and the cloth that had covered the head of Jesus: John is the first to believe that Jesus had to rise from the dead; Peter does not yet comprehend or believe; and while they return home together, Mary Magdalene remains at the tomb weeping. As the other Mary is returning to the tomb with the other women companions, they give no credibility whatsoever to what the other Mary may have told them; they intend to finish their preparing the Lord's body for long-term burial. But they are very surprized to find the stone rolled from the tomb and Mary Magdalene standing there weeping. Mary Magdalene leads the way to look into the tomb, while the others follow her inside, and they find no body; but to their fear and amazement, two angels provide the story of the Lord's resurrection, and give them instructions for Peter and the disciples. Although they were frightened out of their wits and did not discuss the matter even among themselves, they began to experience a certain awe and joy as they ran to tell the disciples, who believed their story to be pure nonsense. Peter, however, again returns to the tomb alone, and running; seeing only the burial clothes, this time he gathers them up and returns home, still not comprehending and utterly amazed. Meanwhile, the chief priests were informed by some of the guards who had been at the tomb about what had happened; and they called a meeting of the elders. They decided to bribe the guards and provided them with a cover-story and they would protect them even if Pontius Pilate should learn of it. That alibi is still making 21st century rounds among atheists and non-believers: the disciples stole him while the guards were sleeping. Mary Magdalene, however, returns to the tomb for her third time, and again she stands outside the tomb weeping. When she looks inside, once more she encounters two angels in white, who again speak to her, as she still believes the Lord's body had been stolen. But when she turns around looking out of the tomb, there is Jesus, whom she believes to be the gardener. The Lord speaks to her as the angels had spoken to her; and she replies just as she had done for the angels, as she pleads for his return so she can take him. She only first recognizes that he is Jesus when he calls her by name, "Mary," and she clings to him as

"Teacher," not wanting to let him go. Jesus provides that he must return to his Father and ours, to his God and ours; for later Jesus would send the Holy Spirit to remind her and the others what he had taught them. Mary Magdalene returns to the disciples to tell them what had happened, but they do not believe her when she tells them that he was alive and she had seen him. Meanwhile, after the Galilean women had left the disciples following their encounter with angels at the tomb, on the road coming towards them, Jesus greets them with one word, "Hello." They are quicker to recognize the Lord, who tells them to tell "my brothers" that they must go to Galilee, and "there they will see me." Sometime after this the Lord also appears to Peter, but two disciples on the road to Emmaus are aware of the morning's report of angels saying that Jesus was "alive," although, from what they knew of events, no one had reported as yet that they had seen him. As the two disciples were talking about everything that had happened, Jesus himself drew near to them and walked by their side, but they failed to recognize him. One of the disciples, Cleopas, finds it perplexing that the stranger could be unaware of the events in Jerusalem, but the two disciples tell Jesus all they knew. In a liturgy of the Word, Jesus began to interpret passages in all of the scriptures that referred to himself, and as evening approached, giving the impression that he was going further on, they invited and insisted that he stay with them, which he does. It was when they were at table, when he took the bread, said the blessing, broke it, and gave it to them, only then they recognized him, in that Eucharist, and at that same moment he disappeared from their sight. Then, in the model for this book, they said to each other, "Didn't our hearts burn within us as he spoke to us on the road and explained the scriptures to us." The two disciples returned to Jerusalem immediately and told the Eleven and the other companions what had happened, but except for Peter and John, the other apostles did not believe them; but they continued talking about these events into the evening in the room where the disciples were, while the doors were locked for their fear of the Jewish authorities. Thomas alone is absent from the Eleven when Jesus suddenly stands in their midst and says, "Peace be with you." They believe him to be a ghost, but he shows them his hands and feet and takes some grilled fish to eat, demonstrating that he is "alive." Their joy becomes unbounded, but their rational mind could not believe it as they were so dumbfounded. In this conclusion of a liturgy of the Word and Eucharist on Sunday, Jesus again gives them peace, just as he had when he first appeared. He tells them, "As the Father has sent me, so I am sending you." And in an initial mini-Pentecost, Jesus breathes on them and tells them, "Receive the Holy Spirit," which is linked immediately to their power through the Holy Spirit to forgive, or to retain, sins. Then Jesus vanishes from their sight. For, the commemoration of the death and resurrection of the Lord in the Eucharist is the celebration of the forgiveness of our sins through Jesus, as his love eventually achieves its perfection in us. In our weakness, God's power is our strength, as we pray for God's help in reflective prayer.

> Readings: John 20:1, Matthew 28:1, Mark 16:1-2, Luke 24:1, Matthew 28:2-4, John 20:2; John 20:3-10; John 20:11a, Mark 16:3-4, Luke 24:2-4, Mark 16:5-7, Matthew 28:5-7, Luke 24:5-8, Mark 16:8, John 20:11b-13; John 20:14-18, Mark 16:9-11, Matthew 28:9-10, 8, Luke 24:9-12; 1 Corinthians 15:5; Matthew 28:11-15; Mark 16:12-13, Luke 24:13-35; Mark 16:14, Luke 24:36-43, John 20:19-25, Acts 10:40-41
>
> Reflective Prayer: Psalms 42-43:1-11, 1-5; 63:1-11; 46:1-11

39. The First Fifty Days in the Lord's New Creation: From Easter Sunday to Pentecost (9th April to 28th May, 30 CE)—Days after the Resurrection of the Lord to the Coming of the Holy Spirit; And Both Resurrection and Pentecost Are Concurrent with Our Baptism into Christ's Death and in the Birth of the Church

The Lord's death, as a grain of wheat, was brought to new life in his resurrection on Easter, the first day of the Lord's New Creation; the fiftieth day, Pentecost, marked seven weeks afterwards, when like the traditional harvest feast, now the Holy Spirit was poured out upon the church to bear spiritual its fruitful harvest for God among men. The chapter begins with a review of the unity of the death and resurrection of Jesus, which we share by baptism in the name of the Trinity. Modern scepticism surrounding the resurrection is linked to the false ideology and idol of secular humanism, as such philosophies place barriers between persons and the spirit of God. To deny the resurrection of Jesus is to deny the forgiveness of sins through the power of God and the person of Jesus Christ. As the risen Lord revealed himself, the position of the Lord's mother, Mary, in the economy of our salvation is unique, primary, and ongoing. Then Mary of Magdala also provides an ideal metaphor and true model for every aspirant Christian. Then the women of Galilee, Peter alone, the two disciples on the road to Emmaus, and the Eleven apostles (less Thomas) were privileged for their Easter experiences of the risen Lord by virtue of their calling by God to love and service in the church, for the Body of Christ. With the Lord's resurrection, many other holy persons also rose from the dead and made their appearances to a large number of people in Jerusalem. Contemporary sceptics may describe such events and the resurrection of the Lord as imaginative projections of the mind under stress, just as materialistic rationalism also may dismiss the apparitions of Our Lady at Fatima, at Lourdes, or at Medjugorje; as sceptics may interpret the conversion of St. Paul, or even reject the apparitions of the "Divine Mercy" to Sister Faustina, or reject Maria Valtorta's Gsopel "visions" and "dictations" as personal constructions during similar times of war or social turbulence. Yet, Mary of the Immaculate Conception figures prominently, from the resurrection, through modern times, and to my personal present. Yet, the scriptures clearly show how God does intervene in human affairs, and that it is possible for persons to experience God today in their life experience, and through the various means God provides for us, if we accept the grace of faith and discern the Spirit of God in our noisy lives. Even so, two of the Lord's staunch disciples, St. Paul and St. Thomas, initially refused to believe. Many of the disciples were fishermen, also very rational and pragmatic persons, with human dispositions and agendas, and they doubted on several occasions; they even thought the risen Lord to be a ghost; or they simply failed to recognize the risen Lord until he presented some sign. After the six distinctive occasions when the risen Christ showed himself to various disciples on Easter Day, he appeared again to the Eleven one week later, when Thomas was present; Thomas then believes, but the Lord presents for all of us, "Blessed are those who have not seen, and yet have believed." For all of us, believers and for sceptics alike, the risen Christ is not to be found by looking backwards into the tomb, of sin and death and our life-tragedies, but is found by the experience of the risen Lord in our personal lives and among the communion of believers. Jesus also reveals himself to seven of the disciples another week later, by the Sea of Galilee, when Jesus directs their fishing, offers them breakfast with him on the shore, and instructs Peter to feed and to look after "my sheep," to "follow me," and for all of them "to abide" in the Lord until he comes. Most likely on the following Sunday, Jesus again meets with the disciples on a mountain in Galilee: all power is his; he directs them to proclaim the gospel, to baptize, and to teach all of his commands; he would be with them to the end of time; this was what he meant that everything written about him in the scriptues was destined to be fulfilled, and Jesus opens their minds to the scriptures; he also leaves them with the central core of the gospel message, as he tells them to remain in the city until they are clothed with the power from on high, "I am sending upon you what the Father has promised." When the disciples return to Jerusalem, they learn that the risen Lord had appeared to "more than five hundred brothers at a single moment," and to "James," the sceptical relative of the Lord, who would be the first bishop of Jerusalem. St. Paul provides the risen Lord's appearance to "all the apostles," those beyond the Twelve, among them, according to St. Ignatious of Loyola, Joseph of Arimathaea. St. Paul describes his own experience of the risen Lord, the last of all, "as if to one born abnormally." Other plausible resurrection appearances of the Lord are suggested in Maria Valtorta's 20th century gospel. On the 40th day of Easter, the Lord rejoins the disciples in Jerusalem, in the upper room; after speaking to them, reminding them of the coming baptism of the Holy Spirit, he takes them out of the city to the Mount of Olives, to the outskirts of Bethany. Some of the disciples are still expecting the Lord to restore the material kingdom to Israel, but regarding the future the Father has estabished his times or dates by his own authority. However, they are to receive the power of the Holy Spirit and be the Lord's witnesses to the ends of the earth. Jesus is taken up to heaven, just as he also will return; and they return to the upper room where they had been staying. Mary, the mother of the Lord, now is central to the core Christian community, some 120 persons, as they waited and prayed together for the coming of the Holy Spirit. Over the ten days before Pentecost, Peter leads the congregation; and they elect Mattias to take the place of Judas Iscariot in his apostolic ministry. When Pentecost arrives with its symbolic manifestations, there is evidenced the very real power of the Holy Spirit for the evangelization of the world. Our final reflective prayer bids us to "never forget" what the Lord has done for "my soul;" to "praise the Lord" in his ascension to the power of God on high; and to "await" and "embrace" the Spirit of the Lord, which the Father and Son send to us, and which renews the face of the earth: to establish God's New Creation, our genesis in Christ.

> Readings: Matthew 27:50-53, Act 10:40-41, 1 Corinthians 15:3-8; John 20:24-31, 21:1-25; Mark 16:14-20, Matthew 28:16-20, Luke 24:44-53, Acts 1:1-14
>
> Readings: Acts 1:15-26, 2:1-13; Proverbs 8:1-36, Genesis 1:1-2, Ephesians 3:14-21; 1 Corinthians 12:4-11
>
> Reflective Prayer: Psalms 103:1-22; 47:1-9; 104:1-35

40. From the Nativity of Our Lord Jesus Christ (Winter Solstice 8 BCE) to the Birth of the Church (The Spring of 30 CE)—the Christian Family and Christian Ecumenism: the Born, the Unborn, and the Reborn

This chapters has two major sections. The first is a retrospective presentation of the Nativity of Jesus and of his infancy and early childhood in Israel and Egypt. The second is the preliminary conclusion of our gospel journey at Pentecost, with the baptism of the church in the Holy Spirit, after its original birth in the Mystical Body of Christ upon his death on the cross, when the Lord also had given Mary to the disciple John to take as its mother and as his mother. The Incarnation of the Son of God, Jesus Christ, and the subsequent coming of the Holy Spirit upon the community of baptized believers at Pentecost are parallel events to each other, and continue the work of the Father's original Creation as God intervenes directly into human history and now most explicitly into our personal lives. The Nativity of Jesus brought direct knowledge of God, the forgiveness of our sins, and the gift of grace (the spirit of God in us). The birth of the church through the coming of the Holy Spirit brings us direct knowledge from God, the power of God's spirit, and divine guidance in truth for our constant implementation of God's love in us, for us to implement God's will in the world. In Part One, the Nativity of Jesus, not incidentally, also involves the child's conception with Mary through the Holy Spirit. Joseph, in his vocation and his relationship with Mary, prefigures the relationship between Christ and his church: so, he took Mary into his home and he cared for her as his wife; but he also had no intercourse with her, to keep her pure and holy perpetually for God. Mary, while pregnant, assists Elizabeth during her pregancy until the birth of John the Baptist; but she returns home to Nazareth and Joseph before making the journey to Bethlehem, where Jesus is born. On Christmas Day, angels proclaim the child's birth to shepherds nearby. One week later, Jesus is circumcised and named at the Temple in Jerusalem, when Simeon praises God, and blesses the child and family, and prophesizes the child's destiny for Israel, for Mary's soul, and the hearts of many. Anna, the prophetess, also speaks to the family and to everyone about the child. The Holy Family remains in Bethlehem for nearly two years, until some magi, royal astrologers from the east, suddenly appear in Jerusalem. The historical context for their visit to Herod the Great is provided, and the "Star" of Bethlehem is explained according to the hypothesis of Michael Molnar, supported by the specific details of Matthew's gospel and by empirical astronomy and Greek astrology of that time. However, Molnar is incorrect about his speculations for the date of the birth of Christ. Molnar's correct explanations for the timing of the magi together with evidence from Maria Valtorta's gospel visions establish the birth of Jesus as on the Winter solstice of 8 BCE. This purposive celestial coordination emphasizes the birth of Jesus as the divine will to our salvation: the great light that shines in our darkness. The Holy Family flees to Egypt to escape the intentions of Herod, who slaughters the children of Bethlehem. After Herod's death in the Spring of 4 BCE, in a dream Joseph is told by an angel to return to Israel, as the Holy Family replicates the exodus from Egypt with its Passover return, but because Archelaus was made king, the family settles in Nazareth. In Egypt, the Holy Family had lived in Matarea, which was part of the ancient city of Heliopolis, the Egyptian center for the cult of Horus the sun-god. Today the location is part of the El Cairo district called Al-Zeitoun, where apparitions of Our Lady were first reported and witnessed by thousands on 2 April 1968; and as recently as 11 December 2009, similar transfigurations have been witnessed in Warraq al-Hadar, Giza, Cairo, apparently within the provenance of Our Lady's vocation as God-bearer, Theotokos, of her divine Son, whose presence evangelized classical Egypt in the context of their "myth of Horus," but who today in Egypt also evangelizes for Christians and Moslems through shared devotion to "Our Lady." For the second part of Chapter 40, we return to the morning of Pentecost, with Peter addressing the crowds of Jerusalem, but each person from throughout the ancient world hearing him speak in their own language. Peter explains, this is what the prophet Joel had meant, "I shall pour out my Spirit upon all humanity." Then Peter preached the crucified Christ, risen from the dead. Cut to the heart, they implored to the brothers what they should do? Peter answered, "Repent and be baptized, in the name of Jesus Christ for the forgiveness of your sins, and you will receive the Holy Spirit." The promise is for themselves and their children and for "whomever the Lord is calling to himself." That day alone, several thousand accepted the message, and they remained faithful: to the teaching of the apostles, to the brotherhood, to the breaking of bread, and to the prayers; and all who shared the faith owned everything in common. Likewise, today, the living Christian community is called to live and share what we possess: our faith and our material possessions. Some persons completely do so as individuals; others have joined themselves to various religious orders and communities; many of us do so by less radical commitments. Likewise we gather for the Word and Eucharist or we join in the prayer of the church. We may share our faith in our own parish communities, in our larger neighborhoods, among our families, in our assistance to anyone, regardless of race, creed or politics. The Holy Spirit will lead each one of us in his way of our repentance, and along his path to our eventual holiness. When we keep our hearts close to the Lord, he supports us by his love, which is beyond our imagination: this Gospel Emmaus is in partial fulfilment of my own calling from the Lord, to whatever purposes Christ seeks to live in your hearts through faith. The Psalm prayer-reflections continue our scriptural meditations on the meaning of the birth of Christ and the coming of the Holy Spirit, both directed towards bringing about the Kingdom of God.

> Readings: Luke 2:1-21, 22-40; Matthew 1:18-25, 2:1-23

> Readings: Acts 2:14-36, 37-47; Acts 10:1-43, 44-48, 11:15-26

> Reflective Prayer: Psalms 2:1-12, 72:1-20, 87:1-7

Part Four (Chapters 41-42): Sin, Faith, and Salvation through Jesus Christ; with Our True Repentance, Mutual Faithfulness, and God's Grace

41. The Gospel (on the Road to) Emmaus: Epilogue

Our Personal Journey of Faith with Christ in Our Time of Grace Cared for by an Intimate and Loving God: Father, Son, and Holy Spirit

Our personal journey in the Gospel is an unpredictable process in us mediated by God according to the divine intention, if we abide in God's will. The specifics for our transformation in love demand from us our present fidelity to God. In the present, our past must not become a preoccupation to weigh us down, but the past must be abandoned to God's mercy; and from the present, because the future is not yet realized in actual clarity, regarding our future we must trust in God's true providence. We cannot know the journey's conclusion, not until it is disclosed to us in eternity; but we do know where the journey must begin: from God's grace, when we make firm our resolution of repetance, as John the Baptist called us to repent in the first chapter. The only uncertain variable in God's equation for our journey is our sometimes very fickle will, when by contrast God's grace and mercy are constant, unless our love of self should overwhelm our love for God. But God provides his increase in us, if we humbly allow ourselves to be purified by the passion and death of Christ, if we also love like Christ, so that we also may rise with him to share in his eternal glory. God intends for us to be remade in the image of his love, which is a divine gift, which no one earns, which we may insult if we refuse it by our hypocrisy; or we may choose to cooperate with God's love. But the only intransigent position for our taking up the journey would be not being open to the "one teacher," who leads us beyond our personal opinions and conclusions to the privilege of the "complete truth" in the "one spirit of God." The Gospel Emmaus journey is not simplistically my human fabrication as an act of existential defiance, although I have expressed "my faith" in God, for if we are called to this particular journey we have been invited to take up the Word and Eucharist with one person: the unrecognized, or recognized Lord, Jesus Christ. The singular gospel of Jesus Christ unites individuals and cultures throughout history, and draws every humble soul to the heart of the One God, who is "love" and "truth," a gospel we must hasten to put into practice. My starting point for this Gospel Emmaus was in a particular moment of repentance and grace, and the mystery is humbling, merciful, and amazing--with only one rule, "embrace God's Spirit and follow it wherever it goes." The journey has been part of God's discipline for me to keep and understand his commands, for if we keep God's word, God's love truly reaches its perfection in us. This practice of God's love is a daily challenge, but the specific applications are known to each of us: through Christ and the Father's love, and by the Spirit who enlightens our minds and inflames our hearts. God's ecumenism embraces everyone broadly, even those who may profess few or no religious principles. Genuine "theophany," or divine revelation, exists fundamentally within the Judeo-Christian tradition and through the Holy Spirit, but also by various means, it includes various mystical traditions within the church and even non-traditional religions. However, the Christian scriptures hold an indespensible place in divine revelation, especially as they are interpreted by the Catholic Church. In my own journey, I have regarded several primarily english translations of the Bible, but I have had access to other language translations and to primary Greek texts. Reading scripture requires a discerning listener: the scriptures are the living word of God for our dialogue with the divine presence (Father, Son, and Holy Spirit) within us. This primarily is a spiritual task, not an academic task, where a personal God reveals himself, or remains hidden, depending upon the grace and mercy of the mystery. Whoever approaches God with some element of faith, God is revealed to them. But Christ is the cornerstone: God is found in love, also within the sharing of human hearts, and when we trust the sacred heart of Jesus and entrust our heart to his, who wishes to come to us. For every person, how God does come to them uniquely reflects the glory of God, whose origen for us is from the cross, as is the 14th September 2003 context for the beginning of this book. For my wife Jane and her son Ralph, who was killed in a motorbike accident eight years ago, they each have or have had their particular paths to the Lord's eventual glory in the way of the cross. My path began from my conception; included a failed first marriage; a journey to Malta eighteen years ago; the providence of my wife Jane, including a civil marriage and our eventual marriage in the church on 8th December 2008; and seven overlapping years for the Gospel Emmaus project to the present moment. My intentions from the beginning were to understand the mind of Christ, whose gospel was my priority. Along the way, the Lord provided me with some additional understanding for me to include biographical and autobiographical narratives within the gospel's original narrative structure. Also, many others, specifically or anonymously, have made their contributions for this gospel journey together with Christ. My mother and my wife Jane have been particularly supportive, but so have been so many others: colleagues, priests, family, friends, and critics. This additional chapter, beyond the original plan, finds its conclusion between Ascension Thursday and Pentecost of 2010, as we are preparing once again for the gift of the Holy Spirit. Christ is head of the church, which is his body: the fullness of him who fills the universe in all its parts. The Spirit God sends to us and the intimacy the Lord makes immediate through the scriptures provide us with vibrancy and life, as the risen Lord animates our being and fill us with his love, by Word and by Eucharist, even as now in this life we are separated from the glory of being with the Lord face to face. But, it may be quite shocking and a revelation from God, for us to discover God as our true friend, companion, and lover, as we humbly enter into the essential relationship God calls us to have with himself: when we pray and take up the scriptures, but essentially when we implement God's love for us in our love for others, when we also become Eucharist in our intimate friendship and union with Christ, as God leads us, including this journey of ours through this gospel on the road to Emmaus. In conclusion, as disciples on the road to Emmaus, we figuratively return to the upper room as we share our experience with the disciples, when Christ suddenly stands in our midst. His words are, "Peace be with you. Why are you frightened, and why do doubts arise in your hearts? Look at my hands and feet; see that it is I myself. Touch me and see; for a ghost does not have flesh and bones as you see that I have." And so it is for us if we touch and see: peace, fearlessness, and joy in our hearts, as the living Lord comes to us in his words, as he opens our minds to understand the scriptures, as we come to understand the words he had spoken, and still speaks to us, in fulfilment of the Law, the prophets, and the psalms; and as believers, we are clothed with "power from on high." May the Holy Spirit bring fire to the earth, and kindle in our hearts the fire of God's love. The final prayer provided is the Divine Praises, which also is my conscious reflection of God's awakening of love in me by music and song, when I was a child of ten. The chapter is concluded on 22nd May 2010, the Vigil of Pentecost, after exactly eighty months for the project: 40 months for the first draft and 40 months for subsequent development and revisions.

> Readings: Genesis 1:1—3:24; John 1:1-18; Revelation 21:1—22:21

42. Faith Post-Pentecost: Lead Us Not into Temptation, but Deliver Us from Presumption and Doubt

Eighty days later, this final post-epilogue chapter was not envisioned by me, but it is a logical progression from the Lord in his actual conclusion for our Gospel Emmaus journey. This journey is derived from the first Pentecost, and from our own Pentecost, with the reality of the coming of the Holy Spirit. Unknown to me initially, this portion of the Gospel Emmaus journey is taken up post Pentecost 2010, as a manifestation of the Holy Spirit; and the chapter is written in twenty days during the 2010 Jewish month of Tishri, originating from Rosh Hashanah, and the chapter concludes at the end of Sukkot. From John's Gospel (John 7:2-39) we are provided with the visible rationale: now, instead of the glory of the Lord leading Israel in the exodus by pillars of cloud or fire (Exodus 13:20-22), today we are led by the Holy Spirit, as a fire in our hearts and as our passion in mind and will for God and as a human instrument of divine love, as God is love. It was at the end of the feast of Sukkot that Christ spoke of the Holy Spirit that he would send into the hearts of believers, "Let anyone who is thirsty come to me, and let the one who believes in me drink, 'Out of the believer's heart shall flow rivers of living water.'" And so, the connection between Sukkot and Pentecost is made, as the Lord leads us through our treacherous wastelands of life by the "fire" of the Holy Spirit, until we may arrive "home" with God, safely face to face in his unapproachable light. This chapter opens with its inter-faith connections, but specifically provides our Jewish roots in Sukkot for the coming of the Spirit (without my awareness yet of this intention of the Holy Spirit for this chapter); yet the writing of the chapter itself becomes a real-time manifestation and explanation of the Spirit, who operates in our lives. This chapter also provides its specific contributions from several other disciples who have been on this Gospel Emmaus journey with me, as they provide us with instruction from Christ, as they have been inspired by the Spirit of truth. Along the way, there will be temptations, and my own journey is no exception; and our journey in faith must be steered between two corrupting forms of sins of pride: away from presumption and away from doubt. In faith, God alone is our divine source; and in faith there is no doubt, but full trust in God. Our faith from God is supported by our humility, our love, and our prayer; and God provides his Holy Spirit to lead us: to preserve us from sin; to bring us to forgive others; to strengthen our love; and ultimately at the end of our lives, to guide us "home" to God. This chapter includes several examples of faith, or our lack of faith; but always these examples are provided to me in the real-time interventions of God through the

Holy Spirit. One such intervention includes one disciple's testimonial of her experience of a visit from the Holy Spirit. Others include the ministry of a priest, who from the Spirit provides "God's Wisdom," and shows the Holy Spirit at work in his ministry to others (and to myself, as one active recepient of that ministry). The beatification of John Henry Newman provides another proximate example to us for our conversion in faith, who himself exemplified the actions of the Holy Spirit, who speaks to us with our hearts. The ordinary processes of our everyday lives are essential to holiness by the nature of love; and these processes are enriched by the actions of the Holy Spirit. Included in these processes are our communications and personal lives entwined with others, our specific relationships as husband and wife together, and our struggles with faith or with enemies of faith (reliance on natural reason, fear, and skepticism). True religion and faith in God naturally bind us together: we are bound to God and bound to each other. Separation from God or divisions from one another is indicative of sin: divisions between husbands and wives, within families, within societies, within the Church, or with actions of hatred or violence directed towards others. Also we sin (or we are without love) in the absence of faith, or when in some degree we lack faith. This chapter provides other living examples of degrees of faith, or degrees of its absence, mostly in the context of myself, my wife, and my family. Yet, God does not impose himself; we are completely free to choose with the parameters of God's gifts, but the gift of faith comes to us from God. When we are justified by the gift of grace from Jesus Christ, God also provides us with his grace for an active faith. True faith is bound to love, as we are espoused to God, who chooses us as his "bride"; but God leaves us totally free to accept or to reject the gift. Our individual confession of faith is manifested by our faithful witness to the Gospel; but it is through the Trinity that we are enabled to do so. The Holy Spirit is sent to us from the Father and the Son, and this "Gospel (on the road to) Emmaus" provides the testimony of its two witnesses: Jesus Christ, whose testimony is true, and the Holy Spirit, the Spirit of Truth, who speak to us in our hearts and through the Church. This chapter specificly ends according to God's chronology (29th September 2010) with the death of my wife's friend, Olga, on the last day of Sukkot after the conclusion of the feast, who in her passing also reminds us of our purpose and final destiny with the Lord. It is the Lord who leads us to him through the Holy Spirit; and if we just persevere in love in active faith, by the gifts of the Spirit, we also will find our way "home" to God. The Holy Spirit goes as it wills; yet, if we are humble and obedient servants of God, the works of the Spirit for the Lord's "New Creation" may be accomplished in us: not by us, but by the Spirit of God, who lives in us as the Trinity of "love." Then we may give true worship to God in Spirit and truth (John 4:23-24), according to the Gospel. Amen. But the final word of the chapter comes one month after it began, finishing on 10th October 2010 with the readings of that Sunday liturgy. The gospel of that day returns to the beginning of this gospel journey, like the leper as I was on my way to the priest. The Lord had healed ten lepers, but only one returned to give thanks. The question for us remains: Do we return our thanks to the Lord after he heals us, or are we like the other nine lepers who fail to do so? The choice is ours; but everything else is grace from God.

Readings: Proverbs 3:1-12, Hebrews 12:1-29, John 7:2-18

Concluding Prayer